# GNU C Library 2.22 Reference Manual 2/2

A catalogue record for this book is available from the Hong Kong Public Libraries.

Published in Hong Kong by Samurai Media Limited.

Email: info@samuraimedia.org

ISBN 978-988-8381-08-1

# Short Contents

# Table of Contents

# 17   Low-Level Terminal Interface ............. 477

# 18   Syslog ................................ 504

# 25   The Basic Program/System Interface..... 705

# 19 Mathematics

This chapter contains information about functions for performing mathematical computations, such as trigonometric functions. Most of these functions have prototypes declared in the header file `math.h`. The complex-valued functions are defined in `complex.h`.

All mathematical functions which take a floating-point argument have three variants, one each for `double`, `float`, and `long double` arguments. The `double` versions are mostly defined in ISO C89. The `float` and `long double` versions are from the numeric extensions to C included in ISO C99.

Which of the three versions of a function should be used depends on the situation. For most calculations, the `float` functions are the fastest. On the other hand, the `long double` functions have the highest precision. `double` is somewhere in between. It is usually wise to pick the narrowest type that can accommodate your data. Not all machines have a distinct `long double` type; it may be the same as `double`.

## 19.1 Predefined Mathematical Constants

The header `math.h` defines several useful mathematical constants. All values are defined as preprocessor macros starting with `M_`. The values provided are:

`M_E`       The base of natural logarithms.

`M_LOG2E`   The logarithm to base 2 of `M_E`.

`M_LOG10E`  The logarithm to base 10 of `M_E`.

`M_LN2`     The natural logarithm of 2.

`M_LN10`    The natural logarithm of 10.

`M_PI`      Pi, the ratio of a circle's circumference to its diameter.

`M_PI_2`    Pi divided by two.

`M_PI_4`    Pi divided by four.

`M_1_PI`    The reciprocal of pi (1/pi)

`M_2_PI`    Two times the reciprocal of pi.

`M_2_SQRTPI`
            Two times the reciprocal of the square root of pi.

`M_SQRT2`   The square root of two.

`M_SQRT1_2`
            The reciprocal of the square root of two (also the square root of $1/2$).

These constants come from the Unix98 standard and were also available in 4.4BSD; therefore they are only defined if `_XOPEN_SOURCE=500`, or a more general feature select macro, is defined. The default set of features includes these constants. See Section 1.3.4 [Feature Test Macros], page 15.

All values are of type `double`. As an extension, the GNU C Library also defines these constants with type `long double`. The `long double` macros have a lowercase 'l' appended to their names: `M_E1`, `M_PI1`, and so forth.  These are only available if `_GNU_SOURCE` is defined.

*Note:* Some programs use a constant named `PI` which has the same value as `M_PI`. This constant is not standard; it may have appeared in some old AT&T headers, and is mentioned in Stroustrup's book on C++. It infringes on the user's name space, so the GNU C Library does not define it.  Fixing programs written to expect it is simple: replace `PI` with `M_PI` throughout, or put '`-DPI=M_PI`' on the compiler command line.

## 19.2 Trigonometric Functions

These are the familiar `sin`, `cos`, and `tan` functions.  The arguments to all of these functions are in units of radians; recall that pi radians equals 180 degrees.

The math library normally defines `M_PI` to a `double` approximation of pi.  If strict ISO and/or POSIX compliance are requested this constant is not defined, but you can easily define it yourself:

```
#define M_PI 3.14159265358979323846264338327
```

You can also compute the value of pi with the expression `acos (-1.0)`.

| | |
|---|---|
| `double sin` (*double x*) | [Function] |
| `float sinf` (*float x*) | [Function] |
| `long double sinl` (*long double x*) | [Function] |

> Preliminary: | MT-Safe | AS-Safe | AC-Safe | See Section 1.2.2.1 [POSIX Safety Concepts], page 2.
>
> These functions return the sine of $x$, where $x$ is given in radians. The return value is in the range -1 to 1.

| | |
|---|---|
| `double cos` (*double x*) | [Function] |
| `float cosf` (*float x*) | [Function] |
| `long double cosl` (*long double x*) | [Function] |

> Preliminary: | MT-Safe | AS-Safe | AC-Safe | See Section 1.2.2.1 [POSIX Safety Concepts], page 2.
>
> These functions return the cosine of $x$, where $x$ is given in radians. The return value is in the range -1 to 1.

| | |
|---|---|
| `double tan` (*double x*) | [Function] |
| `float tanf` (*float x*) | [Function] |
| `long double tanl` (*long double x*) | [Function] |

> Preliminary: | MT-Safe | AS-Safe | AC-Safe | See Section 1.2.2.1 [POSIX Safety Concepts], page 2.
>
> These functions return the tangent of $x$, where $x$ is given in radians.
>
> Mathematically, the tangent function has singularities at odd multiples of pi/2. If the argument $x$ is too close to one of these singularities, `tan` will signal overflow.

In many applications where `sin` and `cos` are used, the sine and cosine of the same angle are needed at the same time.  It is more efficient to compute them simultaneously, so the library provides a function to do that.

void sincos (*double x, double \*sinx, double \*cosx*)                                    [Function]
void sincosf (*float x, float \*sinx, float \*cosx*)                                      [Function]
void sincosl (*long double x, long double \*sinx, long double \*cosx*)                     [Function]
>   Preliminary: | MT-Safe | AS-Safe | AC-Safe | See Section 1.2.2.1 [POSIX Safety
>   Concepts], page 2.
>
>   These functions return the sine of x in \*sinx and the cosine of x in \*cos, where x is
>   given in radians. Both values, \*sinx and \*cosx, are in the range of -1 to 1.
>
>   This function is a GNU extension. Portable programs should be prepared to cope
>   with its absence.

ISO C99 defines variants of the trig functions which work on complex numbers. The
GNU C Library provides these functions, but they are only useful if your compiler supports
the new complex types defined by the standard. (As of this writing GCC supports complex
numbers, but there are bugs in the implementation.)

complex double csin (*complex double z*)                                                  [Function]
complex float csinf (*complex float z*)                                                   [Function]
complex long double csinl (*complex long double z*)                                       [Function]
>   Preliminary: | MT-Safe | AS-Safe | AC-Safe | See Section 1.2.2.1 [POSIX Safety
>   Concepts], page 2.
>
>   These functions return the complex sine of z. The mathematical definition of the
>   complex sine is

$$\sin(z) = \frac{1}{2i}(e^{zi} - e^{-zi})$$

complex double ccos (*complex double z*)                                                  [Function]
complex float ccosf (*complex float z*)                                                   [Function]
complex long double ccosl (*complex long double z*)                                       [Function]
>   Preliminary: | MT-Safe | AS-Safe | AC-Safe | See Section 1.2.2.1 [POSIX Safety
>   Concepts], page 2.
>
>   These functions return the complex cosine of z. The mathematical definition of the
>   complex cosine is

$$\cos(z) = \frac{1}{2}(e^{zi} + e^{-zi})$$

complex double ctan (*complex double z*)                                                  [Function]
complex float ctanf (*complex float z*)                                                   [Function]
complex long double ctanl (*complex long double z*)                                       [Function]
>   Preliminary: | MT-Safe | AS-Safe | AC-Safe | See Section 1.2.2.1 [POSIX Safety
>   Concepts], page 2.
>
>   These functions return the complex tangent of z. The mathematical definition of the
>   complex tangent is

$$\tan(z) = -i \cdot \frac{e^{zi} - e^{-zi}}{e^{zi} + e^{-zi}}$$

The complex tangent has poles at $pi/2 + 2n$, where $n$ is an integer. ctan may signal
overflow if z is too close to a pole.

## 19.3 Inverse Trigonometric Functions

These are the usual arc sine, arc cosine and arc tangent functions, which are the inverses of the sine, cosine and tangent functions respectively.

double asin (*double x*)                                              [Function]
float asinf (*float x*)                                               [Function]
long double asinl (*long double x*)                                   [Function]

> Preliminary: | MT-Safe | AS-Safe | AC-Safe | See Section 1.2.2.1 [POSIX Safety Concepts], page 2.

> These functions compute the arc sine of *x*—that is, the value whose sine is *x*. The value is in units of radians. Mathematically, there are infinitely many such values; the one actually returned is the one between -pi/2 and pi/2 (inclusive).

> The arc sine function is defined mathematically only over the domain -1 to 1. If *x* is outside the domain, asin signals a domain error.

double acos (*double x*)                                              [Function]
float acosf (*float x*)                                               [Function]
long double acosl (*long double x*)                                   [Function]

> Preliminary: | MT-Safe | AS-Safe | AC-Safe | See Section 1.2.2.1 [POSIX Safety Concepts], page 2.

> These functions compute the arc cosine of *x*—that is, the value whose cosine is *x*. The value is in units of radians. Mathematically, there are infinitely many such values; the one actually returned is the one between 0 and pi (inclusive).

> The arc cosine function is defined mathematically only over the domain -1 to 1. If *x* is outside the domain, acos signals a domain error.

double atan (*double x*)                                              [Function]
float atanf (*float x*)                                               [Function]
long double atanl (*long double x*)                                   [Function]

> Preliminary: | MT-Safe | AS-Safe | AC-Safe | See Section 1.2.2.1 [POSIX Safety Concepts], page 2.

> These functions compute the arc tangent of *x*—that is, the value whose tangent is *x*. The value is in units of radians. Mathematically, there are infinitely many such values; the one actually returned is the one between -pi/2 and pi/2 (inclusive).

double atan2 (*double y, double x*)                                   [Function]
float atan2f (*float y, float x*)                                     [Function]
long double atan2l (*long double y, long double x*)                   [Function]

> Preliminary: | MT-Safe | AS-Safe | AC-Safe | See Section 1.2.2.1 [POSIX Safety Concepts], page 2.

> This function computes the arc tangent of *y*/*x*, but the signs of both arguments are used to determine the quadrant of the result, and *x* is permitted to be zero. The return value is given in radians and is in the range -pi to pi, inclusive.

> If *x* and *y* are coordinates of a point in the plane, atan2 returns the signed angle between the line from the origin to that point and the x-axis. Thus, atan2 is useful for converting Cartesian coordinates to polar coordinates. (To compute the radial coordinate, use hypot; see Section 19.4 [Exponentiation and Logarithms], page 515.)

If both $x$ and $y$ are zero, `atan2` returns zero.

ISO C99 defines complex versions of the inverse trig functions.

`complex double casin` (*complex double z*)                             [Function]
`complex float casinf` (*complex float z*)                              [Function]
`complex long double casinl` (*complex long double z*)                  [Function]
> Preliminary: | MT-Safe | AS-Safe | AC-Safe | See Section 1.2.2.1 [POSIX Safety Concepts], page 2.

> These functions compute the complex arc sine of $z$—that is, the value whose sine is $z$. The value returned is in radians.

> Unlike the real-valued functions, `casin` is defined for all values of $z$.

`complex double cacos` (*complex double z*)                             [Function]
`complex float cacosf` (*complex float z*)                              [Function]
`complex long double cacosl` (*complex long double z*)                  [Function]
> Preliminary: | MT-Safe | AS-Safe | AC-Safe | See Section 1.2.2.1 [POSIX Safety Concepts], page 2.

> These functions compute the complex arc cosine of $z$—that is, the value whose cosine is $z$. The value returned is in radians.

> Unlike the real-valued functions, `cacos` is defined for all values of $z$.

`complex double catan` (*complex double z*)                             [Function]
`complex float catanf` (*complex float z*)                              [Function]
`complex long double catanl` (*complex long double z*)                  [Function]
> Preliminary: | MT-Safe | AS-Safe | AC-Safe | See Section 1.2.2.1 [POSIX Safety Concepts], page 2.

> These functions compute the complex arc tangent of $z$—that is, the value whose tangent is $z$. The value is in units of radians.

## 19.4 Exponentiation and Logarithms

`double exp` (*double x*)                                               [Function]
`float expf` (*float x*)                                                [Function]
`long double expl` (*long double x*)                                    [Function]
> Preliminary: | MT-Safe | AS-Safe | AC-Safe | See Section 1.2.2.1 [POSIX Safety Concepts], page 2.

> These functions compute `e` (the base of natural logarithms) raised to the power $x$.

> If the magnitude of the result is too large to be representable, `exp` signals overflow.

`double exp2` (*double x*)                                              [Function]
`float exp2f` (*float x*)                                               [Function]
`long double exp2l` (*long double x*)                                   [Function]
> Preliminary: | MT-Safe | AS-Safe | AC-Safe | See Section 1.2.2.1 [POSIX Safety Concepts], page 2.

> These functions compute 2 raised to the power $x$. Mathematically, `exp2 (x)` is the same as `exp (x * log (2))`.

`double exp10 (`*double x*`)` [Function]
`float exp10f (`*float x*`)` [Function]
`long double exp10l (`*long double x*`)` [Function]
`double pow10 (`*double x*`)` [Function]
`float pow10f (`*float x*`)` [Function]
`long double pow10l (`*long double x*`)` [Function]

Preliminary: | MT-Safe | AS-Safe | AC-Safe | See Section 1.2.2.1 [POSIX Safety Concepts], page 2.

These functions compute 10 raised to the power *x*. Mathematically, `exp10 (x)` is the same as `exp (x * log (10))`.

These functions are GNU extensions. The name `exp10` is preferred, since it is analogous to `exp` and `exp2`.

`double log (`*double x*`)` [Function]
`float logf (`*float x*`)` [Function]
`long double logl (`*long double x*`)` [Function]

Preliminary: | MT-Safe | AS-Safe | AC-Safe | See Section 1.2.2.1 [POSIX Safety Concepts], page 2.

These functions compute the natural logarithm of *x*. `exp (log (x))` equals *x*, exactly in mathematics and approximately in C.

If *x* is negative, `log` signals a domain error. If *x* is zero, it returns negative infinity; if *x* is too close to zero, it may signal overflow.

`double log10 (`*double x*`)` [Function]
`float log10f (`*float x*`)` [Function]
`long double log10l (`*long double x*`)` [Function]

Preliminary: | MT-Safe | AS-Safe | AC-Safe | See Section 1.2.2.1 [POSIX Safety Concepts], page 2.

These functions return the base-10 logarithm of *x*. `log10 (x)` equals `log (x) / log (10)`.

`double log2 (`*double x*`)` [Function]
`float log2f (`*float x*`)` [Function]
`long double log2l (`*long double x*`)` [Function]

Preliminary: | MT-Safe | AS-Safe | AC-Safe | See Section 1.2.2.1 [POSIX Safety Concepts], page 2.

These functions return the base-2 logarithm of *x*. `log2 (x)` equals `log (x) / log (2)`.

`double logb (`*double x*`)` [Function]
`float logbf (`*float x*`)` [Function]
`long double logbl (`*long double x*`)` [Function]

Preliminary: | MT-Safe | AS-Safe | AC-Safe | See Section 1.2.2.1 [POSIX Safety Concepts], page 2.

These functions extract the exponent of *x* and return it as a floating-point value. If `FLT_RADIX` is two, `logb` is equal to `floor (log2 (x))`, except it's probably faster.

If $x$ is de-normalized, `logb` returns the exponent $x$ would have if it were normalized. If $x$ is infinity (positive or negative), `logb` returns $\infty$. If $x$ is zero, `logb` returns $\infty$. It does not signal.

`int ilogb (`*double x*`)`                                                   [Function]
`int ilogbf (`*float x*`)`                                                   [Function]
`int ilogbl (`*long double x*`)`                                             [Function]
> Preliminary: | MT-Safe | AS-Safe | AC-Safe | See Section 1.2.2.1 [POSIX Safety Concepts], page 2.

> These functions are equivalent to the corresponding `logb` functions except that they return signed integer values.

Since integers cannot represent infinity and NaN, `ilogb` instead returns an integer that can't be the exponent of a normal floating-point number. `math.h` defines constants so you can check for this.

`int FP_ILOGB0`                                                             [Macro]
> `ilogb` returns this value if its argument is 0. The numeric value is either `INT_MIN` or `-INT_MAX`.

> This macro is defined in ISO C99.

`int FP_ILOGBNAN`                                                           [Macro]
> `ilogb` returns this value if its argument is NaN. The numeric value is either `INT_MIN` or `INT_MAX`.

> This macro is defined in ISO C99.

These values are system specific. They might even be the same. The proper way to test the result of `ilogb` is as follows:

```
i = ilogb (f);
if (i == FP_ILOGB0 || i == FP_ILOGBNAN)
  {
    if (isnan (f))
      {
        /* Handle NaN.  */
      }
    else if (f  == 0.0)
      {
        /* Handle 0.0.  */
      }
    else
      {
        /* Some other value with large exponent,
           perhaps +Inf.  */
      }
  }
```

`double pow (`*double base, double power*`)`                                [Function]
`float powf (`*float base, float power*`)`                                  [Function]
`long double powl (`*long double base, long double power*`)`                [Function]
> Preliminary: | MT-Safe | AS-Safe | AC-Safe | See Section 1.2.2.1 [POSIX Safety Concepts], page 2.

These are general exponentiation functions, returning *base* raised to *power*.

Mathematically, `pow` would return a complex number when *base* is negative and *power* is not an integral value. `pow` can't do that, so instead it signals a domain error. `pow` may also underflow or overflow the destination type.

double sqrt (*double x*)                              [Function]
float sqrtf (*float x*)                                [Function]
long double sqrtl (*long double x*)             [Function]

> Preliminary: | MT-Safe | AS-Safe | AC-Safe | See Section 1.2.2.1 [POSIX Safety Concepts], page 2.
>
> These functions return the nonnegative square root of *x*.
>
> If *x* is negative, `sqrt` signals a domain error. Mathematically, it should return a complex number.

double cbrt (*double x*)                             [Function]
float cbrtf (*float x*)                              [Function]
long double cbrtl (*long double x*)            [Function]

> Preliminary: | MT-Safe | AS-Safe | AC-Safe | See Section 1.2.2.1 [POSIX Safety Concepts], page 2.
>
> These functions return the cube root of *x*. They cannot fail; every representable real value has a representable real cube root.

double hypot (*double x, double y*)           [Function]
float hypotf (*float x, float y*)              [Function]
long double hypotl (*long double x, long double y*) [Function]

> Preliminary: | MT-Safe | AS-Safe | AC-Safe | See Section 1.2.2.1 [POSIX Safety Concepts], page 2.
>
> These functions return `sqrt (x*x + y*y)`. This is the length of the hypotenuse of a right triangle with sides of length *x* and *y*, or the distance of the point (*x*, *y*) from the origin. Using this function instead of the direct formula is wise, since the error is much smaller. See also the function `cabs` in Section 20.8.1 [Absolute Value], page 574.

double expm1 (*double x*)                          [Function]
float expm1f (*float x*)                           [Function]
long double expm1l (*long double x*)          [Function]

> Preliminary: | MT-Safe | AS-Safe | AC-Safe | See Section 1.2.2.1 [POSIX Safety Concepts], page 2.
>
> These functions return a value equivalent to `exp (x) - 1`. They are computed in a way that is accurate even if *x* is near zero—a case where `exp (x) - 1` would be inaccurate owing to subtraction of two numbers that are nearly equal.

double log1p (*double x*)                          [Function]
float log1pf (*float x*)                           [Function]
long double log1pl (*long double x*)          [Function]

> Preliminary: | MT-Safe | AS-Safe | AC-Safe | See Section 1.2.2.1 [POSIX Safety Concepts], page 2.
>
> These functions returns a value equivalent to `log (1 + x)`. They are computed in a way that is accurate even if *x* is near zero.

ISO C99 defines complex variants of some of the exponentiation and logarithm functions.

`complex double cexp` (*complex double **z***)                                   [Function]
`complex float cexpf` (*complex float **z***)                                    [Function]
`complex long double cexpl` (*complex long double **z***)                        [Function]
    Preliminary: | MT-Safe | AS-Safe | AC-Safe | See Section 1.2.2.1 [POSIX Safety Concepts], page 2.

    These functions return `e` (the base of natural logarithms) raised to the power of *z*. Mathematically, this corresponds to the value

$$\exp(z) = e^z = e^{\mathrm{Re}\, z}(\cos(\mathrm{Im}\, z) + i\sin(\mathrm{Im}\, z))$$

`complex double clog` (*complex double **z***)                                   [Function]
`complex float clogf` (*complex float **z***)                                    [Function]
`complex long double clogl` (*complex long double **z***)                        [Function]
    Preliminary: | MT-Safe | AS-Safe | AC-Safe | See Section 1.2.2.1 [POSIX Safety Concepts], page 2.

    These functions return the natural logarithm of *z*. Mathematically, this corresponds to the value

$$\log(z) = \log|z| + i\arg z$$

    `clog` has a pole at 0, and will signal overflow if *z* equals or is very close to 0. It is well-defined for all other values of *z*.

`complex double clog10` (*complex double **z***)                                 [Function]
`complex float clog10f` (*complex float **z***)                                  [Function]
`complex long double clog10l` (*complex long double **z***)                      [Function]
    Preliminary: | MT-Safe | AS-Safe | AC-Safe | See Section 1.2.2.1 [POSIX Safety Concepts], page 2.

    These functions return the base 10 logarithm of the complex value *z*. Mathematically, this corresponds to the value

$$\log_{10}(z) = \log_{10}|z| + i\arg z$$

    These functions are GNU extensions.

`complex double csqrt` (*complex double **z***)                                  [Function]
`complex float csqrtf` (*complex float **z***)                                   [Function]
`complex long double csqrtl` (*complex long double **z***)                       [Function]
    Preliminary: | MT-Safe | AS-Safe | AC-Safe | See Section 1.2.2.1 [POSIX Safety Concepts], page 2.

    These functions return the complex square root of the argument *z*. Unlike the real-valued functions, they are defined for all values of *z*.

complex double **cpow** (*complex double* **base**, *complex double* **power**)  [Function]
complex float **cpowf** (*complex float* **base**, *complex float* **power**)  [Function]
complex long double **cpowl** (*complex long double* **base**, *complex long*  [Function]
      *double* **power**)

> Preliminary: | MT-Safe | AS-Safe | AC-Safe | See Section 1.2.2.1 [POSIX Safety Concepts], page 2.

> These functions return *base* raised to the power of *power*. This is equivalent to `cexp (y * clog (x))`

## 19.5 Hyperbolic Functions

The functions in this section are related to the exponential functions; see Section 19.4 [Exponentiation and Logarithms], page 515.

double **sinh** (*double* x)  [Function]
float **sinhf** (*float* x)  [Function]
long double **sinhl** (*long double* x)  [Function]

> Preliminary: | MT-Safe | AS-Safe | AC-Safe | See Section 1.2.2.1 [POSIX Safety Concepts], page 2.

> These functions return the hyperbolic sine of x, defined mathematically as `(exp (x) - exp (-x)) / 2`. They may signal overflow if x is too large.

double **cosh** (*double* x)  [Function]
float **coshf** (*float* x)  [Function]
long double **coshl** (*long double* x)  [Function]

> Preliminary: | MT-Safe | AS-Safe | AC-Safe | See Section 1.2.2.1 [POSIX Safety Concepts], page 2.

> These function return the hyperbolic cosine of x, defined mathematically as `(exp (x) + exp (-x)) / 2`. They may signal overflow if x is too large.

double **tanh** (*double* x)  [Function]
float **tanhf** (*float* x)  [Function]
long double **tanhl** (*long double* x)  [Function]

> Preliminary: | MT-Safe | AS-Safe | AC-Safe | See Section 1.2.2.1 [POSIX Safety Concepts], page 2.

> These functions return the hyperbolic tangent of x, defined mathematically as `sinh (x) / cosh (x)`. They may signal overflow if x is too large.

There are counterparts for the hyperbolic functions which take complex arguments.

complex double **csinh** (*complex double* z)  [Function]
complex float **csinhf** (*complex float* z)  [Function]
complex long double **csinhl** (*complex long double* z)  [Function]

> Preliminary: | MT-Safe | AS-Safe | AC-Safe | See Section 1.2.2.1 [POSIX Safety Concepts], page 2.

> These functions return the complex hyperbolic sine of z, defined mathematically as `(exp (z) - exp (-z)) / 2`.

`complex double ccosh` (*complex double z*)                              [Function]
`complex float ccoshf` (*complex float z*)                              [Function]
`complex long double ccoshl` (*complex long double z*)                  [Function]
>    Preliminary: | MT-Safe | AS-Safe | AC-Safe | See Section 1.2.2.1 [POSIX Safety
>    Concepts], page 2.
>
>    These functions return the complex hyperbolic cosine of z, defined mathematically as
>    `(exp (z) + exp (-z)) / 2`.

`complex double ctanh` (*complex double z*)                             [Function]
`complex float ctanhf` (*complex float z*)                             [Function]
`complex long double ctanhl` (*complex long double z*)                 [Function]
>    Preliminary: | MT-Safe | AS-Safe | AC-Safe | See Section 1.2.2.1 [POSIX Safety
>    Concepts], page 2.
>
>    These functions return the complex hyperbolic tangent of z, defined mathematically
>    as `csinh (z) / ccosh (z)`.

`double asinh` (*double x*)                                             [Function]
`float asinhf` (*float x*)                                             [Function]
`long double asinhl` (*long double x*)                                 [Function]
>    Preliminary: | MT-Safe | AS-Safe | AC-Safe | See Section 1.2.2.1 [POSIX Safety
>    Concepts], page 2.
>
>    These functions return the inverse hyperbolic sine of x—the value whose hyperbolic
>    sine is x.

`double acosh` (*double x*)                                             [Function]
`float acoshf` (*float x*)                                             [Function]
`long double acoshl` (*long double x*)                                 [Function]
>    Preliminary: | MT-Safe | AS-Safe | AC-Safe | See Section 1.2.2.1 [POSIX Safety
>    Concepts], page 2.
>
>    These functions return the inverse hyperbolic cosine of x—the value whose hyperbolic
>    cosine is x. If x is less than 1, `acosh` signals a domain error.

`double atanh` (*double x*)                                             [Function]
`float atanhf` (*float x*)                                             [Function]
`long double atanhl` (*long double x*)                                 [Function]
>    Preliminary: | MT-Safe | AS-Safe | AC-Safe | See Section 1.2.2.1 [POSIX Safety
>    Concepts], page 2.
>
>    These functions return the inverse hyperbolic tangent of x—the value whose hyper-
>    bolic tangent is x. If the absolute value of x is greater than 1, `atanh` signals a domain
>    error; if it is equal to 1, `atanh` returns infinity.

`complex double casinh` (*complex double z*)                            [Function]
`complex float casinhf` (*complex float z*)                            [Function]
`complex long double casinhl` (*complex long double z*)                [Function]
>    Preliminary: | MT-Safe | AS-Safe | AC-Safe | See Section 1.2.2.1 [POSIX Safety
>    Concepts], page 2.
>
>    These functions return the inverse complex hyperbolic sine of z—the value whose
>    complex hyperbolic sine is z.

complex double cacosh (*complex double z*)         [Function]
complex float cacoshf (*complex float z*)         [Function]
complex long double cacoshl (*complex long double z*)         [Function]
> Preliminary: | MT-Safe | AS-Safe | AC-Safe | See Section 1.2.2.1 [POSIX Safety Concepts], page 2.

> These functions return the inverse complex hyperbolic cosine of *z*—the value whose complex hyperbolic cosine is *z*. Unlike the real-valued functions, there are no restrictions on the value of *z*.

complex double catanh (*complex double z*)         [Function]
complex float catanhf (*complex float z*)         [Function]
complex long double catanhl (*complex long double z*)         [Function]
> Preliminary: | MT-Safe | AS-Safe | AC-Safe | See Section 1.2.2.1 [POSIX Safety Concepts], page 2.

> These functions return the inverse complex hyperbolic tangent of *z*—the value whose complex hyperbolic tangent is *z*. Unlike the real-valued functions, there are no restrictions on the value of *z*.

## 19.6 Special Functions

These are some more exotic mathematical functions which are sometimes useful. Currently they only have real-valued versions.

double erf (*double x*)         [Function]
float erff (*float x*)         [Function]
long double erfl (*long double x*)         [Function]
> Preliminary: | MT-Safe | AS-Safe | AC-Safe | See Section 1.2.2.1 [POSIX Safety Concepts], page 2.

> erf returns the error function of *x*. The error function is defined as

$$\mathrm{erf}(x) = \frac{2}{\sqrt{\pi}} \cdot \int_0^x e^{-t^2} \, \mathrm{d}t$$

double erfc (*double x*)         [Function]
float erfcf (*float x*)         [Function]
long double erfcl (*long double x*)         [Function]
> Preliminary: | MT-Safe | AS-Safe | AC-Safe | See Section 1.2.2.1 [POSIX Safety Concepts], page 2.

> erfc returns 1.0 - erf(x), but computed in a fashion that avoids round-off error when *x* is large.

double lgamma (*double x*)         [Function]
float lgammaf (*float x*)         [Function]
long double lgammal (*long double x*)         [Function]
> Preliminary: | MT-Unsafe race:signgam | AS-Unsafe | AC-Safe | See Section 1.2.2.1 [POSIX Safety Concepts], page 2.

`lgamma` returns the natural logarithm of the absolute value of the gamma function of
*x*. The gamma function is defined as

$$\Gamma(x) = \int_0^\infty t^{x-1} e^{-t} dt$$

The sign of the gamma function is stored in the global variable *signgam*, which is
declared in `math.h`. It is `1` if the intermediate result was positive or zero, or `-1` if it
was negative.

To compute the real gamma function you can use the `tgamma` function or you can
compute the values as follows:

```
lgam = lgamma(x);
gam  = signgam*exp(lgam);
```

The gamma function has singularities at the non-positive integers. `lgamma` will raise
the zero divide exception if evaluated at a singularity.

double **lgamma_r** (*double x, int *signp*)                                 [Function]
float **lgammaf_r** (*float x, int *signp*)                                  [Function]
long double **lgammal_r** (*long double x, int *signp*)                      [Function]
> Preliminary: | MT-Safe | AS-Safe | AC-Safe | See Section 1.2.2.1 [POSIX Safety
> Concepts], page 2.
>
> `lgamma_r` is just like `lgamma`, but it stores the sign of the intermediate result in
> the variable pointed to by *signp* instead of in the *signgam* global. This means it is
> reentrant.

double **gamma** (*double x*)                                                [Function]
float **gammaf** (*float x*)                                                 [Function]
long double **gammal** (*long double x*)                                     [Function]
> Preliminary: | MT-Unsafe race:signgam | AS-Unsafe | AC-Safe | See Section 1.2.2.1
> [POSIX Safety Concepts], page 2.
>
> These functions exist for compatibility reasons. They are equivalent to `lgamma` etc. It
> is better to use `lgamma` since for one the name reflects better the actual computation,
> moreover `lgamma` is standardized in ISO C99 while **gamma** is not.

double **tgamma** (*double x*)                                               [Function]
float **tgammaf** (*float x*)                                                [Function]
long double **tgammal** (*long double x*)                                    [Function]
> Preliminary: | MT-Safe | AS-Safe | AC-Safe | See Section 1.2.2.1 [POSIX Safety
> Concepts], page 2.
>
> `tgamma` applies the gamma function to *x*. The gamma function is defined as

$$\Gamma(x) = \int_0^\infty t^{x-1} e^{-t} dt$$

> This function was introduced in ISO C99.

**double j0** (*double x*)                                                     [Function]
**float j0f** (*float x*)                                                      [Function]
**long double j0l** (*long double x*)                                          [Function]
>      Preliminary: | MT-Safe | AS-Safe | AC-Safe | See Section 1.2.2.1 [POSIX Safety
>      Concepts], page 2.
>
>      j0 returns the Bessel function of the first kind of order 0 of *x*. It may signal underflow
>      if *x* is too large.

**double j1** (*double x*)                                                     [Function]
**float j1f** (*float x*)                                                      [Function]
**long double j1l** (*long double x*)                                          [Function]
>      Preliminary: | MT-Safe | AS-Safe | AC-Safe | See Section 1.2.2.1 [POSIX Safety
>      Concepts], page 2.
>
>      j1 returns the Bessel function of the first kind of order 1 of *x*. It may signal underflow
>      if *x* is too large.

**double jn** (*int n, double x*)                                              [Function]
**float jnf** (*int n, float x*)                                               [Function]
**long double jnl** (*int n, long double x*)                                   [Function]
>      Preliminary: | MT-Safe | AS-Safe | AC-Safe | See Section 1.2.2.1 [POSIX Safety
>      Concepts], page 2.
>
>      jn returns the Bessel function of the first kind of order *n* of *x*. It may signal underflow
>      if *x* is too large.

**double y0** (*double x*)                                                     [Function]
**float y0f** (*float x*)                                                      [Function]
**long double y0l** (*long double x*)                                          [Function]
>      Preliminary: | MT-Safe | AS-Safe | AC-Safe | See Section 1.2.2.1 [POSIX Safety
>      Concepts], page 2.
>
>      y0 returns the Bessel function of the second kind of order 0 of *x*. It may signal
>      underflow if *x* is too large. If *x* is negative, y0 signals a domain error; if it is zero, y0
>      signals overflow and returns $-\infty$.

**double y1** (*double x*)                                                     [Function]
**float y1f** (*float x*)                                                      [Function]
**long double y1l** (*long double x*)                                          [Function]
>      Preliminary: | MT-Safe | AS-Safe | AC-Safe | See Section 1.2.2.1 [POSIX Safety
>      Concepts], page 2.
>
>      y1 returns the Bessel function of the second kind of order 1 of *x*. It may signal
>      underflow if *x* is too large. If *x* is negative, y1 signals a domain error; if it is zero, y1
>      signals overflow and returns $-\infty$.

**double yn** (*int n, double x*)                                              [Function]
**float ynf** (*int n, float x*)                                               [Function]
**long double ynl** (*int n, long double x*)                                   [Function]
>      Preliminary: | MT-Safe | AS-Safe | AC-Safe | See Section 1.2.2.1 [POSIX Safety
>      Concepts], page 2.

yn returns the Bessel function of the second kind of order $n$ of $x$. It may signal underflow if $x$ is too large. If $x$ is negative, yn signals a domain error; if it is zero, yn signals overflow and returns $-\infty$.

## 19.7 Known Maximum Errors in Math Functions

This section lists the known errors of the functions in the math library. Errors are measured in "units of the last place". This is a measure for the relative error. For a number $z$ with the representation $d.d\dots d{\cdot}2^e$ (we assume IEEE floating-point numbers with base 2) the ULP is represented by

$$\frac{|d.d\dots d - (z/2^e)|}{2^{p-1}}$$

where $p$ is the number of bits in the mantissa of the floating-point number representation. Ideally the error for all functions is always less than 0.5ulps in round-to-nearest mode. Using rounding bits this is also possible and normally implemented for the basic operations. Except for certain functions such as sqrt, fma and rint whose results are fully specified by reference to corresponding IEEE 754 floating-point operations, and conversions between strings and floating point, the GNU C Library does not aim for correctly rounded results for functions in the math library, and does not aim for correctness in whether "inexact" exceptions are raised. Instead, the goals for accuracy of functions without fully specified results are as follows; some functions have bugs meaning they do not meet these goals in all cases. In future, the GNU C Library may provide some other correctly rounding functions under the names such as crsin proposed for an extension to ISO C.

- Each function with a floating-point result behaves as if it computes an infinite-precision result that is within a few ulp (in both real and complex parts, for functions with complex results) of the mathematically correct value of the function (interpreted together with ISO C or POSIX semantics for the function in question) at the exact value passed as the input. Exceptions are raised appropriately for this value and in accordance with IEEE 754 / ISO C / POSIX semantics, and it is then rounded according to the current rounding direction to the result that is returned to the user. errno may also be set (see Section 20.5.4 [Error Reporting by Mathematical Functions], page 569). (The "inexact" exception may be raised, or not raised, even if this is inconsistent with the infinite-precision value.)

- For the IBM long double format, as used on PowerPC GNU/Linux, the accuracy goal is weaker for input values not exactly representable in 106 bits of precision; it is as if the input value is some value within 0.5ulp of the value actually passed, where "ulp" is interpreted in terms of a fixed-precision 106-bit mantissa, but not necessarily the exact value actually passed with discontiguous mantissa bits.

- Functions behave as if the infinite-precision result computed is zero, infinity or NaN if and only if that is the mathematically correct infinite-precision result. They behave as if the infinite-precision result computed always has the same sign as the mathematically correct result.

- If the mathematical result is more than a few ulp above the overflow threshold for the current rounding direction, the value returned is the appropriate overflow value for the current rounding direction, with the overflow exception raised.

- If the mathematical result has magnitude well below half the least subnormal magnitude, the returned value is either zero or the least subnormal (in each case, with the correct sign), according to the current rounding direction and with the underflow exception raised.

- Where the mathematical result underflows (before rounding) and is not exactly representable as a floating-point value, the function does not behave as if the computed infinite-precision result is an exact value in the subnormal range. This means that the underflow exception is raised other than possibly for cases where the mathematical result is very close to the underflow threshold and the function behaves as if it computes an infinite-precision result that does not underflow. (So there may be spurious underflow exceptions in cases where the underflowing result is exact, but not missing underflow exceptions in cases where it is inexact.)

- The GNU C Library does not aim for functions to satisfy other properties of the underlying mathematical function, such as monotonicity, where not implied by the above goals.

- All the above applies to both real and complex parts, for complex functions.

Therefore many of the functions in the math library have errors. The table lists the maximum error for each function which is exposed by one of the existing tests in the test suite. The table tries to cover as much as possible and list the actual maximum error (or at least a ballpark figure) but this is often not achieved due to the large search space.

The table lists the ULP values for different architectures. Different architectures have different results since their hardware support for floating-point operations varies and also the existing hardware support is different.

| Function | aarch64 | Alpha | ARM | Generic | hppa/fpu |
|---|---|---|---|---|---|
| acosf | 1 | 1 | 1 | - | - |
| acos | - | - | - | - | - |
| acosl | - | - | - | - | - |
| acoshf | 2 | 2 | 2 | - | 1 |
| acosh | 1 | 1 | 1 | - | 1 |
| acoshl | 1 | 1 | - | - | - |
| asinf | 1 | 1 | 1 | - | - |
| asin | - | - | - | - | - |
| asinl | 1 | 1 | - | - | - |
| asinhf | 1 | 1 | 1 | - | 1 |
| asinh | 1 | 1 | 1 | - | 1 |
| asinhl | 1 | 1 | - | - | - |
| atanf | 1 | 1 | 1 | - | - |
| atan | 1 | - | - | - | - |
| atanl | 1 | 1 | - | - | - |
| atanhf | 2 | 2 | 2 | - | 1 |
| atanh | 1 | 1 | 1 | - | 1 |
| atanhl | 2 | 2 | - | - | - |
| atan2f | 1 | 1 | 1 | - | 1 |
| atan2 | - | - | - | - | - |
| atan2l | 1 | 1 | - | - | - |
| cabsf | - | - | - | - | - |
| cabs | 1 | 1 | 1 | - | - |
| cabsl | - | - | - | - | - |
| cacosf | 2 + i 2 | 2 + i 2 | 2 + i 2 | - | 2 + i 2 |
| cacos | 1 + i 1 | 1 + i 1 | 1 + i 1 | - | 1 + i 1 |
| cacosl | 2 + i 2 | 2 + i 2 | - | - | - |
| cacoshf | 2 + i 2 | 2 + i 2 | 2 + i 2 | - | 2 + i 2 |
| cacosh | 1 + i 1 | 1 + i 1 | 1 + i 1 | - | 1 + i 1 |
| cacoshl | 2 + i 2 | 2 + i 2 | - | - | - |
| cargf | 1 | 1 | 1 | - | - |
| carg | - | - | - | - | - |
| cargl | 1 | 1 | - | - | - |
| casinf | 1 + i 2 | 1 + i 2 | 1 + i 2 | - | 1 + i 2 |
| casin | 1 + i 1 | 1 + i 1 | 1 + i 1 | - | 1 + i 1 |
| casinl | 2 + i 2 | 2 + i 2 | - | - | 1 + i 0 |
| casinhf | 2 + i 1 | 2 + i 1 | 2 + i 1 | - | 2 + i 1 |
| casinh | 1 + i 1 | 1 + i 1 | 1 + i 1 | - | 5 + i 3 |
| casinhl | 2 + i 2 | 2 + i 2 | - | - | 5 + i 3 |
| catanf | 1 + i 1 | 1 + i 1 | 1 + i 1 | - | 1 + i 1 |
| catan | 0 + i 1 | 0 + i 1 | 0 + i 1 | - | 0 + i 1 |
| catanl | 1 + i 1 | 1 + i 1 | - | - | 0 + i 1 |
| catanhf | 1 + i 1 | 1 + i 1 | 1 + i 1 | - | 1 + i 1 |
| catanh | 1 + i 0 | 1 + i 0 | 1 + i 0 | - | 4 + i 0 |
| catanhl | 1 + i 1 | 1 + i 1 | - | - | 4 + i 0 |
| cbrtf | 1 | 1 | 1 | - | 1 |

| | | | | | |
|---|---|---|---|---|---|
| cbrt | 3 | 3 | 3 | - | 1 |
| cbrtl | 1 | 1 | - | - | 1 |
| ccosf | 1 + i 1 | 1 + i 1 | 1 + i 1 | - | 1 + i 1 |
| ccos | 1 + i 1 | 1 + i 1 | 1 + i 1 | - | 1 + i 1 |
| ccosl | 1 + i 1 | 1 + i 1 | - | - | 1 + i 0 |
| ccoshf | 1 + i 1 | 1 + i 1 | 1 + i 1 | - | 1 + i 1 |
| ccosh | 1 + i 1 | 1 + i 1 | 1 + i 1 | - | 1 + i 1 |
| ccoshl | 1 + i 1 | 1 + i 1 | - | - | 1 + i 0 |
| ceilf | - | - | - | - | - |
| ceil | - | - | - | - | - |
| ceill | - | - | - | - | - |
| cexpf | 1 + i 2 | 1 + i 2 | 1 + i 2 | - | 1 + i 2 |
| cexp | 2 + i 1 | 2 + i 1 | 2 + i 1 | - | 2 + i 1 |
| cexpl | 1 + i 1 | 1 + i 1 | - | - | - |
| cimagf | - | - | - | - | - |
| cimag | - | - | - | - | - |
| cimagl | - | - | - | - | - |
| clogf | 3 + i 1 | 2 + i 1 | 2 + i 1 | - | 1 + i 1 |
| clog | 3 + i 1 | 3 + i 0 | 3 + i 0 | - | 1 + i 0 |
| clogl | 4 + i 1 | 4 + i 1 | - | - | - |
| clog10f | 3 + i 2 | 3 + i 2 | 3 + i 2 | - | 2 + i 1 |
| clog10 | 3 + i 1 | 3 + i 2 | 3 + i 2 | - | 2 + i 1 |
| clog10l | 4 + i 2 | 4 + i 2 | - | - | 0 + i 1 |
| conjf | - | - | - | - | - |
| conj | - | - | - | - | - |
| conjl | - | - | - | - | - |
| copysignf | - | - | - | - | - |
| copysign | - | - | - | - | - |
| copysignl | - | - | - | - | - |
| cosf | 1 | 1 | 1 | - | 1 |
| cos | - | - | - | - | 2 |
| cosl | 1 | 1 | - | - | 2 |
| coshf | 1 | 1 | 1 | - | 1 |
| cosh | 1 | 1 | 1 | - | 1 |
| coshl | 1 | 1 | - | - | - |
| cpowf | 5 + i 2 | 4 + i 2 | 4 + i 2 | - | 4 + i 2 |
| cpow | 2 + i 0 | 2 + i 0 | 2 + i 0 | - | 2 + i 2 |
| cpowl | 4 + i 1 | 4 + i 1 | - | - | 2 + i 2 |
| cprojf | - | - | - | - | - |
| cproj | - | - | - | - | - |
| cprojl | - | - | - | - | - |
| crealf | - | - | - | - | - |
| creal | - | - | - | - | - |
| creall | - | - | - | - | - |
| csinf | 1 + i 0 | 1 + i 0 | 1 + i 0 | - | 1 + i 0 |
| csin | 1 + i 0 | 1 + i 0 | 1 + i 0 | - | 1 + i 0 |
| csinl | 1 + i 1 | 1 + i 1 | - | - | - |

| | | | | | |
|---|---|---|---|---|---|
| csinhf | 1 + i 1 | 1 + i 1 | 1 + i 1 | - | 1 + i 1 |
| csinh | 0 + i 1 | 0 + i 1 | 0 + i 1 | - | 0 + i 1 |
| csinhl | 1 + i 1 | 1 + i 1 | - | - | 0 + i 1 |
| csqrtf | 2 + i 2 | 2 + i 2 | 2 + i 2 | - | 1 + i 1 |
| csqrt | 2 + i 2 | 2 + i 2 | 2 + i 2 | - | 1 + i 1 |
| csqrtl | 1 + i 1 | 1 + i 1 | - | - | - |
| ctanf | 1 + i 1 | 1 + i 1 | 1 + i 1 | - | 1 + i 1 |
| ctan | 1 + i 2 | 1 + i 2 | 1 + i 2 | - | 1 + i 2 |
| ctanl | 3 + i 3 | 3 + i 3 | - | - | 0 + i 1 |
| ctanhf | 2 + i 1 | 1 + i 2 | 1 + i 2 | - | 1 + i 2 |
| ctanh | 2 + i 2 | 2 + i 2 | 2 + i 2 | - | 2 + i 2 |
| ctanhl | 3 + i 3 | 3 + i 3 | - | - | 1 + i 0 |
| erff | 1 | 1 | 1 | - | - |
| erf | 1 | 1 | 1 | - | 1 |
| erfl | 1 | 1 | - | - | 1 |
| erfcf | 2 | 2 | 2 | - | 1 |
| erfc | 2 | 2 | 2 | - | 1 |
| erfcl | 2 | 2 | - | - | 1 |
| expf | - | - | - | - | - |
| exp | - | - | - | - | - |
| expl | - | - | - | - | - |
| exp10f | - | - | - | - | 2 |
| exp10 | 2 | 2 | 2 | - | 6 |
| exp10l | 1 | 1 | - | - | 6 |
| exp2f | - | 1 | 1 | - | - |
| exp2 | 1 | 1 | 1 | - | - |
| exp2l | 1 | 1 | - | - | - |
| expm1f | 1 | 1 | 1 | - | 1 |
| expm1 | 1 | 1 | 1 | - | 1 |
| expm1l | 1 | 1 | - | - | 1 |
| fabsf | - | - | - | - | - |
| fabs | - | - | - | - | - |
| fabsl | - | - | - | - | - |
| fdimf | - | - | - | - | - |
| fdim | - | - | - | - | - |
| fdiml | - | - | - | - | - |
| floorf | - | - | - | - | - |
| floor | - | - | - | - | - |
| floorl | - | - | - | - | - |
| fmaf | - | - | - | - | - |
| fma | - | - | - | - | - |
| fmal | - | - | - | - | - |
| fmaxf | - | - | - | - | - |
| fmax | - | - | - | - | - |
| fmaxl | - | - | - | - | - |
| fminf | - | - | - | - | - |
| fmin | - | - | - | - | - |

| | | | | | |
|---|---|---|---|---|---|
| fminl | - | - | - | - | - |
| fmodf | - | - | - | - | - |
| fmod | - | - | - | - | - |
| fmodl | - | - | - | - | - |
| frexpf | - | - | - | - | - |
| frexp | - | - | - | - | - |
| frexpl | - | - | - | - | - |
| gammaf | 1 | 2 | 2 | - | 2 |
| gamma | 1 | 2 | 2 | - | 1 |
| gammal | 1 | 1 | - | - | - |
| hypotf | - | - | - | - | 1 |
| hypot | 1 | 1 | 1 | - | 1 |
| hypotl | 1 | 1 | - | - | - |
| ilogbf | - | - | - | - | - |
| ilogb | - | - | - | - | - |
| ilogbl | - | - | - | - | - |
| j0f | 2 | 2 | 2 | - | 2 |
| j0 | 2 | 2 | 2 | - | 2 |
| j0l | 2 | 2 | - | - | 2 |
| j1f | 2 | 2 | 2 | - | 2 |
| j1 | 1 | 1 | 1 | - | 1 |
| j1l | 4 | 4 | - | - | 1 |
| jnf | 4 | 4 | 4 | - | 5 |
| jn | 4 | 4 | 4 | - | 4 |
| jnl | 7 | 7 | - | - | 4 |
| lgammaf | 1 | 2 | 2 | - | 2 |
| lgamma | 1 | 2 | 2 | - | 1 |
| lgammal | 1 | 1 | - | - | 1 |
| lrintf | - | - | - | - | - |
| lrint | - | - | - | - | - |
| lrintl | - | - | - | - | - |
| llrintf | - | - | - | - | - |
| llrint | - | - | - | - | - |
| llrintl | - | - | - | - | - |
| logf | 1 | 1 | 1 | - | 1 |
| log | - | - | - | - | - |
| logl | 1 | 1 | - | - | - |
| log10f | 2 | 2 | 2 | - | 2 |
| log10 | 2 | 2 | 2 | - | 1 |
| log10l | 1 | 1 | - | - | 1 |
| log1pf | 1 | 1 | 1 | - | 1 |
| log1p | 1 | 1 | 1 | - | - |
| log1pl | 1 | 1 | - | - | - |
| log2f | 1 | 1 | 1 | - | - |
| log2 | 1 | 2 | 2 | - | - |
| log2l | 1 | 1 | - | - | - |
| logbf | - | - | - | - | - |

| | | | | | |
|---|---|---|---|---|---|
| logb | - | - | - | - | - |
| logbl | - | - | - | - | - |
| lroundf | - | - | - | - | - |
| lround | - | - | - | - | - |
| lroundl | - | - | - | - | - |
| llroundf | - | - | - | - | - |
| llround | - | - | - | - | - |
| llroundl | - | - | - | - | - |
| modff | - | - | - | - | - |
| modf | - | - | - | - | - |
| modfl | - | - | - | - | - |
| nearbyintf | - | - | - | - | - |
| nearbyint | - | - | - | - | - |
| nearbyintl | - | - | - | - | - |
| nextafterf | - | - | - | - | - |
| nextafter | - | - | - | - | - |
| nextafterl | - | - | - | - | - |
| nexttowardf | - | - | - | - | - |
| nexttoward | - | - | - | - | - |
| nexttowardl | - | - | - | - | - |
| powf | 1 | 3 | 3 | - | 1 |
| pow | - | - | - | - | - |
| powl | 1 | 1 | - | - | - |
| remainderf | - | - | - | - | - |
| remainder | - | - | - | - | - |
| remainderl | - | - | - | - | - |
| remquof | - | - | - | - | - |
| remquo | - | - | - | - | - |
| remquol | - | - | - | - | - |
| rintf | - | - | - | - | - |
| rint | - | - | - | - | - |
| rintl | - | - | - | - | - |
| roundf | - | - | - | - | - |
| round | - | - | - | - | - |
| roundl | - | - | - | - | - |
| scalbf | - | - | - | - | - |
| scalb | - | - | - | - | - |
| scalbl | - | - | - | - | - |
| scalbnf | - | - | - | - | - |
| scalbn | - | - | - | - | - |
| scalbnl | - | - | - | - | - |
| scalblnf | - | - | - | - | - |
| scalbln | - | - | - | - | - |
| scalblnl | - | - | - | - | - |
| sinf | 1 | 1 | 1 | - | 1 |
| sin | - | - | - | - | - |
| sinl | 1 | 1 | - | - | - |

| sincosf | 1 | 1 | 1 | - | 1 |
|---|---|---|---|---|---|
| sincos | - | - | - | - | 1 |
| sincosl | 1 | 1 | - | - | 1 |
| sinhf | 2 | 2 | 2 | - | - |
| sinh | 2 | 2 | 2 | - | - |
| sinhl | 1 | 1 | - | - | - |
| sqrtf | - | - | - | - | - |
| sqrt | - | - | - | - | - |
| sqrtl | - | - | - | - | - |
| tanf | 1 | 1 | 1 | - | - |
| tan | - | - | - | - | 1 |
| tanl | - | - | - | - | 1 |
| tanhf | 2 | 2 | 2 | - | - |
| tanh | 2 | 2 | 2 | - | - |
| tanhl | 1 | 1 | - | - | - |
| tgammaf | 3 | 5 | 5 | - | 3 |
| tgamma | 3 | 7 | 3 | - | 4 |
| tgammal | 4 | 4 | - | - | 1 |
| truncf | - | - | - | - | - |
| trunc | - | - | - | - | - |
| truncl | - | - | - | - | - |
| y0f | 1 | 1 | 1 | - | 1 |
| y0 | 2 | 2 | 2 | - | 2 |
| y0l | 3 | 3 | - | - | 2 |
| y1f | 2 | 2 | 2 | - | 2 |
| y1 | 3 | 3 | 3 | - | 3 |
| y1l | 2 | 2 | - | - | 3 |
| ynf | 2 | 2 | 2 | - | 2 |
| yn | 3 | 3 | 3 | - | 3 |
| ynl | 5 | 5 | - | - | 3 |

| Function | ix86 | IA64 | m68k/coldfire/fpu | m68k/m680x0/fpu | microblaze |
|---|---|---|---|---|---|
| acosf | - | - | - | - | - |
| acos | - | - | - | - | - |
| acosl | 1 | - | - | - | - |
| acoshf | - | - | - | 1 | - |
| acosh | - | - | - | 1 | 1 |
| acoshl | 2 | - | - | 1 | - |
| asinf | - | - | - | - | - |
| asin | - | - | - | - | - |
| asinl | 1 | - | - | - | - |
| asinhf | - | - | - | 1 | 1 |
| asinh | - | - | - | 1 | 1 |
| asinhl | 2 | - | - | 1 | - |
| atanf | - | - | - | - | - |
| atan | - | - | - | - | - |
| atanl | 1 | - | - | - | - |

| | | | | | |
|---|---|---|---|---|---|
| atanhf | - | - | 1 | - | 1 |
| atanh | - | - | - | - | - |
| atanhl | 3 | - | - | - | - |
| atan2f | - | - | 1 | 1 | 1 |
| atan2 | - | - | - | - | - |
| atan2l | 1 | - | - | 1 | - |
| cabsf | - | - | - | - | - |
| cabs | - | - | - | 1 | - |
| cabsl | 1 | - | - | 1 | - |
| cacosf | 1 + i 1 | 2 + i 2 | - | 2 + i 1 | 2 + i 2 |
| cacos | 1 + i 1 | 1 + i 1 | - | 1 + i 1 | 1 + i 1 |
| cacosl | 1 + i 2 | 1 + i 2 | - | 1 + i 2 | - |
| cacoshf | 1 + i 1 | 2 + i 2 | 0 + i 1 | 1 + i 2 | 2 + i 2 |
| cacosh | 1 + i 1 | 1 + i 1 | - | 1 + i 1 | 1 + i 1 |
| cacoshl | 2 + i 1 | 2 + i 1 | - | 2 + i 1 | - |
| cargf | - | - | - | 1 | - |
| carg | - | - | - | - | - |
| cargl | 1 | - | - | 1 | - |
| casinf | 1 + i 1 | 1 + i 2 | 1 + i 0 | 1 + i 1 | 1 + i 2 |
| casin | 1 + i 1 | 1 + i 1 | 1 + i 0 | 1 + i 1 | 1 + i 1 |
| casinl | 1 + i 2 | 1 + i 2 | - | 1 + i 2 | - |
| casinhf | 1 + i 1 | 2 + i 1 | 1 + i 6 | 1 + i 1 | 2 + i 1 |
| casinh | 1 + i 1 | 1 + i 1 | 5 + i 3 | 1 + i 1 | 1 + i 1 |
| casinhl | 2 + i 1 | 2 + i 1 | - | 2 + i 1 | - |
| catanf | 0 + i 1 | 0 + i 1 | 0 + i 1 | 0 + i 1 | 1 + i 1 |
| catan | 0 + i 1 | 0 + i 1 | 0 + i 1 | 0 + i 1 | 0 + i 1 |
| catanl | 0 + i 1 | 0 + i 1 | - | 1 + i 1 | - |
| catanhf | 1 + i 0 | 1 + i 0 | - | 1 + i 0 | 1 + i 1 |
| catanh | 1 + i 0 | 1 + i 0 | 4 + i 0 | 1 + i 0 | 1 + i 0 |
| catanhl | 1 + i 0 | 1 + i 0 | - | 1 + i 1 | - |
| cbrtf | - | - | - | 1 | 1 |
| cbrt | 1 | - | 1 | 1 | 1 |
| cbrtl | 1 | - | - | 1 | - |
| ccosf | 1 + i 1 | 0 + i 1 | 1 + i 1 | - | 1 + i 1 |
| ccos | 1 + i 1 | 1 + i 1 | 1 + i 0 | - | 1 + i 1 |
| ccosl | 1 + i 1 | 1 + i 1 | - | 1 + i 1 | - |
| ccoshf | 1 + i 1 | 1 + i 1 | 1 + i 1 | - | 1 + i 1 |
| ccosh | 1 + i 1 | 1 + i 1 | 1 + i 0 | - | 1 + i 1 |
| ccoshl | 1 + i 1 | 0 + i 1 | - | 0 + i 1 | - |
| ceilf | - | - | - | - | - |
| ceil | - | - | - | - | - |
| ceill | - | - | - | - | - |
| cexpf | 1 + i 1 | 1 + i 2 | 1 + i 1 | - | 1 + i 2 |
| cexp | 1 + i 1 | 2 + i 1 | - | - | 2 + i 1 |
| cexpl | 1 + i 1 | 1 + i 1 | - | 1 + i 1 | - |
| cimagf | - | - | - | - | - |
| cimag | - | - | - | - | - |

| | | | | | |
|---|---|---|---|---|---|
| cimagl | - | - | - | - | - |
| clogf | 2 + i 0 | 1 + i 0 | 1 + i 0 | 2 + i 1 | 1 + i 1 |
| clog | 3 + i 1 | 1 + i 1 | - | 3 + i 1 | 1 + i 0 |
| clogl | 4 + i 1 | 1 + i 1 | - | 3 + i 1 | - |
| clog10f | 2 + i 0 | 2 + i 1 | 1 + i 1 | 2 + i 1 | 2 + i 1 |
| clog10 | 2 + i 1 | 2 + i 1 | 0 + i 1 | 2 + i 1 | 2 + i 1 |
| clog10l | 4 + i 2 | 1 + i 1 | - | 3 + i 2 | - |
| conjf | - | - | - | - | - |
| conj | - | - | - | - | - |
| conjl | - | - | - | - | - |
| copysignf | - | - | - | - | - |
| copysign | - | - | - | - | - |
| copysignl | - | - | - | - | - |
| cosf | - | - | 1 | - | 1 |
| cos | - | 1 | 2 | 1 | - |
| cosl | 1 | - | - | - | - |
| coshf | - | - | - | - | 1 |
| cosh | - | - | - | - | 1 |
| coshl | 2 | - | - | - | - |
| cpowf | 5 + i 1 | 5 + i 2 | 4 + i 2 | 3 + i 5 | 4 + i 2 |
| cpow | 2 + i 1 | 2 + i 0 | 2 + i 2 | 1 + i 0 | 2 + i 0 |
| cpowl | 3 + i 4 | 3 + i 4 | - | 3 + i 1 | - |
| cprojf | - | - | - | - | - |
| cproj | - | - | - | - | - |
| cprojl | - | - | - | - | - |
| crealf | - | - | - | - | - |
| creal | - | - | - | - | - |
| creall | - | - | - | - | - |
| csinf | 1 + i 1 | 1 + i 1 | - | - | 1 + i 0 |
| csin | 1 + i 1 | 1 + i 0 | - | - | 1 + i 0 |
| csinl | 1 + i 0 | 1 + i 0 | - | 1 + i 0 | - |
| csinhf | 1 + i 1 | 1 + i 1 | 1 + i 1 | - | 1 + i 1 |
| csinh | 1 + i 1 | 1 + i 1 | 0 + i 1 | - | 0 + i 1 |
| csinhl | 1 + i 1 | 1 + i 0 | - | 1 + i 0 | - |
| csqrtf | - | 1 + i 1 | 1 + i 0 | 1 + i 1 | 1 + i 1 |
| csqrt | 1 + i 1 | 1 + i 1 | - | 1 + i 1 | 1 + i 1 |
| csqrtl | 2 + i 2 | 1 + i 1 | - | 2 + i 2 | - |
| ctanf | 1 + i 1 | 1 + i 1 | - | 1 + i 1 | 1 + i 1 |
| ctan | 1 + i 1 | 1 + i 2 | 0 + i 1 | 1 + i 1 | 1 + i 2 |
| ctanl | 2 + i 1 | 2 + i 2 | - | 2 + i 2 | - |
| ctanhf | 1 + i 1 | 1 + i 1 | 2 + i 1 | 1 + i 2 | 1 + i 2 |
| ctanh | 1 + i 1 | 2 + i 2 | 1 + i 0 | 1 + i 1 | 2 + i 2 |
| ctanhl | 1 + i 2 | 1 + i 2 | - | 2 + i 2 | - |
| erff | 1 | - | - | 1 | - |
| erf | 1 | - | 1 | - | 1 |
| erfl | 1 | - | - | 1 | - |
| erfcf | 1 | - | - | 1 | 1 |

| | | | | | |
|---|---|---|---|---|---|
| erfc | 1 | - | 1 | - | 1 |
| erfcl | 2 | - | - | 2 | - |
| expf | - | - | - | - | - |
| exp | - | - | - | - | - |
| expl | 1 | - | - | - | - |
| exp10f | - | - | 2 | - | - |
| exp10 | - | - | 6 | - | 1 |
| exp10l | 1 | - | - | - | - |
| exp2f | - | - | - | - | - |
| exp2 | 1 | - | - | 1 | - |
| exp2l | 1 | - | - | - | - |
| expm1f | - | - | 1 | - | 1 |
| expm1 | - | - | 1 | - | 1 |
| expm1l | 2 | 1 | - | - | - |
| fabsf | - | - | - | - | - |
| fabs | - | - | - | - | - |
| fabsl | - | - | - | - | - |
| fdimf | - | - | - | - | - |
| fdim | - | - | - | - | - |
| fdiml | - | - | - | - | - |
| floorf | - | - | - | - | - |
| floor | - | - | - | - | - |
| floorl | - | - | - | - | - |
| fmaf | - | - | - | - | - |
| fma | - | - | - | - | - |
| fmal | - | - | - | - | - |
| fmaxf | - | - | - | - | - |
| fmax | - | - | - | - | - |
| fmaxl | - | - | - | - | - |
| fminf | - | - | - | - | - |
| fmin | - | - | - | - | - |
| fminl | - | - | - | - | - |
| fmodf | - | - | - | - | - |
| fmod | - | - | - | - | - |
| fmodl | - | - | - | - | - |
| frexpf | - | - | - | - | - |
| frexp | - | - | - | - | - |
| frexpl | - | - | - | - | - |
| gammaf | 1 | - | - | 1 | 1 |
| gamma | 1 | - | - | - | 1 |
| gammal | 2 | - | - | 2 | - |
| hypotf | - | - | 1 | - | - |
| hypot | - | - | - | 1 | 1 |
| hypotl | 1 | - | - | 1 | - |
| ilogbf | - | - | - | - | - |
| ilogb | - | - | - | - | - |
| ilogbl | - | - | - | - | - |

| | | | | | |
|---|---|---|---|---|---|
| j0f | 1 | 2 | 2 | 2 | 2 |
| j0 | 1 | 2 | 2 | 1 | 2 |
| j0l | 2 | 2 | - | 2 | - |
| j1f | 1 | 2 | 2 | 2 | 2 |
| j1 | 2 | 1 | 1 | - | 1 |
| j1l | 1 | 1 | - | 1 | - |
| jnf | 3 | 4 | 4 | 2 | 4 |
| jn | 2 | 4 | 4 | 2 | 4 |
| jnl | 4 | 4 | - | 4 | - |
| lgammaf | 1 | - | 2 | 1 | 1 |
| lgamma | 1 | - | 1 | - | 1 |
| lgammal | 2 | - | - | 2 | - |
| lrintf | - | - | - | - | - |
| lrint | - | - | - | - | - |
| lrintl | - | - | - | - | - |
| llrintf | - | - | - | - | - |
| llrint | - | - | - | - | - |
| llrintl | - | - | - | - | - |
| logf | - | - | - | - | 1 |
| log | - | - | - | - | - |
| logl | 1 | - | - | - | - |
| log10f | - | - | 2 | - | 2 |
| log10 | - | - | 1 | - | 1 |
| log10l | 1 | - | - | - | - |
| log1pf | - | - | 1 | - | 1 |
| log1p | - | - | - | - | - |
| log1pl | 2 | - | - | - | - |
| log2f | - | - | - | - | - |
| log2 | - | - | - | - | - |
| log2l | 1 | - | - | - | - |
| logbf | - | - | - | - | - |
| logb | - | - | - | - | - |
| logbl | - | - | - | - | - |
| lroundf | - | - | - | - | - |
| lround | - | - | - | - | - |
| lroundl | - | - | - | - | - |
| llroundf | - | - | - | - | - |
| llround | - | - | - | - | - |
| llroundl | - | - | - | - | - |
| modff | - | - | - | - | - |
| modf | - | - | - | - | - |
| modfl | - | - | - | - | - |
| nearbyintf | - | - | - | - | - |
| nearbyint | - | - | - | - | - |
| nearbyintl | - | - | - | - | - |
| nextafterf | - | - | - | - | - |
| nextafter | - | - | - | - | - |

| | | | | | |
|---|---|---|---|---|---|
| nextafterl | - | - | - | - | - |
| nexttowardf | - | - | - | - | - |
| nexttoward | - | - | - | - | - |
| nexttowardl | - | - | - | - | - |
| powf | - | - | - | 7 | 1 |
| pow | - | - | - | 1 | - |
| powl | 1 | - | - | 9 | - |
| remainderf | - | - | - | - | - |
| remainder | - | - | - | - | - |
| remainderl | - | - | - | - | - |
| remquof | - | - | - | - | - |
| remquo | - | - | - | - | - |
| remquol | - | - | - | - | - |
| rintf | - | - | - | - | - |
| rint | - | - | - | - | - |
| rintl | - | - | - | - | - |
| roundf | - | - | - | - | - |
| round | - | - | - | - | - |
| roundl | - | - | - | - | - |
| scalbf | - | - | - | - | - |
| scalb | - | - | - | - | - |
| scalbl | - | - | - | - | - |
| scalbnf | - | - | - | - | - |
| scalbn | - | - | - | - | - |
| scalbnl | - | - | - | - | - |
| scalblnf | - | - | - | - | - |
| scalbln | - | - | - | - | - |
| scalblnl | - | - | - | - | - |
| sinf | - | - | - | - | 1 |
| sin | - | 1 | - | 1 | - |
| sinl | 1 | - | - | - | - |
| sincosf | - | - | 1 | - | 1 |
| sincos | - | 1 | 1 | - | - |
| sincosl | 1 | - | - | - | - |
| sinhf | - | - | - | - | - |
| sinh | - | - | - | - | - |
| sinhl | 2 | - | - | - | - |
| sqrtf | - | - | - | - | - |
| sqrt | - | - | - | - | - |
| sqrtl | - | - | - | - | - |
| tanf | 1 | - | - | - | - |
| tan | - | - | 1 | - | - |
| tanl | 1 | - | - | - | - |
| tanhf | - | - | - | - | - |
| tanh | - | - | - | - | - |
| tanhl | 2 | - | - | - | - |
| tgammaf | 3 | - | 1 | 4 | 3 |

| | mips/mips32 | mips/mips64 | nios2 | PowerPC | powerpc/nofpu |
|---|---|---|---|---|---|
| tgamma | 2 | - | 1 | 1 | 4 |
| tgammal | 3 | 1 | - | 9 | - |
| truncf | - | - | - | - | - |
| trunc | - | - | - | - | - |
| truncl | - | - | - | - | - |
| y0f | 1 | 1 | 1 | 1 | 1 |
| y0 | 1 | 2 | 2 | 1 | 2 |
| y0l | 1 | 1 | - | 1 | - |
| y1f | 2 | 2 | 2 | 3 | 2 |
| y1 | 2 | 3 | 3 | 1 | 3 |
| y1l | 2 | 2 | - | 2 | - |
| ynf | 3 | 3 | 2 | 3 | 2 |
| yn | 2 | 3 | 3 | 2 | 3 |
| ynl | 4 | 2 | - | 4 | - |

| Function | mips/mips32 | mips/mips64 | nios2 | PowerPC | powerpc/nofpu |
|---|---|---|---|---|---|
| acosf | 1 | 1 | 1 | 1 | 1 |
| acos | - | - | - | - | - |
| acosl | - | - | - | 1 | 1 |
| acoshf | 2 | 2 | 2 | 2 | 2 |
| acosh | 1 | 1 | 1 | 1 | 1 |
| acoshl | - | 1 | - | 1 | 1 |
| asinf | 1 | 1 | 1 | 1 | 1 |
| asin | - | - | - | - | - |
| asinl | - | 1 | - | 2 | 2 |
| asinhf | 1 | 1 | 1 | 1 | 1 |
| asinh | 1 | 1 | 1 | 1 | 1 |
| asinhl | - | 1 | - | 2 | 2 |
| atanf | 1 | 1 | 1 | 1 | 1 |
| atan | - | - | - | 1 | - |
| atanl | - | 1 | - | 1 | 1 |
| atanhf | 2 | 2 | 2 | 2 | 2 |
| atanh | 1 | 1 | 1 | 1 | 1 |
| atanhl | - | 2 | - | 2 | 2 |
| atan2f | 1 | 1 | 1 | 1 | 1 |
| atan2 | - | - | - | - | - |
| atan2l | - | 1 | - | 2 | 2 |
| cabsf | - | - | - | - | - |
| cabs | 1 | 1 | 1 | 1 | 1 |
| cabsl | - | - | - | 1 | 1 |
| cacosf | 2 + i 2 | 2 + i 2 | 2 + i 2 | 2 + i 2 | 2 + i 2 |
| cacos | 1 + i 1 | 1 + i 1 | 1 + i 1 | 1 + i 1 | 1 + i 1 |
| cacosl | - | 2 + i 2 | - | 1 + i 2 | 2 + i 1 |
| cacoshf | 2 + i 2 | 2 + i 2 | 2 + i 2 | 2 + i 2 | 2 + i 2 |
| cacosh | 1 + i 1 | 1 + i 1 | 1 + i 1 | 1 + i 1 | 1 + i 1 |
| cacoshl | - | 2 + i 2 | - | 2 + i 1 | 1 + i 2 |
| cargf | 1 | 1 | 1 | 1 | 1 |

| | | | | | |
|---|---|---|---|---|---|
| carg | - | - | - | - | - |
| cargl | - | 1 | - | 1 | 1 |
| casinf | 1 + i 2 | 1 + i 2 | 1 + i 2 | 1 + i 2 | 1 + i 2 |
| casin | 1 + i 1 | 1 + i 1 | 1 + i 1 | 1 + i 1 | 1 + i 1 |
| casinl | - | 2 + i 2 | - | 1 + i 2 | 2 + i 1 |
| casinhf | 2 + i 1 | 2 + i 1 | 2 + i 1 | 2 + i 1 | 2 + i 1 |
| casinh | 1 + i 1 | 1 + i 1 | 1 + i 1 | 1 + i 1 | 1 + i 1 |
| casinhl | - | 2 + i 2 | - | 2 + i 1 | 1 + i 2 |
| catanf | 1 + i 1 | 1 + i 1 | 1 + i 1 | 1 + i 1 | 1 + i 1 |
| catan | 0 + i 1 | 0 + i 1 | 0 + i 1 | 0 + i 1 | 0 + i 1 |
| catanl | - | 1 + i 1 | - | 1 + i 1 | 1 + i 1 |
| catanhf | 1 + i 1 | 1 + i 1 | 1 + i 1 | 1 + i 1 | 1 + i 1 |
| catanh | 1 + i 0 | 1 + i 0 | 1 + i 0 | 1 + i 0 | 1 + i 0 |
| catanhl | - | 1 + i 1 | - | 1 + i 1 | 1 + i 1 |
| cbrtf | 1 | 1 | 1 | 1 | 1 |
| cbrt | 3 | 3 | 3 | 3 | 3 |
| cbrtl | - | 1 | - | 1 | 1 |
| ccosf | 1 + i 1 | 1 + i 1 | 1 + i 1 | 1 + i 1 | 1 + i 1 |
| ccos | 1 + i 1 | 1 + i 1 | 1 + i 1 | 1 + i 1 | 1 + i 1 |
| ccosl | - | 1 + i 1 | - | 1 + i 1 | 1 + i 2 |
| ccoshf | 1 + i 1 | 1 + i 1 | 1 + i 1 | 1 + i 1 | 1 + i 1 |
| ccosh | 1 + i 1 | 1 + i 1 | 1 + i 1 | 1 + i 1 | 1 + i 1 |
| ccoshl | - | 1 + i 1 | - | 1 + i 2 | 1 + i 2 |
| ceilf | - | - | - | - | - |
| ceil | - | - | - | - | - |
| ceill | - | - | - | - | - |
| cexpf | 1 + i 2 | 1 + i 2 | 1 + i 2 | 1 + i 2 | 1 + i 2 |
| cexp | 2 + i 1 | 2 + i 1 | 2 + i 1 | 2 + i 1 | 2 + i 1 |
| cexpl | - | 1 + i 1 | - | 2 + i 2 | 1 + i 1 |
| cimagf | - | - | - | - | - |
| cimag | - | - | - | - | - |
| cimagl | - | - | - | - | - |
| clogf | 2 + i 1 | 2 + i 1 | 2 + i 1 | 3 + i 1 | 2 + i 1 |
| clog | 3 + i 0 | 3 + i 0 | 3 + i 0 | 3 + i 1 | 3 + i 0 |
| clogl | - | 4 + i 1 | - | 5 + i 2 | 5 + i 2 |
| clog10f | 3 + i 2 | 3 + i 2 | 3 + i 2 | 3 + i 2 | 3 + i 2 |
| clog10 | 3 + i 2 | 3 + i 2 | 3 + i 2 | 3 + i 1 | 3 + i 2 |
| clog10l | - | 4 + i 2 | - | 3 + i 2 | 3 + i 2 |
| conjf | - | - | - | - | - |
| conj | - | - | - | - | - |
| conjl | - | - | - | - | - |
| copysignf | - | - | - | - | - |
| copysign | - | - | - | - | - |
| copysignl | - | - | - | - | - |
| cosf | 1 | 1 | 1 | 1 | 1 |
| cos | - | - | - | - | - |
| cosl | - | 1 | - | 4 | 4 |

| | | | | | |
|---|---|---|---|---|---|
| coshf | 1 | 1 | 1 | 1 | 1 |
| cosh | 1 | 1 | 1 | 1 | 1 |
| coshl | - | 1 | - | 3 | 3 |
| cpowf | 4 + i 2 | 4 + i 2 | 4 + i 2 | 5 + i 2 | 4 + i 2 |
| cpow | 2 + i 0 | 2 + i 0 | 2 + i 0 | 2 + i 0 | 2 + i 0 |
| cpowl | - | 4 + i 1 | - | 4 + i 2 | 4 + i 1 |
| cprojf | - | - | - | - | - |
| cproj | - | - | - | - | - |
| cprojl | - | - | - | - | - |
| crealf | - | - | - | - | - |
| creal | - | - | - | - | - |
| creall | - | - | - | - | - |
| csinf | 1 + i 0 | 1 + i 0 | 1 + i 0 | 1 + i 0 | 1 + i 0 |
| csin | 1 + i 0 | 1 + i 0 | 1 + i 0 | 1 + i 0 | 1 + i 0 |
| csinl | - | 1 + i 1 | - | 1 + i 1 | 2 + i 1 |
| csinhf | 1 + i 1 | 1 + i 1 | 1 + i 1 | 1 + i 1 | 1 + i 1 |
| csinh | 0 + i 1 | 0 + i 1 | 0 + i 1 | 0 + i 1 | 0 + i 1 |
| csinhl | - | 1 + i 1 | - | 1 + i 1 | 1 + i 2 |
| csqrtf | 2 + i 2 | 2 + i 2 | 2 + i 2 | 2 + i 2 | 2 + i 2 |
| csqrt | 2 + i 2 | 2 + i 2 | 2 + i 2 | 2 + i 2 | 2 + i 2 |
| csqrtl | - | 1 + i 1 | - | 1 + i 1 | 1 + i 1 |
| ctanf | 1 + i 1 | 1 + i 1 | 1 + i 1 | 1 + i 1 | 1 + i 1 |
| ctan | 1 + i 2 | 1 + i 2 | 1 + i 2 | 1 + i 2 | 1 + i 2 |
| ctanl | - | 3 + i 3 | - | 2 + i 2 | 3 + i 2 |
| ctanhf | 1 + i 2 | 1 + i 2 | 1 + i 2 | 2 + i 1 | 1 + i 2 |
| ctanh | 2 + i 2 | 2 + i 2 | 2 + i 2 | 2 + i 2 | 2 + i 2 |
| ctanhl | - | 3 + i 3 | - | 3 + i 2 | 2 + i 3 |
| erff | 1 | 1 | 1 | 1 | 1 |
| erf | 1 | 1 | 1 | 1 | 1 |
| erfl | - | 1 | - | 1 | 1 |
| erfcf | 2 | 2 | 2 | 2 | 2 |
| erfc | 2 | 2 | 2 | 2 | 2 |
| erfcl | - | 2 | - | 2 | 3 |
| expf | - | - | - | - | - |
| exp | - | - | - | - | - |
| expl | - | - | - | 1 | 1 |
| exp10f | - | - | - | - | - |
| exp10 | 2 | 2 | 2 | 2 | 2 |
| exp10l | - | 1 | - | 1 | 1 |
| exp2f | 1 | 1 | 1 | - | 1 |
| exp2 | 1 | 1 | 1 | 1 | 1 |
| exp2l | - | 1 | - | 1 | 1 |
| expm1f | 1 | 1 | 1 | 1 | 1 |
| expm1 | 1 | 1 | 1 | 1 | 1 |
| expm1l | - | 1 | - | 1 | 1 |
| fabsf | - | - | - | - | - |
| fabs | - | - | - | - | - |

| | | | | | |
|---|---|---|---|---|---|
| fabsl | - | - | - | - | - |
| fdimf | - | - | - | - | - |
| fdim | - | - | - | - | - |
| fdiml | - | - | - | - | - |
| floorf | - | - | - | - | - |
| floor | - | - | - | - | - |
| floorl | - | - | - | - | - |
| fmaf | - | - | - | - | - |
| fma | - | - | - | - | - |
| fmal | - | - | - | 1 | 1 |
| fmaxf | - | - | - | - | - |
| fmax | - | - | - | - | - |
| fmaxl | - | - | - | - | - |
| fminf | - | - | - | - | - |
| fmin | - | - | - | - | - |
| fminl | - | - | - | - | - |
| fmodf | - | - | - | - | - |
| fmod | - | - | - | - | - |
| fmodl | - | - | - | - | - |
| frexpf | - | - | - | - | - |
| frexp | - | - | - | - | - |
| frexpl | - | - | - | - | - |
| gammaf | 2 | 2 | 2 | 1 | 2 |
| gamma | 2 | 2 | 2 | 1 | 2 |
| gammal | - | 1 | - | 1 | 1 |
| hypotf | - | - | - | - | - |
| hypot | 1 | 1 | 1 | 1 | 1 |
| hypotl | - | 1 | - | 1 | 1 |
| ilogbf | - | - | - | - | - |
| ilogb | - | - | - | - | - |
| ilogbl | - | - | - | - | - |
| j0f | 2 | 2 | 2 | 2 | 2 |
| j0 | 2 | 2 | 2 | 2 | 2 |
| j0l | - | 2 | - | 2 | 2 |
| j1f | 2 | 2 | 2 | 2 | 2 |
| j1 | 1 | 1 | 1 | 1 | 1 |
| j1l | - | 4 | - | 1 | 1 |
| jnf | 4 | 4 | 4 | 4 | 4 |
| jn | 4 | 4 | 4 | 4 | 4 |
| jnl | - | 7 | - | 4 | 4 |
| lgammaf | 2 | 2 | 2 | 1 | 2 |
| lgamma | 2 | 2 | 2 | 1 | 2 |
| lgammal | - | 1 | - | 1 | 1 |
| lrintf | - | - | - | - | - |
| lrint | - | - | - | - | - |
| lrintl | - | - | - | - | - |
| llrintf | - | - | - | - | - |

| | | | | | |
|---|---|---|---|---|---|
| llrint | - | - | - | - | - |
| llrintl | - | - | - | - | - |
| logf | 1 | 1 | 1 | 1 | 1 |
| log | - | - | - | - | - |
| logl | - | 1 | - | 1 | 1 |
| log10f | 2 | 2 | 2 | 2 | 2 |
| log10 | 2 | 2 | 2 | 2 | 2 |
| log10l | - | 1 | - | 1 | 1 |
| log1pf | 1 | 1 | 1 | 1 | 1 |
| log1p | 1 | 1 | 1 | 1 | 1 |
| log1pl | - | 1 | - | 1 | 1 |
| log2f | 1 | 1 | 1 | 1 | 1 |
| log2 | 2 | 2 | 2 | 1 | 2 |
| log2l | - | 1 | - | 1 | 1 |
| logbf | - | - | - | - | - |
| logb | - | - | - | - | - |
| logbl | - | - | - | - | - |
| lroundf | - | - | - | - | - |
| lround | - | - | - | - | - |
| lroundl | - | - | - | - | - |
| llroundf | - | - | - | - | - |
| llround | - | - | - | - | - |
| llroundl | - | - | - | - | - |
| modff | - | - | - | - | - |
| modf | - | - | - | - | - |
| modfl | - | - | - | - | - |
| nearbyintf | - | - | - | - | - |
| nearbyint | - | - | - | - | - |
| nearbyintl | - | - | - | - | - |
| nextafterf | - | - | - | - | - |
| nextafter | - | - | - | - | - |
| nextafterl | - | - | - | - | - |
| nexttowardf | - | - | - | - | - |
| nexttoward | - | - | - | - | - |
| nexttowardl | - | - | - | - | - |
| powf | 3 | 3 | 3 | 1 | 3 |
| pow | - | - | - | - | - |
| powl | - | 1 | - | 1 | 1 |
| remainderf | - | - | - | - | - |
| remainder | - | - | - | - | - |
| remainderl | - | - | - | - | - |
| remquof | - | - | - | - | - |
| remquo | - | - | - | - | - |
| remquol | - | - | - | - | - |
| rintf | - | - | - | - | - |
| rint | - | - | - | - | - |
| rintl | - | - | - | - | - |

| Function | S/390 | sh | sparc/fpu | tile | x86_64/fpu |
|---|---|---|---|---|---|
| roundf | - | - | - | - | - |
| round | - | - | - | - | - |
| roundl | - | - | - | - | - |
| scalbf | - | - | - | - | - |
| scalb | - | - | - | - | - |
| scalbl | - | - | - | - | - |
| scalbnf | - | - | - | - | - |
| scalbn | - | - | - | - | - |
| scalbnl | - | - | - | - | - |
| scalblnf | - | - | - | - | - |
| scalbln | - | - | - | - | - |
| scalblnl | - | - | - | - | - |
| sinf | 1 | 1 | 1 | 1 | 1 |
| sin | - | - | - | - | - |
| sinl | - | 1 | - | 1 | 1 |
| sincosf | 1 | 1 | 1 | 1 | 1 |
| sincos | - | - | - | - | - |
| sincosl | - | 1 | - | 1 | 1 |
| sinhf | 2 | 2 | 2 | 2 | 2 |
| sinh | 2 | 2 | 2 | 2 | 2 |
| sinhl | - | 1 | - | 2 | 2 |
| sqrtf | - | - | - | - | - |
| sqrt | - | - | - | - | - |
| sqrtl | - | - | - | 1 | 1 |
| tanf | 1 | 1 | 1 | 1 | 1 |
| tan | - | - | - | - | - |
| tanl | - | - | - | 2 | 2 |
| tanhf | 2 | 2 | 2 | 2 | 2 |
| tanh | 2 | 2 | 2 | 2 | 2 |
| tanhl | - | 1 | - | 1 | 1 |
| tgammaf | 5 | 5 | 5 | 3 | 5 |
| tgamma | 3 | 3 | 4 | 3 | 3 |
| tgammal | - | 4 | - | 5 | 3 |
| truncf | - | - | - | - | - |
| trunc | - | - | - | - | - |
| truncl | - | - | - | - | - |
| y0f | 1 | 1 | 1 | 1 | 1 |
| y0 | 2 | 2 | 2 | 2 | 2 |
| y0l | - | 3 | - | 1 | 1 |
| y1f | 2 | 2 | 2 | 2 | 2 |
| y1 | 3 | 3 | 3 | 3 | 3 |
| y1l | - | 2 | - | 2 | 2 |
| ynf | 2 | 2 | 2 | 2 | 2 |
| yn | 3 | 3 | 3 | 3 | 3 |
| ynl | - | 5 | - | 2 | 2 |

| | | | | | |
|---|---|---|---|---|---|
| acosf | 1 | - | 1 | 1 | 1 |
| acos | - | - | - | - | - |
| acosl | - | - | - | - | 1 |
| acoshf | 2 | - | 2 | 2 | 2 |
| acosh | 1 | 1 | 1 | 1 | 1 |
| acoshl | 1 | - | 1 | - | 2 |
| asinf | 1 | - | 1 | 1 | 1 |
| asin | - | - | - | - | - |
| asinl | 1 | - | 1 | - | 1 |
| asinhf | 1 | 1 | 1 | 1 | 1 |
| asinh | 1 | 1 | 1 | 1 | 1 |
| asinhl | 1 | - | 1 | - | 2 |
| atanf | 1 | - | 1 | 1 | 1 |
| atan | 1 | - | - | - | - |
| atanl | 1 | - | 1 | - | 1 |
| atanhf | 2 | 1 | 2 | 2 | 2 |
| atanh | 1 | - | 1 | 1 | 1 |
| atanhl | 2 | - | 2 | - | 3 |
| atan2f | 1 | 1 | 1 | 1 | 1 |
| atan2 | - | - | - | - | - |
| atan2l | 1 | - | 1 | - | 1 |
| cabsf | - | - | - | - | - |
| cabs | 1 | - | 1 | 1 | 1 |
| cabsl | - | - | - | - | 1 |
| cacosf | 2 + i 2 | 2 + i 2 | 2 + i 2 | 2 + i 2 | 2 + i 2 |
| cacos | 1 + i 1 | 1 + i 1 | 1 + i 1 | 1 + i 1 | 1 + i 1 |
| cacosl | 2 + i 2 | - | 2 + i 2 | - | 1 + i 2 |
| cacoshf | 2 + i 2 | 2 + i 2 | 2 + i 2 | 2 + i 2 | 2 + i 2 |
| cacosh | 1 + i 1 | 1 + i 1 | 1 + i 1 | 1 + i 1 | 1 + i 1 |
| cacoshl | 2 + i 2 | - | 2 + i 2 | - | 2 + i 1 |
| cargf | 1 | - | 1 | 1 | 1 |
| carg | - | - | - | - | - |
| cargl | 1 | - | 1 | - | 1 |
| casinf | 1 + i 2 | 1 + i 2 | 1 + i 2 | 1 + i 2 | 1 + i 2 |
| casin | 1 + i 1 | 1 + i 1 | 1 + i 1 | 1 + i 1 | 1 + i 1 |
| casinl | 2 + i 2 | - | 2 + i 2 | - | 1 + i 2 |
| casinhf | 2 + i 1 | 2 + i 1 | 2 + i 1 | 2 + i 1 | 2 + i 1 |
| casinh | 1 + i 1 | 1 + i 1 | 1 + i 1 | 1 + i 1 | 1 + i 1 |
| casinhl | 2 + i 2 | - | 2 + i 2 | - | 2 + i 1 |
| catanf | 1 + i 1 | 1 + i 1 | 1 + i 1 | 1 + i 1 | 1 + i 1 |
| catan | 0 + i 1 | 0 + i 1 | 0 + i 1 | 0 + i 1 | 0 + i 1 |
| catanl | 1 + i 1 | - | 1 + i 1 | - | 0 + i 1 |
| catanhf | 1 + i 1 | 1 + i 1 | 1 + i 1 | 1 + i 1 | 1 + i 1 |
| catanh | 1 + i 0 | 1 + i 0 | 1 + i 0 | 1 + i 0 | 1 + i 0 |
| catanhl | 1 + i 1 | - | 1 + i 1 | - | 1 + i 0 |
| cbrtf | 1 | 1 | 1 | 1 | 1 |
| cbrt | 3 | 1 | 3 | 3 | 3 |

| | | | | | |
|---|---|---|---|---|---|
| cbrtl | 1 | - | 1 | - | 1 |
| ccosf | 1 + i 1 | 1 + i 1 | 1 + i 1 | 1 + i 1 | 1 + i 1 |
| ccos | 1 + i 1 | 1 + i 1 | 1 + i 1 | 1 + i 1 | 1 + i 1 |
| ccosl | 1 + i 1 | - | 1 + i 1 | - | 1 + i 1 |
| ccoshf | 1 + i 1 | 1 + i 1 | 1 + i 1 | 1 + i 1 | 1 + i 1 |
| ccosh | 1 + i 1 | 1 + i 1 | 1 + i 1 | 1 + i 1 | 1 + i 1 |
| ccoshl | 1 + i 1 | - | 1 + i 1 | - | 1 + i 1 |
| ceilf | - | - | - | - | - |
| ceil | - | - | - | - | - |
| ceill | - | - | - | - | - |
| cexpf | 1 + i 2 | 1 + i 2 | 1 + i 2 | 1 + i 2 | 1 + i 2 |
| cexp | 2 + i 1 | 2 + i 1 | 2 + i 1 | 2 + i 1 | 2 + i 1 |
| cexpl | 1 + i 1 | - | 1 + i 1 | - | 1 + i 1 |
| cimagf | - | - | - | - | - |
| cimag | - | - | - | - | - |
| cimagl | - | - | - | - | - |
| clogf | 3 + i 1 | 1 + i 1 | 2 + i 1 | 2 + i 1 | 2 + i 1 |
| clog | 3 + i 1 | 1 + i 0 | 3 + i 0 | 3 + i 0 | 3 + i 0 |
| clogl | 4 + i 1 | - | 4 + i 1 | - | 4 + i 1 |
| clog10f | 3 + i 2 | 2 + i 1 | 3 + i 2 | 3 + i 2 | 3 + i 2 |
| clog10 | 3 + i 1 | 2 + i 1 | 3 + i 2 | 3 + i 2 | 3 + i 2 |
| clog10l | 4 + i 2 | - | 4 + i 2 | - | 4 + i 2 |
| conjf | - | - | - | - | - |
| conj | - | - | - | - | - |
| conjl | - | - | - | - | - |
| copysignf | - | - | - | - | - |
| copysign | - | - | - | - | - |
| copysignl | - | - | - | - | - |
| cosf | 1 | 1 | 1 | 1 | - |
| cos | - | - | - | - | - |
| cosl | 1 | - | 1 | - | 1 |
| coshf | 1 | 1 | 1 | 1 | 1 |
| cosh | 1 | 1 | 1 | 1 | 1 |
| coshl | 1 | - | 1 | - | 2 |
| cpowf | 5 + i 2 | 4 + i 2 | 4 + i 2 | 4 + i 2 | 5 + i 2 |
| cpow | 2 + i 0 | 2 + i 0 | 2 + i 0 | 2 + i 0 | 2 + i 0 |
| cpowl | 4 + i 1 | - | 4 + i 1 | - | 3 + i 4 |
| cprojf | - | - | - | - | - |
| cproj | - | - | - | - | - |
| cprojl | - | - | - | - | - |
| crealf | - | - | - | - | - |
| creal | - | - | - | - | - |
| creall | - | - | - | - | - |
| csinf | 1 + i 0 | 1 + i 0 | 1 + i 0 | 1 + i 0 | 1 + i 0 |
| csin | 1 + i 0 | 1 + i 0 | 1 + i 0 | 1 + i 0 | 1 + i 0 |
| csinl | 1 + i 1 | - | 1 + i 1 | - | 1 + i 0 |
| csinhf | 1 + i 1 | 1 + i 1 | 1 + i 1 | 1 + i 1 | 1 + i 1 |

| | | | | | |
|---|---|---|---|---|---|
| csinh | 0 + i 1 | 0 + i 1 | 0 + i 1 | 0 + i 1 | 0 + i 1 |
| csinhl | 1 + i 1 | - | 1 + i 1 | - | 1 + i 1 |
| csqrtf | 2 + i 2 | 1 + i 1 | 2 + i 2 | 2 + i 2 | 2 + i 2 |
| csqrt | 2 + i 2 | 1 + i 1 | 2 + i 2 | 2 + i 2 | 2 + i 2 |
| csqrtl | 1 + i 1 | - | 1 + i 1 | - | 2 + i 2 |
| ctanf | 1 + i 1 | 1 + i 1 | 1 + i 1 | 1 + i 1 | 1 + i 2 |
| ctan | 1 + i 2 | 1 + i 2 | 1 + i 2 | 1 + i 2 | 1 + i 2 |
| ctanl | 3 + i 3 | - | 3 + i 3 | - | 2 + i 1 |
| ctanhf | 2 + i 1 | 1 + i 2 | 1 + i 2 | 1 + i 2 | 2 + i 2 |
| ctanh | 2 + i 2 | 2 + i 2 | 2 + i 2 | 2 + i 2 | 2 + i 2 |
| ctanhl | 3 + i 3 | - | 3 + i 3 | - | 1 + i 2 |
| erff | 1 | - | 1 | 1 | 1 |
| erf | 1 | 1 | 1 | 1 | 1 |
| erfl | 1 | - | 1 | - | 1 |
| erfcf | 2 | 1 | 2 | 2 | 2 |
| erfc | 2 | 1 | 2 | 2 | 2 |
| erfcl | 2 | - | 2 | - | 2 |
| expf | - | - | - | - | - |
| exp | - | - | - | - | - |
| expl | - | - | - | - | 1 |
| exp10f | - | - | - | - | - |
| exp10 | 2 | 1 | 2 | 2 | 2 |
| exp10l | 1 | - | 1 | - | 1 |
| exp2f | - | - | 1 | 1 | 1 |
| exp2 | 1 | - | 1 | 1 | 1 |
| exp2l | 1 | - | 1 | - | 1 |
| expm1f | 1 | 1 | 1 | 1 | 1 |
| expm1 | 1 | 1 | 1 | 1 | 1 |
| expm1l | 1 | - | 1 | - | 2 |
| fabsf | - | - | - | - | - |
| fabs | - | - | - | - | - |
| fabsl | - | - | - | - | - |
| fdimf | - | - | - | - | - |
| fdim | - | - | - | - | - |
| fdiml | - | - | - | - | - |
| floorf | - | - | - | - | - |
| floor | - | - | - | - | - |
| floorl | - | - | - | - | - |
| fmaf | - | - | - | - | - |
| fma | - | - | - | - | - |
| fmal | - | - | - | - | - |
| fmaxf | - | - | - | - | - |
| fmax | - | - | - | - | - |
| fmaxl | - | - | - | - | - |
| fminf | - | - | - | - | - |
| fmin | - | - | - | - | - |
| fminl | - | - | - | - | - |

| | | | | | |
|---|---|---|---|---|---|
| fmodf | - | - | - | - | - |
| fmod | - | - | - | - | - |
| fmodl | - | - | - | - | - |
| frexpf | - | - | - | - | - |
| frexp | - | - | - | - | - |
| frexpl | - | - | - | - | - |
| gammaf | 1 | 1 | 2 | 2 | 2 |
| gamma | 1 | 1 | 2 | 2 | 2 |
| gammal | 1 | - | 1 | - | 2 |
| hypotf | - | - | - | - | - |
| hypot | 1 | 1 | 1 | 1 | 1 |
| hypotl | 1 | - | 1 | - | 1 |
| ilogbf | - | - | - | - | - |
| ilogb | - | - | - | - | - |
| ilogbl | - | - | - | - | - |
| j0f | 2 | 2 | 2 | 2 | 2 |
| j0 | 2 | 2 | 2 | 2 | 2 |
| j0l | 2 | - | 2 | - | 2 |
| j1f | 2 | 2 | 2 | 2 | 2 |
| j1 | 1 | 1 | 1 | 1 | 1 |
| j1l | 4 | - | 4 | - | 1 |
| jnf | 4 | 4 | 4 | 4 | 4 |
| jn | 4 | 4 | 4 | 4 | 4 |
| jnl | 7 | - | 7 | - | 4 |
| lgammaf | 1 | 1 | 2 | 2 | 2 |
| lgamma | 1 | 1 | 2 | 2 | 2 |
| lgammal | 1 | - | 1 | - | 2 |
| lrintf | - | - | - | - | - |
| lrint | - | - | - | - | - |
| lrintl | - | - | - | - | - |
| llrintf | - | - | - | - | - |
| llrint | - | - | - | - | - |
| llrintl | - | - | - | - | - |
| logf | 1 | 1 | 1 | 1 | 1 |
| log | - | - | - | - | - |
| logl | 1 | - | 1 | - | 1 |
| log10f | 2 | 2 | 2 | 2 | 2 |
| log10 | 2 | 1 | 2 | 2 | 2 |
| log10l | 1 | - | 1 | - | 1 |
| log1pf | 1 | 1 | 1 | 1 | 1 |
| log1p | 1 | - | 1 | 1 | 1 |
| log1pl | 1 | - | 1 | - | 2 |
| log2f | 1 | - | 1 | 1 | 1 |
| log2 | 1 | - | 2 | 2 | 2 |
| log2l | 1 | - | 1 | - | 1 |
| logbf | - | - | - | - | - |
| logb | - | - | - | - | - |

| | | | | | |
|---|---|---|---|---|---|
| logbl | - | - | - | - | - |
| lroundf | - | - | - | - | - |
| lround | - | - | - | - | - |
| lroundl | - | - | - | - | - |
| llroundf | - | - | - | - | - |
| llround | - | - | - | - | - |
| llroundl | - | - | - | - | - |
| modff | - | - | - | - | - |
| modf | - | - | - | - | - |
| modfl | - | - | - | - | - |
| nearbyintf | - | - | - | - | - |
| nearbyint | - | - | - | - | - |
| nearbyintl | - | - | - | - | - |
| nextafterf | - | - | - | - | - |
| nextafter | - | - | - | - | - |
| nextafterl | - | - | - | - | - |
| nexttowardf | - | - | - | - | - |
| nexttoward | - | - | - | - | - |
| nexttowardl | - | - | - | - | - |
| powf | 1 | 1 | 3 | 3 | 3 |
| pow | - | - | - | - | - |
| powl | 1 | - | 1 | - | 1 |
| remainderf | - | - | - | - | - |
| remainder | - | - | - | - | - |
| remainderl | - | - | - | - | - |
| remquof | - | - | - | - | - |
| remquo | - | - | - | - | - |
| remquol | - | - | - | - | - |
| rintf | - | - | - | - | - |
| rint | - | - | - | - | - |
| rintl | - | - | - | - | - |
| roundf | - | - | - | - | - |
| round | - | - | - | - | - |
| roundl | - | - | - | - | - |
| scalbf | - | - | - | - | - |
| scalb | - | - | - | - | - |
| scalbl | - | - | - | - | - |
| scalbnf | - | - | - | - | - |
| scalbn | - | - | - | - | - |
| scalbnl | - | - | - | - | - |
| scalblnf | - | - | - | - | - |
| scalbln | - | - | - | - | - |
| scalblnl | - | - | - | - | - |
| sinf | 1 | 1 | 1 | 1 | - |
| sin | - | - | - | - | - |
| sinl | 1 | - | 1 | - | 1 |
| sincosf | 1 | 1 | 1 | 1 | - |

| | | | | | |
|---|---|---|---|---|---|
| sincos | - | - | - | - | - |
| sincosl | 1 | - | 1 | - | 1 |
| sinhf | 2 | - | 2 | 2 | 2 |
| sinh | 2 | - | 2 | 2 | 2 |
| sinhl | 1 | - | 1 | - | 2 |
| sqrtf | - | - | - | - | - |
| sqrt | - | - | - | - | - |
| sqrtl | - | - | - | - | - |
| tanf | 1 | - | 1 | 1 | 1 |
| tan | - | - | - | - | - |
| tanl | - | - | - | - | 1 |
| tanhf | 2 | - | 2 | 2 | 2 |
| tanh | 2 | - | 2 | 2 | 2 |
| tanhl | 1 | - | 1 | - | 2 |
| tgammaf | 3 | 3 | 5 | 5 | 5 |
| tgamma | 3 | 4 | 4 | 3 | 4 |
| tgammal | 4 | - | 4 | - | 3 |
| truncf | - | - | - | - | - |
| trunc | - | - | - | - | - |
| truncl | - | - | - | - | - |
| y0f | 1 | 1 | 1 | 1 | 1 |
| y0 | 2 | 2 | 2 | 2 | 2 |
| y0l | 3 | - | 3 | - | 1 |
| y1f | 2 | 2 | 2 | 2 | 2 |
| y1 | 3 | 3 | 3 | 3 | 3 |
| y1l | 2 | - | 2 | - | 2 |
| ynf | 2 | 2 | 2 | 2 | 3 |
| yn | 3 | 3 | 3 | 3 | 3 |
| ynl | 5 | - | 5 | - | 4 |

## 19.8 Pseudo-Random Numbers

This section describes the GNU facilities for generating a series of pseudo-random numbers. The numbers generated are not truly random; typically, they form a sequence that repeats periodically, with a period so large that you can ignore it for ordinary purposes. The random number generator works by remembering a *seed* value which it uses to compute the next random number and also to compute a new seed.

Although the generated numbers look unpredictable within one run of a program, the sequence of numbers is *exactly the same* from one run to the next. This is because the initial seed is always the same. This is convenient when you are debugging a program, but it is unhelpful if you want the program to behave unpredictably. If you want a different pseudo-random series each time your program runs, you must specify a different seed each time. For ordinary purposes, basing the seed on the current time works well.

You can obtain repeatable sequences of numbers on a particular machine type by specifying the same initial seed value for the random number generator. There is no standard meaning for a particular seed value; the same seed, used in different C libraries or on different CPU types, will give you different random numbers.

The GNU C Library supports the standard ISO C random number functions plus two other sets derived from BSD and SVID. The BSD and ISO C functions provide identical, somewhat limited functionality. If only a small number of random bits are required, we recommend you use the ISO C interface, **rand** and **srand**. The SVID functions provide a more flexible interface, which allows better random number generator algorithms, provides more random bits (up to 48) per call, and can provide random floating-point numbers. These functions are required by the XPG standard and therefore will be present in all modern Unix systems.

## 19.8.1 ISO C Random Number Functions

This section describes the random number functions that are part of the ISO C standard.

To use these facilities, you should include the header file **stdlib.h** in your program.

int RAND_MAX                                                                             [Macro]
> The value of this macro is an integer constant representing the largest value the **rand** function can return. In the GNU C Library, it is 2147483647, which is the largest signed integer representable in 32 bits. In other libraries, it may be as low as 32767.

int rand (*void*)                                                                        [Function]
> Preliminary: | MT-Safe | AS-Unsafe lock | AC-Unsafe lock | See Section 1.2.2.1 [POSIX Safety Concepts], page 2.

> The **rand** function returns the next pseudo-random number in the series. The value ranges from 0 to RAND_MAX.

void srand (*unsigned int seed*)                                                         [Function]
> Preliminary: | MT-Safe | AS-Unsafe lock | AC-Unsafe lock | See Section 1.2.2.1 [POSIX Safety Concepts], page 2.

> This function establishes *seed* as the seed for a new series of pseudo-random numbers. If you call **rand** before a seed has been established with **srand**, it uses the value 1 as a default seed.

> To produce a different pseudo-random series each time your program is run, do **srand (time (0))**.

POSIX.1 extended the C standard functions to support reproducible random numbers in multi-threaded programs. However, the extension is badly designed and unsuitable for serious work.

int rand_r (*unsigned int *seed*)                                                        [Function]
> Preliminary: | MT-Safe | AS-Safe | AC-Safe | See Section 1.2.2.1 [POSIX Safety Concepts], page 2.

> This function returns a random number in the range 0 to RAND_MAX just as **rand** does. However, all its state is stored in the *seed* argument. This means the RNG's state can only have as many bits as the type **unsigned int** has. This is far too few to provide a good RNG.

> If your program requires a reentrant RNG, we recommend you use the reentrant GNU extensions to the SVID random number generator. The POSIX.1 interface should only be used when the GNU extensions are not available.

## 19.8.2 BSD Random Number Functions

This section describes a set of random number generation functions that are derived from BSD. There is no advantage to using these functions with the GNU C Library; we support them for BSD compatibility only.

The prototypes for these functions are in `stdlib.h`.

---

**long int random** (*void*)                                                              [Function]
Preliminary: | MT-Safe | AS-Unsafe lock | AC-Unsafe lock | See Section 1.2.2.1 [POSIX Safety Concepts], page 2.

This function returns the next pseudo-random number in the sequence. The value returned ranges from 0 to `2147483647`.

**NB:** Temporarily this function was defined to return a `int32_t` value to indicate that the return value always contains 32 bits even if `long int` is wider. The standard demands it differently. Users must always be aware of the 32-bit limitation, though.

---

**void srandom** (*unsigned int* **seed**)                                                 [Function]
Preliminary: | MT-Safe | AS-Unsafe lock | AC-Unsafe lock | See Section 1.2.2.1 [POSIX Safety Concepts], page 2.

The `srandom` function sets the state of the random number generator based on the integer *seed*. If you supply a *seed* value of `1`, this will cause `random` to reproduce the default set of random numbers.

To produce a different set of pseudo-random numbers each time your program runs, do `srandom (time (0))`.

---

**char * initstate** (*unsigned int* **seed**, *char *state*, *size_t* **size**)            [Function]
Preliminary: | MT-Safe | AS-Unsafe lock | AC-Unsafe lock | See Section 1.2.2.1 [POSIX Safety Concepts], page 2.

The `initstate` function is used to initialize the random number generator state. The argument *state* is an array of *size* bytes, used to hold the state information. It is initialized based on *seed*. The size must be between 8 and 256 bytes, and should be a power of two. The bigger the *state* array, the better.

The return value is the previous value of the state information array. You can use this value later as an argument to `setstate` to restore that state.

---

**char * setstate** (*char *state*)                                                        [Function]
Preliminary: | MT-Safe | AS-Unsafe lock | AC-Unsafe lock | See Section 1.2.2.1 [POSIX Safety Concepts], page 2.

The `setstate` function restores the random number state information *state*. The argument must have been the result of a previous call to *initstate* or *setstate*.

The return value is the previous value of the state information array. You can use this value later as an argument to `setstate` to restore that state.

If the function fails the return value is `NULL`.

---

The four functions described so far in this section all work on a state which is shared by all threads. The state is not directly accessible to the user and can only be modified by these functions. This makes it hard to deal with situations where each thread should have its own pseudo-random number generator.

The GNU C Library contains four additional functions which contain the state as an explicit parameter and therefore make it possible to handle thread-local PRNGs. Beside this there is no difference. In fact, the four functions already discussed are implemented internally using the following interfaces.

The `stdlib.h` header contains a definition of the following type:

**struct random_data**                                                         [Data Type]
Objects of type `struct random_data` contain the information necessary to represent the state of the PRNG. Although a complete definition of the type is present the type should be treated as opaque.

The functions modifying the state follow exactly the already described functions.

**int random_r** (*struct random_data *restrict* **buf**, *int32_t *restrict*          [Function]
    **result**)
Preliminary: | MT-Safe race:buf | AS-Safe | AC-Unsafe corrupt | See Section 1.2.2.1 [POSIX Safety Concepts], page 2.

The `random_r` function behaves exactly like the `random` function except that it uses and modifies the state in the object pointed to by the first parameter instead of the global state.

**int srandom_r** (*unsigned int* **seed**, *struct random_data* **buf**)         [Function]
Preliminary: | MT-Safe race:buf | AS-Safe | AC-Unsafe corrupt | See Section 1.2.2.1 [POSIX Safety Concepts], page 2.

The `srandom_r` function behaves exactly like the `srandom` function except that it uses and modifies the state in the object pointed to by the second parameter instead of the global state.

**int initstate_r** (*unsigned int* **seed**, *char *restrict* **statebuf**, *size_t*     [Function]
    **statelen**, *struct random_data *restrict* **buf**)
Preliminary: | MT-Safe race:buf | AS-Safe | AC-Unsafe corrupt | See Section 1.2.2.1 [POSIX Safety Concepts], page 2.

The `initstate_r` function behaves exactly like the `initstate` function except that it uses and modifies the state in the object pointed to by the fourth parameter instead of the global state.

**int setstate_r** (*char *restrict* **statebuf**, *struct random_data *restrict*      [Function]
    **buf**)
Preliminary: | MT-Safe race:buf | AS-Safe | AC-Unsafe corrupt | See Section 1.2.2.1 [POSIX Safety Concepts], page 2.

The `setstate_r` function behaves exactly like the `setstate` function except that it uses and modifies the state in the object pointed to by the first parameter instead of the global state.

## 19.8.3 SVID Random Number Function

The C library on SVID systems contains yet another kind of random number generator functions. They use a state of 48 bits of data. The user can choose among a collection of functions which return the random bits in different forms.

Generally there are two kinds of function. The first uses a state of the random number generator which is shared among several functions and by all threads of the process. The second requires the user to handle the state.

All functions have in common that they use the same congruential formula with the same constants. The formula is

```
Y = (a * X + c) mod m
```

where $X$ is the state of the generator at the beginning and $Y$ the state at the end. a and c are constants determining the way the generator works. By default they are

```
a = 0x5DEECE66D = 25214903917
c = 0xb = 11
```

but they can also be changed by the user. m is of course $2^{48}$ since the state consists of a 48-bit array.

The prototypes for these functions are in `stdlib.h`.

double drand48 (*void*)                                              [Function]
> Preliminary: | MT-Unsafe race:drand48 | AS-Unsafe | AC-Unsafe corrupt | See Section 1.2.2.1 [POSIX Safety Concepts], page 2.
>
> This function returns a **double** value in the range of 0.0 to 1.0 (exclusive). The random bits are determined by the global state of the random number generator in the C library.
>
> Since the **double** type according to IEEE 754 has a 52-bit mantissa this means 4 bits are not initialized by the random number generator. These are (of course) chosen to be the least significant bits and they are initialized to 0.

double erand48 (*unsigned short int* **xsubi**[*3*])                  [Function]
> Preliminary: | MT-Unsafe race:drand48 | AS-Unsafe | AC-Unsafe corrupt | See Section 1.2.2.1 [POSIX Safety Concepts], page 2.
>
> This function returns a **double** value in the range of 0.0 to 1.0 (exclusive), similarly to **drand48**. The argument is an array describing the state of the random number generator.
>
> This function can be called subsequently since it updates the array to guarantee random numbers. The array should have been initialized before initial use to obtain reproducible results.

long int lrand48 (*void*)                                            [Function]
> Preliminary: | MT-Unsafe race:drand48 | AS-Unsafe | AC-Unsafe corrupt | See Section 1.2.2.1 [POSIX Safety Concepts], page 2.
>
> The **lrand48** function returns an integer value in the range of 0 to $2^{31}$ (exclusive). Even if the size of the **long int** type can take more than 32 bits, no higher numbers are returned. The random bits are determined by the global state of the random number generator in the C library.

**long int nrand48** (*unsigned short int* **xsubi**[*3*])                         [Function]
> Preliminary: | MT-Unsafe race:drand48 | AS-Unsafe | AC-Unsafe corrupt | See
> Section 1.2.2.1 [POSIX Safety Concepts], page 2.
>
> This function is similar to the **lrand48** function in that it returns a number in the
> range of 0 to 2^31 (exclusive) but the state of the random number generator used to
> produce the random bits is determined by the array provided as the parameter to the
> function.
>
> The numbers in the array are updated afterwards so that subsequent calls to this
> function yield different results (as is expected of a random number generator). The
> array should have been initialized before the first call to obtain reproducible results.

**long int mrand48** (*void*)                                                     [Function]
> Preliminary: | MT-Unsafe race:drand48 | AS-Unsafe | AC-Unsafe corrupt | See
> Section 1.2.2.1 [POSIX Safety Concepts], page 2.
>
> The **mrand48** function is similar to **lrand48**. The only difference is that the numbers
> returned are in the range -2^31 to 2^31 (exclusive).

**long int jrand48** (*unsigned short int* **xsubi**[*3*])                         [Function]
> Preliminary: | MT-Unsafe race:drand48 | AS-Unsafe | AC-Unsafe corrupt | See
> Section 1.2.2.1 [POSIX Safety Concepts], page 2.
>
> The **jrand48** function is similar to **nrand48**. The only difference is that the numbers
> returned are in the range -2^31 to 2^31 (exclusive). For the **xsubi** parameter the
> same requirements are necessary.

The internal state of the random number generator can be initialized in several ways.
The methods differ in the completeness of the information provided.

**void srand48** (*long int* **seedval**)                                          [Function]
> Preliminary: | MT-Unsafe race:drand48 | AS-Unsafe | AC-Unsafe corrupt | See
> Section 1.2.2.1 [POSIX Safety Concepts], page 2.
>
> The **srand48** function sets the most significant 32 bits of the internal state of the
> random number generator to the least significant 32 bits of the *seedval* parameter.
> The lower 16 bits are initialized to the value 0x330E. Even if the **long int** type
> contains more than 32 bits only the lower 32 bits are used.
>
> Owing to this limitation, initialization of the state of this function is not very useful.
> But it makes it easy to use a construct like **srand48 (time (0))**.
>
> A side-effect of this function is that the values **a** and **c** from the internal state, which
> are used in the congruential formula, are reset to the default values given above. This
> is of importance once the user has called the **lcong48** function (see below).

**unsigned short int * seed48** (*unsigned short int* **seed16v**[*3*])             [Function]
> Preliminary: | MT-Unsafe race:drand48 | AS-Unsafe | AC-Unsafe corrupt | See
> Section 1.2.2.1 [POSIX Safety Concepts], page 2.
>
> The **seed48** function initializes all 48 bits of the state of the internal random number
> generator from the contents of the parameter *seed16v*. Here the lower 16 bits of the
> first element of *see16v* initialize the least significant 16 bits of the internal state, the

lower 16 bits of *seed16v*[1] initialize the mid-order 16 bits of the state and the 16 lower bits of *seed16v*[2] initialize the most significant 16 bits of the state.

Unlike **srand48** this function lets the user initialize all 48 bits of the state.

The value returned by **seed48** is a pointer to an array containing the values of the internal state before the change. This might be useful to restart the random number generator at a certain state. Otherwise the value can simply be ignored.

As for **srand48**, the values **a** and **c** from the congruential formula are reset to the default values.

There is one more function to initialize the random number generator which enables you to specify even more information by allowing you to change the parameters in the congruential formula.

**void lcong48** (*unsigned short int* **param**[*7*])                                    [Function]
> Preliminary: | MT-Unsafe race:drand48 | AS-Unsafe | AC-Unsafe corrupt | See Section 1.2.2.1 [POSIX Safety Concepts], page 2.
>
> The **lcong48** function allows the user to change the complete state of the random number generator. Unlike **srand48** and **seed48**, this function also changes the constants in the congruential formula.
>
> From the seven elements in the array *param* the least significant 16 bits of the entries **param**[0] to **param**[2] determine the initial state, the least significant 16 bits of **param**[3] to **param**[5] determine the 48 bit constant **a** and **param**[6] determines the 16-bit value **c**.

All the above functions have in common that they use the global parameters for the congruential formula. In multi-threaded programs it might sometimes be useful to have different parameters in different threads. For this reason all the above functions have a counterpart which works on a description of the random number generator in the user-supplied buffer instead of the global state.

Please note that it is no problem if several threads use the global state if all threads use the functions which take a pointer to an array containing the state. The random numbers are computed following the same loop but if the state in the array is different all threads will obtain an individual random number generator.

The user-supplied buffer must be of type **struct drand48_data**. This type should be regarded as opaque and not manipulated directly.

**int drand48_r** (*struct drand48_data* **\*buffer**, *double* **\*result**)                      [Function]
> Preliminary: | MT-Safe race:buffer | AS-Safe | AC-Unsafe corrupt | See Section 1.2.2.1 [POSIX Safety Concepts], page 2.
>
> This function is equivalent to the **drand48** function with the difference that it does not modify the global random number generator parameters but instead the parameters in the buffer supplied through the pointer *buffer*. The random number is returned in the variable pointed to by *result*.
>
> The return value of the function indicates whether the call succeeded. If the value is less than 0 an error occurred and *errno* is set to indicate the problem.
>
> This function is a GNU extension and should not be used in portable programs.

int **erand48_r** (*unsigned short int* **xsubi**[*3*], *struct drand48_data*                [Function]
    ***buffer**, double ***result**)

    Preliminary: | MT-Safe race:buffer | AS-Safe | AC-Unsafe corrupt | See
    Section 1.2.2.1 [POSIX Safety Concepts], page 2.

    The `erand48_r` function works like `erand48`, but in addition it takes an argument
    *buffer* which describes the random number generator. The state of the random num-
    ber generator is taken from the `xsubi` array, the parameters for the congruential
    formula from the global random number generator data. The random number is
    returned in the variable pointed to by *result*.

    The return value is non-negative if the call succeeded.

    This function is a GNU extension and should not be used in portable programs.

int **lrand48_r** (*struct drand48_data* ***buffer**, *long int* ***result**)                [Function]
    Preliminary: | MT-Safe race:buffer | AS-Safe | AC-Unsafe corrupt | See
    Section 1.2.2.1 [POSIX Safety Concepts], page 2.

    This function is similar to `lrand48`, but in addition it takes a pointer to a buffer
    describing the state of the random number generator just like `drand48`.

    If the return value of the function is non-negative the variable pointed to by *result*
    contains the result. Otherwise an error occurred.

    This function is a GNU extension and should not be used in portable programs.

int **nrand48_r** (*unsigned short int* **xsubi**[*3*], *struct drand48_data*                [Function]
    ***buffer**, long int ***result**)

    Preliminary: | MT-Safe race:buffer | AS-Safe | AC-Unsafe corrupt | See
    Section 1.2.2.1 [POSIX Safety Concepts], page 2.

    The `nrand48_r` function works like `nrand48` in that it produces a random number in
    the range 0 to 2^31. But instead of using the global parameters for the congruential
    formula it uses the information from the buffer pointed to by *buffer*. The state is
    described by the values in *xsubi*.

    If the return value is non-negative the variable pointed to by *result* contains the result.

    This function is a GNU extension and should not be used in portable programs.

int **mrand48_r** (*struct drand48_data* ***buffer**, *long int* ***result**)                [Function]
    Preliminary: | MT-Safe race:buffer | AS-Safe | AC-Unsafe corrupt | See
    Section 1.2.2.1 [POSIX Safety Concepts], page 2.

    This function is similar to `mrand48` but like the other reentrant functions it uses the
    random number generator described by the value in the buffer pointed to by *buffer*.

    If the return value is non-negative the variable pointed to by *result* contains the result.

    This function is a GNU extension and should not be used in portable programs.

int **jrand48_r** (*unsigned short int* **xsubi**[*3*], *struct drand48_data*                [Function]
    ***buffer**, long int ***result**)

    Preliminary: | MT-Safe race:buffer | AS-Safe | AC-Unsafe corrupt | See
    Section 1.2.2.1 [POSIX Safety Concepts], page 2.

The `jrand48_r` function is similar to `jrand48`. Like the other reentrant functions of this function family it uses the congruential formula parameters from the buffer pointed to by *buffer*.

If the return value is non-negative the variable pointed to by *result* contains the result.

This function is a GNU extension and should not be used in portable programs.

Before any of the above functions are used the buffer of type `struct drand48_data` should be initialized. The easiest way to do this is to fill the whole buffer with null bytes, e.g. by

```
memset (buffer, '\0', sizeof (struct drand48_data));
```

Using any of the reentrant functions of this family now will automatically initialize the random number generator to the default values for the state and the parameters of the congruential formula.

The other possibility is to use any of the functions which explicitly initialize the buffer. Though it might be obvious how to initialize the buffer from looking at the parameter to the function, it is highly recommended to use these functions since the result might not always be what you expect.

int **srand48_r** (*long int* **seedval**, *struct drand48_data* ***buffer***)        [Function]
    Preliminary: | MT-Safe race:buffer | AS-Safe | AC-Unsafe corrupt | See Section 1.2.2.1 [POSIX Safety Concepts], page 2.

    The description of the random number generator represented by the information in *buffer* is initialized similarly to what the function `srand48` does. The state is initialized from the parameter *seedval* and the parameters for the congruential formula are initialized to their default values.

    If the return value is non-negative the function call succeeded.

    This function is a GNU extension and should not be used in portable programs.

int **seed48_r** (*unsigned short int* **seed16v**[*3*], *struct drand48_data*        [Function]
    ***buffer***)
    Preliminary: | MT-Safe race:buffer | AS-Safe | AC-Unsafe corrupt | See Section 1.2.2.1 [POSIX Safety Concepts], page 2.

    This function is similar to `srand48_r` but like `seed48` it initializes all 48 bits of the state from the parameter *seed16v*.

    If the return value is non-negative the function call succeeded. It does not return a pointer to the previous state of the random number generator like the `seed48` function does. If the user wants to preserve the state for a later re-run s/he can copy the whole buffer pointed to by *buffer*.

    This function is a GNU extension and should not be used in portable programs.

int **lcong48_r** (*unsigned short int* **param**[*7*], *struct drand48_data*        [Function]
    ***buffer***)
    Preliminary: | MT-Safe race:buffer | AS-Safe | AC-Unsafe corrupt | See Section 1.2.2.1 [POSIX Safety Concepts], page 2.

    This function initializes all aspects of the random number generator described in *buffer* with the data in *param*. Here it is especially true that the function does

Chapter 19: Mathematics                                                558

more than just copying the contents of *param* and *buffer*. More work is required and therefore it is important to use this function rather than initializing the random number generator directly.

If the return value is non-negative the function call succeeded.

This function is a GNU extension and should not be used in portable programs.

## 19.9 Is Fast Code or Small Code preferred?

If an application uses many floating point functions it is often the case that the cost of the function calls themselves is not negligible. Modern processors can often execute the operations themselves very fast, but the function call disrupts the instruction pipeline.

For this reason the GNU C Library provides optimizations for many of the frequently-used math functions. When GNU CC is used and the user activates the optimizer, several new inline functions and macros are defined. These new functions and macros have the same names as the library functions and so are used instead of the latter. In the case of inline functions the compiler will decide whether it is reasonable to use them, and this decision is usually correct.

This means that no calls to the library functions may be necessary, and can increase the speed of generated code significantly. The drawback is that code size will increase, and the increase is not always negligible.

There are two kind of inline functions: Those that give the same result as the library functions and others that might not set **errno** and might have a reduced precision and/or argument range in comparison with the library functions. The latter inline functions are only available if the flag **-ffast-math** is given to GNU CC.

In cases where the inline functions and macros are not wanted the symbol **__NO_MATH_ INLINES** should be defined before any system header is included. This will ensure that only library functions are used. Of course, it can be determined for each file in the project whether giving this option is preferable or not.

Not all hardware implements the entire IEEE 754 standard, and even if it does there may be a substantial performance penalty for using some of its features. For example, enabling traps on some processors forces the FPU to run un-pipelined, which can more than double calculation time.

# 20 Arithmetic Functions

This chapter contains information about functions for doing basic arithmetic operations, such as splitting a float into its integer and fractional parts or retrieving the imaginary part of a complex value. These functions are declared in the header files `math.h` and `complex.h`.

## 20.1 Integers

The C language defines several integer data types: integer, short integer, long integer, and character, all in both signed and unsigned varieties. The GNU C compiler extends the language to contain long long integers as well.

The C integer types were intended to allow code to be portable among machines with different inherent data sizes (word sizes), so each type may have different ranges on different machines. The problem with this is that a program often needs to be written for a particular range of integers, and sometimes must be written for a particular size of storage, regardless of what machine the program runs on.

To address this problem, the GNU C Library contains C type definitions you can use to declare integers that meet your exact needs. Because the GNU C Library header files are customized to a specific machine, your program source code doesn't have to be.

These `typedef`s are in `stdint.h`.

If you require that an integer be represented in exactly N bits, use one of the following types, with the obvious mapping to bit size and signedness:

- int8_t
- int16_t
- int32_t
- int64_t
- uint8_t
- uint16_t
- uint32_t
- uint64_t

If your C compiler and target machine do not allow integers of a certain size, the corresponding above type does not exist.

If you don't need a specific storage size, but want the smallest data structure with *at least* N bits, use one of these:

- int_least8_t
- int_least16_t
- int_least32_t
- int_least64_t
- uint_least8_t
- uint_least16_t
- uint_least32_t
- uint_least64_t

If you don't need a specific storage size, but want the data structure that allows the fastest access while having at least N bits (and among data structures with the same access speed, the smallest one), use one of these:

- int_fast8_t
- int_fast16_t
- int_fast32_t
- int_fast64_t
- uint_fast8_t
- uint_fast16_t
- uint_fast32_t
- uint_fast64_t

If you want an integer with the widest range possible on the platform on which it is being used, use one of the following. If you use these, you should write code that takes into account the variable size and range of the integer.

- intmax_t
- uintmax_t

The GNU C Library also provides macros that tell you the maximum and minimum possible values for each integer data type. The macro names follow these examples: `INT32_MAX`, `UINT8_MAX`, `INT_FAST32_MIN`, `INT_LEAST64_MIN`, `UINTMAX_MAX`, `INTMAX_MAX`, `INTMAX_MIN`. Note that there are no macros for unsigned integer minima. These are always zero.

There are similar macros for use with C's built in integer types which should come with your C compiler. These are described in Section A.5 [Data Type Measurements], page 884.

Don't forget you can use the C `sizeof` function with any of these data types to get the number of bytes of storage each uses.

## 20.2 Integer Division

This section describes functions for performing integer division. These functions are redundant when GNU CC is used, because in GNU C the '/' operator always rounds towards zero. But in other C implementations, '/' may round differently with negative arguments. `div` and `ldiv` are useful because they specify how to round the quotient: towards zero. The remainder has the same sign as the numerator.

These functions are specified to return a result $r$ such that the value `r.quot*denominator + r.rem` equals *numerator*.

To use these facilities, you should include the header file `stdlib.h` in your program.

`div_t`                                                                 [Data Type]

    This is a structure type used to hold the result returned by the `div` function. It has the following members:

    `int quot`    The quotient from the division.

    `int rem`    The remainder from the division.

`div_t div` (*int* **numerator**, *int* **denominator**)                    [Function]

> Preliminary: | MT-Safe | AS-Safe | AC-Safe | See Section 1.2.2.1 [POSIX Safety Concepts], page 2.
>
> This function `div` computes the quotient and remainder from the division of *numerator* by *denominator*, returning the result in a structure of type `div_t`.
>
> If the result cannot be represented (as in a division by zero), the behavior is undefined.
>
> Here is an example, albeit not a very useful one.
>
> ```
> div_t result;
> result = div (20, -6);
> ```
>
> Now `result.quot` is -3 and `result.rem` is 2.

`ldiv_t`                                                              [Data Type]

> This is a structure type used to hold the result returned by the `ldiv` function. It has the following members:
>
> `long int quot`
> > The quotient from the division.
>
> `long int rem`
> > The remainder from the division.
>
> (This is identical to `div_t` except that the components are of type `long int` rather than `int`.)

`ldiv_t ldiv` (*long int* **numerator**, *long int* **denominator**)          [Function]

> Preliminary: | MT-Safe | AS-Safe | AC-Safe | See Section 1.2.2.1 [POSIX Safety Concepts], page 2.
>
> The `ldiv` function is similar to `div`, except that the arguments are of type `long int` and the result is returned as a structure of type `ldiv_t`.

`lldiv_t`                                                             [Data Type]

> This is a structure type used to hold the result returned by the `lldiv` function. It has the following members:
>
> `long long int quot`
> > The quotient from the division.
>
> `long long int rem`
> > The remainder from the division.
>
> (This is identical to `div_t` except that the components are of type `long long int` rather than `int`.)

`lldiv_t lldiv` (*long long int* **numerator**, *long long int* **denominator**)     [Function]

> Preliminary: | MT-Safe | AS-Safe | AC-Safe | See Section 1.2.2.1 [POSIX Safety Concepts], page 2.
>
> The `lldiv` function is like the `div` function, but the arguments are of type `long long int` and the result is returned as a structure of type `lldiv_t`.
>
> The `lldiv` function was added in ISO C99.

`imaxdiv_t`                                                                   [Data Type]

> This is a structure type used to hold the result returned by the `imaxdiv` function. It has the following members:

> `intmax_t quot`
>> The quotient from the division.

> `intmax_t rem`
>> The remainder from the division.

> (This is identical to `div_t` except that the components are of type `intmax_t` rather than `int`.)

> See Section 20.1 [Integers], page 559 for a description of the `intmax_t` type.

`imaxdiv_t imaxdiv (`*intmax_t* **numerator**, *intmax_t* **denominator**`)`         [Function]

> Preliminary: | MT-Safe | AS-Safe | AC-Safe | See Section 1.2.2.1 [POSIX Safety Concepts], page 2.

> The `imaxdiv` function is like the `div` function, but the arguments are of type `intmax_t` and the result is returned as a structure of type `imaxdiv_t`.

> See Section 20.1 [Integers], page 559 for a description of the `intmax_t` type.

> The `imaxdiv` function was added in ISO C99.

## 20.3 Floating Point Numbers

Most computer hardware has support for two different kinds of numbers: integers $(\ldots -3, -2, -1, 0, 1, 2, 3 \ldots)$ and floating-point numbers. Floating-point numbers have three parts: the *mantissa*, the *exponent*, and the *sign bit*. The real number represented by a floating-point value is given by $(s\ ?\ -1 : 1) \cdot 2^e \cdot M$ where $s$ is the sign bit, $e$ the exponent, and $M$ the mantissa. See Section A.5.3.1 [Floating Point Representation Concepts], page 887, for details. (It is possible to have a different *base* for the exponent, but all modern hardware uses 2.)

Floating-point numbers can represent a finite subset of the real numbers. While this subset is large enough for most purposes, it is important to remember that the only reals that can be represented exactly are rational numbers that have a terminating binary expansion shorter than the width of the mantissa. Even simple fractions such as 1/5 can only be approximated by floating point.

Mathematical operations and functions frequently need to produce values that are not representable. Often these values can be approximated closely enough for practical purposes, but sometimes they can't. Historically there was no way to tell when the results of a calculation were inaccurate. Modern computers implement the IEEE 754 standard for numerical computations, which defines a framework for indicating to the program when the results of calculation are not trustworthy. This framework consists of a set of *exceptions* that indicate why a result could not be represented, and the special values *infinity* and *not a number* (NaN).

## 20.4 Floating-Point Number Classification Functions

ISO C99 defines macros that let you determine what sort of floating-point number a variable holds.

int fpclassify (*float-type* x)                                    [Macro]
> Preliminary: | MT-Safe | AS-Safe | AC-Safe | See Section 1.2.2.1 [POSIX Safety Concepts], page 2.
>
> This is a generic macro which works on all floating-point types and which returns a value of type int. The possible values are:
>
> FP_NAN   The floating-point number x is "Not a Number" (see Section 20.5.2 [Infinity and NaN], page 566)
>
> FP_INFINITE
> > The value of x is either plus or minus infinity (see Section 20.5.2 [Infinity and NaN], page 566)
>
> FP_ZERO   The value of x is zero. In floating-point formats like IEEE 754, where zero can be signed, this value is also returned if x is negative zero.
>
> FP_SUBNORMAL
> > Numbers whose absolute value is too small to be represented in the normal format are represented in an alternate, *denormalized* format (see Section A.5.3.1 [Floating Point Representation Concepts], page 887). This format is less precise but can represent values closer to zero. fpclassify returns this value for values of x in this alternate format.
>
> FP_NORMAL
> > This value is returned for all other values of x. It indicates that there is nothing special about the number.

fpclassify is most useful if more than one property of a number must be tested. There are more specific macros which only test one property at a time. Generally these macros execute faster than fpclassify, since there is special hardware support for them. You should therefore use the specific macros whenever possible.

int isfinite (*float-type* x)                                    [Macro]
> Preliminary: | MT-Safe | AS-Safe | AC-Safe | See Section 1.2.2.1 [POSIX Safety Concepts], page 2.
>
> This macro returns a nonzero value if x is finite: not plus or minus infinity, and not NaN. It is equivalent to
>
> ```
> (fpclassify (x) != FP_NAN && fpclassify (x) != FP_INFINITE)
> ```
>
> isfinite is implemented as a macro which accepts any floating-point type.

int isnormal (*float-type* x)                                    [Macro]
> Preliminary: | MT-Safe | AS-Safe | AC-Safe | See Section 1.2.2.1 [POSIX Safety Concepts], page 2.
>
> This macro returns a nonzero value if x is finite and normalized. It is equivalent to
>
> ```
> (fpclassify (x) == FP_NORMAL)
> ```

int isnan (*float-type x*)                                                      [Macro]

> Preliminary: | MT-Safe | AS-Safe | AC-Safe | See Section 1.2.2.1 [POSIX Safety Concepts], page 2.
>
> This macro returns a nonzero value if *x* is NaN. It is equivalent to
>
>     (fpclassify (x) == FP_NAN)

int issignaling (*float-type x*)                                                [Macro]

> Preliminary: | MT-Safe | AS-Safe | AC-Safe | See Section 1.2.2.1 [POSIX Safety Concepts], page 2.
>
> This macro returns a nonzero value if *x* is a signaling NaN (sNaN). It is based on draft TS 18661 and currently enabled as a GNU extension.

Another set of floating-point classification functions was provided by BSD. The GNU C Library also supports these functions; however, we recommend that you use the ISO C99 macros in new code. Those are standard and will be available more widely. Also, since they are macros, you do not have to worry about the type of their argument.

int isinf (*double x*)                                                          [Function]
int isinff (*float x*)                                                          [Function]
int isinfl (*long double x*)                                                    [Function]

> Preliminary: | MT-Safe | AS-Safe | AC-Safe | See Section 1.2.2.1 [POSIX Safety Concepts], page 2.
>
> This function returns -1 if *x* represents negative infinity, 1 if *x* represents positive infinity, and 0 otherwise.

int isnan (*double x*)                                                          [Function]
int isnanf (*float x*)                                                          [Function]
int isnanl (*long double x*)                                                    [Function]

> Preliminary: | MT-Safe | AS-Safe | AC-Safe | See Section 1.2.2.1 [POSIX Safety Concepts], page 2.
>
> This function returns a nonzero value if *x* is a "not a number" value, and zero otherwise.
>
> **NB:** The isnan macro defined by ISO C99 overrides the BSD function. This is normally not a problem, because the two routines behave identically. However, if you really need to get the BSD function for some reason, you can write
>
>     (isnan) (x)

int finite (*double x*)                                                         [Function]
int finitef (*float x*)                                                         [Function]
int finitel (*long double x*)                                                   [Function]

> Preliminary: | MT-Safe | AS-Safe | AC-Safe | See Section 1.2.2.1 [POSIX Safety Concepts], page 2.
>
> This function returns a nonzero value if *x* is finite or a "not a number" value, and zero otherwise.

**Portability Note:** The functions listed in this section are BSD extensions.

## 20.5 Errors in Floating-Point Calculations

### 20.5.1 FP Exceptions

The IEEE 754 standard defines five *exceptions* that can occur during a calculation. Each corresponds to a particular sort of error, such as overflow.

When exceptions occur (when exceptions are *raised*, in the language of the standard), one of two things can happen. By default the exception is simply noted in the floating-point *status word*, and the program continues as if nothing had happened. The operation produces a default value, which depends on the exception (see the table below). Your program can check the status word to find out which exceptions happened.

Alternatively, you can enable *traps* for exceptions. In that case, when an exception is raised, your program will receive the SIGFPE signal. The default action for this signal is to terminate the program. See Chapter 24 [Signal Handling], page 661, for how you can change the effect of the signal.

In the System V math library, the user-defined function matherr is called when certain exceptions occur inside math library functions. However, the Unix98 standard deprecates this interface. We support it for historical compatibility, but recommend that you do not use it in new programs. When this interface is used, exceptions may not be raised.

The exceptions defined in IEEE 754 are:

'Invalid Operation'

This exception is raised if the given operands are invalid for the operation to be performed. Examples are (see IEEE 754, section 7):

1. Addition or subtraction: $\infty - \infty$. (But $\infty + \infty = \infty$).

2. Multiplication: $0 \cdot \infty$.

3. Division: $0/0$ or $\infty/\infty$.

4. Remainder: $x$ REM $y$, where $y$ is zero or $x$ is infinite.

5. Square root if the operand is less then zero. More generally, any mathematical function evaluated outside its domain produces this exception.

6. Conversion of a floating-point number to an integer or decimal string, when the number cannot be represented in the target format (due to overflow, infinity, or NaN).

7. Conversion of an unrecognizable input string.

8. Comparison via predicates involving $<$ or $>$, when one or other of the operands is NaN. You can prevent this exception by using the unordered comparison functions instead; see Section 20.8.6 [Floating-Point Comparison Functions], page 580.

If the exception does not trap, the result of the operation is NaN.

'Division by Zero'

This exception is raised when a finite nonzero number is divided by zero. If no trap occurs the result is either $+\infty$ or $-\infty$, depending on the signs of the operands.

'Overflow'

This exception is raised whenever the result cannot be represented as a finite value in the precision format of the destination. If no trap occurs the result depends on the sign of the intermediate result and the current rounding mode (IEEE 754, section 7.3):

1. Round to nearest carries all overflows to $\infty$ with the sign of the intermediate result.

2. Round toward 0 carries all overflows to the largest representable finite number with the sign of the intermediate result.

3. Round toward $-\infty$ carries positive overflows to the largest representable finite number and negative overflows to $-\infty$.

4. Round toward $\infty$ carries negative overflows to the most negative representable finite number and positive overflows to $\infty$.

Whenever the overflow exception is raised, the inexact exception is also raised.

'Underflow'

The underflow exception is raised when an intermediate result is too small to be calculated accurately, or if the operation's result rounded to the destination precision is too small to be normalized.

When no trap is installed for the underflow exception, underflow is signaled (via the underflow flag) only when both tininess and loss of accuracy have been detected. If no trap handler is installed the operation continues with an imprecise small value, or zero if the destination precision cannot hold the small exact result.

'Inexact'   This exception is signalled if a rounded result is not exact (such as when calculating the square root of two) or a result overflows without an overflow trap.

## 20.5.2 Infinity and NaN

IEEE 754 floating point numbers can represent positive or negative infinity, and *NaN* (not a number). These three values arise from calculations whose result is undefined or cannot be represented accurately. You can also deliberately set a floating-point variable to any of them, which is sometimes useful. Some examples of calculations that produce infinity or NaN:

$$\frac{1}{0} = \infty$$

$$\log 0 = -\infty$$

$$\sqrt{-1} = \text{NaN}$$

When a calculation produces any of these values, an exception also occurs; see Section 20.5.1 [FP Exceptions], page 565.

The basic operations and math functions all accept infinity and NaN and produce sensible output. Infinities propagate through calculations as one would expect: for example, $2+\infty = \infty$, $4/\infty = 0$, atan $(\infty) = \pi/2$. NaN, on the other hand, infects any calculation that involves it. Unless the calculation would produce the same result no matter what real value replaced NaN, the result is NaN.

In comparison operations, positive infinity is larger than all values except itself and NaN, and negative infinity is smaller than all values except itself and NaN. NaN is *unordered*: it is not equal to, greater than, or less than anything, *including itself*. x == x is false if the value of x is NaN. You can use this to test whether a value is NaN or not, but the recommended way to test for NaN is with the `isnan` function (see Section 20.4 [Floating-Point Number Classification Functions], page 563). In addition, <, >, <=, and >= will raise an exception when applied to NaNs.

`math.h` defines macros that allow you to explicitly set a variable to infinity or NaN.

float INFINITY                                                                                      [Macro]
>       An expression representing positive infinity. It is equal to the value produced by mathematical operations like `1.0 / 0.0`. `-INFINITY` represents negative infinity.
>
>       You can test whether a floating-point value is infinite by comparing it to this macro. However, this is not recommended; you should use the `isfinite` macro instead. See Section 20.4 [Floating-Point Number Classification Functions], page 563.
>
>       This macro was introduced in the ISO C99 standard.

float NAN                                                                                            [Macro]
>       An expression representing a value which is "not a number". This macro is a GNU extension, available only on machines that support the "not a number" value—that is to say, on all machines that support IEEE floating point.
>
>       You can use '#ifdef NAN' to test whether the machine supports NaN. (Of course, you must arrange for GNU extensions to be visible, such as by defining _GNU_SOURCE, and then you must include `math.h`.)

IEEE 754 also allows for another unusual value: negative zero. This value is produced when you divide a positive number by negative infinity, or when a negative result is smaller than the limits of representation.

## 20.5.3 Examining the FPU status word

ISO C99 defines functions to query and manipulate the floating-point status word. You can use these functions to check for untrapped exceptions when it's convenient, rather than worrying about them in the middle of a calculation.

These constants represent the various IEEE 754 exceptions. Not all FPUs report all the different exceptions. Each constant is defined if and only if the FPU you are compiling for supports that exception, so you can test for FPU support with '#ifdef'. They are defined in `fenv.h`.

FE_INEXACT
>       The inexact exception.

FE_DIVBYZERO
>       The divide by zero exception.

FE_UNDERFLOW
>       The underflow exception.

**FE_OVERFLOW**

> The overflow exception.

**FE_INVALID**

> The invalid exception.

The macro **FE_ALL_EXCEPT** is the bitwise OR of all exception macros which are supported by the FP implementation.

These functions allow you to clear exception flags, test for exceptions, and save and restore the set of exceptions flagged.

**int feclearexcept** (*int excepts*)                                                        [Function]

> Preliminary: | MT-Safe | AS-Safe !posix | AC-Safe !posix | See Section 1.2.2.1 [POSIX Safety Concepts], page 2.
>
> This function clears all of the supported exception flags indicated by *excepts*.
>
> The function returns zero in case the operation was successful, a non-zero value otherwise.

**int feraiseexcept** (*int excepts*)                                                        [Function]

> Preliminary: | MT-Safe | AS-Safe | AC-Safe | See Section 1.2.2.1 [POSIX Safety Concepts], page 2.
>
> This function raises the supported exceptions indicated by *excepts*. If more than one exception bit in *excepts* is set the order in which the exceptions are raised is undefined except that overflow (**FE_OVERFLOW**) or underflow (**FE_UNDERFLOW**) are raised before inexact (**FE_INEXACT**). Whether for overflow or underflow the inexact exception is also raised is also implementation dependent.
>
> The function returns zero in case the operation was successful, a non-zero value otherwise.

**int fetestexcept** (*int excepts*)                                                         [Function]

> Preliminary: | MT-Safe | AS-Safe | AC-Safe | See Section 1.2.2.1 [POSIX Safety Concepts], page 2.
>
> Test whether the exception flags indicated by the parameter *except* are currently set. If any of them are, a nonzero value is returned which specifies which exceptions are set. Otherwise the result is zero.

To understand these functions, imagine that the status word is an integer variable named *status*. **feclearexcept** is then equivalent to '**status &= ~excepts**' and **fetestexcept** is equivalent to '**(status & excepts)**'. The actual implementation may be very different, of course.

Exception flags are only cleared when the program explicitly requests it, by calling **feclearexcept**. If you want to check for exceptions from a set of calculations, you should clear all the flags first. Here is a simple example of the way to use **fetestexcept**:

```
{
    double f;
    int raised;
    feclearexcept (FE_ALL_EXCEPT);
    f = compute ();
    raised = fetestexcept (FE_OVERFLOW | FE_INVALID);
```

```
        if (raised & FE_OVERFLOW) { /* ... */ }
        if (raised & FE_INVALID) { /* ... */ }
        /* ... */
    }
```

You cannot explicitly set bits in the status word. You can, however, save the entire status word and restore it later. This is done with the following functions:

int **fegetexceptflag** (*fexcept_t \*flagp*, *int* **excepts**)                    [Function]
    Preliminary: | MT-Safe | AS-Safe | AC-Safe | See Section 1.2.2.1 [POSIX Safety Concepts], page 2.

    This function stores in the variable pointed to by *flagp* an implementation-defined value representing the current setting of the exception flags indicated by *excepts*.

    The function returns zero in case the operation was successful, a non-zero value otherwise.

int **fesetexceptflag** (*const fexcept_t \*flagp*, *int* **excepts**)               [Function]
    Preliminary: | MT-Safe | AS-Safe | AC-Safe | See Section 1.2.2.1 [POSIX Safety Concepts], page 2.

    This function restores the flags for the exceptions indicated by *excepts* to the values stored in the variable pointed to by *flagp*.

    The function returns zero in case the operation was successful, a non-zero value otherwise.

Note that the value stored in `fexcept_t` bears no resemblance to the bit mask returned by `fetestexcept`. The type may not even be an integer. Do not attempt to modify an `fexcept_t` variable.

## 20.5.4 Error Reporting by Mathematical Functions

Many of the math functions are defined only over a subset of the real or complex numbers. Even if they are mathematically defined, their result may be larger or smaller than the range representable by their return type without loss of accuracy. These are known as *domain errors*, *overflows*, and *underflows*, respectively. Math functions do several things when one of these errors occurs. In this manual we will refer to the complete response as *signalling* a domain error, overflow, or underflow.

When a math function suffers a domain error, it raises the invalid exception and returns NaN. It also sets *errno* to EDOM; this is for compatibility with old systems that do not support IEEE 754 exception handling. Likewise, when overflow occurs, math functions raise the overflow exception and, in the default rounding mode, return $\infty$ or $-\infty$ as appropriate (in other rounding modes, the largest finite value of the appropriate sign is returned when appropriate for that rounding mode). They also set *errno* to ERANGE if returning $\infty$ or $-\infty$; *errno* may or may not be set to ERANGE when a finite value is returned on overflow. When underflow occurs, the underflow exception is raised, and zero (appropriately signed) or a subnormal value, as appropriate for the mathematical result of the function and the rounding mode, is returned. *errno* may be set to ERANGE, but this is not guaranteed; it is intended that the GNU C Library should set it when the underflow is to an appropriately signed zero, but not necessarily for other underflows.

Some of the math functions are defined mathematically to result in a complex value over parts of their domains. The most familiar example of this is taking the square root of a negative number. The complex math functions, such as `csqrt`, will return the appropriate complex value in this case. The real-valued functions, such as `sqrt`, will signal a domain error.

Some older hardware does not support infinities. On that hardware, overflows instead return a particular very large number (usually the largest representable number). `math.h` defines macros you can use to test for overflow on both old and new hardware.

`double HUGE_VAL`                                                            [Macro]

`float HUGE_VALF`                                                            [Macro]

`long double HUGE_VALL`                                                      [Macro]

>   An expression representing a particular very large number. On machines that use IEEE 754 floating point format, `HUGE_VAL` is infinity. On other machines, it's typically the largest positive number that can be represented.
>
>   Mathematical functions return the appropriately typed version of `HUGE_VAL` or −`HUGE_VAL` when the result is too large to be represented.

## 20.6 Rounding Modes

Floating-point calculations are carried out internally with extra precision, and then rounded to fit into the destination type. This ensures that results are as precise as the input data. IEEE 754 defines four possible rounding modes:

Round to nearest.

>   This is the default mode. It should be used unless there is a specific need for one of the others. In this mode results are rounded to the nearest representable value. If the result is midway between two representable values, the even representable is chosen. *Even* here means the lowest-order bit is zero. This rounding mode prevents statistical bias and guarantees numeric stability: round-off errors in a lengthy calculation will remain smaller than half of `FLT_EPSILON`.

Round toward plus Infinity.

>   All results are rounded to the smallest representable value which is greater than the result.

Round toward minus Infinity.

>   All results are rounded to the largest representable value which is less than the result.

Round toward zero.

>   All results are rounded to the largest representable value whose magnitude is less than that of the result. In other words, if the result is negative it is rounded up; if it is positive, it is rounded down.

`fenv.h` defines constants which you can use to refer to the various rounding modes. Each one will be defined if and only if the FPU supports the corresponding rounding mode.

`FE_TONEAREST`

>   Round to nearest.

`FE_UPWARD`

>  Round toward $+\infty$.

`FE_DOWNWARD`

>  Round toward $-\infty$.

`FE_TOWARDZERO`

>  Round toward zero.

Underflow is an unusual case. Normally, IEEE 754 floating point numbers are always normalized (see Section A.5.3.1 [Floating Point Representation Concepts], page 887). Numbers smaller than $2^r$ (where $r$ is the minimum exponent, `FLT_MIN_RADIX-1` for *float*) cannot be represented as normalized numbers. Rounding all such numbers to zero or $2^r$ would cause some algorithms to fail at 0. Therefore, they are left in denormalized form. That produces loss of precision, since some bits of the mantissa are stolen to indicate the decimal point.

If a result is too small to be represented as a denormalized number, it is rounded to zero. However, the sign of the result is preserved; if the calculation was negative, the result is *negative zero*. Negative zero can also result from some operations on infinity, such as $4/-\infty$.

At any time one of the above four rounding modes is selected. You can find out which one with this function:

`int fegetround (`*void*`)`                                                 [Function]

>  Preliminary: | MT-Safe | AS-Safe | AC-Safe | See Section 1.2.2.1 [POSIX Safety Concepts], page 2.
>
>  Returns the currently selected rounding mode, represented by one of the values of the defined rounding mode macros.

To change the rounding mode, use this function:

`int fesetround (`*int* `round`)`                                           [Function]

>  Preliminary: | MT-Safe | AS-Safe | AC-Safe | See Section 1.2.2.1 [POSIX Safety Concepts], page 2.
>
>  Changes the currently selected rounding mode to *round*. If *round* does not correspond to one of the supported rounding modes nothing is changed. `fesetround` returns zero if it changed the rounding mode, a nonzero value if the mode is not supported.

You should avoid changing the rounding mode if possible. It can be an expensive operation; also, some hardware requires you to compile your program differently for it to work. The resulting code may run slower. See your compiler documentation for details.

## 20.7 Floating-Point Control Functions

IEEE 754 floating-point implementations allow the programmer to decide whether traps will occur for each of the exceptions, by setting bits in the *control word*. In C, traps result in the program receiving the `SIGFPE` signal; see Chapter 24 [Signal Handling], page 661.

**NB:** IEEE 754 says that trap handlers are given details of the exceptional situation, and can set the result value. C signals do not provide any mechanism to pass this information back and forth. Trapping exceptions in C is therefore not very useful.

It is sometimes necessary to save the state of the floating-point unit while you perform some calculation. The library provides functions which save and restore the exception flags, the set of exceptions that generate traps, and the rounding mode. This information is known as the *floating-point environment*.

The functions to save and restore the floating-point environment all use a variable of type `fenv_t` to store information. This type is defined in `fenv.h`. Its size and contents are implementation-defined. You should not attempt to manipulate a variable of this type directly.

To save the state of the FPU, use one of these functions:

**int fegetenv** (*fenv_t* **\*envp**)                                                    [Function]
> Preliminary: | MT-Safe | AS-Safe | AC-Safe | See Section 1.2.2.1 [POSIX Safety Concepts], page 2.
>
> Store the floating-point environment in the variable pointed to by *envp*.
>
> The function returns zero in case the operation was successful, a non-zero value otherwise.

**int feholdexcept** (*fenv_t* **\*envp**)                                                [Function]
> Preliminary: | MT-Safe | AS-Safe | AC-Safe | See Section 1.2.2.1 [POSIX Safety Concepts], page 2.
>
> Store the current floating-point environment in the object pointed to by *envp*. Then clear all exception flags, and set the FPU to trap no exceptions. Not all FPUs support trapping no exceptions; if `feholdexcept` cannot set this mode, it returns nonzero value. If it succeeds, it returns zero.

The functions which restore the floating-point environment can take these kinds of arguments:

- Pointers to `fenv_t` objects, which were initialized previously by a call to `fegetenv` or `feholdexcept`.

- The special macro `FE_DFL_ENV` which represents the floating-point environment as it was available at program start.

- Implementation defined macros with names starting with `FE_` and having type `fenv_t *`.

  If possible, the GNU C Library defines a macro `FE_NOMASK_ENV` which represents an environment where every exception raised causes a trap to occur. You can test for this macro using `#ifdef`. It is only defined if `_GNU_SOURCE` is defined.

  Some platforms might define other predefined environments.

To set the floating-point environment, you can use either of these functions:

**int fesetenv** (*const fenv_t* **\*envp**)                                              [Function]
> Preliminary: | MT-Safe | AS-Safe | AC-Safe | See Section 1.2.2.1 [POSIX Safety Concepts], page 2.
>
> Set the floating-point environment to that described by *envp*.
>
> The function returns zero in case the operation was successful, a non-zero value otherwise.

`int feupdateenv` (*const fenv_t \*envp*)                              [Function]
> Preliminary: | MT-Safe | AS-Safe | AC-Safe | See Section 1.2.2.1 [POSIX Safety
> Concepts], page 2.
>
> Like `fesetenv`, this function sets the floating-point environment to that described by
> *envp*. However, if any exceptions were flagged in the status word before `feupdateenv`
> was called, they remain flagged after the call. In other words, after `feupdateenv` is
> called, the status word is the bitwise OR of the previous status word and the one
> saved in *envp*.
>
> The function returns zero in case the operation was successful, a non-zero value oth-
> erwise.

To control for individual exceptions if raising them causes a trap to occur, you can use the
following two functions.

**Portability Note:** These functions are all GNU extensions.

`int feenableexcept` (*int excepts*)                                  [Function]
> Preliminary: | MT-Safe | AS-Safe | AC-Safe | See Section 1.2.2.1 [POSIX Safety
> Concepts], page 2.
>
> This functions enables traps for each of the exceptions as indicated by the parameter
> *except*. The individual exceptions are described in Section 20.5.3 [Examining the
> FPU status word], page 567. Only the specified exceptions are enabled, the status of
> the other exceptions is not changed.
>
> The function returns the previous enabled exceptions in case the operation was suc-
> cessful, -1 otherwise.

`int fedisableexcept` (*int excepts*)                                 [Function]
> Preliminary: | MT-Safe | AS-Safe | AC-Safe | See Section 1.2.2.1 [POSIX Safety
> Concepts], page 2.
>
> This functions disables traps for each of the exceptions as indicated by the parameter
> *except*. The individual exceptions are described in Section 20.5.3 [Examining the
> FPU status word], page 567. Only the specified exceptions are disabled, the status of
> the other exceptions is not changed.
>
> The function returns the previous enabled exceptions in case the operation was suc-
> cessful, -1 otherwise.

`int fegetexcept` (*void*)                                            [Function]
> Preliminary: | MT-Safe | AS-Safe | AC-Safe | See Section 1.2.2.1 [POSIX Safety
> Concepts], page 2.
>
> The function returns a bitmask of all currently enabled exceptions. It returns -1 in
> case of failure.

## 20.8 Arithmetic Functions

The C library provides functions to do basic operations on floating-point numbers. These
include absolute value, maximum and minimum, normalization, bit twiddling, rounding,
and a few others.

### 20.8.1 Absolute Value

These functions are provided for obtaining the *absolute value* (or *magnitude*) of a number. The absolute value of a real number $x$ is $x$ if $x$ is positive, $-x$ if $x$ is negative. For a complex number $z$, whose real part is $x$ and whose imaginary part is $y$, the absolute value is `sqrt (x*x + y*y)`.

Prototypes for `abs`, `labs` and `llabs` are in `stdlib.h`; `imaxabs` is declared in `inttypes.h`; `fabs`, `fabsf` and `fabsl` are declared in `math.h`. `cabs`, `cabsf` and `cabsl` are declared in `complex.h`.

`int abs` (*int* `number`)                                                  [Function]
`long int labs` (*long int* `number`)                                        [Function]
`long long int llabs` (*long long int* `number`)                             [Function]
`intmax_t imaxabs` (*intmax_t* `number`)                                     [Function]

> Preliminary: | MT-Safe | AS-Safe | AC-Safe | See Section 1.2.2.1 [POSIX Safety Concepts], page 2.
>
> These functions return the absolute value of *number*.
>
> Most computers use a two's complement integer representation, in which the absolute value of `INT_MIN` (the smallest possible `int`) cannot be represented; thus, `abs (INT_MIN)` is not defined.
>
> `llabs` and `imaxdiv` are new to ISO C99.
>
> See Section 20.1 [Integers], page 559 for a description of the `intmax_t` type.

`double fabs` (*double* `number`)                                           [Function]
`float fabsf` (*float* `number`)                                             [Function]
`long double fabsl` (*long double* `number`)                                 [Function]

> Preliminary: | MT-Safe | AS-Safe | AC-Safe | See Section 1.2.2.1 [POSIX Safety Concepts], page 2.
>
> This function returns the absolute value of the floating-point number *number*.

`double cabs` (*complex double* `z`)                                        [Function]
`float cabsf` (*complex float* `z`)                                          [Function]
`long double cabsl` (*complex long double* `z`)                             [Function]

> Preliminary: | MT-Safe | AS-Safe | AC-Safe | See Section 1.2.2.1 [POSIX Safety Concepts], page 2.
>
> These functions return the absolute value of the complex number $z$ (see Section 20.9 [Complex Numbers], page 583). The absolute value of a complex number is:
>
> > `sqrt (creal (z) * creal (z) + cimag (z) * cimag (z))`
>
> This function should always be used instead of the direct formula because it takes special care to avoid losing precision. It may also take advantage of hardware support for this operation. See `hypot` in Section 19.4 [Exponentiation and Logarithms], page 515.

### 20.8.2 Normalization Functions

The functions described in this section are primarily provided as a way to efficiently perform certain low-level manipulations on floating point numbers that are represented internally using a binary radix; see Section A.5.3.1 [Floating Point Representation Concepts], page 887.

These functions are required to have equivalent behavior even if the representation does not use a radix of 2, but of course they are unlikely to be particularly efficient in those cases.

All these functions are declared in `math.h`.

double frexp (*double* **value**, *int* **\*exponent**)                         [Function]
float frexpf (*float* **value**, *int* **\*exponent**)                          [Function]
long double frexpl (*long double* **value**, *int* **\*exponent**)              [Function]
> Preliminary: | MT-Safe | AS-Safe | AC-Safe | See Section 1.2.2.1 [POSIX Safety Concepts], page 2.
>
> These functions are used to split the number *value* into a normalized fraction and an exponent.
>
> If the argument *value* is not zero, the return value is *value* times a power of two, and its magnitude is always in the range 1/2 (inclusive) to 1 (exclusive). The corresponding exponent is stored in *\*exponent*; the return value multiplied by 2 raised to this exponent equals the original number *value*.
>
> For example, `frexp (12.8, &exponent)` returns `0.8` and stores `4` in `exponent`.
>
> If *value* is zero, then the return value is zero and zero is stored in *\*exponent*.

double ldexp (*double* **value**, *int* **exponent**)                           [Function]
float ldexpf (*float* **value**, *int* **exponent**)                            [Function]
long double ldexpl (*long double* **value**, *int* **exponent**)                [Function]
> Preliminary: | MT-Safe | AS-Safe | AC-Safe | See Section 1.2.2.1 [POSIX Safety Concepts], page 2.
>
> These functions return the result of multiplying the floating-point number *value* by 2 raised to the power *exponent*. (It can be used to reassemble floating-point numbers that were taken apart by `frexp`.)
>
> For example, `ldexp (0.8, 4)` returns `12.8`.

The following functions, which come from BSD, provide facilities equivalent to those of `ldexp` and `frexp`. See also the ISO C function `logb` which originally also appeared in BSD.

double scalb (*double* **value**, *double* **exponent**)                        [Function]
float scalbf (*float* **value**, *float* **exponent**)                          [Function]
long double scalbl (*long double* **value**, *long double* **exponent**)        [Function]
> Preliminary: | MT-Safe | AS-Safe | AC-Safe | See Section 1.2.2.1 [POSIX Safety Concepts], page 2.
>
> The `scalb` function is the BSD name for `ldexp`.

double scalbn (*double* **x**, *int* **n**)                                     [Function]
float scalbnf (*float* **x**, *int* **n**)                                      [Function]
long double scalbnl (*long double* **x**, *int* **n**)                          [Function]
> Preliminary: | MT-Safe | AS-Safe | AC-Safe | See Section 1.2.2.1 [POSIX Safety Concepts], page 2.
>
> `scalbn` is identical to `scalb`, except that the exponent *n* is an `int` instead of a floating-point number.

`double scalbln` (*double x, long int n*)                                  [Function]
`float scalblnf` (*float x, long int n*)                                    [Function]
`long double scalblnl` (*long double x, long int n*)                        [Function]
> Preliminary: | MT-Safe | AS-Safe | AC-Safe | See Section 1.2.2.1 [POSIX Safety Concepts], page 2.

> `scalbln` is identical to `scalb`, except that the exponent *n* is a `long int` instead of a floating-point number.

`double significand` (*double x*)                                           [Function]
`float significandf` (*float x*)                                            [Function]
`long double significandl` (*long double x*)                                [Function]
> Preliminary: | MT-Safe | AS-Safe | AC-Safe | See Section 1.2.2.1 [POSIX Safety Concepts], page 2.

> `significand` returns the mantissa of *x* scaled to the range $[1, 2)$. It is equivalent to `scalb (x, (double) -ilogb (x))`.

> This function exists mainly for use in certain standardized tests of IEEE 754 conformance.

## 20.8.3 Rounding Functions

The functions listed here perform operations such as rounding and truncation of floating-point values. Some of these functions convert floating point numbers to integer values. They are all declared in `math.h`.

You can also convert floating-point numbers to integers simply by casting them to `int`. This discards the fractional part, effectively rounding towards zero. However, this only works if the result can actually be represented as an `int`—for very large numbers, this is impossible. The functions listed here return the result as a `double` instead to get around this problem.

`double ceil` (*double x*)                                                  [Function]
`float ceilf` (*float x*)                                                    [Function]
`long double ceill` (*long double x*)                                        [Function]
> Preliminary: | MT-Safe | AS-Safe | AC-Safe | See Section 1.2.2.1 [POSIX Safety Concepts], page 2.

> These functions round *x* upwards to the nearest integer, returning that value as a `double`. Thus, `ceil (1.5)` is `2.0`.

`double floor` (*double x*)                                                 [Function]
`float floorf` (*float x*)                                                   [Function]
`long double floorl` (*long double x*)                                       [Function]
> Preliminary: | MT-Safe | AS-Safe | AC-Safe | See Section 1.2.2.1 [POSIX Safety Concepts], page 2.

> These functions round *x* downwards to the nearest integer, returning that value as a `double`. Thus, `floor (1.5)` is `1.0` and `floor (-1.5)` is `-2.0`.

`double trunc` (*double x*)                                                 [Function]
`float truncf` (*float x*)                                                   [Function]

`long double trunc1` (*long double x*)                                        [Function]
> Preliminary: | MT-Safe | AS-Safe | AC-Safe | See Section 1.2.2.1 [POSIX Safety Concepts], page 2.
>
> The `trunc` functions round *x* towards zero to the nearest integer (returned in floating-point format). Thus, `trunc (1.5)` is `1.0` and `trunc (-1.5)` is `-1.0`.

`double rint` (*double x*)                                                    [Function]
`float rintf` (*float x*)                                                     [Function]
`long double rintl` (*long double x*)                                         [Function]
> Preliminary: | MT-Safe | AS-Safe | AC-Safe | See Section 1.2.2.1 [POSIX Safety Concepts], page 2.
>
> These functions round *x* to an integer value according to the current rounding mode. See Section A.5.3.2 [Floating Point Parameters], page 888, for information about the various rounding modes. The default rounding mode is to round to the nearest integer; some machines support other modes, but round-to-nearest is always used unless you explicitly select another.
>
> If *x* was not initially an integer, these functions raise the inexact exception.

`double nearbyint` (*double x*)                                               [Function]
`float nearbyintf` (*float x*)                                                [Function]
`long double nearbyintl` (*long double x*)                                    [Function]
> Preliminary: | MT-Safe | AS-Safe | AC-Safe | See Section 1.2.2.1 [POSIX Safety Concepts], page 2.
>
> These functions return the same value as the `rint` functions, but do not raise the inexact exception if *x* is not an integer.

`double round` (*double x*)                                                   [Function]
`float roundf` (*float x*)                                                    [Function]
`long double roundl` (*long double x*)                                        [Function]
> Preliminary: | MT-Safe | AS-Safe | AC-Safe | See Section 1.2.2.1 [POSIX Safety Concepts], page 2.
>
> These functions are similar to `rint`, but they round halfway cases away from zero instead of to the nearest integer (or other current rounding mode).

`long int lrint` (*double x*)                                                 [Function]
`long int lrintf` (*float x*)                                                 [Function]
`long int lrintl` (*long double x*)                                           [Function]
> Preliminary: | MT-Safe | AS-Safe | AC-Safe | See Section 1.2.2.1 [POSIX Safety Concepts], page 2.
>
> These functions are just like `rint`, but they return a `long int` instead of a floating-point number.

`long long int llrint` (*double x*)                                           [Function]
`long long int llrintf` (*float x*)                                           [Function]
`long long int llrintl` (*long double x*)                                     [Function]
> Preliminary: | MT-Safe | AS-Safe | AC-Safe | See Section 1.2.2.1 [POSIX Safety Concepts], page 2.

These functions are just like `rint`, but they return a `long long int` instead of a floating-point number.

`long int lround (double x)` [Function]
`long int lroundf (float x)` [Function]
`long int lroundl (long double x)` [Function]
> Preliminary: | MT-Safe | AS-Safe | AC-Safe | See Section 1.2.2.1 [POSIX Safety Concepts], page 2.

> These functions are just like `round`, but they return a `long int` instead of a floating-point number.

`long long int llround (double x)` [Function]
`long long int llroundf (float x)` [Function]
`long long int llroundl (long double x)` [Function]
> Preliminary: | MT-Safe | AS-Safe | AC-Safe | See Section 1.2.2.1 [POSIX Safety Concepts], page 2.

> These functions are just like `round`, but they return a `long long int` instead of a floating-point number.

`double modf (double value, double *integer-part)` [Function]
`float modff (float value, float *integer-part)` [Function]
`long double modfl (long double value, long double *integer-part)` [Function]
> Preliminary: | MT-Safe | AS-Safe | AC-Safe | See Section 1.2.2.1 [POSIX Safety Concepts], page 2.

> These functions break the argument *value* into an integer part and a fractional part (between -1 and 1, exclusive). Their sum equals *value*. Each of the parts has the same sign as *value*, and the integer part is always rounded toward zero.

> `modf` stores the integer part in `*integer-part`, and returns the fractional part. For example, `modf (2.5, &intpart)` returns 0.5 and stores 2.0 into `intpart`.

## 20.8.4 Remainder Functions

The functions in this section compute the remainder on division of two floating-point numbers. Each is a little different; pick the one that suits your problem.

`double fmod (double numerator, double denominator)` [Function]
`float fmodf (float numerator, float denominator)` [Function]
`long double fmodl (long double numerator, long double denominator)` [Function]
> Preliminary: | MT-Safe | AS-Safe | AC-Safe | See Section 1.2.2.1 [POSIX Safety Concepts], page 2.

> These functions compute the remainder from the division of *numerator* by *denominator*. Specifically, the return value is `numerator - n * denominator`, where *n* is the quotient of *numerator* divided by *denominator*, rounded towards zero to an integer. Thus, `fmod (6.5, 2.3)` returns 1.9, which is 6.5 minus 4.6.

> The result has the same sign as the *numerator* and has magnitude less than the magnitude of the *denominator*.

> If *denominator* is zero, `fmod` signals a domain error.

double drem (*double* numerator, *double* denominator)                        [Function]
float dremf (*float* numerator, *float* denominator)                          [Function]
long double dreml (*long double* numerator, *long double*                     [Function]
    denominator)
> Preliminary: | MT-Safe | AS-Safe | AC-Safe | See Section 1.2.2.1 [POSIX Safety
> Concepts], page 2.

> These functions are like fmod except that they round the internal quotient *n* to the
> nearest integer instead of towards zero to an integer. For example, drem (6.5, 2.3)
> returns -0.4, which is 6.5 minus 6.9.

> The absolute value of the result is less than or equal to half the absolute value of the
> *denominator*. The difference between fmod (numerator, denominator) and drem
> (numerator, denominator) is always either *denominator*, minus *denominator*, or
> zero.

> If *denominator* is zero, drem signals a domain error.

double remainder (*double* numerator, *double* denominator)                   [Function]
float remainderf (*float* numerator, *float* denominator)                     [Function]
long double remainderl (*long double* numerator, *long double*                [Function]
    denominator)
> Preliminary: | MT-Safe | AS-Safe | AC-Safe | See Section 1.2.2.1 [POSIX Safety
> Concepts], page 2.

> This function is another name for drem.

## 20.8.5 Setting and modifying single bits of FP values

There are some operations that are too complicated or expensive to perform by hand on
floating-point numbers. ISO C99 defines functions to do these operations, which mostly
involve changing single bits.

double copysign (*double x, double y*)                                        [Function]
float copysignf (*float x, float y*)                                          [Function]
long double copysignl (*long double x, long double y*)                        [Function]
> Preliminary: | MT-Safe | AS-Safe | AC-Safe | See Section 1.2.2.1 [POSIX Safety
> Concepts], page 2.

> These functions return *x* but with the sign of *y*. They work even if *x* or *y* are NaN
> or zero. Both of these can carry a sign (although not all implementations support it)
> and this is one of the few operations that can tell the difference.

> copysign never raises an exception.

> This function is defined in IEC 559 (and the appendix with recommended functions
> in IEEE 754/IEEE 854).

int signbit (*float-type x*)                                                  [Function]
> Preliminary: | MT-Safe | AS-Safe | AC-Safe | See Section 1.2.2.1 [POSIX Safety
> Concepts], page 2.

> signbit is a generic macro which can work on all floating-point types. It returns a
> nonzero value if the value of *x* has its sign bit set.

This is not the same as `x < 0.0`, because IEEE 754 floating point allows zero to be signed. The comparison `-0.0 < 0.0` is false, but `signbit (-0.0)` will return a nonzero value.

| | |
|---|---|
| **double nextafter** (*double x, double y*) | [Function] |
| **float nextafterf** (*float x, float y*) | [Function] |
| **long double nextafterl** (*long double x, long double y*) | [Function] |

    Preliminary: | MT-Safe | AS-Safe | AC-Safe | See Section 1.2.2.1 [POSIX Safety Concepts], page 2.

    The `nextafter` function returns the next representable neighbor of *x* in the direction towards *y*. The size of the step between *x* and the result depends on the type of the result. If $x = y$ the function simply returns *y*. If either value is NaN, NaN is returned. Otherwise a value corresponding to the value of the least significant bit in the mantissa is added or subtracted, depending on the direction. `nextafter` will signal overflow or underflow if the result goes outside of the range of normalized numbers.

    This function is defined in IEC 559 (and the appendix with recommended functions in IEEE 754/IEEE 854).

| | |
|---|---|
| **double nexttoward** (*double x, long double y*) | [Function] |
| **float nexttowardf** (*float x, long double y*) | [Function] |
| **long double nexttowardl** (*long double x, long double y*) | [Function] |

    Preliminary: | MT-Safe | AS-Safe | AC-Safe | See Section 1.2.2.1 [POSIX Safety Concepts], page 2.

    These functions are identical to the corresponding versions of `nextafter` except that their second argument is a `long double`.

| | |
|---|---|
| **double nan** (*const char \*tagp*) | [Function] |
| **float nanf** (*const char \*tagp*) | [Function] |
| **long double nanl** (*const char \*tagp*) | [Function] |

    Preliminary: | MT-Safe locale | AS-Safe | AC-Safe | See Section 1.2.2.1 [POSIX Safety Concepts], page 2.

    The `nan` function returns a representation of NaN, provided that NaN is supported by the target platform. `nan ("n-char-sequence")` is equivalent to `strtod ("NAN(n-char-sequence)")`.

    The argument *tagp* is used in an unspecified manner. On IEEE 754 systems, there are many representations of NaN, and *tagp* selects one. On other systems it may do nothing.

### 20.8.6 Floating-Point Comparison Functions

The standard C comparison operators provoke exceptions when one or other of the operands is NaN. For example,

```
int v = a < 1.0;
```

will raise an exception if *a* is NaN. (This does *not* happen with `==` and `!=`; those merely return false and true, respectively, when NaN is examined.) Frequently this exception is undesirable. ISO C99 therefore defines comparison functions that do not raise exceptions when NaN is examined. All of the functions are implemented as macros which allow their arguments to be of any floating-point type. The macros are guaranteed to evaluate their arguments only once.

**int isgreater** (*real-floating x, real-floating y*)                     [Macro]
    Preliminary: | MT-Safe | AS-Safe | AC-Safe | See Section 1.2.2.1 [POSIX Safety Concepts], page 2.

    This macro determines whether the argument $x$ is greater than $y$. It is equivalent to $(x) > (y)$, but no exception is raised if $x$ or $y$ are NaN.

**int isgreaterequal** (*real-floating x, real-floating y*)               [Macro]
    Preliminary: | MT-Safe | AS-Safe | AC-Safe | See Section 1.2.2.1 [POSIX Safety Concepts], page 2.

    This macro determines whether the argument $x$ is greater than or equal to $y$. It is equivalent to $(x) >= (y)$, but no exception is raised if $x$ or $y$ are NaN.

**int isless** (*real-floating x, real-floating y*)                       [Macro]
    Preliminary: | MT-Safe | AS-Safe | AC-Safe | See Section 1.2.2.1 [POSIX Safety Concepts], page 2.

    This macro determines whether the argument $x$ is less than $y$. It is equivalent to $(x) < (y)$, but no exception is raised if $x$ or $y$ are NaN.

**int islessequal** (*real-floating x, real-floating y*)                  [Macro]
    Preliminary: | MT-Safe | AS-Safe | AC-Safe | See Section 1.2.2.1 [POSIX Safety Concepts], page 2.

    This macro determines whether the argument $x$ is less than or equal to $y$. It is equivalent to $(x) <= (y)$, but no exception is raised if $x$ or $y$ are NaN.

**int islessgreater** (*real-floating x, real-floating y*)                [Macro]
    Preliminary: | MT-Safe | AS-Safe | AC-Safe | See Section 1.2.2.1 [POSIX Safety Concepts], page 2.

    This macro determines whether the argument $x$ is less or greater than $y$. It is equivalent to $(x) < (y)$ || $(x) > (y)$ (although it only evaluates $x$ and $y$ once), but no exception is raised if $x$ or $y$ are NaN.

    This macro is not equivalent to $x$ != $y$, because that expression is true if $x$ or $y$ are NaN.

**int isunordered** (*real-floating x, real-floating y*)                  [Macro]
    Preliminary: | MT-Safe | AS-Safe | AC-Safe | See Section 1.2.2.1 [POSIX Safety Concepts], page 2.

    This macro determines whether its arguments are unordered. In other words, it is true if $x$ or $y$ are NaN, and false otherwise.

Not all machines provide hardware support for these operations. On machines that don't, the macros can be very slow. Therefore, you should not use these functions when NaN is not a concern.

**NB:** There are no macros `isequal` or `isunequal`. They are unnecessary, because the `==` and `!=` operators do *not* throw an exception if one or both of the operands are NaN.

### 20.8.7 Miscellaneous FP arithmetic functions

The functions in this section perform miscellaneous but common operations that are awkward to express with C operators. On some processors these functions can use special machine instructions to perform these operations faster than the equivalent C code.

| | |
|---|---|
| double fmin (*double x, double y*) | [Function] |
| float fminf (*float x, float y*) | [Function] |
| long double fminl (*long double x, long double y*) | [Function] |

Preliminary: | MT-Safe | AS-Safe | AC-Safe | See Section 1.2.2.1 [POSIX Safety Concepts], page 2.

The fmin function returns the lesser of the two values *x* and *y*. It is similar to the expression

```
((x) < (y) ? (x) : (y))
```

except that *x* and *y* are only evaluated once.

If an argument is NaN, the other argument is returned. If both arguments are NaN, NaN is returned.

| | |
|---|---|
| double fmax (*double x, double y*) | [Function] |
| float fmaxf (*float x, float y*) | [Function] |
| long double fmaxl (*long double x, long double y*) | [Function] |

Preliminary: | MT-Safe | AS-Safe | AC-Safe | See Section 1.2.2.1 [POSIX Safety Concepts], page 2.

The fmax function returns the greater of the two values *x* and *y*.

If an argument is NaN, the other argument is returned. If both arguments are NaN, NaN is returned.

| | |
|---|---|
| double fdim (*double x, double y*) | [Function] |
| float fdimf (*float x, float y*) | [Function] |
| long double fdiml (*long double x, long double y*) | [Function] |

Preliminary: | MT-Safe | AS-Safe | AC-Safe | See Section 1.2.2.1 [POSIX Safety Concepts], page 2.

The fdim function returns the positive difference between *x* and *y*. The positive difference is $x - y$ if *x* is greater than *y*, and 0 otherwise.

If *x*, *y*, or both are NaN, NaN is returned.

| | |
|---|---|
| double fma (*double x, double y, double z*) | [Function] |
| float fmaf (*float x, float y, float z*) | [Function] |
| long double fmal (*long double x, long double y, long double z*) | [Function] |

Preliminary: | MT-Safe | AS-Safe | AC-Safe | See Section 1.2.2.1 [POSIX Safety Concepts], page 2.

The fma function performs floating-point multiply-add. This is the operation $(x \cdot y) + z$, but the intermediate result is not rounded to the destination type. This can sometimes improve the precision of a calculation.

This function was introduced because some processors have a special instruction to perform multiply-add. The C compiler cannot use it directly, because the expression 'x*y + z' is defined to round the intermediate result. `fma` lets you choose when you want to round only once.

On processors which do not implement multiply-add in hardware, `fma` can be very slow since it must avoid intermediate rounding. `math.h` defines the symbols `FP_FAST_FMA`, `FP_FAST_FMAF`, and `FP_FAST_FMAL` when the corresponding version of `fma` is no slower than the expression 'x*y + z'. In the GNU C Library, this always means the operation is implemented in hardware.

## 20.9 Complex Numbers

ISO C99 introduces support for complex numbers in C. This is done with a new type qualifier, `complex`. It is a keyword if and only if `complex.h` has been included. There are three complex types, corresponding to the three real types: `float complex`, `double complex`, and `long double complex`.

To construct complex numbers you need a way to indicate the imaginary part of a number. There is no standard notation for an imaginary floating point constant. Instead, `complex.h` defines two macros that can be used to create complex numbers.

**const float complex _Complex_I**                                              [Macro]

    This macro is a representation of the complex number "$0 + 1i$". Multiplying a real floating-point value by `_Complex_I` gives a complex number whose value is purely imaginary. You can use this to construct complex constants:

        3.0  +  4.0*i = 3.0 + 4.0 * _Complex_I

    Note that `_Complex_I * _Complex_I` has the value **-1**, but the type of that value is `complex`.

`_Complex_I` is a bit of a mouthful. `complex.h` also defines a shorter name for the same constant.

**const float complex I**                                                       [Macro]

    This macro has exactly the same value as `_Complex_I`. Most of the time it is preferable. However, it causes problems if you want to use the identifier `I` for something else. You can safely write

        `#include <complex.h>`
        `#undef I`

    if you need `I` for your own purposes. (In that case we recommend you also define some other short name for `_Complex_I`, such as J.)

## 20.10 Projections, Conjugates, and Decomposing of Complex Numbers

ISO C99 also defines functions that perform basic operations on complex numbers, such as decomposition and conjugation. The prototypes for all these functions are in `complex.h`. All functions are available in three variants, one for each of the three complex types.

**double creal** (*complex double z*)                                           [Function]
**float crealf** (*complex float z*)                                            [Function]

long double creall (*complex long double z*)                                          [Function]
>     Preliminary: | MT-Safe | AS-Safe | AC-Safe | See Section 1.2.2.1 [POSIX Safety
>     Concepts], page 2.

>     These functions return the real part of the complex number *z*.

double cimag (*complex double z*)                                                     [Function]
float cimagf (*complex float z*)                                                      [Function]
long double cimagl (*complex long double z*)                                          [Function]
>     Preliminary: | MT-Safe | AS-Safe | AC-Safe | See Section 1.2.2.1 [POSIX Safety
>     Concepts], page 2.

>     These functions return the imaginary part of the complex number *z*.

complex double conj (*complex double z*)                                              [Function]
complex float conjf (*complex float z*)                                               [Function]
complex long double conjl (*complex long double z*)                                   [Function]
>     Preliminary: | MT-Safe | AS-Safe | AC-Safe | See Section 1.2.2.1 [POSIX Safety
>     Concepts], page 2.

>     These functions return the conjugate value of the complex number *z*. The conjugate
>     of a complex number has the same real part and a negated imaginary part. In other
>     words, 'conj(a + bi) = a + -bi'.

double carg (*complex double z*)                                                      [Function]
float cargf (*complex float z*)                                                       [Function]
long double cargl (*complex long double z*)                                           [Function]
>     Preliminary: | MT-Safe | AS-Safe | AC-Safe | See Section 1.2.2.1 [POSIX Safety
>     Concepts], page 2.

>     These functions return the argument of the complex number *z*. The argument of a
>     complex number is the angle in the complex plane between the positive real axis and
>     a line passing through zero and the number. This angle is measured in the usual
>     fashion and ranges from $-\pi$ to $\pi$.

>     carg has a branch cut along the negative real axis.

complex double cproj (*complex double z*)                                             [Function]
complex float cprojf (*complex float z*)                                              [Function]
complex long double cprojl (*complex long double z*)                                  [Function]
>     Preliminary: | MT-Safe | AS-Safe | AC-Safe | See Section 1.2.2.1 [POSIX Safety
>     Concepts], page 2.

>     These functions return the projection of the complex value *z* onto the Riemann sphere.
>     Values with an infinite imaginary part are projected to positive infinity on the real
>     axis, even if the real part is NaN. If the real part is infinite, the result is equivalent to
>
>         INFINITY + I * copysign (0.0, cimag (z))

## 20.11 Parsing of Numbers

This section describes functions for "reading" integer and floating-point numbers from a
string. It may be more convenient in some cases to use **sscanf** or one of the related
functions; see Section 12.14 [Formatted Input], page 292. But often you can make a program

more robust by finding the tokens in the string by hand, then converting the numbers one by one.

## 20.11.1 Parsing of Integers

The 'str' functions are declared in **stdlib.h** and those beginning with 'wcs' are declared in **wchar.h**. One might wonder about the use of **restrict** in the prototypes of the functions in this section. It is seemingly useless but the ISO C standard uses it (for the functions defined there) so we have to do it as well.

**long int strtol** (*const char \*restrict* **string**, *char \*\*restrict* **tailptr**,      [Function]
      *int* **base**)

Preliminary: | MT-Safe locale | AS-Safe  | AC-Safe  | See Section 1.2.2.1 [POSIX Safety Concepts], page 2.

The **strtol** ("string-to-long") function converts the initial part of *string* to a signed integer, which is returned as a value of type **long int**.

This function attempts to decompose *string* as follows:

- A (possibly empty) sequence of whitespace characters. Which characters are whitespace is determined by the **isspace** function (see Section 4.1 [Classification of Characters], page 77). These are discarded.

- An optional plus or minus sign ('+' or '-').

- A nonempty sequence of digits in the radix specified by *base*.

  If *base* is zero, decimal radix is assumed unless the series of digits begins with '0' (specifying octal radix), or '0x' or '0X' (specifying hexadecimal radix); in other words, the same syntax used for integer constants in C.

  Otherwise *base* must have a value between 2 and 36. If *base* is 16, the digits may optionally be preceded by '0x' or '0X'. If base has no legal value the value returned is 0l and the global variable **errno** is set to EINVAL.

- Any remaining characters in the string. If *tailptr* is not a null pointer, **strtol** stores a pointer to this tail in *\*tailptr*.

If the string is empty, contains only whitespace, or does not contain an initial substring that has the expected syntax for an integer in the specified *base*, no conversion is performed. In this case, **strtol** returns a value of zero and the value stored in *\*tailptr* is the value of *string*.

In a locale other than the standard "C" locale, this function may recognize additional implementation-dependent syntax.

If the string has valid syntax for an integer but the value is not representable because of overflow, **strtol** returns either LONG_MAX or LONG_MIN (see Section A.5.2 [Range of an Integer Type], page 885), as appropriate for the sign of the value. It also sets **errno** to ERANGE to indicate there was overflow.

You should not check for errors by examining the return value of **strtol**, because the string might be a valid representation of 0l, LONG_MAX, or LONG_MIN. Instead, check whether *tailptr* points to what you expect after the number (e.g. '\0' if the string should end after the number). You also need to clear *errno* before the call and check it afterward, in case there was overflow.

There is an example at the end of this section.

**long int wcstol** (*const wchar_t \*restrict* **string**, *wchar_t \*\*restrict*        [Function]
    **tailptr**, *int* **base**)

Preliminary: | MT-Safe locale | AS-Safe | AC-Safe | See Section 1.2.2.1 [POSIX Safety Concepts], page 2.

The **wcstol** function is equivalent to the **strtol** function in nearly all aspects but handles wide character strings.

The **wcstol** function was introduced in Amendment 1 of ISO C90.

**unsigned long int strtoul** (*const char \*retrict* **string**, *char*        [Function]
    *\*\*restrict* **tailptr**, *int* **base**)

Preliminary: | MT-Safe locale | AS-Safe | AC-Safe | See Section 1.2.2.1 [POSIX Safety Concepts], page 2.

The **strtoul** ("string-to-unsigned-long") function is like **strtol** except it converts to an **unsigned long int** value. The syntax is the same as described above for **strtol**. The value returned on overflow is **ULONG_MAX** (see Section A.5.2 [Range of an Integer Type], page 885).

If *string* depicts a negative number, **strtoul** acts the same as *strtol* but casts the result to an unsigned integer. That means for example that **strtoul** on "-1" returns **ULONG_MAX** and an input more negative than **LONG_MIN** returns (**ULONG_MAX** + 1) / 2.

**strtoul** sets *errno* to **EINVAL** if *base* is out of range, or **ERANGE** on overflow.

**unsigned long int wcstoul** (*const wchar_t \*restrict* **string**, *wchar_t*        [Function]
    *\*\*restrict* **tailptr**, *int* **base**)

Preliminary: | MT-Safe locale | AS-Safe | AC-Safe | See Section 1.2.2.1 [POSIX Safety Concepts], page 2.

The **wcstoul** function is equivalent to the **strtoul** function in nearly all aspects but handles wide character strings.

The **wcstoul** function was introduced in Amendment 1 of ISO C90.

**long long int strtoll** (*const char \*restrict* **string**, *char \*\*restrict*        [Function]
    **tailptr**, *int* **base**)

Preliminary: | MT-Safe locale | AS-Safe | AC-Safe | See Section 1.2.2.1 [POSIX Safety Concepts], page 2.

The **strtoll** function is like **strtol** except that it returns a **long long int** value, and accepts numbers with a correspondingly larger range.

If the string has valid syntax for an integer but the value is not representable because of overflow, **strtoll** returns either **LLONG_MAX** or **LLONG_MIN** (see Section A.5.2 [Range of an Integer Type], page 885), as appropriate for the sign of the value. It also sets **errno** to **ERANGE** to indicate there was overflow.

The **strtoll** function was introduced in ISO C99.

**long long int wcstoll** (*const wchar_t \*restrict* **string**, *wchar_t*        [Function]
    *\*\*restrict* **tailptr**, *int* **base**)

Preliminary: | MT-Safe locale | AS-Safe | AC-Safe | See Section 1.2.2.1 [POSIX Safety Concepts], page 2.

The `wcstoll` function is equivalent to the `strtoll` function in nearly all aspects but handles wide character strings.

The `wcstoll` function was introduced in Amendment 1 of ISO C90.

`long long int strtoq` (*const char \*restrict* **string**, *char \*\*restrict*     [Function]
    **tailptr**, *int* **base**)
Preliminary: | MT-Safe locale | AS-Safe | AC-Safe | See Section 1.2.2.1 [POSIX Safety Concepts], page 2.

`strtoq` ("string-to-quad-word") is the BSD name for `strtoll`.

`long long int wcstoq` (*const wchar_t \*restrict* **string**, *wchar_t*     [Function]
    *\*\*restrict* **tailptr**, *int* **base**)
Preliminary: | MT-Safe locale | AS-Safe | AC-Safe | See Section 1.2.2.1 [POSIX Safety Concepts], page 2.

The `wcstoq` function is equivalent to the `strtoq` function in nearly all aspects but handles wide character strings.

The `wcstoq` function is a GNU extension.

`unsigned long long int strtoull` (*const char \*restrict* **string**, *char*     [Function]
    *\*\*restrict* **tailptr**, *int* **base**)
Preliminary: | MT-Safe locale | AS-Safe | AC-Safe | See Section 1.2.2.1 [POSIX Safety Concepts], page 2.

The `strtoull` function is related to `strtoll` the same way `strtoul` is related to `strtol`.

The `strtoull` function was introduced in ISO C99.

`unsigned long long int wcstoull` (*const wchar_t \*restrict* **string**,     [Function]
    *wchar_t \*\*restrict* **tailptr**, *int* **base**)
Preliminary: | MT-Safe locale | AS-Safe | AC-Safe | See Section 1.2.2.1 [POSIX Safety Concepts], page 2.

The `wcstoull` function is equivalent to the `strtoull` function in nearly all aspects but handles wide character strings.

The `wcstoull` function was introduced in Amendment 1 of ISO C90.

`unsigned long long int strtouq` (*const char \*restrict* **string**, *char*     [Function]
    *\*\*restrict* **tailptr**, *int* **base**)
Preliminary: | MT-Safe locale | AS-Safe | AC-Safe | See Section 1.2.2.1 [POSIX Safety Concepts], page 2.

`strtouq` is the BSD name for `strtoull`.

`unsigned long long int wcstouq` (*const wchar_t \*restrict* **string**,     [Function]
    *wchar_t \*\*restrict* **tailptr**, *int* **base**)
Preliminary: | MT-Safe locale | AS-Safe | AC-Safe | See Section 1.2.2.1 [POSIX Safety Concepts], page 2.

The `wcstouq` function is equivalent to the `strtouq` function in nearly all aspects but handles wide character strings.

The `wcstouq` function is a GNU extension.

`intmax_t strtoimax` (*const char \*restrict* **string**, *char \*\*restrict*          [Function]
      **tailptr**, *int* **base**)

Preliminary: | MT-Safe locale | AS-Safe | AC-Safe | See Section 1.2.2.1 [POSIX Safety Concepts], page 2.

The `strtoimax` function is like `strtol` except that it returns a `intmax_t` value, and accepts numbers of a corresponding range.

If the string has valid syntax for an integer but the value is not representable because of overflow, `strtoimax` returns either `INTMAX_MAX` or `INTMAX_MIN` (see Section 20.1 [Integers], page 559), as appropriate for the sign of the value. It also sets `errno` to `ERANGE` to indicate there was overflow.

See Section 20.1 [Integers], page 559 for a description of the `intmax_t` type. The `strtoimax` function was introduced in ISO C99.

`intmax_t wcstoimax` (*const wchar_t \*restrict* **string**, *wchar_t \*\*restrict*    [Function]
      **tailptr**, *int* **base**)

Preliminary: | MT-Safe locale | AS-Safe | AC-Safe | See Section 1.2.2.1 [POSIX Safety Concepts], page 2.

The `wcstoimax` function is equivalent to the `strtoimax` function in nearly all aspects but handles wide character strings.

The `wcstoimax` function was introduced in ISO C99.

`uintmax_t strtoumax` (*const char \*restrict* **string**, *char \*\*restrict*          [Function]
      **tailptr**, *int* **base**)

Preliminary: | MT-Safe locale | AS-Safe | AC-Safe | See Section 1.2.2.1 [POSIX Safety Concepts], page 2.

The `strtoumax` function is related to `strtoimax` the same way that `strtoul` is related to `strtol`.

See Section 20.1 [Integers], page 559 for a description of the `intmax_t` type. The `strtoumax` function was introduced in ISO C99.

`uintmax_t wcstoumax` (*const wchar_t \*restrict* **string**, *wchar_t*                [Function]
      *\*\*restrict* **tailptr**, *int* **base**)

Preliminary: | MT-Safe locale | AS-Safe | AC-Safe | See Section 1.2.2.1 [POSIX Safety Concepts], page 2.

The `wcstoumax` function is equivalent to the `strtoumax` function in nearly all aspects but handles wide character strings.

The `wcstoumax` function was introduced in ISO C99.

`long int atol` (*const char \**string*)                                             [Function]

Preliminary: | MT-Safe locale | AS-Safe | AC-Safe | See Section 1.2.2.1 [POSIX Safety Concepts], page 2.

This function is similar to the `strtol` function with a *base* argument of `10`, except that it need not detect overflow errors. The `atol` function is provided mostly for compatibility with existing code; using `strtol` is more robust.

`int atoi (const char *string)`                                    [Function]
> Preliminary: | MT-Safe locale | AS-Safe | AC-Safe | See Section 1.2.2.1 [POSIX Safety Concepts], page 2.
>
> This function is like `atol`, except that it returns an `int`. The `atoi` function is also considered obsolete; use `strtol` instead.

`long long int atoll (const char *string)`                          [Function]
> Preliminary: | MT-Safe locale | AS-Safe | AC-Safe | See Section 1.2.2.1 [POSIX Safety Concepts], page 2.
>
> This function is similar to `atol`, except it returns a `long long int`.
>
> The `atoll` function was introduced in ISO C99. It too is obsolete (despite having just been added); use `strtoll` instead.

All the functions mentioned in this section so far do not handle alternative representations of characters as described in the locale data. Some locales specify thousands separator and the way they have to be used which can help to make large numbers more readable. To read such numbers one has to use the `scanf` functions with the ' ' ' flag.

Here is a function which parses a string as a sequence of integers and returns the sum of them:

```
int
sum_ints_from_string (char *string)
{
  int sum = 0;

  while (1) {
    char *tail;
    int next;

    /* Skip whitespace by hand, to detect the end.  */
    while (isspace (*string)) string++;
    if (*string == 0)
      break;

    /* There is more nonwhitespace,  */
    /* so it ought to be another number.  */
    errno = 0;
    /* Parse it.  */
    next = strtol (string, &tail, 0);
    /* Add it in, if not overflow.  */
    if (errno)
      printf ("Overflow\n");
    else
      sum += next;
    /* Advance past it.  */
    string = tail;
  }

  return sum;
}
```

## 20.11.2 Parsing of Floats

The 'str' functions are declared in `stdlib.h` and those beginning with 'wcs' are declared in `wchar.h`. One might wonder about the use of `restrict` in the prototypes of the functions in this section. It is seemingly useless but the ISO C standard uses it (for the functions defined there) so we have to do it as well.

**double strtod** (*const char \*restrict* **string**, *char \*\*restrict* **tailptr**)      [Function]
Preliminary: | MT-Safe locale | AS-Safe | AC-Safe | See Section 1.2.2.1 [POSIX Safety Concepts], page 2.

The **strtod** ("string-to-double") function converts the initial part of *string* to a floating-point number, which is returned as a value of type **double**.

This function attempts to decompose *string* as follows:

- A (possibly empty) sequence of whitespace characters. Which characters are whitespace is determined by the **isspace** function (see Section 4.1 [Classification of Characters], page 77). These are discarded.
- An optional plus or minus sign ('+' or '-').
- A floating point number in decimal or hexadecimal format. The decimal format is:
  - A nonempty sequence of digits optionally containing a decimal-point character—normally '.', but it depends on the locale (see Section 7.7.1.1 [Generic Numeric Formatting Parameters], page 175).
  - An optional exponent part, consisting of a character 'e' or 'E', an optional sign, and a sequence of digits.

  The hexadecimal format is as follows:
  - A 0x or 0X followed by a nonempty sequence of hexadecimal digits optionally containing a decimal-point character—normally '.', but it depends on the locale (see Section 7.7.1.1 [Generic Numeric Formatting Parameters], page 175).
  - An optional binary-exponent part, consisting of a character 'p' or 'P', an optional sign, and a sequence of digits.
- Any remaining characters in the string. If *tailptr* is not a null pointer, a pointer to this tail of the string is stored in *\*tailptr*.

If the string is empty, contains only whitespace, or does not contain an initial substring that has the expected syntax for a floating-point number, no conversion is performed. In this case, **strtod** returns a value of zero and the value returned in *\*tailptr* is the value of *string*.

In a locale other than the standard "C" or "POSIX" locales, this function may recognize additional locale-dependent syntax.

If the string has valid syntax for a floating-point number but the value is outside the range of a **double**, **strtod** will signal overflow or underflow as described in Section 20.5.4 [Error Reporting by Mathematical Functions], page 569.

**strtod** recognizes four special input strings. The strings "inf" and "infinity" are converted to ∞, or to the largest representable value if the floating-point format doesn't support infinities. You can prepend a "+" or "-" to specify the sign. Case is ignored when scanning these strings.

The strings `"nan"` and `"nan(chars...)"` are converted to NaN. Again, case is ignored. If *chars...* are provided, they are used in some unspecified fashion to select a particular representation of NaN (there can be several).

Since zero is a valid result as well as the value returned on error, you should check for errors in the same way as for `strtol`, by examining *errno* and *tailptr*.

**float strtof** (*const char \*string, char \*\*tailptr*)                         [Function]
**long double strtold** (*const char \*string, char \*\*tailptr*)              [Function]
> Preliminary: | MT-Safe locale | AS-Safe | AC-Safe | See Section 1.2.2.1 [POSIX Safety Concepts], page 2.
>
> These functions are analogous to `strtod`, but return `float` and `long double` values respectively. They report errors in the same way as `strtod`. `strtof` can be substantially faster than `strtod`, but has less precision; conversely, `strtold` can be much slower but has more precision (on systems where `long double` is a separate type).
>
> These functions have been GNU extensions and are new to ISO C99.

**double wcstod** (*const wchar_t \*restrict string, wchar_t \*\*restrict*      [Function]
> *tailptr*)
**float wcstof** (*const wchar_t \*string, wchar_t \*\*tailptr*)                 [Function]
**long double wcstold** (*const wchar_t \*string, wchar_t \*\*tailptr*)      [Function]
> Preliminary: | MT-Safe locale | AS-Safe | AC-Safe | See Section 1.2.2.1 [POSIX Safety Concepts], page 2.
>
> The `wcstod`, `wcstof`, and `wcstol` functions are equivalent in nearly all aspect to the `strtod`, `strtof`, and `strtold` functions but it handles wide character string.
>
> The `wcstod` function was introduced in Amendment 1 of ISO C90. The `wcstof` and `wcstold` functions were introduced in ISO C99.

**double atof** (*const char \*string*)                                           [Function]
> Preliminary: | MT-Safe locale | AS-Safe | AC-Safe | See Section 1.2.2.1 [POSIX Safety Concepts], page 2.
>
> This function is similar to the `strtod` function, except that it need not detect overflow and underflow errors. The `atof` function is provided mostly for compatibility with existing code; using `strtod` is more robust.

The GNU C Library also provides '`_l`' versions of these functions, which take an additional argument, the locale to use in conversion.

See also Section 20.11.1 [Parsing of Integers], page 585.

## 20.12 Old-fashioned System V number-to-string functions

The old System V C library provided three functions to convert numbers to strings, with unusual and hard-to-use semantics. The GNU C Library also provides these functions and some natural extensions.

These functions are only available in the GNU C Library and on systems descended from AT&T Unix. Therefore, unless these functions do precisely what you need, it is better to use `sprintf`, which is standard.

All these functions are defined in `stdlib.h`.

char * ecvt (*double* **value**, *int* **ndigit**, *int* **\*decpt**, *int* **\*neg**)                          [Function]
    Preliminary: | MT-Unsafe race:ecvt | AS-Unsafe | AC-Safe | See Section 1.2.2.1
    [POSIX Safety Concepts], page 2.

    The function ecvt converts the floating-point number *value* to a string with at most
    *ndigit* decimal digits. The returned string contains no decimal point or sign. The
    first digit of the string is non-zero (unless *value* is actually zero) and the last digit is
    rounded to nearest. *decpt* is set to the index in the string of the first digit after the
    decimal point. *neg* is set to a nonzero value if *value* is negative, zero otherwise.

    If *ndigit* decimal digits would exceed the precision of a double it is reduced to a
    system-specific value.

    The returned string is statically allocated and overwritten by each call to ecvt.

    If *value* is zero, it is implementation defined whether *decpt* is 0 or 1.

    For example: ecvt (12.3, 5, &d, &n) returns "12300" and sets *d* to 2 and *n* to 0.

char * fcvt (*double* **value**, *int* **ndigit**, *int* **\*decpt**, *int* **\*neg**)                          [Function]
    Preliminary: | MT-Unsafe race:fcvt | AS-Unsafe heap | AC-Unsafe mem | See
    Section 1.2.2.1 [POSIX Safety Concepts], page 2.

    The function fcvt is like ecvt, but *ndigit* specifies the number of digits after the
    decimal point. If *ndigit* is less than zero, *value* is rounded to the *ndigit* + 1'th place
    to the left of the decimal point. For example, if *ndigit* is -1, *value* will be rounded to
    the nearest 10. If *ndigit* is negative and larger than the number of digits to the left
    of the decimal point in *value*, *value* will be rounded to one significant digit.

    If *ndigit* decimal digits would exceed the precision of a double it is reduced to a
    system-specific value.

    The returned string is statically allocated and overwritten by each call to fcvt.

char * gcvt (*double* **value**, *int* **ndigit**, *char* **\*buf**)                          [Function]
    Preliminary: | MT-Safe | AS-Safe | AC-Safe | See Section 1.2.2.1 [POSIX Safety
    Concepts], page 2.

    gcvt is functionally equivalent to 'sprintf(buf, "%*g", ndigit, value'. It is pro-
    vided only for compatibility's sake. It returns *buf*.

    If *ndigit* decimal digits would exceed the precision of a double it is reduced to a
    system-specific value.

   As extensions, the GNU C Library provides versions of these three functions that take
long double arguments.

char * qecvt (*long double* **value**, *int* **ndigit**, *int* **\*decpt**, *int* **\*neg**)                          [Function]
    Preliminary: | MT-Unsafe race:qecvt | AS-Unsafe | AC-Safe | See Section 1.2.2.1
    [POSIX Safety Concepts], page 2.

    This function is equivalent to ecvt except that it takes a long double for the first
    parameter and that *ndigit* is restricted by the precision of a long double.

char * qfcvt (*long double* **value**, *int* **ndigit**, *int* **\*decpt**, *int* **\*neg**)                          [Function]
    Preliminary: | MT-Unsafe race:qfcvt | AS-Unsafe heap | AC-Unsafe mem | See
    Section 1.2.2.1 [POSIX Safety Concepts], page 2.

This function is equivalent to `fcvt` except that it takes a `long double` for the first parameter and that *ndigit* is restricted by the precision of a `long double`.

`char * qgcvt` (*long double* **value**, *int* **ndigit**, *char* *\*buf*)                    [Function]
Preliminary: | MT-Safe | AS-Safe | AC-Safe | See Section 1.2.2.1 [POSIX Safety Concepts], page 2.

This function is equivalent to `gcvt` except that it takes a `long double` for the first parameter and that *ndigit* is restricted by the precision of a `long double`.

The `ecvt` and `fcvt` functions, and their `long double` equivalents, all return a string located in a static buffer which is overwritten by the next call to the function. The GNU C Library provides another set of extended functions which write the converted string into a user-supplied buffer. These have the conventional `_r` suffix.

`gcvt_r` is not necessary, because `gcvt` already uses a user-supplied buffer.

`int ecvt_r` (*double* **value**, *int* **ndigit**, *int* *\*decpt*, *int* *\*neg*, *char* *\*buf*,    [Function]
        *size_t* **len**)
Preliminary: | MT-Safe | AS-Safe | AC-Safe | See Section 1.2.2.1 [POSIX Safety Concepts], page 2.

The `ecvt_r` function is the same as `ecvt`, except that it places its result into the user-specified buffer pointed to by *buf*, with length *len*. The return value is −1 in case of an error and zero otherwise.

This function is a GNU extension.

`int fcvt_r` (*double* **value**, *int* **ndigit**, *int* *\*decpt*, *int* *\*neg*, *char* *\*buf*,    [Function]
        *size_t* **len**)
Preliminary: | MT-Safe | AS-Safe | AC-Safe | See Section 1.2.2.1 [POSIX Safety Concepts], page 2.

The `fcvt_r` function is the same as `fcvt`, except that it places its result into the user-specified buffer pointed to by *buf*, with length *len*. The return value is −1 in case of an error and zero otherwise.

This function is a GNU extension.

`int qecvt_r` (*long double* **value**, *int* **ndigit**, *int* *\*decpt*, *int* *\*neg*, *char*    [Function]
        *\*buf*, *size_t* **len**)
Preliminary: | MT-Safe | AS-Safe | AC-Safe | See Section 1.2.2.1 [POSIX Safety Concepts], page 2.

The `qecvt_r` function is the same as `qecvt`, except that it places its result into the user-specified buffer pointed to by *buf*, with length *len*. The return value is −1 in case of an error and zero otherwise.

This function is a GNU extension.

`int qfcvt_r` (*long double* **value**, *int* **ndigit**, *int* *\*decpt*, *int* *\*neg*, *char*    [Function]
        *\*buf*, *size_t* **len**)
Preliminary: | MT-Safe | AS-Safe | AC-Safe | See Section 1.2.2.1 [POSIX Safety Concepts], page 2.

The `qfcvt_r` function is the same as `qfcvt`, except that it places its result into the user-specified buffer pointed to by *buf*, with length *len*. The return value is -1 in case of an error and zero otherwise.

This function is a GNU extension.

# 21 Date and Time

This chapter describes functions for manipulating dates and times, including functions for determining what time it is and conversion between different time representations.

## 21.1 Time Basics

Discussing time in a technical manual can be difficult because the word "time" in English refers to lots of different things. In this manual, we use a rigorous terminology to avoid confusion, and the only thing we use the simple word "time" for is to talk about the abstract concept.

A *calendar time* is a point in the time continuum, for example November 4, 1990 at 18:02.5 UTC. Sometimes this is called "absolute time".

We don't speak of a "date", because that is inherent in a calendar time.

An *interval* is a contiguous part of the time continuum between two calendar times, for example the hour between 9:00 and 10:00 on July 4, 1980.

An *elapsed time* is the length of an interval, for example, 35 minutes. People sometimes sloppily use the word "interval" to refer to the elapsed time of some interval.

An *amount of time* is a sum of elapsed times, which need not be of any specific intervals. For example, the amount of time it takes to read a book might be 9 hours, independently of when and in how many sittings it is read.

A *period* is the elapsed time of an interval between two events, especially when they are part of a sequence of regularly repeating events.

*CPU time* is like calendar time, except that it is based on the subset of the time continuum when a particular process is actively using a CPU. CPU time is, therefore, relative to a process.

*Processor time* is an amount of time that a CPU is in use. In fact, it's a basic system resource, since there's a limit to how much can exist in any given interval (that limit is the elapsed time of the interval times the number of CPUs in the processor). People often call this CPU time, but we reserve the latter term in this manual for the definition above.

## 21.2 Elapsed Time

One way to represent an elapsed time is with a simple arithmetic data type, as with the following function to compute the elapsed time between two calendar times. This function is declared in `time.h`.

`double difftime` (*time_t time1*, *time_t time0*)                              [Function]

> Preliminary: | MT-Safe | AS-Safe | AC-Safe | See Section 1.2.2.1 [POSIX Safety Concepts], page 2.

> The `difftime` function returns the number of seconds of elapsed time between calendar time *time1* and calendar time *time0*, as a value of type `double`. The difference ignores leap seconds unless leap second support is enabled.

> In the GNU C Library, you can simply subtract `time_t` values. But on other systems, the `time_t` data type might use some other encoding where subtraction doesn't work directly.

The GNU C Library provides two data types specifically for representing an elapsed time. They are used by various GNU C Library functions, and you can use them for your own purposes too. They're exactly the same except that one has a resolution in microseconds, and the other, newer one, is in nanoseconds.

**struct timeval**                                                              [Data Type]

The **struct timeval** structure represents an elapsed time. It is declared in **sys/time.h** and has the following members:

**time_t tv_sec**

This represents the number of whole seconds of elapsed time.

**long int tv_usec**

This is the rest of the elapsed time (a fraction of a second), represented as the number of microseconds. It is always less than one million.

**struct timespec**                                                            [Data Type]

The **struct timespec** structure represents an elapsed time. It is declared in **time.h** and has the following members:

**time_t tv_sec**

This represents the number of whole seconds of elapsed time.

**long int tv_nsec**

This is the rest of the elapsed time (a fraction of a second), represented as the number of nanoseconds. It is always less than one billion.

It is often necessary to subtract two values of type **struct timeval** or **struct timespec**. Here is the best way to do this. It works even on some peculiar operating systems where the **tv_sec** member has an unsigned type.

```
/* Subtract the 'struct timeval' values X and Y,
   storing the result in RESULT.
   Return 1 if the difference is negative, otherwise 0. */

int
timeval_subtract (result, x, y)
     struct timeval *result, *x, *y;
{
  /* Perform the carry for the later subtraction by updating y. */
  if (x->tv_usec < y->tv_usec) {
    int nsec = (y->tv_usec - x->tv_usec) / 1000000 + 1;
    y->tv_usec -= 1000000 * nsec;
    y->tv_sec += nsec;
  }
  if (x->tv_usec - y->tv_usec > 1000000) {
    int nsec = (x->tv_usec - y->tv_usec) / 1000000;
    y->tv_usec += 1000000 * nsec;
    y->tv_sec -= nsec;
  }

  /* Compute the time remaining to wait.
     tv_usec is certainly positive. */
  result->tv_sec = x->tv_sec - y->tv_sec;
  result->tv_usec = x->tv_usec - y->tv_usec;
```

```
    /* Return 1 if result is negative. */
    return x->tv_sec < y->tv_sec;
}
```

Common functions that use **struct timeval** are **gettimeofday** and **settimeofday**.

There are no GNU C Library functions specifically oriented toward dealing with elapsed times, but the calendar time, processor time, and alarm and sleeping functions have a lot to do with them.

## 21.3 Processor And CPU Time

If you're trying to optimize your program or measure its efficiency, it's very useful to know how much processor time it uses. For that, calendar time and elapsed times are useless because a process may spend time waiting for I/O or for other processes to use the CPU. However, you can get the information with the functions in this section.

CPU time (see Section 21.1 [Time Basics], page 595) is represented by the data type **clock_t**, which is a number of *clock ticks*. It gives the total amount of time a process has actively used a CPU since some arbitrary event. On GNU systems, that event is the creation of the process. While arbitrary in general, the event is always the same event for any particular process, so you can always measure how much time on the CPU a particular computation takes by examining the process' CPU time before and after the computation.

On GNU/Linux and GNU/Hurd systems, **clock_t** is equivalent to **long int** and **CLOCKS_PER_SEC** is an integer value. But in other systems, both **clock_t** and the macro **CLOCKS_PER_SEC** can be either integer or floating-point types. Casting CPU time values to **double**, as in the example above, makes sure that operations such as arithmetic and printing work properly and consistently no matter what the underlying representation is.

Note that the clock can wrap around. On a 32bit system with **CLOCKS_PER_SEC** set to one million this function will return the same value approximately every 72 minutes.

For additional functions to examine a process' use of processor time, and to control it, see Chapter 22 [Resource Usage And Limitation], page 630.

### 21.3.1 CPU Time Inquiry

To get a process' CPU time, you can use the **clock** function. This facility is declared in the header file **time.h**.

In typical usage, you call the **clock** function at the beginning and end of the interval you want to time, subtract the values, and then divide by **CLOCKS_PER_SEC** (the number of clock ticks per second) to get processor time, like this:

```
#include <time.h>

clock_t start, end;
double cpu_time_used;

start = clock();
... /* Do the work. */
end = clock();
cpu_time_used = ((double) (end - start)) / CLOCKS_PER_SEC;
```

Do not use a single CPU time as an amount of time; it doesn't work that way. Either do a subtraction as shown above or query processor time directly. See Section 21.3.2 [Processor Time Inquiry], page 598.

Different computers and operating systems vary wildly in how they keep track of CPU time. It's common for the internal processor clock to have a resolution somewhere between a hundredth and millionth of a second.

int CLOCKS_PER_SEC                                                [Macro]
    The value of this macro is the number of clock ticks per second measured by the clock function. POSIX requires that this value be one million independent of the actual resolution.

clock_t                                                        [Data Type]
    This is the type of the value returned by the clock function. Values of type clock_t are numbers of clock ticks.

clock_t clock (*void*)                                          [Function]
    Preliminary: | MT-Safe | AS-Safe | AC-Safe | See Section 1.2.2.1 [POSIX Safety Concepts], page 2.

    This function returns the calling process' current CPU time. If the CPU time is not available or cannot be represented, clock returns the value (clock_t)(-1).

## 21.3.2 Processor Time Inquiry

The times function returns information about a process' consumption of processor time in a struct tms object, in addition to the process' CPU time. See Section 21.1 [Time Basics], page 595. You should include the header file sys/times.h to use this facility.

struct tms                                                     [Data Type]
    The tms structure is used to return information about process times. It contains at least the following members:

    clock_t tms_utime
            This is the total processor time the calling process has used in executing the instructions of its program.

    clock_t tms_stime
            This is the processor time the system has used on behalf of the calling process.

    clock_t tms_cutime
            This is the sum of the tms_utime values and the tms_cutime values of all terminated child processes of the calling process, whose status has been reported to the parent process by wait or waitpid; see Section 26.6 [Process Completion], page 755. In other words, it represents the total processor time used in executing the instructions of all the terminated child processes of the calling process, excluding child processes which have not yet been reported by wait or waitpid.

```
clock_t tms_cstime
```
> This is similar to `tms_cutime`, but represents the total processor time system has used on behalf of all the terminated child processes of the calling process.

All of the times are given in numbers of clock ticks. Unlike CPU time, these are the actual amounts of time; not relative to any event. See Section 26.4 [Creating a Process], page 751.

`int CLK_TCK`                                                                          [Macro]
> This is an obsolete name for the number of clock ticks per second. Use `sysconf (_SC_CLK_TCK)` instead.

`clock_t times (struct tms *buffer)`                                                   [Function]
> Preliminary: | MT-Safe | AS-Safe | AC-Safe | See Section 1.2.2.1 [POSIX Safety Concepts], page 2.
>
> The `times` function stores the processor time information for the calling process in *buffer*.
>
> The return value is the number of clock ticks since an arbitrary point in the past, e.g. since system start-up. `times` returns `(clock_t)(-1)` to indicate failure.

**Portability Note:** The `clock` function described in Section 21.3.1 [CPU Time Inquiry], page 597 is specified by the ISO C standard. The `times` function is a feature of POSIX.1. On GNU systems, the CPU time is defined to be equivalent to the sum of the `tms_utime` and `tms_stime` fields returned by `times`.

## 21.4 Calendar Time

This section describes facilities for keeping track of calendar time. See Section 21.1 [Time Basics], page 595.

The GNU C Library represents calendar time three ways:

- *Simple time* (the `time_t` data type) is a compact representation, typically giving the number of seconds of elapsed time since some implementation-specific base time.

- There is also a "high-resolution time" representation. Like simple time, this represents a calendar time as an elapsed time since a base time, but instead of measuring in whole seconds, it uses a `struct timeval` data type, which includes fractions of a second. Use this time representation instead of simple time when you need greater precision.

- *Local time* or *broken-down time* (the `struct tm` data type) represents a calendar time as a set of components specifying the year, month, and so on in the Gregorian calendar, for a specific time zone. This calendar time representation is usually used only to communicate with people.

### 21.4.1 Simple Calendar Time

This section describes the `time_t` data type for representing calendar time as simple time, and the functions which operate on simple time objects. These facilities are declared in the header file `time.h`.

**time_t**                                                                      [Data Type]

This is the data type used to represent simple time. Sometimes, it also represents an elapsed time. When interpreted as a calendar time value, it represents the number of seconds elapsed since 00:00:00 on January 1, 1970, Coordinated Universal Time. (This calendar time is sometimes referred to as the *epoch*.) POSIX requires that this count not include leap seconds, but on some systems this count includes leap seconds if you set TZ to certain values (see Section 21.4.7 [Specifying the Time Zone with TZ], page 622).

Note that a simple time has no concept of local time zone. Calendar Time $T$ is the same instant in time regardless of where on the globe the computer is.

In the GNU C Library, time_t is equivalent to **long int**. In other systems, time_t might be either an integer or floating-point type.

The function **difftime** tells you the elapsed time between two simple calendar times, which is not always as easy to compute as just subtracting. See Section 21.2 [Elapsed Time], page 595.

**time_t time** (*time_t *result*)                                              [Function]

Preliminary: | MT-Safe | AS-Safe | AC-Safe | See Section 1.2.2.1 [POSIX Safety Concepts], page 2.

The **time** function returns the current calendar time as a value of type **time_t**. If the argument *result* is not a null pointer, the calendar time value is also stored in ***result**. If the current calendar time is not available, the value **(time_t)(-1)** is returned.

**int stime** (*const time_t *newtime*)                                         [Function]

Preliminary: | MT-Safe | AS-Safe | AC-Safe | See Section 1.2.2.1 [POSIX Safety Concepts], page 2.

**stime** sets the system clock, i.e., it tells the system that the current calendar time is *newtime*, where **newtime** is interpreted as described in the above definition of **time_t**.

**settimeofday** is a newer function which sets the system clock to better than one second precision. **settimeofday** is generally a better choice than **stime**. See Section 21.4.2 [High-Resolution Calendar], page 600.

Only the superuser can set the system clock.

If the function succeeds, the return value is zero. Otherwise, it is **-1** and **errno** is set accordingly:

EPERM       The process is not superuser.

## 21.4.2 High-Resolution Calendar

The **time_t** data type used to represent simple times has a resolution of only one second. Some applications need more precision.

So, the GNU C Library also contains functions which are capable of representing calendar times to a higher resolution than one second. The functions and the associated data types described in this section are declared in **sys/time.h**.

`struct timezone`                                                                      [Data Type]

> The `struct timezone` structure is used to hold minimal information about the local time zone. It has the following members:
>
> `int tz_minuteswest`
>> This is the number of minutes west of UTC.
>
> `int tz_dsttime`
>> If nonzero, Daylight Saving Time applies during some part of the year.
>
> The `struct timezone` type is obsolete and should never be used. Instead, use the facilities described in Section 21.4.8 [Functions and Variables for Time Zones], page 624.

`int gettimeofday` (*struct timeval \*tp, struct timezone \*tzp*)                   [Function]

> Preliminary: | MT-Safe | AS-Safe | AC-Safe | See Section 1.2.2.1 [POSIX Safety Concepts], page 2.
>
> The `gettimeofday` function returns the current calendar time as the elapsed time since the epoch in the `struct timeval` structure indicated by *tp*. (see Section 21.2 [Elapsed Time], page 595 for a description of `struct timeval`). Information about the time zone is returned in the structure pointed at *tzp*. If the *tzp* argument is a null pointer, time zone information is ignored.
>
> The return value is 0 on success and -1 on failure. The following `errno` error condition is defined for this function:
>
> `ENOSYS`   The operating system does not support getting time zone information, and *tzp* is not a null pointer. GNU systems do not support using `struct timezone` to represent time zone information; that is an obsolete feature of 4.3 BSD. Instead, use the facilities described in Section 21.4.8 [Functions and Variables for Time Zones], page 624.

`int settimeofday` (*const struct timeval \*tp, const struct timezone \*tzp*)       [Function]

> Preliminary: | MT-Safe | AS-Safe | AC-Safe | See Section 1.2.2.1 [POSIX Safety Concepts], page 2.
>
> The `settimeofday` function sets the current calendar time in the system clock according to the arguments. As for `gettimeofday`, the calendar time is represented as the elapsed time since the epoch. As for `gettimeofday`, time zone information is ignored if *tzp* is a null pointer.
>
> You must be a privileged user in order to use `settimeofday`.
>
> Some kernels automatically set the system clock from some source such as a hardware clock when they start up. Others, including Linux, place the system clock in an "invalid" state (in which attempts to read the clock fail). A call of `stime` removes the system clock from an invalid state, and system startup scripts typically run a program that calls `stime`.
>
> `settimeofday` causes a sudden jump forwards or backwards, which can cause a variety of problems in a system. Use `adjtime` (below) to make a smooth transition from one time to another by temporarily speeding up or slowing down the clock.
>
> With a Linux kernel, `adjtimex` does the same thing and can also make permanent changes to the speed of the system clock so it doesn't need to be corrected as often.

The return value is 0 on success and -1 on failure. The following **errno** error conditions are defined for this function:

EPERM        This process cannot set the clock because it is not privileged.

ENOSYS       The operating system does not support setting time zone information, and *tzp* is not a null pointer.

**int adjtime** (*const struct timeval *delta, struct timeval *olddelta*)        [Function]
Preliminary: | MT-Safe | AS-Safe | AC-Safe | See Section 1.2.2.1 [POSIX Safety Concepts], page 2.

This function speeds up or slows down the system clock in order to make a gradual adjustment. This ensures that the calendar time reported by the system clock is always monotonically increasing, which might not happen if you simply set the clock.

The *delta* argument specifies a relative adjustment to be made to the clock time. If negative, the system clock is slowed down for a while until it has lost this much elapsed time. If positive, the system clock is speeded up for a while.

If the *olddelta* argument is not a null pointer, the **adjtime** function returns information about any previous time adjustment that has not yet completed.

This function is typically used to synchronize the clocks of computers in a local network. You must be a privileged user to use it.

With a Linux kernel, you can use the **adjtimex** function to permanently change the clock speed.

The return value is 0 on success and -1 on failure. The following **errno** error condition is defined for this function:

EPERM        You do not have privilege to set the time.

**Portability Note:** The **gettimeofday**, **settimeofday**, and **adjtime** functions are derived from BSD.

Symbols for the following function are declared in **sys/timex.h**.

**int adjtimex** (*struct timex *timex*)        [Function]
Preliminary: | MT-Safe | AS-Safe | AC-Safe | See Section 1.2.2.1 [POSIX Safety Concepts], page 2.

**adjtimex** is functionally identical to **ntp_adjtime**. See Section 21.4.4 [High Accuracy Clock], page 605.

This function is present only with a Linux kernel.

## 21.4.3 Broken-down Time

Calendar time is represented by the usual GNU C Library functions as an elapsed time since a fixed base calendar time. This is convenient for computation, but has no relation to the way people normally think of calendar time. By contrast, *broken-down time* is a binary representation of calendar time separated into year, month, day, and so on. Broken-down time values are not useful for calculations, but they are useful for printing human readable time information.

A broken-down time value is always relative to a choice of time zone, and it also indicates which time zone that is.

The symbols in this section are declared in the header file **time.h**.

`struct tm`                                                    [Data Type]

>   This is the data type used to represent a broken-down time. The structure contains
>   at least the following members, which can appear in any order.

> `int tm_sec`
>
>>   This is the number of full seconds since the top of the minute (normally
>>   in the range 0 through 59, but the actual upper limit is 60, to allow for
>>   leap seconds if leap second support is available).

> `int tm_min`
>
>>   This is the number of full minutes since the top of the hour (in the range
>>   0 through 59).

> `int tm_hour`
>
>>   This is the number of full hours past midnight (in the range 0 through
>>   23).

> `int tm_mday`
>
>>   This is the ordinal day of the month (in the range 1 through 31). Watch
>>   out for this one! As the only ordinal number in the structure, it is incon-
>>   sistent with the rest of the structure.

> `int tm_mon`
>
>>   This is the number of full calendar months since the beginning of the year
>>   (in the range 0 through 11). Watch out for this one! People usually use
>>   ordinal numbers for month-of-year (where January = 1).

> `int tm_year`
>
>>   This is the number of full calendar years since 1900.

> `int tm_wday`
>
>>   This is the number of full days since Sunday (in the range 0 through 6).

> `int tm_yday`
>
>>   This is the number of full days since the beginning of the year (in the
>>   range 0 through 365).

> `int tm_isdst`
>
>>   This is a flag that indicates whether Daylight Saving Time is (or was, or
>>   will be) in effect at the time described. The value is positive if Daylight
>>   Saving Time is in effect, zero if it is not, and negative if the information
>>   is not available.

> `long int tm_gmtoff`
>
>>   This field describes the time zone that was used to compute this broken-
>>   down time value, including any adjustment for daylight saving; it is the
>>   number of seconds that you must add to UTC to get local time. You can
>>   also think of this as the number of seconds east of UTC. For example,
>>   for U.S. Eastern Standard Time, the value is -5*60*60. The `tm_gmtoff`
>>   field is derived from BSD and is a GNU library extension; it is not visible
>>   in a strict ISO C environment.

```
const char *tm_zone
```
This field is the name for the time zone that was used to compute this broken-down time value. Like `tm_gmtoff`, this field is a BSD and GNU extension, and is not visible in a strict ISO C environment.

`struct tm * localtime` (*const time_t *time*)                              [Function]
Preliminary: | MT-Unsafe race:tmbuf env locale | AS-Unsafe heap lock | AC-Unsafe lock mem fd | See Section 1.2.2.1 [POSIX Safety Concepts], page 2.

The `localtime` function converts the simple time pointed to by *time* to broken-down time representation, expressed relative to the user's specified time zone.

The return value is a pointer to a static broken-down time structure, which might be overwritten by subsequent calls to `ctime`, `gmtime`, or `localtime`. (But no other library function overwrites the contents of this object.)

The return value is the null pointer if *time* cannot be represented as a broken-down time; typically this is because the year cannot fit into an `int`.

Calling `localtime` also sets the current time zone as if `tzset` were called. See Section 21.4.8 [Functions and Variables for Time Zones], page 624.

Using the `localtime` function is a big problem in multi-threaded programs. The result is returned in a static buffer and this is used in all threads. POSIX.1c introduced a variant of this function.

`struct tm * localtime_r` (*const time_t *time, struct tm *resultp*)       [Function]
Preliminary: | MT-Safe env locale | AS-Unsafe heap lock | AC-Unsafe lock mem fd | See Section 1.2.2.1 [POSIX Safety Concepts], page 2.

The `localtime_r` function works just like the `localtime` function. It takes a pointer to a variable containing a simple time and converts it to the broken-down time format.

But the result is not placed in a static buffer. Instead it is placed in the object of type `struct tm` to which the parameter *resultp* points.

If the conversion is successful the function returns a pointer to the object the result was written into, i.e., it returns *resultp*.

`struct tm * gmtime` (*const time_t *time*)                                 [Function]
Preliminary: | MT-Unsafe race:tmbuf env locale | AS-Unsafe heap lock | AC-Unsafe lock mem fd | See Section 1.2.2.1 [POSIX Safety Concepts], page 2.

This function is similar to `localtime`, except that the broken-down time is expressed as Coordinated Universal Time (UTC) (formerly called Greenwich Mean Time (GMT)) rather than relative to a local time zone.

As for the `localtime` function we have the problem that the result is placed in a static variable. POSIX.1c also provides a replacement for `gmtime`.

`struct tm * gmtime_r` (*const time_t *time, struct tm *resultp*)          [Function]
Preliminary: | MT-Safe env locale | AS-Unsafe heap lock | AC-Unsafe lock mem fd | See Section 1.2.2.1 [POSIX Safety Concepts], page 2.

This function is similar to `localtime_r`, except that it converts just like `gmtime` the given time as Coordinated Universal Time.

If the conversion is successful the function returns a pointer to the object the result was written into, i.e., it returns *resultp*.

**time_t mktime** (*struct tm \*brokentime*)                                     [Function]
  Preliminary: | MT-Safe env locale | AS-Unsafe heap lock | AC-Unsafe lock mem fd
  | See Section 1.2.2.1 [POSIX Safety Concepts], page 2.

  The mktime function converts a broken-down time structure to a simple time representation. It also normalizes the contents of the broken-down time structure, and fills in some components based on the values of the others.

  The mktime function ignores the specified contents of the tm_wday, tm_yday, tm_gmtoff, and tm_zone members of the broken-down time structure. It uses the values of the other components to determine the calendar time; it's permissible for these components to have unnormalized values outside their normal ranges. The last thing that mktime does is adjust the components of the *brokentime* structure, including the members that were initially ignored.

  If the specified broken-down time cannot be represented as a simple time, mktime returns a value of (time_t)(-1) and does not modify the contents of *brokentime*.

  Calling mktime also sets the current time zone as if tzset were called; mktime uses this information instead of *brokentime*'s initial tm_gmtoff and tm_zone members. See Section 21.4.8 [Functions and Variables for Time Zones], page 624.

**time_t timelocal** (*struct tm \*brokentime*)                                     [Function]
  Preliminary: | MT-Safe env locale | AS-Unsafe heap lock | AC-Unsafe lock mem fd
  | See Section 1.2.2.1 [POSIX Safety Concepts], page 2.

  timelocal is functionally identical to mktime, but more mnemonically named. Note that it is the inverse of the localtime function.

  **Portability note:** mktime is essentially universally available. timelocal is rather rare.

**time_t timegm** (*struct tm \*brokentime*)                                     [Function]
  Preliminary: | MT-Safe env locale | AS-Unsafe heap lock | AC-Unsafe lock mem fd
  | See Section 1.2.2.1 [POSIX Safety Concepts], page 2.

  timegm is functionally identical to mktime except it always takes the input values to be Coordinated Universal Time (UTC) regardless of any local time zone setting.

  Note that timegm is the inverse of gmtime.

  **Portability note:** mktime is essentially universally available. timegm is rather rare. For the most portable conversion from a UTC broken-down time to a simple time, set the TZ environment variable to UTC, call mktime, then set TZ back.

## 21.4.4 High Accuracy Clock

The ntp_gettime and ntp_adjtime functions provide an interface to monitor and manipulate the system clock to maintain high accuracy time. For example, you can fine tune the speed of the clock or synchronize it with another time source.

A typical use of these functions is by a server implementing the Network Time Protocol to synchronize the clocks of multiple systems and high precision clocks.

These functions are declared in sys/timex.h.

`struct ntptimeval`                                                    [Data Type]

This structure is used for information about the system clock. It contains the following members:

`struct timeval time`

>    This is the current calendar time, expressed as the elapsed time since the epoch. The `struct timeval` data type is described in Section 21.2 [Elapsed Time], page 595.

`long int maxerror`

>    This is the maximum error, measured in microseconds. Unless updated via `ntp_adjtime` periodically, this value will reach some platform-specific maximum value.

`long int esterror`

>    This is the estimated error, measured in microseconds. This value can be set by `ntp_adjtime` to indicate the estimated offset of the system clock from the true calendar time.

`int ntp_gettime` (*struct ntptimeval *tptr*)                         [Function]

Preliminary: | MT-Safe | AS-Safe | AC-Safe | See Section 1.2.2.1 [POSIX Safety Concepts], page 2.

The `ntp_gettime` function sets the structure pointed to by *tptr* to current values. The elements of the structure afterwards contain the values the timer implementation in the kernel assumes. They might or might not be correct. If they are not a `ntp_adjtime` call is necessary.

The return value is 0 on success and other values on failure. The following `errno` error conditions are defined for this function:

`TIME_ERROR`

>    The precision clock model is not properly set up at the moment, thus the clock must be considered unsynchronized, and the values should be treated with care.

`struct timex`                                                        [Data Type]

This structure is used to control and monitor the system clock. It contains the following members:

`unsigned int modes`

>    This variable controls whether and which values are set. Several symbolic constants have to be combined with *binary or* to specify the effective mode. These constants start with `MOD_`.

`long int offset`

>    This value indicates the current offset of the system clock from the true calendar time. The value is given in microseconds. If bit `MOD_OFFSET` is set in `modes`, the offset (and possibly other dependent values) can be set. The offset's absolute value must not exceed `MAXPHASE`.

`long int frequency`

>    This value indicates the difference in frequency between the true calendar time and the system clock. The value is expressed as scaled PPM (parts

per million, 0.0001%). The scaling is `1 << SHIFT_USEC`. The value can be set with bit `MOD_FREQUENCY`, but the absolute value must not exceed `MAXFREQ`.

`long int maxerror`

This is the maximum error, measured in microseconds. A new value can be set using bit `MOD_MAXERROR`. Unless updated via `ntp_adjtime` periodically, this value will increase steadily and reach some platform-specific maximum value.

`long int esterror`

This is the estimated error, measured in microseconds. This value can be set using bit `MOD_ESTERROR`.

`int status`

This variable reflects the various states of the clock machinery. There are symbolic constants for the significant bits, starting with `STA_`. Some of these flags can be updated using the `MOD_STATUS` bit.

`long int constant`

This value represents the bandwidth or stiffness of the PLL (phase locked loop) implemented in the kernel. The value can be changed using bit `MOD_TIMECONST`.

`long int precision`

This value represents the accuracy or the maximum error when reading the system clock. The value is expressed in microseconds.

`long int tolerance`

This value represents the maximum frequency error of the system clock in scaled PPM. This value is used to increase the `maxerror` every second.

`struct timeval time`

The current calendar time.

`long int tick`

The elapsed time between clock ticks in microseconds. A clock tick is a periodic timer interrupt on which the system clock is based.

`long int ppsfreq`

This is the first of a few optional variables that are present only if the system clock can use a PPS (pulse per second) signal to discipline the system clock. The value is expressed in scaled PPM and it denotes the difference in frequency between the system clock and the PPS signal.

`long int jitter`

This value expresses a median filtered average of the PPS signal's dispersion in microseconds.

`int shift` This value is a binary exponent for the duration of the PPS calibration interval, ranging from `PPS_SHIFT` to `PPS_SHIFTMAX`.

`long int stabil`

This value represents the median filtered dispersion of the PPS frequency in scaled PPM.

`long int jitcnt`

> This counter represents the number of pulses where the jitter exceeded the allowed maximum `MAXTIME`.

`long int calcnt`

> This counter reflects the number of successful calibration intervals.

`long int errcnt`

> This counter represents the number of calibration errors (caused by large offsets or jitter).

`long int stbcnt`

> This counter denotes the number of calibrations where the stability exceeded the threshold.

`int ntp_adjtime` (*struct timex \*tptr*)                                      [Function]
> Preliminary: | MT-Safe | AS-Safe | AC-Safe | See Section 1.2.2.1 [POSIX Safety Concepts], page 2.

The `ntp_adjtime` function sets the structure specified by *tptr* to current values.

In addition, `ntp_adjtime` updates some settings to match what you pass to it in \**tptr*. Use the `modes` element of \**tptr* to select what settings to update. You can set `offset`, `freq`, `maxerror`, `esterror`, `status`, `constant`, and `tick`.

`modes` = zero means set nothing.

Only the superuser can update settings.

The return value is 0 on success and other values on failure. The following `errno` error conditions are defined for this function:

`TIME_ERROR`

> The high accuracy clock model is not properly set up at the moment, thus the clock must be considered unsynchronized, and the values should be treated with care. Another reason could be that the specified new values are not allowed.

`EPERM`     The process specified a settings update, but is not superuser.

For more details see RFC1305 (Network Time Protocol, Version 3) and related documents.

**Portability note:** Early versions of the GNU C Library did not have this function but did have the synonymous `adjtimex`.

## 21.4.5 Formatting Calendar Time

The functions described in this section format calendar time values as strings. These functions are declared in the header file `time.h`.

`char * asctime` (*const struct tm \*brokentime*)                              [Function]
> Preliminary: | MT-Unsafe race:asctime locale | AS-Unsafe | AC-Safe | See Section 1.2.2.1 [POSIX Safety Concepts], page 2.

The `asctime` function converts the broken-down time value that *brokentime* points to into a string in a standard format:

```
"Tue May 21 13:46:22 1991\n"
```

The abbreviations for the days of week are: 'Sun', 'Mon', 'Tue', 'Wed', 'Thu', 'Fri', and 'Sat'.

The abbreviations for the months are: 'Jan', 'Feb', 'Mar', 'Apr', 'May', 'Jun', 'Jul', 'Aug', 'Sep', 'Oct', 'Nov', and 'Dec'.

The return value points to a statically allocated string, which might be overwritten by subsequent calls to `asctime` or `ctime`. (But no other library function overwrites the contents of this string.)

`char * asctime_r` (*const struct tm \*brokentime, char \*buffer*)                    [Function]
Preliminary: | MT-Safe locale | AS-Safe | AC-Safe | See Section 1.2.2.1 [POSIX Safety Concepts], page 2.

This function is similar to `asctime` but instead of placing the result in a static buffer it writes the string in the buffer pointed to by the parameter *buffer*. This buffer should have room for at least 26 bytes, including the terminating null.

If no error occurred the function returns a pointer to the string the result was written into, i.e., it returns *buffer*. Otherwise return `NULL`.

`char * ctime` (*const time_t \*time*)                                              [Function]
Preliminary: | MT-Unsafe race:tmbuf race:asctime env locale | AS-Unsafe heap lock | AC-Unsafe lock mem fd | See Section 1.2.2.1 [POSIX Safety Concepts], page 2.

The `ctime` function is similar to `asctime`, except that you specify the calendar time argument as a `time_t` simple time value rather than in broken-down local time format. It is equivalent to

```
asctime (localtime (time))
```

Calling `ctime` also sets the current time zone as if `tzset` were called. See Section 21.4.8 [Functions and Variables for Time Zones], page 624.

`char * ctime_r` (*const time_t \*time, char \*buffer*)                               [Function]
Preliminary: | MT-Safe env locale | AS-Unsafe heap lock | AC-Unsafe lock mem fd | See Section 1.2.2.1 [POSIX Safety Concepts], page 2.

This function is similar to `ctime`, but places the result in the string pointed to by *buffer*. It is equivalent to (written using gcc extensions, see Section "Statement Exprs" in *Porting and Using gcc*):

```
({ struct tm tm; asctime_r (localtime_r (time, &tm), buf); })
```

If no error occurred the function returns a pointer to the string the result was written into, i.e., it returns *buffer*. Otherwise return `NULL`.

`size_t strftime` (*char \*s, size_t size, const char \*template, const*            [Function]
      *struct tm \*brokentime*)
Preliminary: | MT-Safe env locale | AS-Unsafe corrupt heap lock dlopen | AC-Unsafe corrupt lock mem fd | See Section 1.2.2.1 [POSIX Safety Concepts], page 2.

This function is similar to the `sprintf` function (see Section 12.14 [Formatted Input], page 292), but the conversion specifications that can appear in the format template *template* are specialized for printing components of the date and time *brokentime* according to the locale currently specified for time conversion (see Chapter 7 [Locales and Internationalization], page 169) and the current time zone (see Section 21.4.8 [Functions and Variables for Time Zones], page 624).

Ordinary characters appearing in the *template* are copied to the output string *s*; this can include multibyte character sequences. Conversion specifiers are introduced by a '%' character, followed by an optional flag which can be one of the following. These flags are all GNU extensions. The first three affect only the output of numbers:

_           The number is padded with spaces.

−           The number is not padded at all.

0           The number is padded with zeros even if the format specifies padding with spaces.

^           The output uses uppercase characters, but only if this is possible (see Section 4.2 [Case Conversion], page 79).

The default action is to pad the number with zeros to keep it a constant width. Numbers that do not have a range indicated below are never padded, since there is no natural width for them.

Following the flag an optional specification of the width is possible. This is specified in decimal notation. If the natural size of the output is of the field has less than the specified number of characters, the result is written right adjusted and space padded to the given size.

An optional modifier can follow the optional flag and width specification. The modifiers, which were first standardized by POSIX.2-1992 and by ISO C99, are:

E           Use the locale's alternate representation for date and time. This modifier applies to the %c, %C, %x, %X, %y and %Y format specifiers. In a Japanese locale, for example, %Ex might yield a date format based on the Japanese Emperors' reigns.

O           Use the locale's alternate numeric symbols for numbers. This modifier applies only to numeric format specifiers.

If the format supports the modifier but no alternate representation is available, it is ignored.

The conversion specifier ends with a format specifier taken from the following list. The whole '%' sequence is replaced in the output string as follows:

%a          The abbreviated weekday name according to the current locale.

%A          The full weekday name according to the current locale.

%b          The abbreviated month name according to the current locale.

%B          The full month name according to the current locale.

            Using %B together with %d produces grammatically incorrect results for some locales.

%c          The preferred calendar time representation for the current locale.

%C          The century of the year. This is equivalent to the greatest integer not
            greater than the year divided by 100.

            This format was first standardized by POSIX.2-1992 and by ISO C99.

%d          The day of the month as a decimal number (range 01 through 31).

%D          The date using the format %m/%d/%y.

            This format was first standardized by POSIX.2-1992 and by ISO C99.

%e          The day of the month like with %d, but padded with blank (range  1
            through 31).

            This format was first standardized by POSIX.2-1992 and by ISO C99.

%F          The date using the format %Y-%m-%d. This is the form specified in the
            ISO 8601 standard and is the preferred form for all uses.

            This format was first standardized by ISO C99 and by POSIX.1-2001.

%g          The year corresponding to the ISO week number, but without the century
            (range 00 through 99). This has the same format and value as %y, except
            that if the ISO week number (see %V) belongs to the previous or next
            year, that year is used instead.

            This format was first standardized by ISO C99 and by POSIX.1-2001.

%G          The year corresponding to the ISO week number. This has the same
            format and value as %Y, except that if the ISO week number (see %V)
            belongs to the previous or next year, that year is used instead.

            This format was first standardized by ISO C99 and by POSIX.1-2001 but
            was previously available as a GNU extension.

%h          The abbreviated month name according to the current locale. The action
            is the same as for %b.

            This format was first standardized by POSIX.2-1992 and by ISO C99.

%H          The hour as a decimal number, using a 24-hour clock (range 00 through
            23).

%I          The hour as a decimal number, using a 12-hour clock (range 01 through
            12).

%j          The day of the year as a decimal number (range 001 through 366).

%k          The hour as a decimal number, using a 24-hour clock like %H, but padded
            with blank (range  0 through 23).

            This format is a GNU extension.

%l          The hour as a decimal number, using a 12-hour clock like %I, but padded
            with blank (range  1 through 12).

            This format is a GNU extension.

%m          The month as a decimal number (range 01 through 12).

%M          The minute as a decimal number (range 00 through 59).

%n        A single '\n' (newline) character.

          This format was first standardized by POSIX.2-1992 and by ISO C99.

%p        Either 'AM' or 'PM', according to the given time value; or the corresponding
          strings for the current locale. Noon is treated as 'PM' and midnight as
          'AM'. In most locales 'AM'/'PM' format is not supported, in such cases "%p"
          yields an empty string.

%P        Either 'am' or 'pm', according to the given time value; or the corresponding
          strings for the current locale, printed in lowercase characters. Noon is
          treated as 'pm' and midnight as 'am'. In most locales 'AM'/'PM' format is
          not supported, in such cases "%P" yields an empty string.

          This format is a GNU extension.

%r        The complete calendar time using the AM/PM format of the current
          locale.

          This format was first standardized by POSIX.2-1992 and by ISO C99. In
          the POSIX locale, this format is equivalent to %I:%M:%S %p.

%R        The hour and minute in decimal numbers using the format %H:%M.

          This format was first standardized by ISO C99 and by POSIX.1-2001 but
          was previously available as a GNU extension.

%s        The number of seconds since the epoch, i.e., since 1970-01-01 00:00:00
          UTC. Leap seconds are not counted unless leap second support is avail-
          able.

          This format is a GNU extension.

%S        The seconds as a decimal number (range 00 through 60).

%t        A single '\t' (tabulator) character.

          This format was first standardized by POSIX.2-1992 and by ISO C99.

%T        The time of day using decimal numbers using the format %H:%M:%S.

          This format was first standardized by POSIX.2-1992 and by ISO C99.

%u        The day of the week as a decimal number (range 1 through 7), Monday
          being 1.

          This format was first standardized by POSIX.2-1992 and by ISO C99.

%U        The week number of the current year as a decimal number (range 00
          through 53), starting with the first Sunday as the first day of the first
          week. Days preceding the first Sunday in the year are considered to be
          in week 00.

%V        The ISO 8601:1988 week number as a decimal number (range 01 through
          53). ISO weeks start with Monday and end with Sunday. Week 01 of a
          year is the first week which has the majority of its days in that year; this
          is equivalent to the week containing the year's first Thursday, and it is
          also equivalent to the week containing January 4. Week 01 of a year can
          contain days from the previous year. The week before week 01 of a year

is the last week (52 or 53) of the previous year even if it contains days from the new year.

This format was first standardized by POSIX.2-1992 and by ISO C99.

%w    The day of the week as a decimal number (range 0 through 6), Sunday being 0.

%W    The week number of the current year as a decimal number (range 00 through 53), starting with the first Monday as the first day of the first week. All days preceding the first Monday in the year are considered to be in week 00.

%x    The preferred date representation for the current locale.

%X    The preferred time of day representation for the current locale.

%y    The year without a century as a decimal number (range 00 through 99). This is equivalent to the year modulo 100.

%Y    The year as a decimal number, using the Gregorian calendar. Years before the year 1 are numbered 0, -1, and so on.

%z    RFC 822/ISO 8601:1988 style numeric time zone (e.g., -0600 or +0100), or nothing if no time zone is determinable.

      This format was first standardized by ISO C99 and by POSIX.1-2001 but was previously available as a GNU extension.

      In the POSIX locale, a full RFC 822 timestamp is generated by the format '"%a, %d %b %Y %H:%M:%S %z"' (or the equivalent '"%a, %d %b %Y %T %z"').

%Z    The time zone abbreviation (empty if the time zone can't be determined).

%%    A literal '%' character.

The *size* parameter can be used to specify the maximum number of characters to be stored in the array *s*, including the terminating null character. If the formatted time requires more than *size* characters, **strftime** returns zero and the contents of the array *s* are undefined. Otherwise the return value indicates the number of characters placed in the array *s*, not including the terminating null character.

*Warning:* This convention for the return value which is prescribed in ISO C can lead to problems in some situations. For certain format strings and certain locales the output really can be the empty string and this cannot be discovered by testing the return value only. E.g., in most locales the AM/PM time format is not supported (most of the world uses the 24 hour time representation). In such locales "%p" will return the empty string, i.e., the return value is zero. To detect situations like this something similar to the following code should be used:

```
buf[0] = '\1';
len = strftime (buf, bufsize, format, tp);
if (len == 0 && buf[0] != '\0')
  {
    /* Something went wrong in the strftime call.  */
    ...
  }
```

If *s* is a null pointer, `strftime` does not actually write anything, but instead returns the number of characters it would have written.

Calling `strftime` also sets the current time zone as if `tzset` were called; `strftime` uses this information instead of *brokentime*'s `tm_gmtoff` and `tm_zone` members. See Section 21.4.8 [Functions and Variables for Time Zones], page 624.

For an example of `strftime`, see Section 21.4.9 [Time Functions Example], page 625.

**size_t wcsftime** (*wchar_t \*s*, *size_t* `size`, *const wchar_t \*`template`*,          [Function]
        *const struct tm \*`brokentime`*)

Preliminary: | MT-Safe env locale | AS-Unsafe corrupt heap lock dlopen | AC-Unsafe corrupt lock mem fd | See Section 1.2.2.1 [POSIX Safety Concepts], page 2.

The `wcsftime` function is equivalent to the `strftime` function with the difference that it operates on wide character strings. The buffer where the result is stored, pointed to by *s*, must be an array of wide characters. The parameter *size* which specifies the size of the output buffer gives the number of wide character, not the number of bytes.

Also the format string *template* is a wide character string. Since all characters needed to specify the format string are in the basic character set it is portably possible to write format strings in the C source code using the `L"..."` notation. The parameter *brokentime* has the same meaning as in the `strftime` call.

The `wcsftime` function supports the same flags, modifiers, and format specifiers as the `strftime` function.

The return value of `wcsftime` is the number of wide characters stored in `s`. When more characters would have to be written than can be placed in the buffer *s* the return value is zero, with the same problems indicated in the `strftime` documentation.

## 21.4.6 Convert textual time and date information back

The ISO C standard does not specify any functions which can convert the output of the `strftime` function back into a binary format. This led to a variety of more-or-less successful implementations with different interfaces over the years. Then the Unix standard was extended by the addition of two functions: `strptime` and `getdate`. Both have strange interfaces but at least they are widely available.

### 21.4.6.1 Interpret string according to given format

The first function is rather low-level. It is nevertheless frequently used in software since it is better known. Its interface and implementation are heavily influenced by the `getdate` function, which is defined and implemented in terms of calls to `strptime`.

**char \* strptime** (*const char \*s*, *const char \*fmt*, *struct tm \*tp*)          [Function]

Preliminary: | MT-Safe env locale | AS-Unsafe heap lock | AC-Unsafe lock mem fd | See Section 1.2.2.1 [POSIX Safety Concepts], page 2.

The `strptime` function parses the input string *s* according to the format string *fmt* and stores its results in the structure *tp*.

The input string could be generated by a `strftime` call or obtained any other way. It does not need to be in a human-recognizable format; e.g. a date passed as `"02:1999:9"` is acceptable, even though it is ambiguous without context. As long as the format string *fmt* matches the input string the function will succeed.

The user has to make sure, though, that the input can be parsed in a unambiguous way. The string "1999112" can be parsed using the format "%Y%m%d" as 1999-1-12, 1999-11-2, or even 19991-1-2. It is necessary to add appropriate separators to reliably get results.

The format string consists of the same components as the format string of the strftime function. The only difference is that the flags _, -, 0, and ^ are not allowed. Several of the distinct formats of strftime do the same work in strptime since differences like case of the input do not matter. For reasons of symmetry all formats are supported, though.

The modifiers E and O are also allowed everywhere the strftime function allows them.

The formats are:

%a

%A    The weekday name according to the current locale, in abbreviated form or the full name.

%b

%B

%h    The month name according to the current locale, in abbreviated form or the full name.

%c    The date and time representation for the current locale.

%Ec   Like %c but the locale's alternative date and time format is used.

%C    The century of the year.

      It makes sense to use this format only if the format string also contains the %y format.

%EC   The locale's representation of the period.

      Unlike %C it sometimes makes sense to use this format since some cultures represent years relative to the beginning of eras instead of using the Gregorian years.

%d

%e    The day of the month as a decimal number (range 1 through 31). Leading zeroes are permitted but not required.

%Od

%Oe   Same as %d but using the locale's alternative numeric symbols.

      Leading zeroes are permitted but not required.

%D    Equivalent to %m/%d/%y.

%F    Equivalent to %Y-%m-%d, which is the ISO 8601 date format.

      This is a GNU extension following an ISO C99 extension to strftime.

%g    The year corresponding to the ISO week number, but without the century (range 00 through 99).

      *Note:* Currently, this is not fully implemented. The format is recognized, input is consumed but no field in *tm* is set.

      This format is a GNU extension following a GNU extension of strftime.

%G        The year corresponding to the ISO week number.

          *Note:* Currently, this is not fully implemented. The format is recognized, input is consumed but no field in *tm* is set.

          This format is a GNU extension following a GNU extension of `strftime`.

%H

%k        The hour as a decimal number, using a 24-hour clock (range 00 through 23).

          %k is a GNU extension following a GNU extension of `strftime`.

%OH       Same as %H but using the locale's alternative numeric symbols.

%I

%1        The hour as a decimal number, using a 12-hour clock (range 01 through 12).

          %1 is a GNU extension following a GNU extension of `strftime`.

%OI       Same as %I but using the locale's alternative numeric symbols.

%j        The day of the year as a decimal number (range 1 through 366).

          Leading zeroes are permitted but not required.

%m        The month as a decimal number (range 1 through 12).

          Leading zeroes are permitted but not required.

%Om       Same as %m but using the locale's alternative numeric symbols.

%M        The minute as a decimal number (range 0 through 59).

          Leading zeroes are permitted but not required.

%OM       Same as %M but using the locale's alternative numeric symbols.

%n

%t        Matches any white space.

%p

%P        The locale-dependent equivalent to 'AM' or 'PM'.

          This format is not useful unless %I or %1 is also used. Another complication is that the locale might not define these values at all and therefore the conversion fails.

          %P is a GNU extension following a GNU extension to `strftime`.

%r        The complete time using the AM/PM format of the current locale.

          A complication is that the locale might not define this format at all and therefore the conversion fails.

%R        The hour and minute in decimal numbers using the format %H:%M.

          %R is a GNU extension following a GNU extension to `strftime`.

%s        The number of seconds since the epoch, i.e., since 1970-01-01 00:00:00 UTC. Leap seconds are not counted unless leap second support is available.

          %s is a GNU extension following a GNU extension to `strftime`.

| | |
|---|---|
| %S | The seconds as a decimal number (range 0 through 60). |
| | Leading zeroes are permitted but not required. |
| | **NB:** The Unix specification says the upper bound on this value is 61, a result of a decision to allow double leap seconds. You will not see the value 61 because no minute has more than one leap second, but the myth persists. |
| %OS | Same as %S but using the locale's alternative numeric symbols. |
| %T | Equivalent to the use of %H:%M:%S in this place. |
| %u | The day of the week as a decimal number (range 1 through 7), Monday being 1. |
| | Leading zeroes are permitted but not required. |
| | *Note:* Currently, this is not fully implemented. The format is recognized, input is consumed but no field in *tm* is set. |
| %U | The week number of the current year as a decimal number (range 0 through 53). |
| | Leading zeroes are permitted but not required. |
| %OU | Same as %U but using the locale's alternative numeric symbols. |
| %V | The ISO 8601:1988 week number as a decimal number (range 1 through 53). |
| | Leading zeroes are permitted but not required. |
| | *Note:* Currently, this is not fully implemented. The format is recognized, input is consumed but no field in *tm* is set. |
| %w | The day of the week as a decimal number (range 0 through 6), Sunday being 0. |
| | Leading zeroes are permitted but not required. |
| | *Note:* Currently, this is not fully implemented. The format is recognized, input is consumed but no field in *tm* is set. |
| %Ow | Same as %w but using the locale's alternative numeric symbols. |
| %W | The week number of the current year as a decimal number (range 0 through 53). |
| | Leading zeroes are permitted but not required. |
| | *Note:* Currently, this is not fully implemented. The format is recognized, input is consumed but no field in *tm* is set. |
| %OW | Same as %W but using the locale's alternative numeric symbols. |
| %x | The date using the locale's date format. |
| %Ex | Like %x but the locale's alternative data representation is used. |
| %X | The time using the locale's time format. |
| %EX | Like %X but the locale's alternative time representation is used. |

%y          The year without a century as a decimal number (range 0 through 99).
            Leading zeroes are permitted but not required.

            Note that it is questionable to use this format without the %C format.
            The `strptime` function does regard input values in the range 68 to 99 as
            the years 1969 to 1999 and the values 0 to 68 as the years 2000 to 2068.
            But maybe this heuristic fails for some input data.

            Therefore it is best to avoid %y completely and use %Y instead.

%Ey         The offset from %EC in the locale's alternative representation.

%Oy         The offset of the year (from %C) using the locale's alternative numeric
            symbols.

%Y          The year as a decimal number, using the Gregorian calendar.

%EY         The full alternative year representation.

%z          The offset from GMT in ISO 8601/RFC822 format.

%Z          The timezone name.

            *Note:* Currently, this is not fully implemented. The format is recognized,
            input is consumed but no field in *tm* is set.

%%          A literal '%' character.

All other characters in the format string must have a matching character in the input
string. Exceptions are white spaces in the input string which can match zero or more
whitespace characters in the format string.

**Portability Note:** The XPG standard advises applications to use at least one whitespace character (as specified by `isspace`) or other non-alphanumeric characters between any two conversion specifications. The GNU C Library does not have this limitation but other libraries might have trouble parsing formats like `"%d%m%Y%H%M%S"`.

The `strptime` function processes the input string from right to left. Each of the
three possible input elements (white space, literal, or format) are handled one after
the other. If the input cannot be matched to the format string the function stops.
The remainder of the format and input strings are not processed.

The function returns a pointer to the first character it was unable to process. If the
input string contains more characters than required by the format string the return
value points right after the last consumed input character. If the whole input string
is consumed the return value points to the `NULL` byte at the end of the string. If
an error occurs, i.e., `strptime` fails to match all of the format string, the function
returns `NULL`.

The specification of the function in the XPG standard is rather vague, leaving out a
few important pieces of information. Most importantly, it does not specify what happens
to those elements of *tm* which are not directly initialized by the different formats. The
implementations on different Unix systems vary here.

The GNU C Library implementation does not touch those fields which are not directly
initialized. Exceptions are the `tm_wday` and `tm_yday` elements, which are recomputed if any
of the year, month, or date elements changed. This has two implications:

- Before calling the `strptime` function for a new input string, you should prepare the *tm* structure you pass. Normally this will mean initializing all values are to zero. Alternatively, you can set all fields to values like `INT_MAX`, allowing you to determine which elements were set by the function call. Zero does not work here since it is a valid value for many of the fields.

  Careful initialization is necessary if you want to find out whether a certain field in *tm* was initialized by the function call.

- You can construct a `struct tm` value with several consecutive `strptime` calls. A useful application of this is e.g. the parsing of two separate strings, one containing date information and the other time information. By parsing one after the other without clearing the structure in-between, you can construct a complete broken-down time.

The following example shows a function which parses a string which is contains the date information in either US style or ISO 8601 form:

```
const char *
parse_date (const char *input, struct tm *tm)
{
  const char *cp;

  /* First clear the result structure.  */
  memset (tm, '\0', sizeof (*tm));

  /* Try the ISO format first.  */
  cp = strptime (input, "%F", tm);
  if (cp == NULL)
    {
      /* Does not match.  Try the US form.  */
      cp = strptime (input, "%D", tm);
    }

  return cp;
}
```

## 21.4.6.2 A More User-friendly Way to Parse Times and Dates

The Unix standard defines another function for parsing date strings. The interface is weird, but if the function happens to suit your application it is just fine. It is problematic to use this function in multi-threaded programs or libraries, since it returns a pointer to a static variable, and uses a global variable and global state (an environment variable).

getdate_err                                                                    [Variable]
> This variable of type `int` contains the error code of the last unsuccessful call to `getdate`. Defined values are:

> 1       The environment variable `DATEMSK` is not defined or null.

> 2       The template file denoted by the `DATEMSK` environment variable cannot be opened.

> 3       Information about the template file cannot retrieved.

> 4       The template file is not a regular file.

> 5       An I/O error occurred while reading the template file.

6           Not enough memory available to execute the function.

7           The template file contains no matching template.

8           The input date is invalid, but would match a template otherwise. This
            includes dates like February 31st, and dates which cannot be represented
            in a `time_t` variable.

**struct tm \* getdate** (*const char \*string*)                              [Function]
Preliminary: | MT-Unsafe race:getdate env locale | AS-Unsafe heap lock | AC-Unsafe
lock mem fd | See Section 1.2.2.1 [POSIX Safety Concepts], page 2.

The interface to `getdate` is the simplest possible for a function to parse a string and
return the value. *string* is the input string and the result is returned in a statically-
allocated variable.

The details about how the string is processed are hidden from the user. In fact, they
can be outside the control of the program. Which formats are recognized is controlled
by the file named by the environment variable `DATEMSK`. This file should contain lines
of valid format strings which could be passed to `strptime`.

The `getdate` function reads these format strings one after the other and tries to
match the input string. The first line which completely matches the input string is
used.

Elements not initialized through the format string retain the values present at the
time of the `getdate` function call.

The formats recognized by `getdate` are the same as for `strptime`. See above for an
explanation. There are only a few extensions to the `strptime` behavior:

- If the `%Z` format is given the broken-down time is based on the current time of
  the timezone matched, not of the current timezone of the runtime environment.

  *Note*: This is not implemented (currently). The problem is that timezone names
  are not unique. If a fixed timezone is assumed for a given string (say **EST** meaning
  US East Coast time), then uses for countries other than the USA will fail. So far
  we have found no good solution to this.

- If only the weekday is specified the selected day depends on the current date. If
  the current weekday is greater or equal to the `tm_wday` value the current week's
  day is chosen, otherwise the day next week is chosen.

- A similar heuristic is used when only the month is given and not the year. If the
  month is greater than or equal to the current month, then the current year is
  used. Otherwise it wraps to next year. The first day of the month is assumed if
  one is not explicitly specified.

- The current hour, minute, and second are used if the appropriate value is not set
  through the format.

- If no date is given tomorrow's date is used if the time is smaller than the current
  time. Otherwise today's date is taken.

It should be noted that the format in the template file need not only contain format
elements. The following is a list of possible format strings (taken from the Unix
standard):

```
%m
%A %B %d, %Y %H:%M:%S
%A
%B
%m/%d/%y %I %p
%d,%m,%Y %H:%M
at %A the %dst of %B in %Y
run job at %I %p,%B %dnd
%A den %d. %B %Y %H.%M Uhr
```

As you can see, the template list can contain very specific strings like `run job at %I`
`%p,%B %dnd`. Using the above list of templates and assuming the current time is Mon
Sep 22 12:19:47 EDT 1986 we can obtain the following results for the given input.

| Input | Match | Result |
|-------|-------|--------|
| Mon | %a | Mon Sep 22 12:19:47 EDT 1986 |
| Sun | %a | Sun Sep 28 12:19:47 EDT 1986 |
| Fri | %a | Fri Sep 26 12:19:47 EDT 1986 |
| September | %B | Mon Sep 1 12:19:47 EDT 1986 |
| January | %B | Thu Jan 1 12:19:47 EST 1987 |
| December | %B | Mon Dec 1 12:19:47 EST 1986 |
| Sep Mon | %b %a | Mon Sep 1 12:19:47 EDT 1986 |
| Jan Fri | %b %a | Fri Jan 2 12:19:47 EST 1987 |
| Dec Mon | %b %a | Mon Dec 1 12:19:47 EST 1986 |
| Jan Wed 1989 | %b %a %Y | Wed Jan 4 12:19:47 EST 1989 |
| Fri 9 | %a %H | Fri Sep 26 09:00:00 EDT 1986 |
| Feb 10:30 | %b %H:%S | Sun Feb 1 10:00:30 EST 1987 |
| 10:30 | %H:%M | Tue Sep 23 10:30:00 EDT 1986 |
| 13:30 | %H:%M | Mon Sep 22 13:30:00 EDT 1986 |

The return value of the function is a pointer to a static variable of type `struct tm`,
or a null pointer if an error occurred. The result is only valid until the next `getdate`
call, making this function unusable in multi-threaded applications.

The `errno` variable is *not* changed. Error conditions are stored in the global variable
`getdate_err`. See the description above for a list of the possible error values.

*Warning:* The `getdate` function should *never* be used in SUID-programs. The reason
is obvious: using the `DATEMSK` environment variable you can get the function to open
any arbitrary file and chances are high that with some bogus input (such as a binary
file) the program will crash.

**int getdate_r** (*const char* **\*string**, *struct tm* **\*tp**)                                      [Function]
Preliminary: | MT-Safe env locale | AS-Unsafe heap lock | AC-Unsafe lock mem fd
| See Section 1.2.2.1 [POSIX Safety Concepts], page 2.

The `getdate_r` function is the reentrant counterpart of `getdate`. It does not use
the global variable `getdate_err` to signal an error, but instead returns an error code.
The same error codes as described in the `getdate_err` documentation above are used,
with 0 meaning success.

Moreover, `getdate_r` stores the broken-down time in the variable of type `struct tm`
pointed to by the second argument, rather than in a static variable.

This function is not defined in the Unix standard. Nevertheless it is available on some other Unix systems as well.

The warning against using `getdate` in SUID-programs applies to `getdate_r` as well.

## 21.4.7 Specifying the Time Zone with `TZ`

In POSIX systems, a user can specify the time zone by means of the `TZ` environment variable. For information about how to set environment variables, see Section 25.4 [Environment Variables], page 738. The functions for accessing the time zone are declared in `time.h`.

You should not normally need to set `TZ`. If the system is configured properly, the default time zone will be correct. You might set `TZ` if you are using a computer over a network from a different time zone, and would like times reported to you in the time zone local to you, rather than what is local to the computer.

In POSIX.1 systems the value of the `TZ` variable can be in one of three formats. With the GNU C Library, the most common format is the last one, which can specify a selection from a large database of time zone information for many regions of the world. The first two formats are used to describe the time zone information directly, which is both more cumbersome and less precise. But the POSIX.1 standard only specifies the details of the first two formats, so it is good to be familiar with them in case you come across a POSIX.1 system that doesn't support a time zone information database.

The first format is used when there is no Daylight Saving Time (or summer time) in the local time zone:

> *std offset*

The *std* string specifies the name of the time zone. It must be three or more characters long and must not contain a leading colon, embedded digits, commas, nor plus and minus signs. There is no space character separating the time zone name from the *offset*, so these restrictions are necessary to parse the specification correctly.

The *offset* specifies the time value you must add to the local time to get a Coordinated Universal Time value. It has syntax like [+|-]*hh*[:*mm*[:*ss*]]. This is positive if the local time zone is west of the Prime Meridian and negative if it is east. The hour must be between 0 and 24, and the minute and seconds between 0 and 59.

For example, here is how we would specify Eastern Standard Time, but without any Daylight Saving Time alternative:

> `EST+5`

The second format is used when there is Daylight Saving Time:

> *std offset dst* [*offset*],*start*[/*time*],*end*[/*time*]

The initial *std* and *offset* specify the standard time zone, as described above. The *dst* string and *offset* specify the name and offset for the corresponding Daylight Saving Time zone; if the *offset* is omitted, it defaults to one hour ahead of standard time.

The remainder of the specification describes when Daylight Saving Time is in effect. The *start* field is when Daylight Saving Time goes into effect and the *end* field is when the change is made back to standard time. The following formats are recognized for these fields:

`Jn`          This specifies the Julian day, with *n* between 1 and 365. February 29 is never counted, even in leap years.

*n*           This specifies the Julian day, with *n* between 0 and 365. February 29 is counted
            in leap years.

`Mm.w.d`   This specifies day *d* of week *w* of month *m*. The day *d* must be between 0
            (Sunday) and 6. The week *w* must be between 1 and 5; week 1 is the first week
            in which day *d* occurs, and week 5 specifies the *last d* day in the month. The
            month *m* should be between 1 and 12.

The *time* fields specify when, in the local time currently in effect, the change to the
other time occurs. If omitted, the default is 02:00:00. The hours part of the time fields
can range from −167 through 167; this is an extension to POSIX.1, which allows only the
range 0 through 24.

Here are some example TZ values, including the appropriate Daylight Saving Time and
its dates of applicability. In North American Eastern Standard Time (EST) and Eastern
Daylight Time (EDT), the normal offset from UTC is 5 hours; since this is west of the prime
meridian, the sign is positive. Summer time begins on March's second Sunday at 2:00am,
and ends on November's first Sunday at 2:00am.

        `EST+5EDT,M3.2.0/2,M11.1.0/2`

Israel Standard Time (IST) and Israel Daylight Time (IDT) are 2 hours ahead of the
prime meridian in winter, springing forward an hour on March's fourth Thursday at 26:00
(i.e., 02:00 on the first Friday on or after March 23), and falling back on October's last
Sunday at 02:00.

        `IST-2IDT,M3.4.4/26,M10.5.0`

Western Argentina Summer Time (WARST) is 3 hours behind the prime meridian all
year. There is a dummy fall-back transition on December 31 at 25:00 daylight saving
time (i.e., 24:00 standard time, equivalent to January 1 at 00:00 standard time), and a
simultaneous spring-forward transition on January 1 at 00:00 standard time, so daylight
saving time is in effect all year and the initial WART is a placeholder.

        `WART4WARST,J1/0,J365/25`

Western Greenland Time (WGT) and Western Greenland Summer Time (WGST) are 3
hours behind UTC in the winter. Its clocks follow the European Union rules of springing
forward by one hour on March's last Sunday at 01:00 UTC (−02:00 local time) and falling
back on October's last Sunday at 01:00 UTC (−01:00 local time).

        `WGT3WGST,M3.5.0/-2,M10.5.0/-1`

The schedule of Daylight Saving Time in any particular jurisdiction has changed over
the years. To be strictly correct, the conversion of dates and times in the past should be
based on the schedule that was in effect then. However, this format has no facilities to let
you specify how the schedule has changed from year to year. The most you can do is specify
one particular schedule—usually the present day schedule—and this is used to convert any
date, no matter when. For precise time zone specifications, it is best to use the time zone
information database (see below).

The third format looks like this:

        `:characters`

Each operating system interprets this format differently; in the GNU C Library, *characters* is the name of a file which describes the time zone.

If the TZ environment variable does not have a value, the operation chooses a time zone by default. In the GNU C Library, the default time zone is like the specification 'TZ=:/etc/localtime' (or 'TZ=:/usr/local/etc/localtime', depending on how the GNU C Library was configured; see Appendix C [Installing the GNU C Library], page 995). Other C libraries use their own rule for choosing the default time zone, so there is little we can say about them.

If *characters* begins with a slash, it is an absolute file name; otherwise the library looks for the file /usr/share/zoneinfo/*characters*. The zoneinfo directory contains data files describing local time zones in many different parts of the world. The names represent major cities, with subdirectories for geographical areas; for example, America/New_York, Europe/London, Asia/Hong_Kong. These data files are installed by the system administrator, who also sets /etc/localtime to point to the data file for the local time zone. The files typically come from the Time Zone Database (http://www.iana.org/time-zones) of time zone and daylight saving time information for most regions of the world, which is maintained by a community of volunteers and put in the public domain.

## 21.4.8 Functions and Variables for Time Zones

char * tzname [2]                                                              [Variable]

> The array tzname contains two strings, which are the standard names of the pair of time zones (standard and Daylight Saving) that the user has selected. tzname[0] is the name of the standard time zone (for example, "EST"), and tzname[1] is the name for the time zone when Daylight Saving Time is in use (for example, "EDT"). These correspond to the *std* and *dst* strings (respectively) from the TZ environment variable. If Daylight Saving Time is never used, tzname[1] is the empty string.
>
> The tzname array is initialized from the TZ environment variable whenever tzset, ctime, strftime, mktime, or localtime is called. If multiple abbreviations have been used (e.g. "EWT" and "EDT" for U.S. Eastern War Time and Eastern Daylight Time), the array contains the most recent abbreviation.
>
> The tzname array is required for POSIX.1 compatibility, but in GNU programs it is better to use the tm_zone member of the broken-down time structure, since tm_zone reports the correct abbreviation even when it is not the latest one.
>
> Though the strings are declared as char * the user must refrain from modifying these strings. Modifying the strings will almost certainly lead to trouble.

void tzset (*void*)                                                            [Function]

> Preliminary: | MT-Safe env locale | AS-Unsafe heap lock | AC-Unsafe lock mem fd | See Section 1.2.2.1 [POSIX Safety Concepts], page 2.
>
> The tzset function initializes the tzname variable from the value of the TZ environment variable. It is not usually necessary for your program to call this function, because it is called automatically when you use the other time conversion functions that depend on the time zone.

The following variables are defined for compatibility with System V Unix. Like tzname, these variables are set by calling tzset or the other time conversion functions.

**long int timezone** [Variable]

This contains the difference between UTC and the latest local standard time, in seconds west of UTC. For example, in the U.S. Eastern time zone, the value is 5*60*60. Unlike the `tm_gmtoff` member of the broken-down time structure, this value is not adjusted for daylight saving, and its sign is reversed. In GNU programs it is better to use `tm_gmtoff`, since it contains the correct offset even when it is not the latest one.

**int daylight** [Variable]

This variable has a nonzero value if Daylight Saving Time rules apply. A nonzero value does not necessarily mean that Daylight Saving Time is now in effect; it means only that Daylight Saving Time is sometimes in effect.

### 21.4.9 Time Functions Example

Here is an example program showing the use of some of the calendar time functions.

```
#include <time.h>
#include <stdio.h>

#define SIZE 256

int
main (void)
{
  char buffer[SIZE];
  time_t curtime;
  struct tm *loctime;

  /* Get the current time. */
  curtime = time (NULL);

  /* Convert it to local time representation. */
  loctime = localtime (&curtime);

  /* Print out the date and time in the standard format. */
  fputs (asctime (loctime), stdout);

  /* Print it out in a nice format. */
  strftime (buffer, SIZE, "Today is %A, %B %d.\n", loctime);
  fputs (buffer, stdout);
  strftime (buffer, SIZE, "The time is %I:%M %p.\n", loctime);
  fputs (buffer, stdout);

  return 0;
}
```

It produces output like this:
```
Wed Jul 31 13:02:36 1991
Today is Wednesday, July 31.
The time is 01:02 PM.
```

## 21.5 Setting an Alarm

The `alarm` and `setitimer` functions provide a mechanism for a process to interrupt itself in the future. They do this by setting a timer; when the timer expires, the process receives a signal.

Each process has three independent interval timers available:

- A real-time timer that counts elapsed time. This timer sends a `SIGALRM` signal to the process when it expires.

- A virtual timer that counts processor time used by the process. This timer sends a `SIGVTALRM` signal to the process when it expires.

- A profiling timer that counts both processor time used by the process, and processor time spent in system calls on behalf of the process. This timer sends a `SIGPROF` signal to the process when it expires.

  This timer is useful for profiling in interpreters. The interval timer mechanism does not have the fine granularity necessary for profiling native code.

You can only have one timer of each kind set at any given time. If you set a timer that has not yet expired, that timer is simply reset to the new value.

You should establish a handler for the appropriate alarm signal using `signal` or `sigaction` before issuing a call to `setitimer` or `alarm`. Otherwise, an unusual chain of events could cause the timer to expire before your program establishes the handler. In this case it would be terminated, since termination is the default action for the alarm signals. See Chapter 24 [Signal Handling], page 661.

To be able to use the alarm function to interrupt a system call which might block otherwise indefinitely it is important to *not* set the `SA_RESTART` flag when registering the signal handler using `sigaction`. When not using `sigaction` things get even uglier: the `signal` function has to fixed semantics with respect to restarts. The BSD semantics for this function is to set the flag. Therefore, if `sigaction` for whatever reason cannot be used, it is necessary to use `sysv_signal` and not `signal`.

The `setitimer` function is the primary means for setting an alarm. This facility is declared in the header file `sys/time.h`. The `alarm` function, declared in `unistd.h`, provides a somewhat simpler interface for setting the real-time timer.

`struct itimerval`                                                           [Data Type]

> This structure is used to specify when a timer should expire. It contains the following members:
>
> `struct timeval it_interval`
>
> > This is the period between successive timer interrupts. If zero, the alarm will only be sent once.
>
> `struct timeval it_value`
>
> > This is the period between now and the first timer interrupt. If zero, the alarm is disabled.
>
> The `struct timeval` data type is described in Section 21.2 [Elapsed Time], page 595.

`int setitimer` (*int* ***which***, *const struct itimerval* ***\*new***, *struct itimerval*          [Function]
           *\*old*)

> Preliminary: | MT-Safe timer | AS-Safe | AC-Safe | See Section 1.2.2.1 [POSIX Safety Concepts], page 2.
>
> The `setitimer` function sets the timer specified by *which* according to *new*. The *which* argument can have a value of `ITIMER_REAL`, `ITIMER_VIRTUAL`, or `ITIMER_PROF`.

If *old* is not a null pointer, `setitimer` returns information about any previous unexpired timer of the same kind in the structure it points to.

The return value is 0 on success and -1 on failure. The following `errno` error conditions are defined for this function:

EINVAL      The timer period is too large.

int getitimer (*int which, struct itimerval \*old*)                                    [Function]
Preliminary: | MT-Safe | AS-Safe | AC-Safe | See Section 1.2.2.1 [POSIX Safety Concepts], page 2.

The `getitimer` function stores information about the timer specified by *which* in the structure pointed at by *old*.

The return value and error conditions are the same as for `setitimer`.

ITIMER_REAL

This constant can be used as the *which* argument to the `setitimer` and `getitimer` functions to specify the real-time timer.

ITIMER_VIRTUAL

This constant can be used as the *which* argument to the `setitimer` and `getitimer` functions to specify the virtual timer.

ITIMER_PROF

This constant can be used as the *which* argument to the `setitimer` and `getitimer` functions to specify the profiling timer.

unsigned int alarm (*unsigned int seconds*)                                    [Function]
Preliminary: | MT-Safe timer | AS-Safe | AC-Safe | See Section 1.2.2.1 [POSIX Safety Concepts], page 2.

The `alarm` function sets the real-time timer to expire in *seconds* seconds. If you want to cancel any existing alarm, you can do this by calling `alarm` with a *seconds* argument of zero.

The return value indicates how many seconds remain before the previous alarm would have been sent. If there is no previous alarm, `alarm` returns zero.

The `alarm` function could be defined in terms of `setitimer` like this:

```
unsigned int
alarm (unsigned int seconds)
{
  struct itimerval old, new;
  new.it_interval.tv_usec = 0;
  new.it_interval.tv_sec = 0;
  new.it_value.tv_usec = 0;
  new.it_value.tv_sec = (long int) seconds;
  if (setitimer (ITIMER_REAL, &new, &old) < 0)
    return 0;
  else
    return old.it_value.tv_sec;
}
```

There is an example showing the use of the `alarm` function in Section 24.4.1 [Signal Handlers that Return], page 678.

If you simply want your process to wait for a given number of seconds, you should use the `sleep` function. See Section 21.6 [Sleeping], page 628.

You shouldn't count on the signal arriving precisely when the timer expires. In a multi-processing environment there is typically some amount of delay involved.

**Portability Note:** The `setitimer` and `getitimer` functions are derived from BSD Unix, while the `alarm` function is specified by the POSIX.1 standard. `setitimer` is more powerful than `alarm`, but `alarm` is more widely used.

## 21.6 Sleeping

The function `sleep` gives a simple way to make the program wait for a short interval. If your program doesn't use signals (except to terminate), then you can expect `sleep` to wait reliably throughout the specified interval. Otherwise, `sleep` can return sooner if a signal arrives; if you want to wait for a given interval regardless of signals, use `select` (see Section 13.8 [Waiting for Input or Output], page 342) and don't specify any descriptors to wait for.

`unsigned int sleep (`*unsigned int* `seconds)`                                              [Function]
> Preliminary: | MT-Unsafe sig:SIGCHLD/linux | AS-Unsafe | AC-Unsafe | See Section 1.2.2.1 [POSIX Safety Concepts], page 2.
>
> The `sleep` function waits for *seconds* or until a signal is delivered, whichever happens first.
>
> If `sleep` function returns because the requested interval is over, it returns a value of zero. If it returns because of delivery of a signal, its return value is the remaining time in the sleep interval.
>
> The `sleep` function is declared in `unistd.h`.

Resist the temptation to implement a sleep for a fixed amount of time by using the return value of `sleep`, when nonzero, to call `sleep` again. This will work with a certain amount of accuracy as long as signals arrive infrequently. But each signal can cause the eventual wakeup time to be off by an additional second or so. Suppose a few signals happen to arrive in rapid succession by bad luck—there is no limit on how much this could shorten or lengthen the wait.

Instead, compute the calendar time at which the program should stop waiting, and keep trying to wait until that calendar time. This won't be off by more than a second. With just a little more work, you can use `select` and make the waiting period quite accurate. (Of course, heavy system load can cause additional unavoidable delays—unless the machine is dedicated to one application, there is no way you can avoid this.)

On some systems, `sleep` can do strange things if your program uses `SIGALRM` explicitly. Even if `SIGALRM` signals are being ignored or blocked when `sleep` is called, `sleep` might return prematurely on delivery of a `SIGALRM` signal. If you have established a handler for `SIGALRM` signals and a `SIGALRM` signal is delivered while the process is sleeping, the action taken might be just to cause `sleep` to return instead of invoking your handler. And, if `sleep` is interrupted by delivery of a signal whose handler requests an alarm or alters the handling of `SIGALRM`, this handler and `sleep` will interfere.

On GNU systems, it is safe to use `sleep` and `SIGALRM` in the same program, because `sleep` does not work by means of `SIGALRM`.

**int nanosleep** (*const struct timespec *requested_time, struct*                [Function]
        *timespec *remaining*)

> Preliminary: | MT-Safe | AS-Safe | AC-Safe | See Section 1.2.2.1 [POSIX Safety Concepts], page 2.
>
> If resolution to seconds is not enough the **nanosleep** function can be used. As the name suggests the sleep interval can be specified in nanoseconds. The actual elapsed time of the sleep interval might be longer since the system rounds the elapsed time you request up to the next integer multiple of the actual resolution the system can deliver.
>
> *requested_time is the elapsed time of the interval you want to sleep.
>
> The function returns as *remaining the elapsed time left in the interval for which you requested to sleep. If the interval completed without getting interrupted by a signal, this is zero.
>
> **struct timespec** is described in See Section 21.2 [Elapsed Time], page 595.
>
> If the function returns because the interval is over the return value is zero. If the function returns −1 the global variable *errno* is set to the following values:
>
> EINTR       The call was interrupted because a signal was delivered to the thread. If the *remaining* parameter is not the null pointer the structure pointed to by *remaining* is updated to contain the remaining elapsed time.
>
> EINVAL      The nanosecond value in the *requested_time* parameter contains an illegal value. Either the value is negative or greater than or equal to 1000 million.
>
> This function is a cancellation point in multi-threaded programs. This is a problem if the thread allocates some resources (like memory, file descriptors, semaphores or whatever) at the time **nanosleep** is called. If the thread gets canceled these resources stay allocated until the program ends. To avoid this calls to **nanosleep** should be protected using cancellation handlers.
>
> The **nanosleep** function is declared in **time.h**.

# 22  Resource Usage And Limitation

This chapter describes functions for examining how much of various kinds of resources (CPU time, memory, etc.) a process has used and getting and setting limits on future usage.

## 22.1  Resource Usage

The function **getrusage** and the data type **struct rusage** are used to examine the resource usage of a process. They are declared in **sys/resource.h**.

**int getrusage** (*int processes*, *struct rusage *****rusage***)                           [Function]
>    Preliminary: | MT-Safe | AS-Safe | AC-Safe | See Section 1.2.2.1 [POSIX Safety Concepts], page 2.
>
>    This function reports resource usage totals for processes specified by *processes*, storing the information in ***rusage***.
>
>    In most systems, *processes* has only two valid values:
>
>    RUSAGE_SELF
>>           Just the current process.
>
>    RUSAGE_CHILDREN
>>           All child processes (direct and indirect) that have already terminated.
>
>    The return value of **getrusage** is zero for success, and **-1** for failure.
>
>    EINVAL     The argument *processes* is not valid.

>    One way of getting resource usage for a particular child process is with the function **wait4**, which returns totals for a child when it terminates. See Section 26.8 [BSD Process Wait Functions], page 758.

**struct rusage**                                                          [Data Type]
>    This data type stores various resource usage statistics. It has the following members, and possibly others:
>
>    struct timeval ru_utime
>>           Time spent executing user instructions.
>
>    struct timeval ru_stime
>>           Time spent in operating system code on behalf of *processes*.
>
>    long int ru_maxrss
>>           The maximum resident set size used, in kilobytes. That is, the maximum number of kilobytes of physical memory that *processes* used simultaneously.
>
>    long int ru_ixrss
>>           An integral value expressed in kilobytes times ticks of execution, which indicates the amount of memory used by text that was shared with other processes.
>
>    long int ru_idrss
>>           An integral value expressed the same way, which is the amount of unshared memory used for data.

`long int ru_isrss`
> An integral value expressed the same way, which is the amount of un-shared memory used for stack space.

`long int ru_minflt`
> The number of page faults which were serviced without requiring any I/O.

`long int ru_majflt`
> The number of page faults which were serviced by doing I/O.

`long int ru_nswap`
> The number of times *processes* was swapped entirely out of main memory.

`long int ru_inblock`
> The number of times the file system had to read from the disk on behalf of *processes*.

`long int ru_oublock`
> The number of times the file system had to write to the disk on behalf of *processes*.

`long int ru_msgsnd`
> Number of IPC messages sent.

`long int ru_msgrcv`
> Number of IPC messages received.

`long int ru_nsignals`
> Number of signals received.

`long int ru_nvcsw`
> The number of times *processes* voluntarily invoked a context switch (usually to wait for some service).

`long int ru_nivcsw`
> The number of times an involuntary context switch took place (because a time slice expired, or another process of higher priority was scheduled).

`vtimes` is a historical function that does some of what `getrusage` does. `getrusage` is a better choice.

`vtimes` and its `vtimes` data structure are declared in `sys/vtimes.h`.

`int` `vtimes` (*struct vtimes *`current`, struct vtimes *`child`*)        [Function]
> Preliminary: | MT-Safe | AS-Safe | AC-Safe | See Section 1.2.2.1 [POSIX Safety Concepts], page 2.

`vtimes` reports resource usage totals for a process.

If *current* is non-null, `vtimes` stores resource usage totals for the invoking process alone in the structure to which it points. If *child* is non-null, `vtimes` stores resource usage totals for all past children (which have terminated) of the invoking process in the structure to which it points.

`struct vtimes`                                                                   [Data Type]

> This data type contains information about the resource usage of a process. Each member corresponds to a member of the **struct rusage** data type described above.

`vm_utime`    User CPU time. Analogous to `ru_utime` in `struct rusage`

`vm_stime`    System CPU time. Analogous to `ru_stime` in `struct rusage`

`vm_idsrss`
> Data and stack memory. The sum of the values that would be reported as `ru_idrss` and `ru_isrss` in `struct rusage`

`vm_ixrss`    Shared memory. Analogous to `ru_ixrss` in `struct rusage`

`vm_maxrss`
> Maximent resident set size. Analogous to `ru_maxrss` in `struct rusage`

`vm_majflt`
> Major page faults. Analogous to `ru_majflt` in `struct rusage`

`vm_minflt`
> Minor page faults. Analogous to `ru_minflt` in `struct rusage`

`vm_nswap`    Swap count. Analogous to `ru_nswap` in `struct rusage`

`vm_inblk`    Disk reads. Analogous to `ru_inblk` in `struct rusage`

`vm_oublk`    Disk writes. Analogous to `ru_oublk` in `struct rusage`

> The return value is zero if the function succeeds; `-1` otherwise.

An additional historical function for examining resource usage, `vtimes`, is supported but not documented here. It is declared in `sys/vtimes.h`.

## 22.2  Limiting Resource Usage

You can specify limits for the resource usage of a process. When the process tries to exceed a limit, it may get a signal, or the system call by which it tried to do so may fail, depending on the resource. Each process initially inherits its limit values from its parent, but it can subsequently change them.

There are two per-process limits associated with a resource:

*current limit*
> The current limit is the value the system will not allow usage to exceed. It is also called the "soft limit" because the process being limited can generally raise the current limit at will.

*maximum limit*
> The maximum limit is the maximum value to which a process is allowed to set its current limit. It is also called the "hard limit" because there is no way for a process to get around it. A process may lower its own maximum limit, but only the superuser may increase a maximum limit.

The symbols for use with `getrlimit`, `setrlimit`, `getrlimit64`, and `setrlimit64` are
defined in `sys/resource.h`.

int getrlimit (*int **resource**, struct rlimit \*`rlp`*)                                  [Function]
> Preliminary: | MT-Safe | AS-Safe | AC-Safe | See Section 1.2.2.1 [POSIX Safety
> Concepts], page 2.
>
> Read the current and maximum limits for the resource *resource* and store them in
> `*rlp`.
>
> The return value is 0 on success and -1 on failure. The only possible `errno` error
> condition is `EFAULT`.
>
> When the sources are compiled with `_FILE_OFFSET_BITS == 64` on a 32-bit system
> this function is in fact `getrlimit64`. Thus, the LFS interface transparently replaces
> the old interface.

int getrlimit64 (*int **resource**, struct rlimit64 \*`rlp`*)                              [Function]
> Preliminary: | MT-Safe | AS-Safe | AC-Safe | See Section 1.2.2.1 [POSIX Safety
> Concepts], page 2.
>
> This function is similar to `getrlimit` but its second parameter is a pointer to a
> variable of type `struct rlimit64`, which allows it to read values which wouldn't fit
> in the member of a `struct rlimit`.
>
> If the sources are compiled with `_FILE_OFFSET_BITS == 64` on a 32-bit machine, this
> function is available under the name `getrlimit` and so transparently replaces the old
> interface.

int setrlimit (*int **resource**, const struct rlimit \*`rlp`*)                            [Function]
> Preliminary: | MT-Safe | AS-Safe | AC-Safe | See Section 1.2.2.1 [POSIX Safety
> Concepts], page 2.
>
> Store the current and maximum limits for the resource *resource* in `*rlp`.
>
> The return value is 0 on success and -1 on failure. The following `errno` error condition
> is possible:
>
> `EPERM`
>> • The process tried to raise a current limit beyond the maximum limit.
>>
>> • The process tried to raise a maximum limit, but is not superuser.
>
> When the sources are compiled with `_FILE_OFFSET_BITS == 64` on a 32-bit system
> this function is in fact `setrlimit64`. Thus, the LFS interface transparently replaces
> the old interface.

int setrlimit64 (*int **resource**, const struct rlimit64 \*`rlp`*)                        [Function]
> Preliminary: | MT-Safe | AS-Safe | AC-Safe | See Section 1.2.2.1 [POSIX Safety
> Concepts], page 2.
>
> This function is similar to `setrlimit` but its second parameter is a pointer to a
> variable of type `struct rlimit64` which allows it to set values which wouldn't fit in
> the member of a `struct rlimit`.
>
> If the sources are compiled with `_FILE_OFFSET_BITS == 64` on a 32-bit machine this
> function is available under the name `setrlimit` and so transparently replaces the old
> interface.

`struct rlimit`                                                                    [Data Type]

This structure is used with `getrlimit` to receive limit values, and with `setrlimit` to specify limit values for a particular process and resource. It has two fields:

`rlim_t rlim_cur`

The current limit

`rlim_t rlim_max`

The maximum limit.

For `getrlimit`, the structure is an output; it receives the current values. For `setrlimit`, it specifies the new values.

For the LFS functions a similar type is defined in `sys/resource.h`.

`struct rlimit64`                                                                  [Data Type]

This structure is analogous to the `rlimit` structure above, but its components have wider ranges. It has two fields:

`rlim64_t rlim_cur`

This is analogous to `rlimit.rlim_cur`, but with a different type.

`rlim64_t rlim_max`

This is analogous to `rlimit.rlim_max`, but with a different type.

Here is a list of resources for which you can specify a limit. Memory and file sizes are measured in bytes.

`RLIMIT_CPU`

The maximum amount of CPU time the process can use. If it runs for longer than this, it gets a signal: `SIGXCPU`. The value is measured in seconds. See Section 24.2.6 [Operation Error Signals], page 669.

`RLIMIT_FSIZE`

The maximum size of file the process can create. Trying to write a larger file causes a signal: `SIGXFSZ`. See Section 24.2.6 [Operation Error Signals], page 669.

`RLIMIT_DATA`

The maximum size of data memory for the process. If the process tries to allocate data memory beyond this amount, the allocation function fails.

`RLIMIT_STACK`

The maximum stack size for the process. If the process tries to extend its stack past this size, it gets a `SIGSEGV` signal. See Section 24.2.1 [Program Error Signals], page 663.

`RLIMIT_CORE`

The maximum size core file that this process can create. If the process terminates and would dump a core file larger than this, then no core file is created. So setting this limit to zero prevents core files from ever being created.

`RLIMIT_RSS`

The maximum amount of physical memory that this process should get. This parameter is a guide for the system's scheduler and memory allocator; the system may give the process more memory when there is a surplus.

RLIMIT_MEMLOCK

> The maximum amount of memory that can be locked into physical memory (so it will never be paged out).

RLIMIT_NPROC

> The maximum number of processes that can be created with the same user ID. If you have reached the limit for your user ID, fork will fail with EAGAIN. See Section 26.4 [Creating a Process], page 751.

RLIMIT_NOFILE
RLIMIT_OFILE

> The maximum number of files that the process can open. If it tries to open more files than this, its open attempt fails with errno EMFILE. See Section 2.2 [Error Codes], page 23. Not all systems support this limit; GNU does, and 4.4 BSD does.

RLIMIT_AS

> The maximum size of total memory that this process should get. If the process tries to allocate more memory beyond this amount with, for example, brk, malloc, mmap or sbrk, the allocation function fails.

RLIM_NLIMITS

> The number of different resource limits. Any valid *resource* operand must be less than RLIM_NLIMITS.

rlim_t RLIM_INFINITY                                                          [Constant]

> This constant stands for a value of "infinity" when supplied as the limit value in setrlimit.

The following are historical functions to do some of what the functions above do. The functions above are better choices.

ulimit and the command symbols are declared in ulimit.h.

long int ulimit (*int cmd, ...*)                                              [Function]

> Preliminary: | MT-Safe | AS-Safe | AC-Safe | See Section 1.2.2.1 [POSIX Safety Concepts], page 2.
>
> ulimit gets the current limit or sets the current and maximum limit for a particular resource for the calling process according to the command *cmd*.a
>
> If you are getting a limit, the command argument is the only argument. If you are setting a limit, there is a second argument: long int *limit* which is the value to which you are setting the limit.
>
> The *cmd* values and the operations they specify are:
>
> GETFSIZE    Get the current limit on the size of a file, in units of 512 bytes.
>
> SETFSIZE    Set the current and maximum limit on the size of a file to *limit* * 512 bytes.
>
> There are also some other *cmd* values that may do things on some systems, but they are not supported.
>
> Only the superuser may increase a maximum limit.

When you successfully get a limit, the return value of `ulimit` is that limit, which is never negative. When you successfully set a limit, the return value is zero. When the function fails, the return value is -1 and `errno` is set according to the reason:

EPERM        A process tried to increase a maximum limit, but is not superuser.

`vlimit` and its resource symbols are declared in `sys/vlimit.h`.

`int vlimit (int resource, int limit)`                                   [Function]
    Preliminary: | MT-Unsafe race:setrlimit | AS-Unsafe | AC-Safe | See Section 1.2.2.1 [POSIX Safety Concepts], page 2.

    `vlimit` sets the current limit for a resource for a process.

    *resource* identifies the resource:

    LIM_CPU      Maximum CPU time. Same as `RLIMIT_CPU` for `setrlimit`.

    LIM_FSIZE
                 Maximum file size. Same as `RLIMIT_FSIZE` for `setrlimit`.

    LIM_DATA     Maximum data memory. Same as `RLIMIT_DATA` for `setrlimit`.

    LIM_STACK
                 Maximum stack size. Same as `RLIMIT_STACK` for `setrlimit`.

    LIM_CORE     Maximum core file size. Same as `RLIMIT_COR` for `setrlimit`.

    LIM_MAXRSS
                 Maximum physical memory. Same as `RLIMIT_RSS` for `setrlimit`.

    The return value is zero for success, and -1 with `errno` set accordingly for failure:

    EPERM        The process tried to set its current limit beyond its maximum limit.

## 22.3 Process CPU Priority And Scheduling

When multiple processes simultaneously require CPU time, the system's scheduling policy and process CPU priorities determine which processes get it. This section describes how that determination is made and GNU C Library functions to control it.

It is common to refer to CPU scheduling simply as scheduling and a process' CPU priority simply as the process' priority, with the CPU resource being implied. Bear in mind, though, that CPU time is not the only resource a process uses or that processes contend for. In some cases, it is not even particularly important. Giving a process a high "priority" may have very little effect on how fast a process runs with respect to other processes. The priorities discussed in this section apply only to CPU time.

CPU scheduling is a complex issue and different systems do it in wildly different ways. New ideas continually develop and find their way into the intricacies of the various systems' scheduling algorithms. This section discusses the general concepts, some specifics of systems that commonly use the GNU C Library, and some standards.

For simplicity, we talk about CPU contention as if there is only one CPU in the system. But all the same principles apply when a processor has multiple CPUs, and knowing that the number of processes that can run at any one time is equal to the number of CPUs, you can easily extrapolate the information.

The functions described in this section are all defined by the POSIX.1 and POSIX.1b standards (the `sched...` functions are POSIX.1b). However, POSIX does not define any semantics for the values that these functions get and set. In this chapter, the semantics are based on the Linux kernel's implementation of the POSIX standard. As you will see, the Linux implementation is quite the inverse of what the authors of the POSIX syntax had in mind.

## 22.3.1 Absolute Priority

Every process has an absolute priority, and it is represented by a number. The higher the number, the higher the absolute priority.

On systems of the past, and most systems today, all processes have absolute priority 0 and this section is irrelevant. In that case, See Section 22.3.4 [Traditional Scheduling], page 642. Absolute priorities were invented to accommodate realtime systems, in which it is vital that certain processes be able to respond to external events happening in real time, which means they cannot wait around while some other process that *wants to*, but doesn't *need to* run occupies the CPU.

When two processes are in contention to use the CPU at any instant, the one with the higher absolute priority always gets it. This is true even if the process with the lower priority is already using the CPU (i.e., the scheduling is preemptive). Of course, we're only talking about processes that are running or "ready to run," which means they are ready to execute instructions right now. When a process blocks to wait for something like I/O, its absolute priority is irrelevant.

**NB:** The term "runnable" is a synonym for "ready to run."

When two processes are running or ready to run and both have the same absolute priority, it's more interesting. In that case, who gets the CPU is determined by the scheduling policy. If the processes have absolute priority 0, the traditional scheduling policy described in Section 22.3.4 [Traditional Scheduling], page 642 applies. Otherwise, the policies described in Section 22.3.2 [Realtime Scheduling], page 638 apply.

You normally give an absolute priority above 0 only to a process that can be trusted not to hog the CPU. Such processes are designed to block (or terminate) after relatively short CPU runs.

A process begins life with the same absolute priority as its parent process. Functions described in Section 22.3.3 [Basic Scheduling Functions], page 639 can change it.

Only a privileged process can change a process' absolute priority to something other than 0. Only a privileged process or the target process' owner can change its absolute priority at all.

POSIX requires absolute priority values used with the realtime scheduling policies to be consecutive with a range of at least 32. On Linux, they are 1 through 99. The functions `sched_get_priority_max` and `sched_set_priority_min` portably tell you what the range is on a particular system.

## 22.3.1.1 Using Absolute Priority

One thing you must keep in mind when designing real time applications is that having higher absolute priority than any other process doesn't guarantee the process can run continuously. Two things that can wreck a good CPU run are interrupts and page faults.

Interrupt handlers live in that limbo between processes. The CPU is executing instructions, but they aren't part of any process. An interrupt will stop even the highest priority process. So you must allow for slight delays and make sure that no device in the system has an interrupt handler that could cause too long a delay between instructions for your process.

Similarly, a page fault causes what looks like a straightforward sequence of instructions to take a long time. The fact that other processes get to run while the page faults in is of no consequence, because as soon as the I/O is complete, the high priority process will kick them out and run again, but the wait for the I/O itself could be a problem. To neutralize this threat, use `mlock` or `mlockall`.

There are a few ramifications of the absoluteness of this priority on a single-CPU system that you need to keep in mind when you choose to set a priority and also when you're working on a program that runs with high absolute priority. Consider a process that has higher absolute priority than any other process in the system and due to a bug in its program, it gets into an infinite loop. It will never cede the CPU. You can't run a command to kill it because your command would need to get the CPU in order to run. The errant program is in complete control. It controls the vertical, it controls the horizontal.

There are two ways to avoid this: 1) keep a shell running somewhere with a higher absolute priority. 2) keep a controlling terminal attached to the high priority process group. All the priority in the world won't stop an interrupt handler from running and delivering a signal to the process if you hit Control-C.

Some systems use absolute priority as a means of allocating a fixed percentage of CPU time to a process. To do this, a super high priority privileged process constantly monitors the process' CPU usage and raises its absolute priority when the process isn't getting its entitled share and lowers it when the process is exceeding it.

**NB:** The absolute priority is sometimes called the "static priority." We don't use that term in this manual because it misses the most important feature of the absolute priority: its absoluteness.

## 22.3.2 Realtime Scheduling

Whenever two processes with the same absolute priority are ready to run, the kernel has a decision to make, because only one can run at a time. If the processes have absolute priority 0, the kernel makes this decision as described in Section 22.3.4 [Traditional Scheduling], page 642. Otherwise, the decision is as described in this section.

If two processes are ready to run but have different absolute priorities, the decision is much simpler, and is described in Section 22.3.1 [Absolute Priority], page 637.

Each process has a scheduling policy. For processes with absolute priority other than zero, there are two available:

1. First Come First Served
2. Round Robin

The most sensible case is where all the processes with a certain absolute priority have the same scheduling policy. We'll discuss that first.

In Round Robin, processes share the CPU, each one running for a small quantum of time ("time slice") and then yielding to another in a circular fashion. Of course, only processes that are ready to run and have the same absolute priority are in this circle.

In First Come First Served, the process that has been waiting the longest to run gets the CPU, and it keeps it until it voluntarily relinquishes the CPU, runs out of things to do (blocks), or gets preempted by a higher priority process.

First Come First Served, along with maximal absolute priority and careful control of interrupts and page faults, is the one to use when a process absolutely, positively has to run at full CPU speed or not at all.

Judicious use of `sched_yield` function invocations by processes with First Come First Served scheduling policy forms a good compromise between Round Robin and First Come First Served.

To understand how scheduling works when processes of different scheduling policies occupy the same absolute priority, you have to know the nitty gritty details of how processes enter and exit the ready to run list:

In both cases, the ready to run list is organized as a true queue, where a process gets pushed onto the tail when it becomes ready to run and is popped off the head when the scheduler decides to run it. Note that ready to run and running are two mutually exclusive states. When the scheduler runs a process, that process is no longer ready to run and no longer in the ready to run list. When the process stops running, it may go back to being ready to run again.

The only difference between a process that is assigned the Round Robin scheduling policy and a process that is assigned First Come First Serve is that in the former case, the process is automatically booted off the CPU after a certain amount of time. When that happens, the process goes back to being ready to run, which means it enters the queue at the tail. The time quantum we're talking about is small. Really small. This is not your father's timesharing. For example, with the Linux kernel, the round robin time slice is a thousand times shorter than its typical time slice for traditional scheduling.

A process begins life with the same scheduling policy as its parent process. Functions described in Section 22.3.3 [Basic Scheduling Functions], page 639 can change it.

Only a privileged process can set the scheduling policy of a process that has absolute priority higher than 0.

## 22.3.3 Basic Scheduling Functions

This section describes functions in the GNU C Library for setting the absolute priority and scheduling policy of a process.

**Portability Note:** On systems that have the functions in this section, the macro _POSIX_PRIORITY_SCHEDULING is defined in `<unistd.h>`.

For the case that the scheduling policy is traditional scheduling, more functions to fine tune the scheduling are in Section 22.3.4 [Traditional Scheduling], page 642.

Don't try to make too much out of the naming and structure of these functions. They don't match the concepts described in this manual because the functions are as defined by POSIX.1b, but the implementation on systems that use the GNU C Library is the inverse of what the POSIX structure contemplates. The POSIX scheme assumes that the primary scheduling parameter is the scheduling policy and that the priority value, if any, is a parameter of the scheduling policy. In the implementation, though, the priority value is king and the scheduling policy, if anything, only fine tunes the effect of that priority.

The symbols in this section are declared by including file `sched.h`.

`struct sched_param`                                              [Data Type]
>    This structure describes an absolute priority.

>    `int sched_priority`
>>            absolute priority value

`int sched_setscheduler` (*pid_t* `pid`, *int* `policy`, *const struct*    [Function]
>        *sched_param* `*param`)
>    Preliminary: | MT-Safe | AS-Safe | AC-Safe | See Section 1.2.2.1 [POSIX Safety
>    Concepts], page 2.

>    This function sets both the absolute priority and the scheduling policy for a process.

>    It assigns the absolute priority value given by *param* and the scheduling policy *policy*
>    to the process with Process ID *pid*, or the calling process if *pid* is zero. If *policy* is
>    negative, `sched_setscheduler` keeps the existing scheduling policy.

>    The following macros represent the valid values for *policy*:

>    `SCHED_OTHER`
>>            Traditional Scheduling

>    `SCHED_FIFO`
>>            First In First Out

>    `SCHED_RR`    Round Robin

>    On success, the return value is 0. Otherwise, it is -1 and `ERRNO` is set accordingly.
>    The `errno` values specific to this function are:

>    `EPERM`
>>    - The calling process does not have `CAP_SYS_NICE` permission and *policy* is not `SCHED_OTHER` (or it's negative and the existing policy is not `SCHED_OTHER`.
>>    - The calling process does not have `CAP_SYS_NICE` permission and its owner is not the target process' owner. I.e., the effective uid of the calling process is neither the effective nor the real uid of process *pid*.

>    `ESRCH`    There is no process with pid *pid* and *pid* is not zero.

>    `EINVAL`
>>    - *policy* does not identify an existing scheduling policy.
>>    - The absolute priority value identified by *param* is outside the valid range for the scheduling policy *policy* (or the existing scheduling policy if *policy* is negative) or *param* is null. `sched_get_priority_max` and `sched_get_priority_min` tell you what the valid range is.
>>    - *pid* is negative.

`int sched_getscheduler` (*pid_t* `pid`)                          [Function]
>    Preliminary: | MT-Safe | AS-Safe | AC-Safe | See Section 1.2.2.1 [POSIX Safety
>    Concepts], page 2.

>    This function returns the scheduling policy assigned to the process with Process ID
>    (pid) *pid*, or the calling process if *pid* is zero.

The return value is the scheduling policy. See `sched_setscheduler` for the possible values.

If the function fails, the return value is instead -1 and `errno` is set accordingly.

The `errno` values specific to this function are:

ESRCH      There is no process with pid *pid* and it is not zero.

EINVAL     *pid* is negative.

Note that this function is not an exact mate to `sched_setscheduler` because while that function sets the scheduling policy and the absolute priority, this function gets only the scheduling policy. To get the absolute priority, use `sched_getparam`.

int **sched_setparam** (*pid_t* **pid**, *const struct sched_param* **\*param**)     [Function]
Preliminary: | MT-Safe | AS-Safe | AC-Safe | See Section 1.2.2.1 [POSIX Safety Concepts], page 2.

This function sets a process' absolute priority.

It is functionally identical to `sched_setscheduler` with *policy* = -1.

int **sched_getparam** (*pid_t* **pid**, *struct sched_param* **\*param**)     [Function]
Preliminary: | MT-Safe | AS-Safe | AC-Safe | See Section 1.2.2.1 [POSIX Safety Concepts], page 2.

This function returns a process' absolute priority.

*pid* is the Process ID (pid) of the process whose absolute priority you want to know.

*param* is a pointer to a structure in which the function stores the absolute priority of the process.

On success, the return value is 0. Otherwise, it is -1 and ERRNO is set accordingly. The `errno` values specific to this function are:

ESRCH      There is no process with pid *pid* and it is not zero.

EINVAL     *pid* is negative.

int **sched_get_priority_min** (*int* **policy**)     [Function]
Preliminary: | MT-Safe | AS-Safe | AC-Safe | See Section 1.2.2.1 [POSIX Safety Concepts], page 2.

This function returns the lowest absolute priority value that is allowable for a process with scheduling policy *policy*.

On Linux, it is 0 for SCHED_OTHER and 1 for everything else.

On success, the return value is 0. Otherwise, it is -1 and ERRNO is set accordingly. The `errno` values specific to this function are:

EINVAL     *policy* does not identify an existing scheduling policy.

int **sched_get_priority_max** (*int* **policy**)     [Function]
Preliminary: | MT-Safe | AS-Safe | AC-Safe | See Section 1.2.2.1 [POSIX Safety Concepts], page 2.

This function returns the highest absolute priority value that is allowable for a process that with scheduling policy *policy*.

On Linux, it is 0 for SCHED_OTHER and 99 for everything else.

On success, the return value is 0. Otherwise, it is -1 and ERRNO is set accordingly. The errno values specific to this function are:

EINVAL        *policy* does not identify an existing scheduling policy.

**int sched_rr_get_interval** (*pid_t* **pid**, *struct timespec* **\*interval**)        [Function]
Preliminary: | MT-Safe | AS-Safe | AC-Safe | See Section 1.2.2.1 [POSIX Safety Concepts], page 2.

This function returns the length of the quantum (time slice) used with the Round Robin scheduling policy, if it is used, for the process with Process ID *pid*.

It returns the length of time as *interval*.

With a Linux kernel, the round robin time slice is always 150 microseconds, and *pid* need not even be a real pid.

The return value is 0 on success and in the pathological case that it fails, the return value is -1 and errno is set accordingly. There is nothing specific that can go wrong with this function, so there are no specific errno values.

**int sched_yield** (*void*)                                        [Function]
Preliminary: | MT-Safe | AS-Safe | AC-Safe | See Section 1.2.2.1 [POSIX Safety Concepts], page 2.

This function voluntarily gives up the process' claim on the CPU.

Technically, sched_yield causes the calling process to be made immediately ready to run (as opposed to running, which is what it was before). This means that if it has absolute priority higher than 0, it gets pushed onto the tail of the queue of processes that share its absolute priority and are ready to run, and it will run again when its turn next arrives. If its absolute priority is 0, it is more complicated, but still has the effect of yielding the CPU to other processes.

If there are no other processes that share the calling process' absolute priority, this function doesn't have any effect.

To the extent that the containing program is oblivious to what other processes in the system are doing and how fast it executes, this function appears as a no-op.

The return value is 0 on success and in the pathological case that it fails, the return value is -1 and errno is set accordingly. There is nothing specific that can go wrong with this function, so there are no specific errno values.

## 22.3.4 Traditional Scheduling

This section is about the scheduling among processes whose absolute priority is 0. When the system hands out the scraps of CPU time that are left over after the processes with higher absolute priority have taken all they want, the scheduling described herein determines who among the great unwashed processes gets them.

## 22.3.4.1 Introduction To Traditional Scheduling

Long before there was absolute priority (See Section 22.3.1 [Absolute Priority], page 637), Unix systems were scheduling the CPU using this system. When Posix came in like the Romans and imposed absolute priorities to accommodate the needs of realtime processing, it left the indigenous Absolute Priority Zero processes to govern themselves by their own familiar scheduling policy.

Indeed, absolute priorities higher than zero are not available on many systems today and are not typically used when they are, being intended mainly for computers that do realtime processing. So this section describes the only scheduling many programmers need to be concerned about.

But just to be clear about the scope of this scheduling: Any time a process with an absolute priority of 0 and a process with an absolute priority higher than 0 are ready to run at the same time, the one with absolute priority 0 does not run. If it's already running when the higher priority ready-to-run process comes into existence, it stops immediately.

In addition to its absolute priority of zero, every process has another priority, which we will refer to as "dynamic priority" because it changes over time. The dynamic priority is meaningless for processes with an absolute priority higher than zero.

The dynamic priority sometimes determines who gets the next turn on the CPU. Sometimes it determines how long turns last. Sometimes it determines whether a process can kick another off the CPU.

In Linux, the value is a combination of these things, but mostly it is just determines the length of the time slice. The higher a process' dynamic priority, the longer a shot it gets on the CPU when it gets one. If it doesn't use up its time slice before giving up the CPU to do something like wait for I/O, it is favored for getting the CPU back when it's ready for it, to finish out its time slice. Other than that, selection of processes for new time slices is basically round robin. But the scheduler does throw a bone to the low priority processes: A process' dynamic priority rises every time it is snubbed in the scheduling process. In Linux, even the fat kid gets to play.

The fluctuation of a process' dynamic priority is regulated by another value: The "nice" value. The nice value is an integer, usually in the range -20 to 20, and represents an upper limit on a process' dynamic priority. The higher the nice number, the lower that limit.

On a typical Linux system, for example, a process with a nice value of 20 can get only 10 milliseconds on the CPU at a time, whereas a process with a nice value of -20 can achieve a high enough priority to get 400 milliseconds.

The idea of the nice value is deferential courtesy. In the beginning, in the Unix garden of Eden, all processes shared equally in the bounty of the computer system. But not all processes really need the same share of CPU time, so the nice value gave a courteous process the ability to refuse its equal share of CPU time that others might prosper. Hence, the higher a process' nice value, the nicer the process is. (Then a snake came along and offered some process a negative nice value and the system became the crass resource allocation system we know today).

Dynamic priorities tend upward and downward with an objective of smoothing out allocation of CPU time and giving quick response time to infrequent requests. But they never exceed their nice limits, so on a heavily loaded CPU, the nice value effectively determines how fast a process runs.

In keeping with the socialistic heritage of Unix process priority, a process begins life with the same nice value as its parent process and can raise it at will. A process can also raise the nice value of any other process owned by the same user (or effective user). But only a privileged process can lower its nice value. A privileged process can also raise or lower another process' nice value.

GNU C Library functions for getting and setting nice values are described in See Section 22.3.4.2 [Functions For Traditional Scheduling], page 644.

## 22.3.4.2 Functions For Traditional Scheduling

This section describes how you can read and set the nice value of a process. All these symbols are declared in `sys/resource.h`.

The function and macro names are defined by POSIX, and refer to "priority," but the functions actually have to do with nice values, as the terms are used both in the manual and POSIX.

The range of valid nice values depends on the kernel, but typically it runs from -20 to 20. A lower nice value corresponds to higher priority for the process. These constants describe the range of priority values:

PRIO_MIN    The lowest valid nice value.

PRIO_MAX    The highest valid nice value.

int getpriority (*int* `class`, *int* `id`)                                     [Function]
> Preliminary: | MT-Safe | AS-Safe | AC-Safe | See Section 1.2.2.1 [POSIX Safety Concepts], page 2.

> Return the nice value of a set of processes; *class* and *id* specify which ones (see below). If the processes specified do not all have the same nice value, this returns the lowest value that any of them has.

> On success, the return value is 0. Otherwise, it is -1 and ERRNO is set accordingly. The `errno` values specific to this function are:

> ESRCH       The combination of *class* and *id* does not match any existing process.

> EINVAL      The value of *class* is not valid.

> If the return value is -1, it could indicate failure, or it could be the nice value. The only way to make certain is to set `errno = 0` before calling `getpriority`, then use `errno != 0` afterward as the criterion for failure.

int setpriority (*int* `class`, *int* `id`, *int* `niceval`)                    [Function]
> Preliminary: | MT-Safe | AS-Safe | AC-Safe | See Section 1.2.2.1 [POSIX Safety Concepts], page 2.

> Set the nice value of a set of processes to *niceval*; *class* and *id* specify which ones (see below).

> The return value is 0 on success, and -1 on failure. The following `errno` error condition are possible for this function:

> ESRCH       The combination of *class* and *id* does not match any existing process.

> EINVAL      The value of *class* is not valid.

> EPERM       The call would set the nice value of a process which is owned by a different user than the calling process (i.e., the target process' real or effective uid does not match the calling process' effective uid) and the calling process does not have CAP_SYS_NICE permission.

EACCES          The call would lower the process' nice value and the process does not
                have CAP_SYS_NICE permission.

The arguments *class* and *id* together specify a set of processes in which you are interested.
These are the possible values of *class*:

PRIO_PROCESS
                One particular process. The argument *id* is a process ID (pid).

PRIO_PGRP
                All the processes in a particular process group. The argument *id* is a process
                group ID (pgid).

PRIO_USER
                All the processes owned by a particular user (i.e., whose real uid indicates the
                user). The argument *id* is a user ID (uid).

If the argument *id* is 0, it stands for the calling process, its process group, or its owner
(real uid), according to *class*.

int nice (*int increment*)                                                    [Function]
        Preliminary:   |  MT-Unsafe race:setpriority  |  AS-Unsafe   |  AC-Safe   |  See
        Section 1.2.2.1 [POSIX Safety Concepts], page 2.

        Increment the nice value of the calling process by *increment*. The return value is the
        new nice value on success, and -1 on failure. In the case of failure, errno will be set
        to the same values as for setpriority.

        Here is an equivalent definition of nice:

```
int
nice (int increment)
{
  int result, old = getpriority (PRIO_PROCESS, 0);
  result = setpriority (PRIO_PROCESS, 0, old + increment);
  if (result != -1)
      return old + increment;
  else
      return -1;
}
```

## 22.3.5 Limiting execution to certain CPUs

On a multi-processor system the operating system usually distributes the different processes
which are runnable on all available CPUs in a way which allows the system to work most
efficiently. Which processes and threads run can be to some extend be control with the
scheduling functionality described in the last sections. But which CPU finally executes
which process or thread is not covered.

There are a number of reasons why a program might want to have control over this
aspect of the system as well:

- One thread or process is responsible for absolutely critical work which under no circumstances must be interrupted or hindered from making process by other process or
  threads using CPU resources. In this case the special process would be confined to a
  CPU which no other process or thread is allowed to use.

- The access to certain resources (RAM, I/O ports) has different costs from different CPUs. This is the case in NUMA (Non-Uniform Memory Architecture) machines. Preferably memory should be accessed locally but this requirement is usually not visible to the scheduler. Therefore forcing a process or thread to the CPUs which have local access to the mostly used memory helps to significantly boost the performance.

- In controlled runtimes resource allocation and book-keeping work (for instance garbage collection) is performance local to processors. This can help to reduce locking costs if the resources do not have to be protected from concurrent accesses from different processors.

The POSIX standard up to this date is of not much help to solve this problem. The Linux kernel provides a set of interfaces to allow specifying *affinity sets* for a process. The scheduler will schedule the thread or process on CPUs specified by the affinity masks. The interfaces which the GNU C Library define follow to some extend the Linux kernel interface.

**cpu_set_t**          [Data Type]

This data set is a bitset where each bit represents a CPU. How the system's CPUs are mapped to bits in the bitset is system dependent. The data type has a fixed size; in the unlikely case that the number of bits are not sufficient to describe the CPUs of the system a different interface has to be used.

This type is a GNU extension and is defined in **sched.h**.

To manipulate the bitset, to set and reset bits, a number of macros is defined. Some of the macros take a CPU number as a parameter. Here it is important to never exceed the size of the bitset. The following macro specifies the number of bits in the **cpu_set_t** bitset.

**int CPU_SETSIZE**          [Macro]

The value of this macro is the maximum number of CPUs which can be handled with a **cpu_set_t** object.

The type **cpu_set_t** should be considered opaque; all manipulation should happen via the next four macros.

**void CPU_ZERO** (*cpu_set_t \*set*)          [Macro]

Preliminary: | MT-Safe | AS-Safe | AC-Safe | See Section 1.2.2.1 [POSIX Safety Concepts], page 2.

This macro initializes the CPU set *set* to be the empty set.

This macro is a GNU extension and is defined in **sched.h**.

**void CPU_SET** (*int cpu*, *cpu_set_t \*set*)          [Macro]

Preliminary: | MT-Safe | AS-Safe | AC-Safe | See Section 1.2.2.1 [POSIX Safety Concepts], page 2.

This macro adds *cpu* to the CPU set *set*.

The *cpu* parameter must not have side effects since it is evaluated more than once.

This macro is a GNU extension and is defined in **sched.h**.

void **CPU_CLR** (*int* **cpu**, *cpu_set_t* ***set***)                                          [Macro]
> Preliminary: | MT-Safe | AS-Safe | AC-Safe | See Section 1.2.2.1 [POSIX Safety Concepts], page 2.
>
> This macro removes *cpu* from the CPU set *set*.
>
> The *cpu* parameter must not have side effects since it is evaluated more than once.
>
> This macro is a GNU extension and is defined in **sched.h**.

int **CPU_ISSET** (*int* **cpu**, *const cpu_set_t* ***set***)                              [Macro]
> Preliminary: | MT-Safe | AS-Safe | AC-Safe | See Section 1.2.2.1 [POSIX Safety Concepts], page 2.
>
> This macro returns a nonzero value (true) if *cpu* is a member of the CPU set *set*, and zero (false) otherwise.
>
> The *cpu* parameter must not have side effects since it is evaluated more than once.
>
> This macro is a GNU extension and is defined in **sched.h**.

CPU bitsets can be constructed from scratch or the currently installed affinity mask can be retrieved from the system.

int **sched_getaffinity** (*pid_t* **pid**, *size_t* **cpusetsize**, *cpu_set_t*          [Function]
    ***cpuset***)
> Preliminary: | MT-Safe | AS-Safe | AC-Safe | See Section 1.2.2.1 [POSIX Safety Concepts], page 2.
>
> This functions stores the CPU affinity mask for the process or thread with the ID *pid* in the *cpusetsize* bytes long bitmap pointed to by *cpuset*. If successful, the function always initializes all bits in the **cpu_set_t** object and returns zero.
>
> If *pid* does not correspond to a process or thread on the system the or the function fails for some other reason, it returns -1 and **errno** is set to represent the error condition.
>
> **ESRCH**      No process or thread with the given ID found.
>
> **EFAULT**     The pointer *cpuset* is does not point to a valid object.
>
> This function is a GNU extension and is declared in **sched.h**.

Note that it is not portably possible to use this information to retrieve the information for different POSIX threads. A separate interface must be provided for that.

int **sched_setaffinity** (*pid_t* **pid**, *size_t* **cpusetsize**, *const cpu_set_t*     [Function]
    ***cpuset***)
> Preliminary: | MT-Safe | AS-Safe | AC-Safe | See Section 1.2.2.1 [POSIX Safety Concepts], page 2.
>
> This function installs the *cpusetsize* bytes long affinity mask pointed to by *cpuset* for the process or thread with the ID *pid*. If successful the function returns zero and the scheduler will in future take the affinity information into account.
>
> If the function fails it will return -1 and **errno** is set to the error code:
>
> **ESRCH**      No process or thread with the given ID found.

EFAULT    The pointer *cpuset* is does not point to a valid object.

EINVAL    The bitset is not valid. This might mean that the affinity set might not leave a processor for the process or thread to run on.

This function is a GNU extension and is declared in `sched.h`.

## 22.4 Querying memory available resources

The amount of memory available in the system and the way it is organized determines oftentimes the way programs can and have to work. For functions like `mmap` it is necessary to know about the size of individual memory pages and knowing how much memory is available enables a program to select appropriate sizes for, say, caches. Before we get into these details a few words about memory subsystems in traditional Unix systems will be given.

### 22.4.1 Overview about traditional Unix memory handling

Unix systems normally provide processes virtual address spaces. This means that the addresses of the memory regions do not have to correspond directly to the addresses of the actual physical memory which stores the data. An extra level of indirection is introduced which translates virtual addresses into physical addresses. This is normally done by the hardware of the processor.

Using a virtual address space has several advantage. The most important is process isolation. The different processes running on the system cannot interfere directly with each other. No process can write into the address space of another process (except when shared memory is used but then it is wanted and controlled).

Another advantage of virtual memory is that the address space the processes see can actually be larger than the physical memory available. The physical memory can be extended by storage on an external media where the content of currently unused memory regions is stored. The address translation can then intercept accesses to these memory regions and make memory content available again by loading the data back into memory. This concept makes it necessary that programs which have to use lots of memory know the difference between available virtual address space and available physical memory. If the working set of virtual memory of all the processes is larger than the available physical memory the system will slow down dramatically due to constant swapping of memory content from the memory to the storage media and back. This is called "thrashing".

A final aspect of virtual memory which is important and follows from what is said in the last paragraph is the granularity of the virtual address space handling. When we said that the virtual address handling stores memory content externally it cannot do this on a byte-by-byte basis. The administrative overhead does not allow this (leaving alone the processor hardware). Instead several thousand bytes are handled together and form a *page*. The size of each page is always a power of two byte. The smallest page size in use today is 4096, with 8192, 16384, and 65536 being other popular sizes.

### 22.4.2 How to get information about the memory subsystem?

The page size of the virtual memory the process sees is essential to know in several situations. Some programming interface (e.g., `mmap`, see Section 13.7 [Memory-mapped I/O], page 337) require the user to provide information adjusted to the page size. In the case of `mmap` is it necessary to provide a length argument which is a multiple of the page size. Another place where the knowledge about the page size is useful is in memory allocation. If one allocates pieces of memory in larger chunks which are then subdivided by the application code it is useful to adjust the size of the larger blocks to the page size. If the total memory requirement for the block is close (but not larger) to a multiple of the page size the kernel's memory handling can work more effectively since it only has to allocate memory pages which are fully used. (To do this optimization it is necessary to know a bit about the memory allocator which will require a bit of memory itself for each block and this overhead must not push the total size over the page size multiple.)

The page size traditionally was a compile time constant. But recent development of processors changed this. Processors now support different page sizes and they can possibly even vary among different processes on the same system. Therefore the system should be queried at runtime about the current page size and no assumptions (except about it being a power of two) should be made.

The correct interface to query about the page size is `sysconf` (see Section 32.4.1 [Definition of `sysconf`], page 841) with the parameter `_SC_PAGESIZE`. There is a much older interface available, too.

`int getpagesize (`*void*`)`                                                                 [Function]
> Preliminary: | MT-Safe | AS-Safe | AC-Safe | See Section 1.2.2.1 [POSIX Safety Concepts], page 2.
>
> The `getpagesize` function returns the page size of the process. This value is fixed for the runtime of the process but can vary in different runs of the application.
>
> The function is declared in `unistd.h`.

Widely available on System V derived systems is a method to get information about the physical memory the system has. The call

    sysconf (_SC_PHYS_PAGES)

returns the total number of pages of physical the system has. This does not mean all this memory is available. This information can be found using

    sysconf (_SC_AVPHYS_PAGES)

These two values help to optimize applications. The value returned for `_SC_AVPHYS_PAGES` is the amount of memory the application can use without hindering any other process (given that no other process increases its memory usage). The value returned for `_SC_PHYS_PAGES` is more or less a hard limit for the working set. If all applications together constantly use more than that amount of memory the system is in trouble.

The GNU C Library provides in addition to these already described way to get this information two functions. They are declared in the file `sys/sysinfo.h`. Programmers should prefer to use the `sysconf` method described above.

`long int get_phys_pages (`*void*`)`                                                          [Function]
> Preliminary: | MT-Safe | AS-Unsafe heap lock | AC-Unsafe lock fd mem | See Section 1.2.2.1 [POSIX Safety Concepts], page 2.
>
> The `get_phys_pages` function returns the total number of pages of physical the system has. To get the amount of memory this number has to be multiplied by the page size.

This function is a GNU extension.

**long int get_avphys_pages** (*void*)                                    [Function]

> Preliminary: | MT-Safe | AS-Unsafe heap lock | AC-Unsafe lock fd mem | See Section 1.2.2.1 [POSIX Safety Concepts], page 2.
>
> The **get_avphys_pages** function returns the number of available pages of physical the system has. To get the amount of memory this number has to be multiplied by the page size.
>
> This function is a GNU extension.

## 22.5 Learn about the processors available

The use of threads or processes with shared memory allows an application to take advantage of all the processing power a system can provide. If the task can be parallelized the optimal way to write an application is to have at any time as many processes running as there are processors. To determine the number of processors available to the system one can run

>     sysconf (_SC_NPROCESSORS_CONF)

which returns the number of processors the operating system configured. But it might be possible for the operating system to disable individual processors and so the call

>     sysconf (_SC_NPROCESSORS_ONLN)

returns the number of processors which are currently online (i.e., available).

For these two pieces of information the GNU C Library also provides functions to get the information directly. The functions are declared in **sys/sysinfo.h**.

**int get_nprocs_conf** (*void*)                                    [Function]

> Preliminary: | MT-Safe | AS-Unsafe heap lock | AC-Unsafe lock fd mem | See Section 1.2.2.1 [POSIX Safety Concepts], page 2.
>
> The **get_nprocs_conf** function returns the number of processors the operating system configured.
>
> This function is a GNU extension.

**int get_nprocs** (*void*)                                    [Function]

> Preliminary: | MT-Safe | AS-Safe | AC-Safe fd | See Section 1.2.2.1 [POSIX Safety Concepts], page 2.
>
> The **get_nprocs** function returns the number of available processors.
>
> This function is a GNU extension.

Before starting more threads it should be checked whether the processors are not already overused. Unix systems calculate something called the *load average*. This is a number indicating how many processes were running. This number is average over different periods of times (normally 1, 5, and 15 minutes).

**int getloadavg** (*double* **loadavg**[], *int* **nelem**)                                    [Function]

> Preliminary: | MT-Safe | AS-Safe | AC-Safe fd | See Section 1.2.2.1 [POSIX Safety Concepts], page 2.
>
> This function gets the 1, 5 and 15 minute load averages of the system. The values are placed in *loadavg*. **getloadavg** will place at most *nelem* elements into the array but

never more than three elements. The return value is the number of elements written to *loadavg*, or -1 on error.

This function is declared in `stdlib.h`.

# 23 Non-Local Exits

Sometimes when your program detects an unusual situation inside a deeply nested set of function calls, you would like to be able to immediately return to an outer level of control. This section describes how you can do such *non-local exits* using the `setjmp` and `longjmp` functions.

## 23.1 Introduction to Non-Local Exits

As an example of a situation where a non-local exit can be useful, suppose you have an interactive program that has a "main loop" that prompts for and executes commands. Suppose the "read" command reads input from a file, doing some lexical analysis and parsing of the input while processing it. If a low-level input error is detected, it would be useful to be able to return immediately to the "main loop" instead of having to make each of the lexical analysis, parsing, and processing phases all have to explicitly deal with error situations initially detected by nested calls.

(On the other hand, if each of these phases has to do a substantial amount of cleanup when it exits—such as closing files, deallocating buffers or other data structures, and the like—then it can be more appropriate to do a normal return and have each phase do its own cleanup, because a non-local exit would bypass the intervening phases and their associated cleanup code entirely. Alternatively, you could use a non-local exit but do the cleanup explicitly either before or after returning to the "main loop".)

In some ways, a non-local exit is similar to using the 'return' statement to return from a function. But while 'return' abandons only a single function call, transferring control back to the point at which it was called, a non-local exit can potentially abandon many levels of nested function calls.

You identify return points for non-local exits by calling the function `setjmp`. This function saves information about the execution environment in which the call to `setjmp` appears in an object of type `jmp_buf`. Execution of the program continues normally after the call to `setjmp`, but if an exit is later made to this return point by calling `longjmp` with the corresponding `jmp_buf` object, control is transferred back to the point where `setjmp` was called. The return value from `setjmp` is used to distinguish between an ordinary return and a return made by a call to `longjmp`, so calls to `setjmp` usually appear in an 'if' statement.

Here is how the example program described above might be set up:

```
#include <setjmp.h>
#include <stdlib.h>
#include <stdio.h>

jmp_buf main_loop;

void
abort_to_main_loop (int status)
{
  longjmp (main_loop, status);
}

int
main (void)
```

```
{
  while (1)
    if (setjmp (main_loop))
      puts ("Back at main loop....");
    else
      do_command ();
}


void
do_command (void)
{
  char buffer[128];
  if (fgets (buffer, 128, stdin) == NULL)
    abort_to_main_loop (-1);
  else
    exit (EXIT_SUCCESS);
}
```

The function `abort_to_main_loop` causes an immediate transfer of control back to the main loop of the program, no matter where it is called from.

The flow of control inside the `main` function may appear a little mysterious at first, but it is actually a common idiom with `setjmp`. A normal call to `setjmp` returns zero, so the "else" clause of the conditional is executed. If `abort_to_main_loop` is called somewhere within the execution of `do_command`, then it actually appears as if the *same* call to `setjmp` in `main` were returning a second time with a value of `-1`.

So, the general pattern for using `setjmp` looks something like:

```
if (setjmp (buffer))
  /* Code to clean up after premature return. */
  ...
else
  /* Code to be executed normally after setting up the return point. */
  ...
```

## 23.2 Details of Non-Local Exits

Here are the details on the functions and data structures used for performing non-local exits. These facilities are declared in `setjmp.h`.

`jmp_buf`                                                                    [Data Type]
> Objects of type `jmp_buf` hold the state information to be restored by a non-local exit. The contents of a `jmp_buf` identify a specific place to return to.

`int setjmp (`*jmp_buf* `state)`                                             [Macro]
> Preliminary: | MT-Safe | AS-Safe | AC-Safe | See Section 1.2.2.1 [POSIX Safety Concepts], page 2.
>
> When called normally, `setjmp` stores information about the execution state of the program in *state* and returns zero. If `longjmp` is later used to perform a non-local exit to this *state*, `setjmp` returns a nonzero value.

`void longjmp (`*jmp_buf* `state, int` `value)`                             [Function]
> Preliminary: | MT-Safe | AS-Unsafe plugin corrupt lock/hurd | AC-Unsafe corrupt lock/hurd | See Section 1.2.2.1 [POSIX Safety Concepts], page 2.

This function restores current execution to the state saved in *state*, and continues execution from the call to `setjmp` that established that return point. Returning from `setjmp` by means of `longjmp` returns the *value* argument that was passed to `longjmp`, rather than 0. (But if *value* is given as 0, `setjmp` returns 1).

There are a lot of obscure but important restrictions on the use of `setjmp` and `longjmp`. Most of these restrictions are present because non-local exits require a fair amount of magic on the part of the C compiler and can interact with other parts of the language in strange ways.

The `setjmp` function is actually a macro without an actual function definition, so you shouldn't try to '#undef' it or take its address. In addition, calls to `setjmp` are safe in only the following contexts:

- As the test expression of a selection or iteration statement (such as 'if', 'switch', or 'while').

- As one operand of an equality or comparison operator that appears as the test expression of a selection or iteration statement. The other operand must be an integer constant expression.

- As the operand of a unary '!' operator, that appears as the test expression of a selection or iteration statement.

- By itself as an expression statement.

Return points are valid only during the dynamic extent of the function that called `setjmp` to establish them. If you `longjmp` to a return point that was established in a function that has already returned, unpredictable and disastrous things are likely to happen.

You should use a nonzero *value* argument to `longjmp`. While `longjmp` refuses to pass back a zero argument as the return value from `setjmp`, this is intended as a safety net against accidental misuse and is not really good programming style.

When you perform a non-local exit, accessible objects generally retain whatever values they had at the time `longjmp` was called. The exception is that the values of automatic variables local to the function containing the `setjmp` call that have been changed since the call to `setjmp` are indeterminate, unless you have declared them `volatile`.

## 23.3 Non-Local Exits and Signals

In BSD Unix systems, `setjmp` and `longjmp` also save and restore the set of blocked signals; see Section 24.7 [Blocking Signals], page 692. However, the POSIX.1 standard requires `setjmp` and `longjmp` not to change the set of blocked signals, and provides an additional pair of functions (`sigsetjmp` and `siglongjmp`) to get the BSD behavior.

The behavior of `setjmp` and `longjmp` in the GNU C Library is controlled by feature test macros; see Section 1.3.4 [Feature Test Macros], page 15. The default in the GNU C Library is the POSIX.1 behavior rather than the BSD behavior.

The facilities in this section are declared in the header file `setjmp.h`.

`sigjmp_buf`                                                                [Data Type]
This is similar to `jmp_buf`, except that it can also store state information about the set of blocked signals.

`int sigsetjmp` (*sigjmp_buf* `state`, *int* `savesigs`)                                    [Function]
> Preliminary: | MT-Safe | AS-Unsafe lock/hurd | AC-Unsafe lock/hurd | See
> Section 1.2.2.1 [POSIX Safety Concepts], page 2.
>
> This is similar to `setjmp`. If *savesigs* is nonzero, the set of blocked signals is saved in
> *state* and will be restored if a `siglongjmp` is later performed with this *state*.

`void siglongjmp` (*sigjmp_buf* `state`, *int* `value`)                                     [Function]
> Preliminary: | MT-Safe | AS-Unsafe plugin corrupt lock/hurd | AC-Unsafe corrupt
> lock/hurd | See Section 1.2.2.1 [POSIX Safety Concepts], page 2.
>
> This is similar to `longjmp` except for the type of its *state* argument. If the `sigsetjmp`
> call that set this *state* used a nonzero *savesigs* flag, `siglongjmp` also restores the set
> of blocked signals.

## 23.4 Complete Context Control

The Unix standard provides one more set of functions to control the execution path and
these functions are more powerful than those discussed in this chapter so far. These function
were part of the original System V API and by this route were added to the Unix API.
Beside on branded Unix implementations these interfaces are not widely available. Not all
platforms and/or architectures the GNU C Library is available on provide this interface.
Use `configure` to detect the availability.

Similar to the `jmp_buf` and `sigjmp_buf` types used for the variables to contain the state
of the `longjmp` functions the interfaces of interest here have an appropriate type as well.
Objects of this type are normally much larger since more information is contained. The
type is also used in a few more places as we will see. The types and functions described in
this section are all defined and declared respectively in the `ucontext.h` header file.

`ucontext_t`                                                                              [Data Type]
> The `ucontext_t` type is defined as a structure with at least the following elements:
>
> `ucontext_t *uc_link`
>> This is a pointer to the next context structure which is used if the context
>> described in the current structure returns.
>
> `sigset_t uc_sigmask`
>> Set of signals which are blocked when this context is used.
>
> `stack_t uc_stack`
>> Stack used for this context. The value need not be (and normally is
>> not) the stack pointer. See Section 24.9 [Using a Separate Signal Stack],
>> page 701.
>
> `mcontext_t uc_mcontext`
>> This element contains the actual state of the process. The `mcontext_t`
>> type is also defined in this header but the definition should be treated
>> as opaque. Any use of knowledge of the type makes applications less
>> portable.

Objects of this type have to be created by the user. The initialization and modification
happens through one of the following functions:

**int getcontext** (*ucontext_t *ucp*)                                                  [Function]
    Preliminary: | MT-Safe race:ucp | AS-Safe | AC-Safe | See Section 1.2.2.1 [POSIX Safety Concepts], page 2.

    The `getcontext` function initializes the variable pointed to by *ucp* with the context of the calling thread. The context contains the content of the registers, the signal mask, and the current stack. Executing the contents would start at the point where the `getcontext` call just returned.

    The function returns 0 if successful. Otherwise it returns −1 and sets *errno* accordingly.

The `getcontext` function is similar to `setjmp` but it does not provide an indication of whether `getcontext` is returning for the first time or whether an initialized context has just been restored. If this is necessary the user has to determine this herself. This must be done carefully since the context contains registers which might contain register variables. This is a good situation to define variables with `volatile`.

Once the context variable is initialized it can be used as is or it can be modified using the `makecontext` function. The latter is normally done when implementing co-routines or similar constructs.

**void makecontext** (*ucontext_t *ucp, void (*func) (void), int argc, . . .*)     [Function]
    Preliminary: | MT-Safe race:ucp | AS-Safe | AC-Safe | See Section 1.2.2.1 [POSIX Safety Concepts], page 2.

    The *ucp* parameter passed to `makecontext` shall be initialized by a call to `getcontext`. The context will be modified in a way such that if the context is resumed it will start by calling the function `func` which gets *argc* integer arguments passed. The integer arguments which are to be passed should follow the *argc* parameter in the call to `makecontext`.

    Before the call to this function the `uc_stack` and `uc_link` element of the *ucp* structure should be initialized. The `uc_stack` element describes the stack which is used for this context. No two contexts which are used at the same time should use the same memory region for a stack.

    The `uc_link` element of the object pointed to by *ucp* should be a pointer to the context to be executed when the function *func* returns or it should be a null pointer. See `setcontext` for more information about the exact use.

While allocating the memory for the stack one has to be careful. Most modern processors keep track of whether a certain memory region is allowed to contain code which is executed or not. Data segments and heap memory are normally not tagged to allow this. The result is that programs would fail. Examples for such code include the calling sequences the GNU C compiler generates for calls to nested functions. Safe ways to allocate stacks correctly include using memory on the original threads stack or explicitly allocate memory tagged for execution using (see Section 13.7 [Memory-mapped I/O], page 337).

**Compatibility note:** The current Unix standard is very imprecise about the way the stack is allocated. All implementations seem to agree that the `uc_stack` element must be used but the values stored in the elements of the `stack_t` value are unclear. The GNU C Library and most other Unix implementations require the `ss_sp` value of the `uc_stack` element to point to the base of the memory region allocated for the stack and the size of the memory region is stored in `ss_size`. There are implements out there which require `ss_sp` to be set to the value the stack pointer will have (which can, depending on the direction the stack grows, be different). This difference makes the `makecontext` function hard to use and it requires detection of the platform at compile time.

int **setcontext** (*const ucontext_t *ucp*)                                           [Function]
    Preliminary: | MT-Safe race:ucp | AS-Unsafe corrupt | AC-Unsafe corrupt | See Section 1.2.2.1 [POSIX Safety Concepts], page 2.

    The `setcontext` function restores the context described by *ucp*. The context is not modified and can be reused as often as wanted.

    If the context was created by `getcontext` execution resumes with the registers filled with the same values and the same stack as if the `getcontext` call just returned.

    If the context was modified with a call to `makecontext` execution continues with the function passed to `makecontext` which gets the specified parameters passed. If this function returns execution is resumed in the context which was referenced by the `uc_link` element of the context structure passed to `makecontext` at the time of the call. If `uc_link` was a null pointer the application terminates normally with an exit status value of `EXIT_SUCCESS` (see Section 25.7 [Program Termination], page 744).

    If the context was created by a call to a signal handler or from any other source then the behaviour of `setcontext` is unspecified.

    Since the context contains information about the stack no two threads should use the same context at the same time. The result in most cases would be disastrous.

    The `setcontext` function does not return unless an error occurred in which case it returns `-1`.

   The `setcontext` function simply replaces the current context with the one described by the *ucp* parameter. This is often useful but there are situations where the current context has to be preserved.

int **swapcontext** (*ucontext_t *restrict oucp, const ucontext_t *restrict*        [Function]
    *ucp*)
    Preliminary: | MT-Safe race:oucp race:ucp | AS-Unsafe corrupt | AC-Unsafe corrupt | See Section 1.2.2.1 [POSIX Safety Concepts], page 2.

    The `swapcontext` function is similar to `setcontext` but instead of just replacing the current context the latter is first saved in the object pointed to by *oucp* as if this was a call to `getcontext`. The saved context would resume after the call to `swapcontext`.

    Once the current context is saved the context described in *ucp* is installed and execution continues as described in this context.

    If `swapcontext` succeeds the function does not return unless the context *oucp* is used without prior modification by `makecontext`. The return value in this case is 0. If the function fails it returns `-1` and sets *errno* accordingly.

## Example for SVID Context Handling

The easiest way to use the context handling functions is as a replacement for `setjmp` and `longjmp`. The context contains on most platforms more information which may lead to fewer surprises but this also means using these functions is more expensive (besides being less portable).

```
int
random_search (int n, int (*fp) (int, ucontext_t *))
{
  volatile int cnt = 0;
  ucontext_t uc;

  /* Safe current context.  */
  if (getcontext (&uc) < 0)
    return -1;

  /* If we have not tried n times try again.  */
  if (cnt++ < n)
    /* Call the function with a new random number
       and the context.  */
    if (fp (rand (), &uc) != 0)
      /* We found what we were looking for.  */
      return 1;

  /* Not found.  */
  return 0;
}
```

Using contexts in such a way enables emulating exception handling. The search functions passed in the *fp* parameter could be very large, nested, and complex which would make it complicated (or at least would require a lot of code) to leave the function with an error value which has to be passed down to the caller. By using the context it is possible to leave the search function in one step and allow restarting the search which also has the nice side effect that it can be significantly faster.

Something which is harder to implement with `setjmp` and `longjmp` is to switch temporarily to a different execution path and then resume where execution was stopped.

```
#include <signal.h>
#include <stdio.h>
#include <stdlib.h>
#include <ucontext.h>
#include <sys/time.h>

/* Set by the signal handler. */
static volatile int expired;

/* The contexts. */
static ucontext_t uc[3];

/* We do only a certain number of switches. */
static int switches;


/* This is the function doing the work.  It is just a
   skeleton, real code has to be filled in. */
static void
```

```
f (int n)
{
  int m = 0;
  while (1)
    {
      /* This is where the work would be done. */
      if (++m % 100 == 0)
        {
          putchar ('.');
          fflush (stdout);
        }

      /* Regularly the expire variable must be checked. */
      if (expired)
        {
          /* We do not want the program to run forever. */
          if (++switches == 20)
            return;

          printf ("\nswitching from %d to %d\n", n, 3 - n);
          expired = 0;
          /* Switch to the other context, saving the current one. */
          swapcontext (&uc[n], &uc[3 - n]);
        }
    }
}

/* This is the signal handler which simply set the variable. */
void
handler (int signal)
{
  expired = 1;
}


int
main (void)
{
  struct sigaction sa;
  struct itimerval it;
  char st1[8192];
  char st2[8192];

  /* Initialize the data structures for the interval timer. */
  sa.sa_flags = SA_RESTART;
  sigfillset (&sa.sa_mask);
  sa.sa_handler = handler;
  it.it_interval.tv_sec = 0;
  it.it_interval.tv_usec = 1;
  it.it_value = it.it_interval;

  /* Install the timer and get the context we can manipulate. */
  if (sigaction (SIGPROF, &sa, NULL) < 0
      || setitimer (ITIMER_PROF, &it, NULL) < 0
      || getcontext (&uc[1]) == -1
      || getcontext (&uc[2]) == -1)
    abort ();
```

```
      /* Create a context with a separate stack which causes the
         function f to be call with the parameter 1.
         Note that the uc_link points to the main context
         which will cause the program to terminate once the function
         return. */
      uc[1].uc_link = &uc[0];
      uc[1].uc_stack.ss_sp = st1;
      uc[1].uc_stack.ss_size = sizeof st1;
      makecontext (&uc[1], (void (*) (void)) f, 1, 1);

      /* Similarly, but 2 is passed as the parameter to f. */
      uc[2].uc_link = &uc[0];
      uc[2].uc_stack.ss_sp = st2;
      uc[2].uc_stack.ss_size = sizeof st2;
      makecontext (&uc[2], (void (*) (void)) f, 1, 2);

      /* Start running. */
      swapcontext (&uc[0], &uc[1]);
      putchar ('\n');

      return 0;
    }
```

This an example how the context functions can be used to implement co-routines or cooperative multi-threading. All that has to be done is to call every once in a while **swapcontext** to continue running a different context. It is not recommended to do the context switching from the signal handler directly since leaving the signal handler via **setcontext** if the signal was delivered during code that was not asynchronous signal safe could lead to problems. Setting a variable in the signal handler and checking it in the body of the functions which are executed is a safer approach. Since **swapcontext** is saving the current context it is possible to have multiple different scheduling points in the code. Execution will always resume where it was left.

# 24 Signal Handling

A *signal* is a software interrupt delivered to a process. The operating system uses signals to report exceptional situations to an executing program. Some signals report errors such as references to invalid memory addresses; others report asynchronous events, such as disconnection of a phone line.

The GNU C Library defines a variety of signal types, each for a particular kind of event. Some kinds of events make it inadvisable or impossible for the program to proceed as usual, and the corresponding signals normally abort the program. Other kinds of signals that report harmless events are ignored by default.

If you anticipate an event that causes signals, you can define a handler function and tell the operating system to run it when that particular type of signal arrives.

Finally, one process can send a signal to another process; this allows a parent process to abort a child, or two related processes to communicate and synchronize.

## 24.1 Basic Concepts of Signals

This section explains basic concepts of how signals are generated, what happens after a signal is delivered, and how programs can handle signals.

### 24.1.1 Some Kinds of Signals

A signal reports the occurrence of an exceptional event. These are some of the events that can cause (or *generate*, or *raise*) a signal:

- A program error such as dividing by zero or issuing an address outside the valid range.

- A user request to interrupt or terminate the program. Most environments are set up to let a user suspend the program by typing *C-z*, or terminate it with *C-c*. Whatever key sequence is used, the operating system sends the proper signal to interrupt the process.

- The termination of a child process.

- Expiration of a timer or alarm.

- A call to `kill` or `raise` by the same process.

- A call to `kill` from another process. Signals are a limited but useful form of interprocess communication.

- An attempt to perform an I/O operation that cannot be done. Examples are reading from a pipe that has no writer (see Chapter 15 [Pipes and FIFOs], page 424), and reading or writing to a terminal in certain situations (see Chapter 28 [Job Control], page 763).

Each of these kinds of events (excepting explicit calls to `kill` and `raise`) generates its own particular kind of signal. The various kinds of signals are listed and described in detail in Section 24.2 [Standard Signals], page 663.

### 24.1.2 Concepts of Signal Generation

In general, the events that generate signals fall into three major categories: errors, external events, and explicit requests.

An error means that a program has done something invalid and cannot continue execution. But not all kinds of errors generate signals—in fact, most do not. For example, opening a nonexistent file is an error, but it does not raise a signal; instead, **open** returns -1. In general, errors that are necessarily associated with certain library functions are reported by returning a value that indicates an error. The errors which raise signals are those which can happen anywhere in the program, not just in library calls. These include division by zero and invalid memory addresses.

An external event generally has to do with I/O or other processes. These include the arrival of input, the expiration of a timer, and the termination of a child process.

An explicit request means the use of a library function such as **kill** whose purpose is specifically to generate a signal.

Signals may be generated *synchronously* or *asynchronously*. A synchronous signal pertains to a specific action in the program, and is delivered (unless blocked) during that action. Most errors generate signals synchronously, and so do explicit requests by a process to generate a signal for that same process. On some machines, certain kinds of hardware errors (usually floating-point exceptions) are not reported completely synchronously, but may arrive a few instructions later.

Asynchronous signals are generated by events outside the control of the process that receives them. These signals arrive at unpredictable times during execution. External events generate signals asynchronously, and so do explicit requests that apply to some other process.

A given type of signal is either typically synchronous or typically asynchronous. For example, signals for errors are typically synchronous because errors generate signals synchronously. But any type of signal can be generated synchronously or asynchronously with an explicit request.

## 24.1.3 How Signals Are Delivered

When a signal is generated, it becomes *pending*. Normally it remains pending for just a short period of time and then is *delivered* to the process that was signaled. However, if that kind of signal is currently *blocked*, it may remain pending indefinitely—until signals of that kind are *unblocked*. Once unblocked, it will be delivered immediately. See Section 24.7 [Blocking Signals], page 692.

When the signal is delivered, whether right away or after a long delay, the *specified action* for that signal is taken. For certain signals, such as SIGKILL and SIGSTOP, the action is fixed, but for most signals, the program has a choice: ignore the signal, specify a *handler function*, or accept the *default action* for that kind of signal. The program specifies its choice using functions such as **signal** or **sigaction** (see Section 24.3 [Specifying Signal Actions], page 671). We sometimes say that a handler *catches* the signal. While the handler is running, that particular signal is normally blocked.

If the specified action for a kind of signal is to ignore it, then any such signal which is generated is discarded immediately. This happens even if the signal is also blocked at the time. A signal discarded in this way will never be delivered, not even if the program subsequently specifies a different action for that kind of signal and then unblocks it.

If a signal arrives which the program has neither handled nor ignored, its *default action* takes place. Each kind of signal has its own default action, documented below (see

Section 24.2 [Standard Signals], page 663). For most kinds of signals, the default action is to terminate the process. For certain kinds of signals that represent "harmless" events, the default action is to do nothing.

When a signal terminates a process, its parent process can determine the cause of termination by examining the termination status code reported by the `wait` or `waitpid` functions. (This is discussed in more detail in Section 26.6 [Process Completion], page 755.) The information it can get includes the fact that termination was due to a signal and the kind of signal involved. If a program you run from a shell is terminated by a signal, the shell typically prints some kind of error message.

The signals that normally represent program errors have a special property: when one of these signals terminates the process, it also writes a *core dump file* which records the state of the process at the time of termination. You can examine the core dump with a debugger to investigate what caused the error.

If you raise a "program error" signal by explicit request, and this terminates the process, it makes a core dump file just as if the signal had been due directly to an error.

## 24.2 Standard Signals

This section lists the names for various standard kinds of signals and describes what kind of event they mean. Each signal name is a macro which stands for a positive integer—the *signal number* for that kind of signal. Your programs should never make assumptions about the numeric code for a particular kind of signal, but rather refer to them always by the names defined here. This is because the number for a given kind of signal can vary from system to system, but the meanings of the names are standardized and fairly uniform.

The signal names are defined in the header file `signal.h`.

int NSIG                                                                                          [Macro]
> The value of this symbolic constant is the total number of signals defined. Since the signal numbers are allocated consecutively, `NSIG` is also one greater than the largest defined signal number.

### 24.2.1 Program Error Signals

The following signals are generated when a serious program error is detected by the operating system or the computer itself. In general, all of these signals are indications that your program is seriously broken in some way, and there's usually no way to continue the computation which encountered the error.

Some programs handle program error signals in order to tidy up before terminating; for example, programs that turn off echoing of terminal input should handle program error signals in order to turn echoing back on. The handler should end by specifying the default action for the signal that happened and then reraising it; this will cause the program to terminate with that signal, as if it had not had a handler. (See Section 24.4.2 [Handlers That Terminate the Process], page 679.)

Termination is the sensible ultimate outcome from a program error in most programs. However, programming systems such as Lisp that can load compiled user programs might need to keep executing even if a user program incurs an error. These programs have handlers which use `longjmp` to return control to the command level.

The default action for all of these signals is to cause the process to terminate. If you block or ignore these signals or establish handlers for them that return normally, your program will probably break horribly when such signals happen, unless they are generated by `raise` or `kill` instead of a real error.

When one of these program error signals terminates a process, it also writes a *core dump file* which records the state of the process at the time of termination. The core dump file is named `core` and is written in whichever directory is current in the process at the time. (On GNU/Hurd systems, you can specify the file name for core dumps with the environment variable `COREFILE`.) The purpose of core dump files is so that you can examine them with a debugger to investigate what caused the error.

`int SIGFPE`                                                          [Macro]

> The `SIGFPE` signal reports a fatal arithmetic error. Although the name is derived from "floating-point exception", this signal actually covers all arithmetic errors, including division by zero and overflow. If a program stores integer data in a location which is then used in a floating-point operation, this often causes an "invalid operation" exception, because the processor cannot recognize the data as a floating-point number.

> Actual floating-point exceptions are a complicated subject because there are many types of exceptions with subtly different meanings, and the `SIGFPE` signal doesn't distinguish between them. The *IEEE Standard for Binary Floating-Point Arithmetic (ANSI/IEEE Std 754-1985 and ANSI/IEEE Std 854-1987)* defines various floating-point exceptions and requires conforming computer systems to report their occurrences. However, this standard does not specify how the exceptions are reported, or what kinds of handling and control the operating system can offer to the programmer.

BSD systems provide the `SIGFPE` handler with an extra argument that distinguishes various causes of the exception. In order to access this argument, you must define the handler to accept two arguments, which means you must cast it to a one-argument function type in order to establish the handler. The GNU C Library does provide this extra argument, but the value is meaningful only on operating systems that provide the information (BSD systems and GNU systems).

`FPE_INTOVF_TRAP`

> Integer overflow (impossible in a C program unless you enable overflow trapping in a hardware-specific fashion).

`FPE_INTDIV_TRAP`

> Integer division by zero.

`FPE_SUBRNG_TRAP`

> Subscript-range (something that C programs never check for).

`FPE_FLTOVF_TRAP`

> Floating overflow trap.

`FPE_FLTDIV_TRAP`

> Floating/decimal division by zero.

`FPE_FLTUND_TRAP`

> Floating underflow trap. (Trapping on floating underflow is not normally enabled.)

`FPE_DECOVF_TRAP`

> Decimal overflow trap. (Only a few machines have decimal arithmetic and C never uses it.)

`int SIGILL` [Macro]

> The name of this signal is derived from "illegal instruction"; it usually means your program is trying to execute garbage or a privileged instruction. Since the C compiler generates only valid instructions, `SIGILL` typically indicates that the executable file is corrupted, or that you are trying to execute data. Some common ways of getting into the latter situation are by passing an invalid object where a pointer to a function was expected, or by writing past the end of an automatic array (or similar problems with pointers to automatic variables) and corrupting other data on the stack such as the return address of a stack frame.

> `SIGILL` can also be generated when the stack overflows, or when the system has trouble running the handler for a signal.

`int SIGSEGV` [Macro]

> This signal is generated when a program tries to read or write outside the memory that is allocated for it, or to write memory that can only be read. (Actually, the signals only occur when the program goes far enough outside to be detected by the system's memory protection mechanism.) The name is an abbreviation for "segmentation violation".

> Common ways of getting a `SIGSEGV` condition include dereferencing a null or uninitialized pointer, or when you use a pointer to step through an array, but fail to check for the end of the array. It varies among systems whether dereferencing a null pointer generates `SIGSEGV` or `SIGBUS`.

`int SIGBUS` [Macro]

> This signal is generated when an invalid pointer is dereferenced. Like `SIGSEGV`, this signal is typically the result of dereferencing an uninitialized pointer. The difference between the two is that `SIGSEGV` indicates an invalid access to valid memory, while `SIGBUS` indicates an access to an invalid address. In particular, `SIGBUS` signals often result from dereferencing a misaligned pointer, such as referring to a four-word integer at an address not divisible by four. (Each kind of computer has its own requirements for address alignment.)

> The name of this signal is an abbreviation for "bus error".

`int SIGABRT` [Macro]

> This signal indicates an error detected by the program itself and reported by calling `abort`. See Section 25.7.4 [Aborting a Program], page 747.

`int SIGIOT` [Macro]

> Generated by the PDP-11 "iot" instruction. On most machines, this is just another name for `SIGABRT`.

**int SIGTRAP**                                                                                    [Macro]

Generated by the machine's breakpoint instruction, and possibly other trap instructions. This signal is used by debuggers. Your program will probably only see SIGTRAP if it is somehow executing bad instructions.

**int SIGEMT**                                                                                     [Macro]

Emulator trap; this results from certain unimplemented instructions which might be emulated in software, or the operating system's failure to properly emulate them.

**int SIGSYS**                                                                                     [Macro]

Bad system call; that is to say, the instruction to trap to the operating system was executed, but the code number for the system call to perform was invalid.

## 24.2.2 Termination Signals

These signals are all used to tell a process to terminate, in one way or another. They have different names because they're used for slightly different purposes, and programs might want to handle them differently.

The reason for handling these signals is usually so your program can tidy up as appropriate before actually terminating. For example, you might want to save state information, delete temporary files, or restore the previous terminal modes. Such a handler should end by specifying the default action for the signal that happened and then reraising it; this will cause the program to terminate with that signal, as if it had not had a handler. (See Section 24.4.2 [Handlers That Terminate the Process], page 679.)

The (obvious) default action for all of these signals is to cause the process to terminate.

**int SIGTERM**                                                                                    [Macro]

The SIGTERM signal is a generic signal used to cause program termination. Unlike SIGKILL, this signal can be blocked, handled, and ignored. It is the normal way to politely ask a program to terminate.

The shell command `kill` generates SIGTERM by default.

**int SIGINT**                                                                                     [Macro]

The SIGINT ("program interrupt") signal is sent when the user types the INTR character (normally C-c). See Section 17.4.9 [Special Characters], page 490, for information about terminal driver support for C-c.

**int SIGQUIT**                                                                                    [Macro]

The SIGQUIT signal is similar to SIGINT, except that it's controlled by a different key—the QUIT character, usually C-\—and produces a core dump when it terminates the process, just like a program error signal. You can think of this as a program error condition "detected" by the user.

See Section 24.2.1 [Program Error Signals], page 663, for information about core dumps. See Section 17.4.9 [Special Characters], page 490, for information about terminal driver support.

Certain kinds of cleanups are best omitted in handling SIGQUIT. For example, if the program creates temporary files, it should handle the other termination requests by deleting the temporary files. But it is better for SIGQUIT not to delete them, so that the user can examine them in conjunction with the core dump.

`int` `SIGKILL`                                                                      [Macro]

> The `SIGKILL` signal is used to cause immediate program termination. It cannot be
> handled or ignored, and is therefore always fatal. It is also not possible to block this
> signal.
>
> This signal is usually generated only by explicit request. Since it cannot be handled,
> you should generate it only as a last resort, after first trying a less drastic method such
> as `C-c` or `SIGTERM`. If a process does not respond to any other termination signals,
> sending it a `SIGKILL` signal will almost always cause it to go away.
>
> In fact, if `SIGKILL` fails to terminate a process, that by itself constitutes an operating
> system bug which you should report.
>
> The system will generate `SIGKILL` for a process itself under some unusual conditions
> where the program cannot possibly continue to run (even to run a signal handler).

`int` `SIGHUP`                                                                       [Macro]

> The `SIGHUP` ("hang-up") signal is used to report that the user's terminal is discon-
> nected, perhaps because a network or telephone connection was broken. For more
> information about this, see Section 17.4.6 [Control Modes], page 485.
>
> This signal is also used to report the termination of the controlling process on a
> terminal to jobs associated with that session; this termination effectively disconnects
> all processes in the session from the controlling terminal. For more information, see
> Section 25.7.5 [Termination Internals], page 747.

## 24.2.3 Alarm Signals

These signals are used to indicate the expiration of timers. See Section 21.5 [Setting an
Alarm], page 625, for information about functions that cause these signals to be sent.

The default behavior for these signals is to cause program termination. This default is
rarely useful, but no other default would be useful; most of the ways of using these signals
would require handler functions in any case.

`int` `SIGALRM`                                                                      [Macro]

> This signal typically indicates expiration of a timer that measures real or clock time.
> It is used by the **alarm** function, for example.

`int` `SIGVTALRM`                                                                    [Macro]

> This signal typically indicates expiration of a timer that measures CPU time used by
> the current process. The name is an abbreviation for "virtual time alarm".

`int` `SIGPROF`                                                                      [Macro]

> This signal typically indicates expiration of a timer that measures both CPU time
> used by the current process, and CPU time expended on behalf of the process by the
> system. Such a timer is used to implement code profiling facilities, hence the name
> of this signal.

## 24.2.4 Asynchronous I/O Signals

The signals listed in this section are used in conjunction with asynchronous I/O facilities.
You have to take explicit action by calling **fcntl** to enable a particular file descriptor to
generate these signals (see Section 13.18 [Interrupt-Driven Input], page 375). The default
action for these signals is to ignore them.

`int SIGIO`                                                                                    [Macro]

> This signal is sent when a file descriptor is ready to perform input or output.
>
> On most operating systems, terminals and sockets are the only kinds of files that can generate `SIGIO`; other kinds, including ordinary files, never generate `SIGIO` even if you ask them to.
>
> On GNU systems `SIGIO` will always be generated properly if you successfully set asynchronous mode with `fcntl`.

`int SIGURG`                                                                                   [Macro]

> This signal is sent when "urgent" or out-of-band data arrives on a socket. See Section 16.9.8 [Out-of-Band Data], page 464.

`int SIGPOLL`                                                                                  [Macro]

> This is a System V signal name, more or less similar to `SIGIO`. It is defined only for compatibility.

## 24.2.5 Job Control Signals

These signals are used to support job control. If your system doesn't support job control, then these macros are defined but the signals themselves can't be raised or handled.

You should generally leave these signals alone unless you really understand how job control works. See Chapter 28 [Job Control], page 763.

`int SIGCHLD`                                                                                  [Macro]

> This signal is sent to a parent process whenever one of its child processes terminates or stops.
>
> The default action for this signal is to ignore it. If you establish a handler for this signal while there are child processes that have terminated but not reported their status via `wait` or `waitpid` (see Section 26.6 [Process Completion], page 755), whether your new handler applies to those processes or not depends on the particular operating system.

`int SIGCLD`                                                                                   [Macro]

> This is an obsolete name for `SIGCHLD`.

`int SIGCONT`                                                                                  [Macro]

> You can send a `SIGCONT` signal to a process to make it continue. This signal is special—it always makes the process continue if it is stopped, before the signal is delivered. The default behavior is to do nothing else. You cannot block this signal. You can set a handler, but `SIGCONT` always makes the process continue regardless.
>
> Most programs have no reason to handle `SIGCONT`; they simply resume execution without realizing they were ever stopped. You can use a handler for `SIGCONT` to make a program do something special when it is stopped and continued—for example, to reprint a prompt when it is suspended while waiting for input.

`int SIGSTOP`                                                                                  [Macro]

> The `SIGSTOP` signal stops the process. It cannot be handled, ignored, or blocked.

int SIGTSTP                                                                                [Macro]

    The SIGTSTP signal is an interactive stop signal. Unlike SIGSTOP, this signal can be
handled and ignored.

    Your program should handle this signal if you have a special need to leave files or
system tables in a secure state when a process is stopped. For example, programs
that turn off echoing should handle SIGTSTP so they can turn echoing back on before
stopping.

    This signal is generated when the user types the SUSP character (normally C-z). For
more information about terminal driver support, see Section 17.4.9 [Special Charac-
ters], page 490.

int SIGTTIN                                                                                [Macro]

    A process cannot read from the user's terminal while it is running as a background
job. When any process in a background job tries to read from the terminal, all of the
processes in the job are sent a SIGTTIN signal. The default action for this signal is
to stop the process. For more information about how this interacts with the terminal
driver, see Section 28.4 [Access to the Controlling Terminal], page 764.

int SIGTTOU                                                                                [Macro]

    This is similar to SIGTTIN, but is generated when a process in a background job
attempts to write to the terminal or set its modes. Again, the default action is to
stop the process. SIGTTOU is only generated for an attempt to write to the terminal
if the TOSTOP output mode is set; see Section 17.4.5 [Output Modes], page 484.

    While a process is stopped, no more signals can be delivered to it until it is continued,
except SIGKILL signals and (obviously) SIGCONT signals. The signals are marked as pending,
but not delivered until the process is continued. The SIGKILL signal always causes termination of the process and can't be blocked, handled or ignored. You can ignore SIGCONT, but it
always causes the process to be continued anyway if it is stopped. Sending a SIGCONT signal
to a process causes any pending stop signals for that process to be discarded. Likewise, any
pending SIGCONT signals for a process are discarded when it receives a stop signal.

    When a process in an orphaned process group (see Section 28.5 [Orphaned Process
Groups], page 765) receives a SIGTSTP, SIGTTIN, or SIGTTOU signal and does not handle
it, the process does not stop. Stopping the process would probably not be very useful,
since there is no shell program that will notice it stop and allow the user to continue it.
What happens instead depends on the operating system you are using. Some systems
may do nothing; others may deliver another signal instead, such as SIGKILL or SIGHUP.
On GNU/Hurd systems, the process dies with SIGKILL; this avoids the problem of many
stopped, orphaned processes lying around the system.

## 24.2.6 Operation Error Signals

These signals are used to report various errors generated by an operation done by the
program. They do not necessarily indicate a programming error in the program, but an
error that prevents an operating system call from completing. The default action for all of
them is to cause the process to terminate.

`int SIGPIPE`                                                                    [Macro]

> Broken pipe. If you use pipes or FIFOs, you have to design your application so that one process opens the pipe for reading before another starts writing. If the reading process never starts, or terminates unexpectedly, writing to the pipe or FIFO raises a `SIGPIPE` signal. If `SIGPIPE` is blocked, handled or ignored, the offending call fails with `EPIPE` instead.
>
> Pipes and FIFO special files are discussed in more detail in Chapter 15 [Pipes and FIFOs], page 424.
>
> Another cause of `SIGPIPE` is when you try to output to a socket that isn't connected. See Section 16.9.5.1 [Sending Data], page 459.

`int SIGLOST`                                                                    [Macro]

> Resource lost. This signal is generated when you have an advisory lock on an NFS file, and the NFS server reboots and forgets about your lock.
>
> On GNU/Hurd systems, `SIGLOST` is generated when any server program dies unexpectedly. It is usually fine to ignore the signal; whatever call was made to the server that died just returns an error.

`int SIGXCPU`                                                                    [Macro]

> CPU time limit exceeded. This signal is generated when the process exceeds its soft resource limit on CPU time. See Section 22.2 [Limiting Resource Usage], page 632.

`int SIGXFSZ`                                                                    [Macro]

> File size limit exceeded. This signal is generated when the process attempts to extend a file so it exceeds the process's soft resource limit on file size. See Section 22.2 [Limiting Resource Usage], page 632.

### 24.2.7 Miscellaneous Signals

These signals are used for various other purposes. In general, they will not affect your program unless it explicitly uses them for something.

`int SIGUSR1`                                                                    [Macro]
`int SIGUSR2`                                                                    [Macro]

> The `SIGUSR1` and `SIGUSR2` signals are set aside for you to use any way you want. They're useful for simple interprocess communication, if you write a signal handler for them in the program that receives the signal.
>
> There is an example showing the use of `SIGUSR1` and `SIGUSR2` in Section 24.6.2 [Signaling Another Process], page 689.
>
> The default action is to terminate the process.

`int SIGWINCH`                                                                   [Macro]

> Window size change. This is generated on some systems (including GNU) when the terminal driver's record of the number of rows and columns on the screen is changed. The default action is to ignore it.
>
> If a program does full-screen display, it should handle `SIGWINCH`. When the signal arrives, it should fetch the new screen size and reformat its display accordingly.

`int` **SIGINFO**                                                                          [Macro]

> Information request. On 4.4 BSD and GNU/Hurd systems, this signal is sent to all
> the processes in the foreground process group of the controlling terminal when the
> user types the STATUS character in canonical mode; see Section 17.4.9.2 [Characters
> that Cause Signals], page 492.
>
> If the process is the leader of the process group, the default action is to print some
> status information about the system and what the process is doing. Otherwise the
> default is to do nothing.

### 24.2.8 Signal Messages

We mentioned above that the shell prints a message describing the signal that terminated
a child process. The clean way to print a message describing a signal is to use the functions
**strsignal** and **psignal**. These functions use a signal number to specify which kind of
signal to describe. The signal number may come from the termination status of a child
process (see Section 26.6 [Process Completion], page 755) or it may come from a signal
handler in the same process.

`char * ` **strsignal** `(int signum)`                                                    [Function]

> Preliminary: | MT-Unsafe race:strsignal locale | AS-Unsafe init i18n corrupt heap |
> AC-Unsafe init corrupt mem | See Section 1.2.2.1 [POSIX Safety Concepts], page 2.
>
> This function returns a pointer to a statically-allocated string containing a message
> describing the signal signum. You should not modify the contents of this string; and,
> since it can be rewritten on subsequent calls, you should save a copy of it if you need
> to reference it later.
>
> This function is a GNU extension, declared in the header file **string.h**.

`void ` **psignal** `(int signum, const char *message)`                                     [Function]

> Preliminary: | MT-Safe locale | AS-Unsafe corrupt i18n heap | AC-Unsafe lock
> corrupt mem | See Section 1.2.2.1 [POSIX Safety Concepts], page 2.
>
> This function prints a message describing the signal signum to the standard error
> output stream **stderr**; see Section 12.2 [Standard Streams], page 248.
>
> If you call **psignal** with a message that is either a null pointer or an empty string,
> **psignal** just prints the message corresponding to signum, adding a trailing newline.
>
> If you supply a non-null message argument, then **psignal** prefixes its output with
> this string. It adds a colon and a space character to separate the message from the
> string corresponding to signum.
>
> This function is a BSD feature, declared in the header file **signal.h**.

There is also an array **sys_siglist** which contains the messages for the various signal
codes. This array exists on BSD systems, unlike **strsignal**.

### 24.3 Specifying Signal Actions

The simplest way to change the action for a signal is to use the **signal** function. You can
specify a built-in action (such as to ignore the signal), or you can establish a handler.

The GNU C Library also implements the more versatile **sigaction** facility. This section
describes both facilities and gives suggestions on which to use when.

## 24.3.1 Basic Signal Handling

The **signal** function provides a simple interface for establishing an action for a particular signal. The function and associated macros are declared in the header file **signal.h**.

**sighandler_t** [Data Type]

This is the type of signal handler functions. Signal handlers take one integer argument specifying the signal number, and have return type **void**. So, you should define handler functions like this:

```
void handler (int signum) { ... }
```

The name **sighandler_t** for this data type is a GNU extension.

**sighandler_t signal** (*int signum*, *sighandler_t action*) [Function]

Preliminary: | MT-Safe sigintr | AS-Safe | AC-Safe | See Section 1.2.2.1 [POSIX Safety Concepts], page 2.

The **signal** function establishes *action* as the action for the signal *signum*.

The first argument, *signum*, identifies the signal whose behavior you want to control, and should be a signal number. The proper way to specify a signal number is with one of the symbolic signal names (see Section 24.2 [Standard Signals], page 663)—don't use an explicit number, because the numerical code for a given kind of signal may vary from operating system to operating system.

The second argument, *action*, specifies the action to use for the signal *signum*. This can be one of the following:

SIG_DFL     SIG_DFL specifies the default action for the particular signal. The default actions for various kinds of signals are stated in Section 24.2 [Standard Signals], page 663.

SIG_IGN     SIG_IGN specifies that the signal should be ignored.

Your program generally should not ignore signals that represent serious events or that are normally used to request termination. You cannot ignore the SIGKILL or SIGSTOP signals at all. You can ignore program error signals like SIGSEGV, but ignoring the error won't enable the program to continue executing meaningfully. Ignoring user requests such as SIGINT, SIGQUIT, and SIGTSTP is unfriendly.

When you do not wish signals to be delivered during a certain part of the program, the thing to do is to block them, not ignore them. See Section 24.7 [Blocking Signals], page 692.

*handler*     Supply the address of a handler function in your program, to specify running this handler as the way to deliver the signal.

For more information about defining signal handler functions, see Section 24.4 [Defining Signal Handlers], page 678.

If you set the action for a signal to SIG_IGN, or if you set it to SIG_DFL and the default action is to ignore that signal, then any pending signals of that type are discarded (even if they are blocked). Discarding the pending signals means that they will never be delivered, not even if you subsequently specify another action and unblock this kind of signal.

The **signal** function returns the action that was previously in effect for the specified *signum*. You can save this value and restore it later by calling **signal** again.

If **signal** can't honor the request, it returns **SIG_ERR** instead. The following **errno** error conditions are defined for this function:

EINVAL       You specified an invalid *signum*; or you tried to ignore or provide a handler for **SIGKILL** or **SIGSTOP**.

**Compatibility Note:** A problem encountered when working with the **signal** function is that it has different semantics on BSD and SVID systems. The difference is that on SVID systems the signal handler is deinstalled after signal delivery. On BSD systems the handler must be explicitly deinstalled. In the GNU C Library we use the BSD version by default. To use the SVID version you can either use the function **sysv_signal** (see below) or use the **_XOPEN_SOURCE** feature select macro (see Section 1.3.4 [Feature Test Macros], page 15). In general, use of these functions should be avoided because of compatibility problems. It is better to use **sigaction** if it is available since the results are much more reliable.

Here is a simple example of setting up a handler to delete temporary files when certain fatal signals happen:

```
#include <signal.h>

void
termination_handler (int signum)
{
  struct temp_file *p;

  for (p = temp_file_list; p; p = p->next)
    unlink (p->name);
}

int
main (void)
{
  ...
  if (signal (SIGINT, termination_handler) == SIG_IGN)
    signal (SIGINT, SIG_IGN);
  if (signal (SIGHUP, termination_handler) == SIG_IGN)
    signal (SIGHUP, SIG_IGN);
  if (signal (SIGTERM, termination_handler) == SIG_IGN)
    signal (SIGTERM, SIG_IGN);
  ...
}
```

Note that if a given signal was previously set to be ignored, this code avoids altering that setting. This is because non-job-control shells often ignore certain signals when starting children, and it is important for the children to respect this.

We do not handle **SIGQUIT** or the program error signals in this example because these are designed to provide information for debugging (a core dump), and the temporary files may give useful information.

**sighandler_t sysv_signal** (*int signum*, *sighandler_t action*)                    [Function]
    Preliminary: | MT-Safe | AS-Safe | AC-Safe | See Section 1.2.2.1 [POSIX Safety Concepts], page 2.

The `sysv_signal` implements the behavior of the standard `signal` function as found on SVID systems. The difference to BSD systems is that the handler is deinstalled after a delivery of a signal.

**Compatibility Note:** As said above for `signal`, this function should be avoided when possible. `sigaction` is the preferred method.

sighandler_t ssignal (*int* `signum`, *sighandler_t* `action`)                    [Function]
> Preliminary: | MT-Safe sigintr | AS-Safe | AC-Safe | See Section 1.2.2.1 [POSIX Safety Concepts], page 2.

> The `ssignal` function does the same thing as `signal`; it is provided only for compatibility with SVID.

sighandler_t SIG_ERR                                                              [Macro]
> The value of this macro is used as the return value from `signal` to indicate an error.

## 24.3.2 Advanced Signal Handling

The `sigaction` function has the same basic effect as `signal`: to specify how a signal should be handled by the process. However, `sigaction` offers more control, at the expense of more complexity. In particular, `sigaction` allows you to specify additional flags to control when the signal is generated and how the handler is invoked.

The `sigaction` function is declared in `signal.h`.

struct sigaction                                                                  [Data Type]
> Structures of type `struct sigaction` are used in the `sigaction` function to specify all the information about how to handle a particular signal. This structure contains at least the following members:

> sighandler_t sa_handler
> > This is used in the same way as the *action* argument to the `signal` function. The value can be `SIG_DFL`, `SIG_IGN`, or a function pointer. See Section 24.3.1 [Basic Signal Handling], page 672.

> sigset_t sa_mask
> > This specifies a set of signals to be blocked while the handler runs. Blocking is explained in Section 24.7.5 [Blocking Signals for a Handler], page 696. Note that the signal that was delivered is automatically blocked by default before its handler is started; this is true regardless of the value in `sa_mask`. If you want that signal not to be blocked within its handler, you must write code in the handler to unblock it.

> int sa_flags
> > This specifies various flags which can affect the behavior of the signal. These are described in more detail in Section 24.3.5 [Flags for `sigaction`], page 676.

int sigaction (*int* `signum`, *const struct sigaction \*restrict* `action`,        [Function]
        *struct sigaction \*restrict* `old-action`)
> Preliminary: | MT-Safe | AS-Safe | AC-Safe | See Section 1.2.2.1 [POSIX Safety Concepts], page 2.

The *action* argument is used to set up a new action for the signal *signum*, while the *old-action* argument is used to return information about the action previously associated with this symbol. (In other words, *old-action* has the same purpose as the `signal` function's return value—you can check to see what the old action in effect for the signal was, and restore it later if you want.)

Either *action* or *old-action* can be a null pointer. If *old-action* is a null pointer, this simply suppresses the return of information about the old action. If *action* is a null pointer, the action associated with the signal *signum* is unchanged; this allows you to inquire about how a signal is being handled without changing that handling.

The return value from `sigaction` is zero if it succeeds, and `-1` on failure. The following `errno` error conditions are defined for this function:

EINVAL      The *signum* argument is not valid, or you are trying to trap or ignore `SIGKILL` or `SIGSTOP`.

### 24.3.3 Interaction of `signal` and `sigaction`

It's possible to use both the `signal` and `sigaction` functions within a single program, but you have to be careful because they can interact in slightly strange ways.

The `sigaction` function specifies more information than the `signal` function, so the return value from `signal` cannot express the full range of `sigaction` possibilities. Therefore, if you use `signal` to save and later reestablish an action, it may not be able to reestablish properly a handler that was established with `sigaction`.

To avoid having problems as a result, always use `sigaction` to save and restore a handler if your program uses `sigaction` at all. Since `sigaction` is more general, it can properly save and reestablish any action, regardless of whether it was established originally with `signal` or `sigaction`.

On some systems if you establish an action with `signal` and then examine it with `sigaction`, the handler address that you get may not be the same as what you specified with `signal`. It may not even be suitable for use as an action argument with `signal`. But you can rely on using it as an argument to `sigaction`. This problem never happens on GNU systems.

So, you're better off using one or the other of the mechanisms consistently within a single program.

**Portability Note:** The basic `signal` function is a feature of ISO C, while `sigaction` is part of the POSIX.1 standard. If you are concerned about portability to non-POSIX systems, then you should use the `signal` function instead.

### 24.3.4 `sigaction` Function Example

In Section 24.3.1 [Basic Signal Handling], page 672, we gave an example of establishing a simple handler for termination signals using `signal`. Here is an equivalent example using `sigaction`:

```
#include <signal.h>

void
termination_handler (int signum)
{
```

```
      struct temp_file *p;

      for (p = temp_file_list; p; p = p->next)
        unlink (p->name);
    }

    int
    main (void)
    {
      ...
      struct sigaction new_action, old_action;

      /* Set up the structure to specify the new action. */
      new_action.sa_handler = termination_handler;
      sigemptyset (&new_action.sa_mask);
      new_action.sa_flags = 0;

      sigaction (SIGINT, NULL, &old_action);
      if (old_action.sa_handler != SIG_IGN)
        sigaction (SIGINT, &new_action, NULL);
      sigaction (SIGHUP, NULL, &old_action);
      if (old_action.sa_handler != SIG_IGN)
        sigaction (SIGHUP, &new_action, NULL);
      sigaction (SIGTERM, NULL, &old_action);
      if (old_action.sa_handler != SIG_IGN)
        sigaction (SIGTERM, &new_action, NULL);
      ...
    }
```

The program just loads the **new_action** structure with the desired parameters and passes it in the **sigaction** call. The usage of **sigemptyset** is described later; see Section 24.7 [Blocking Signals], page 692.

As in the example using **signal**, we avoid handling signals previously set to be ignored. Here we can avoid altering the signal handler even momentarily, by using the feature of **sigaction** that lets us examine the current action without specifying a new one.

Here is another example. It retrieves information about the current action for **SIGINT** without changing that action.

```
    struct sigaction query_action;

    if (sigaction (SIGINT, NULL, &query_action) < 0)
      /* sigaction returns -1 in case of error. */
    else if (query_action.sa_handler == SIG_DFL)
      /* SIGINT is handled in the default, fatal manner. */
    else if (query_action.sa_handler == SIG_IGN)
      /* SIGINT is ignored. */
    else
      /* A programmer-defined signal handler is in effect. */
```

## 24.3.5 Flags for `sigaction`

The **sa_flags** member of the **sigaction** structure is a catch-all for special features. Most of the time, **SA_RESTART** is a good value to use for this field.

The value of **sa_flags** is interpreted as a bit mask. Thus, you should choose the flags you want to set, OR those flags together, and store the result in the **sa_flags** member of your **sigaction** structure.

Each signal number has its own set of flags. Each call to `sigaction` affects one particular signal number, and the flags that you specify apply only to that particular signal.

In the GNU C Library, establishing a handler with `signal` sets all the flags to zero except for `SA_RESTART`, whose value depends on the settings you have made with `siginterrupt`. See Section 24.5 [Primitives Interrupted by Signals], page 687, to see what this is about.

These macros are defined in the header file `signal.h`.

int **SA_NOCLDSTOP**                                            [Macro]

> This flag is meaningful only for the `SIGCHLD` signal. When the flag is set, the system delivers the signal for a terminated child process but not for one that is stopped. By default, `SIGCHLD` is delivered for both terminated children and stopped children.
>
> Setting this flag for a signal other than `SIGCHLD` has no effect.

int **SA_ONSTACK**                                              [Macro]

> If this flag is set for a particular signal number, the system uses the signal stack when delivering that kind of signal. See Section 24.9 [Using a Separate Signal Stack], page 701. If a signal with this flag arrives and you have not set a signal stack, the system terminates the program with `SIGILL`.

int **SA_RESTART**                                              [Macro]

> This flag controls what happens when a signal is delivered during certain primitives (such as `open`, `read` or `write`), and the signal handler returns normally. There are two alternatives: the library function can resume, or it can return failure with error code `EINTR`.
>
> The choice is controlled by the `SA_RESTART` flag for the particular kind of signal that was delivered. If the flag is set, returning from a handler resumes the library function. If the flag is clear, returning from a handler makes the function fail. See Section 24.5 [Primitives Interrupted by Signals], page 687.

## 24.3.6 Initial Signal Actions

When a new process is created (see Section 26.4 [Creating a Process], page 751), it inherits handling of signals from its parent process. However, when you load a new process image using the `exec` function (see Section 26.5 [Executing a File], page 752), any signals that you've defined your own handlers for revert to their `SIG_DFL` handling. (If you think about it a little, this makes sense; the handler functions from the old program are specific to that program, and aren't even present in the address space of the new program image.) Of course, the new program can establish its own handlers.

When a program is run by a shell, the shell normally sets the initial actions for the child process to `SIG_DFL` or `SIG_IGN`, as appropriate. It's a good idea to check to make sure that the shell has not set up an initial action of `SIG_IGN` before you establish your own signal handlers.

Here is an example of how to establish a handler for `SIGHUP`, but not if `SIGHUP` is currently ignored:

```
...
struct sigaction temp;

sigaction (SIGHUP, NULL, &temp);

if (temp.sa_handler != SIG_IGN)
  {
    temp.sa_handler = handle_sighup;
    sigemptyset (&temp.sa_mask);
    sigaction (SIGHUP, &temp, NULL);
  }
```

## 24.4 Defining Signal Handlers

This section describes how to write a signal handler function that can be established with the **signal** or **sigaction** functions.

A signal handler is just a function that you compile together with the rest of the program. Instead of directly invoking the function, you use **signal** or **sigaction** to tell the operating system to call it when a signal arrives. This is known as *establishing* the handler. See Section 24.3 [Specifying Signal Actions], page 671.

There are two basic strategies you can use in signal handler functions:

- You can have the handler function note that the signal arrived by tweaking some global data structures, and then return normally.

- You can have the handler function terminate the program or transfer control to a point where it can recover from the situation that caused the signal.

You need to take special care in writing handler functions because they can be called asynchronously. That is, a handler might be called at any point in the program, unpredictably. If two signals arrive during a very short interval, one handler can run within another. This section describes what your handler should do, and what you should avoid.

### 24.4.1 Signal Handlers that Return

Handlers which return normally are usually used for signals such as **SIGALRM** and the I/O and interprocess communication signals. But a handler for **SIGINT** might also return normally after setting a flag that tells the program to exit at a convenient time.

It is not safe to return normally from the handler for a program error signal, because the behavior of the program when the handler function returns is not defined after a program error. See Section 24.2.1 [Program Error Signals], page 663.

Handlers that return normally must modify some global variable in order to have any effect. Typically, the variable is one that is examined periodically by the program during normal operation. Its data type should be **sig_atomic_t** for reasons described in Section 24.4.7 [Atomic Data Access and Signal Handling], page 685.

Here is a simple example of such a program. It executes the body of the loop until it has noticed that a **SIGALRM** signal has arrived. This technique is useful because it allows the iteration in progress when the signal arrives to complete before the loop exits.

```
#include <signal.h>
#include <stdio.h>
#include <stdlib.h>
```

```
/* This flag controls termination of the main loop. */
volatile sig_atomic_t keep_going = 1;

/* The signal handler just clears the flag and re-enables itself. */
void
catch_alarm (int sig)
{
  keep_going = 0;
  signal (sig, catch_alarm);
}

void
do_stuff (void)
{
  puts ("Doing stuff while waiting for alarm....");
}

int
main (void)
{
  /* Establish a handler for SIGALRM signals. */
  signal (SIGALRM, catch_alarm);

  /* Set an alarm to go off in a little while. */
  alarm (2);

  /* Check the flag once in a while to see when to quit. */
  while (keep_going)
    do_stuff ();

  return EXIT_SUCCESS;
}
```

## 24.4.2 Handlers That Terminate the Process

Handler functions that terminate the program are typically used to cause orderly cleanup or recovery from program error signals and interactive interrupts.

The cleanest way for a handler to terminate the process is to raise the same signal that ran the handler in the first place. Here is how to do this:

```
volatile sig_atomic_t fatal_error_in_progress = 0;

void
fatal_error_signal (int sig)
{
  /* Since this handler is established for more than one kind of signal,
       it might still get invoked recursively by delivery of some other kind
       of signal.  Use a static variable to keep track of that. */
  if (fatal_error_in_progress)
    raise (sig);
  fatal_error_in_progress = 1;

  /* Now do the clean up actions:
       - reset terminal modes
       - kill child processes
       - remove lock files */
  ...
```

```
  /* Now reraise the signal.  We reactivate the signal's
     default handling, which is to terminate the process.
     We could just call exit or abort,
     but reraising the signal sets the return status
     from the process correctly. */
  signal (sig, SIG_DFL);
  raise (sig);
}
```

## 24.4.3 Nonlocal Control Transfer in Handlers

You can do a nonlocal transfer of control out of a signal handler using the `setjmp` and `longjmp` facilities (see Chapter 23 [Non-Local Exits], page 652).

When the handler does a nonlocal control transfer, the part of the program that was running will not continue. If this part of the program was in the middle of updating an important data structure, the data structure will remain inconsistent. Since the program does not terminate, the inconsistency is likely to be noticed later on.

There are two ways to avoid this problem. One is to block the signal for the parts of the program that update important data structures. Blocking the signal delays its delivery until it is unblocked, once the critical updating is finished. See Section 24.7 [Blocking Signals], page 692.

The other way is to re-initialize the crucial data structures in the signal handler, or to make their values consistent.

Here is a rather schematic example showing the reinitialization of one global variable.

```
#include <signal.h>
#include <setjmp.h>

jmp_buf return_to_top_level;

volatile sig_atomic_t waiting_for_input;

void
handle_sigint (int signum)
{
  /* We may have been waiting for input when the signal arrived,
     but we are no longer waiting once we transfer control. */
  waiting_for_input = 0;
  longjmp (return_to_top_level, 1);
}

int
main (void)
{
  ...
  signal (SIGINT, sigint_handler);
  ...
  while (1) {
    prepare_for_command ();
    if (setjmp (return_to_top_level) == 0)
      read_and_execute_command ();
  }
}
```

```
/* Imagine this is a subroutine used by various commands. */
char *
read_data ()
{
  if (input_from_terminal) {
    waiting_for_input = 1;
    ...
    waiting_for_input = 0;
  } else {
    ...
  }
}
```

## 24.4.4 Signals Arriving While a Handler Runs

What happens if another signal arrives while your signal handler function is running?

When the handler for a particular signal is invoked, that signal is automatically blocked until the handler returns. That means that if two signals of the same kind arrive close together, the second one will be held until the first has been handled. (The handler can explicitly unblock the signal using `sigprocmask`, if you want to allow more signals of this type to arrive; see Section 24.7.3 [Process Signal Mask], page 694.)

However, your handler can still be interrupted by delivery of another kind of signal. To avoid this, you can use the `sa_mask` member of the action structure passed to `sigaction` to explicitly specify which signals should be blocked while the signal handler runs. These signals are in addition to the signal for which the handler was invoked, and any other signals that are normally blocked by the process. See Section 24.7.5 [Blocking Signals for a Handler], page 696.

When the handler returns, the set of blocked signals is restored to the value it had before the handler ran. So using `sigprocmask` inside the handler only affects what signals can arrive during the execution of the handler itself, not what signals can arrive once the handler returns.

**Portability Note:** Always use `sigaction` to establish a handler for a signal that you expect to receive asynchronously, if you want your program to work properly on System V Unix. On this system, the handling of a signal whose handler was established with `signal` automatically sets the signal's action back to `SIG_DFL`, and the handler must re-establish itself each time it runs. This practice, while inconvenient, does work when signals cannot arrive in succession. However, if another signal can arrive right away, it may arrive before the handler can re-establish itself. Then the second signal would receive the default handling, which could terminate the process.

## 24.4.5 Signals Close Together Merge into One

If multiple signals of the same type are delivered to your process before your signal handler has a chance to be invoked at all, the handler may only be invoked once, as if only a single signal had arrived. In effect, the signals merge into one. This situation can arise when the signal is blocked, or in a multiprocessing environment where the system is busy running some other processes while the signals are delivered. This means, for example, that you cannot reliably use a signal handler to count signals. The only distinction you can reliably make is whether at least one signal has arrived since a given time in the past.

Here is an example of a handler for SIGCHLD that compensates for the fact that the number of signals received may not equal the number of child processes that generate them. It assumes that the program keeps track of all the child processes with a chain of structures as follows:

```
struct process
{
  struct process *next;
  /* The process ID of this child.  */
  int pid;
  /* The descriptor of the pipe or pseudo terminal
     on which output comes from this child.  */
  int input_descriptor;
  /* Nonzero if this process has stopped or terminated.  */
  sig_atomic_t have_status;
  /* The status of this child; 0 if running,
     otherwise a status value from waitpid.  */
  int status;
};
```

```
struct process *process_list;
```

This example also uses a flag to indicate whether signals have arrived since some time in the past—whenever the program last cleared it to zero.

```
/* Nonzero means some child's status has changed
   so look at process_list for the details.  */
int process_status_change;
```

Here is the handler itself:

```
void
sigchld_handler (int signo)
{
  int old_errno = errno;

  while (1) {
    register int pid;
    int w;
    struct process *p;

    /* Keep asking for a status until we get a definitive result.  */
    do
      {
        errno = 0;
        pid = waitpid (WAIT_ANY, &w, WNOHANG | WUNTRACED);
      }
    while (pid <= 0 && errno == EINTR);

    if (pid <= 0) {
      /* A real failure means there are no more
         stopped or terminated child processes, so return.  */
      errno = old_errno;
      return;
    }

    /* Find the process that signaled us, and record its status.  */

    for (p = process_list; p; p = p->next)
      if (p->pid == pid) {
        p->status = w;
```

```
    /* Indicate that the status field
       has data to look at.  We do this only after storing it.  */
    p->have_status = 1;

    /* If process has terminated, stop waiting for its output.  */
    if (WIFSIGNALED (w) || WIFEXITED (w))
      if (p->input_descriptor)
        FD_CLR (p->input_descriptor, &input_wait_mask);

    /* The program should check this flag from time to time
       to see if there is any news in process_list.  */
    ++process_status_change;
  }

  /* Loop around to handle all the processes
     that have something to tell us.  */
}
}
```

Here is the proper way to check the flag `process_status_change`:

```
if (process_status_change) {
  struct process *p;
  process_status_change = 0;
  for (p = process_list; p; p = p->next)
    if (p->have_status) {
      ... Examine p->status ...
    }
}
```

It is vital to clear the flag before examining the list; otherwise, if a signal were delivered just before the clearing of the flag, and after the appropriate element of the process list had been checked, the status change would go unnoticed until the next signal arrived to set the flag again. You could, of course, avoid this problem by blocking the signal while scanning the list, but it is much more elegant to guarantee correctness by doing things in the right order.

The loop which checks process status avoids examining `p->status` until it sees that status has been validly stored. This is to make sure that the status cannot change in the middle of accessing it. Once `p->have_status` is set, it means that the child process is stopped or terminated, and in either case, it cannot stop or terminate again until the program has taken notice. See Section 24.4.7.3 [Atomic Usage Patterns], page 687, for more information about coping with interruptions during accesses of a variable.

Here is another way you can test whether the handler has run since the last time you checked. This technique uses a counter which is never changed outside the handler. Instead of clearing the count, the program remembers the previous value and sees whether it has changed since the previous check. The advantage of this method is that different parts of the program can check independently, each part checking whether there has been a signal since that part last checked.

```
sig_atomic_t process_status_change;

sig_atomic_t last_process_status_change;

...
{
  sig_atomic_t prev = last_process_status_change;
```

```
        last_process_status_change = process_status_change;
        if (last_process_status_change != prev) {
          struct process *p;
          for (p = process_list; p; p = p->next)
            if (p->have_status) {
                ... Examine p->status ...
            }
        }
      }
```

## 24.4.6 Signal Handling and Nonreentrant Functions

Handler functions usually don't do very much. The best practice is to write a handler that does nothing but set an external variable that the program checks regularly, and leave all serious work to the program. This is best because the handler can be called asynchronously, at unpredictable times—perhaps in the middle of a primitive function, or even between the beginning and the end of a C operator that requires multiple instructions. The data structures being manipulated might therefore be in an inconsistent state when the handler function is invoked. Even copying one **int** variable into another can take two instructions on most machines.

This means you have to be very careful about what you do in a signal handler.

- If your handler needs to access any global variables from your program, declare those variables **volatile**. This tells the compiler that the value of the variable might change asynchronously, and inhibits certain optimizations that would be invalidated by such modifications.

- If you call a function in the handler, make sure it is *reentrant* with respect to signals, or else make sure that the signal cannot interrupt a call to a related function.

A function can be non-reentrant if it uses memory that is not on the stack.

- If a function uses a static variable or a global variable, or a dynamically-allocated object that it finds for itself, then it is non-reentrant and any two calls to the function can interfere.

  For example, suppose that the signal handler uses **gethostbyname**. This function returns its value in a static object, reusing the same object each time. If the signal happens to arrive during a call to **gethostbyname**, or even after one (while the program is still using the value), it will clobber the value that the program asked for.

  However, if the program does not use **gethostbyname** or any other function that returns information in the same object, or if it always blocks signals around each use, then you are safe.

  There are a large number of library functions that return values in a fixed object, always reusing the same object in this fashion, and all of them cause the same problem. Function descriptions in this manual always mention this behavior.

- If a function uses and modifies an object that you supply, then it is potentially non-reentrant; two calls can interfere if they use the same object.

  This case arises when you do I/O using streams. Suppose that the signal handler prints a message with **fprintf**. Suppose that the program was in the middle of an **fprintf** call using the same stream when the signal was delivered. Both the signal handler's message and the program's data could be corrupted, because both calls operate on the same data structure—the stream itself.

However, if you know that the stream that the handler uses cannot possibly be used by the program at a time when signals can arrive, then you are safe. It is no problem if the program uses some other stream.

- On most systems, `malloc` and `free` are not reentrant, because they use a static data structure which records what memory blocks are free. As a result, no library functions that allocate or free memory are reentrant. This includes functions that allocate space to store a result.

The best way to avoid the need to allocate memory in a handler is to allocate in advance space for signal handlers to use.

The best way to avoid freeing memory in a handler is to flag or record the objects to be freed, and have the program check from time to time whether anything is waiting to be freed. But this must be done with care, because placing an object on a chain is not atomic, and if it is interrupted by another signal handler that does the same thing, you could "lose" one of the objects.

- Any function that modifies `errno` is non-reentrant, but you can correct for this: in the handler, save the original value of `errno` and restore it before returning normally. This prevents errors that occur within the signal handler from being confused with errors from system calls at the point the program is interrupted to run the handler.

This technique is generally applicable; if you want to call in a handler a function that modifies a particular object in memory, you can make this safe by saving and restoring that object.

- Merely reading from a memory object is safe provided that you can deal with any of the values that might appear in the object at a time when the signal can be delivered. Keep in mind that assignment to some data types requires more than one instruction, which means that the handler could run "in the middle of" an assignment to the variable if its type is not atomic. See Section 24.4.7 [Atomic Data Access and Signal Handling], page 685.

- Merely writing into a memory object is safe as long as a sudden change in the value, at any time when the handler might run, will not disturb anything.

## 24.4.7 Atomic Data Access and Signal Handling

Whether the data in your application concerns atoms, or mere text, you have to be careful about the fact that access to a single datum is not necessarily *atomic*. This means that it can take more than one instruction to read or write a single object. In such cases, a signal handler might be invoked in the middle of reading or writing the object.

There are three ways you can cope with this problem. You can use data types that are always accessed atomically; you can carefully arrange that nothing untoward happens if an access is interrupted, or you can block all signals around any access that had better not be interrupted (see Section 24.7 [Blocking Signals], page 692).

### 24.4.7.1 Problems with Non-Atomic Access

Here is an example which shows what can happen if a signal handler runs in the middle of modifying a variable. (Interrupting the reading of a variable can also lead to paradoxical results, but here we only show writing.)

```
#include <signal.h>
#include <stdio.h>

volatile struct two_words { int a, b; } memory;

void
handler(int signum)
{
   printf ("%d,%d\n", memory.a, memory.b);
   alarm (1);
}

int
main (void)
{
   static struct two_words zeros = { 0, 0 }, ones = { 1, 1 };
   signal (SIGALRM, handler);
   memory = zeros;
   alarm (1);
   while (1)
     {
       memory = zeros;
       memory = ones;
     }
}
```

This program fills memory with zeros, ones, zeros, ones, alternating forever; meanwhile, once per second, the alarm signal handler prints the current contents. (Calling printf in the handler is safe in this program because it is certainly not being called outside the handler when the signal happens.)

Clearly, this program can print a pair of zeros or a pair of ones. But that's not all it can do! On most machines, it takes several instructions to store a new value in memory, and the value is stored one word at a time. If the signal is delivered in between these instructions, the handler might find that memory.a is zero and memory.b is one (or vice versa).

On some machines it may be possible to store a new value in memory with just one instruction that cannot be interrupted. On these machines, the handler will always print two zeros or two ones.

### 24.4.7.2 Atomic Types

To avoid uncertainty about interrupting access to a variable, you can use a particular data type for which access is always atomic: sig_atomic_t. Reading and writing this data type is guaranteed to happen in a single instruction, so there's no way for a handler to run "in the middle" of an access.

The type sig_atomic_t is always an integer data type, but which one it is, and how many bits it contains, may vary from machine to machine.

sig_atomic_t                                                    [Data Type]
   This is an integer data type. Objects of this type are always accessed atomically.

In practice, you can assume that `int` is atomic. You can also assume that pointer types are atomic; that is very convenient. Both of these assumptions are true on all of the machines that the GNU C Library supports and on all POSIX systems we know of.

### 24.4.7.3 Atomic Usage Patterns

Certain patterns of access avoid any problem even if an access is interrupted. For example, a flag which is set by the handler, and tested and cleared by the main program from time to time, is always safe even if access actually requires two instructions. To show that this is so, we must consider each access that could be interrupted, and show that there is no problem if it is interrupted.

An interrupt in the middle of testing the flag is safe because either it's recognized to be nonzero, in which case the precise value doesn't matter, or it will be seen to be nonzero the next time it's tested.

An interrupt in the middle of clearing the flag is no problem because either the value ends up zero, which is what happens if a signal comes in just before the flag is cleared, or the value ends up nonzero, and subsequent events occur as if the signal had come in just after the flag was cleared. As long as the code handles both of these cases properly, it can also handle a signal in the middle of clearing the flag. (This is an example of the sort of reasoning you need to do to figure out whether non-atomic usage is safe.)

Sometimes you can insure uninterrupted access to one object by protecting its use with another object, perhaps one whose type guarantees atomicity. See Section 24.4.5 [Signals Close Together Merge into One], page 681, for an example.

## 24.5 Primitives Interrupted by Signals

A signal can arrive and be handled while an I/O primitive such as `open` or `read` is waiting for an I/O device. If the signal handler returns, the system faces the question: what should happen next?

POSIX specifies one approach: make the primitive fail right away. The error code for this kind of failure is `EINTR`. This is flexible, but usually inconvenient. Typically, POSIX applications that use signal handlers must check for `EINTR` after each library function that can return it, in order to try the call again. Often programmers forget to check, which is a common source of error.

The GNU C Library provides a convenient way to retry a call after a temporary failure, with the macro `TEMP_FAILURE_RETRY`:

`TEMP_FAILURE_RETRY (expression)`                                  [Macro]
> This macro evaluates *expression* once, and examines its value as type `long int`. If the value equals `-1`, that indicates a failure and `errno` should be set to show what kind of failure. If it fails and reports error code `EINTR`, `TEMP_FAILURE_RETRY` evaluates it again, and over and over until the result is not a temporary failure.
>
> The value returned by `TEMP_FAILURE_RETRY` is whatever value *expression* produced.

BSD avoids `EINTR` entirely and provides a more convenient approach: to restart the interrupted primitive, instead of making it fail. If you choose this approach, you need not be concerned with `EINTR`.

You can choose either approach with the GNU C Library. If you use **sigaction** to establish a signal handler, you can specify how that handler should behave. If you specify the **SA_RESTART** flag, return from that handler will resume a primitive; otherwise, return from that handler will cause **EINTR**. See Section 24.3.5 [Flags for **sigaction**], page 676.

Another way to specify the choice is with the **siginterrupt** function. See Section 24.10 [BSD Signal Handling], page 703.

When you don't specify with **sigaction** or **siginterrupt** what a particular handler should do, it uses a default choice. The default choice in the GNU C Library is to make primitives fail with **EINTR**.

The description of each primitive affected by this issue lists **EINTR** among the error codes it can return.

There is one situation where resumption never happens no matter which choice you make: when a data-transfer function such as **read** or **write** is interrupted by a signal after transferring part of the data. In this case, the function returns the number of bytes already transferred, indicating partial success.

This might at first appear to cause unreliable behavior on record-oriented devices (including datagram sockets; see Section 16.10 [Datagram Socket Operations], page 467), where splitting one **read** or **write** into two would read or write two records. Actually, there is no problem, because interruption after a partial transfer cannot happen on such devices; they always transfer an entire record in one burst, with no waiting once data transfer has started.

## 24.6 Generating Signals

Besides signals that are generated as a result of a hardware trap or interrupt, your program can explicitly send signals to itself or to another process.

### 24.6.1 Signaling Yourself

A process can send itself a signal with the **raise** function. This function is declared in **signal.h**.

int **raise** (*int signum*)                                                          [Function]
>    Preliminary: | MT-Safe | AS-Safe | AC-Safe | See Section 1.2.2.1 [POSIX Safety
>    Concepts], page 2.
>
>    The **raise** function sends the signal *signum* to the calling process. It returns zero if
>    successful and a nonzero value if it fails. About the only reason for failure would be
>    if the value of *signum* is invalid.

int **gsignal** (*int signum*)                                                        [Function]
>    Preliminary: | MT-Safe | AS-Safe | AC-Safe | See Section 1.2.2.1 [POSIX Safety
>    Concepts], page 2.
>
>    The **gsignal** function does the same thing as **raise**; it is provided only for compati-
>    bility with SVID.

One convenient use for **raise** is to reproduce the default behavior of a signal that you have trapped. For instance, suppose a user of your program types the SUSP character (usually *C-z*; see Section 17.4.9 [Special Characters], page 490) to send it an interactive stop signal (`SIGTSTP`), and you want to clean up some internal data buffers before stopping. You might set this up like this:

```
#include <signal.h>

/* When a stop signal arrives, set the action back to the default
   and then resend the signal after doing cleanup actions. */

void
tstp_handler (int sig)
{
  signal (SIGTSTP, SIG_DFL);
  /* Do cleanup actions here. */
  ...
  raise (SIGTSTP);
}

/* When the process is continued again, restore the signal handler. */

void
cont_handler (int sig)
{
  signal (SIGCONT, cont_handler);
  signal (SIGTSTP, tstp_handler);
}

/* Enable both handlers during program initialization. */

int
main (void)
{
  signal (SIGCONT, cont_handler);
  signal (SIGTSTP, tstp_handler);
  ...
}
```

**Portability note:** `raise` was invented by the ISO C committee. Older systems may not support it, so using `kill` may be more portable. See Section 24.6.2 [Signaling Another Process], page 689.

## 24.6.2 Signaling Another Process

The `kill` function can be used to send a signal to another process. In spite of its name, it can be used for a lot of things other than causing a process to terminate. Some examples of situations where you might want to send signals between processes are:

- A parent process starts a child to perform a task—perhaps having the child running an infinite loop—and then terminates the child when the task is no longer needed.

- A process executes as part of a group, and needs to terminate or notify the other processes in the group when an error or other event occurs.

- Two processes need to synchronize while working together.

This section assumes that you know a little bit about how processes work. For more information on this subject, see Chapter 26 [Processes], page 749.

The `kill` function is declared in `signal.h`.

**int kill** (*pid_t pid*, *int signum*) [Function]
> Preliminary: | MT-Safe | AS-Safe | AC-Safe | See Section 1.2.2.1 [POSIX Safety Concepts], page 2.
>
> The **kill** function sends the signal *signum* to the process or process group specified by *pid*. Besides the signals listed in Section 24.2 [Standard Signals], page 663, *signum* can also have a value of zero to check the validity of the *pid*.
>
> The *pid* specifies the process or process group to receive the signal:
>
> *pid* > 0    The process whose identifier is *pid*.
>
> *pid* == 0    All processes in the same process group as the sender.
>
> *pid* < -1    The process group whose identifier is −*pid*.
>
> *pid* == -1    If the process is privileged, send the signal to all processes except for some special system processes. Otherwise, send the signal to all processes with the same effective user ID.
>
> A process can send a signal to itself with a call like **kill (getpid(), signum)**. If **kill** is used by a process to send a signal to itself, and the signal is not blocked, then **kill** delivers at least one signal (which might be some other pending unblocked signal instead of the signal *signum*) to that process before it returns.
>
> The return value from **kill** is zero if the signal can be sent successfully. Otherwise, no signal is sent, and a value of **-1** is returned. If *pid* specifies sending a signal to several processes, **kill** succeeds if it can send the signal to at least one of them. There's no way you can tell which of the processes got the signal or whether all of them did.
>
> The following **errno** error conditions are defined for this function:
>
> **EINVAL**    The *signum* argument is an invalid or unsupported number.
>
> **EPERM**    You do not have the privilege to send a signal to the process or any of the processes in the process group named by *pid*.
>
> **ESRCH**    The *pid* argument does not refer to an existing process or group.

**int killpg** (*int pgid*, *int signum*) [Function]
> Preliminary: | MT-Safe | AS-Safe | AC-Safe | See Section 1.2.2.1 [POSIX Safety Concepts], page 2.
>
> This is similar to **kill**, but sends signal *signum* to the process group *pgid*. This function is provided for compatibility with BSD; using **kill** to do this is more portable.

As a simple example of **kill**, the call **kill (getpid (), sig)** has the same effect as **raise (sig)**.

### 24.6.3 Permission for using kill

There are restrictions that prevent you from using **kill** to send signals to any random process. These are intended to prevent antisocial behavior such as arbitrarily killing off processes belonging to another user. In typical use, **kill** is used to pass signals between parent, child, and sibling processes, and in these situations you normally do have permission to send signals. The only common exception is when you run a setuid program in a child process; if the program changes its real UID as well as its effective UID, you may not have permission to send a signal. The `su` program does this.

Whether a process has permission to send a signal to another process is determined by the user IDs of the two processes. This concept is discussed in detail in Section 30.2 [The Persona of a Process], page 791.

Generally, for a process to be able to send a signal to another process, either the sending process must belong to a privileged user (like 'root'), or the real or effective user ID of the sending process must match the real or effective user ID of the receiving process. If the receiving process has changed its effective user ID from the set-user-ID mode bit on its process image file, then the owner of the process image file is used in place of its current effective user ID. In some implementations, a parent process might be able to send signals to a child process even if the user ID's don't match, and other implementations might enforce other restrictions.

The `SIGCONT` signal is a special case. It can be sent if the sender is part of the same session as the receiver, regardless of user IDs.

## 24.6.4 Using `kill` for Communication

Here is a longer example showing how signals can be used for interprocess communication. This is what the `SIGUSR1` and `SIGUSR2` signals are provided for. Since these signals are fatal by default, the process that is supposed to receive them must trap them through `signal` or `sigaction`.

In this example, a parent process forks a child process and then waits for the child to complete its initialization. The child process tells the parent when it is ready by sending it a `SIGUSR1` signal, using the `kill` function.

```
#include <signal.h>
#include <stdio.h>
#include <sys/types.h>
#include <unistd.h>

/* When a SIGUSR1 signal arrives, set this variable. */
volatile sig_atomic_t usr_interrupt = 0;

void
synch_signal (int sig)
{
  usr_interrupt = 1;
}

/* The child process executes this function. */
void
child_function (void)
{
  /* Perform initialization. */
  printf ("I'm here!!!  My pid is %d.\n", (int) getpid ());

  /* Let parent know you're done. */
  kill (getppid (), SIGUSR1);

  /* Continue with execution. */
  puts ("Bye, now....");
```

```
      exit (0);
}

int
main (void)
{
  struct sigaction usr_action;
  sigset_t block_mask;
  pid_t child_id;

  /* Establish the signal handler. */
  sigfillset (&block_mask);
  usr_action.sa_handler = synch_signal;
  usr_action.sa_mask = block_mask;
  usr_action.sa_flags = 0;
  sigaction (SIGUSR1, &usr_action, NULL);

  /* Create the child process. */
  child_id = fork ();
  if (child_id == 0)
    child_function ();              /* Does not return. */

  /* Busy wait for the child to send a signal. */
  while (!usr_interrupt)
    ;

  /* Now continue execution. */
  puts ("That's all, folks!");

  return 0;
}
```

This example uses a busy wait, which is bad, because it wastes CPU cycles that other programs could otherwise use. It is better to ask the system to wait until the signal arrives. See the example in Section 24.8 [Waiting for a Signal], page 699.

## 24.7 Blocking Signals

Blocking a signal means telling the operating system to hold it and deliver it later. Generally, a program does not block signals indefinitely—it might as well ignore them by setting their actions to SIG_IGN. But it is useful to block signals briefly, to prevent them from interrupting sensitive operations. For instance:

- You can use the sigprocmask function to block signals while you modify global variables that are also modified by the handlers for these signals.
- You can set sa_mask in your sigaction call to block certain signals while a particular signal handler runs. This way, the signal handler can run without being interrupted itself by signals.

### 24.7.1 Why Blocking Signals is Useful

Temporary blocking of signals with sigprocmask gives you a way to prevent interrupts during critical parts of your code. If signals arrive in that part of the program, they are delivered later, after you unblock them.

One example where this is useful is for sharing data between a signal handler and the rest of the program. If the type of the data is not sig_atomic_t (see Section 24.4.7 [Atomic

Data Access and Signal Handling], page 685), then the signal handler could run when the rest of the program has only half finished reading or writing the data. This would lead to confusing consequences.

To make the program reliable, you can prevent the signal handler from running while the rest of the program is examining or modifying that data—by blocking the appropriate signal around the parts of the program that touch the data.

Blocking signals is also necessary when you want to perform a certain action only if a signal has not arrived. Suppose that the handler for the signal sets a flag of type `sig_atomic_t`; you would like to test the flag and perform the action if the flag is not set. This is unreliable. Suppose the signal is delivered immediately after you test the flag, but before the consequent action: then the program will perform the action even though the signal has arrived.

The only way to test reliably for whether a signal has yet arrived is to test while the signal is blocked.

## 24.7.2 Signal Sets

All of the signal blocking functions use a data structure called a *signal set* to specify what signals are affected. Thus, every activity involves two stages: creating the signal set, and then passing it as an argument to a library function.

These facilities are declared in the header file `signal.h`.

`sigset_t`                                                                        [Data Type]

> The `sigset_t` data type is used to represent a signal set. Internally, it may be implemented as either an integer or structure type.
>
> For portability, use only the functions described in this section to initialize, change, and retrieve information from `sigset_t` objects—don't try to manipulate them directly.

There are two ways to initialize a signal set. You can initially specify it to be empty with `sigemptyset` and then add specified signals individually. Or you can specify it to be full with `sigfillset` and then delete specified signals individually.

You must always initialize the signal set with one of these two functions before using it in any other way. Don't try to set all the signals explicitly because the `sigset_t` object might include some other information (like a version field) that needs to be initialized as well. (In addition, it's not wise to put into your program an assumption that the system has no signals aside from the ones you know about.)

`int sigemptyset (`*sigset_t \*set*`)`                                              [Function]

> Preliminary: | MT-Safe | AS-Safe | AC-Safe | See Section 1.2.2.1 [POSIX Safety Concepts], page 2.
>
> This function initializes the signal set *set* to exclude all of the defined signals. It always returns 0.

`int sigfillset (`*sigset_t \*set*`)`                                               [Function]

> Preliminary: | MT-Safe | AS-Safe | AC-Safe | See Section 1.2.2.1 [POSIX Safety Concepts], page 2.

This function initializes the signal set *set* to include all of the defined signals. Again, the return value is 0.

**int sigaddset** (*sigset_t \*set*, *int* **signum**)                                    [Function]
Preliminary: | MT-Safe | AS-Safe | AC-Safe | See Section 1.2.2.1 [POSIX Safety Concepts], page 2.

This function adds the signal *signum* to the signal set *set*. All **sigaddset** does is modify *set*; it does not block or unblock any signals.

The return value is 0 on success and −1 on failure. The following **errno** error condition is defined for this function:

EINVAL     The *signum* argument doesn't specify a valid signal.

**int sigdelset** (*sigset_t \*set*, *int* **signum**)                                    [Function]
Preliminary: | MT-Safe | AS-Safe | AC-Safe | See Section 1.2.2.1 [POSIX Safety Concepts], page 2.

This function removes the signal *signum* from the signal set *set*. All **sigdelset** does is modify *set*; it does not block or unblock any signals. The return value and error conditions are the same as for **sigaddset**.

Finally, there is a function to test what signals are in a signal set:

**int sigismember** (*const sigset_t \*set*, *int* **signum**)                            [Function]
Preliminary: | MT-Safe | AS-Safe | AC-Safe | See Section 1.2.2.1 [POSIX Safety Concepts], page 2.

The **sigismember** function tests whether the signal *signum* is a member of the signal set *set*. It returns 1 if the signal is in the set, 0 if not, and −1 if there is an error.

The following **errno** error condition is defined for this function:

EINVAL     The *signum* argument doesn't specify a valid signal.

## 24.7.3 Process Signal Mask

The collection of signals that are currently blocked is called the *signal mask*. Each process has its own signal mask. When you create a new process (see Section 26.4 [Creating a Process], page 751), it inherits its parent's mask. You can block or unblock signals with total flexibility by modifying the signal mask.

The prototype for the **sigprocmask** function is in **signal.h**.

Note that you must not use **sigprocmask** in multi-threaded processes, because each thread has its own signal mask and there is no single process signal mask. According to POSIX, the behavior of **sigprocmask** in a multi-threaded process is "unspecified". Instead, use **pthread_sigmask**.

**int sigprocmask** (*int* **how**, *const sigset_t \*restrict* **set**, *sigset_t \*restrict*    [Function]
    **oldset**)
Preliminary: | MT-Unsafe race:sigprocmask/bsd(SIG_UNBLOCK) | AS-Unsafe lock/hurd | AC-Unsafe lock/hurd | See Section 1.2.2.1 [POSIX Safety Concepts], page 2.

The `sigprocmask` function is used to examine or change the calling process's signal mask. The *how* argument determines how the signal mask is changed, and must be one of the following values:

SIG_BLOCK

Block the signals in `set`—add them to the existing mask. In other words, the new mask is the union of the existing mask and *set*.

SIG_UNBLOCK

Unblock the signals in *set*—remove them from the existing mask.

SIG_SETMASK

Use *set* for the mask; ignore the previous value of the mask.

The last argument, *oldset*, is used to return information about the old process signal mask. If you just want to change the mask without looking at it, pass a null pointer as the *oldset* argument. Similarly, if you want to know what's in the mask without changing it, pass a null pointer for *set* (in this case the *how* argument is not significant). The *oldset* argument is often used to remember the previous signal mask in order to restore it later. (Since the signal mask is inherited over `fork` and `exec` calls, you can't predict what its contents are when your program starts running.)

If invoking `sigprocmask` causes any pending signals to be unblocked, at least one of those signals is delivered to the process before `sigprocmask` returns. The order in which pending signals are delivered is not specified, but you can control the order explicitly by making multiple `sigprocmask` calls to unblock various signals one at a time.

The `sigprocmask` function returns 0 if successful, and -1 to indicate an error. The following `errno` error conditions are defined for this function:

EINVAL    The *how* argument is invalid.

You can't block the `SIGKILL` and `SIGSTOP` signals, but if the signal set includes these, `sigprocmask` just ignores them instead of returning an error status.

Remember, too, that blocking program error signals such as `SIGFPE` leads to undesirable results for signals generated by an actual program error (as opposed to signals sent with `raise` or `kill`). This is because your program may be too broken to be able to continue executing to a point where the signal is unblocked again. See Section 24.2.1 [Program Error Signals], page 663.

## 24.7.4 Blocking to Test for Delivery of a Signal

Now for a simple example. Suppose you establish a handler for `SIGALRM` signals that sets a flag whenever a signal arrives, and your main program checks this flag from time to time and then resets it. You can prevent additional `SIGALRM` signals from arriving in the meantime by wrapping the critical part of the code with calls to `sigprocmask`, like this:

```
/* This variable is set by the SIGALRM signal handler. */
volatile sig_atomic_t flag = 0;

int
main (void)
{
```

```
        sigset_t block_alarm;

        ...

        /* Initialize the signal mask. */
        sigemptyset (&block_alarm);
        sigaddset (&block_alarm, SIGALRM);

        while (1)
          {
            /* Check if a signal has arrived; if so, reset the flag. */
            sigprocmask (SIG_BLOCK, &block_alarm, NULL);
            if (flag)
              {
                actions-if-not-arrived
                flag = 0;
              }
            sigprocmask (SIG_UNBLOCK, &block_alarm, NULL);

            ...
          }
      }
```

## 24.7.5 Blocking Signals for a Handler

When a signal handler is invoked, you usually want it to be able to finish without being interrupted by another signal. From the moment the handler starts until the moment it finishes, you must block signals that might confuse it or corrupt its data.

When a handler function is invoked on a signal, that signal is automatically blocked (in addition to any other signals that are already in the process's signal mask) during the time the handler is running. If you set up a handler for SIGTSTP, for instance, then the arrival of that signal forces further SIGTSTP signals to wait during the execution of the handler.

However, by default, other kinds of signals are not blocked; they can arrive during handler execution.

The reliable way to block other kinds of signals during the execution of the handler is to use the **sa_mask** member of the **sigaction** structure.

Here is an example:

```
#include <signal.h>
#include <stddef.h>

void catch_stop ();

void
install_handler (void)
{
  struct sigaction setup_action;
  sigset_t block_mask;

  sigemptyset (&block_mask);
  /* Block other terminal-generated signals while handler runs. */
  sigaddset (&block_mask, SIGINT);
  sigaddset (&block_mask, SIGQUIT);
  setup_action.sa_handler = catch_stop;
  setup_action.sa_mask = block_mask;
```

```
    setup_action.sa_flags = 0;
    sigaction (SIGTSTP, &setup_action, NULL);
}
```

This is more reliable than blocking the other signals explicitly in the code for the handler. If you block signals explicitly in the handler, you can't avoid at least a short interval at the beginning of the handler where they are not yet blocked.

You cannot remove signals from the process's current mask using this mechanism. However, you can make calls to `sigprocmask` within your handler to block or unblock signals as you wish.

In any case, when the handler returns, the system restores the mask that was in place before the handler was entered. If any signals that become unblocked by this restoration are pending, the process will receive those signals immediately, before returning to the code that was interrupted.

## 24.7.6 Checking for Pending Signals

You can find out which signals are pending at any time by calling `sigpending`. This function is declared in `signal.h`.

`int sigpending (`*sigset_t *set*`)` [Function]

> Preliminary: | MT-Safe | AS-Unsafe lock/hurd | AC-Unsafe lock/hurd | See Section 1.2.2.1 [POSIX Safety Concepts], page 2.
>
> The `sigpending` function stores information about pending signals in *set*. If there is a pending signal that is blocked from delivery, then that signal is a member of the returned set. (You can test whether a particular signal is a member of this set using `sigismember`; see Section 24.7.2 [Signal Sets], page 693.)
>
> The return value is 0 if successful, and -1 on failure.

Testing whether a signal is pending is not often useful. Testing when that signal is not blocked is almost certainly bad design.

Here is an example.

```
#include <signal.h>
#include <stddef.h>

sigset_t base_mask, waiting_mask;

sigemptyset (&base_mask);
sigaddset (&base_mask, SIGINT);
sigaddset (&base_mask, SIGTSTP);

/* Block user interrupts while doing other processing. */
sigprocmask (SIG_SETMASK, &base_mask, NULL);
...

/* After a while, check to see whether any signals are pending. */
sigpending (&waiting_mask);
if (sigismember (&waiting_mask, SIGINT)) {
  /* User has tried to kill the process. */
}
else if (sigismember (&waiting_mask, SIGTSTP)) {
  /* User has tried to stop the process. */
```

```
  }
```

Remember that if there is a particular signal pending for your process, additional signals of that same type that arrive in the meantime might be discarded. For example, if a `SIGINT` signal is pending when another `SIGINT` signal arrives, your program will probably only see one of them when you unblock this signal.

**Portability Note:** The `sigpending` function is new in POSIX.1. Older systems have no equivalent facility.

### 24.7.7 Remembering a Signal to Act On Later

Instead of blocking a signal using the library facilities, you can get almost the same results by making the handler set a flag to be tested later, when you "unblock". Here is an example:

```
/* If this flag is nonzero, don't handle the signal right away. */
volatile sig_atomic_t signal_pending;

/* This is nonzero if a signal arrived and was not handled. */
volatile sig_atomic_t defer_signal;

void
handler (int signum)
{
  if (defer_signal)
    signal_pending = signum;
  else
    ... /* "Really" handle the signal. */
}

...

void
update_mumble (int frob)
{
  /* Prevent signals from having immediate effect. */
  defer_signal++;
  /* Now update mumble, without worrying about interruption. */
  mumble.a = 1;
  mumble.b = hack ();
  mumble.c = frob;
  /* We have updated mumble.  Handle any signal that came in. */
  defer_signal--;
  if (defer_signal == 0 && signal_pending != 0)
    raise (signal_pending);
}
```

Note how the particular signal that arrives is stored in `signal_pending`. That way, we can handle several types of inconvenient signals with the same mechanism.

We increment and decrement `defer_signal` so that nested critical sections will work properly; thus, if `update_mumble` were called with `signal_pending` already nonzero, signals would be deferred not only within `update_mumble`, but also within the caller. This is also why we do not check `signal_pending` if `defer_signal` is still nonzero.

The incrementing and decrementing of `defer_signal` each require more than one instruction; it is possible for a signal to happen in the middle. But that does not cause any problem. If the signal happens early enough to see the value from before the increment or decrement, that is equivalent to a signal which came before the beginning of the increment or decrement, which is a case that works properly.

It is absolutely vital to decrement `defer_signal` before testing `signal_pending`, because this avoids a subtle bug. If we did these things in the other order, like this,

```
if (defer_signal == 1 && signal_pending != 0)
   raise (signal_pending);
defer_signal--;
```

then a signal arriving in between the `if` statement and the decrement would be effectively "lost" for an indefinite amount of time. The handler would merely set `defer_signal`, but the program having already tested this variable, it would not test the variable again.

Bugs like these are called *timing errors*. They are especially bad because they happen only rarely and are nearly impossible to reproduce. You can't expect to find them with a debugger as you would find a reproducible bug. So it is worth being especially careful to avoid them.

(You would not be tempted to write the code in this order, given the use of `defer_signal` as a counter which must be tested along with `signal_pending`. After all, testing for zero is cleaner than testing for one. But if you did not use `defer_signal` as a counter, and gave it values of zero and one only, then either order might seem equally simple. This is a further advantage of using a counter for `defer_signal`: it will reduce the chance you will write the code in the wrong order and create a subtle bug.)

## 24.8 Waiting for a Signal

If your program is driven by external events, or uses signals for synchronization, then when it has nothing to do it should probably wait until a signal arrives.

### 24.8.1 Using pause

The simple way to wait until a signal arrives is to call **pause**. Please read about its disadvantages, in the following section, before you use it.

`int pause` (*void*)                                                              [Function]

> Preliminary: | MT-Unsafe race:sigprocmask/!bsd!linux | AS-Unsafe lock/hurd | AC-Unsafe lock/hurd | See Section 1.2.2.1 [POSIX Safety Concepts], page 2.
>
> The **pause** function suspends program execution until a signal arrives whose action is either to execute a handler function, or to terminate the process.
>
> If the signal causes a handler function to be executed, then **pause** returns. This is considered an unsuccessful return (since "successful" behavior would be to suspend the program forever), so the return value is -1. Even if you specify that other primitives should resume when a system handler returns (see Section 24.5 [Primitives Interrupted by Signals], page 687), this has no effect on **pause**; it always fails when a signal is handled.
>
> The following **errno** error conditions are defined for this function:
>
> EINTR     The function was interrupted by delivery of a signal.
>
> If the signal causes program termination, **pause** doesn't return (obviously).
>
> This function is a cancellation point in multithreaded programs. This is a problem if the thread allocates some resources (like memory, file descriptors, semaphores or

whatever) at the time `pause` is called. If the thread gets cancelled these resources stay allocated until the program ends. To avoid this calls to `pause` should be protected using cancellation handlers.

The `pause` function is declared in `unistd.h`.

## 24.8.2 Problems with pause

The simplicity of `pause` can conceal serious timing errors that can make a program hang mysteriously.

It is safe to use `pause` if the real work of your program is done by the signal handlers themselves, and the "main program" does nothing but call `pause`. Each time a signal is delivered, the handler will do the next batch of work that is to be done, and then return, so that the main loop of the program can call `pause` again.

You can't safely use `pause` to wait until one more signal arrives, and then resume real work. Even if you arrange for the signal handler to cooperate by setting a flag, you still can't use `pause` reliably. Here is an example of this problem:

```
/* usr_interrupt is set by the signal handler.  */
if (!usr_interrupt)
  pause ();

/* Do work once the signal arrives.  */
...
```

This has a bug: the signal could arrive after the variable `usr_interrupt` is checked, but before the call to `pause`. If no further signals arrive, the process would never wake up again.

You can put an upper limit on the excess waiting by using `sleep` in a loop, instead of using `pause`. (See Section 21.6 [Sleeping], page 628, for more about `sleep`.) Here is what this looks like:

```
/* usr_interrupt is set by the signal handler.
while (!usr_interrupt)
  sleep (1);

/* Do work once the signal arrives.  */
...
```

For some purposes, that is good enough. But with a little more complexity, you can wait reliably until a particular signal handler is run, using `sigsuspend`.

## 24.8.3 Using sigsuspend

The clean and reliable way to wait for a signal to arrive is to block it and then use `sigsuspend`. By using `sigsuspend` in a loop, you can wait for certain kinds of signals, while letting other kinds of signals be handled by their handlers.

**int sigsuspend** (*const sigset_t *set*)                                            [Function]
> Preliminary: | MT-Unsafe race:sigprocmask/!bsd!linux | AS-Unsafe lock/hurd | AC-Unsafe lock/hurd | See Section 1.2.2.1 [POSIX Safety Concepts], page 2.
>
> This function replaces the process's signal mask with *set* and then suspends the process until a signal is delivered whose action is either to terminate the process or invoke a signal handling function. In other words, the program is effectively suspended until one of the signals that is not a member of *set* arrives.

If the process is woken up by delivery of a signal that invokes a handler function, and the handler function returns, then `sigsuspend` also returns.

The mask remains *set* only as long as `sigsuspend` is waiting. The function `sigsuspend` always restores the previous signal mask when it returns.

The return value and error conditions are the same as for `pause`.

With `sigsuspend`, you can replace the `pause` or `sleep` loop in the previous section with something completely reliable:

```
sigset_t mask, oldmask;

...

/* Set up the mask of signals to temporarily block. */
sigemptyset (&mask);
sigaddset (&mask, SIGUSR1);

...

/* Wait for a signal to arrive. */
sigprocmask (SIG_BLOCK, &mask, &oldmask);
while (!usr_interrupt)
  sigsuspend (&oldmask);
sigprocmask (SIG_UNBLOCK, &mask, NULL);
```

This last piece of code is a little tricky. The key point to remember here is that when `sigsuspend` returns, it resets the process's signal mask to the original value, the value from before the call to `sigsuspend`—in this case, the `SIGUSR1` signal is once again blocked. The second call to `sigprocmask` is necessary to explicitly unblock this signal.

One other point: you may be wondering why the `while` loop is necessary at all, since the program is apparently only waiting for one `SIGUSR1` signal. The answer is that the mask passed to `sigsuspend` permits the process to be woken up by the delivery of other kinds of signals, as well—for example, job control signals. If the process is woken up by a signal that doesn't set `usr_interrupt`, it just suspends itself again until the "right" kind of signal eventually arrives.

This technique takes a few more lines of preparation, but that is needed just once for each kind of wait criterion you want to use. The code that actually waits is just four lines.

## 24.9 Using a Separate Signal Stack

A signal stack is a special area of memory to be used as the execution stack during signal handlers. It should be fairly large, to avoid any danger that it will overflow in turn; the macro `SIGSTKSZ` is defined to a canonical size for signal stacks. You can use `malloc` to allocate the space for the stack. Then call `sigaltstack` or `sigstack` to tell the system to use that space for the signal stack.

You don't need to write signal handlers differently in order to use a signal stack. Switching from one stack to the other happens automatically. (Some non-GNU debuggers on some machines may get confused if you examine a stack trace while a handler that uses the signal stack is running.)

There are two interfaces for telling the system to use a separate signal stack. `sigstack` is the older interface, which comes from 4.2 BSD. `sigaltstack` is the newer interface, and comes from 4.4 BSD. The `sigaltstack` interface has the advantage that it does not require your program to know which direction the stack grows, which depends on the specific machine and operating system.

`stack_t`                                                                                      [Data Type]

This structure describes a signal stack. It contains the following members:

`void *ss_sp`

This points to the base of the signal stack.

`size_t ss_size`

This is the size (in bytes) of the signal stack which '`ss_sp`' points to. You should set this to however much space you allocated for the stack.

There are two macros defined in **signal.h** that you should use in calculating this size:

SIGSTKSZ   This is the canonical size for a signal stack. It is judged to be sufficient for normal uses.

MINSIGSTKSZ

This is the amount of signal stack space the operating system needs just to implement signal delivery. The size of a signal stack **must** be greater than this.

For most cases, just using SIGSTKSZ for `ss_size` is sufficient. But if you know how much stack space your program's signal handlers will need, you may want to use a different size. In this case, you should allocate MINSIGSTKSZ additional bytes for the signal stack and increase `ss_size` accordingly.

`int ss_flags`

This field contains the bitwise OR of these flags:

SS_DISABLE

This tells the system that it should not use the signal stack.

SS_ONSTACK

This is set by the system, and indicates that the signal stack is currently in use. If this bit is not set, then signals will be delivered on the normal user stack.

`int sigaltstack (const stack_t *restrict stack, stack_t *restrict`                            [Function]
`        oldstack)`

Preliminary:  | MT-Safe  | AS-Unsafe lock/hurd | AC-Unsafe lock/hurd | See Section 1.2.2.1 [POSIX Safety Concepts], page 2.

The `sigaltstack` function specifies an alternate stack for use during signal handling. When a signal is received by the process and its action indicates that the signal stack is used, the system arranges a switch to the currently installed signal stack while the handler for that signal is executed.

If *oldstack* is not a null pointer, information about the currently installed signal stack is returned in the location it points to. If *stack* is not a null pointer, then this is installed as the new stack for use by signal handlers.

The return value is 0 on success and -1 on failure. If `sigaltstack` fails, it sets `errno` to one of these values:

EINVAL        You tried to disable a stack that was in fact currently in use.

ENOMEM        The size of the alternate stack was too small. It must be greater than `MINSIGSTKSZ`.

Here is the older `sigstack` interface. You should use `sigaltstack` instead on systems that have it.

**struct sigstack**                                                      [Data Type]
    This structure describes a signal stack. It contains the following members:

    **void *ss_sp**
                This is the stack pointer. If the stack grows downwards on your machine, this should point to the top of the area you allocated. If the stack grows upwards, it should point to the bottom.

    **int ss_onstack**
                This field is true if the process is currently using this stack.

**int sigstack** (*struct sigstack* ***stack**, *struct sigstack* ***oldstack**)       [Function]
    Preliminary:  |  MT-Safe   |  AS-Unsafe lock/hurd  |  AC-Unsafe lock/hurd  |  See Section 1.2.2.1 [POSIX Safety Concepts], page 2.

    The `sigstack` function specifies an alternate stack for use during signal handling. When a signal is received by the process and its action indicates that the signal stack is used, the system arranges a switch to the currently installed signal stack while the handler for that signal is executed.

    If *oldstack* is not a null pointer, information about the currently installed signal stack is returned in the location it points to. If *stack* is not a null pointer, then this is installed as the new stack for use by signal handlers.

    The return value is 0 on success and -1 on failure.

## 24.10 BSD Signal Handling

This section describes alternative signal handling functions derived from BSD Unix. These facilities were an advance, in their time; today, they are mostly obsolete, and supported mainly for compatibility with BSD Unix.

There are many similarities between the BSD and POSIX signal handling facilities, because the POSIX facilities were inspired by the BSD facilities. Besides having different names for all the functions to avoid conflicts, the main difference between the two is that BSD Unix represents signal masks as an `int` bit mask, rather than as a `sigset_t` object.

The BSD facilities are declared in `signal.h`.

**int siginterrupt** (*int* ***signum**, *int* ***failflag**)                     [Function]
    Preliminary:  |  MT-Unsafe const:sigintr  |  AS-Unsafe  |  AC-Unsafe corrupt  |  See Section 1.2.2.1 [POSIX Safety Concepts], page 2.

    This function specifies which approach to use when certain primitives are interrupted by handling signal *signum*. If *failflag* is false, signal *signum* restarts primitives. If *failflag* is true, handling *signum* causes these primitives to fail with error code `EINTR`. See Section 24.5 [Primitives Interrupted by Signals], page 687.

`int sigmask (`*int signum*`)` [Macro]

Preliminary: | MT-Safe | AS-Safe | AC-Safe | See Section 1.2.2.1 [POSIX Safety Concepts], page 2.

This macro returns a signal mask that has the bit for signal *signum* set. You can bitwise-OR the results of several calls to `sigmask` together to specify more than one signal. For example,

```
(sigmask (SIGTSTP) | sigmask (SIGSTOP)
 | sigmask (SIGTTIN) | sigmask (SIGTTOU))
```

specifies a mask that includes all the job-control stop signals.

`int sigblock (`*int mask*`)` [Function]

Preliminary: | MT-Safe | AS-Unsafe lock/hurd | AC-Unsafe lock/hurd | See Section 1.2.2.1 [POSIX Safety Concepts], page 2.

This function is equivalent to `sigprocmask` (see Section 24.7.3 [Process Signal Mask], page 694) with a *how* argument of `SIG_BLOCK`: it adds the signals specified by *mask* to the calling process's set of blocked signals. The return value is the previous set of blocked signals.

`int sigsetmask (`*int mask*`)` [Function]

Preliminary: | MT-Safe | AS-Unsafe lock/hurd | AC-Unsafe lock/hurd | See Section 1.2.2.1 [POSIX Safety Concepts], page 2.

This function equivalent to `sigprocmask` (see Section 24.7.3 [Process Signal Mask], page 694) with a *how* argument of `SIG_SETMASK`: it sets the calling process's signal mask to *mask*. The return value is the previous set of blocked signals.

`int sigpause (`*int mask*`)` [Function]

Preliminary: | MT-Unsafe race:sigprocmask/!bsd!linux | AS-Unsafe lock/hurd | AC-Unsafe lock/hurd | See Section 1.2.2.1 [POSIX Safety Concepts], page 2.

This function is the equivalent of `sigsuspend` (see Section 24.8 [Waiting for a Signal], page 699): it sets the calling process's signal mask to *mask*, and waits for a signal to arrive. On return the previous set of blocked signals is restored.

# 25 The Basic Program/System Interface

*Processes* are the primitive units for allocation of system resources. Each process has its own address space and (usually) one thread of control. A process executes a program; you can have multiple processes executing the same program, but each process has its own copy of the program within its own address space and executes it independently of the other copies. Though it may have multiple threads of control within the same program and a program may be composed of multiple logically separate modules, a process always executes exactly one program.

Note that we are using a specific definition of "program" for the purposes of this manual, which corresponds to a common definition in the context of Unix system. In popular usage, "program" enjoys a much broader definition; it can refer for example to a system's kernel, an editor macro, a complex package of software, or a discrete section of code executing within a process.

Writing the program is what this manual is all about. This chapter explains the most basic interface between your program and the system that runs, or calls, it. This includes passing of parameters (arguments and environment) from the system, requesting basic services from the system, and telling the system the program is done.

A program starts another program with the **exec** family of system calls. This chapter looks at program startup from the execee's point of view. To see the event from the execor's point of view, see Section 26.5 [Executing a File], page 752.

## 25.1 Program Arguments

The system starts a C program by calling the function **main**. It is up to you to write a function named **main**—otherwise, you won't even be able to link your program without errors.

In ISO C you can define **main** either to take no arguments, or to take two arguments that represent the command line arguments to the program, like this:

```
int main (int argc, char *argv[])
```

The command line arguments are the whitespace-separated tokens given in the shell command used to invoke the program; thus, in 'cat foo bar', the arguments are 'foo' and 'bar'. The only way a program can look at its command line arguments is via the arguments of **main**. If **main** doesn't take arguments, then you cannot get at the command line.

The value of the *argc* argument is the number of command line arguments. The *argv* argument is a vector of C strings; its elements are the individual command line argument strings. The file name of the program being run is also included in the vector as the first element; the value of *argc* counts this element. A null pointer always follows the last element: **argv[argc]** is this null pointer.

For the command 'cat foo bar', *argc* is 3 and *argv* has three elements, "cat", "foo" and "bar".

In Unix systems you can define **main** a third way, using three arguments:

```
int main (int argc, char *argv[], char *envp[])
```

The first two arguments are just the same. The third argument *envp* gives the program's environment; it is the same as the value of **environ**. See Section 25.4 [Environment Variables], page 738. POSIX.1 does not allow this three-argument form, so to be portable it is best to write **main** to take two arguments, and use the value of **environ**.

## 25.1.1 Program Argument Syntax Conventions

POSIX recommends these conventions for command line arguments. **getopt** (see Section 25.2 [Parsing program options using **getopt**], page 707) and **argp_parse** (see Section 25.3 [Parsing Program Options with Argp], page 714) make it easy to implement them.

- Arguments are options if they begin with a hyphen delimiter ('-').

- Multiple options may follow a hyphen delimiter in a single token if the options do not take arguments. Thus, '-abc' is equivalent to '-a -b -c'.

- Option names are single alphanumeric characters (as for **isalnum**; see Section 4.1 [Classification of Characters], page 77).

- Certain options require an argument. For example, the '-o' command of the **ld** command requires an argument—an output file name.

- An option and its argument may or may not appear as separate tokens. (In other words, the whitespace separating them is optional.) Thus, '-o foo' and '-ofoo' are equivalent.

- Options typically precede other non-option arguments.

  The implementations of **getopt** and **argp_parse** in the GNU C Library normally make it appear as if all the option arguments were specified before all the non-option arguments for the purposes of parsing, even if the user of your program intermixed option and non-option arguments. They do this by reordering the elements of the *argv* array. This behavior is nonstandard; if you want to suppress it, define the **_POSIX_OPTION_ORDER** environment variable. See Section 25.4.2 [Standard Environment Variables], page 741.

- The argument '--' terminates all options; any following arguments are treated as non-option arguments, even if they begin with a hyphen.

- A token consisting of a single hyphen character is interpreted as an ordinary non-option argument. By convention, it is used to specify input from or output to the standard input and output streams.

- Options may be supplied in any order, or appear multiple times. The interpretation is left up to the particular application program.

GNU adds *long options* to these conventions. Long options consist of '--' followed by a name made of alphanumeric characters and dashes. Option names are typically one to three words long, with hyphens to separate words. Users can abbreviate the option names as long as the abbreviations are unique.

To specify an argument for a long option, write '--*name*=*value*'. This syntax enables a long option to accept an argument that is itself optional.

Eventually, GNU systems will provide completion for long option names in the shell.

## 25.1.2 Parsing Program Arguments

If the syntax for the command line arguments to your program is simple enough, you can simply pick the arguments off from *argv* by hand. But unless your program takes a fixed number of arguments, or all of the arguments are interpreted in the same way (as file names, for example), you are usually better off using `getopt` (see Section 25.2 [Parsing program options using `getopt`], page 707) or `argp_parse` (see Section 25.3 [Parsing Program Options with Argp], page 714) to do the parsing.

`getopt` is more standard (the short-option only version of it is a part of the POSIX standard), but using `argp_parse` is often easier, both for very simple and very complex option structures, because it does more of the dirty work for you.

## 25.2 Parsing program options using `getopt`

The `getopt` and `getopt_long` functions automate some of the chore involved in parsing typical unix command line options.

### 25.2.1 Using the `getopt` function

Here are the details about how to call the `getopt` function. To use this facility, your program must include the header file `unistd.h`.

`int opterr`                                                              [Variable]

> If the value of this variable is nonzero, then `getopt` prints an error message to the standard error stream if it encounters an unknown option character or an option with a missing required argument. This is the default behavior. If you set this variable to zero, `getopt` does not print any messages, but it still returns the character `?` to indicate an error.

`int optopt`                                                              [Variable]

> When `getopt` encounters an unknown option character or an option with a missing required argument, it stores that option character in this variable. You can use this for providing your own diagnostic messages.

`int optind`                                                              [Variable]

> This variable is set by `getopt` to the index of the next element of the *argv* array to be processed. Once `getopt` has found all of the option arguments, you can use this variable to determine where the remaining non-option arguments begin. The initial value of this variable is `1`.

`char * optarg`                                                           [Variable]

> This variable is set by `getopt` to point at the value of the option argument, for those options that accept arguments.

`int getopt (int argc, char *const *argv, const char *options)`          [Function]

> Preliminary: | MT-Unsafe race:getopt env | AS-Unsafe heap i18n lock corrupt | AC-Unsafe mem lock corrupt | See Section 1.2.2.1 [POSIX Safety Concepts], page 2.
>
> The `getopt` function gets the next option argument from the argument list specified by the *argv* and *argc* arguments. Normally these values come directly from the arguments received by `main`.
>
> The *options* argument is a string that specifies the option characters that are valid for this program. An option character in this string can be followed by a colon (':')

to indicate that it takes a required argument. If an option character is followed by two colons ('::'), its argument is optional; this is a GNU extension.

`getopt` has three ways to deal with options that follow non-options *argv* elements. The special argument '--' forces in all cases the end of option scanning.

- The default is to permute the contents of *argv* while scanning it so that eventually all the non-options are at the end. This allows options to be given in any order, even with programs that were not written to expect this.

- If the *options* argument string begins with a hyphen ('-'), this is treated specially. It permits arguments that are not options to be returned as if they were associated with option character '\1'.

- POSIX demands the following behavior: The first non-option stops option processing. This mode is selected by either setting the environment variable `POSIXLY_CORRECT` or beginning the *options* argument string with a plus sign ('+').

The `getopt` function returns the option character for the next command line option. When no more option arguments are available, it returns -1. There may still be more non-option arguments; you must compare the external variable `optind` against the *argc* parameter to check this.

If the option has an argument, `getopt` returns the argument by storing it in the variable *optarg*. You don't ordinarily need to copy the `optarg` string, since it is a pointer into the original *argv* array, not into a static area that might be overwritten.

If `getopt` finds an option character in *argv* that was not included in *options*, or a missing option argument, it returns '?' and sets the external variable `optopt` to the actual option character. If the first character of *options* is a colon (':'), then `getopt` returns ':' instead of '?' to indicate a missing option argument. In addition, if the external variable `opterr` is nonzero (which is the default), `getopt` prints an error message.

## 25.2.2 Example of Parsing Arguments with `getopt`

Here is an example showing how `getopt` is typically used. The key points to notice are:

- Normally, `getopt` is called in a loop. When `getopt` returns -1, indicating no more options are present, the loop terminates.

- A `switch` statement is used to dispatch on the return value from `getopt`. In typical use, each case just sets a variable that is used later in the program.

- A second loop is used to process the remaining non-option arguments.

```
#include <ctype.h>
#include <stdio.h>
#include <stdlib.h>
#include <unistd.h>

int
main (int argc, char **argv)
{
  int aflag = 0;
  int bflag = 0;
  char *cvalue = NULL;
  int index;
  int c;

  opterr = 0;

  while ((c = getopt (argc, argv, "abc:")) != -1)
    switch (c)
      {
      case 'a':
        aflag = 1;
        break;
      case 'b':
        bflag = 1;
        break;
      case 'c':
        cvalue = optarg;
        break;
      case '?':
        if (optopt == 'c')
          fprintf (stderr, "Option -%c requires an argument.\n", optopt);
        else if (isprint (optopt))
          fprintf (stderr, "Unknown option '-%c'.\n", optopt);
        else
          fprintf (stderr,
                   "Unknown option character '\\x%x'.\n",
                   optopt);
        return 1;
      default:
        abort ();
      }

  printf ("aflag = %d, bflag = %d, cvalue = %s\n",
          aflag, bflag, cvalue);

  for (index = optind; index < argc; index++)
    printf ("Non-option argument %s\n", argv[index]);
  return 0;
}
```

Here are some examples showing what this program prints with different combinations of arguments:

```
% testopt
aflag = 0, bflag = 0, cvalue = (null)

% testopt -a -b
aflag = 1, bflag = 1, cvalue = (null)
```

```
% testopt -ab
aflag = 1, bflag = 1, cvalue = (null)

% testopt -c foo
aflag = 0, bflag = 0, cvalue = foo

% testopt -cfoo
aflag = 0, bflag = 0, cvalue = foo

% testopt arg1
aflag = 0, bflag = 0, cvalue = (null)
Non-option argument arg1

% testopt -a arg1
aflag = 1, bflag = 0, cvalue = (null)
Non-option argument arg1

% testopt -c foo arg1
aflag = 0, bflag = 0, cvalue = foo
Non-option argument arg1

% testopt -a -- -b
aflag = 1, bflag = 0, cvalue = (null)
Non-option argument -b

% testopt -a -
aflag = 1, bflag = 0, cvalue = (null)
Non-option argument -
```

## 25.2.3 Parsing Long Options with `getopt_long`

To accept GNU-style long options as well as single-character options, use `getopt_long` instead of `getopt`. This function is declared in `getopt.h`, not `unistd.h`. You should make every program accept long options if it uses any options, for this takes little extra work and helps beginners remember how to use the program.

**struct option**                                                                              [Data Type]

This structure describes a single long option name for the sake of `getopt_long`. The argument *longopts* must be an array of these structures, one for each long option. Terminate the array with an element containing all zeros.

The **struct option** structure has these fields:

**const char \*name**

This field is the name of the option. It is a string.

**int has_arg**

This field says whether the option takes an argument. It is an integer, and there are three legitimate values: `no_argument`, `required_argument` and `optional_argument`.

**int \*flag**
**int val**   These fields control how to report or act on the option when it occurs.

If `flag` is a null pointer, then the `val` is a value which identifies this option. Often these values are chosen to uniquely identify particular long options.

If `flag` is not a null pointer, it should be the address of an `int` variable which is the flag for this option. The value in `val` is the value to store in the flag to indicate that the option was seen.

**int getopt_long** (*int* `argc`, *char \*const \**`argv`, *const char \**`shortopts`,    [Function]
    *const struct option \**`longopts`, *int \**`indexptr`)

Preliminary: | MT-Unsafe race:getopt env | AS-Unsafe heap i18n lock corrupt | AC-Unsafe mem lock corrupt | See Section 1.2.2.1 [POSIX Safety Concepts], page 2.

Decode options from the vector *argv* (whose length is *argc*). The argument *shortopts* describes the short options to accept, just as it does in `getopt`. The argument *longopts* describes the long options to accept (see above).

When `getopt_long` encounters a short option, it does the same thing that `getopt` would do: it returns the character code for the option, and stores the options argument (if it has one) in `optarg`.

When `getopt_long` encounters a long option, it takes actions based on the `flag` and `val` fields of the definition of that option.

If `flag` is a null pointer, then `getopt_long` returns the contents of `val` to indicate which option it found. You should arrange distinct values in the `val` field for options with different meanings, so you can decode these values after `getopt_long` returns. If the long option is equivalent to a short option, you can use the short option's character code in `val`.

If `flag` is not a null pointer, that means this option should just set a flag in the program. The flag is a variable of type `int` that you define. Put the address of the flag in the `flag` field. Put in the `val` field the value you would like this option to store in the flag. In this case, `getopt_long` returns 0.

For any long option, `getopt_long` tells you the index in the array *longopts* of the options definition, by storing it into *\*indexptr*. You can get the name of the option with *longopts[\*indexptr]*.name. So you can distinguish among long options either by the values in their `val` fields or by their indices. You can also distinguish in this way among long options that set flags.

When a long option has an argument, `getopt_long` puts the argument value in the variable `optarg` before returning. When the option has no argument, the value in `optarg` is a null pointer. This is how you can tell whether an optional argument was supplied.

When `getopt_long` has no more options to handle, it returns −1, and leaves in the variable `optind` the index in *argv* of the next remaining argument.

Since long option names were used before the `getopt_long` options was invented there are program interfaces which require programs to recognize options like '-option value' instead of '--option value'. To enable these programs to use the GNU getopt functionality there is one more function available.

**int getopt_long_only** (*int* `argc`, *char \*const \**`argv`, *const char*    [Function]
    *\**`shortopts`, *const struct option \**`longopts`, *int \**`indexptr`)

Preliminary: | MT-Unsafe race:getopt env | AS-Unsafe heap i18n lock corrupt | AC-Unsafe mem lock corrupt | See Section 1.2.2.1 [POSIX Safety Concepts], page 2.

The `getopt_long_only` function is equivalent to the `getopt_long` function but it allows to specify the user of the application to pass long options with only '-' instead of '--'. The '--' prefix is still recognized but instead of looking through the short options if a '-' is seen it is first tried whether this parameter names a long option. If not, it is parsed as a short option.

Assuming `getopt_long_only` is used starting an application with

        app -foo

the `getopt_long_only` will first look for a long option named 'foo'. If this is not found, the short options 'f', 'o', and again 'o' are recognized.

## 25.2.4 Example of Parsing Long Options with getopt_long

```
#include <stdio.h>
#include <stdlib.h>
#include <getopt.h>

/* Flag set by '--verbose'. */
static int verbose_flag;

int
main (int argc, char **argv)
{
  int c;

  while (1)
    {
      static struct option long_options[] =
        {
          /* These options set a flag. */
          {"verbose", no_argument,       &verbose_flag, 1},
          {"brief",   no_argument,       &verbose_flag, 0},
          /* These options don't set a flag.
          We distinguish them by their indices. */
          {"add",     no_argument,       0, 'a'},
          {"append",  no_argument,       0, 'b'},
          {"delete",  required_argument, 0, 'd'},
          {"create",  required_argument, 0, 'c'},
          {"file",    required_argument, 0, 'f'},
          {0, 0, 0, 0}
        };
      /* getopt_long stores the option index here. */
      int option_index = 0;

      c = getopt_long (argc, argv, "abc:d:f:",
                       long_options, &option_index);

      /* Detect the end of the options. */
      if (c == -1)
        break;

      switch (c)
        {
        case 0:
          /* If this option set a flag, do nothing else now. */
          if (long_options[option_index].flag != 0)
```

```
                  break;
              printf ("option %s", long_options[option_index].name);
              if (optarg)
                printf (" with arg %s", optarg);
              printf ("\n");
              break;

          case 'a':
            puts ("option -a\n");
            break;

          case 'b':
            puts ("option -b\n");
            break;

          case 'c':
            printf ("option -c with value '%s'\n", optarg);
            break;

          case 'd':
            printf ("option -d with value '%s'\n", optarg);
            break;

          case 'f':
            printf ("option -f with value '%s'\n", optarg);
            break;

          case '?':
            /* getopt_long already printed an error message. */
            break;

          default:
            abort ();
          }
      }

  /* Instead of reporting '--verbose'
     and '--brief' as they are encountered,
     we report the final status resulting from them. */
  if (verbose_flag)
    puts ("verbose flag is set");

  /* Print any remaining command line arguments (not options). */
  if (optind < argc)
    {
      printf ("non-option ARGV-elements: ");
      while (optind < argc)
        printf ("%s ", argv[optind++]);
      putchar ('\n');
    }

  exit (0);
}
```

## 25.3 Parsing Program Options with Argp

*Argp* is an interface for parsing unix-style argument vectors. See Section 25.1 [Program Arguments], page 705.

Argp provides features unavailable in the more commonly used `getopt` interface. These features include automatically producing output in response to the '`--help`' and '`--version`' options, as described in the GNU coding standards. Using argp makes it less likely that programmers will neglect to implement these additional options or keep them up to date.

Argp also provides the ability to merge several independently defined option parsers into one, mediating conflicts between them and making the result appear seamless. A library can export an argp option parser that user programs might employ in conjunction with their own option parsers, resulting in less work for the user programs. Some programs may use only argument parsers exported by libraries, thereby achieving consistent and efficient option-parsing for abstractions implemented by the libraries.

The header file `<argp.h>` should be included to use argp.

### 25.3.1 The `argp_parse` Function

The main interface to argp is the `argp_parse` function. In many cases, calling `argp_parse` is the only argument-parsing code needed in `main`. See Section 25.1 [Program Arguments], page 705.

`error_t argp_parse` (*const struct argp* `*argp`, *int* `argc`, *char* `**argv`,          [Function]
          *unsigned* `flags`, *int* `*arg_index`, *void* `*input`)

Preliminary: | MT-Unsafe race:argpbuf locale env | AS-Unsafe heap i18n lock corrupt | AC-Unsafe mem lock corrupt | See Section 1.2.2.1 [POSIX Safety Concepts], page 2.

The `argp_parse` function parses the arguments in *argv*, of length *argc*, using the argp parser *argp*. See Section 25.3.3 [Specifying Argp Parsers], page 715. Passing a null pointer for *argp* is the same as using a `struct argp` containing all zeros.

*flags* is a set of flag bits that modify the parsing behavior. See Section 25.3.7 [Flags for `argp_parse`], page 724. *input* is passed through to the argp parser *argp*, and has meaning defined by *argp*. A typical usage is to pass a pointer to a structure which is used for specifying parameters to the parser and passing back the results.

Unless the `ARGP_NO_EXIT` or `ARGP_NO_HELP` flags are included in *flags*, calling `argp_parse` may result in the program exiting. This behavior is true if an error is detected, or when an unknown option is encountered. See Section 25.7 [Program Termination], page 744.

If *arg_index* is non-null, the index of the first unparsed option in *argv* is returned as a value.

The return value is zero for successful parsing, or an error code (see Section 2.2 [Error Codes], page 23) if an error is detected. Different argp parsers may return arbitrary error codes, but the standard error codes are: `ENOMEM` if a memory allocation error occurred, or `EINVAL` if an unknown option or option argument is encountered.

## 25.3.2 Argp Global Variables

These variables make it easy for user programs to implement the '--version' option and provide a bug-reporting address in the '--help' output. These are implemented in argp by default.

`const char * argp_program_version`                                 [Variable]

> If defined or set by the user program to a non-zero value, then a '--version' option is added when parsing with `argp_parse`, which will print the '--version' string followed by a newline and exit. The exception to this is if the `ARGP_NO_EXIT` flag is used.

`const char * argp_program_bug_address`                              [Variable]

> If defined or set by the user program to a non-zero value, `argp_program_bug_address` should point to a string that will be printed at the end of the standard output for the '--help' option, embedded in a sentence that says 'Report bugs to *address*.'.

`argp_program_version_hook`                                          [Variable]

> If defined or set by the user program to a non-zero value, a '--version' option is added when parsing with `arg_parse`, which prints the program version and exits with a status of zero. This is not the case if the `ARGP_NO_HELP` flag is used. If the `ARGP_NO_EXIT` flag is set, the exit behavior of the program is suppressed or modified, as when the argp parser is going to be used by other programs.
>
> It should point to a function with this type of signature:
>
> > `void *print-version* (FILE *stream*, struct argp_state *state*)`
>
> See Section 25.3.5.2 [Argp Parsing State], page 721, for an explanation of *state*.
>
> This variable takes precedence over `argp_program_version`, and is useful if a program has version information not easily expressed in a simple string.

`error_t argp_err_exit_status`                                       [Variable]

> This is the exit status used when argp exits due to a parsing error. If not defined or set by the user program, this defaults to: `EX_USAGE` from `<sysexits.h>`.

## 25.3.3 Specifying Argp Parsers

The first argument to the `argp_parse` function is a pointer to a `struct argp`, which is known as an *argp parser*:

`struct argp`                                                        [Data Type]

> This structure specifies how to parse a given set of options and arguments, perhaps in conjunction with other argp parsers. It has the following fields:
>
> `const struct argp_option *options`
>
> > A pointer to a vector of `argp_option` structures specifying which options this argp parser understands; it may be zero if there are no options at all. See Section 25.3.4 [Specifying Options in an Argp Parser], page 716.
>
> `argp_parser_t parser`
>
> > A pointer to a function that defines actions for this parser; it is called for each option parsed, and at other well-defined points in the parsing

process. A value of zero is the same as a pointer to a function that always returns `ARGP_ERR_UNKNOWN`. See Section 25.3.5 [Argp Parser Functions], page 718.

`const char *args_doc`

If non-zero, a string describing what non-option arguments are called by this parser. This is only used to print the 'Usage:' message. If it contains newlines, the strings separated by them are considered alternative usage patterns and printed on separate lines. Lines after the first are prefixed by ' or: ' instead of 'Usage:'.

`const char *doc`

If non-zero, a string containing extra text to be printed before and after the options in a long help message, with the two sections separated by a vertical tab ('\v', '\013') character. By convention, the documentation before the options is just a short string explaining what the program does. Documentation printed after the options describe behavior in more detail.

`const struct argp_child *children`

A pointer to a vector of `argp_children` structures. This pointer specifies which additional argp parsers should be combined with this one. See Section 25.3.6 [Combining Multiple Argp Parsers], page 724.

`char *(*help_filter)(int key, const char *text, void *input)`

If non-zero, a pointer to a function that filters the output of help messages. See Section 25.3.8 [Customizing Argp Help Output], page 725.

`const char *argp_domain`

If non-zero, the strings used in the argp library are translated using the domain described by this string. If zero, the current default domain is used.

Of the above group, `options`, `parser`, `args_doc`, and the `doc` fields are usually all that are needed. If an argp parser is defined as an initialized C variable, only the fields used need be specified in the initializer. The rest will default to zero due to the way C structure initialization works. This design is exploited in most argp structures; the most-used fields are grouped near the beginning, the unused fields left unspecified.

## 25.3.4 Specifying Options in an Argp Parser

The `options` field in a `struct argp` points to a vector of `struct argp_option` structures, each of which specifies an option that the argp parser supports. Multiple entries may be used for a single option provided it has multiple names. This should be terminated by an entry with zero in all fields. Note that when using an initialized C array for options, writing `{ 0 }` is enough to achieve this.

`struct argp_option`                                                        [Data Type]

This structure specifies a single option that an argp parser understands, as well as how to parse and document that option. It has the following fields:

`const char *name`

The long name for this option, corresponding to the long option '`--name`'; this field may be zero if this option *only* has a short name. To specify multiple names for an option, additional entries may follow this one, with the `OPTION_ALIAS` flag set. See Section 25.3.4.1 [Flags for Argp Options], page 717.

int key
The integer key provided by the current option to the option parser. If *key* has a value that is a printable ASCII character (i.e., `isascii (key)` is true), it *also* specifies a short option '-*char*', where *char* is the ASCII character with the code *key*.

const char *arg
If non-zero, this is the name of an argument associated with this option, which must be provided (e.g., with the '--*name*=*value*' or '-*char value*' syntaxes), unless the `OPTION_ARG_OPTIONAL` flag (see Section 25.3.4.1 [Flags for Argp Options], page 717) is set, in which case it *may* be provided.

int flags
Flags associated with this option, some of which are referred to above. See Section 25.3.4.1 [Flags for Argp Options], page 717.

const char *doc
A documentation string for this option, for printing in help messages.

If both the **name** and **key** fields are zero, this string will be printed tabbed left from the normal option column, making it useful as a group header. This will be the first thing printed in its group. In this usage, it's conventional to end the string with a ':' character.

int group
Group identity for this option.

In a long help message, options are sorted alphabetically within each group, and the groups presented in the order 0, 1, 2, ..., $n$, $-m$, ..., $-2$, $-1$.

Every entry in an options array with this field 0 will inherit the group number of the previous entry, or zero if it's the first one. If it's a group header with **name** and **key** fields both zero, the previous entry + 1 is the default. Automagic options such as '--help' are put into group $-1$.

Note that because of C structure initialization rules, this field often need not be specified, because 0 is the correct value.

## 25.3.4.1 Flags for Argp Options

The following flags may be or'd together in the **flags** field of a **struct argp_option**. These flags control various aspects of how that option is parsed or displayed in help messages:

OPTION_ARG_OPTIONAL
The argument associated with this option is optional.

OPTION_HIDDEN
This option isn't displayed in any help messages.

OPTION_ALIAS
This option is an alias for the closest previous non-alias option. This means that it will be displayed in the same help entry, and will inherit fields other than **name** and **key** from the option being aliased.

OPTION_DOC

> This option isn't actually an option and should be ignored by the actual option parser. It is an arbitrary section of documentation that should be displayed in much the same manner as the options. This is known as a *documentation option*.
>
> If this flag is set, then the option **name** field is displayed unmodified (e.g., no '--' prefix is added) at the left-margin where a *short* option would normally be displayed, and this documentation string is left in it's usual place. For purposes of sorting, any leading whitespace and punctuation is ignored, unless the first non-whitespace character is '-'. This entry is displayed after all options, after **OPTION_DOC** entries with a leading '-', in the same group.

OPTION_NO_USAGE

> This option shouldn't be included in 'long' usage messages, but should still be included in other help messages. This is intended for options that are completely documented in an argp's **args_doc** field. See Section 25.3.3 [Specifying Argp Parsers], page 715. Including this option in the generic usage list would be redundant, and should be avoided.
>
> For instance, if **args_doc** is "FOO BAR\n-x BLAH", and the '-x' option's purpose is to distinguish these two cases, '-x' should probably be marked OPTION_NO_ USAGE.

## 25.3.5  Argp Parser Functions

The function pointed to by the **parser** field in a **struct argp** (see Section 25.3.3 [Specifying Argp Parsers], page 715) defines what actions take place in response to each option or argument parsed. It is also used as a hook, allowing a parser to perform tasks at certain other points during parsing.

Argp parser functions have the following type signature:

```
error_t parser (int key, char *arg, struct argp_state *state)
```

where the arguments are as follows:

*key*    For each option that is parsed, *parser* is called with a value of *key* from that option's **key** field in the option vector. See Section 25.3.4 [Specifying Options in an Argp Parser], page 716. *parser* is also called at other times with special reserved keys, such as **ARGP_KEY_ARG** for non-option arguments. See Section 25.3.5.1 [Special Keys for Argp Parser Functions], page 719.

*arg*    If *key* is an option, *arg* is its given value. This defaults to zero if no value is specified. Only options that have a non-zero **arg** field can ever have a value. These must *always* have a value unless the **OPTION_ARG_OPTIONAL** flag is specified. If the input being parsed specifies a value for an option that doesn't allow one, an error results before *parser* ever gets called.

If *key* is **ARGP_KEY_ARG**, *arg* is a non-option argument. Other special keys always have a zero *arg*.

*state*   *state* points to a **struct argp_state**, containing useful information about the current parsing state for use by *parser*. See Section 25.3.5.2 [Argp Parsing State], page 721.

When *parser* is called, it should perform whatever action is appropriate for *key*, and return 0 for success, `ARGP_ERR_UNKNOWN` if the value of *key* is not handled by this parser function, or a unix error code if a real error occurred. See Section 2.2 [Error Codes], page 23.

`int ARGP_ERR_UNKNOWN`                                                    [Macro]

> Argp parser functions should return `ARGP_ERR_UNKNOWN` for any *key* value they do not recognize, or for non-option arguments (`key == ARGP_KEY_ARG`) that they are not equipped to handle.

A typical parser function uses a switch statement on *key*:

```
error_t
parse_opt (int key, char *arg, struct argp_state *state)
{
  switch (key)
    {
    case option_key:
      action
      break;
    ...
    default:
      return ARGP_ERR_UNKNOWN;
    }
  return 0;
}
```

## 25.3.5.1 Special Keys for Argp Parser Functions

In addition to key values corresponding to user options, the *key* argument to argp parser functions may have a number of other special values. In the following example *arg* and *state* refer to parser function arguments. See Section 25.3.5 [Argp Parser Functions], page 718.

`ARGP_KEY_ARG`

> This is not an option at all, but rather a command line argument, whose value is pointed to by *arg*.
>
> When there are multiple parser functions in play due to argp parsers being combined, it's impossible to know which one will handle a specific argument. Each is called until one returns 0 or an error other than `ARGP_ERR_UNKNOWN`; if an argument is not handled, **argp_parse** immediately returns success, without parsing any more arguments.
>
> Once a parser function returns success for this key, that fact is recorded, and the `ARGP_KEY_NO_ARGS` case won't be used. *However*, if while processing the argument a parser function decrements the **next** field of its *state* argument, the option won't be considered processed; this is to allow you to actually modify the argument, perhaps into an option, and have it processed again.

`ARGP_KEY_ARGS`

> If a parser function returns `ARGP_ERR_UNKNOWN` for `ARGP_KEY_ARG`, it is immediately called again with the key `ARGP_KEY_ARGS`, which has a similar meaning, but is slightly more convenient for consuming all remaining arguments. *arg* is 0, and the tail of the argument vector may be found at **state->argv + state->next**. If success is returned for this key, and **state->next** is unchanged, all remaining arguments are considered to have been consumed. Otherwise, the

amount by which `state->next` has been adjusted indicates how many were used. Here's an example that uses both, for different args:

```
...
case ARGP_KEY_ARG:
  if (state->arg_num == 0)
    /* First argument */
    first_arg = arg;
  else
    /* Let the next case parse it.  */
    return ARGP_KEY_UNKNOWN;
  break;
case ARGP_KEY_ARGS:
  remaining_args = state->argv + state->next;
  num_remaining_args = state->argc - state->next;
  break;
```

ARGP_KEY_END

> This indicates that there are no more command line arguments. Parser functions are called in a different order, children first. This allows each parser to clean up its state for the parent.

ARGP_KEY_NO_ARGS

> Because it's common to do some special processing if there aren't any non-option args, parser functions are called with this key if they didn't successfully process any non-option arguments. This is called just before `ARGP_KEY_END`, where more general validity checks on previously parsed arguments take place.

ARGP_KEY_INIT

> This is passed in before any parsing is done. Afterwards, the values of each element of the `child_input` field of *state*, if any, are copied to each child's state to be the initial value of the **input** when *their* parsers are called.

ARGP_KEY_SUCCESS

> Passed in when parsing has successfully been completed, even if arguments remain.

ARGP_KEY_ERROR

> Passed in if an error has occurred and parsing is terminated. In this case a call with a key of `ARGP_KEY_SUCCESS` is never made.

ARGP_KEY_FINI

> The final key ever seen by any parser, even after `ARGP_KEY_SUCCESS` and `ARGP_KEY_ERROR`. Any resources allocated by `ARGP_KEY_INIT` may be freed here. At times, certain resources allocated are to be returned to the caller after a successful parse. In that case, those particular resources can be freed in the `ARGP_KEY_ERROR` case.

In all cases, `ARGP_KEY_INIT` is the first key seen by parser functions, and `ARGP_KEY_FINI` the last, unless an error was returned by the parser for `ARGP_KEY_INIT`. Other keys can occur in one the following orders. *opt* refers to an arbitrary option key:

*opt*... ARGP_KEY_NO_ARGS ARGP_KEY_END ARGP_KEY_SUCCESS

> The arguments being parsed did not contain any non-option arguments.

( *opt* | `ARGP_KEY_ARG` )... `ARGP_KEY_END ARGP_KEY_SUCCESS`

>    All non-option arguments were successfully handled by a parser function. There may be multiple parser functions if multiple argp parsers were combined.

( *opt* | `ARGP_KEY_ARG` )... `ARGP_KEY_SUCCESS`

>    Some non-option argument went unrecognized.
>
>    This occurs when every parser function returns `ARGP_KEY_UNKNOWN` for an argument, in which case parsing stops at that argument if *arg_index* is a null pointer. Otherwise an error occurs.

In all cases, if a non-null value for *arg_index* gets passed to **argp_parse**, the index of the first unparsed command-line argument is passed back in that value.

If an error occurs and is either detected by argp or because a parser function returned an error value, each parser is called with `ARGP_KEY_ERROR`. No further calls are made, except the final call with `ARGP_KEY_FINI`.

## 25.3.5.2 Argp Parsing State

The third argument to argp parser functions (see Section 25.3.5 [Argp Parser Functions], page 718) is a pointer to a **struct argp_state**, which contains information about the state of the option parsing.

`struct argp_state`                                                       [Data Type]

>    This structure has the following fields, which may be modified as noted:

>    `const struct argp *const root_argp`
>
>    >    The top level argp parser being parsed. Note that this is often *not* the same **struct argp** passed into **argp_parse** by the invoking program. See Section 25.3 [Parsing Program Options with Argp], page 714. It is an internal argp parser that contains options implemented by **argp_parse** itself, such as '`--help`'.

>    `int argc`
>    `char **argv`
>
>    >    The argument vector being parsed. This may be modified.

>    `int next`  The index in **argv** of the next argument to be parsed. This may be modified.
>
>    >    One way to consume all remaining arguments in the input is to set `state->next = state->argc`, perhaps after recording the value of the next field to find the consumed arguments. The current option can be re-parsed immediately by decrementing this field, then modifying `state->argv[state->next]` to reflect the option that should be reexamined.

>    `unsigned flags`
>
>    >    The flags supplied to **argp_parse**. These may be modified, although some flags may only take effect when **argp_parse** is first invoked. See Section 25.3.7 [Flags for **argp_parse**], page 724.

unsigned arg_num

> While calling a parsing function with the *key* argument `ARGP_KEY_ARG`, this represents the number of the current arg, starting at 0. It is incremented after each `ARGP_KEY_ARG` call returns. At all other times, this is the number of `ARGP_KEY_ARG` arguments that have been processed.

int quoted

> If non-zero, the index in `argv` of the first argument following a special '`--`' argument. This prevents anything that follows from being interpreted as an option. It is only set after argument parsing has proceeded past this point.

void *input

> An arbitrary pointer passed in from the caller of `argp_parse`, in the *input* argument.

void **child_inputs

> These are values that will be passed to child parsers. This vector will be the same length as the number of children in the current parser. Each child parser will be given the value of **state->child_inputs[i]** as *its* **state->input** field, where *i* is the index of the child in the this parser's **children** field. See Section 25.3.6 [Combining Multiple Argp Parsers], page 724.

void *hook

> For the parser function's use. Initialized to 0, but otherwise ignored by argp.

char *name

> The name used when printing messages. This is initialized to `argv[0]`, or `program_invocation_name` if `argv[0]` is unavailable.

FILE *err_stream
FILE *out_stream

> The stdio streams used when argp prints. Error messages are printed to `err_stream`, all other output, such as '`--help`' output) to `out_stream`. These are initialized to `stderr` and `stdout` respectively. See Section 12.2 [Standard Streams], page 248.

void *pstate

> Private, for use by the argp implementation.

### 25.3.5.3 Functions For Use in Argp Parsers

Argp provides a number of functions available to the user of argp (see Section 25.3.5 [Argp Parser Functions], page 718), mostly for producing error messages. These take as their first argument the *state* argument to the parser function. See Section 25.3.5.2 [Argp Parsing State], page 721.

void **argp_usage** (*const struct argp_state *state*)                        [Function]

> Preliminary: | MT-Unsafe race:argpbuf env locale | AS-Unsafe heap i18n corrupt | AC-Unsafe mem corrupt lock | See Section 1.2.2.1 [POSIX Safety Concepts], page 2.

Outputs the standard usage message for the argp parser referred to by *state* to
`state->err_stream` and terminate the program with `exit (argp_err_exit_`
`status)`. See Section 25.3.2 [Argp Global Variables], page 715.

void `argp_error` (*const struct argp_state \*state, const char \*fmt, ...*)    [Function]
Preliminary: | MT-Unsafe race:argpbuf env locale | AS-Unsafe heap i18n corrupt |
AC-Unsafe mem corrupt lock | See Section 1.2.2.1 [POSIX Safety Concepts], page 2.

Prints the printf format string *fmt* and following args, preceded by the program name
and ':', and followed by a 'Try ... --help' message, and terminates the program with
an exit status of `argp_err_exit_status`. See Section 25.3.2 [Argp Global Variables],
page 715.

void `argp_failure` (*const struct argp_state \*state, int* `status`, *int*         [Function]
      `errnum`, *const char \*fmt, ...*)
Preliminary: | MT-Safe | AS-Unsafe corrupt heap | AC-Unsafe lock corrupt mem
| See Section 1.2.2.1 [POSIX Safety Concepts], page 2.

Similar to the standard gnu error-reporting function `error`, this prints the program
name and ':', the printf format string *fmt*, and the appropriate following args. If it
is non-zero, the standard unix error text for *errnum* is printed. If *status* is non-zero,
it terminates the program with that value as its exit status.

The difference between `argp_failure` and `argp_error` is that `argp_error` is for
*parsing errors*, whereas `argp_failure` is for other problems that occur during parsing
but don't reflect a syntactic problem with the input, such as illegal values for options,
bad phase of the moon, etc.

void `argp_state_help` (*const struct argp_state \*state, FILE \*stream,*       [Function]
      *unsigned* `flags`)
Preliminary: | MT-Unsafe race:argpbuf env locale | AS-Unsafe heap i18n corrupt |
AC-Unsafe mem corrupt lock | See Section 1.2.2.1 [POSIX Safety Concepts], page 2.

Outputs a help message for the argp parser referred to by *state*, to *stream*. The *flags*
argument determines what sort of help message is produced. See Section 25.3.10
[Flags for the `argp_help` Function], page 726.

Error output is sent to `state->err_stream`, and the program name printed is
`state->name`.

The output or program termination behavior of these functions may be suppressed if the
`ARGP_NO_EXIT` or `ARGP_NO_ERRS` flags are passed to `argp_parse`. See Section 25.3.7 [Flags
for `argp_parse`], page 724.

This behavior is useful if an argp parser is exported for use by other programs (e.g., by
a library), and may be used in a context where it is not desirable to terminate the program
in response to parsing errors. In argp parsers intended for such general use, and for the case
where the program *doesn't* terminate, calls to any of these functions should be followed by
code that returns the appropriate error code:

```
if (bad argument syntax)
  {
    argp_usage (state);
    return EINVAL;
  }
```

If a parser function will *only* be used when `ARGP_NO_EXIT` is not set, the return may be omitted.

## 25.3.6 Combining Multiple Argp Parsers

The `children` field in a `struct argp` enables other argp parsers to be combined with the referencing one for the parsing of a single set of arguments. This field should point to a vector of `struct argp_child`, which is terminated by an entry having a value of zero in the `argp` field.

Where conflicts between combined parsers arise, as when two specify an option with the same name, the parser conflicts are resolved in favor of the parent argp parser(s), or the earlier of the argp parsers in the list of children.

`struct argp_child`                                                    [Data Type]

> An entry in the list of subsidiary argp parsers pointed to by the `children` field in a `struct argp`. The fields are as follows:

> `const struct argp *argp`
>> The child argp parser, or zero to end of the list.

> `int flags`  Flags for this child.

> `const char *header`
>> If non-zero, this is an optional header to be printed within help output before the child options. As a side-effect, a non-zero value forces the child options to be grouped together. To achieve this effect without actually printing a header string, use a value of `""`. As with header strings specified in an option entry, the conventional value of the last character is ':'. See Section 25.3.4 [Specifying Options in an Argp Parser], page 716.

> `int group`  This is where the child options are grouped relative to the other 'consolidated' options in the parent argp parser. The values are the same as the `group` field in `struct argp_option`. See Section 25.3.4 [Specifying Options in an Argp Parser], page 716. All child-groupings follow parent options at a particular group level. If both this field and `header` are zero, then the child's options aren't grouped together, they are merged with parent options at the parent option group level.

## 25.3.7 Flags for `argp_parse`

The default behavior of `argp_parse` is designed to be convenient for the most common case of parsing program command line argument. To modify these defaults, the following flags may be or'd together in the *flags* argument to `argp_parse`:

`ARGP_PARSE_ARGV0`
> Don't ignore the first element of the *argv* argument to `argp_parse`. Unless `ARGP_NO_ERRS` is set, the first element of the argument vector is skipped for option parsing purposes, as it corresponds to the program name in a command line.

`ARGP_NO_ERRS`
> Don't print error messages for unknown options to `stderr`; unless this flag is set, `ARGP_PARSE_ARGV0` is ignored, as `argv[0]` is used as the program name

in the error messages. This flag implies `ARGP_NO_EXIT`. This is based on the assumption that silent exiting upon errors is bad behavior.

**ARGP_NO_ARGS**

Don't parse any non-option args. Normally these are parsed by calling the parse functions with a key of `ARGP_KEY_ARG`, the actual argument being the value. This flag needn't normally be set, as the default behavior is to stop parsing as soon as an argument fails to be parsed. See Section 25.3.5 [Argp Parser Functions], page 718.

**ARGP_IN_ORDER**

Parse options and arguments in the same order they occur on the command line. Normally they're rearranged so that all options come first.

**ARGP_NO_HELP**

Don't provide the standard long option '`--help`', which ordinarily causes usage and option help information to be output to `stdout` and `exit (0)`.

**ARGP_NO_EXIT**

Don't exit on errors, although they may still result in error messages.

**ARGP_LONG_ONLY**

Use the gnu getopt 'long-only' rules for parsing arguments. This allows long-options to be recognized with only a single '`-`' (i.e., '`-help`'). This results in a less useful interface, and its use is discouraged as it conflicts with the way most GNU programs work as well as the GNU coding standards.

**ARGP_SILENT**

Turns off any message-printing/exiting options, specifically `ARGP_NO_EXIT`, `ARGP_NO_ERRS`, and `ARGP_NO_HELP`.

## 25.3.8 Customizing Argp Help Output

The `help_filter` field in a `struct argp` is a pointer to a function that filters the text of help messages before displaying them. They have a function signature like:

```
char *help-filter (int key, const char *text, void *input)
```

Where *key* is either a key from an option, in which case *text* is that option's help text. See Section 25.3.4 [Specifying Options in an Argp Parser], page 716. Alternately, one of the special keys with names beginning with '`ARGP_KEY_HELP_`' might be used, describing which other help text *text* will contain. See Section 25.3.8.1 [Special Keys for Argp Help Filter Functions], page 725.

The function should return either *text* if it remains as-is, or a replacement string allocated using `malloc`. This will be either be freed by argp or zero, which prints nothing. The value of *text* is supplied *after* any translation has been done, so if any of the replacement text needs translation, it will be done by the filter function. *input* is either the input supplied to `argp_parse` or it is zero, if `argp_help` was called directly by the user.

## 25.3.8.1 Special Keys for Argp Help Filter Functions

The following special values may be passed to an argp help filter function as the first argument in addition to key values for user options. They specify which help text the *text* argument contains:

`ARGP_KEY_HELP_PRE_DOC`
> The help text preceding options.

`ARGP_KEY_HELP_POST_DOC`
> The help text following options.

`ARGP_KEY_HELP_HEADER`
> The option header string.

`ARGP_KEY_HELP_EXTRA`
> This is used after all other documentation; *text* is zero for this key.

`ARGP_KEY_HELP_DUP_ARGS_NOTE`
> The explanatory note printed when duplicate option arguments have been suppressed.

`ARGP_KEY_HELP_ARGS_DOC`
> The argument doc string; formally the **args_doc** field from the argp parser. See Section 25.3.3 [Specifying Argp Parsers], page 715.

### 25.3.9 The `argp_help` Function

Normally programs using argp need not be written with particular printing argument-usage-type help messages in mind as the standard '--help' option is handled automatically by argp. Typical error cases can be handled using **argp_usage** and **argp_error**. See Section 25.3.5.3 [Functions For Use in Argp Parsers], page 722. However, if it's desirable to print a help message in some context other than parsing the program options, argp offers the **argp_help** interface.

void **argp_help** (*const struct argp* \***argp**, *FILE* \***stream**, *unsigned*                [Function]
    **flags**, *char* \***name**)
> Preliminary: | MT-Unsafe race:argpbuf env locale | AS-Unsafe heap i18n corrupt | AC-Unsafe mem corrupt lock | See Section 1.2.2.1 [POSIX Safety Concepts], page 2.
>
> This outputs a help message for the argp parser *argp* to *stream*. The type of messages printed will be determined by *flags*.
>
> Any options such as '--help' that are implemented automatically by argp itself will *not* be present in the help output; for this reason it is best to use **argp_state_help** if calling from within an argp parser function. See Section 25.3.5.3 [Functions For Use in Argp Parsers], page 722.

### 25.3.10 Flags for the `argp_help` Function

When calling **argp_help** (see Section 25.3.9 [The **argp_help** Function], page 726) or **argp_state_help** (see Section 25.3.5.3 [Functions For Use in Argp Parsers], page 722) the exact output is determined by the *flags* argument. This should consist of any of the following flags, or'd together:

`ARGP_HELP_USAGE`
> A unix 'Usage:' message that explicitly lists all options.

`ARGP_HELP_SHORT_USAGE`
> A unix 'Usage:' message that displays an appropriate placeholder to indicate where the options go; useful for showing the non-option argument syntax.

ARGP_HELP_SEE

A 'Try ... for more help' message; '...' contains the program name and '--help'.

ARGP_HELP_LONG

A verbose option help message that gives each option available along with its documentation string.

ARGP_HELP_PRE_DOC

The part of the argp parser doc string preceding the verbose option help.

ARGP_HELP_POST_DOC

The part of the argp parser doc string that following the verbose option help.

ARGP_HELP_DOC

(ARGP_HELP_PRE_DOC | ARGP_HELP_POST_DOC)

ARGP_HELP_BUG_ADDR

A message that prints where to report bugs for this program, if the argp_program_bug_address variable contains this information.

ARGP_HELP_LONG_ONLY

This will modify any output to reflect the ARGP_LONG_ONLY mode.

The following flags are only understood when used with argp_state_help. They control whether the function returns after printing its output, or terminates the program:

ARGP_HELP_EXIT_ERR

This will terminate the program with exit (argp_err_exit_status).

ARGP_HELP_EXIT_OK

This will terminate the program with exit (0).

The following flags are combinations of the basic flags for printing standard messages:

ARGP_HELP_STD_ERR

Assuming that an error message for a parsing error has printed, this prints a message on how to get help, and terminates the program with an error.

ARGP_HELP_STD_USAGE

This prints a standard usage message and terminates the program with an error. This is used when no other specific error messages are appropriate or available.

ARGP_HELP_STD_HELP

This prints the standard response for a '--help' option, and terminates the program successfully.

## 25.3.11 Argp Examples

These example programs demonstrate the basic usage of argp.

## 25.3.11.1 A Minimal Program Using Argp

This is perhaps the smallest program possible that uses argp. It won't do much except give an error messages and exit when there are any arguments, and prints a rather pointless message for '--help'.

```
/* This is (probably) the smallest possible program that
   uses argp.  It won't do much except give an error
   messages and exit when there are any arguments, and print
   a (rather pointless) messages for –help. */

#include <stdlib.h>
#include <argp.h>

int
main (int argc, char **argv)
{
  argp_parse (0, argc, argv, 0, 0, 0);
  exit (0);
}
```

## 25.3.11.2 A Program Using Argp with Only Default Options

This program doesn't use any options or arguments, it uses argp to be compliant with the GNU standard command line format.

In addition to giving no arguments and implementing a '`--help`' option, this example has a '`--version`' option, which will put the given documentation string and bug address in the '`--help`' output, as per GNU standards.

The variable **argp** contains the argument parser specification. Adding fields to this structure is the way most parameters are passed to **argp_parse**. The first three fields are normally used, but they are not in this small program. There are also two global variables that argp can use defined here, **argp_program_version** and **argp_program_bug_address**. They are considered global variables because they will almost always be constant for a given program, even if they use different argument parsers for various tasks.

```
/* This program doesn't use any options or arguments, but uses
   argp to be compliant with the GNU standard command line
   format.

   In addition to making sure no arguments are given, and
   implementing a –help option, this example will have a
   –version option, and will put the given documentation string
   and bug address in the –help output, as per GNU standards.

   The variable ARGP contains the argument parser specification;
   adding fields to this structure is the way most parameters are
   passed to argp_parse (the first three fields are usually used,
   but not in this small program).  There are also two global
   variables that argp knows about defined here,
   ARGP_PROGRAM_VERSION and ARGP_PROGRAM_BUG_ADDRESS (they are
   global variables because they will almost always be constant
   for a given program, even if it uses different argument
   parsers for various tasks). */

#include <stdlib.h>
#include <argp.h>

const char *argp_program_version =
  "argp-ex2 1.0";
const char *argp_program_bug_address =
```

```
    "<bug-gnu-utils@gnu.org>";

/* Program documentation. */
static char doc[] =
  "Argp example #2 -- a pretty minimal program using argp";

/* Our argument parser.  The options, parser, and
   args_doc fields are zero because we have neither options or
   arguments; doc and argp_program_bug_address will be
   used in the output for '--help', and the '--version'
   option will print out argp_program_version. */
static struct argp argp = { 0, 0, 0, doc };

int
main (int argc, char **argv)
{
  argp_parse (&argp, argc, argv, 0, 0, 0);
  exit (0);
}
```

## 25.3.11.3 A Program Using Argp with User Options

This program uses the same features as example 2, adding user options and arguments.

We now use the first four fields in `argp` (see Section 25.3.3 [Specifying Argp Parsers], page 715) and specify `parse_opt` as the parser function. See Section 25.3.5 [Argp Parser Functions], page 718.

Note that in this example, `main` uses a structure to communicate with the `parse_opt` function, a pointer to which it passes in the `input` argument to `argp_parse`. See Section 25.3 [Parsing Program Options with Argp], page 714. It is retrieved by `parse_opt` through the `input` field in its `state` argument. See Section 25.3.5.2 [Argp Parsing State], page 721. Of course, it's also possible to use global variables instead, but using a structure like this is somewhat more flexible and clean.

```
/* This program uses the same features as example 2, and uses options and
   arguments.

   We now use the first four fields in ARGP, so here's a description of them:
     OPTIONS  - A pointer to a vector of struct argp_option (see below)
     PARSER   - A function to parse a single option, called by argp
     ARGS_DOC - A string describing how the non-option arguments should look
     DOC      - A descriptive string about this program; if it contains a
                vertical tab character (\v), the part after it will be
                printed *following* the options

   The function PARSER takes the following arguments:
     KEY  - An integer specifying which option this is (taken
            from the KEY field in each struct argp_option), or
            a special key specifying something else; the only
            special keys we use here are ARGP_KEY_ARG, meaning
            a non-option argument, and ARGP_KEY_END, meaning
            that all arguments have been parsed
     ARG  - For an option KEY, the string value of its
            argument, or NULL if it has none
     STATE- A pointer to a struct argp_state, containing
            various useful information about the parsing state; used here
            are the INPUT field, which reflects the INPUT argument to
```

argp_parse, and the ARG_NUM field, which is the number of the
current non-option argument being parsed
It should return either 0, meaning success, ARGP_ERR_UNKNOWN, meaning the
given KEY wasn't recognized, or an errno value indicating some other
error.

Note that in this example, main uses a structure to communicate with the
parse_opt function, a pointer to which it passes in the INPUT argument to
argp_parse. Of course, it's also possible to use global variables
instead, but this is somewhat more flexible.

The OPTIONS field contains a pointer to a vector of struct argp_option's;
that structure has the following fields (if you assign your option
structures using array initialization like this example, unspecified
fields will be defaulted to 0, and need not be specified):
   NAME   – The name of this option's long option (may be zero)
   KEY    – The KEY to pass to the PARSER function when parsing this option,
           *and* the name of this option's short option, if it is a
           printable ascii character
   ARG    – The name of this option's argument, if any
   FLAGS – Flags describing this option; some of them are:
           OPTION_ARG_OPTIONAL – The argument to this option is optional
           OPTION_ALIAS     – This option is an alias for the
                      previous option
           OPTION_HIDDEN     – Don't show this option in –help output
   DOC    – A documentation string for this option, shown in –help output

An options vector should be terminated by an option with all fields zero. */

```
#include <stdlib.h>
#include <argp.h>

const char *argp_program_version =
  "argp-ex3 1.0";
const char *argp_program_bug_address =
  "<bug-gnu-utils@gnu.org>";

/* Program documentation. */
static char doc[] =
  "Argp example #3 -- a program with options and arguments using argp";

/* A description of the arguments we accept. */
static char args_doc[] = "ARG1 ARG2";

/* The options we understand. */
static struct argp_option options[] = {
  {"verbose",  'v', 0,      0,  "Produce verbose output" },
  {"quiet",    'q', 0,      0,  "Don't produce any output" },
  {"silent",   's', 0,      OPTION_ALIAS },
  {"output",   'o', "FILE", 0,
   "Output to FILE instead of standard output" },
  { 0 }
};

/* Used by main to communicate with parse_opt. */
struct arguments
{
  char *args[2];                 /* arg1 & arg2 */
```

```
    int silent, verbose;
    char *output_file;
};

/* Parse a single option. */
static error_t
parse_opt (int key, char *arg, struct argp_state *state)
{
    /* Get the input argument from argp_parse, which we
       know is a pointer to our arguments structure. */
    struct arguments *arguments = state->input;

    switch (key)
      {
      case 'q': case 's':
        arguments->silent = 1;
        break;
      case 'v':
        arguments->verbose = 1;
        break;
      case 'o':
        arguments->output_file = arg;
        break;

      case ARGP_KEY_ARG:
        if (state->arg_num >= 2)
          /* Too many arguments. */
          argp_usage (state);

        arguments->args[state->arg_num] = arg;

        break;

      case ARGP_KEY_END:
        if (state->arg_num < 2)
          /* Not enough arguments. */
          argp_usage (state);
        break;

      default:
        return ARGP_ERR_UNKNOWN;
      }
    return 0;
}

/* Our argp parser. */
static struct argp argp = { options, parse_opt, args_doc, doc };

int
main (int argc, char **argv)
{
    struct arguments arguments;

    /* Default values. */
    arguments.silent = 0;
    arguments.verbose = 0;
    arguments.output_file = "-";
```

```
/* Parse our arguments; every option seen by parse_opt will
   be reflected in arguments. */
argp_parse (&argp, argc, argv, 0, 0, &arguments);

printf ("ARG1 = %s\nARG2 = %s\nOUTPUT_FILE = %s\n"
        "VERBOSE = %s\nSILENT = %s\n",
        arguments.args[0], arguments.args[1],
        arguments.output_file,
        arguments.verbose ? "yes" : "no",
        arguments.silent ? "yes" : "no");

exit (0);
}
```

## 25.3.11.4 A Program Using Multiple Combined Argp Parsers

This program uses the same features as example 3, but has more options, and presents more structure in the '--help' output. It also illustrates how you can 'steal' the remainder of the input arguments past a certain point for programs that accept a list of items. It also illustrates the *key* value ARGP_KEY_NO_ARGS, which is only given if no non-option arguments were supplied to the program. See Section 25.3.5.1 [Special Keys for Argp Parser Functions], page 719.

For structuring help output, two features are used: *headers* and a two part option string. The *headers* are entries in the options vector. See Section 25.3.4 [Specifying Options in an Argp Parser], page 716. The first four fields are zero. The two part documentation string are in the variable doc, which allows documentation both before and after the options. See Section 25.3.3 [Specifying Argp Parsers], page 715, the two parts of doc are separated by a vertical-tab character ('\v', or '\013'). By convention, the documentation before the options is a short string stating what the program does, and after any options it is longer, describing the behavior in more detail. All documentation strings are automatically filled for output, although newlines may be included to force a line break at a particular point. In addition, documentation strings are passed to the gettext function, for possible translation into the current locale.

```
/* This program uses the same features as example 3, but has more
   options, and somewhat more structure in the -help output.  It
   also shows how you can 'steal' the remainder of the input
   arguments past a certain point, for programs that accept a
   list of items.  It also shows the special argp KEY value
   ARGP_KEY_NO_ARGS, which is only given if no non-option
   arguments were supplied to the program.

   For structuring the help output, two features are used,
   *headers* which are entries in the options vector with the
   first four fields being zero, and a two part documentation
   string (in the variable DOC), which allows documentation both
   before and after the options; the two parts of DOC are
   separated by a vertical-tab character ('\v', or '\013').  By
   convention, the documentation before the options is just a
   short string saying what the program does, and that afterwards
   is longer, describing the behavior in more detail.  All
   documentation strings are automatically filled for output,
   although newlines may be included to force a line break at a
   particular point.  All documentation strings are also passed to
```

the 'gettext' function, for possible translation into the
current locale. */

```
#include <stdlib.h>
#include <error.h>
#include <argp.h>

const char *argp_program_version =
  "argp-ex4 1.0";
const char *argp_program_bug_address =
  "<bug-gnu-utils@prep.ai.mit.edu>";

/* Program documentation. */
static char doc[] =
  "Argp example #4 -- a program with somewhat more complicated\
options\
\vThis part of the documentation comes *after* the options;\
 note that the text is automatically filled, but it's possible\
 to force a line-break, e.g.\n<-- here.";

/* A description of the arguments we accept. */
static char args_doc[] = "ARG1 [STRING...]";

/* Keys for options without short-options. */
#define OPT_ABORT  1              /* –abort */

/* The options we understand. */
static struct argp_option options[] = {
  {"verbose",  'v', 0,       0, "Produce verbose output" },
  {"quiet",    'q', 0,       0, "Don't produce any output" },
  {"silent",   's', 0,       OPTION_ALIAS },
  {"output",   'o', "FILE",  0,
   "Output to FILE instead of standard output" },

  {0,0,0,0, "The following options should be grouped together:" },
  {"repeat",   'r', "COUNT", OPTION_ARG_OPTIONAL,
   "Repeat the output COUNT (default 10) times"},
  {"abort",    OPT_ABORT, 0, 0, "Abort before showing any output"},

  { 0 }
};

/* Used by main to communicate with parse_opt. */
struct arguments
{
  char *arg1;                  /* arg1 */
  char **strings;              /* [string...] */
  int silent, verbose, abort;  /* '-s', '-v', '--abort' */
  char *output_file;           /* file arg to '--output' */
  int repeat_count;            /* count arg to '--repeat' */
};

/* Parse a single option. */
static error_t
parse_opt (int key, char *arg, struct argp_state *state)
{
  /* Get the input argument from argp_parse, which we
     know is a pointer to our arguments structure. */
```

```
        struct arguments *arguments = state->input;

    switch (key)
      {
      case 'q': case 's':
        arguments->silent = 1;
        break;
      case 'v':
        arguments->verbose = 1;
        break;
      case 'o':
        arguments->output_file = arg;
        break;
      case 'r':
        arguments->repeat_count = arg ? atoi (arg) : 10;
        break;
      case OPT_ABORT:
        arguments->abort = 1;
        break;

      case ARGP_KEY_NO_ARGS:
        argp_usage (state);

      case ARGP_KEY_ARG:
        /* Here we know that state->arg_num == 0, since we
        force argument parsing to end before any more arguments can
        get here. */
        arguments->arg1 = arg;

        /* Now we consume all the rest of the arguments.
        state->next is the index in state->argv of the
        next argument to be parsed, which is the first string
        we're interested in, so we can just use
        &state->argv[state->next] as the value for
        arguments->strings.

        In addition, by setting state->next to the end
        of the arguments, we can force argp to stop parsing here and
        return. */
        arguments->strings = &state->argv[state->next];
        state->next = state->argc;

        break;

      default:
        return ARGP_ERR_UNKNOWN;
      }
    return 0;
}

/* Our argp parser. */
static struct argp argp = { options, parse_opt, args_doc, doc };

int
main (int argc, char **argv)
{
  int i, j;
  struct arguments arguments;
```

```
/* Default values. */
arguments.silent = 0;
arguments.verbose = 0;
arguments.output_file = "-";
arguments.repeat_count = 1;
arguments.abort = 0;

/* Parse our arguments; every option seen by parse_opt will be
   reflected in arguments. */
argp_parse (&argp, argc, argv, 0, 0, &arguments);

if (arguments.abort)
  error (10, 0, "ABORTED");

for (i = 0; i < arguments.repeat_count; i++)
  {
    printf ("ARG1 = %s\n", arguments.arg1);
    printf ("STRINGS = ");
    for (j = 0; arguments.strings[j]; j++)
      printf (j == 0 ? "%s" : ", %s", arguments.strings[j]);
    printf ("\n");
    printf ("OUTPUT_FILE = %s\nVERBOSE = %s\nSILENT = %s\n",
            arguments.output_file,
            arguments.verbose ? "yes" : "no",
            arguments.silent ? "yes" : "no");
  }

exit (0);
}
```

## 25.3.12 Argp User Customization

The formatting of argp '--help' output may be controlled to some extent by a program's users, by setting the ARGP_HELP_FMT environment variable to a comma-separated list of tokens. Whitespace is ignored:

'dup-args'
'no-dup-args'

> These turn *duplicate-argument-mode* on or off. In duplicate argument mode, if an option that accepts an argument has multiple names, the argument is shown for each name. Otherwise, it is only shown for the first long option. A note is subsequently printed so the user knows that it applies to other names as well. The default is 'no-dup-args', which is less consistent, but prettier.

'dup-args-note'
'no-dup-args-note'

> These will enable or disable the note informing the user of suppressed option argument duplication. The default is 'dup-args-note'.

'short-opt-col=n'

> This prints the first short option in column $n$. The default is 2.

'long-opt-col=n'

> This prints the first long option in column $n$. The default is 6.

`doc-opt-col=n`
> This prints 'documentation options' (see Section 25.3.4.1 [Flags for Argp Options], page 717) in column n. The default is 2.

`opt-doc-col=n`
> This prints the documentation for options starting in column n. The default is 29.

`header-col=n`
> This will indent the group headers that document groups of options to column n. The default is 1.

`usage-indent=n`
> This will indent continuation lines in 'Usage:' messages to column n. The default is 12.

`rmargin=n`
> This will word wrap help output at or before column n. The default is 79.

## 25.3.12.1 Parsing of Suboptions

Having a single level of options is sometimes not enough. There might be too many options which have to be available or a set of options is closely related.

For this case some programs use suboptions. One of the most prominent programs is certainly mount(8). The -o option take one argument which itself is a comma separated list of options. To ease the programming of code like this the function getsubopt is available.

**int getsubopt** (*char \*\*optionp, char \*const \*tokens, char \*\*valuep*)    [Function]
> Preliminary: | MT-Safe | AS-Safe | AC-Safe | See Section 1.2.2.1 [POSIX Safety Concepts], page 2.

> The *optionp* parameter must be a pointer to a variable containing the address of the string to process. When the function returns the reference is updated to point to the next suboption or to the terminating '\0' character if there is no more suboption available.

> The *tokens* parameter references an array of strings containing the known suboptions. All strings must be '\0' terminated and to mark the end a null pointer must be stored. When getsubopt finds a possible legal suboption it compares it with all strings available in the *tokens* array and returns the index in the string as the indicator.

> In case the suboption has an associated value introduced by a '=' character, a pointer to the value is returned in *valuep*. The string is '\0' terminated. If no argument is available *valuep* is set to the null pointer. By doing this the caller can check whether a necessary value is given or whether no unexpected value is present.

> In case the next suboption in the string is not mentioned in the *tokens* array the starting address of the suboption including a possible value is returned in *valuep* and the return value of the function is '-1'.

## 25.3.13 Parsing of Suboptions Example

The code which might appear in the mount(8) program is a perfect example of the use of getsubopt:

```
#include <stdio.h>
#include <stdlib.h>
#include <unistd.h>

int do_all;
const char *type;
int read_size;
int write_size;
int read_only;

enum
{
  RO_OPTION = 0,
  RW_OPTION,
  READ_SIZE_OPTION,
  WRITE_SIZE_OPTION,
  THE_END
};

const char *mount_opts[] =
{
  [RO_OPTION] = "ro",
  [RW_OPTION] = "rw",
  [READ_SIZE_OPTION] = "rsize",
  [WRITE_SIZE_OPTION] = "wsize",
  [THE_END] = NULL
};

int
main (int argc, char **argv)
{
  char *subopts, *value;
  int opt;

  while ((opt = getopt (argc, argv, "at:o:")) != -1)
    switch (opt)
      {
      case 'a':
        do_all = 1;
        break;
      case 't':
        type = optarg;
        break;
      case 'o':
        subopts = optarg;
        while (*subopts != '\0')
          switch (getsubopt (&subopts, mount_opts, &value))
            {
            case RO_OPTION:
              read_only = 1;
              break;
            case RW_OPTION:
              read_only = 0;
              break;
            case READ_SIZE_OPTION:
              if (value == NULL)
                abort ();
```

```
              read_size = atoi (value);
              break;
            case WRITE_SIZE_OPTION:
              if (value == NULL)
                abort ();
              write_size = atoi (value);
              break;
            default:
              /* Unknown suboption. */
              printf ("Unknown suboption '%s'\n", value);
              break;
            }
          break;
        default:
          abort ();
        }

    /* Do the real work. */

    return 0;
}
```

## 25.4 Environment Variables

When a program is executed, it receives information about the context in which it was invoked in two ways. The first mechanism uses the *argv* and *argc* arguments to its **main** function, and is discussed in Section 25.1 [Program Arguments], page 705. The second mechanism uses *environment variables* and is discussed in this section.

The *argv* mechanism is typically used to pass command-line arguments specific to the particular program being invoked. The environment, on the other hand, keeps track of information that is shared by many programs, changes infrequently, and that is less frequently used.

The environment variables discussed in this section are the same environment variables that you set using assignments and the **export** command in the shell. Programs executed from the shell inherit all of the environment variables from the shell.

Standard environment variables are used for information about the user's home directory, terminal type, current locale, and so on; you can define additional variables for other purposes. The set of all environment variables that have values is collectively known as the *environment*.

Names of environment variables are case-sensitive and must not contain the character '='. System-defined environment variables are invariably uppercase.

The values of environment variables can be anything that can be represented as a string. A value must not contain an embedded null character, since this is assumed to terminate the string.

### 25.4.1 Environment Access

The value of an environment variable can be accessed with the **getenv** function. This is declared in the header file **stdlib.h**.

Libraries should use **secure_getenv** instead of **getenv**, so that they do not accidentally use untrusted environment variables. Modifications of environment variables are not allowed in multi-threaded programs. The `getenv` and `secure_getenv` functions can be safely used in multi-threaded programs.

`char * getenv (const char *name)` [Function]
Preliminary: | MT-Safe env | AS-Safe | AC-Safe | See Section 1.2.2.1 [POSIX Safety Concepts], page 2.

This function returns a string that is the value of the environment variable *name*. You must not modify this string. In some non-Unix systems not using the GNU C Library, it might be overwritten by subsequent calls to `getenv` (but not by any other library function). If the environment variable *name* is not defined, the value is a null pointer.

`char * secure_getenv (const char *name)` [Function]
Preliminary: | MT-Safe env | AS-Safe | AC-Safe | See Section 1.2.2.1 [POSIX Safety Concepts], page 2.

This function is similar to `getenv`, but it returns a null pointer if the environment is untrusted. This happens when the program file has SUID or SGID bits set. General-purpose libraries should always prefer this function over `getenv` to avoid vulnerabilities if the library is referenced from a SUID/SGID program.

This function is a GNU extension.

`int putenv (char *string)` [Function]
Preliminary: | MT-Unsafe const:env | AS-Unsafe heap lock | AC-Unsafe corrupt lock mem | See Section 1.2.2.1 [POSIX Safety Concepts], page 2.

The `putenv` function adds or removes definitions from the environment. If the *string* is of the form '`name=value`', the definition is added to the environment. Otherwise, the *string* is interpreted as the name of an environment variable, and any definition for this variable in the environment is removed.

If the function is successful it returns `0`. Otherwise the return value is nonzero and `errno` is set to indicate the error.

The difference to the `setenv` function is that the exact string given as the parameter *string* is put into the environment. If the user should change the string after the `putenv` call this will reflect automatically in the environment. This also requires that *string* not be an automatic variable whose scope is left before the variable is removed from the environment. The same applies of course to dynamically allocated variables which are freed later.

This function is part of the extended Unix interface. You should define *_XOPEN_SOURCE* before including any header.

`int setenv (const char *name, const char *value, int replace)` [Function]
Preliminary: | MT-Unsafe const:env | AS-Unsafe heap lock | AC-Unsafe corrupt lock mem | See Section 1.2.2.1 [POSIX Safety Concepts], page 2.

The `setenv` function can be used to add a new definition to the environment. The entry with the name *name* is replaced by the value '`name=value`'. Please note that this is also true if *value* is the empty string. To do this a new string is created and the strings *name* and *value* are copied. A null pointer for the *value* parameter is illegal.

If the environment already contains an entry with key *name* the *replace* parameter controls the action. If replace is zero, nothing happens. Otherwise the old entry is replaced by the new one.

Please note that you cannot remove an entry completely using this function.

If the function is successful it returns 0. Otherwise the environment is unchanged and the return value is -1 and `errno` is set.

This function was originally part of the BSD library but is now part of the Unix standard.

**int unsetenv** (*const char* **\*name**)                                                    [Function]
> Preliminary: | MT-Unsafe const:env | AS-Unsafe lock | AC-Unsafe lock | See Section 1.2.2.1 [POSIX Safety Concepts], page 2.
>
> Using this function one can remove an entry completely from the environment. If the environment contains an entry with the key *name* this whole entry is removed. A call to this function is equivalent to a call to `putenv` when the *value* part of the string is empty.
>
> The function return -1 if *name* is a null pointer, points to an empty string, or points to a string containing a = character. It returns 0 if the call succeeded.
>
> This function was originally part of the BSD library but is now part of the Unix standard. The BSD version had no return value, though.

There is one more function to modify the whole environment. This function is said to be used in the POSIX.9 (POSIX bindings for Fortran 77) and so one should expect it did made it into POSIX.1. But this never happened. But we still provide this function as a GNU extension to enable writing standard compliant Fortran environments.

**int clearenv** (*void*)                                                                      [Function]
> Preliminary: | MT-Unsafe const:env | AS-Unsafe heap lock | AC-Unsafe lock mem | See Section 1.2.2.1 [POSIX Safety Concepts], page 2.
>
> The `clearenv` function removes all entries from the environment. Using `putenv` and `setenv` new entries can be added again later.
>
> If the function is successful it returns 0. Otherwise the return value is nonzero.

You can deal directly with the underlying representation of environment objects to add more variables to the environment (for example, to communicate with another program you are about to execute; see Section 26.5 [Executing a File], page 752).

**char \*\* environ**                                                                          [Variable]
> The environment is represented as an array of strings. Each string is of the format '*name=value*'. The order in which strings appear in the environment is not significant, but the same *name* must not appear more than once. The last element of the array is a null pointer.
>
> This variable is declared in the header file `unistd.h`.
>
> If you just want to get the value of an environment variable, use `getenv`.

Unix systems, and GNU systems, pass the initial value of `environ` as the third argument to `main`. See Section 25.1 [Program Arguments], page 705.

## 25.4.2 Standard Environment Variables

These environment variables have standard meanings. This doesn't mean that they are always present in the environment; but if these variables *are* present, they have these meanings. You shouldn't try to use these environment variable names for some other purpose.

HOME

This is a string representing the user's *home directory*, or initial default working directory.

The user can set HOME to any value. If you need to make sure to obtain the proper home directory for a particular user, you should not use HOME; instead, look up the user's name in the user database (see Section 30.13 [User Database], page 810).

For most purposes, it is better to use HOME, precisely because this lets the user specify the value.

LOGNAME

This is the name that the user used to log in. Since the value in the environment can be tweaked arbitrarily, this is not a reliable way to identify the user who is running a program; a function like getlogin (see Section 30.11 [Identifying Who Logged In], page 801) is better for that purpose.

For most purposes, it is better to use LOGNAME, precisely because this lets the user specify the value.

PATH

A *path* is a sequence of directory names which is used for searching for a file. The variable PATH holds a path used for searching for programs to be run.

The execlp and execvp functions (see Section 26.5 [Executing a File], page 752) use this environment variable, as do many shells and other utilities which are implemented in terms of those functions.

The syntax of a path is a sequence of directory names separated by colons. An empty string instead of a directory name stands for the current directory (see Section 14.1 [Working Directory], page 377).

A typical value for this environment variable might be a string like:

```
:/bin:/etc:/usr/bin:/usr/new/X11:/usr/new:/usr/local/bin
```

This means that if the user tries to execute a program named foo, the system will look for files named foo, /bin/foo, /etc/foo, and so on. The first of these files that exists is the one that is executed.

TERM

This specifies the kind of terminal that is receiving program output. Some programs can make use of this information to take advantage of special escape sequences or terminal modes supported by particular kinds of terminals. Many programs which use the termcap library (see Section "Finding a Terminal Description" in *The Termcap Library Manual*) use the TERM environment variable, for example.

TZ

>This specifies the time zone. See Section 21.4.7 [Specifying the Time Zone with TZ], page 622, for information about the format of this string and how it is used.

LANG

>This specifies the default locale to use for attribute categories where neither LC_ ALL nor the specific environment variable for that category is set. See Chapter 7 [Locales and Internationalization], page 169, for more information about locales.

LC_ALL

>If this environment variable is set it overrides the selection for all the locales done using the other LC_* environment variables. The value of the other LC_* environment variables is simply ignored in this case.

LC_COLLATE

>This specifies what locale to use for string sorting.

LC_CTYPE

>This specifies what locale to use for character sets and character classification.

LC_MESSAGES

>This specifies what locale to use for printing messages and to parse responses.

LC_MONETARY

>This specifies what locale to use for formatting monetary values.

LC_NUMERIC

>This specifies what locale to use for formatting numbers.

LC_TIME

>This specifies what locale to use for formatting date/time values.

NLSPATH

>This specifies the directories in which the **catopen** function looks for message translation catalogs.

_POSIX_OPTION_ORDER

>If this environment variable is defined, it suppresses the usual reordering of command line arguments by **getopt** and **argp_parse**. See Section 25.1.1 [Program Argument Syntax Conventions], page 706.

## 25.5 Auxiliary Vector

When a program is executed, it receives information from the operating system about the environment in which it is operating. The form of this information is a table of key-value pairs, where the keys are from the set of 'AT_' values in **elf.h**. Some of the data is provided by the kernel for libc consumption, and may be obtained by ordinary interfaces, such as **sysconf**. However, on a platform-by-platform basis there may be information that is not available any other way.

### 25.5.1 Definition of getauxval

unsigned long int getauxval (*unsigned long int type*)                    [Function]
> Preliminary: | MT-Safe | AS-Safe | AC-Safe | See Section 1.2.2.1 [POSIX Safety Concepts], page 2.

> This function is used to inquire about the entries in the auxiliary vector. The *type* argument should be one of the 'AT_' symbols defined in elf.h. If a matching entry is found, the value is returned; if the entry is not found, zero is returned and errno is set to ENOENT.

For some platforms, the key AT_HWCAP is the easiest way to inquire about any instruction set extensions available at runtime. In this case, there will (of necessity) be a platform-specific set of 'HWCAP_' values masked together that describe the capabilities of the cpu on which the program is being executed.

## 25.6 System Calls

A system call is a request for service that a program makes of the kernel. The service is generally something that only the kernel has the privilege to do, such as doing I/O. Programmers don't normally need to be concerned with system calls because there are functions in the GNU C Library to do virtually everything that system calls do. These functions work by making system calls themselves. For example, there is a system call that changes the permissions of a file, but you don't need to know about it because you can just use the GNU C Library's chmod function.

System calls are sometimes called kernel calls.

However, there are times when you want to make a system call explicitly, and for that, the GNU C Library provides the syscall function. syscall is harder to use and less portable than functions like chmod, but easier and more portable than coding the system call in assembler instructions.

syscall is most useful when you are working with a system call which is special to your system or is newer than the GNU C Library you are using. syscall is implemented in an entirely generic way; the function does not know anything about what a particular system call does or even if it is valid.

The description of syscall in this section assumes a certain protocol for system calls on the various platforms on which the GNU C Library runs. That protocol is not defined by any strong authority, but we won't describe it here either because anyone who is coding syscall probably won't accept anything less than kernel and C library source code as a specification of the interface between them anyway.

syscall is declared in unistd.h.

long int syscall (*long int sysno, ...*)                         [Function]
> Preliminary: | MT-Safe | AS-Safe | AC-Safe | See Section 1.2.2.1 [POSIX Safety Concepts], page 2.

> syscall performs a generic system call.

> *sysno* is the system call number. Each kind of system call is identified by a number. Macros for all the possible system call numbers are defined in sys/syscall.h

The remaining arguments are the arguments for the system call, in order, and their meanings depend on the kind of system call. Each kind of system call has a definite number of arguments, from zero to five. If you code more arguments than the system call takes, the extra ones to the right are ignored.

The return value is the return value from the system call, unless the system call failed. In that case, `syscall` returns -1 and sets `errno` to an error code that the system call returned. Note that system calls do not return -1 when they succeed.

If you specify an invalid *sysno*, `syscall` returns -1 with `errno` = ENOSYS.

Example:

```
#include <unistd.h>
#include <sys/syscall.h>
#include <errno.h>

...

int rc;

rc = syscall(SYS_chmod, "/etc/passwd", 0444);

if (rc == -1)
    fprintf(stderr, "chmod failed, errno = %d\n", errno);
```

This, if all the compatibility stars are aligned, is equivalent to the following preferable code:

```
#include <sys/types.h>
#include <sys/stat.h>
#include <errno.h>

...

int rc;

rc = chmod("/etc/passwd", 0444);
if (rc == -1)
    fprintf(stderr, "chmod failed, errno = %d\n", errno);
```

## 25.7 Program Termination

The usual way for a program to terminate is simply for its `main` function to return. The *exit status value* returned from the `main` function is used to report information back to the process's parent process or shell.

A program can also terminate normally by calling the `exit` function.

In addition, programs can be terminated by signals; this is discussed in more detail in Chapter 24 [Signal Handling], page 661. The `abort` function causes a signal that kills the program.

## 25.7.1 Normal Termination

A process terminates normally when its program signals it is done by calling `exit`. Returning from `main` is equivalent to calling `exit`, and the value that `main` returns is used as the argument to `exit`.

<pre>void exit (int status)                                              [Function]</pre>
> Preliminary: | MT-Unsafe race:exit | AS-Unsafe corrupt | AC-Unsafe corrupt lock | See Section 1.2.2.1 [POSIX Safety Concepts], page 2.
>
> The `exit` function tells the system that the program is done, which causes it to terminate the process.
>
> *status* is the program's exit status, which becomes part of the process' termination status. This function does not return.

Normal termination causes the following actions:

1. Functions that were registered with the `atexit` or `on_exit` functions are called in the reverse order of their registration. This mechanism allows your application to specify its own "cleanup" actions to be performed at program termination. Typically, this is used to do things like saving program state information in a file, or unlocking locks in shared data bases.

2. All open streams are closed, writing out any buffered output data. See Section 12.4 [Closing Streams], page 253. In addition, temporary files opened with the `tmpfile` function are removed; see Section 14.11 [Temporary Files], page 419.

3. `_exit` is called, terminating the program. See Section 25.7.5 [Termination Internals], page 747.

## 25.7.2 Exit Status

When a program exits, it can return to the parent process a small amount of information about the cause of termination, using the *exit status*. This is a value between 0 and 255 that the exiting process passes as an argument to `exit`.

Normally you should use the exit status to report very broad information about success or failure. You can't provide a lot of detail about the reasons for the failure, and most parent processes would not want much detail anyway.

There are conventions for what sorts of status values certain programs should return. The most common convention is simply 0 for success and 1 for failure. Programs that perform comparison use a different convention: they use status 1 to indicate a mismatch, and status 2 to indicate an inability to compare. Your program should follow an existing convention if an existing convention makes sense for it.

A general convention reserves status values 128 and up for special purposes. In particular, the value 128 is used to indicate failure to execute another program in a subprocess. This convention is not universally obeyed, but it is a good idea to follow it in your programs.

**Warning:** Don't try to use the number of errors as the exit status. This is actually not very useful; a parent process would generally not care how many errors occurred. Worse than that, it does not work, because the status value is truncated to eight bits. Thus, if the program tried to report 256 errors, the parent would receive a report of 0 errors—that is, success.

For the same reason, it does not work to use the value of **errno** as the exit status—these can exceed 255.

**Portability note:** Some non-POSIX systems use different conventions for exit status values. For greater portability, you can use the macros **EXIT_SUCCESS** and **EXIT_FAILURE** for the conventional status value for success and failure, respectively. They are declared in the file **stdlib.h**.

**int EXIT_SUCCESS** [Macro]

This macro can be used with the **exit** function to indicate successful program completion.

On POSIX systems, the value of this macro is 0. On other systems, the value might be some other (possibly non-constant) integer expression.

**int EXIT_FAILURE** [Macro]

This macro can be used with the **exit** function to indicate unsuccessful program completion in a general sense.

On POSIX systems, the value of this macro is 1. On other systems, the value might be some other (possibly non-constant) integer expression. Other nonzero status values also indicate failures. Certain programs use different nonzero status values to indicate particular kinds of "non-success". For example, **diff** uses status value 1 to mean that the files are different, and 2 or more to mean that there was difficulty in opening the files.

Don't confuse a program's exit status with a process' termination status. There are lots of ways a process can terminate besides having its program finish. In the event that the process termination *is* caused by program termination (i.e., **exit**), though, the program's exit status becomes part of the process' termination status.

### 25.7.3 Cleanups on Exit

Your program can arrange to run its own cleanup functions if normal termination happens. If you are writing a library for use in various application programs, then it is unreliable to insist that all applications call the library's cleanup functions explicitly before exiting. It is much more robust to make the cleanup invisible to the application, by setting up a cleanup function in the library itself using **atexit** or **on_exit**.

**int atexit** (*void* (**function*) (*void*)) [Function]

Preliminary: | MT-Safe | AS-Unsafe heap lock | AC-Unsafe lock mem | See Section 1.2.2.1 [POSIX Safety Concepts], page 2.

The **atexit** function registers the function *function* to be called at normal program termination. The *function* is called with no arguments.

The return value from **atexit** is zero on success and nonzero if the function cannot be registered.

**int on_exit** (*void* (**function*)(*int* **status**, *void* **arg*), *void* **arg*) [Function]

Preliminary: | MT-Safe | AS-Unsafe heap lock | AC-Unsafe lock mem | See Section 1.2.2.1 [POSIX Safety Concepts], page 2.

This function is a somewhat more powerful variant of `atexit`. It accepts two arguments, a function *function* and an arbitrary pointer *arg*. At normal program termination, the *function* is called with two arguments: the *status* value passed to `exit`, and the *arg*.

This function is included in the GNU C Library only for compatibility for SunOS, and may not be supported by other implementations.

Here's a trivial program that illustrates the use of `exit` and `atexit`:

```
#include <stdio.h>
#include <stdlib.h>

void
bye (void)
{
  puts ("Goodbye, cruel world....");
}

int
main (void)
{
  atexit (bye);
  exit (EXIT_SUCCESS);
}
```

When this program is executed, it just prints the message and exits.

## 25.7.4 Aborting a Program

You can abort your program using the `abort` function. The prototype for this function is in `stdlib.h`.

`void abort` (*void*)                                              [Function]
> Preliminary:  | MT-Safe  | AS-Unsafe corrupt  | AC-Unsafe lock corrupt | See Section 1.2.2.1 [POSIX Safety Concepts], page 2.
>
> The `abort` function causes abnormal program termination. This does not execute cleanup functions registered with `atexit` or `on_exit`.
>
> This function actually terminates the process by raising a `SIGABRT` signal, and your program can include a handler to intercept this signal; see Chapter 24 [Signal Handling], page 661.

> **Future Change Warning:** Proposed Federal censorship regulations may prohibit us from giving you information about the possibility of calling this function. We would be required to say that this is not an acceptable way of terminating a program.

## 25.7.5 Termination Internals

The `_exit` function is the primitive used for process termination by `exit`. It is declared in the header file `unistd.h`.

`void _exit (int status)`                                                [Function]
> Preliminary: | MT-Safe | AS-Safe | AC-Safe | See Section 1.2.2.1 [POSIX Safety Concepts], page 2.
>
> The `_exit` function is the primitive for causing a process to terminate with status *status*. Calling this function does not execute cleanup functions registered with `atexit` or `on_exit`.

`void _Exit (int status)`                                                [Function]
> Preliminary: | MT-Safe | AS-Safe | AC-Safe | See Section 1.2.2.1 [POSIX Safety Concepts], page 2.
>
> The `_Exit` function is the ISO C equivalent to `_exit`. The ISO C committee members were not sure whether the definitions of `_exit` and `_Exit` were compatible so they have not used the POSIX name.
>
> This function was introduced in ISO C99 and is declared in `stdlib.h`.

When a process terminates for any reason—either because the program terminates, or as a result of a signal—the following things happen:

- All open file descriptors in the process are closed. See Chapter 13 [Low-Level Input/Output], page 323. Note that streams are not flushed automatically when the process terminates; see Chapter 12 [Input/Output on Streams], page 248.

- A process exit status is saved to be reported back to the parent process via `wait` or `waitpid`; see Section 26.6 [Process Completion], page 755. If the program exited, this status includes as its low-order 8 bits the program exit status.

- Any child processes of the process being terminated are assigned a new parent process. (On most systems, including GNU, this is the `init` process, with process ID 1.)

- A `SIGCHLD` signal is sent to the parent process.

- If the process is a session leader that has a controlling terminal, then a `SIGHUP` signal is sent to each process in the foreground job, and the controlling terminal is disassociated from that session. See Chapter 28 [Job Control], page 763.

- If termination of a process causes a process group to become orphaned, and any member of that process group is stopped, then a `SIGHUP` signal and a `SIGCONT` signal are sent to each process in the group. See Chapter 28 [Job Control], page 763.

# 26 Processes

*Processes* are the primitive units for allocation of system resources. Each process has its own address space and (usually) one thread of control. A process executes a program; you can have multiple processes executing the same program, but each process has its own copy of the program within its own address space and executes it independently of the other copies.

Processes are organized hierarchically. Each process has a *parent process* which explicitly arranged to create it. The processes created by a given parent are called its *child processes*. A child inherits many of its attributes from the parent process.

This chapter describes how a program can create, terminate, and control child processes. Actually, there are three distinct operations involved: creating a new child process, causing the new process to execute a program, and coordinating the completion of the child process with the original program.

The `system` function provides a simple, portable mechanism for running another program; it does all three steps automatically. If you need more control over the details of how this is done, you can use the primitive functions to do each step individually instead.

## 26.1 Running a Command

The easy way to run another program is to use the `system` function. This function does all the work of running a subprogram, but it doesn't give you much control over the details: you have to wait until the subprogram terminates before you can do anything else.

`int system` (*const char *command*)                                    [Function]
> Preliminary: | MT-Safe | AS-Unsafe plugin heap lock | AC-Unsafe lock mem | See Section 1.2.2.1 [POSIX Safety Concepts], page 2.
>
> This function executes *command* as a shell command. In the GNU C Library, it always uses the default shell `sh` to run the command. In particular, it searches the directories in `PATH` to find programs to execute. The return value is `-1` if it wasn't possible to create the shell process, and otherwise is the status of the shell process. See Section 26.6 [Process Completion], page 755, for details on how this status code can be interpreted.
>
> If the *command* argument is a null pointer, a return value of zero indicates that no command processor is available.
>
> This function is a cancellation point in multi-threaded programs. This is a problem if the thread allocates some resources (like memory, file descriptors, semaphores or whatever) at the time `system` is called. If the thread gets canceled these resources stay allocated until the program ends. To avoid this calls to `system` should be protected using cancellation handlers.
>
> The `system` function is declared in the header file `stdlib.h`.

**Portability Note:** Some C implementations may not have any notion of a command processor that can execute other programs. You can determine whether a command processor exists by executing `system (NULL)`; if the return value is nonzero, a command processor is available.

The `popen` and `pclose` functions (see Section 15.2 [Pipe to a Subprocess], page 426) are closely related to the `system` function. They allow the parent process to communicate with the standard input and output channels of the command being executed.

## 26.2 Process Creation Concepts

This section gives an overview of processes and of the steps involved in creating a process and making it run another program.

Each process is named by a *process ID* number. A unique process ID is allocated to each process when it is created. The *lifetime* of a process ends when its termination is reported to its parent process; at that time, all of the process resources, including its process ID, are freed.

Processes are created with the `fork` system call (so the operation of creating a new process is sometimes called *forking* a process). The *child process* created by `fork` is a copy of the original *parent process*, except that it has its own process ID.

After forking a child process, both the parent and child processes continue to execute normally. If you want your program to wait for a child process to finish executing before continuing, you must do this explicitly after the fork operation, by calling `wait` or `waitpid` (see Section 26.6 [Process Completion], page 755). These functions give you limited information about why the child terminated—for example, its exit status code.

A newly forked child process continues to execute the same program as its parent process, at the point where the `fork` call returns. You can use the return value from `fork` to tell whether the program is running in the parent process or the child.

Having several processes run the same program is only occasionally useful. But the child can execute another program using one of the `exec` functions; see Section 26.5 [Executing a File], page 752. The program that the process is executing is called its *process image*. Starting execution of a new program causes the process to forget all about its previous process image; when the new program exits, the process exits too, instead of returning to the previous process image.

## 26.3 Process Identification

The `pid_t` data type represents process IDs. You can get the process ID of a process by calling `getpid`. The function `getppid` returns the process ID of the parent of the current process (this is also known as the *parent process ID*). Your program should include the header files `unistd.h` and `sys/types.h` to use these functions.

`pid_t`                                                                    [Data Type]
> The `pid_t` data type is a signed integer type which is capable of representing a process ID. In the GNU C Library, this is an `int`.

`pid_t getpid` (*void*)                                                    [Function]
> Preliminary: | MT-Safe | AS-Safe | AC-Safe | See Section 1.2.2.1 [POSIX Safety Concepts], page 2.

> The `getpid` function returns the process ID of the current process.

`pid_t getppid` (*void*)                                                          [Function]
> Preliminary: | MT-Safe | AS-Safe | AC-Safe | See Section 1.2.2.1 [POSIX Safety Concepts], page 2.

> The `getppid` function returns the process ID of the parent of the current process.

## 26.4 Creating a Process

The `fork` function is the primitive for creating a process. It is declared in the header file `unistd.h`.

`pid_t fork` (*void*)                                                             [Function]
> Preliminary: | MT-Safe | AS-Unsafe plugin | AC-Unsafe lock | See Section 1.2.2.1 [POSIX Safety Concepts], page 2.

> The `fork` function creates a new process.

> If the operation is successful, there are then both parent and child processes and both see `fork` return, but with different values: it returns a value of `0` in the child process and returns the child's process ID in the parent process.

> If process creation failed, `fork` returns a value of `-1` in the parent process. The following `errno` error conditions are defined for `fork`:

> `EAGAIN`     There aren't enough system resources to create another process, or the user already has too many processes running. This means exceeding the `RLIMIT_NPROC` resource limit, which can usually be increased; see Section 22.2 [Limiting Resource Usage], page 632.

> `ENOMEM`     The process requires more space than the system can supply.

The specific attributes of the child process that differ from the parent process are:

- The child process has its own unique process ID.

- The parent process ID of the child process is the process ID of its parent process.

- The child process gets its own copies of the parent process's open file descriptors. Subsequently changing attributes of the file descriptors in the parent process won't affect the file descriptors in the child, and vice versa. See Section 13.11 [Control Operations on Files], page 359. However, the file position associated with each descriptor is shared by both processes; see Section 11.1.2 [File Position], page 244.

- The elapsed processor times for the child process are set to zero; see Section 21.3.2 [Processor Time Inquiry], page 598.

- The child doesn't inherit file locks set by the parent process. See Section 13.11 [Control Operations on Files], page 359.

- The child doesn't inherit alarms set by the parent process. See Section 21.5 [Setting an Alarm], page 625.

- The set of pending signals (see Section 24.1.3 [How Signals Are Delivered], page 662) for the child process is cleared. (The child process inherits its mask of blocked signals and signal actions from the parent process.)

**pid_t vfork** (*void*)                                                              [Function]
> Preliminary: | MT-Safe | AS-Unsafe plugin | AC-Unsafe lock | See Section 1.2.2.1 [POSIX Safety Concepts], page 2.
>
> The **vfork** function is similar to **fork** but on some systems it is more efficient; however, there are restrictions you must follow to use it safely.
>
> While **fork** makes a complete copy of the calling process's address space and allows both the parent and child to execute independently, **vfork** does not make this copy. Instead, the child process created with **vfork** shares its parent's address space until it calls **_exit** or one of the **exec** functions. In the meantime, the parent process suspends execution.
>
> You must be very careful not to allow the child process created with **vfork** to modify any global data or even local variables shared with the parent. Furthermore, the child process cannot return from (or do a long jump out of) the function that called **vfork**! This would leave the parent process's control information very confused. If in doubt, use **fork** instead.
>
> Some operating systems don't really implement **vfork**. The GNU C Library permits you to use **vfork** on all systems, but actually executes **fork** if **vfork** isn't available. If you follow the proper precautions for using **vfork**, your program will still work even if the system uses **fork** instead.

## 26.5 Executing a File

This section describes the **exec** family of functions, for executing a file as a process image. You can use these functions to make a child process execute a new program after it has been forked.

To see the effects of **exec** from the point of view of the called program, see Chapter 25 [The Basic Program/System Interface], page 705.

The functions in this family differ in how you specify the arguments, but otherwise they all do the same thing. They are declared in the header file **unistd.h**.

**int execv** (*const char \*filename, char \*const* **argv**[])                       [Function]
> Preliminary: | MT-Safe | AS-Safe | AC-Safe | See Section 1.2.2.1 [POSIX Safety Concepts], page 2.
>
> The **execv** function executes the file named by *filename* as a new process image.
>
> The *argv* argument is an array of null-terminated strings that is used to provide a value for the **argv** argument to the **main** function of the program to be executed. The last element of this array must be a null pointer. By convention, the first element of this array is the file name of the program sans directory names. See Section 25.1 [Program Arguments], page 705, for full details on how programs can access these arguments.
>
> The environment for the new process image is taken from the **environ** variable of the current process image; see Section 25.4 [Environment Variables], page 738, for information about environments.

**int execl** (*const char \*filename, const char \*arg0, ...*)                       [Function]
> Preliminary: | MT-Safe | AS-Unsafe heap | AC-Unsafe mem | See Section 1.2.2.1 [POSIX Safety Concepts], page 2.

This is similar to `execv`, but the *argv* strings are specified individually instead of as an array. A null pointer must be passed as the last such argument.

`int execve (const char *filename, char *const argv[], char *const`      [Function]
     `env[])`
     Preliminary: | MT-Safe | AS-Safe | AC-Safe | See Section 1.2.2.1 [POSIX Safety Concepts], page 2.

     This is similar to `execv`, but permits you to specify the environment for the new program explicitly as the *env* argument. This should be an array of strings in the same format as for the `environ` variable; see Section 25.4.1 [Environment Access], page 738.

`int execle (const char *filename, const char *arg0, ..., char *const`      [Function]
     `env[])`
     Preliminary: | MT-Safe | AS-Unsafe heap | AC-Unsafe mem | See Section 1.2.2.1 [POSIX Safety Concepts], page 2.

     This is similar to `execl`, but permits you to specify the environment for the new program explicitly. The environment argument is passed following the null pointer that marks the last *argv* argument, and should be an array of strings in the same format as for the `environ` variable.

`int execvp (const char *filename, char *const argv[])`      [Function]
     Preliminary: | MT-Safe env | AS-Unsafe heap | AC-Unsafe mem | See Section 1.2.2.1 [POSIX Safety Concepts], page 2.

     The `execvp` function is similar to `execv`, except that it searches the directories listed in the `PATH` environment variable (see Section 25.4.2 [Standard Environment Variables], page 741) to find the full file name of a file from *filename* if *filename* does not contain a slash.

     This function is useful for executing system utility programs, because it looks for them in the places that the user has chosen. Shells use it to run the commands that users type.

`int execlp (const char *filename, const char *arg0, ...)`      [Function]
     Preliminary: | MT-Safe env | AS-Unsafe heap | AC-Unsafe mem | See Section 1.2.2.1 [POSIX Safety Concepts], page 2.

     This function is like `execl`, except that it performs the same file name searching as the `execvp` function.

The size of the argument list and environment list taken together must not be greater than `ARG_MAX` bytes. See Section 32.1 [General Capacity Limits], page 838. On GNU/Hurd systems, the size (which compares against `ARG_MAX`) includes, for each string, the number of characters in the string, plus the size of a `char *`, plus one, rounded up to a multiple of the size of a `char *`. Other systems may have somewhat different rules for counting.

These functions normally don't return, since execution of a new program causes the currently executing program to go away completely. A value of -1 is returned in the event of a failure. In addition to the usual file name errors (see Section 11.2.3 [File Name Errors], page 246), the following `errno` error conditions are defined for these functions:

E2BIG      The combined size of the new program's argument list and environment list is
           larger than `ARG_MAX` bytes. GNU/Hurd systems have no specific limit on the
           argument list size, so this error code cannot result, but you may get `ENOMEM`
           instead if the arguments are too big for available memory.

ENOEXEC    The specified file can't be executed because it isn't in the right format.

ENOMEM     Executing the specified file requires more storage than is available.

If execution of the new file succeeds, it updates the access time field of the file as if the
file had been read. See Section 14.9.9 [File Times], page 413, for more details about access
times of files.

The point at which the file is closed again is not specified, but is at some point before
the process exits or before another process image is executed.

Executing a new process image completely changes the contents of memory, copying only
the argument and environment strings to new locations. But many other attributes of the
process are unchanged:

- The process ID and the parent process ID. See Section 26.2 [Process Creation Concepts],
  page 750.

- Session and process group membership. See Section 28.1 [Concepts of Job Control],
  page 763.

- Real user ID and group ID, and supplementary group IDs. See Section 30.2 [The
  Persona of a Process], page 791.

- Pending alarms. See Section 21.5 [Setting an Alarm], page 625.

- Current working directory and root directory. See Section 14.1 [Working Directory],
  page 377. On GNU/Hurd systems, the root directory is not copied when executing a
  setuid program; instead the system default root directory is used for the new program.

- File mode creation mask. See Section 14.9.7 [Assigning File Permissions], page 410.

- Process signal mask; see Section 24.7.3 [Process Signal Mask], page 694.

- Pending signals; see Section 24.7 [Blocking Signals], page 692.

- Elapsed processor time associated with the process; see Section 21.3.2 [Processor Time
  Inquiry], page 598.

If the set-user-ID and set-group-ID mode bits of the process image file are set, this affects
the effective user ID and effective group ID (respectively) of the process. These concepts
are discussed in detail in Section 30.2 [The Persona of a Process], page 791.

Signals that are set to be ignored in the existing process image are also set to be ignored
in the new process image. All other signals are set to the default action in the new process
image. For more information about signals, see Chapter 24 [Signal Handling], page 661.

File descriptors open in the existing process image remain open in the new process image,
unless they have the `FD_CLOEXEC` (close-on-exec) flag set. The files that remain open inherit
all attributes of the open file description from the existing process image, including file
locks. File descriptors are discussed in Chapter 13 [Low-Level Input/Output], page 323.

Streams, by contrast, cannot survive through **exec** functions, because they are located
in the memory of the process itself. The new process image has no streams except those it
creates afresh. Each of the streams in the pre-**exec** process image has a descriptor inside

it, and these descriptors do survive through `exec` (provided that they do not have `FD_CLOEXEC` set). The new process image can reconnect these to new streams using `fdopen` (see Section 13.4 [Descriptors and Streams], page 333).

## 26.6 Process Completion

The functions described in this section are used to wait for a child process to terminate or stop, and determine its status. These functions are declared in the header file `sys/wait.h`.

`pid_t waitpid` (*pid_t pid*, *int \*status-ptr*, *int options*)                    [Function]
    Preliminary: | MT-Safe | AS-Safe | AC-Safe | See Section 1.2.2.1 [POSIX Safety Concepts], page 2.

The `waitpid` function is used to request status information from a child process whose process ID is *pid*. Normally, the calling process is suspended until the child process makes status information available by terminating.

Other values for the *pid* argument have special interpretations. A value of `-1` or `WAIT_ANY` requests status information for any child process; a value of 0 or `WAIT_MYPGRP` requests information for any child process in the same process group as the calling process; and any other negative value − *pgid* requests information for any child process whose process group ID is *pgid*.

If status information for a child process is available immediately, this function returns immediately without waiting. If more than one eligible child process has status information available, one of them is chosen randomly, and its status is returned immediately. To get the status from the other eligible child processes, you need to call `waitpid` again.

The *options* argument is a bit mask. Its value should be the bitwise OR (that is, the '|' operator) of zero or more of the `WNOHANG` and `WUNTRACED` flags. You can use the `WNOHANG` flag to indicate that the parent process shouldn't wait; and the `WUNTRACED` flag to request status information from stopped processes as well as processes that have terminated.

The status information from the child process is stored in the object that *status-ptr* points to, unless *status-ptr* is a null pointer.

This function is a cancellation point in multi-threaded programs. This is a problem if the thread allocates some resources (like memory, file descriptors, semaphores or whatever) at the time `waitpid` is called. If the thread gets canceled these resources stay allocated until the program ends. To avoid this calls to `waitpid` should be protected using cancellation handlers.

The return value is normally the process ID of the child process whose status is reported. If there are child processes but none of them is waiting to be noticed, `waitpid` will block until one is. However, if the `WNOHANG` option was specified, `waitpid` will return zero instead of blocking.

If a specific PID to wait for was given to `waitpid`, it will ignore all other children (if any). Therefore if there are children waiting to be noticed but the child whose PID was specified is not one of them, `waitpid` will block or return zero as described above.

A value of -1 is returned in case of error. The following **errno** error conditions are defined for this function:

EINTR      The function was interrupted by delivery of a signal to the calling process. See Section 24.5 [Primitives Interrupted by Signals], page 687.

ECHILD     There are no child processes to wait for, or the specified *pid* is not a child of the calling process.

EINVAL     An invalid value was provided for the *options* argument.

These symbolic constants are defined as values for the *pid* argument to the **waitpid** function.

WAIT_ANY

> This constant macro (whose value is -1) specifies that **waitpid** should return status information about any child process.

WAIT_MYPGRP

> This constant (with value 0) specifies that **waitpid** should return status information about any child process in the same process group as the calling process.

These symbolic constants are defined as flags for the *options* argument to the **waitpid** function. You can bitwise-OR the flags together to obtain a value to use as the argument.

WNOHANG

> This flag specifies that **waitpid** should return immediately instead of waiting, if there is no child process ready to be noticed.

WUNTRACED

> This flag specifies that **waitpid** should report the status of any child processes that have been stopped as well as those that have terminated.

**pid_t wait** (*int \*status-ptr*)                                            [Function]
> Preliminary: | MT-Safe | AS-Safe | AC-Safe | See Section 1.2.2.1 [POSIX Safety Concepts], page 2.
>
> This is a simplified version of **waitpid**, and is used to wait until any one child process terminates. The call:
>
>> `wait (&status)`
>
> is exactly equivalent to:
>
>> `waitpid (-1, &status, 0)`
>
> This function is a cancellation point in multi-threaded programs. This is a problem if the thread allocates some resources (like memory, file descriptors, semaphores or whatever) at the time **wait** is called. If the thread gets canceled these resources stay allocated until the program ends. To avoid this calls to **wait** should be protected using cancellation handlers.

**pid_t wait4** (*pid_t pid*, *int \*status-ptr*, *int options*, *struct rusage*          [Function]
  *\*usage*)
> Preliminary: | MT-Safe | AS-Safe | AC-Safe | See Section 1.2.2.1 [POSIX Safety Concepts], page 2.

If *usage* is a null pointer, `wait4` is equivalent to `waitpid (pid, status-ptr, options)`.

If *usage* is not null, `wait4` stores usage figures for the child process in *\*rusage* (but only if the child has terminated, not if it has stopped). See Section 22.1 [Resource Usage], page 630.

This function is a BSD extension.

Here's an example of how to use `waitpid` to get the status from all child processes that have terminated, without ever waiting. This function is designed to be a handler for `SIGCHLD`, the signal that indicates that at least one child process has terminated.

```
void
sigchld_handler (int signum)
{
  int pid, status, serrno;
  serrno = errno;
  while (1)
    {
      pid = waitpid (WAIT_ANY, &status, WNOHANG);
      if (pid < 0)
        {
          perror ("waitpid");
          break;
        }
      if (pid == 0)
        break;
      notice_termination (pid, status);
    }
  errno = serrno;
}
```

## 26.7 Process Completion Status

If the exit status value (see Section 25.7 [Program Termination], page 744) of the child process is zero, then the status value reported by `waitpid` or `wait` is also zero. You can test for other kinds of information encoded in the returned status value using the following macros. These macros are defined in the header file `sys/wait.h`.

int WIFEXITED (*int status*)                                            [Macro]
> Preliminary: | MT-Safe | AS-Safe | AC-Safe | See Section 1.2.2.1 [POSIX Safety Concepts], page 2.
>
> This macro returns a nonzero value if the child process terminated normally with `exit` or `_exit`.

int WEXITSTATUS (*int status*)                                          [Macro]
> Preliminary: | MT-Safe | AS-Safe | AC-Safe | See Section 1.2.2.1 [POSIX Safety Concepts], page 2.
>
> If `WIFEXITED` is true of *status*, this macro returns the low-order 8 bits of the exit status value from the child process. See Section 25.7.2 [Exit Status], page 745.

int WIFSIGNALED (*int status*)                                          [Macro]
> Preliminary: | MT-Safe | AS-Safe | AC-Safe | See Section 1.2.2.1 [POSIX Safety Concepts], page 2.

This macro returns a nonzero value if the child process terminated because it received a signal that was not handled. See Chapter 24 [Signal Handling], page 661.

int **WTERMSIG** (*int status*)                                                              [Macro]

> Preliminary: | MT-Safe | AS-Safe | AC-Safe | See Section 1.2.2.1 [POSIX Safety Concepts], page 2.
>
> If `WIFSIGNALED` is true of *status*, this macro returns the signal number of the signal that terminated the child process.

int **WCOREDUMP** (*int status*)                                                             [Macro]

> Preliminary: | MT-Safe | AS-Safe | AC-Safe | See Section 1.2.2.1 [POSIX Safety Concepts], page 2.
>
> This macro returns a nonzero value if the child process terminated and produced a core dump.

int **WIFSTOPPED** (*int status*)                                                            [Macro]

> Preliminary: | MT-Safe | AS-Safe | AC-Safe | See Section 1.2.2.1 [POSIX Safety Concepts], page 2.
>
> This macro returns a nonzero value if the child process is stopped.

int **WSTOPSIG** (*int status*)                                                              [Macro]

> Preliminary: | MT-Safe | AS-Safe | AC-Safe | See Section 1.2.2.1 [POSIX Safety Concepts], page 2.
>
> If `WIFSTOPPED` is true of *status*, this macro returns the signal number of the signal that caused the child process to stop.

## 26.8 BSD Process Wait Functions

The GNU C Library also provides these related facilities for compatibility with BSD Unix. BSD uses the `union wait` data type to represent status values rather than an `int`. The two representations are actually interchangeable; they describe the same bit patterns. The GNU C Library defines macros such as `WEXITSTATUS` so that they will work on either kind of object, and the `wait` function is defined to accept either type of pointer as its *status-ptr* argument.

These functions are declared in `sys/wait.h`.

union **wait**                                                                               [Data Type]

> This data type represents program termination status values. It has the following members:
>
> int w_termsig
>
>> The value of this member is the same as that of the `WTERMSIG` macro.
>
> int w_coredump
>
>> The value of this member is the same as that of the `WCOREDUMP` macro.
>
> int w_retcode
>
>> The value of this member is the same as that of the `WEXITSTATUS` macro.
>
> int w_stopsig
>
>> The value of this member is the same as that of the `WSTOPSIG` macro.

Instead of accessing these members directly, you should use the equivalent macros.

The `wait3` function is the predecessor to `wait4`, which is more flexible. `wait3` is now obsolete.

`pid_t wait3` (*union wait \*status-ptr*, *int* `options`, *struct rusage*          [Function]
     `*usage`)

Preliminary: | MT-Safe | AS-Safe | AC-Safe | See Section 1.2.2.1 [POSIX Safety Concepts], page 2.

If *usage* is a null pointer, `wait3` is equivalent to `waitpid` (-1, *status-ptr*, *options*).

If *usage* is not null, `wait3` stores usage figures for the child process in `*rusage` (but only if the child has terminated, not if it has stopped). See Section 22.1 [Resource Usage], page 630.

## 26.9 Process Creation Example

Here is an example program showing how you might write a function similar to the built-in `system`. It executes its *command* argument using the equivalent of 'sh -c *command*'.

```
#include <stddef.h>
#include <stdlib.h>
#include <unistd.h>
#include <sys/types.h>
#include <sys/wait.h>

/* Execute the command using this shell program.  */
#define SHELL "/bin/sh"

int
my_system (const char *command)
{
  int status;
  pid_t pid;

  pid = fork ();
  if (pid == 0)
    {
      /* This is the child process. Execute the shell command. */
      execl (SHELL, SHELL, "-c", command, NULL);
      _exit (EXIT_FAILURE);
    }
  else if (pid < 0)
    /* The fork failed. Report failure.  */
    status = -1;
  else
    /* This is the parent process. Wait for the child to complete.  */
    if (waitpid (pid, &status, 0) != pid)
      status = -1;
  return status;
}
```

There are a couple of things you should pay attention to in this example.

Remember that the first `argv` argument supplied to the program represents the name of the program being executed. That is why, in the call to `execl`, SHELL is supplied once to name the program to execute and a second time to supply a value for `argv[0]`.

The `execl` call in the child process doesn't return if it is successful. If it fails, you must do something to make the child process terminate. Just returning a bad status code with `return` would leave two processes running the original program. Instead, the right behavior is for the child process to report failure to its parent process.

Call `_exit` to accomplish this. The reason for using `_exit` instead of `exit` is to avoid flushing fully buffered streams such as `stdout`. The buffers of these streams probably contain data that was copied from the parent process by the `fork`, data that will be output eventually by the parent process. Calling `exit` in the child would output the data twice. See Section 25.7.5 [Termination Internals], page 747.

# 27 Inter-Process Communication

This chapter describes the GNU C Library inter-process communication primitives.

## 27.1 Semaphores

The GNU C Library implements the semaphore APIs as defined in POSIX and System V. Semaphores can be used by multiple processes to coordinate shared resources. The following is a complete list of the semaphore functions provided by the GNU C Library.

### 27.1.1 System V Semaphores

int semctl (*int* **semid**, *int* **semnum**, *int* **cmd**);                    [Function]
    Preliminary: | MT-Safe | AS-Safe | AC-Unsafe corrupt/linux | See Section 1.2.2.1 [POSIX Safety Concepts], page 2.

int semget (*key_t* **key**, *int* **nsems**, *int* **semflg**);                    [Function]
    Preliminary: | MT-Safe | AS-Safe | AC-Safe | See Section 1.2.2.1 [POSIX Safety Concepts], page 2.

int semop (*int* **semid**, *struct sembuf* ***sops**, *size_t* **nsops**);                    [Function]
    Preliminary: | MT-Safe | AS-Safe | AC-Safe | See Section 1.2.2.1 [POSIX Safety Concepts], page 2.

int semtimedop (*int* **semid**, *struct sembuf* ***sops**, *size_t* **nsops**, *const*                    [Function]
        *struct timespec* ***timeout**);
    Preliminary: | MT-Safe | AS-Safe | AC-Safe | See Section 1.2.2.1 [POSIX Safety Concepts], page 2.

### 27.1.2 POSIX Semaphores

int sem_init (*sem_t* ***sem**, *int* **pshared**, *unsigned int* **value**);                    [Function]
    Preliminary: | MT-Safe | AS-Safe | AC-Unsafe corrupt | See Section 1.2.2.1 [POSIX Safety Concepts], page 2.

int sem_destroy (*sem_t* ***sem**);                    [Function]
    Preliminary: | MT-Safe | AS-Safe | AC-Safe | See Section 1.2.2.1 [POSIX Safety Concepts], page 2.

sem_t *sem_open (*const char* ***name**, *int* **oflag**, ...);                    [Function]
    Preliminary: | MT-Safe | AS-Unsafe init | AC-Unsafe init | See Section 1.2.2.1 [POSIX Safety Concepts], page 2.

int sem_close (*sem_t* ***sem**);                    [Function]
    Preliminary: | MT-Safe | AS-Unsafe lock | AC-Unsafe lock | See Section 1.2.2.1 [POSIX Safety Concepts], page 2.

int sem_unlink (*const char* ***name**);                    [Function]
    Preliminary: | MT-Safe | AS-Unsafe init | AC-Unsafe corrupt | See Section 1.2.2.1 [POSIX Safety Concepts], page 2.

int **sem_wait** (*sem_t* \***sem**);                                      [Function]
> Preliminary: | MT-Safe | AS-Safe | AC-Unsafe corrupt | See Section 1.2.2.1 [POSIX Safety Concepts], page 2.

int **sem_timedwait** (*sem_t* \***sem**, *const struct timespec* \***abstime**);        [Function]
> Preliminary: | MT-Safe | AS-Safe | AC-Unsafe corrupt | See Section 1.2.2.1 [POSIX Safety Concepts], page 2.

int **sem_trywait** (*sem_t* \***sem**);                                   [Function]
> Preliminary: | MT-Safe | AS-Safe | AC-Safe | See Section 1.2.2.1 [POSIX Safety Concepts], page 2.

int **sem_post** (*sem_t* \***sem**);                                      [Function]
> Preliminary: | MT-Safe | AS-Safe | AC-Safe | See Section 1.2.2.1 [POSIX Safety Concepts], page 2.

int **sem_getvalue** (*sem_t* \***sem**, *int* \***sval**);                [Function]
> Preliminary: | MT-Safe | AS-Safe | AC-Safe | See Section 1.2.2.1 [POSIX Safety Concepts], page 2.

# 28 Job Control

*Job control* refers to the protocol for allowing a user to move between multiple *process groups* (or *jobs*) within a single *login session*. The job control facilities are set up so that appropriate behavior for most programs happens automatically and they need not do anything special about job control. So you can probably ignore the material in this chapter unless you are writing a shell or login program.

You need to be familiar with concepts relating to process creation (see Section 26.2 [Process Creation Concepts], page 750) and signal handling (see Chapter 24 [Signal Handling], page 661) in order to understand this material presented in this chapter.

## 28.1 Concepts of Job Control

The fundamental purpose of an interactive shell is to read commands from the user's terminal and create processes to execute the programs specified by those commands. It can do this using the `fork` (see Section 26.4 [Creating a Process], page 751) and `exec` (see Section 26.5 [Executing a File], page 752) functions.

A single command may run just one process—but often one command uses several processes. If you use the '|' operator in a shell command, you explicitly request several programs in their own processes. But even if you run just one program, it can use multiple processes internally. For example, a single compilation command such as 'cc -c foo.c' typically uses four processes (though normally only two at any given time). If you run `make`, its job is to run other programs in separate processes.

The processes belonging to a single command are called a *process group* or *job*. This is so that you can operate on all of them at once. For example, typing *C-c* sends the signal `SIGINT` to terminate all the processes in the foreground process group.

A *session* is a larger group of processes. Normally all the processes that stem from a single login belong to the same session.

Every process belongs to a process group. When a process is created, it becomes a member of the same process group and session as its parent process. You can put it in another process group using the `setpgid` function, provided the process group belongs to the same session.

The only way to put a process in a different session is to make it the initial process of a new session, or a *session leader*, using the `setsid` function. This also puts the session leader into a new process group, and you can't move it out of that process group again.

Usually, new sessions are created by the system login program, and the session leader is the process running the user's login shell.

A shell that supports job control must arrange to control which job can use the terminal at any time. Otherwise there might be multiple jobs trying to read from the terminal at once, and confusion about which process should receive the input typed by the user. To prevent this, the shell must cooperate with the terminal driver using the protocol described in this chapter.

The shell can give unlimited access to the controlling terminal to only one process group at a time. This is called the *foreground job* on that controlling terminal. Other process groups managed by the shell that are executing without such access to the terminal are called *background jobs.*

If a background job needs to read from its controlling terminal, it is *stopped* by the terminal driver; if the TOSTOP mode is set, likewise for writing. The user can stop a foreground job by typing the SUSP character (see Section 17.4.9 [Special Characters], page 490) and a program can stop any job by sending it a SIGSTOP signal. It's the responsibility of the shell to notice when jobs stop, to notify the user about them, and to provide mechanisms for allowing the user to interactively continue stopped jobs and switch jobs between foreground and background.

See Section 28.4 [Access to the Controlling Terminal], page 764, for more information about I/O to the controlling terminal,

## 28.2 Job Control is Optional

Not all operating systems support job control. GNU systems do support job control, but if you are using the GNU C Library on some other system, that system may not support job control itself.

You can use the _POSIX_JOB_CONTROL macro to test at compile-time whether the system supports job control. See Section 32.2 [Overall System Options], page 839.

If job control is not supported, then there can be only one process group per session, which behaves as if it were always in the foreground. The functions for creating additional process groups simply fail with the error code ENOSYS.

The macros naming the various job control signals (see Section 24.2.5 [Job Control Signals], page 668) are defined even if job control is not supported. However, the system never generates these signals, and attempts to send a job control signal or examine or specify their actions report errors or do nothing.

## 28.3 Controlling Terminal of a Process

One of the attributes of a process is its controlling terminal. Child processes created with fork inherit the controlling terminal from their parent process. In this way, all the processes in a session inherit the controlling terminal from the session leader. A session leader that has control of a terminal is called the *controlling process* of that terminal.

You generally do not need to worry about the exact mechanism used to allocate a controlling terminal to a session, since it is done for you by the system when you log in.

An individual process disconnects from its controlling terminal when it calls setsid to become the leader of a new session. See Section 28.7.2 [Process Group Functions], page 778.

## 28.4 Access to the Controlling Terminal

Processes in the foreground job of a controlling terminal have unrestricted access to that terminal; background processes do not. This section describes in more detail what happens when a process in a background job tries to access its controlling terminal.

When a process in a background job tries to read from its controlling terminal, the process group is usually sent a SIGTTIN signal. This normally causes all of the processes in that group to stop (unless they handle the signal and don't stop themselves). However, if the reading process is ignoring or blocking this signal, then **read** fails with an **EIO** error instead.

Similarly, when a process in a background job tries to write to its controlling terminal, the default behavior is to send a **SIGTTOU** signal to the process group. However, the behavior is modified by the **TOSTOP** bit of the local modes flags (see Section 17.4.7 [Local Modes], page 486). If this bit is not set (which is the default), then writing to the controlling terminal is always permitted without sending a signal. Writing is also permitted if the **SIGTTOU** signal is being ignored or blocked by the writing process.

Most other terminal operations that a program can do are treated as reading or as writing. (The description of each operation should say which.)

For more information about the primitive **read** and **write** functions, see Section 13.2 [Input and Output Primitives], page 326.

## 28.5 Orphaned Process Groups

When a controlling process terminates, its terminal becomes free and a new session can be established on it. (In fact, another user could log in on the terminal.) This could cause a problem if any processes from the old session are still trying to use that terminal.

To prevent problems, process groups that continue running even after the session leader has terminated are marked as *orphaned process groups*.

When a process group becomes an orphan, its processes are sent a **SIGHUP** signal. Ordinarily, this causes the processes to terminate. However, if a program ignores this signal or establishes a handler for it (see Chapter 24 [Signal Handling], page 661), it can continue running as in the orphan process group even after its controlling process terminates; but it still cannot access the terminal any more.

## 28.6 Implementing a Job Control Shell

This section describes what a shell must do to implement job control, by presenting an extensive sample program to illustrate the concepts involved.

## 28.6.1 Data Structures for the Shell

All of the program examples included in this chapter are part of a simple shell program. This section presents data structures and utility functions which are used throughout the example.

The sample shell deals mainly with two data structures. The `job` type contains information about a job, which is a set of subprocesses linked together with pipes. The `process` type holds information about a single subprocess. Here are the relevant data structure declarations:

```c
/* A process is a single process.  */
typedef struct process
{
  struct process *next;       /* next process in pipeline */
  char **argv;                /* for exec */
  pid_t pid;                  /* process ID */
  char completed;             /* true if process has completed */
  char stopped;               /* true if process has stopped */
  int status;                 /* reported status value */
} process;

/* A job is a pipeline of processes.  */
typedef struct job
{
  struct job *next;           /* next active job */
  char *command;              /* command line, used for messages */
  process *first_process;     /* list of processes in this job */
  pid_t pgid;                 /* process group ID */
  char notified;              /* true if user told about stopped job */
  struct termios tmodes;      /* saved terminal modes */
  int stdin, stdout, stderr;  /* standard i/o channels */
} job;

/* The active jobs are linked into a list. This is its head.  */
job *first_job = NULL;
```

Here are some utility functions that are used for operating on `job` objects.

```c
/* Find the active job with the indicated pgid.  */
job *
find_job (pid_t pgid)
{
  job *j;

  for (j = first_job; j; j = j->next)
    if (j->pgid == pgid)
      return j;
  return NULL;
}
```

```
/* Return true if all processes in the job have stopped or completed.  */
int
job_is_stopped (job *j)
{
  process *p;

  for (p = j->first_process; p; p = p->next)
    if (!p->completed && !p->stopped)
      return 0;
  return 1;
}

/* Return true if all processes in the job have completed.  */
int
job_is_completed (job *j)
{
  process *p;

  for (p = j->first_process; p; p = p->next)
    if (!p->completed)
      return 0;
  return 1;
}
```

## 28.6.2 Initializing the Shell

When a shell program that normally performs job control is started, it has to be careful in case it has been invoked from another shell that is already doing its own job control.

A subshell that runs interactively has to ensure that it has been placed in the foreground by its parent shell before it can enable job control itself. It does this by getting its initial process group ID with the getpgrp function, and comparing it to the process group ID of the current foreground job associated with its controlling terminal (which can be retrieved using the tcgetpgrp function).

If the subshell is not running as a foreground job, it must stop itself by sending a SIGTTIN signal to its own process group. It may not arbitrarily put itself into the foreground; it must wait for the user to tell the parent shell to do this. If the subshell is continued again, it should repeat the check and stop itself again if it is still not in the foreground.

Once the subshell has been placed into the foreground by its parent shell, it can enable its own job control. It does this by calling setpgid to put itself into its own process group, and then calling tcsetpgrp to place this process group into the foreground.

When a shell enables job control, it should set itself to ignore all the job control stop signals so that it doesn't accidentally stop itself. You can do this by setting the action for all the stop signals to SIG_IGN.

A subshell that runs non-interactively cannot and should not support job control. It must leave all processes it creates in the same process group as the shell itself; this allows the non-interactive shell and its child processes to be treated as a single job by the parent shell. This is easy to do—just don't use any of the job control primitives—but you must remember to make the shell do it.

Here is the initialization code for the sample shell that shows how to do all of this.

```
/* Keep track of attributes of the shell.  */
```

```
#include <sys/types.h>
#include <termios.h>
#include <unistd.h>

pid_t shell_pgid;
struct termios shell_tmodes;
int shell_terminal;
int shell_is_interactive;


/* Make sure the shell is running interactively as the foreground job
   before proceeding. */

void
init_shell ()
{

  /* See if we are running interactively.  */
  shell_terminal = STDIN_FILENO;
  shell_is_interactive = isatty (shell_terminal);

  if (shell_is_interactive)
    {
      /* Loop until we are in the foreground.  */
      while (tcgetpgrp (shell_terminal) != (shell_pgid = getpgrp ()))
        kill (- shell_pgid, SIGTTIN);

      /* Ignore interactive and job-control signals.  */
      signal (SIGINT, SIG_IGN);
      signal (SIGQUIT, SIG_IGN);
      signal (SIGTSTP, SIG_IGN);
      signal (SIGTTIN, SIG_IGN);
      signal (SIGTTOU, SIG_IGN);
      signal (SIGCHLD, SIG_IGN);

      /* Put ourselves in our own process group.  */
      shell_pgid = getpid ();
      if (setpgid (shell_pgid, shell_pgid) < 0)
        {
          perror ("Couldn't put the shell in its own process group");
          exit (1);
        }

      /* Grab control of the terminal.  */
      tcsetpgrp (shell_terminal, shell_pgid);

      /* Save default terminal attributes for shell.  */
      tcgetattr (shell_terminal, &shell_tmodes);
    }
}
```

## 28.6.3 Launching Jobs

Once the shell has taken responsibility for performing job control on its controlling terminal, it can launch jobs in response to commands typed by the user.

To create the processes in a process group, you use the same **fork** and **exec** functions described in Section 26.2 [Process Creation Concepts], page 750. Since there are multiple child processes involved, though, things are a little more complicated and you must be careful to do things in the right order. Otherwise, nasty race conditions can result.

You have two choices for how to structure the tree of parent-child relationships among the processes. You can either make all the processes in the process group be children of the shell process, or you can make one process in group be the ancestor of all the other processes in that group. The sample shell program presented in this chapter uses the first approach because it makes bookkeeping somewhat simpler.

As each process is forked, it should put itself in the new process group by calling `setpgid`; see Section 28.7.2 [Process Group Functions], page 778. The first process in the new group becomes its *process group leader*, and its process ID becomes the *process group ID* for the group.

The shell should also call `setpgid` to put each of its child processes into the new process group. This is because there is a potential timing problem: each child process must be put in the process group before it begins executing a new program, and the shell depends on having all the child processes in the group before it continues executing. If both the child processes and the shell call `setpgid`, this ensures that the right things happen no matter which process gets to it first.

If the job is being launched as a foreground job, the new process group also needs to be put into the foreground on the controlling terminal using `tcsetpgrp`. Again, this should be done by the shell as well as by each of its child processes, to avoid race conditions.

The next thing each child process should do is to reset its signal actions.

During initialization, the shell process set itself to ignore job control signals; see Section 28.6.2 [Initializing the Shell], page 767. As a result, any child processes it creates also ignore these signals by inheritance. This is definitely undesirable, so each child process should explicitly set the actions for these signals back to `SIG_DFL` just after it is forked.

Since shells follow this convention, applications can assume that they inherit the correct handling of these signals from the parent process. But every application has a responsibility not to mess up the handling of stop signals. Applications that disable the normal interpretation of the SUSP character should provide some other mechanism for the user to stop the job. When the user invokes this mechanism, the program should send a `SIGTSTP` signal to the process group of the process, not just to the process itself. See Section 24.6.2 [Signaling Another Process], page 689.

Finally, each child process should call `exec` in the normal way. This is also the point at which redirection of the standard input and output channels should be handled. See Section 13.12 [Duplicating Descriptors], page 360, for an explanation of how to do this.

Here is the function from the sample shell program that is responsible for launching a program. The function is executed by each child process immediately after it has been forked by the shell, and never returns.

```
void
launch_process (process *p, pid_t pgid,
                int infile, int outfile, int errfile,
                int foreground)
{
  pid_t pid;

  if (shell_is_interactive)
```

```
      {
        /* Put the process into the process group and give the process group
           the terminal, if appropriate.
           This has to be done both by the shell and in the individual
           child processes because of potential race conditions.   */
        pid = getpid ();
        if (pgid == 0) pgid = pid;
        setpgid (pid, pgid);
        if (foreground)
          tcsetpgrp (shell_terminal, pgid);

        /* Set the handling for job control signals back to the default.   */
        signal (SIGINT, SIG_DFL);
        signal (SIGQUIT, SIG_DFL);
        signal (SIGTSTP, SIG_DFL);
        signal (SIGTTIN, SIG_DFL);
        signal (SIGTTOU, SIG_DFL);
        signal (SIGCHLD, SIG_DFL);
      }

  /* Set the standard input/output channels of the new process.   */
  if (infile != STDIN_FILENO)
    {
      dup2 (infile, STDIN_FILENO);
      close (infile);
    }
  if (outfile != STDOUT_FILENO)
    {
      dup2 (outfile, STDOUT_FILENO);
      close (outfile);
    }
  if (errfile != STDERR_FILENO)
    {
      dup2 (errfile, STDERR_FILENO);
      close (errfile);
    }

  /* Exec the new process.  Make sure we exit.   */
  execvp (p->argv[0], p->argv);
  perror ("execvp");
  exit (1);
}
```

If the shell is not running interactively, this function does not do anything with process groups or signals. Remember that a shell not performing job control must keep all of its subprocesses in the same process group as the shell itself.

Next, here is the function that actually launches a complete job. After creating the child processes, this function calls some other functions to put the newly created job into the foreground or background; these are discussed in Section 28.6.4 [Foreground and Background], page 772.

```
void
launch_job (job *j, int foreground)
{
  process *p;
  pid_t pid;
  int mypipe[2], infile, outfile;
```

```
          infile = j->stdin;
          for (p = j->first_process; p; p = p->next)
            {
              /* Set up pipes, if necessary.  */
              if (p->next)
                {
                  if (pipe (mypipe) < 0)
                    {
                      perror ("pipe");
                      exit (1);
                    }
                  outfile = mypipe[1];
                }
              else
                outfile = j->stdout;

              /* Fork the child processes.  */
              pid = fork ();
              if (pid == 0)
                /* This is the child process.  */
                launch_process (p, j->pgid, infile,
                                outfile, j->stderr, foreground);
              else if (pid < 0)
                {
                  /* The fork failed.  */
                  perror ("fork");
                  exit (1);
                }
              else
                {
                  /* This is the parent process.  */
                  p->pid = pid;
                  if (shell_is_interactive)
                    {
                      if (!j->pgid)
                        j->pgid = pid;
                      setpgid (pid, j->pgid);
                    }
                }

              /* Clean up after pipes.  */
              if (infile != j->stdin)
                close (infile);
              if (outfile != j->stdout)
                close (outfile);
              infile = mypipe[0];
            }

          format_job_info (j, "launched");

          if (!shell_is_interactive)
            wait_for_job (j);
          else if (foreground)
            put_job_in_foreground (j, 0);
          else
            put_job_in_background (j, 0);
        }
```

## 28.6.4 Foreground and Background

Now let's consider what actions must be taken by the shell when it launches a job into the foreground, and how this differs from what must be done when a background job is launched.

When a foreground job is launched, the shell must first give it access to the controlling terminal by calling `tcsetpgrp`. Then, the shell should wait for processes in that process group to terminate or stop. This is discussed in more detail in Section 28.6.5 [Stopped and Terminated Jobs], page 773.

When all of the processes in the group have either completed or stopped, the shell should regain control of the terminal for its own process group by calling `tcsetpgrp` again. Since stop signals caused by I/O from a background process or a SUSP character typed by the user are sent to the process group, normally all the processes in the job stop together.

The foreground job may have left the terminal in a strange state, so the shell should restore its own saved terminal modes before continuing. In case the job is merely stopped, the shell should first save the current terminal modes so that it can restore them later if the job is continued. The functions for dealing with terminal modes are `tcgetattr` and `tcsetattr`; these are described in Section 17.4 [Terminal Modes], page 479.

Here is the sample shell's function for doing all of this.

```
/* Put job j in the foreground.  If cont is nonzero,
   restore the saved terminal modes and send the process group a
   SIGCONT signal to wake it up before we block.  */

void
put_job_in_foreground (job *j, int cont)
{
  /* Put the job into the foreground.  */
  tcsetpgrp (shell_terminal, j->pgid);

  /* Send the job a continue signal, if necessary.  */
  if (cont)
    {
      tcsetattr (shell_terminal, TCSADRAIN, &j->tmodes);
      if (kill (- j->pgid, SIGCONT) < 0)
        perror ("kill (SIGCONT)");
    }

  /* Wait for it to report.  */
  wait_for_job (j);

  /* Put the shell back in the foreground.  */
  tcsetpgrp (shell_terminal, shell_pgid);

  /* Restore the shell's terminal modes.  */
  tcgetattr (shell_terminal, &j->tmodes);
  tcsetattr (shell_terminal, TCSADRAIN, &shell_tmodes);
}
```

If the process group is launched as a background job, the shell should remain in the foreground itself and continue to read commands from the terminal.

In the sample shell, there is not much that needs to be done to put a job into the background. Here is the function it uses:

```
/* Put a job in the background.  If the cont argument is true, send
   the process group a SIGCONT signal to wake it up.   */

void
put_job_in_background (job *j, int cont)
{
  /* Send the job a continue signal, if necessary.   */
  if (cont)
    if (kill (-j->pgid, SIGCONT) < 0)
      perror ("kill (SIGCONT)");
}
```

## 28.6.5 Stopped and Terminated Jobs

When a foreground process is launched, the shell must block until all of the processes in that job have either terminated or stopped. It can do this by calling the `waitpid` function; see Section 26.6 [Process Completion], page 755. Use the `WUNTRACED` option so that status is reported for processes that stop as well as processes that terminate.

The shell must also check on the status of background jobs so that it can report terminated and stopped jobs to the user; this can be done by calling `waitpid` with the `WNOHANG` option. A good place to put a such a check for terminated and stopped jobs is just before prompting for a new command.

The shell can also receive asynchronous notification that there is status information available for a child process by establishing a handler for `SIGCHLD` signals. See Chapter 24 [Signal Handling], page 661.

In the sample shell program, the `SIGCHLD` signal is normally ignored. This is to avoid reentrancy problems involving the global data structures the shell manipulates. But at specific times when the shell is not using these data structures—such as when it is waiting for input on the terminal—it makes sense to enable a handler for `SIGCHLD`. The same function that is used to do the synchronous status checks (`do_job_notification`, in this case) can also be called from within this handler.

Here are the parts of the sample shell program that deal with checking the status of jobs and reporting the information to the user.

```
/* Store the status of the process pid that was returned by waitpid.
   Return 0 if all went well, nonzero otherwise.   */

int
mark_process_status (pid_t pid, int status)
{
  job *j;
  process *p;
```

```
    if (pid > 0)
      {
        /* Update the record for the process.  */
        for (j = first_job; j; j = j->next)
          for (p = j->first_process; p; p = p->next)
            if (p->pid == pid)
              {
                p->status = status;
                if (WIFSTOPPED (status))
                  p->stopped = 1;
                else
                  {
                    p->completed = 1;
                    if (WIFSIGNALED (status))
                      fprintf (stderr, "%d: Terminated by signal %d.\n",
                               (int) pid, WTERMSIG (p->status));
                  }
                return 0;
              }
        fprintf (stderr, "No child process %d.\n", pid);
        return -1;
      }
    else if (pid == 0 || errno == ECHILD)
      /* No processes ready to report.  */
      return -1;
    else {
      /* Other weird errors.  */
      perror ("waitpid");
      return -1;
    }
}

/* Check for processes that have status information available,
   without blocking.  */

void
update_status (void)
{
  int status;
  pid_t pid;

  do
    pid = waitpid (WAIT_ANY, &status, WUNTRACED|WNOHANG);
  while (!mark_process_status (pid, status));
}
```

```
/* Check for processes that have status information available,
     blocking until all processes in the given job have reported.   */

void
wait_for_job (job *j)
{
  int status;
  pid_t pid;

  do
    pid = waitpid (WAIT_ANY, &status, WUNTRACED);
  while (!mark_process_status (pid, status)
         && !job_is_stopped (j)
         && !job_is_completed (j));
}

/* Format information about job status for the user to look at.   */

void
format_job_info (job *j, const char *status)
{
  fprintf (stderr, "%ld (%s): %s\n", (long)j->pgid, status, j->command);
}
```

```
/* Notify the user about stopped or terminated jobs.
   Delete terminated jobs from the active job list.  */

void
do_job_notification (void)
{
  job *j, *jlast, *jnext;
  process *p;

  /* Update status information for child processes.  */
  update_status ();

  jlast = NULL;
  for (j = first_job; j; j = jnext)
    {
      jnext = j->next;

      /* If all processes have completed, tell the user the job has
         completed and delete it from the list of active jobs.  */
      if (job_is_completed (j)) {
        format_job_info (j, "completed");
        if (jlast)
          jlast->next = jnext;
        else
          first_job = jnext;
        free_job (j);
      }

      /* Notify the user about stopped jobs,
         marking them so that we won't do this more than once.  */
      else if (job_is_stopped (j) && !j->notified) {
        format_job_info (j, "stopped");
        j->notified = 1;
        jlast = j;
      }

      /* Don't say anything about jobs that are still running.  */
      else
        jlast = j;
    }
}
```

## 28.6.6 Continuing Stopped Jobs

The shell can continue a stopped job by sending a SIGCONT signal to its process group. If the job is being continued in the foreground, the shell should first invoke tcsetpgrp to give the job access to the terminal, and restore the saved terminal settings. After continuing a job in the foreground, the shell should wait for the job to stop or complete, as if the job had just been launched in the foreground.

The sample shell program handles both newly created and continued jobs with the same pair of functions, put_job_in_foreground and put_job_in_background. The definitions of these functions were given in Section 28.6.4 [Foreground and Background], page 772. When continuing a stopped job, a nonzero value is passed as the *cont* argument to ensure that the SIGCONT signal is sent and the terminal modes reset, as appropriate.

This leaves only a function for updating the shell's internal bookkeeping about the job being continued:

```
/* Mark a stopped job J as being running again.  */

void
mark_job_as_running (job *j)
{
  Process *p;

  for (p = j->first_process; p; p = p->next)
    p->stopped = 0;
  j->notified = 0;
}

/* Continue the job J.  */

void
continue_job (job *j, int foreground)
{
  mark_job_as_running (j);
  if (foreground)
    put_job_in_foreground (j, 1);
  else
    put_job_in_background (j, 1);
}
```

## 28.6.7 The Missing Pieces

The code extracts for the sample shell included in this chapter are only a part of the entire shell program. In particular, nothing at all has been said about how job and program data structures are allocated and initialized.

Most real shells provide a complex user interface that has support for a command language; variables; abbreviations, substitutions, and pattern matching on file names; and the like. All of this is far too complicated to explain here! Instead, we have concentrated on showing how to implement the core process creation and job control functions that can be called from such a shell.

Here is a table summarizing the major entry points we have presented:

void init_shell (void)
> Initialize the shell's internal state. See Section 28.6.2 [Initializing the Shell], page 767.

void launch_job (job *j, int *foreground*)
> Launch the job j as either a foreground or background job. See Section 28.6.3 [Launching Jobs], page 768.

void do_job_notification (void)
> Check for and report any jobs that have terminated or stopped. Can be called synchronously or within a handler for SIGCHLD signals. See Section 28.6.5 [Stopped and Terminated Jobs], page 773.

void continue_job (job *j, int *foreground*)
> Continue the job j. See Section 28.6.6 [Continuing Stopped Jobs], page 776.

Of course, a real shell would also want to provide other functions for managing jobs. For example, it would be useful to have commands to list all active jobs or to send a signal (such as SIGKILL) to a job.

## 28.7 Functions for Job Control

This section contains detailed descriptions of the functions relating to job control.

### 28.7.1 Identifying the Controlling Terminal

You can use the ctermid function to get a file name that you can use to open the controlling terminal. In the GNU C Library, it returns the same string all the time: "/dev/tty". That is a special "magic" file name that refers to the controlling terminal of the current process (if it has one). To find the name of the specific terminal device, use ttyname; see Section 17.1 [Identifying Terminals], page 477.

The function ctermid is declared in the header file stdio.h.

char * ctermid (char *string)                                              [Function]
    Preliminary: | MT-Safe !posix/!string | AS-Safe | AC-Safe | See Section 1.2.2.1 [POSIX Safety Concepts], page 2.

    The ctermid function returns a string containing the file name of the controlling terminal for the current process. If string is not a null pointer, it should be an array that can hold at least L_ctermid characters; the string is returned in this array. Otherwise, a pointer to a string in a static area is returned, which might get overwritten on subsequent calls to this function.

    An empty string is returned if the file name cannot be determined for any reason. Even if a file name is returned, access to the file it represents is not guaranteed.

int L_ctermid                                                              [Macro]
    The value of this macro is an integer constant expression that represents the size of a string large enough to hold the file name returned by ctermid.

See also the isatty and ttyname functions, in Section 17.1 [Identifying Terminals], page 477.

### 28.7.2 Process Group Functions

Here are descriptions of the functions for manipulating process groups. Your program should include the header files sys/types.h and unistd.h to use these functions.

pid_t setsid (void)                                                        [Function]
    Preliminary: | MT-Safe | AS-Safe | AC-Safe | See Section 1.2.2.1 [POSIX Safety Concepts], page 2.

    The setsid function creates a new session. The calling process becomes the session leader, and is put in a new process group whose process group ID is the same as the process ID of that process. There are initially no other processes in the new process group, and no other process groups in the new session.

    This function also makes the calling process have no controlling terminal.

The `setsid` function returns the new process group ID of the calling process if successful. A return value of -1 indicates an error. The following `errno` error conditions are defined for this function:

EPERM          The calling process is already a process group leader, or there is already another process group around that has the same process group ID.

pid_t getsid (*pid_t* `pid`)                                                          [Function]
    Preliminary: | MT-Safe | AS-Safe | AC-Safe | See Section 1.2.2.1 [POSIX Safety Concepts], page 2.

    The `getsid` function returns the process group ID of the session leader of the specified process. If a *pid* is 0, the process group ID of the session leader of the current process is returned.

    In case of error -1 is returned and `errno` is set. The following `errno` error conditions are defined for this function:

    ESRCH          There is no process with the given process ID *pid*.

    EPERM          The calling process and the process specified by *pid* are in different sessions, and the implementation doesn't allow to access the process group ID of the session leader of the process with ID *pid* from the calling process.

pid_t getpgrp (*void*)                                                               [Function]
    Preliminary: | MT-Safe | AS-Safe | AC-Safe | See Section 1.2.2.1 [POSIX Safety Concepts], page 2.

    The `getpgrp` function returns the process group ID of the calling process.

int getpgid (*pid_t* `pid`)                                                          [Function]
    Preliminary: | MT-Safe | AS-Safe | AC-Safe | See Section 1.2.2.1 [POSIX Safety Concepts], page 2.

    The `getpgid` function returns the process group ID of the process *pid*. You can supply a value of 0 for the *pid* argument to get information about the calling process.

    In case of error -1 is returned and `errno` is set. The following `errno` error conditions are defined for this function:

    ESRCH          There is no process with the given process ID *pid*. The calling process and the process specified by *pid* are in different sessions, and the implementation doesn't allow to access the process group ID of the process with ID *pid* from the calling process.

int setpgid (*pid_t* `pid`, *pid_t* `pgid`)                                          [Function]
    Preliminary: | MT-Safe | AS-Safe | AC-Safe | See Section 1.2.2.1 [POSIX Safety Concepts], page 2.

    The `setpgid` function puts the process *pid* into the process group *pgid*. As a special case, either *pid* or *pgid* can be zero to indicate the process ID of the calling process.

    This function fails on a system that does not support job control. See Section 28.2 [Job Control is Optional], page 764, for more information.

    If the operation is successful, `setpgid` returns zero. Otherwise it returns -1. The following `errno` error conditions are defined for this function:

EACCES     The child process named by *pid* has executed an **exec** function since it was forked.

EINVAL     The value of the *pgid* is not valid.

ENOSYS     The system doesn't support job control.

EPERM      The process indicated by the *pid* argument is a session leader, or is not in the same session as the calling process, or the value of the *pgid* argument doesn't match a process group ID in the same session as the calling process.

ESRCH      The process indicated by the *pid* argument is not the calling process or a child of the calling process.

**int setpgrp** (*pid_t* **pid**, *pid_t* **pgid**)                                    [Function]
   Preliminary: | MT-Safe | AS-Safe | AC-Safe | See Section 1.2.2.1 [POSIX Safety Concepts], page 2.

   This is the BSD Unix name for **setpgid**. Both functions do exactly the same thing.

## 28.7.3 Functions for Controlling Terminal Access

These are the functions for reading or setting the foreground process group of a terminal. You should include the header files **sys/types.h** and **unistd.h** in your application to use these functions.

Although these functions take a file descriptor argument to specify the terminal device, the foreground job is associated with the terminal file itself and not a particular open file descriptor.

**pid_t tcgetpgrp** (*int* **filedes**)                                             [Function]
   Preliminary: | MT-Safe | AS-Safe | AC-Safe | See Section 1.2.2.1 [POSIX Safety Concepts], page 2.

   This function returns the process group ID of the foreground process group associated with the terminal open on descriptor *filedes*.

   If there is no foreground process group, the return value is a number greater than 1 that does not match the process group ID of any existing process group. This can happen if all of the processes in the job that was formerly the foreground job have terminated, and no other job has yet been moved into the foreground.

   In case of an error, a value of -1 is returned. The following **errno** error conditions are defined for this function:

   EBADF      The *filedes* argument is not a valid file descriptor.

   ENOSYS     The system doesn't support job control.

   ENOTTY     The terminal file associated with the *filedes* argument isn't the controlling terminal of the calling process.

**int tcsetpgrp** (*int* **filedes**, *pid_t* **pgid**)                              [Function]
   Preliminary: | MT-Safe | AS-Safe | AC-Safe | See Section 1.2.2.1 [POSIX Safety Concepts], page 2.

This function is used to set a terminal's foreground process group ID. The argument *filedes* is a descriptor which specifies the terminal; *pgid* specifies the process group. The calling process must be a member of the same session as *pgid* and must have the same controlling terminal.

For terminal access purposes, this function is treated as output. If it is called from a background process on its controlling terminal, normally all processes in the process group are sent a `SIGTTOU` signal. The exception is if the calling process itself is ignoring or blocking `SIGTTOU` signals, in which case the operation is performed and no signal is sent.

If successful, `tcsetpgrp` returns 0. A return value of `-1` indicates an error. The following `errno` error conditions are defined for this function:

EBADF       The *filedes* argument is not a valid file descriptor.

EINVAL      The *pgid* argument is not valid.

ENOSYS      The system doesn't support job control.

ENOTTY      The *filedes* isn't the controlling terminal of the calling process.

EPERM       The *pgid* isn't a process group in the same session as the calling process.

**pid_t tcgetsid (*int filedes*)** [Function]
Preliminary: | MT-Safe | AS-Safe | AC-Safe | See Section 1.2.2.1 [POSIX Safety Concepts], page 2.

This function is used to obtain the process group ID of the session for which the terminal specified by *fildes* is the controlling terminal. If the call is successful the group ID is returned. Otherwise the return value is (`pid_t`) `-1` and the global variable *errno* is set to the following value:

EBADF       The *filedes* argument is not a valid file descriptor.

ENOTTY      The calling process does not have a controlling terminal, or the file is not the controlling terminal.

# 29 System Databases and Name Service Switch

Various functions in the C Library need to be configured to work correctly in the local environment. Traditionally, this was done by using files (e.g., /etc/passwd), but other nameservices (like the Network Information Service (NIS) and the Domain Name Service (DNS)) became popular, and were hacked into the C library, usually with a fixed search order.

The GNU C Library contains a cleaner solution of this problem. It is designed after a method used by Sun Microsystems in the C library of Solaris 2. The GNU C Library follows their name and calls this scheme *Name Service Switch* (NSS).

Though the interface might be similar to Sun's version there is no common code. We never saw any source code of Sun's implementation and so the internal interface is incompatible. This also manifests in the file names we use as we will see later.

## 29.1 NSS Basics

The basic idea is to put the implementation of the different services offered to access the databases in separate modules. This has some advantages:

1. Contributors can add new services without adding them to the GNU C Library.
2. The modules can be updated separately.
3. The C library image is smaller.

To fulfill the first goal above the ABI of the modules will be described below. For getting the implementation of a new service right it is important to understand how the functions in the modules get called. They are in no way designed to be used by the programmer directly. Instead the programmer should only use the documented and standardized functions to access the databases.

The databases available in the NSS are

aliases     Mail aliases

ethers      Ethernet numbers,

group       Groups of users, see Section 30.14 [Group Database], page 814.

hosts       Host names and numbers, see Section 16.6.2.4 [Host Names], page 443.

netgroup    Network wide list of host and users, see Section 30.16 [Netgroup Database], page 818.

networks    Network names and numbers, see Section 16.13 [Networks Database], page 475.

protocols
            Network protocols, see Section 16.6.6 [Protocols Database], page 450.

passwd      User passwords, see Section 30.13 [User Database], page 810.

rpc         Remote procedure call names and numbers,

services    Network services, see Section 16.6.4 [The Services Database], page 448.

shadow      Shadow user passwords,

There will be some more added later (automount, bootparams, netmasks, and publickey).

## 29.2 The NSS Configuration File

Somehow the NSS code must be told about the wishes of the user. For this reason there is the file /etc/nsswitch.conf. For each database this file contain a specification how the lookup process should work. The file could look like this:

```
# /etc/nsswitch.conf
#
# Name Service Switch configuration file.
#

passwd:     db files nis
shadow:     files
group:      db files nis

hosts:      files nisplus nis dns
networks:   nisplus [NOTFOUND=return] files

ethers:     nisplus [NOTFOUND=return] db files
protocols:  nisplus [NOTFOUND=return] db files
rpc:        nisplus [NOTFOUND=return] db files
services:   nisplus [NOTFOUND=return] db files
```

The first column is the database as you can guess from the table above. The rest of the line specifies how the lookup process works. Please note that you specify the way it works for each database individually. This cannot be done with the old way of a monolithic implementation.

The configuration specification for each database can contain two different items:

- the service specification like files, db, or nis.

- the reaction on lookup result like [NOTFOUND=return].

### 29.2.1 Services in the NSS configuration File

The above example file mentions five different services: files, db, dns, nis, and nisplus. This does not mean these services are available on all sites and it does also not mean these are all the services which will ever be available.

In fact, these names are simply strings which the NSS code uses to find the implicitly addressed functions. The internal interface will be described later. Visible to the user are the modules which implement an individual service.

Assume the service *name* shall be used for a lookup. The code for this service is implemented in a module called libnss_*name*. On a system supporting shared libraries this is in fact a shared library with the name (for example) libnss_*name*.so.2. The number at the end is the currently used version of the interface which will not change frequently. Normally the user should not have to be cognizant of these files since they should be placed in a directory where they are found automatically. Only the names of all available services are important.

## 29.2.2 Actions in the NSS configuration

The second item in the specification gives the user much finer control on the lookup process. Action items are placed between two service names and are written within brackets. The general form is

        [ ( !? *status* = *action* )+ ]

where

        *status* ⇒ success | notfound | unavail | tryagain
        *action* ⇒ return | continue

The case of the keywords is insignificant. The *status* values are the results of a call to a lookup function of a specific service. They mean

'success'       No error occurred and the wanted entry is returned. The default action for this is **return**.

'notfound'

                The lookup process works ok but the needed value was not found. The default action is **continue**.

'unavail'       The service is permanently unavailable. This can either mean the needed file is not available, or, for DNS, the server is not available or does not allow queries. The default action is **continue**.

'tryagain'

                The service is temporarily unavailable. This could mean a file is locked or a server currently cannot accept more connections. The default action is **continue**.

If we have a line like

        ethers: nisplus [NOTFOUND=return] db files

this is equivalent to

        ethers: nisplus [SUCCESS=return NOTFOUND=return UNAVAIL=continue
                         TRYAGAIN=continue]
                db      [SUCCESS=return NOTFOUND=continue UNAVAIL=continue
                         TRYAGAIN=continue]
                files

(except that it would have to be written on one line). The default value for the actions are normally what you want, and only need to be changed in exceptional cases.

If the optional ! is placed before the *status* this means the following action is used for all statuses but *status* itself. I.e., ! is negation as in the C language (and others).

Before we explain the exception which makes this action item necessary one more remark: obviously it makes no sense to add another action item after the **files** service. Since there is no other service following the action *always* is **return**.

Now, why is this [NOTFOUND=return] action useful? To understand this we should know that the **nisplus** service is often complete; i.e., if an entry is not available in the NIS+ tables it is not available anywhere else. This is what is expressed by this action item: it is useless to examine further services since they will not give us a result.

The situation would be different if the NIS+ service is not available because the machine is booting. In this case the return value of the lookup function is not **notfound** but instead unavail. And as you can see in the complete form above: in this situation the db and files services are used. Neat, isn't it? The system administrator need not pay special care for the time the system is not completely ready to work (while booting or shutdown or network problems).

### 29.2.3 Notes on the NSS Configuration File

Finally a few more hints. The NSS implementation is not completely helpless if /etc/nsswitch.conf does not exist. For all supported databases there is a default value so it should normally be possible to get the system running even if the file is corrupted or missing.

For the hosts and networks databases the default value is dns [!UNAVAIL=return] files. I.e., the system is prepared for the DNS service not to be available but if it is available the answer it returns is definitive.

The passwd, group, and shadow databases are traditionally handled in a special way. The appropriate files in the /etc directory are read but if an entry with a name starting with a + character is found NIS is used. This kind of lookup remains possible by using the special lookup service compat and the default value for the three databases above is compat [NOTFOUND=return] files.

For all other databases the default value is nis [NOTFOUND=return] files. This solution give the best chance to be correct since NIS and file based lookup is used.

A second point is that the user should try to optimize the lookup process. The different service have different response times. A simple file look up on a local file could be fast, but if the file is long and the needed entry is near the end of the file this may take quite some time. In this case it might be better to use the db service which allows fast local access to large data sets.

Often the situation is that some global information like NIS must be used. So it is unavoidable to use service entries like nis etc. But one should avoid slow services like this if possible.

## 29.3 NSS Module Internals

Now it is time to describe what the modules look like. The functions contained in a module are identified by their names. I.e., there is no jump table or the like. How this is done is of no interest here; those interested in this topic should read about Dynamic Linking.

### 29.3.1 The Naming Scheme of the NSS Modules

The name of each function consist of various parts:

  _nss_*service*_*function*

*service* of course corresponds to the name of the module this function is found in.[1] The *function* part is derived from the interface function in the C library itself. If the user calls the function gethostbyname and the service used is files the function

        _nss_files_gethostbyname_r

in the module

---

[1] Now you might ask why this information is duplicated. The answer is that we want to make it possible to link directly with these shared objects.

```
libnss_files.so.2
```

is used. You see, what is explained above in not the whole truth. In fact the NSS modules only contain reentrant versions of the lookup functions. I.e., if the user would call the `gethostbyname_r` function this also would end in the above function. For all user interface functions the C library maps this call to a call to the reentrant function. For reentrant functions this is trivial since the interface is (nearly) the same. For the non-reentrant version The library keeps internal buffers which are used to replace the user supplied buffer.

I.e., the reentrant functions *can* have counterparts. No service module is forced to have functions for all databases and all kinds to access them. If a function is not available it is simply treated as if the function would return `unavail` (see Section 29.2.2 [Actions in the NSS configuration], page 784).

The file name `libnss_files.so.2` would be on a Solaris 2 system `nss_files.so.2`. This is the difference mentioned above. Sun's NSS modules are usable as modules which get indirectly loaded only.

The NSS modules in the GNU C Library are prepared to be used as normal libraries themselves. This is *not* true at the moment, though. However, the organization of the name space in the modules does not make it impossible like it is for Solaris. Now you can see why the modules are still libraries.[2]

## 29.3.2 The Interface of the Function in NSS Modules

Now we know about the functions contained in the modules. It is now time to describe the types. When we mentioned the reentrant versions of the functions above, this means there are some additional arguments (compared with the standard, non-reentrant version). The prototypes for the non-reentrant and reentrant versions of our function above are:

```
struct hostent *gethostbyname (const char *name)

int gethostbyname_r (const char *name, struct hostent *result_buf,
                     char *buf, size_t buflen, struct hostent **result,
                     int *h_errnop)
```

The actual prototype of the function in the NSS modules in this case is

```
enum nss_status _nss_files_gethostbyname_r (const char *name,
                                            struct hostent *result_buf,
                                            char *buf, size_t buflen,
                                            int *errnop, int *h_errnop)
```

I.e., the interface function is in fact the reentrant function with the change of the return value and the omission of the *result* parameter. While the user-level function returns a pointer to the result the reentrant function return an `enum nss_status` value:

`NSS_STATUS_TRYAGAIN`
> numeric value -2

`NSS_STATUS_UNAVAIL`
> numeric value -1

`NSS_STATUS_NOTFOUND`
> numeric value 0

---

[2] There is a second explanation: we were too lazy to change the Makefiles to allow the generation of shared objects not starting with `lib` but don't tell this to anybody.

`NSS_STATUS_SUCCESS`
> numeric value 1

Now you see where the action items of the `/etc/nsswitch.conf` file are used.

If you study the source code you will find there is a fifth value: `NSS_STATUS_RETURN`. This is an internal use only value, used by a few functions in places where none of the above value can be used. If necessary the source code should be examined to learn about the details.

In case the interface function has to return an error it is important that the correct error code is stored in *errnop*. Some return status value have only one associated error code, others have more.

| `NSS_STATUS_TRYAGAIN` | `EAGAIN` | One of the functions used ran temporarily out of resources or a service is currently not available. |
| | `ERANGE` | The provided buffer is not large enough. The function should be called again with a larger buffer. |
| `NSS_STATUS_UNAVAIL` | `ENOENT` | A necessary input file cannot be found. |
| `NSS_STATUS_NOTFOUND` | `ENOENT` | The requested entry is not available. |

These are proposed values. There can be other error codes and the described error codes can have different meaning. **With one exception:** when returning `NSS_STATUS_TRYAGAIN` the error code `ERANGE` *must* mean that the user provided buffer is too small. Everything is non-critical.

The above function has something special which is missing for almost all the other module functions. There is an argument *h_errnop*. This points to a variable which will be filled with the error code in case the execution of the function fails for some reason. The reentrant function cannot use the global variable *h_errno*; `gethostbyname` calls `gethostbyname_r` with the last argument set to `&h_errno`.

The get*XXX*by*YYY* functions are the most important functions in the NSS modules. But there are others which implement the other ways to access system databases (say for the password database, there are `setpwent`, `getpwent`, and `endpwent`). These will be described in more detail later. Here we give a general way to determine the signature of the module function:

- the return value is `int`;
- the name is as explained in see Section 29.3.1 [The Naming Scheme of the NSS Modules], page 785;
- the first arguments are identical to the arguments of the non-reentrant function;
- the next three arguments are:

`STRUCT_TYPE *result_buf`
> pointer to buffer where the result is stored. `STRUCT_TYPE` is normally a struct which corresponds to the database.

`char *buffer`
> pointer to a buffer where the function can store additional data for the result etc.

```
size_t buflen
```
> length of the buffer pointed to by *buffer*.

- possibly a last argument *h_errnop*, for the host name and network name lookup functions.

This table is correct for all functions but the `set...ent` and `end...ent` functions.

## 29.4 Extending NSS

One of the advantages of NSS mentioned above is that it can be extended quite easily. There are two ways in which the extension can happen: adding another database or adding another service. The former is normally done only by the C library developers. It is here only important to remember that adding another database is independent from adding another service because a service need not support all databases or lookup functions.

A designer/implementor of a new service is therefore free to choose the databases s/he is interested in and leave the rest for later (or completely aside).

### 29.4.1 Adding another Service to NSS

The sources for a new service need not (and should not) be part of the GNU C Library itself. The developer retains complete control over the sources and its development. The links between the C library and the new service module consists solely of the interface functions.

Each module is designed following a specific interface specification. For now the version is 2 (the interface in version 1 was not adequate) and this manifests in the version number of the shared library object of the NSS modules: they have the extension `.2`. If the interface changes again in an incompatible way, this number will be increased. Modules using the old interface will still be usable.

Developers of a new service will have to make sure that their module is created using the correct interface number. This means the file itself must have the correct name and on ELF systems the *soname* (Shared Object Name) must also have this number. Building a module from a bunch of object files on an ELF system using GNU CC could be done like this:

```
gcc -shared -o libnss_NAME.so.2 -Wl,-soname,libnss_NAME.so.2 OBJECTS
```

Section "Link Options" in *GNU CC*, to learn more about this command line.

To use the new module the library must be able to find it. This can be achieved by using options for the dynamic linker so that it will search the directory where the binary is placed. For an ELF system this could be done by adding the wanted directory to the value of `LD_LIBRARY_PATH`.

But this is not always possible since some programs (those which run under IDs which do not belong to the user) ignore this variable. Therefore the stable version of the module should be placed into a directory which is searched by the dynamic linker. Normally this should be the directory `$prefix/lib`, where `$prefix` corresponds to the value given to configure using the `--prefix` option. But be careful: this should only be done if it is clear the module does not cause any harm. System administrators should be careful.

## 29.4.2 Internals of the NSS Module Functions

Until now we only provided the syntactic interface for the functions in the NSS module. In fact there is not much more we can say since the implementation obviously is different for each function. But a few general rules must be followed by all functions.

In fact there are four kinds of different functions which may appear in the interface. All derive from the traditional ones for system databases. *db* in the following table is normally an abbreviation for the database (e.g., it is `pw` for the password database).

enum nss_status _nss_*database*_setd*b*ent (void)
> This function prepares the service for following operations. For a simple file based lookup this means files could be opened, for other services this function simply is a noop.
>
> One special case for this function is that it takes an additional argument for some *databases* (i.e., the interface is `int setdbent (int)`). Section 16.6.2.4 [Host Names], page 443, which describes the `sethostent` function.
>
> The return value should be *NSS_STATUS_SUCCESS* or according to the table above in case of an error (see Section 29.3.2 [The Interface of the Function in NSS Modules], page 786).

enum nss_status _nss_*database*_endd*b*ent (void)
> This function simply closes all files which are still open or removes buffer caches. If there are no files or buffers to remove this is again a simple noop.
>
> There normally is no return value different to *NSS_STATUS_SUCCESS*.

enum nss_status _nss_*database*_getd*b*ent_r (*STRUCTURE* *result, char *buffer, size_t buflen, int *errnop)
> Since this function will be called several times in a row to retrieve one entry after the other it must keep some kind of state. But this also means the functions are not really reentrant. They are reentrant only in that simultaneous calls to this function will not try to write the retrieved data in the same place (as it would be the case for the non-reentrant functions); instead, it writes to the structure pointed to by the *result* parameter. But the calls share a common state and in the case of a file access this means they return neighboring entries in the file.
>
> The buffer of length *buflen* pointed to by *buffer* can be used for storing some additional data for the result. It is *not* guaranteed that the same buffer will be passed for the next call of this function. Therefore one must not misuse this buffer to save some state information from one call to another.
>
> Before the function returns the implementation should store the value of the local *errno* variable in the variable pointed to be *errnop*. This is important to guarantee the module working in statically linked programs.
>
> As explained above this function could also have an additional last argument. This depends on the database used; it happens only for `host` and `networks`.
>
> The function shall return `NSS_STATUS_SUCCESS` as long as there are more entries. When the last entry was read it should return `NSS_STATUS_NOTFOUND`. When the buffer given as an argument is too small for the data to be returned `NSS_STATUS_TRYAGAIN` should be returned. When the service was not formerly

initialized by a call to _nss_*DATABASE*_setdbent all return value allowed for this function can also be returned here.

enum nss_status _nss_*DATABASE*_getdbby*XX*_r (*PARAMS*, *STRUCTURE* *result, char *buffer, size_t buflen, int *errnop)

This function shall return the entry from the database which is addressed by the *PARAMS*. The type and number of these arguments vary. It must be individually determined by looking to the user-level interface functions. All arguments given to the non-reentrant version are here described by *PARAMS*.

The result must be stored in the structure pointed to by *result*. If there is additional data to return (say strings, where the *result* structure only contains pointers) the function must use the *buffer* or length *buflen*. There must not be any references to non-constant global data.

The implementation of this function should honor the *stayopen* flag set by the set*DB*ent function whenever this makes sense.

Before the function returns the implementation should store the value of the local *errno* variable in the variable pointed to be *errnop*. This is important to guarantee the module working in statically linked programs.

Again, this function takes an additional last argument for the host and networks database.

The return value should as always follow the rules given above (see Section 29.3.2 [The Interface of the Function in NSS Modules], page 786).

# 30 Users and Groups

Every user who can log in on the system is identified by a unique number called the *user ID*. Each process has an effective user ID which says which user's access permissions it has.

Users are classified into *groups* for access control purposes. Each process has one or more *group ID values* which say which groups the process can use for access to files.

The effective user and group IDs of a process collectively form its *persona*. This determines which files the process can access. Normally, a process inherits its persona from the parent process, but under special circumstances a process can change its persona and thus change its access permissions.

Each file in the system also has a user ID and a group ID. Access control works by comparing the user and group IDs of the file with those of the running process.

The system keeps a database of all the registered users, and another database of all the defined groups. There are library functions you can use to examine these databases.

## 30.1 User and Group IDs

Each user account on a computer system is identified by a *user name* (or *login name*) and *user ID*. Normally, each user name has a unique user ID, but it is possible for several login names to have the same user ID. The user names and corresponding user IDs are stored in a data base which you can access as described in Section 30.13 [User Database], page 810.

Users are classified in *groups*. Each user name belongs to one *default group* and may also belong to any number of *supplementary groups*. Users who are members of the same group can share resources (such as files) that are not accessible to users who are not a member of that group. Each group has a *group name* and *group ID*. See Section 30.14 [Group Database], page 814, for how to find information about a group ID or group name.

## 30.2 The Persona of a Process

At any time, each process has an *effective user ID*, a *effective group ID*, and a set of *supplementary group IDs*. These IDs determine the privileges of the process. They are collectively called the *persona* of the process, because they determine "who it is" for purposes of access control.

Your login shell starts out with a persona which consists of your user ID, your default group ID, and your supplementary group IDs (if you are in more than one group). In normal circumstances, all your other processes inherit these values.

A process also has a *real user ID* which identifies the user who created the process, and a *real group ID* which identifies that user's default group. These values do not play a role in access control, so we do not consider them part of the persona. But they are also important.

Both the real and effective user ID can be changed during the lifetime of a process. See Section 30.3 [Why Change the Persona of a Process?], page 792.

For details on how a process's effective user ID and group IDs affect its permission to access files, see Section 14.9.6 [How Your Access to a File is Decided], page 409.

The effective user ID of a process also controls permissions for sending signals using the `kill` function. See Section 24.6.2 [Signaling Another Process], page 689.

Finally, there are many operations which can only be performed by a process whose effective user ID is zero. A process with this user ID is a *privileged process*. Commonly the user name `root` is associated with user ID 0, but there may be other user names with this ID.

## 30.3 Why Change the Persona of a Process?

The most obvious situation where it is necessary for a process to change its user and/or group IDs is the `login` program. When `login` starts running, its user ID is `root`. Its job is to start a shell whose user and group IDs are those of the user who is logging in. (To accomplish this fully, `login` must set the real user and group IDs as well as its persona. But this is a special case.)

The more common case of changing persona is when an ordinary user program needs access to a resource that wouldn't ordinarily be accessible to the user actually running it.

For example, you may have a file that is controlled by your program but that shouldn't be read or modified directly by other users, either because it implements some kind of locking protocol, or because you want to preserve the integrity or privacy of the information it contains. This kind of restricted access can be implemented by having the program change its effective user or group ID to match that of the resource.

Thus, imagine a game program that saves scores in a file. The game program itself needs to be able to update this file no matter who is running it, but if users can write the file without going through the game, they can give themselves any scores they like. Some people consider this undesirable, or even reprehensible. It can be prevented by creating a new user ID and login name (say, `games`) to own the scores file, and make the file writable only by this user. Then, when the game program wants to update this file, it can change its effective user ID to be that for `games`. In effect, the program must adopt the persona of `games` so it can write the scores file.

## 30.4 How an Application Can Change Persona

The ability to change the persona of a process can be a source of unintentional privacy violations, or even intentional abuse. Because of the potential for problems, changing persona is restricted to special circumstances.

You can't arbitrarily set your user ID or group ID to anything you want; only privileged processes can do that. Instead, the normal way for a program to change its persona is that it has been set up in advance to change to a particular user or group. This is the function of the setuid and setgid bits of a file's access mode. See Section 14.9.5 [The Mode Bits for Access Permission], page 408.

When the setuid bit of an executable file is on, executing that file gives the process a third user ID: the *file user ID*. This ID is set to the owner ID of the file. The system then changes the effective user ID to the file user ID. The real user ID remains as it was. Likewise, if the setgid bit is on, the process is given a *file group ID* equal to the group ID of the file, and its effective group ID is changed to the file group ID.

If a process has a file ID (user or group), then it can at any time change its effective ID to its real ID and back to its file ID. Programs use this feature to relinquish their special privileges except when they actually need them. This makes it less likely that they can be tricked into doing something inappropriate with their privileges.

**Portability Note:** Older systems do not have file IDs. To determine if a system has this feature, you can test the compiler define `_POSIX_SAVED_IDS`. (In the POSIX standard, file IDs are known as saved IDs.)

See Section 14.9 [File Attributes], page 399, for a more general discussion of file modes and accessibility.

## 30.5 Reading the Persona of a Process

Here are detailed descriptions of the functions for reading the user and group IDs of a process, both real and effective. To use these facilities, you must include the header files `sys/types.h` and `unistd.h`.

`uid_t`                                                                              [Data Type]
> This is an integer data type used to represent user IDs. In the GNU C Library, this is an alias for `unsigned int`.

`gid_t`                                                                              [Data Type]
> This is an integer data type used to represent group IDs. In the GNU C Library, this is an alias for `unsigned int`.

`uid_t getuid (void)`                                                                [Function]
> Preliminary: | MT-Safe | AS-Safe | AC-Safe | See Section 1.2.2.1 [POSIX Safety Concepts], page 2.
>
> The `getuid` function returns the real user ID of the process.

`gid_t getgid (void)`                                                                [Function]
> Preliminary: | MT-Safe | AS-Safe | AC-Safe | See Section 1.2.2.1 [POSIX Safety Concepts], page 2.
>
> The `getgid` function returns the real group ID of the process.

`uid_t geteuid (void)`                                                               [Function]
> Preliminary: | MT-Safe | AS-Safe | AC-Safe | See Section 1.2.2.1 [POSIX Safety Concepts], page 2.
>
> The `geteuid` function returns the effective user ID of the process.

`gid_t getegid (void)`                                                               [Function]
> Preliminary: | MT-Safe | AS-Safe | AC-Safe | See Section 1.2.2.1 [POSIX Safety Concepts], page 2.
>
> The `getegid` function returns the effective group ID of the process.

`int getgroups (int count, gid_t *groups)`                                           [Function]
> Preliminary: | MT-Safe | AS-Safe | AC-Safe | See Section 1.2.2.1 [POSIX Safety Concepts], page 2.
>
> The `getgroups` function is used to inquire about the supplementary group IDs of the process. Up to *count* of these group IDs are stored in the array *groups*; the return value from the function is the number of group IDs actually stored. If *count* is smaller than the total number of supplementary group IDs, then `getgroups` returns a value of -1 and `errno` is set to `EINVAL`.

If *count* is zero, then `getgroups` just returns the total number of supplementary group IDs. On systems that do not support supplementary groups, this will always be zero.

Here's how to use `getgroups` to read all the supplementary group IDs:

```
gid_t *
read_all_groups (void)
{
  int ngroups = getgroups (0, NULL);
  gid_t *groups
    = (gid_t *) xmalloc (ngroups * sizeof (gid_t));
  int val = getgroups (ngroups, groups);
  if (val < 0)
    {
      free (groups);
      return NULL;
    }
  return groups;
}
```

## 30.6 Setting the User ID

This section describes the functions for altering the user ID (real and/or effective) of a process. To use these facilities, you must include the header files `sys/types.h` and `unistd.h`.

int seteuid (*uid_t neweuid*)                                                    [Function]
> Preliminary: | MT-Safe | AS-Unsafe lock | AC-Unsafe lock | See Section 1.2.2.1 [POSIX Safety Concepts], page 2.
>
> This function sets the effective user ID of a process to *neweuid*, provided that the process is allowed to change its effective user ID. A privileged process (effective user ID zero) can change its effective user ID to any legal value. An unprivileged process with a file user ID can change its effective user ID to its real user ID or to its file user ID. Otherwise, a process may not change its effective user ID at all.
>
> The `seteuid` function returns a value of 0 to indicate successful completion, and a value of -1 to indicate an error. The following `errno` error conditions are defined for this function:
>
> EINVAL      The value of the *neweuid* argument is invalid.
>
> EPERM       The process may not change to the specified ID.
>
> Older systems (those without the `_POSIX_SAVED_IDS` feature) do not have this function.

int setuid (*uid_t newuid*)                                                      [Function]
> Preliminary: | MT-Safe | AS-Unsafe lock | AC-Unsafe lock | See Section 1.2.2.1 [POSIX Safety Concepts], page 2.
>
> If the calling process is privileged, this function sets both the real and effective user ID of the process to *newuid*. It also deletes the file user ID of the process, if any. *newuid* may be any legal value. (Once this has been done, there is no way to recover the old effective user ID.)
>
> If the process is not privileged, and the system supports the `_POSIX_SAVED_IDS` feature, then this function behaves like `seteuid`.

The return values and error conditions are the same as for `seteuid`.

**`int setreuid (uid_t ruid, uid_t euid)`** [Function]

Preliminary: | MT-Safe | AS-Unsafe lock | AC-Unsafe lock | See Section 1.2.2.1 [POSIX Safety Concepts], page 2.

This function sets the real user ID of the process to *ruid* and the effective user ID to *euid*. If *ruid* is -1, it means not to change the real user ID; likewise if *euid* is -1, it means not to change the effective user ID.

The `setreuid` function exists for compatibility with 4.3 BSD Unix, which does not support file IDs. You can use this function to swap the effective and real user IDs of the process. (Privileged processes are not limited to this particular usage.) If file IDs are supported, you should use that feature instead of this function. See Section 30.8 [Enabling and Disabling Setuid Access], page 797.

The return value is 0 on success and -1 on failure. The following `errno` error conditions are defined for this function:

`EPERM`       The process does not have the appropriate privileges; you do not have permission to change to the specified ID.

## 30.7 Setting the Group IDs

This section describes the functions for altering the group IDs (real and effective) of a process. To use these facilities, you must include the header files `sys/types.h` and `unistd.h`.

**`int setegid (gid_t newgid)`** [Function]

Preliminary: | MT-Safe | AS-Unsafe lock | AC-Unsafe lock | See Section 1.2.2.1 [POSIX Safety Concepts], page 2.

This function sets the effective group ID of the process to *newgid*, provided that the process is allowed to change its group ID. Just as with `seteuid`, if the process is privileged it may change its effective group ID to any value; if it isn't, but it has a file group ID, then it may change to its real group ID or file group ID; otherwise it may not change its effective group ID.

Note that a process is only privileged if its effective *user* ID is zero. The effective group ID only affects access permissions.

The return values and error conditions for `setegid` are the same as those for `seteuid`.

This function is only present if `_POSIX_SAVED_IDS` is defined.

**`int setgid (gid_t newgid)`** [Function]

Preliminary: | MT-Safe | AS-Unsafe lock | AC-Unsafe lock | See Section 1.2.2.1 [POSIX Safety Concepts], page 2.

This function sets both the real and effective group ID of the process to *newgid*, provided that the process is privileged. It also deletes the file group ID, if any.

If the process is not privileged, then `setgid` behaves like `setegid`.

The return values and error conditions for `setgid` are the same as those for `seteuid`.

**int setregid** (*gid_t* **rgid**, *gid_t* **egid**)                              [Function]
>    Preliminary: | MT-Safe | AS-Unsafe lock | AC-Unsafe lock | See Section 1.2.2.1
>    [POSIX Safety Concepts], page 2.
>
>    This function sets the real group ID of the process to *rgid* and the effective group ID
>    to *egid*. If *rgid* is -1, it means not to change the real group ID; likewise if *egid* is -1,
>    it means not to change the effective group ID.
>
>    The **setregid** function is provided for compatibility with 4.3 BSD Unix, which does
>    not support file IDs. You can use this function to swap the effective and real group
>    IDs of the process. (Privileged processes are not limited to this usage.) If file IDs are
>    supported, you should use that feature instead of using this function. See Section 30.8
>    [Enabling and Disabling Setuid Access], page 797.
>
>    The return values and error conditions for **setregid** are the same as those for
>    **setreuid**.

**setuid** and **setgid** behave differently depending on whether the effective user ID at the
time is zero. If it is not zero, they behave like **seteuid** and **setegid**. If it is, they change
both effective and real IDs and delete the file ID. To avoid confusion, we recommend you
always use **seteuid** and **setegid** except when you know the effective user ID is zero and
your intent is to change the persona permanently. This case is rare—most of the programs
that need it, such as **login** and **su**, have already been written.

Note that if your program is setuid to some user other than **root**, there is no way to
drop privileges permanently.

The system also lets privileged processes change their supplementary group IDs. To use
**setgroups** or **initgroups**, your programs should include the header file **grp.h**.

**int setgroups** (*size_t* **count**, *const gid_t* **\*groups**)                        [Function]
>    Preliminary: | MT-Safe | AS-Unsafe lock | AC-Unsafe lock | See Section 1.2.2.1
>    [POSIX Safety Concepts], page 2.
>
>    This function sets the process's supplementary group IDs. It can only be called from
>    privileged processes. The *count* argument specifies the number of group IDs in the
>    array *groups*.
>
>    This function returns 0 if successful and -1 on error. The following **errno** error
>    conditions are defined for this function:
>
>    EPERM        The calling process is not privileged.

**int initgroups** (*const char* **\*user**, *gid_t* **group**)                          [Function]
>    Preliminary: | MT-Safe locale | AS-Unsafe dlopen plugin heap lock | AC-Unsafe
>    corrupt mem fd lock | See Section 1.2.2.1 [POSIX Safety Concepts], page 2.
>
>    The **initgroups** function sets the process's supplementary group IDs to be the normal
>    default for the user name *user*. The group *group* is automatically included.
>
>    This function works by scanning the group database for all the groups *user* belongs
>    to. It then calls **setgroups** with the list it has constructed.
>
>    The return values and error conditions are the same as for **setgroups**.

If you are interested in the groups a particular user belongs to, but do not want to change
the process's supplementary group IDs, you can use **getgrouplist**. To use **getgrouplist**,
your programs should include the header file **grp.h**.

int getgrouplist (*const char \*user, gid_t group, gid_t \*groups, int*      [Function]
        *\*ngroups*)

> Preliminary: | MT-Safe locale | AS-Unsafe dlopen plugin heap lock | AC-Unsafe
> corrupt mem fd lock | See Section 1.2.2.1 [POSIX Safety Concepts], page 2.

> The `getgrouplist` function scans the group database for all the groups *user* belongs
> to. Up to *\*ngroups* group IDs corresponding to these groups are stored in the array
> *groups*; the return value from the function is the number of group IDs actually stored.
> If *\*ngroups* is smaller than the total number of groups found, then `getgrouplist`
> returns a value of −1 and stores the actual number of groups in *\*ngroups*. The group
> *group* is automatically included in the list of groups returned by `getgrouplist`.

> Here's how to use `getgrouplist` to read all supplementary groups for *user*:

```
gid_t *
supplementary_groups (char *user)
{
  int ngroups = 16;
  gid_t *groups
    = (gid_t *) xmalloc (ngroups * sizeof (gid_t));
  struct passwd *pw = getpwnam (user);

  if (pw == NULL)
    return NULL;

  if (getgrouplist (pw->pw_name, pw->pw_gid, groups, &ngroups) < 0)
    {
      groups = xrealloc (ngroups * sizeof (gid_t));
      getgrouplist (pw->pw_name, pw->pw_gid, groups, &ngroups);
    }
  return groups;
}
```

## 30.8 Enabling and Disabling Setuid Access

A typical setuid program does not need its special access all of the time. It's a good idea
to turn off this access when it isn't needed, so it can't possibly give unintended access.

If the system supports the `_POSIX_SAVED_IDS` feature, you can accomplish this with
`seteuid`. When the game program starts, its real user ID is `jdoe`, its effective user ID is
`games`, and its saved user ID is also `games`. The program should record both user ID values
once at the beginning, like this:

```
user_user_id = getuid ();
game_user_id = geteuid ();
```

Then it can turn off game file access with

```
seteuid (user_user_id);
```

and turn it on with

```
seteuid (game_user_id);
```

Throughout this process, the real user ID remains `jdoe` and the file user ID remains `games`,
so the program can always set its effective user ID to either one.

On other systems that don't support file user IDs, you can turn setuid access on and off
by using `setreuid` to swap the real and effective user IDs of the process, as follows:

```
setreuid (geteuid (), getuid ());
```

This special case is always allowed—it cannot fail.

Why does this have the effect of toggling the setuid access? Suppose a game program has just started, and its real user ID is jdoe while its effective user ID is games. In this state, the game can write the scores file. If it swaps the two uids, the real becomes games and the effective becomes jdoe; now the program has only jdoe access. Another swap brings games back to the effective user ID and restores access to the scores file.

In order to handle both kinds of systems, test for the saved user ID feature with a preprocessor conditional, like this:

```
#ifdef _POSIX_SAVED_IDS
  seteuid (user_user_id);
#else
  setreuid (geteuid (), getuid ());
#endif
```

## 30.9 Setuid Program Example

Here's an example showing how to set up a program that changes its effective user ID.

This is part of a game program called caber-toss that manipulates a file scores that should be writable only by the game program itself. The program assumes that its executable file will be installed with the setuid bit set and owned by the same user as the scores file. Typically, a system administrator will set up an account like games for this purpose.

The executable file is given mode 4755, so that doing an 'ls -l' on it produces output like:

```
-rwsr-xr-x   1 games    184422 Jul 30 15:17 caber-toss
```

The setuid bit shows up in the file modes as the 's'.

The scores file is given mode 644, and doing an 'ls -l' on it shows:

```
-rw-r--r--  1 games           0 Jul 31 15:33 scores
```

Here are the parts of the program that show how to set up the changed user ID. This program is conditionalized so that it makes use of the file IDs feature if it is supported, and otherwise uses setreuid to swap the effective and real user IDs.

```
#include <stdio.h>
#include <sys/types.h>
#include <unistd.h>
#include <stdlib.h>


/* Remember the effective and real UIDs. */

static uid_t euid, ruid;


/* Restore the effective UID to its original value. */

void
do_setuid (void)
{
  int status;
```

```
#ifdef _POSIX_SAVED_IDS
  status = seteuid (euid);
#else
  status = setreuid (ruid, euid);
#endif
  if (status < 0) {
    fprintf (stderr, "Couldn't set uid.\n");
    exit (status);
    }
}


/* Set the effective UID to the real UID. */

void
undo_setuid (void)
{
  int status;

#ifdef _POSIX_SAVED_IDS
  status = seteuid (ruid);
#else
  status = setreuid (euid, ruid);
#endif
  if (status < 0) {
    fprintf (stderr, "Couldn't set uid.\n");
    exit (status);
    }
}

/* Main program. */

int
main (void)
{
  /* Remember the real and effective user IDs.  */
  ruid = getuid ();
  euid = geteuid ();
  undo_setuid ();

  /* Do the game and record the score.  */
  ...
}
```

Notice how the first thing the **main** function does is to set the effective user ID back to
the real user ID. This is so that any other file accesses that are performed while the user is
playing the game use the real user ID for determining permissions. Only when the program
needs to open the scores file does it switch back to the file user ID, like this:

```
/* Record the score. */

int
record_score (int score)
{
  FILE *stream;
  char *myname;

  /* Open the scores file. */
  do_setuid ();
```

```
stream = fopen (SCORES_FILE, "a");
undo_setuid ();

/* Write the score to the file. */
if (stream)
  {
    myname = cuserid (NULL);
    if (score < 0)
      fprintf (stream, "%10s: Couldn't lift the caber.\n", myname);
    else
      fprintf (stream, "%10s: %d feet.\n", myname, score);
    fclose (stream);
    return 0;
  }
else
  return -1;
}
```

## 30.10 Tips for Writing Setuid Programs

It is easy for setuid programs to give the user access that isn't intended—in fact, if you want to avoid this, you need to be careful. Here are some guidelines for preventing unintended access and minimizing its consequences when it does occur:

- Don't have **setuid** programs with privileged user IDs such as **root** unless it is absolutely necessary. If the resource is specific to your particular program, it's better to define a new, nonprivileged user ID or group ID just to manage that resource. It's better if you can write your program to use a special group than a special user.

- Be cautious about using the **exec** functions in combination with changing the effective user ID. Don't let users of your program execute arbitrary programs under a changed user ID. Executing a shell is especially bad news. Less obviously, the **execlp** and **execvp** functions are a potential risk (since the program they execute depends on the user's **PATH** environment variable).

  If you must **exec** another program under a changed ID, specify an absolute file name (see Section 11.2.2 [File Name Resolution], page 246) for the executable, and make sure that the protections on that executable and *all* containing directories are such that ordinary users cannot replace it with some other program.

  You should also check the arguments passed to the program to make sure they do not have unexpected effects. Likewise, you should examine the environment variables. Decide which arguments and variables are safe, and reject all others.

  You should never use **system** in a privileged program, because it invokes a shell.

- Only use the user ID controlling the resource in the part of the program that actually uses that resource. When you're finished with it, restore the effective user ID back to the actual user's user ID. See Section 30.8 [Enabling and Disabling Setuid Access], page 797.

- If the **setuid** part of your program needs to access other files besides the controlled resource, it should verify that the real user would ordinarily have permission to access those files. You can use the **access** function (see Section 14.9.6 [How Your Access to a File is Decided], page 409) to check this; it uses the real user and group IDs, rather than the effective IDs.

## 30.11 Identifying Who Logged In

You can use the functions listed in this section to determine the login name of the user who is running a process, and the name of the user who logged in the current session. See also the function getuid and friends (see Section 30.5 [Reading the Persona of a Process], page 793). How this information is collected by the system and how to control/add/remove information from the background storage is described in Section 30.12 [The User Accounting Database], page 802.

The getlogin function is declared in unistd.h, while cuserid and L_cuserid are declared in stdio.h.

char * getlogin (*void*)                                                    [Function]
    Preliminary: | MT-Unsafe race:getlogin race:utent sig:ALRM timer locale | AS-Unsafe dlopen plugin heap lock | AC-Unsafe corrupt lock fd mem | See Section 1.2.2.1 [POSIX Safety Concepts], page 2.

    The getlogin function returns a pointer to a string containing the name of the user logged in on the controlling terminal of the process, or a null pointer if this information cannot be determined. The string is statically allocated and might be overwritten on subsequent calls to this function or to cuserid.

char * cuserid (*char *string*)                                             [Function]
    Preliminary: | MT-Unsafe race:cuserid/!string locale | AS-Unsafe dlopen plugin heap lock | AC-Unsafe corrupt lock fd mem | See Section 1.2.2.1 [POSIX Safety Concepts], page 2.

    The cuserid function returns a pointer to a string containing a user name associated with the effective ID of the process. If *string* is not a null pointer, it should be an array that can hold at least L_cuserid characters; the string is returned in this array. Otherwise, a pointer to a string in a static area is returned. This string is statically allocated and might be overwritten on subsequent calls to this function or to getlogin.

    The use of this function is deprecated since it is marked to be withdrawn in XPG4.2 and has already been removed from newer revisions of POSIX.1.

int L_cuserid                                                               [Macro]
    An integer constant that indicates how long an array you might need to store a user name.

These functions let your program identify positively the user who is running or the user who logged in this session. (These can differ when setuid programs are involved; see Section 30.2 [The Persona of a Process], page 791.) The user cannot do anything to fool these functions.

For most purposes, it is more useful to use the environment variable LOGNAME to find out who the user is. This is more flexible precisely because the user can set LOGNAME arbitrarily. See Section 25.4.2 [Standard Environment Variables], page 741.

## 30.12 The User Accounting Database

Most Unix-like operating systems keep track of logged in users by maintaining a user accounting database. This user accounting database stores for each terminal, who has logged on, at what time, the process ID of the user's login shell, etc., etc., but also stores information about the run level of the system, the time of the last system reboot, and possibly more.

The user accounting database typically lives in /etc/utmp, /var/adm/utmp or /var/run/utmp. However, these files should **never** be accessed directly. For reading information from and writing information to the user accounting database, the functions described in this section should be used.

### 30.12.1 Manipulating the User Accounting Database

These functions and the corresponding data structures are declared in the header file utmp.h.

struct exit_status                                                       [Data Type]
> The exit_status data structure is used to hold information about the exit status of processes marked as DEAD_PROCESS in the user accounting database.

> short int e_termination
>> The exit status of the process.

> short int e_exit
>> The exit status of the process.

struct utmp                                                              [Data Type]
> The utmp data structure is used to hold information about entries in the user accounting database. On GNU systems it has the following members:

> short int ut_type
>> Specifies the type of login; one of EMPTY, RUN_LVL, BOOT_TIME, OLD_TIME, NEW_TIME, INIT_PROCESS, LOGIN_PROCESS, USER_PROCESS, DEAD_PROCESS or ACCOUNTING.

> pid_t ut_pid
>> The process ID number of the login process.

> char ut_line[]
>> The device name of the tty (without /dev/).

> char ut_id[]
>> The inittab ID of the process.

> char ut_user[]
>> The user's login name.

> char ut_host[]
>> The name of the host from which the user logged in.

> struct exit_status ut_exit
>> The exit status of a process marked as DEAD_PROCESS.

long ut_session
> The Session ID, used for windowing.

struct timeval ut_tv
> Time the entry was made. For entries of type OLD_TIME this is the time
> when the system clock changed, and for entries of type NEW_TIME this is
> the time the system clock was set to.

int32_t ut_addr_v6[4]
> The Internet address of a remote host.

The ut_type, ut_pid, ut_id, ut_tv, and ut_host fields are not available on all systems. Portable applications therefore should be prepared for these situations. To help doing this the utmp.h header provides macros _HAVE_UT_TYPE, _HAVE_UT_PID, _HAVE_UT_ID, _HAVE_UT_TV, and _HAVE_UT_HOST if the respective field is available. The programmer can handle the situations by using #ifdef in the program code.

The following macros are defined for use as values for the ut_type member of the utmp structure. The values are integer constants.

EMPTY
> This macro is used to indicate that the entry contains no valid user accounting information.

RUN_LVL
> This macro is used to identify the systems runlevel.

BOOT_TIME
> This macro is used to identify the time of system boot.

OLD_TIME
> This macro is used to identify the time when the system clock changed.

NEW_TIME
> This macro is used to identify the time after the system changed.

INIT_PROCESS
> This macro is used to identify a process spawned by the init process.

LOGIN_PROCESS
> This macro is used to identify the session leader of a logged in user.

USER_PROCESS
> This macro is used to identify a user process.

DEAD_PROCESS
> This macro is used to identify a terminated process.

ACCOUNTING
> ???

The size of the ut_line, ut_id, ut_user and ut_host arrays can be found using the sizeof operator.

Many older systems have, instead of an ut_tv member, an ut_time member, usually of type time_t, for representing the time associated with the entry. Therefore, for backwards compatibility only, utmp.h defines ut_time as an alias for ut_tv.tv_sec.

void setutent (void)                                                    [Function]
> Preliminary: | MT-Unsafe race:utent | AS-Unsafe lock | AC-Unsafe lock fd | See
> Section 1.2.2.1 [POSIX Safety Concepts], page 2.

This function opens the user accounting database to begin scanning it. You can then call `getutent`, `getutid` or `getutline` to read entries and `pututline` to write entries.

If the database is already open, it resets the input to the beginning of the database.

**struct utmp * getutent** (*void*)                                    [Function]
Preliminary: | MT-Unsafe init race:utent race:utentbuf sig:ALRM timer | AS-Unsafe heap lock | AC-Unsafe lock fd mem | See Section 1.2.2.1 [POSIX Safety Concepts], page 2.

The `getutent` function reads the next entry from the user accounting database. It returns a pointer to the entry, which is statically allocated and may be overwritten by subsequent calls to `getutent`. You must copy the contents of the structure if you wish to save the information or you can use the `getutent_r` function which stores the data in a user-provided buffer.

A null pointer is returned in case no further entry is available.

**void endutent** (*void*)                                             [Function]
Preliminary: | MT-Unsafe race:utent | AS-Unsafe lock | AC-Unsafe lock fd | See Section 1.2.2.1 [POSIX Safety Concepts], page 2.

This function closes the user accounting database.

**struct utmp * getutid** (*const struct utmp \*id*)                    [Function]
Preliminary: | MT-Unsafe init race:utent sig:ALRM timer | AS-Unsafe lock heap | AC-Unsafe lock mem fd | See Section 1.2.2.1 [POSIX Safety Concepts], page 2.

This function searches forward from the current point in the database for an entry that matches *id*. If the `ut_type` member of the *id* structure is one of `RUN_LVL`, `BOOT_TIME`, `OLD_TIME` or `NEW_TIME` the entries match if the `ut_type` members are identical. If the `ut_type` member of the *id* structure is `INIT_PROCESS`, `LOGIN_PROCESS`, `USER_PROCESS` or `DEAD_PROCESS`, the entries match if the `ut_type` member of the entry read from the database is one of these four, and the `ut_id` members match. However if the `ut_id` member of either the *id* structure or the entry read from the database is empty it checks if the `ut_line` members match instead. If a matching entry is found, `getutid` returns a pointer to the entry, which is statically allocated, and may be overwritten by a subsequent call to `getutent`, `getutid` or `getutline`. You must copy the contents of the structure if you wish to save the information.

A null pointer is returned in case the end of the database is reached without a match.

The `getutid` function may cache the last read entry. Therefore, if you are using `getutid` to search for multiple occurrences, it is necessary to zero out the static data after each call. Otherwise `getutid` could just return a pointer to the same entry over and over again.

**struct utmp * getutline** (*const struct utmp \*line*)               [Function]
Preliminary: | MT-Unsafe init race:utent sig:ALRM timer | AS-Unsafe heap lock | AC-Unsafe lock fd mem | See Section 1.2.2.1 [POSIX Safety Concepts], page 2.

This function searches forward from the current point in the database until it finds an entry whose `ut_type` value is `LOGIN_PROCESS` or `USER_PROCESS`, and whose `ut_line` member matches the `ut_line` member of the *line* structure. If it finds such an entry, it returns a pointer to the entry which is statically allocated, and may be overwritten by a subsequent call to `getutent`, `getutid` or `getutline`. You must copy the contents of the structure if you wish to save the information.

A null pointer is returned in case the end of the database is reached without a match.

The `getutline` function may cache the last read entry. Therefore if you are using `getutline` to search for multiple occurrences, it is necessary to zero out the static data after each call. Otherwise `getutline` could just return a pointer to the same entry over and over again.

**struct utmp \* pututline** (*const struct utmp \*utmp*)                              [Function]
    Preliminary: | MT-Unsafe race:utent sig:ALRM timer | AS-Unsafe lock | AC-Unsafe lock fd | See Section 1.2.2.1 [POSIX Safety Concepts], page 2.

    The `pututline` function inserts the entry *\*utmp* at the appropriate place in the user accounting database. If it finds that it is not already at the correct place in the database, it uses `getutid` to search for the position to insert the entry, however this will not modify the static structure returned by `getutent`, `getutid` and `getutline`. If this search fails, the entry is appended to the database.

    The `pututline` function returns a pointer to a copy of the entry inserted in the user accounting database, or a null pointer if the entry could not be added. The following `errno` error conditions are defined for this function:

    EPERM      The process does not have the appropriate privileges; you cannot modify the user accounting database.

All the `get*` functions mentioned before store the information they return in a static buffer. This can be a problem in multi-threaded programs since the data returned for the request is overwritten by the return value data in another thread. Therefore the GNU C Library provides as extensions three more functions which return the data in a user-provided buffer.

**int getutent_r** (*struct utmp \*buffer, struct utmp \*\*result*)                    [Function]
    Preliminary: | MT-Unsafe race:utent sig:ALRM timer | AS-Unsafe lock | AC-Unsafe lock fd | See Section 1.2.2.1 [POSIX Safety Concepts], page 2.

    The `getutent_r` is equivalent to the `getutent` function. It returns the next entry from the database. But instead of storing the information in a static buffer it stores it in the buffer pointed to by the parameter *buffer*.

    If the call was successful, the function returns 0 and the pointer variable pointed to by the parameter *result* contains a pointer to the buffer which contains the result (this is most probably the same value as *buffer*). If something went wrong during the execution of `getutent_r` the function returns -1.

    This function is a GNU extension.

**int getutid_r** (*const struct utmp \*id, struct utmp \*buffer, struct*           [Function]
        *utmp \*\*result*)
    Preliminary: | MT-Unsafe race:utent sig:ALRM timer | AS-Unsafe lock | AC-Unsafe lock fd | See Section 1.2.2.1 [POSIX Safety Concepts], page 2.

This function retrieves just like `getutid` the next entry matching the information stored in *id*. But the result is stored in the buffer pointed to by the parameter *buffer*.

If successful the function returns 0 and the pointer variable pointed to by the parameter *result* contains a pointer to the buffer with the result (probably the same as *result*. If not successful the function return -1.

This function is a GNU extension.

---

int **getutline_r** (*const struct utmp *line, struct utmp *buffer*,              [Function]
    *struct utmp **result*)

Preliminary: | MT-Unsafe race:utent sig:ALRM timer | AS-Unsafe lock | AC-Unsafe lock fd | See Section 1.2.2.1 [POSIX Safety Concepts], page 2.

This function retrieves just like `getutline` the next entry matching the information stored in *line*. But the result is stored in the buffer pointed to by the parameter *buffer*.

If successful the function returns 0 and the pointer variable pointed to by the parameter *result* contains a pointer to the buffer with the result (probably the same as *result*. If not successful the function return -1.

This function is a GNU extension.

---

In addition to the user accounting database, most systems keep a number of similar databases. For example most systems keep a log file with all previous logins (usually in `/etc/wtmp` or `/var/log/wtmp`).

For specifying which database to examine, the following function should be used.

---

int **utmpname** (*const char *file*)                                              [Function]

Preliminary: | MT-Unsafe race:utent | AS-Unsafe lock heap | AC-Unsafe lock mem | See Section 1.2.2.1 [POSIX Safety Concepts], page 2.

The **utmpname** function changes the name of the database to be examined to *file*, and closes any previously opened database. By default `getutent`, `getutid`, `getutline` and `pututline` read from and write to the user accounting database.

The following macros are defined for use as the *file* argument:

---

char * **_PATH_UTMP**                                                              [Macro]

This macro is used to specify the user accounting database.

---

char * **_PATH_WTMP**                                                              [Macro]

This macro is used to specify the user accounting log file.

---

The **utmpname** function returns a value of 0 if the new name was successfully stored, and a value of -1 to indicate an error. Note that **utmpname** does not try to open the database, and that therefore the return value does not say anything about whether the database can be successfully opened.

Specially for maintaining log-like databases the GNU C Library provides the following function:

**void updwtmp** (*const char \*wtmp_file, const struct utmp \*utmp*)          [Function]
> Preliminary: | MT-Unsafe sig:ALRM timer | AS-Unsafe | AC-Unsafe fd | See
> Section 1.2.2.1 [POSIX Safety Concepts], page 2.
>
> The updwtmp function appends the entry *\*utmp* to the database specified by
> *wtmp_file*. For possible values for the *wtmp_file* argument see the utmpname
> function.

**Portability Note:** Although many operating systems provide a subset of these functions, they are not standardized. There are often subtle differences in the return types, and there are considerable differences between the various definitions of struct utmp. When programming for the GNU C Library, it is probably best to stick with the functions described in this section. If however, you want your program to be portable, consider using the XPG functions described in Section 30.12.2 [XPG User Accounting Database Functions], page 807, or take a look at the BSD compatible functions in Section 30.12.3 [Logging In and Out], page 809.

## 30.12.2 XPG User Accounting Database Functions

These functions, described in the X/Open Portability Guide, are declared in the header file utmpx.h.

**struct utmpx**                                                          [Data Type]
> The utmpx data structure contains at least the following members:
>
> **short int ut_type**
> > Specifies the type of login; one of EMPTY, RUN_LVL, BOOT_TIME, OLD_TIME, NEW_TIME, INIT_PROCESS, LOGIN_PROCESS, USER_PROCESS or DEAD_PROCESS.
>
> **pid_t ut_pid**
> > The process ID number of the login process.
>
> **char ut_line[]**
> > The device name of the tty (without /dev/).
>
> **char ut_id[]**
> > The inittab ID of the process.
>
> **char ut_user[]**
> > The user's login name.
>
> **struct timeval ut_tv**
> > Time the entry was made. For entries of type OLD_TIME this is the time when the system clock changed, and for entries of type NEW_TIME this is the time the system clock was set to.
>
> In the GNU C Library, struct utmpx is identical to struct utmp except for the fact that including utmpx.h does not make visible the declaration of struct exit_status.

The following macros are defined for use as values for the ut_type member of the utmpx structure. The values are integer constants and are, in the GNU C Library, identical to the definitions in utmp.h.

**EMPTY**       This macro is used to indicate that the entry contains no valid user accounting information.

**RUN_LVL**    This macro is used to identify the systems runlevel.

**BOOT_TIME**
               This macro is used to identify the time of system boot.

**OLD_TIME**   This macro is used to identify the time when the system clock changed.

**NEW_TIME**   This macro is used to identify the time after the system changed.

**INIT_PROCESS**
               This macro is used to identify a process spawned by the init process.

**LOGIN_PROCESS**
               This macro is used to identify the session leader of a logged in user.

**USER_PROCESS**
               This macro is used to identify a user process.

**DEAD_PROCESS**
               This macro is used to identify a terminated process.

The size of the `ut_line`, `ut_id` and `ut_user` arrays can be found using the `sizeof` operator.

**void setutxent** (*void*)                                                     [Function]
> Preliminary: | MT-Unsafe race:utent | AS-Unsafe lock | AC-Unsafe lock fd | See Section 1.2.2.1 [POSIX Safety Concepts], page 2.

> This function is similar to `setutent`. In the GNU C Library it is simply an alias for `setutent`.

**struct utmpx \* getutxent** (*void*)                                          [Function]
> Preliminary: | MT-Unsafe init race:utent sig:ALRM timer | AS-Unsafe heap lock | AC-Unsafe lock fd mem | See Section 1.2.2.1 [POSIX Safety Concepts], page 2.

> The `getutxent` function is similar to `getutent`, but returns a pointer to a `struct utmpx` instead of `struct utmp`. In the GNU C Library it simply is an alias for `getutent`.

**void endutxent** (*void*)                                                     [Function]
> Preliminary: | MT-Unsafe race:utent | AS-Unsafe lock | AC-Unsafe lock | See Section 1.2.2.1 [POSIX Safety Concepts], page 2.

> This function is similar to `endutent`. In the GNU C Library it is simply an alias for `endutent`.

**struct utmpx \* getutxid** (*const struct utmpx \*id*)                          [Function]
> Preliminary: | MT-Unsafe init race:utent sig:ALRM timer | AS-Unsafe lock heap | AC-Unsafe lock mem fd | See Section 1.2.2.1 [POSIX Safety Concepts], page 2.

> This function is similar to `getutid`, but uses `struct utmpx` instead of `struct utmp`. In the GNU C Library it is simply an alias for `getutid`.

**struct utmpx \* getutxline** (*const struct utmpx \*line*)                  [Function]
    Preliminary: | MT-Unsafe init race:utent sig:ALRM timer | AS-Unsafe heap lock |
    AC-Unsafe lock fd mem | See Section 1.2.2.1 [POSIX Safety Concepts], page 2.

    This function is similar to **getutid**, but uses **struct utmpx** instead of **struct utmp**.
    In the GNU C Library it is simply an alias for **getutline**.

**struct utmpx \* pututxline** (*const struct utmpx \*utmp*)                  [Function]
    Preliminary: | MT-Unsafe race:utent sig:ALRM timer | AS-Unsafe lock | AC-Unsafe
    lock fd | See Section 1.2.2.1 [POSIX Safety Concepts], page 2.

    The **pututxline** function is functionally identical to **pututline**, but uses **struct
    utmpx** instead of **struct utmp**. In the GNU C Library, **pututxline** is simply an alias
    for **pututline**.

**int utmpxname** (*const char \*file*)                  [Function]
    Preliminary: | MT-Unsafe race:utent | AS-Unsafe lock heap | AC-Unsafe lock mem
    | See Section 1.2.2.1 [POSIX Safety Concepts], page 2.

    The **utmpxname** function is functionally identical to **utmpname**. In the GNU C Library,
    **utmpxname** is simply an alias for **utmpname**.

You can translate between a traditional **struct utmp** and an XPG **struct utmpx** with
the following functions. In the GNU C Library, these functions are merely copies, since the
two structures are identical.

**int getutmp** (*const struct utmpx \*utmpx, struct utmp \*utmp*)                  [Function]
    Preliminary: | MT-Safe | AS-Safe | AC-Safe | See Section 1.2.2.1 [POSIX Safety
    Concepts], page 2.

    **getutmp** copies the information, insofar as the structures are compatible, from *utmpx*
    to *utmp*.

**int getutmpx** (*const struct utmp \*utmp, struct utmpx \*utmpx*)                  [Function]
    Preliminary: | MT-Safe | AS-Safe | AC-Safe | See Section 1.2.2.1 [POSIX Safety
    Concepts], page 2.

    **getutmpx** copies the information, insofar as the structures are compatible, from *utmp*
    to *utmpx*.

## 30.12.3 Logging In and Out

These functions, derived from BSD, are available in the separate **libutil** library, and
declared in **utmp.h**.

Note that the **ut_user** member of **struct utmp** is called **ut_name** in BSD. Therefore,
**ut_name** is defined as an alias for **ut_user** in **utmp.h**.

**int login_tty** (*int filedes*)                  [Function]
    Preliminary: | MT-Unsafe race:ttyname | AS-Unsafe heap lock | AC-Unsafe lock fd
    mem | See Section 1.2.2.1 [POSIX Safety Concepts], page 2.

    This function makes *filedes* the controlling terminal of the current process, redirects
    standard input, standard output and standard error output to this terminal, and
    closes *filedes*.

    This function returns 0 on successful completion, and -1 on error.

**void login** (*const struct utmp *entry*)                              [Function]
> Preliminary: | MT-Unsafe race:utent sig:ALRM timer | AS-Unsafe lock heap | AC-Unsafe lock corrupt fd mem | See Section 1.2.2.1 [POSIX Safety Concepts], page 2.
>
> The `login` functions inserts an entry into the user accounting database. The `ut_line` member is set to the name of the terminal on standard input. If standard input is not a terminal `login` uses standard output or standard error output to determine the name of the terminal. If `struct utmp` has a `ut_type` member, `login` sets it to `USER_PROCESS`, and if there is an `ut_pid` member, it will be set to the process ID of the current process. The remaining entries are copied from *entry*.
>
> A copy of the entry is written to the user accounting log file.

**int logout** (*const char *ut_line*)                                   [Function]
> Preliminary: | MT-Unsafe race:utent sig:ALRM timer | AS-Unsafe lock heap | AC-Unsafe lock fd mem | See Section 1.2.2.1 [POSIX Safety Concepts], page 2.
>
> This function modifies the user accounting database to indicate that the user on *ut_line* has logged out.
>
> The `logout` function returns 1 if the entry was successfully written to the database, or 0 on error.

**void logwtmp** (*const char *ut_line, const char *ut_name, const char*     [Function]
> *ut_host*)
>
> Preliminary: | MT-Unsafe sig:ALRM timer | AS-Unsafe  | AC-Unsafe fd | See Section 1.2.2.1 [POSIX Safety Concepts], page 2.
>
> The `logwtmp` function appends an entry to the user accounting log file, for the current time and the information provided in the *ut_line*, *ut_name* and *ut_host* arguments.

**Portability Note:** The BSD `struct utmp` only has the `ut_line`, `ut_name`, `ut_host` and `ut_time` members. Older systems do not even have the `ut_host` member.

## 30.13 User Database

This section describes how to search and scan the database of registered users. The database itself is kept in the file `/etc/passwd` on most systems, but on some systems a special network server gives access to it.

### 30.13.1 The Data Structure that Describes a User

The functions and data structures for accessing the system user database are declared in the header file `pwd.h`.

**struct passwd**                                                        [Data Type]
> The `passwd` data structure is used to hold information about entries in the system user data base. It has at least the following members:
>
> char *pw_name
> > The user's login name.
>
> char *pw_passwd.
> > The encrypted password string.

`uid_t pw_uid`

> The user ID number.

`gid_t pw_gid`

> The user's default group ID number.

`char *pw_gecos`

> A string typically containing the user's real name, and possibly other information such as a phone number.

`char *pw_dir`

> The user's home directory, or initial working directory. This might be a null pointer, in which case the interpretation is system-dependent.

`char *pw_shell`

> The user's default shell, or the initial program run when the user logs in. This might be a null pointer, indicating that the system default should be used.

## 30.13.2 Looking Up One User

You can search the system user database for information about a specific user using `getpwuid` or `getpwnam`. These functions are declared in `pwd.h`.

`struct passwd * getpwuid (`*uid_t* `uid)`                                        [Function]

> Preliminary: | MT-Unsafe race:pwuid locale | AS-Unsafe dlopen plugin heap lock | AC-Unsafe corrupt lock fd mem | See Section 1.2.2.1 [POSIX Safety Concepts], page 2.
>
> This function returns a pointer to a statically-allocated structure containing information about the user whose user ID is *uid*. This structure may be overwritten on subsequent calls to `getpwuid`.
>
> A null pointer value indicates there is no user in the data base with user ID *uid*.

`int getpwuid_r (`*uid_t* `uid,` *struct passwd* `*result_buf,` *char* `*buffer,`      [Function]
     *size_t* `buflen,` *struct passwd* `**result)`

> Preliminary: | MT-Safe locale | AS-Unsafe dlopen plugin heap lock | AC-Unsafe corrupt lock fd mem | See Section 1.2.2.1 [POSIX Safety Concepts], page 2.
>
> This function is similar to `getpwuid` in that it returns information about the user whose user ID is *uid*. However, it fills the user supplied structure pointed to by *result_buf* with the information instead of using a static buffer. The first *buflen* bytes of the additional buffer pointed to by *buffer* are used to contain additional information, normally strings which are pointed to by the elements of the result structure.
>
> If a user with ID *uid* is found, the pointer returned in *result* points to the record which contains the wanted data (i.e., *result* contains the value *result_buf*). If no user is found or if an error occurred, the pointer returned in *result* is a null pointer. The function returns zero or an error code. If the buffer *buffer* is too small to contain all the needed information, the error code `ERANGE` is returned and *errno* is set to `ERANGE`.

**struct passwd * getpwnam** (*const char \*name*)                    [Function]
> Preliminary: | MT-Unsafe race:pwnam locale | AS-Unsafe dlopen plugin heap lock | AC-Unsafe corrupt lock fd mem | See Section 1.2.2.1 [POSIX Safety Concepts], page 2.
>
> This function returns a pointer to a statically-allocated structure containing information about the user whose user name is *name*. This structure may be overwritten on subsequent calls to getpwnam.
>
> A null pointer return indicates there is no user named *name*.

**int getpwnam_r** (*const char \*name, struct passwd \*result_buf, char*           [Function]
> *\*buffer, size_t buflen, struct passwd \*\*result*)
> Preliminary: | MT-Safe locale | AS-Unsafe dlopen plugin heap lock | AC-Unsafe corrupt lock fd mem | See Section 1.2.2.1 [POSIX Safety Concepts], page 2.
>
> This function is similar to getpwnam in that is returns information about the user whose user name is *name*. However, like getpwuid_r, it fills the user supplied buffers in *result_buf* and *buffer* with the information instead of using a static buffer.
>
> The return values are the same as for getpwuid_r.

### 30.13.3 Scanning the List of All Users

This section explains how a program can read the list of all users in the system, one user at a time. The functions described here are declared in pwd.h.

You can use the fgetpwent function to read user entries from a particular file.

**struct passwd * fgetpwent** (*FILE \*stream*)                              [Function]
> Preliminary: | MT-Unsafe race:fpwent | AS-Unsafe corrupt lock | AC-Unsafe corrupt lock | See Section 1.2.2.1 [POSIX Safety Concepts], page 2.
>
> This function reads the next user entry from *stream* and returns a pointer to the entry. The structure is statically allocated and is rewritten on subsequent calls to fgetpwent. You must copy the contents of the structure if you wish to save the information.
>
> The stream must correspond to a file in the same format as the standard password database file.

**int fgetpwent_r** (*FILE \*stream, struct passwd \*result_buf, char*              [Function]
> *\*buffer, size_t buflen, struct passwd \*\*result*)
> Preliminary: | MT-Safe | AS-Unsafe corrupt | AC-Unsafe corrupt lock | See Section 1.2.2.1 [POSIX Safety Concepts], page 2.
>
> This function is similar to fgetpwent in that it reads the next user entry from *stream*. But the result is returned in the structure pointed to by *result_buf*. The first *buflen* bytes of the additional buffer pointed to by *buffer* are used to contain additional information, normally strings which are pointed to by the elements of the result structure.
>
> The stream must correspond to a file in the same format as the standard password database file.
>
> If the function returns zero *result* points to the structure with the wanted data (normally this is in *result_buf*). If errors occurred the return value is nonzero and *result* contains a null pointer.

The way to scan all the entries in the user database is with `setpwent`, `getpwent`, and `endpwent`.

void setpwent (*void*)                                                     [Function]
> Preliminary: | MT-Unsafe race:pwent locale | AS-Unsafe dlopen plugin heap lock | AC-Unsafe corrupt lock fd mem | See Section 1.2.2.1 [POSIX Safety Concepts], page 2.
>
> This function initializes a stream which `getpwent` and `getpwent_r` use to read the user database.

struct passwd * getpwent (*void*)                                          [Function]
> Preliminary: | MT-Unsafe race:pwent race:pwentbuf locale | AS-Unsafe dlopen plugin heap lock | AC-Unsafe corrupt lock fd mem | See Section 1.2.2.1 [POSIX Safety Concepts], page 2.
>
> The `getpwent` function reads the next entry from the stream initialized by `setpwent`. It returns a pointer to the entry. The structure is statically allocated and is rewritten on subsequent calls to `getpwent`. You must copy the contents of the structure if you wish to save the information.
>
> A null pointer is returned when no more entries are available.

int getpwent_r (*struct passwd *result_buf, char *buffer, size_t buflen, struct passwd **result*)                                                     [Function]
> Preliminary: | MT-Unsafe race:pwent locale | AS-Unsafe dlopen plugin heap lock | AC-Unsafe corrupt lock fd mem | See Section 1.2.2.1 [POSIX Safety Concepts], page 2.
>
> This function is similar to `getpwent` in that it returns the next entry from the stream initialized by `setpwent`. Like `fgetpwent_r`, it uses the user-supplied buffers in *result_buf* and *buffer* to return the information requested.
>
> The return values are the same as for `fgetpwent_r`.

void endpwent (*void*)                                                     [Function]
> Preliminary: | MT-Unsafe race:pwent locale | AS-Unsafe dlopen plugin heap lock | AC-Unsafe corrupt lock fd mem | See Section 1.2.2.1 [POSIX Safety Concepts], page 2.
>
> This function closes the internal stream used by `getpwent` or `getpwent_r`.

## 30.13.4 Writing a User Entry

int putpwent (*const struct passwd *p, FILE *stream*)                      [Function]
> Preliminary: | MT-Safe locale | AS-Unsafe corrupt | AC-Unsafe lock corrupt | See Section 1.2.2.1 [POSIX Safety Concepts], page 2.
>
> This function writes the user entry *\*p* to the stream *stream*, in the format used for the standard user database file. The return value is zero on success and nonzero on failure.
>
> This function exists for compatibility with SVID. We recommend that you avoid using it, because it makes sense only on the assumption that the `struct passwd` structure has no members except the standard ones; on a system which merges the traditional

Unix data base with other extended information about users, adding an entry using this function would inevitably leave out much of the important information.

The group and user ID fields are left empty if the group or user name starts with a - or +.

The function `putpwent` is declared in `pwd.h`.

## 30.14 Group Database

This section describes how to search and scan the database of registered groups. The database itself is kept in the file /etc/group on most systems, but on some systems a special network service provides access to it.

### 30.14.1 The Data Structure for a Group

The functions and data structures for accessing the system group database are declared in the header file `grp.h`.

`struct group`                                                          [Data Type]

> The `group` structure is used to hold information about an entry in the system group database. It has at least the following members:
>
> `char *gr_name`
>> The name of the group.
>
> `gid_t gr_gid`
>> The group ID of the group.
>
> `char **gr_mem`
>> A vector of pointers to the names of users in the group. Each user name is a null-terminated string, and the vector itself is terminated by a null pointer.

### 30.14.2 Looking Up One Group

You can search the group database for information about a specific group using `getgrgid` or `getgrnam`. These functions are declared in `grp.h`.

`struct group * getgrgid` (gid_t gid)                                    [Function]

> Preliminary: | MT-Unsafe race:grgid locale | AS-Unsafe dlopen plugin heap lock | AC-Unsafe corrupt lock fd mem | See Section 1.2.2.1 [POSIX Safety Concepts], page 2.
>
> This function returns a pointer to a statically-allocated structure containing information about the group whose group ID is gid. This structure may be overwritten by subsequent calls to `getgrgid`.
>
> A null pointer indicates there is no group with ID gid.

`int getgrgid_r` (gid_t gid, struct group *result_buf, char *buffer,     [Function]
        size_t buflen, struct group **result)

> Preliminary: | MT-Safe locale | AS-Unsafe dlopen plugin heap lock | AC-Unsafe corrupt lock fd mem | See Section 1.2.2.1 [POSIX Safety Concepts], page 2.

This function is similar to `getgrgid` in that it returns information about the group whose group ID is *gid*. However, it fills the user supplied structure pointed to by *result_buf* with the information instead of using a static buffer. The first *buflen* bytes of the additional buffer pointed to by *buffer* are used to contain additional information, normally strings which are pointed to by the elements of the result structure.

If a group with ID *gid* is found, the pointer returned in *result* points to the record which contains the wanted data (i.e., *result* contains the value *result_buf*). If no group is found or if an error occurred, the pointer returned in *result* is a null pointer. The function returns zero or an error code. If the buffer *buffer* is too small to contain all the needed information, the error code `ERANGE` is returned and *errno* is set to `ERANGE`.

**struct group * getgrnam** (*const char *`name`*)                                [Function]
> Preliminary: | MT-Unsafe race:grnam locale | AS-Unsafe dlopen plugin heap lock | AC-Unsafe corrupt lock fd mem | See Section 1.2.2.1 [POSIX Safety Concepts], page 2.

> This function returns a pointer to a statically-allocated structure containing information about the group whose group name is *name*. This structure may be overwritten by subsequent calls to `getgrnam`.

> A null pointer indicates there is no group named *name*.

**int getgrnam_r** (*const char *`name`, struct group *`result_buf`, char*   [Function]
> *`*buffer`, size_t `buflen`, struct group **`result`*)
> Preliminary: | MT-Safe locale | AS-Unsafe dlopen plugin heap lock | AC-Unsafe corrupt lock fd mem | See Section 1.2.2.1 [POSIX Safety Concepts], page 2.

> This function is similar to `getgrnam` in that is returns information about the group whose group name is *name*. Like `getgrgid_r`, it uses the user supplied buffers in *result_buf* and *buffer*, not a static buffer.

> The return values are the same as for `getgrgid_r ERANGE`.

## 30.14.3 Scanning the List of All Groups

This section explains how a program can read the list of all groups in the system, one group at a time. The functions described here are declared in `grp.h`.

You can use the `fgetgrent` function to read group entries from a particular file.

**struct group * fgetgrent** (*FILE *`stream`*)                                [Function]
> Preliminary: | MT-Unsafe race:fgrent | AS-Unsafe corrupt lock | AC-Unsafe corrupt lock | See Section 1.2.2.1 [POSIX Safety Concepts], page 2.

> The `fgetgrent` function reads the next entry from *stream*. It returns a pointer to the entry. The structure is statically allocated and is overwritten on subsequent calls to `fgetgrent`. You must copy the contents of the structure if you wish to save the information.

> The stream must correspond to a file in the same format as the standard group database file.

`int fgetgrent_r (FILE *stream, struct group *result_buf, char`          [Function]
        `*buffer, size_t buflen, struct group **result)`
> Preliminary: | MT-Safe | AS-Unsafe corrupt | AC-Unsafe corrupt lock | See Section 1.2.2.1 [POSIX Safety Concepts], page 2.

> This function is similar to `fgetgrent` in that it reads the next user entry from *stream*. But the result is returned in the structure pointed to by *result_buf*. The first *buflen* bytes of the additional buffer pointed to by *buffer* are used to contain additional information, normally strings which are pointed to by the elements of the result structure.

> This stream must correspond to a file in the same format as the standard group database file.

> If the function returns zero *result* points to the structure with the wanted data (normally this is in *result_buf*). If errors occurred the return value is non-zero and *result* contains a null pointer.

The way to scan all the entries in the group database is with `setgrent`, `getgrent`, and `endgrent`.

`void setgrent (void)`                                                    [Function]
> Preliminary: | MT-Unsafe race:grent locale | AS-Unsafe dlopen plugin heap lock | AC-Unsafe corrupt lock fd mem | See Section 1.2.2.1 [POSIX Safety Concepts], page 2.

> This function initializes a stream for reading from the group data base. You use this stream by calling `getgrent` or `getgrent_r`.

`struct group * getgrent (void)`                                          [Function]
> Preliminary: | MT-Unsafe race:grent race:grentbuf locale | AS-Unsafe dlopen plugin heap lock | AC-Unsafe corrupt lock fd mem | See Section 1.2.2.1 [POSIX Safety Concepts], page 2.

> The `getgrent` function reads the next entry from the stream initialized by `setgrent`. It returns a pointer to the entry. The structure is statically allocated and is overwritten on subsequent calls to `getgrent`. You must copy the contents of the structure if you wish to save the information.

`int getgrent_r (struct group *result_buf, char *buffer, size_t`          [Function]
        `buflen, struct group **result)`
> Preliminary: | MT-Unsafe race:grent locale | AS-Unsafe dlopen plugin heap lock | AC-Unsafe corrupt lock fd mem | See Section 1.2.2.1 [POSIX Safety Concepts], page 2.

> This function is similar to `getgrent` in that it returns the next entry from the stream initialized by `setgrent`. Like `fgetgrent_r`, it places the result in user-supplied buffers pointed to *result_buf* and *buffer*.

> If the function returns zero *result* contains a pointer to the data (normally equal to *result_buf*). If errors occurred the return value is non-zero and *result* contains a null pointer.

void **endgrent** (*void*)                                                                [Function]
    Preliminary: | MT-Unsafe race:grent locale | AS-Unsafe dlopen plugin heap lock
    | AC-Unsafe corrupt lock fd mem | See Section 1.2.2.1 [POSIX Safety Concepts],
    page 2.

    This function closes the internal stream used by `getgrent` or `getgrent_r`.

## 30.15 User and Group Database Example

Here is an example program showing the use of the system database inquiry functions. The
program prints some information about the user running the program.

```
#include <grp.h>
#include <pwd.h>
#include <sys/types.h>
#include <unistd.h>
#include <stdlib.h>

int
main (void)
{
  uid_t me;
  struct passwd *my_passwd;
  struct group *my_group;
  char **members;

  /* Get information about the user ID. */
  me = getuid ();
  my_passwd = getpwuid (me);
  if (!my_passwd)
    {
      printf ("Couldn't find out about user %d.\n", (int) me);
      exit (EXIT_FAILURE);
    }

  /* Print the information. */
  printf ("I am %s.\n", my_passwd->pw_gecos);
  printf ("My login name is %s.\n", my_passwd->pw_name);
  printf ("My uid is %d.\n", (int) (my_passwd->pw_uid));
  printf ("My home directory is %s.\n", my_passwd->pw_dir);
  printf ("My default shell is %s.\n", my_passwd->pw_shell);

  /* Get information about the default group ID. */
  my_group = getgrgid (my_passwd->pw_gid);
  if (!my_group)
    {
      printf ("Couldn't find out about group %d.\n",
              (int) my_passwd->pw_gid);
      exit (EXIT_FAILURE);
    }

  /* Print the information. */
  printf ("My default group is %s (%d).\n",
          my_group->gr_name, (int) (my_passwd->pw_gid));
  printf ("The members of this group are:\n");
  members = my_group->gr_mem;
  while (*members)
```

```
      {
        printf ("  %s\n", *(members));
        members++;
      }

    return EXIT_SUCCESS;
  }
```

Here is some output from this program:

```
I am Throckmorton Snurd.
My login name is snurd.
My uid is 31093.
My home directory is /home/fsg/snurd.
My default shell is /bin/sh.
My default group is guest (12).
The members of this group are:
  friedman
  tami
```

## 30.16  Netgroup Database

### 30.16.1  Netgroup Data

Sometimes it is useful to group users according to other criteria (see Section 30.14 [Group Database], page 814). E.g., it is useful to associate a certain group of users with a certain machine. On the other hand grouping of host names is not supported so far.

In Sun Microsystems SunOS appeared a new kind of database, the netgroup database. It allows grouping hosts, users, and domains freely, giving them individual names. To be more concrete, a netgroup is a list of triples consisting of a host name, a user name, and a domain name where any of the entries can be a wildcard entry matching all inputs. A last possibility is that names of other netgroups can also be given in the list specifying a netgroup. So one can construct arbitrary hierarchies without loops.

Sun's implementation allows netgroups only for the **nis** or **nisplus** service, see Section 29.2.1 [Services in the NSS configuration File], page 783. The implementation in the GNU C Library has no such restriction. An entry in either of the input services must have the following form:

```
groupname ( groupname | (hostname,username,domainname) )+
```

Any of the fields in the triple can be empty which means anything matches. While describing the functions we will see that the opposite case is useful as well. I.e., there may be entries which will not match any input. For entries like this, a name consisting of the single character - shall be used.

### 30.16.2  Looking up one Netgroup

The lookup functions for netgroups are a bit different to all other system database handling functions. Since a single netgroup can contain many entries a two-step process is needed. First a single netgroup is selected and then one can iterate over all entries in this netgroup. These functions are declared in **netdb.h**.

`int setnetgrent (`*`const char *netgroup`*`)`                                  [Function]

> Preliminary: | MT-Unsafe race:netgrent locale | AS-Unsafe dlopen plugin heap lock
> | AC-Unsafe corrupt lock fd mem | See Section 1.2.2.1 [POSIX Safety Concepts],
> page 2.

> A call to this function initializes the internal state of the library to allow following calls
> of the `getnetgrent` to iterate over all entries in the netgroup with name *netgroup*.

> When the call is successful (i.e., when a netgroup with this name exists) the return
> value is `1`. When the return value is `0` no netgroup of this name is known or some
> other error occurred.

It is important to remember that there is only one single state for iterating the netgroups.
Even if the programmer uses the `getnetgrent_r` function the result is not really reentrant
since always only one single netgroup at a time can be processed. If the program needs
to process more than one netgroup simultaneously she must protect this by using external
locking. This problem was introduced in the original netgroups implementation in SunOS
and since we must stay compatible it is not possible to change this.

Some other functions also use the netgroups state. Currently these are the `innetgr`
function and parts of the implementation of the `compat` service part of the NSS implementation.

`int getnetgrent (`*`char **hostp, char **userp, char **domainp`*`)`          [Function]

> Preliminary: | MT-Unsafe race:netgrent race:netgrentbuf locale | AS-Unsafe dlopen
> plugin heap lock | AC-Unsafe corrupt lock fd mem | See Section 1.2.2.1 [POSIX
> Safety Concepts], page 2.

> This function returns the next unprocessed entry of the currently selected netgroup.
> The string pointers, in which addresses are passed in the arguments *hostp*, *userp*, and
> *domainp*, will contain after a successful call pointers to appropriate strings. If the
> string in the next entry is empty the pointer has the value `NULL`. The returned string
> pointers are only valid if none of the netgroup related functions are called.

> The return value is `1` if the next entry was successfully read. A value of `0` means no
> further entries exist or internal errors occurred.

`int getnetgrent_r (`*`char **hostp, char **userp, char **domainp,`*          [Function]
        *`char *buffer, size_t buflen`*`)`

> Preliminary: | MT-Unsafe race:netgrent locale | AS-Unsafe dlopen plugin heap lock
> | AC-Unsafe corrupt lock fd mem | See Section 1.2.2.1 [POSIX Safety Concepts],
> page 2.

> This function is similar to `getnetgrent` with only one exception: the strings the three
> string pointers *hostp*, *userp*, and *domainp* point to, are placed in the buffer of *buflen*
> bytes starting at *buffer*. This means the returned values are valid even after other
> netgroup related functions are called.

> The return value is `1` if the next entry was successfully read and the buffer contains
> enough room to place the strings in it. `0` is returned in case no more entries are found,
> the buffer is too small, or internal errors occurred.

> This function is a GNU extension. The original implementation in the SunOS libc
> does not provide this function.

**void endnetgrent** (*void*)                                              [Function]
> Preliminary: | MT-Unsafe race:netgrent | AS-Unsafe dlopen plugin heap lock | AC-Unsafe corrupt lock fd mem | See Section 1.2.2.1 [POSIX Safety Concepts], page 2.

> This function frees all buffers which were allocated to process the last selected netgroup. As a result all string pointers returned by calls to **getnetgrent** are invalid afterwards.

## 30.16.3 Testing for Netgroup Membership

It is often not necessary to scan the whole netgroup since often the only interesting question is whether a given entry is part of the selected netgroup.

**int innetgr** (*const char \*netgroup, const char \*host, const char*      [Function]
      *\*user, const char \*domain*)
> Preliminary: | MT-Unsafe race:netgrent locale | AS-Unsafe dlopen plugin heap lock | AC-Unsafe corrupt lock fd mem | See Section 1.2.2.1 [POSIX Safety Concepts], page 2.

> This function tests whether the triple specified by the parameters *hostp*, *userp*, and *domainp* is part of the netgroup *netgroup*. Using this function has the advantage that

> 1. no other netgroup function can use the global netgroup state since internal locking is used and

> 2. the function is implemented more efficiently than successive calls to the other **set/get/endnetgrent** functions.

> Any of the pointers *hostp*, *userp*, and *domainp* can be **NULL** which means any value is accepted in this position. This is also true for the name – which should not match any other string otherwise.

> The return value is 1 if an entry matching the given triple is found in the netgroup. The return value is 0 if the netgroup itself is not found, the netgroup does not contain the triple or internal errors occurred.

# 31 System Management

This chapter describes facilities for controlling the system that underlies a process (including the operating system and hardware) and for getting information about it. Anyone can generally use the informational facilities, but usually only a properly privileged process can make changes.

To get information on parameters of the system that are built into the system, such as the maximum length of a filename, Chapter 32 [System Configuration Parameters], page 838.

## 31.1 Host Identification

This section explains how to identify the particular system on which your program is running. First, let's review the various ways computer systems are named, which is a little complicated because of the history of the development of the Internet.

Every Unix system (also known as a host) has a host name, whether it's connected to a network or not. In its simplest form, as used before computer networks were an issue, it's just a word like 'chicken'.

But any system attached to the Internet or any network like it conforms to a more rigorous naming convention as part of the Domain Name System (DNS). In DNS, every host name is composed of two parts:

1. hostname

2. domain name

You will note that "hostname" looks a lot like "host name", but is not the same thing, and that people often incorrectly refer to entire host names as "domain names."

In DNS, the full host name is properly called the FQDN (Fully Qualified Domain Name) and consists of the hostname, then a period, then the domain name. The domain name itself usually has multiple components separated by periods. So for example, a system's hostname may be 'chicken' and its domain name might be 'ai.mit.edu', so its FQDN (which is its host name) is 'chicken.ai.mit.edu'.

Adding to the confusion, though, is that DNS is not the only name space in which a computer needs to be known. Another name space is the NIS (aka YP) name space. For NIS purposes, there is another domain name, which is called the NIS domain name or the YP domain name. It need not have anything to do with the DNS domain name.

Confusing things even more is the fact that in DNS, it is possible for multiple FQDNs to refer to the same system. However, there is always exactly one of them that is the true host name, and it is called the canonical FQDN.

In some contexts, the host name is called a "node name."

For more information on DNS host naming, see Section 16.6.2.4 [Host Names], page 443.

Prototypes for these functions appear in `unistd.h`.

The programs `hostname`, `hostid`, and `domainname` work by calling these functions.

`int gethostname (char *name, size_t size)`                                    [Function]
    Preliminary: | MT-Safe | AS-Safe | AC-Safe | See Section 1.2.2.1 [POSIX Safety Concepts], page 2.

This function returns the host name of the system on which it is called, in the array *name*. The *size* argument specifies the size of this array, in bytes. Note that this is *not* the DNS hostname. If the system participates in DNS, this is the FQDN (see above).

The return value is 0 on success and -1 on failure. In the GNU C Library, `gethostname` fails if *size* is not large enough; then you can try again with a larger array. The following `errno` error condition is defined for this function:

ENAMETOOLONG
> The *size* argument is less than the size of the host name plus one.

On some systems, there is a symbol for the maximum possible host name length: `MAXHOSTNAMELEN`. It is defined in `sys/param.h`. But you can't count on this to exist, so it is cleaner to handle failure and try again.

`gethostname` stores the beginning of the host name in *name* even if the host name won't entirely fit. For some purposes, a truncated host name is good enough. If it is, you can ignore the error code.

**int sethostname** (*const char \*name*, *size_t* **length**)                              [Function]
> Preliminary: | MT-Safe | AS-Safe | AC-Safe | See Section 1.2.2.1 [POSIX Safety Concepts], page 2.

> The `sethostname` function sets the host name of the system that calls it to *name*, a string with length *length*. Only privileged processes are permitted to do this.

> Usually `sethostname` gets called just once, at system boot time. Often, the program that calls it sets it to the value it finds in the file `/etc/hostname`.

> Be sure to set the host name to the full host name, not just the DNS hostname (see above).

> The return value is 0 on success and -1 on failure. The following `errno` error condition is defined for this function:

> EPERM      This process cannot set the host name because it is not privileged.

**int getdomainnname** (*char \*name*, *size_t* **length**)                              [Function]
> Preliminary: | MT-Safe | AS-Safe | AC-Safe | See Section 1.2.2.1 [POSIX Safety Concepts], page 2.

> `getdomainname` returns the NIS (aka YP) domain name of the system on which it is called. Note that this is not the more popular DNS domain name. Get that with `gethostname`.

> The specifics of this function are analogous to `gethostname`, above.

**int setdomainname** (*const char \*name*, *size_t* **length**)                              [Function]
> Preliminary: | MT-Safe | AS-Safe | AC-Safe | See Section 1.2.2.1 [POSIX Safety Concepts], page 2.

> `getdomainname` sets the NIS (aka YP) domain name of the system on which it is called. Note that this is not the more popular DNS domain name. Set that with `sethostname`.

> The specifics of this function are analogous to `sethostname`, above.

**long int gethostid** (*void*) [Function]

    Preliminary: | MT-Safe hostid env locale | AS-Unsafe dlopen plugin corrupt heap lock | AC-Unsafe lock corrupt mem fd | See Section 1.2.2.1 [POSIX Safety Concepts], page 2.

    This function returns the "host ID" of the machine the program is running on. By convention, this is usually the primary Internet IP address of that machine, converted to a **long int**. However, on some systems it is a meaningless but unique number which is hard-coded for each machine.

    This is not widely used. It arose in BSD 4.2, but was dropped in BSD 4.4. It is not required by POSIX.

    The proper way to query the IP address is to use **gethostbyname** on the results of **gethostname**. For more information on IP addresses, See Section 16.6.2 [Host Addresses], page 439.

**int sethostid** (*long int id*) [Function]

    Preliminary: | MT-Unsafe const:hostid | AS-Unsafe | AC-Unsafe corrupt fd | See Section 1.2.2.1 [POSIX Safety Concepts], page 2.

    The **sethostid** function sets the "host ID" of the host machine to *id*. Only privileged processes are permitted to do this. Usually it happens just once, at system boot time.

    The proper way to establish the primary IP address of a system is to configure the IP address resolver to associate that IP address with the system's host name as returned by **gethostname**. For example, put a record for the system in **/etc/hosts**.

    See **gethostid** above for more information on host ids.

    The return value is **0** on success and **-1** on failure. The following **errno** error conditions are defined for this function:

    **EPERM**    This process cannot set the host name because it is not privileged.

    **ENOSYS**    The operating system does not support setting the host ID. On some systems, the host ID is a meaningless but unique number hard-coded for each machine.

## 31.2 Platform Type Identification

You can use the **uname** function to find out some information about the type of computer your program is running on. This function and the associated data type are declared in the header file **sys/utsname.h**.

    As a bonus, **uname** also gives some information identifying the particular system your program is running on. This is the same information which you can get with functions targeted to this purpose described in Section 31.1 [Host Identification], page 821.

**struct utsname** [Data Type]

    The **utsname** structure is used to hold information returned by the **uname** function. It has the following members:

    **char sysname[]**

        This is the name of the operating system in use.

`char release[]`

> This is the current release level of the operating system implementation.

`char version[]`

> This is the current version level within the release of the operating system.

`char machine[]`

> This is a description of the type of hardware that is in use.
>
> Some systems provide a mechanism to interrogate the kernel directly for this information. On systems without such a mechanism, the GNU C Library fills in this field based on the configuration name that was specified when building and installing the library.
>
> GNU uses a three-part name to describe a system configuration; the three parts are *cpu*, *manufacturer* and *system-type*, and they are separated with dashes. Any possible combination of three names is potentially meaningful, but most such combinations are meaningless in practice and even the meaningful ones are not necessarily supported by any particular GNU program.
>
> Since the value in `machine` is supposed to describe just the hardware, it consists of the first two parts of the configuration name: '`cpu-manufacturer`'. For example, it might be one of these:
>
> > `"sparc-sun"`, `"i386-anything"`, `"m68k-hp"`, `"m68k-sony"`,
> > `"m68k-sun"`, `"mips-dec"`

`char nodename[]`

> This is the host name of this particular computer. In the GNU C Library, the value is the same as that returned by `gethostname`; see Section 31.1 [Host Identification], page 821.
>
> gethostname() is implemented with a call to uname().

`char domainname[]`

> This is the NIS or YP domain name. It is the same value returned by `getdomainname`; see Section 31.1 [Host Identification], page 821. This element is a relatively recent invention and use of it is not as portable as use of the rest of the structure.

`int uname` (*struct utsname \*info*)                                    [Function]
> Preliminary: | MT-Safe | AS-Safe | AC-Safe | See Section 1.2.2.1 [POSIX Safety Concepts], page 2.

The `uname` function fills in the structure pointed to by *info* with information about the operating system and host machine. A non-negative value indicates that the data was successfully stored.

`-1` as the value indicates an error. The only error possible is `EFAULT`, which we normally don't mention as it is always a possibility.

## 31.3 Controlling and Querying Mounts

All files are in filesystems, and before you can access any file, its filesystem must be mounted. Because of Unix's concept of *Everything is a file*, mounting of filesystems is central to doing almost anything. This section explains how to find out what filesystems are currently mounted and what filesystems are available for mounting, and how to change what is mounted.

The classic filesystem is the contents of a disk drive. The concept is considerably more abstract, though, and lots of things other than disk drives can be mounted.

Some block devices don't correspond to traditional devices like disk drives. For example, a loop device is a block device whose driver uses a regular file in another filesystem as its medium. So if that regular file contains appropriate data for a filesystem, you can by mounting the loop device essentially mount a regular file.

Some filesystems aren't based on a device of any kind. The "proc" filesystem, for example, contains files whose data is made up by the filesystem driver on the fly whenever you ask for it. And when you write to it, the data you write causes changes in the system. No data gets stored.

## 31.3.1 Mount Information

For some programs it is desirable and necessary to access information about whether a certain filesystem is mounted and, if it is, where, or simply to get lists of all the available filesystems. The GNU C Library provides some functions to retrieve this information portably.

Traditionally Unix systems have a file named /etc/fstab which describes all possibly mounted filesystems. The mount program uses this file to mount at startup time of the system all the necessary filesystems. The information about all the filesystems actually mounted is normally kept in a file named either /var/run/mtab or /etc/mtab. Both files share the same syntax and it is crucial that this syntax is followed all the time. Therefore it is best to never directly write the files. The functions described in this section can do this and they also provide the functionality to convert the external textual representation to the internal representation.

Note that the fstab and mtab files are maintained on a system by *convention*. It is possible for the files not to exist or not to be consistent with what is really mounted or available to mount, if the system's administration policy allows it. But programs that mount and unmount filesystems typically maintain and use these files as described herein.

The filenames given above should never be used directly. The portable way to handle these file is to use the macro _PATH_FSTAB, defined in fstab.h, or _PATH_MNTTAB, defined in mntent.h and paths.h, for fstab; and the macro _PATH_MOUNTED, also defined in mntent.h and paths.h, for mtab. There are also two alternate macro names FSTAB, MNTTAB, and MOUNTED defined but these names are deprecated and kept only for backward compatibility. The names _PATH_MNTTAB and _PATH_MOUNTED should always be used.

### 31.3.1.1 The fstab file

The internal representation for entries of the file is struct fstab, defined in fstab.h.

struct fstab                                                                  [Data Type]
> This structure is used with the getfsent, getfsspec, and getfsfile functions.

> char *fs_spec
>> This element describes the device from which the filesystem is mounted. Normally this is the name of a special device, such as a hard disk partition,

but it could also be a more or less generic string. For *NFS* it would be a hostname and directory name combination.

Even though the element is not declared `const` it shouldn't be modified. The missing `const` has historic reasons, since this function predates ISO C. The same is true for the other string elements of this structure.

`char *fs_file`

This describes the mount point on the local system. I.e., accessing any file in this filesystem has implicitly or explicitly this string as a prefix.

`char *fs_vfstype`

This is the type of the filesystem. Depending on what the underlying kernel understands it can be any string.

`char *fs_mntops`

This is a string containing options passed to the kernel with the `mount` call. Again, this can be almost anything. There can be more than one option, separated from the others by a comma. Each option consists of a name and an optional value part, introduced by an = character.

If the value of this element must be processed it should ideally be done using the `getsubopt` function; see Section 25.3.12.1 [Parsing of Suboptions], page 736.

`const char *fs_type`

This name is poorly chosen. This element points to a string (possibly in the `fs_mntops` string) which describes the modes with which the filesystem is mounted. `fstab` defines five macros to describe the possible values:

`FSTAB_RW`   The filesystems gets mounted with read and write enabled.

`FSTAB_RQ`   The filesystems gets mounted with read and write enabled. Write access is restricted by quotas.

`FSTAB_RO`   The filesystem gets mounted read-only.

`FSTAB_SW`   This is not a real filesystem, it is a swap device.

`FSTAB_XX`   This entry from the `fstab` file is totally ignored.

Testing for equality with these value must happen using `strcmp` since these are all strings. Comparing the pointer will probably always fail.

`int fs_freq`

This element describes the dump frequency in days.

`int fs_passno`

This element describes the pass number on parallel dumps. It is closely related to the `dump` utility used on Unix systems.

To read the entire content of the of the `fstab` file the GNU C Library contains a set of three functions which are designed in the usual way.

`int setfsent` (*void*)                                                                       [Function]
Preliminary: | MT-Unsafe race:fsent | AS-Unsafe heap corrupt lock | AC-Unsafe corrupt lock mem fd | See Section 1.2.2.1 [POSIX Safety Concepts], page 2.

This function makes sure that the internal read pointer for the `fstab` file is at the beginning of the file. This is done by either opening the file or resetting the read pointer.

Since the file handle is internal to the libc this function is not thread-safe.

This function returns a non-zero value if the operation was successful and the `getfs*` functions can be used to read the entries of the file.

**void endfsent** (*void*)                                                          [Function]
    Preliminary: | MT-Unsafe race:fsent | AS-Unsafe heap corrupt lock | AC-Unsafe corrupt lock mem fd | See Section 1.2.2.1 [POSIX Safety Concepts], page 2.

    This function makes sure that all resources acquired by a prior call to `setfsent` (explicitly or implicitly by calling `getfsent`) are freed.

**struct fstab \* getfsent** (*void*)                                               [Function]
    Preliminary: | MT-Unsafe race:fsent locale | AS-Unsafe corrupt heap lock | AC-Unsafe corrupt lock mem | See Section 1.2.2.1 [POSIX Safety Concepts], page 2.

    This function returns the next entry of the `fstab` file. If this is the first call to any of the functions handling `fstab` since program start or the last call of `endfsent`, the file will be opened.

    The function returns a pointer to a variable of type `struct fstab`. This variable is shared by all threads and therefore this function is not thread-safe. If an error occurred `getfsent` returns a `NULL` pointer.

**struct fstab \* getfsspec** (*const char \*name*)                                 [Function]
    Preliminary: | MT-Unsafe race:fsent locale | AS-Unsafe corrupt heap lock | AC-Unsafe corrupt lock mem | See Section 1.2.2.1 [POSIX Safety Concepts], page 2.

    This function returns the next entry of the `fstab` file which has a string equal to *name* pointed to by the `fs_spec` element. Since there is normally exactly one entry for each special device it makes no sense to call this function more than once for the same argument. If this is the first call to any of the functions handling `fstab` since program start or the last call of `endfsent`, the file will be opened.

    The function returns a pointer to a variable of type `struct fstab`. This variable is shared by all threads and therefore this function is not thread-safe. If an error occurred `getfsent` returns a `NULL` pointer.

**struct fstab \* getfsfile** (*const char \*name*)                                 [Function]
    Preliminary: | MT-Unsafe race:fsent locale | AS-Unsafe corrupt heap lock | AC-Unsafe corrupt lock mem | See Section 1.2.2.1 [POSIX Safety Concepts], page 2.

    This function returns the next entry of the `fstab` file which has a string equal to *name* pointed to by the `fs_file` element. Since there is normally exactly one entry for each mount point it makes no sense to call this function more than once for the same argument. If this is the first call to any of the functions handling `fstab` since program start or the last call of `endfsent`, the file will be opened.

    The function returns a pointer to a variable of type `struct fstab`. This variable is shared by all threads and therefore this function is not thread-safe. If an error occurred `getfsent` returns a `NULL` pointer.

### 31.3.1.2 The `mtab` file

The following functions and data structure access the `mtab` file.

**struct mntent** [Data Type]

This structure is used with the `getmntent`, `getmntent_t`, `addmntent`, and `hasmntopt` functions.

`char *mnt_fsname`

This element contains a pointer to a string describing the name of the special device from which the filesystem is mounted. It corresponds to the `fs_spec` element in `struct fstab`.

`char *mnt_dir`

This element points to a string describing the mount point of the filesystem. It corresponds to the `fs_file` element in `struct fstab`.

`char *mnt_type`

`mnt_type` describes the filesystem type and is therefore equivalent to `fs_vfstype` in `struct fstab`. `mntent.h` defines a few symbolic names for some of the values this string can have. But since the kernel can support arbitrary filesystems it does not make much sense to give them symbolic names. If one knows the symbol name one also knows the filesystem name. Nevertheless here follows the list of the symbols provided in `mntent.h`.

`MNTTYPE_IGNORE`

This symbol expands to `"ignore"`. The value is sometime used in `fstab` files to make sure entries are not used without removing them.

`MNTTYPE_NFS`

Expands to `"nfs"`. Using this macro sometimes could make sense since it names the default NFS implementation, in case both version 2 and 3 are supported.

`MNTTYPE_SWAP`

This symbol expands to `"swap"`. It names the special `fstab` entry which names one of the possibly multiple swap partitions.

`char *mnt_opts`

The element contains a string describing the options used while mounting the filesystem. As for the equivalent element `fs_mntops` of `struct fstab` it is best to use the function `getsubopt` (see Section 25.3.12.1 [Parsing of Suboptions], page 736) to access the parts of this string.

The `mntent.h` file defines a number of macros with string values which correspond to some of the options understood by the kernel. There might be many more options which are possible so it doesn't make much sense to rely on these macros but to be consistent here is the list:

MNTOPT_DEFAULTS

> Expands to "defaults". This option should be used alone since it indicates all values for the customizable values are chosen to be the default.

MNTOPT_RO

> Expands to "ro". See the FSTAB_RO value, it means the filesystem is mounted read-only.

MNTOPT_RW

> Expand to "rw". See the FSTAB_RW value, it means the filesystem is mounted with read and write permissions.

MNTOPT_SUID

> Expands to "suid". This means that the SUID bit (see Section 30.4 [How an Application Can Change Persona], page 792) is respected when a program from the filesystem is started.

MNTOPT_NOSUID

> Expands to "nosuid". This is the opposite of MNTOPT_SUID, the SUID bit for all files from the filesystem is ignored.

MNTOPT_NOAUTO

> Expands to "noauto". At startup time the mount program will ignore this entry if it is started with the -a option to mount all filesystems mentioned in the fstab file.

> As for the FSTAB_* entries introduced above it is important to use strcmp to check for equality.

mnt_freq  This elements corresponds to fs_freq and also specifies the frequency in days in which dumps are made.

mnt_passno

> This element is equivalent to fs_passno with the same meaning which is uninteresting for all programs beside dump.

For accessing the mtab file there is again a set of three functions to access all entries in a row. Unlike the functions to handle fstab these functions do not access a fixed file and there is even a thread safe variant of the get function. Beside this the GNU C Librarycontains functions to alter the file and test for specific options.

FILE * setmntent (const char *file, const char *mode)                              [Function]
> Preliminary: | MT-Safe | AS-Unsafe heap lock | AC-Unsafe mem fd lock | See Section 1.2.2.1 [POSIX Safety Concepts], page 2.

> The setmntent function prepares the file named FILE which must be in the format of a fstab and mtab file for the upcoming processing through the other functions of the family. The mode parameter can be chosen in the way the opentype parameter for fopen (see Section 12.3 [Opening Streams], page 249) can be chosen. If the file is opened for writing the file is also allowed to be empty.

> If the file was successfully opened setmntent returns a file descriptor for future use. Otherwise the return value is NULL and errno is set accordingly.

**int endmntent** (*FILE \*stream*)                                          [Function]
>  Preliminary: | MT-Safe | AS-Unsafe heap lock | AC-Unsafe lock mem fd | See
>  Section 1.2.2.1 [POSIX Safety Concepts], page 2.

>  This function takes for the *stream* parameter a file handle which previously was
>  returned from the `setmntent` call. `endmntent` closes the stream and frees all resources.

>  The return value is 1 unless an error occurred in which case it is 0.

**struct mntent \* getmntent** (*FILE \*stream*)                              [Function]
>  Preliminary: | MT-Unsafe race:mntentbuf locale | AS-Unsafe corrupt heap init |
>  AC-Unsafe init corrupt lock mem | See Section 1.2.2.1 [POSIX Safety Concepts],
>  page 2.

>  The `getmntent` function takes as the parameter a file handle previously returned by
>  successful call to `setmntent`. It returns a pointer to a static variable of type `struct`
>  `mntent` which is filled with the information from the next entry from the file currently
>  read.

>  The file format used prescribes the use of spaces or tab characters to separate the
>  fields. This makes it harder to use name containing one of these characters (e.g.,
>  mount points using spaces). Therefore these characters are encoded in the files and
>  the `getmntent` function takes care of the decoding while reading the entries back in.
>  `'\040'` is used to encode a space character, `'\011'` to encode a tab character, `'\012'`
>  to encode a newline character, and `'\\'` to encode a backslash.

>  If there was an error or the end of the file is reached the return value is `NULL`.

>  This function is not thread-safe since all calls to this function return a pointer to
>  the same static variable. `getmntent_r` should be used in situations where multiple
>  threads access the file.

**struct mntent \* getmntent_r** (*FILE \*stream*, *struct mntent*          [Function]
>     *\*result*, *char \*buffer*, *int bufsize*)
>  Preliminary: | MT-Safe locale | AS-Unsafe corrupt heap | AC-Unsafe corrupt lock
>  mem | See Section 1.2.2.1 [POSIX Safety Concepts], page 2.

>  The `getmntent_r` function is the reentrant variant of `getmntent`. It also returns the
>  next entry from the file and returns a pointer. The actual variable the values are
>  stored in is not static, though. Instead the function stores the values in the variable
>  pointed to by the *result* parameter. Additional information (e.g., the strings pointed
>  to by the elements of the result) are kept in the buffer of size *bufsize* pointed to by
>  *buffer*.

>  Escaped characters (space, tab, backslash) are converted back in the same way as it
>  happens for `getmentent`.

>  The function returns a `NULL` pointer in error cases. Errors could be:
>  - error while reading the file,
>  - end of file reached,
>  - *bufsize* is too small for reading a complete new entry.

**int addmntent** (*FILE \*stream*, *const struct mntent \*mnt*)             [Function]
>  Preliminary: | MT-Safe race:stream locale | AS-Unsafe corrupt | AC-Unsafe corrupt
>  | See Section 1.2.2.1 [POSIX Safety Concepts], page 2.

The `addmntent` function allows adding a new entry to the file previously opened with `setmntent`. The new entries are always appended. I.e., even if the position of the file descriptor is not at the end of the file this function does not overwrite an existing entry following the current position.

The implication of this is that to remove an entry from a file one has to create a new file while leaving out the entry to be removed and after closing the file remove the old one and rename the new file to the chosen name.

This function takes care of spaces and tab characters in the names to be written to the file. It converts them and the backslash character into the format describe in the `getmntent` description above.

This function returns 0 in case the operation was successful. Otherwise the return value is 1 and `errno` is set appropriately.

`char * hasmntopt` (*const struct mntent \*mnt, const char \*opt*)                    [Function]
Preliminary: | MT-Safe | AS-Safe | AC-Safe | See Section 1.2.2.1 [POSIX Safety Concepts], page 2.

This function can be used to check whether the string pointed to by the `mnt_opts` element of the variable pointed to by *mnt* contains the option *opt*. If this is true a pointer to the beginning of the option in the `mnt_opts` element is returned. If no such option exists the function returns `NULL`.

This function is useful to test whether a specific option is present but when all options have to be processed one is better off with using the `getsubopt` function to iterate over all options in the string.

### 31.3.1.3 Other (Non-libc) Sources of Mount Information

On a system with a Linux kernel and the `proc` filesystem, you can get information on currently mounted filesystems from the file `mounts` in the `proc` filesystem. Its format is similar to that of the `mtab` file, but represents what is truly mounted without relying on facilities outside the kernel to keep `mtab` up to date.

### 31.3.2 Mount, Unmount, Remount

This section describes the functions for mounting, unmounting, and remounting filesystems.

Only the superuser can mount, unmount, or remount a filesystem.

These functions do not access the `fstab` and `mtab` files. You should maintain and use these separately. See Section 31.3.1 [Mount Information], page 825.

The symbols in this section are declared in `sys/mount.h`.

`int mount` (*const char \*special_file, const char \*dir, const char*                  [Function]
     *\*fstype, unsigned long int options, const void \*data*)
Preliminary: | MT-Safe | AS-Safe | AC-Safe | See Section 1.2.2.1 [POSIX Safety Concepts], page 2.

`mount` mounts or remounts a filesystem. The two operations are quite different and are merged rather unnaturally into this one function. The `MS_REMOUNT` option, explained below, determines whether `mount` mounts or remounts.

For a mount, the filesystem on the block device represented by the device special file named *special_file* gets mounted over the mount point *dir*. This means that the directory *dir* (along with any files in it) is no longer visible; in its place (and still with the name *dir*) is the root directory of the filesystem on the device.

As an exception, if the filesystem type (see below) is one which is not based on a device (e.g. "proc"), `mount` instantiates a filesystem and mounts it over *dir* and ignores *special_file*.

For a remount, *dir* specifies the mount point where the filesystem to be remounted is (and remains) mounted and *special_file* is ignored. Remounting a filesystem means changing the options that control operations on the filesystem while it is mounted. It does not mean unmounting and mounting again.

For a mount, you must identify the type of the filesystem as *fstype*. This type tells the kernel how to access the filesystem and can be thought of as the name of a filesystem driver. The acceptable values are system dependent. On a system with a Linux kernel and the `proc` filesystem, the list of possible values is in the file `filesystems` in the `proc` filesystem (e.g. type `cat /proc/filesystems` to see the list). With a Linux kernel, the types of filesystems that `mount` can mount, and their type names, depends on what filesystem drivers are configured into the kernel or loaded as loadable kernel modules. An example of a common value for *fstype* is `ext2`.

For a remount, `mount` ignores *fstype*.

*options* specifies a variety of options that apply until the filesystem is unmounted or remounted. The precise meaning of an option depends on the filesystem and with some filesystems, an option may have no effect at all. Furthermore, for some filesystems, some of these options (but never `MS_RDONLY`) can be overridden for individual file accesses via `ioctl`.

*options* is a bit string with bit fields defined using the following mask and masked value macros:

`MS_MGC_MASK`
> This multibit field contains a magic number. If it does not have the value `MS_MGC_VAL`, `mount` assumes all the following bits are zero and the *data* argument is a null string, regardless of their actual values.

`MS_REMOUNT`
> This bit on means to remount the filesystem. Off means to mount it.

`MS_RDONLY`
> This bit on specifies that no writing to the filesystem shall be allowed while it is mounted. This cannot be overridden by `ioctl`. This option is available on nearly all filesystems.

`S_IMMUTABLE`
> This bit on specifies that no writing to the files in the filesystem shall be allowed while it is mounted. This can be overridden for a particular file access by a properly privileged call to `ioctl`. This option is a relatively new invention and is not available on many filesystems.

`S_APPEND` This bit on specifies that the only file writing that shall be allowed while the filesystem is mounted is appending. Some filesystems allow this to be overridden for a particular process by a properly privileged call to `ioctl`. This is a relatively new invention and is not available on many filesystems.

MS_NOSUID

> This bit on specifies that Setuid and Setgid permissions on files in the filesystem shall be ignored while it is mounted.

MS_NOEXEC

> This bit on specifies that no files in the filesystem shall be executed while the filesystem is mounted.

MS_NODEV  This bit on specifies that no device special files in the filesystem shall be accessible while the filesystem is mounted.

MS_SYNCHRONOUS

> This bit on specifies that all writes to the filesystem while it is mounted shall be synchronous; i.e., data shall be synced before each write completes rather than held in the buffer cache.

MS_MANDLOCK

> This bit on specifies that mandatory locks on files shall be permitted while the filesystem is mounted.

MS_NOATIME

> This bit on specifies that access times of files shall not be updated when the files are accessed while the filesystem is mounted.

MS_NODIRATIME

> This bit on specifies that access times of directories shall not be updated when the directories are accessed while the filesystem in mounted.

Any bits not covered by the above masks should be set off; otherwise, results are undefined.

The meaning of *data* depends on the filesystem type and is controlled entirely by the filesystem driver in the kernel.

Example:

```
#include <sys/mount.h>

mount("/dev/hdb", "/cdrom", MS_MGC_VAL | MS_RDONLY | MS_NOSUID, "");

mount("/dev/hda2", "/mnt", MS_MGC_VAL | MS_REMOUNT, "");
```

Appropriate arguments for `mount` are conventionally recorded in the `fstab` table. See Section 31.3.1 [Mount Information], page 825.

The return value is zero if the mount or remount is successful. Otherwise, it is `-1` and **errno** is set appropriately. The values of **errno** are filesystem dependent, but here is a general list:

EPERM     The process is not superuser.

ENODEV    The file system type *fstype* is not known to the kernel.

ENOTBLK    The file *dev* is not a block device special file.

EBUSY

- The device is already mounted.

- The mount point is busy. (E.g. it is some process' working directory or has a filesystem mounted on it already).

- The request is to remount read-only, but there are files open for write.

EINVAL

- A remount was attempted, but there is no filesystem mounted over the specified mount point.

- The supposed filesystem has an invalid superblock.

EACCES

- The filesystem is inherently read-only (possibly due to a switch on the device) and the process attempted to mount it read/write (by setting the `MS_RDONLY` bit off).

- *special_file* or *dir* is not accessible due to file permissions.

- *special_file* is not accessible because it is in a filesystem that is mounted with the `MS_NODEV` option.

EM_FILE    The table of dummy devices is full. `mount` needs to create a dummy device (aka "unnamed" device) if the filesystem being mounted is not one that uses a device.

int **umount2** (*const char \*file*, *int flags*)                                          [Function]
Preliminary: | MT-Safe | AS-Safe | AC-Safe | See Section 1.2.2.1 [POSIX Safety Concepts], page 2.

**umount2** unmounts a filesystem.

You can identify the filesystem to unmount either by the device special file that contains the filesystem or by the mount point. The effect is the same. Specify either as the string *file*.

*flags* contains the one-bit field identified by the following mask macro:

MNT_FORCE

This bit on means to force the unmounting even if the filesystem is busy, by making it unbusy first. If the bit is off and the filesystem is busy, **umount2** fails with `errno` = `EBUSY`. Depending on the filesystem, this may override all, some, or no busy conditions.

All other bits in *flags* should be set to zero; otherwise, the result is undefined.

Example:

```
#include <sys/mount.h>

umount2("/mnt", MNT_FORCE);

umount2("/dev/hdd1", 0);
```

After the filesystem is unmounted, the directory that was the mount point is visible, as are any files in it.

As part of unmounting, `umount2` syncs the filesystem.

If the unmounting is successful, the return value is zero. Otherwise, it is -1 and `errno` is set accordingly:

EPERM      The process is not superuser.

EBUSY      The filesystem cannot be unmounted because it is busy. E.g. it contains a directory that is some process's working directory or a file that some process has open. With some filesystems in some cases, you can avoid this failure with the `MNT_FORCE` option.

EINVAL      *file* validly refers to a file, but that file is neither a mount point nor a device special file of a currently mounted filesystem.

This function is not available on all systems.

`int umount (const char *file)`        [Function]
     Preliminary: | MT-Safe | AS-Safe | AC-Safe | See Section 1.2.2.1 [POSIX Safety Concepts], page 2.

     `umount` does the same thing as `umount2` with *flags* set to zeroes. It is more widely available than `umount2` but since it lacks the possibility to forcefully unmount a filesystem is deprecated when `umount2` is also available.

## 31.4 System Parameters

This section describes the `sysctl` function, which gets and sets a variety of system parameters.

     The symbols used in this section are declared in the file `sys/sysctl.h`.

`int sysctl (int *names, int nlen, void *oldval, size_t *oldlenp, void`        [Function]
       `*newval, size_t newlen)`
     Preliminary: | MT-Safe | AS-Safe | AC-Safe | See Section 1.2.2.1 [POSIX Safety Concepts], page 2.

     `sysctl` gets or sets a specified system parameter. There are so many of these parameters that it is not practical to list them all here, but here are some examples:

     • network domain name

     • paging parameters

     • network Address Resolution Protocol timeout time

     • maximum number of files that may be open

     • root filesystem device

     • when kernel was built

The set of available parameters depends on the kernel configuration and can change while the system is running, particularly when you load and unload loadable kernel modules.

The system parameters with which **syslog** is concerned are arranged in a hierarchical structure like a hierarchical filesystem. To identify a particular parameter, you specify a path through the structure in a way analogous to specifying the pathname of a file. Each component of the path is specified by an integer and each of these integers has a macro defined for it by **sys/sysctl.h**. *names* is the path, in the form of an array of integers. Each component of the path is one element of the array, in order. *nlen* is the number of components in the path.

For example, the first component of the path for all the paging parameters is the value **CTL_VM**. For the free page thresholds, the second component of the path is **VM_FREEPG**. So to get the free page threshold values, make *names* an array containing the two elements **CTL_VM** and **VM_FREEPG** and make *nlen* = 2.

The format of the value of a parameter depends on the parameter. Sometimes it is an integer; sometimes it is an ASCII string; sometimes it is an elaborate structure. In the case of the free page thresholds used in the example above, the parameter value is a structure containing several integers.

In any case, you identify a place to return the parameter's value with *oldval* and specify the amount of storage available at that location as *\*oldlenp*. *\*oldlenp* does double duty because it is also the output location that contains the actual length of the returned value.

If you don't want the parameter value returned, specify a null pointer for *oldval*.

To set the parameter, specify the address and length of the new value as *newval* and *newlen*. If you don't want to set the parameter, specify a null pointer as *newval*.

If you get and set a parameter in the same **sysctl** call, the value returned is the value of the parameter before it was set.

Each system parameter has a set of permissions similar to the permissions for a file (including the permissions on directories in its path) that determine whether you may get or set it. For the purposes of these permissions, every parameter is considered to be owned by the superuser and Group 0 so processes with that effective uid or gid may have more access to system parameters. Unlike with files, the superuser does not invariably have full permission to all system parameters, because some of them are designed not to be changed ever.

**sysctl** returns a zero return value if it succeeds. Otherwise, it returns -1 and sets **errno** appropriately. Besides the failures that apply to all system calls, the following are the **errno** codes for all possible failures:

EPERM        The process is not permitted to access one of the components of the path of the system parameter or is not permitted to access the system parameter itself in the way (read or write) that it requested.

ENOTDIR      There is no system parameter corresponding to *name*.

EFAULT       *oldval* is not null, which means the process wanted to read the parameter, but *\*oldlenp* is zero, so there is no place to return it.

EINVAL

  - The process attempted to set a system parameter to a value that is not valid for that parameter.

- The space provided for the return of the system parameter is not the right size for that parameter.

ENOMEM      This value may be returned instead of the more correct `EINVAL` in some cases where the space provided for the return of the system parameter is too small.

If you have a Linux kernel with the `proc` filesystem, you can get and set most of the same parameters by reading and writing to files in the `sys` directory of the `proc` filesystem. In the `sys` directory, the directory structure represents the hierarchical structure of the parameters. E.g. you can display the free page thresholds with

```
cat /proc/sys/vm/freepages
```

Some more traditional and more widely available, though less general, GNU C Library functions for getting and setting some of the same system parameters are:

- `getdomainname, setdomainname`
- `gethostname, sethostname` (See Section 31.1 [Host Identification], page 821.)
- `uname` (See Section 31.2 [Platform Type Identification], page 823.)
- `bdflush`

# 32 System Configuration Parameters

The functions and macros listed in this chapter give information about configuration parameters of the operating system—for example, capacity limits, presence of optional POSIX features, and the default path for executable files (see Section 32.12 [String-Valued Parameters], page 856).

## 32.1 General Capacity Limits

The POSIX.1 and POSIX.2 standards specify a number of parameters that describe capacity limitations of the system. These limits can be fixed constants for a given operating system, or they can vary from machine to machine. For example, some limit values may be configurable by the system administrator, either at run time or by rebuilding the kernel, and this should not require recompiling application programs.

Each of the following limit parameters has a macro that is defined in `limits.h` only if the system has a fixed, uniform limit for the parameter in question. If the system allows different file systems or files to have different limits, then the macro is undefined; use `sysconf` to find out the limit that applies at a particular time on a particular machine. See Section 32.4 [Using `sysconf`], page 841.

Each of these parameters also has another macro, with a name starting with '_POSIX', which gives the lowest value that the limit is allowed to have on *any* POSIX system. See Section 32.5 [Minimum Values for General Capacity Limits], page 849.

int ARG_MAX                                                          [Macro]
    If defined, the unvarying maximum combined length of the *argv* and *environ* arguments that can be passed to the `exec` functions.

int CHILD_MAX                                                        [Macro]
    If defined, the unvarying maximum number of processes that can exist with the same real user ID at any one time. In BSD and GNU, this is controlled by the `RLIMIT_NPROC` resource limit; see Section 22.2 [Limiting Resource Usage], page 632.

int OPEN_MAX                                                         [Macro]
    If defined, the unvarying maximum number of files that a single process can have open simultaneously. In BSD and GNU, this is controlled by the `RLIMIT_NOFILE` resource limit; see Section 22.2 [Limiting Resource Usage], page 632.

int STREAM_MAX                                                       [Macro]
    If defined, the unvarying maximum number of streams that a single process can have open simultaneously. See Section 12.3 [Opening Streams], page 249.

int TZNAME_MAX                                                       [Macro]
    If defined, the unvarying maximum length of a time zone name. See Section 21.4.8 [Functions and Variables for Time Zones], page 624.

These limit macros are always defined in `limits.h`.

`int NGROUPS_MAX` [Macro]

> The maximum number of supplementary group IDs that one process can have.
>
> The value of this macro is actually a lower bound for the maximum. That is, you can count on being able to have that many supplementary group IDs, but a particular machine might let you have even more. You can use `sysconf` to see whether a particular machine will let you have more (see Section 32.4 [Using `sysconf`], page 841).

`ssize_t SSIZE_MAX` [Macro]

> The largest value that can fit in an object of type `ssize_t`. Effectively, this is the limit on the number of bytes that can be read or written in a single operation.
>
> This macro is defined in all POSIX systems because this limit is never configurable.

`int RE_DUP_MAX` [Macro]

> The largest number of repetitions you are guaranteed is allowed in the construct '\{min,max\}' in a regular expression.
>
> The value of this macro is actually a lower bound for the maximum. That is, you can count on being able to have that many repetitions, but a particular machine might let you have even more. You can use `sysconf` to see whether a particular machine will let you have more (see Section 32.4 [Using `sysconf`], page 841). And even the value that `sysconf` tells you is just a lower bound—larger values might work.
>
> This macro is defined in all POSIX.2 systems, because POSIX.2 says it should always be defined even if there is no specific imposed limit.

## 32.2 Overall System Options

POSIX defines certain system-specific options that not all POSIX systems support. Since these options are provided in the kernel, not in the library, simply using the GNU C Library does not guarantee any of these features is supported; it depends on the system you are using.

You can test for the availability of a given option using the macros in this section, together with the function `sysconf`. The macros are defined only if you include `unistd.h`.

For the following macros, if the macro is defined in `unistd.h`, then the option is supported. Otherwise, the option may or may not be supported; use `sysconf` to find out. See Section 32.4 [Using `sysconf`], page 841.

`int _POSIX_JOB_CONTROL` [Macro]

> If this symbol is defined, it indicates that the system supports job control. Otherwise, the implementation behaves as if all processes within a session belong to a single process group. See Chapter 28 [Job Control], page 763.

`int _POSIX_SAVED_IDS` [Macro]

> If this symbol is defined, it indicates that the system remembers the effective user and group IDs of a process before it executes an executable file with the set-user-ID or set-group-ID bits set, and that explicitly changing the effective user or group IDs back to these values is permitted. If this option is not defined, then if a nonprivileged process changes its effective user or group ID to the real user or group ID of the process, it can't change it back again. See Section 30.8 [Enabling and Disabling Setuid Access], page 797.

For the following macros, if the macro is defined in `unistd.h`, then its value indicates whether the option is supported. A value of -1 means no, and any other value means yes. If the macro is not defined, then the option may or may not be supported; use `sysconf` to find out. See Section 32.4 [Using `sysconf`], page 841.

int _POSIX2_C_DEV                                                          [Macro]

> If this symbol is defined, it indicates that the system has the POSIX.2 C compiler command, `c89`. The GNU C Library always defines this as 1, on the assumption that you would not have installed it if you didn't have a C compiler.

int _POSIX2_FORT_DEV                                                       [Macro]

> If this symbol is defined, it indicates that the system has the POSIX.2 Fortran compiler command, `fort77`. The GNU C Library never defines this, because we don't know what the system has.

int _POSIX2_FORT_RUN                                                       [Macro]

> If this symbol is defined, it indicates that the system has the POSIX.2 `asa` command to interpret Fortran carriage control. The GNU C Library never defines this, because we don't know what the system has.

int _POSIX2_LOCALEDEF                                                      [Macro]

> If this symbol is defined, it indicates that the system has the POSIX.2 `localedef` command. The GNU C Library never defines this, because we don't know what the system has.

int _POSIX2_SW_DEV                                                         [Macro]

> If this symbol is defined, it indicates that the system has the POSIX.2 commands `ar`, `make`, and `strip`. The GNU C Library always defines this as 1, on the assumption that you had to have `ar` and `make` to install the library, and it's unlikely that `strip` would be absent when those are present.

## 32.3 Which Version of POSIX is Supported

long int _POSIX_VERSION                                                    [Macro]

> This constant represents the version of the POSIX.1 standard to which the implementation conforms. For an implementation conforming to the 1995 POSIX.1 standard, the value is the integer 199506L.
>
> `_POSIX_VERSION` is always defined (in `unistd.h`) in any POSIX system.
>
> **Usage Note:** Don't try to test whether the system supports POSIX by including `unistd.h` and then checking whether `_POSIX_VERSION` is defined. On a non-POSIX system, this will probably fail because there is no `unistd.h`. We do not know of *any* way you can reliably test at compilation time whether your target system supports POSIX or whether `unistd.h` exists.

long int _POSIX2_C_VERSION                                                 [Macro]

> This constant represents the version of the POSIX.2 standard which the library and system kernel support. We don't know what value this will be for the first version of the POSIX.2 standard, because the value is based on the year and month in which the standard is officially adopted.

The value of this symbol says nothing about the utilities installed on the system.

**Usage Note:** You can use this macro to tell whether a POSIX.1 system library supports POSIX.2 as well. Any POSIX.1 system contains `unistd.h`, so include that file and then test `defined (_POSIX2_C_VERSION)`.

## 32.4 Using `sysconf`

When your system has configurable system limits, you can use the `sysconf` function to find out the value that applies to any particular machine. The function and the associated *parameter* constants are declared in the header file `unistd.h`.

### 32.4.1 Definition of `sysconf`

`long int sysconf (`*`int parameter`*`)`                                    [Function]
> Preliminary: | MT-Safe env | AS-Unsafe lock heap | AC-Unsafe lock mem fd | See Section 1.2.2.1 [POSIX Safety Concepts], page 2.
>
> This function is used to inquire about runtime system parameters. The *parameter* argument should be one of the '`_SC_`' symbols listed below.
>
> The normal return value from `sysconf` is the value you requested. A value of −1 is returned both if the implementation does not impose a limit, and in case of an error.
>
> The following `errno` error conditions are defined for this function:
>
> `EINVAL`       The value of the *parameter* is invalid.

### 32.4.2 Constants for `sysconf` Parameters

Here are the symbolic constants for use as the *parameter* argument to `sysconf`. The values are all integer constants (more specifically, enumeration type values).

`_SC_ARG_MAX`
> Inquire about the parameter corresponding to `ARG_MAX`.

`_SC_CHILD_MAX`
> Inquire about the parameter corresponding to `CHILD_MAX`.

`_SC_OPEN_MAX`
> Inquire about the parameter corresponding to `OPEN_MAX`.

`_SC_STREAM_MAX`
> Inquire about the parameter corresponding to `STREAM_MAX`.

`_SC_TZNAME_MAX`
> Inquire about the parameter corresponding to `TZNAME_MAX`.

`_SC_NGROUPS_MAX`
> Inquire about the parameter corresponding to `NGROUPS_MAX`.

`_SC_JOB_CONTROL`
> Inquire about the parameter corresponding to `_POSIX_JOB_CONTROL`.

`_SC_SAVED_IDS`
> Inquire about the parameter corresponding to `_POSIX_SAVED_IDS`.

_SC_VERSION

> Inquire about the parameter corresponding to _POSIX_VERSION.

_SC_CLK_TCK

> Inquire about the number of clock ticks per second; see Section 21.3.1 [CPU Time Inquiry], page 597. The corresponding parameter CLK_TCK is obsolete.

_SC_CHARCLASS_NAME_MAX

> Inquire about the parameter corresponding to maximal length allowed for a character class name in an extended locale specification. These extensions are not yet standardized and so this option is not standardized as well.

_SC_REALTIME_SIGNALS

> Inquire about the parameter corresponding to _POSIX_REALTIME_SIGNALS.

_SC_PRIORITY_SCHEDULING

> Inquire about the parameter corresponding to _POSIX_PRIORITY_SCHEDULING.

_SC_TIMERS

> Inquire about the parameter corresponding to _POSIX_TIMERS.

_SC_ASYNCHRONOUS_IO

> Inquire about the parameter corresponding to _POSIX_ASYNCHRONOUS_IO.

_SC_PRIORITIZED_IO

> Inquire about the parameter corresponding to _POSIX_PRIORITIZED_IO.

_SC_SYNCHRONIZED_IO

> Inquire about the parameter corresponding to _POSIX_SYNCHRONIZED_IO.

_SC_FSYNC

> Inquire about the parameter corresponding to _POSIX_FSYNC.

_SC_MAPPED_FILES

> Inquire about the parameter corresponding to _POSIX_MAPPED_FILES.

_SC_MEMLOCK

> Inquire about the parameter corresponding to _POSIX_MEMLOCK.

_SC_MEMLOCK_RANGE

> Inquire about the parameter corresponding to _POSIX_MEMLOCK_RANGE.

_SC_MEMORY_PROTECTION

> Inquire about the parameter corresponding to _POSIX_MEMORY_PROTECTION.

_SC_MESSAGE_PASSING

> Inquire about the parameter corresponding to _POSIX_MESSAGE_PASSING.

_SC_SEMAPHORES

> Inquire about the parameter corresponding to _POSIX_SEMAPHORES.

_SC_SHARED_MEMORY_OBJECTS

> Inquire about the parameter corresponding to
> _POSIX_SHARED_MEMORY_OBJECTS.

_SC_AIO_LISTIO_MAX

> Inquire about the parameter corresponding to _POSIX_AIO_LISTIO_MAX.

`_SC_AIO_MAX`
>  Inquire about the parameter corresponding to `_POSIX_AIO_MAX`.

`_SC_AIO_PRIO_DELTA_MAX`
>  Inquire the value by which a process can decrease its asynchronous I/O priority level from its own scheduling priority. This corresponds to the run-time invariant value `AIO_PRIO_DELTA_MAX`.

`_SC_DELAYTIMER_MAX`
>  Inquire about the parameter corresponding to `_POSIX_DELAYTIMER_MAX`.

`_SC_MQ_OPEN_MAX`
>  Inquire about the parameter corresponding to `_POSIX_MQ_OPEN_MAX`.

`_SC_MQ_PRIO_MAX`
>  Inquire about the parameter corresponding to `_POSIX_MQ_PRIO_MAX`.

`_SC_RTSIG_MAX`
>  Inquire about the parameter corresponding to `_POSIX_RTSIG_MAX`.

`_SC_SEM_NSEMS_MAX`
>  Inquire about the parameter corresponding to `_POSIX_SEM_NSEMS_MAX`.

`_SC_SEM_VALUE_MAX`
>  Inquire about the parameter corresponding to `_POSIX_SEM_VALUE_MAX`.

`_SC_SIGQUEUE_MAX`
>  Inquire about the parameter corresponding to `_POSIX_SIGQUEUE_MAX`.

`_SC_TIMER_MAX`
>  Inquire about the parameter corresponding to `_POSIX_TIMER_MAX`.

`_SC_PII`    Inquire about the parameter corresponding to `_POSIX_PII`.

`_SC_PII_XTI`
>  Inquire about the parameter corresponding to `_POSIX_PII_XTI`.

`_SC_PII_SOCKET`
>  Inquire about the parameter corresponding to `_POSIX_PII_SOCKET`.

`_SC_PII_INTERNET`
>  Inquire about the parameter corresponding to `_POSIX_PII_INTERNET`.

`_SC_PII_OSI`
>  Inquire about the parameter corresponding to `_POSIX_PII_OSI`.

`_SC_SELECT`
>  Inquire about the parameter corresponding to `_POSIX_SELECT`.

`_SC_UIO_MAXIOV`
>  Inquire about the parameter corresponding to `_POSIX_UIO_MAXIOV`.

`_SC_PII_INTERNET_STREAM`
>  Inquire about the parameter corresponding to `_POSIX_PII_INTERNET_STREAM`.

`_SC_PII_INTERNET_DGRAM`
>  Inquire about the parameter corresponding to `_POSIX_PII_INTERNET_DGRAM`.

`_SC_PII_OSI_COTS`

> Inquire about the parameter corresponding to `_POSIX_PII_OSI_COTS`.

`_SC_PII_OSI_CLTS`

> Inquire about the parameter corresponding to `_POSIX_PII_OSI_CLTS`.

`_SC_PII_OSI_M`

> Inquire about the parameter corresponding to `_POSIX_PII_OSI_M`.

`_SC_T_IOV_MAX`

> Inquire the value of the value associated with the `T_IOV_MAX` variable.

`_SC_THREADS`

> Inquire about the parameter corresponding to `_POSIX_THREADS`.

`_SC_THREAD_SAFE_FUNCTIONS`

> Inquire about the parameter corresponding to
> `_POSIX_THREAD_SAFE_FUNCTIONS`.

`_SC_GETGR_R_SIZE_MAX`

> Inquire about the parameter corresponding to `_POSIX_GETGR_R_SIZE_MAX`.

`_SC_GETPW_R_SIZE_MAX`

> Inquire about the parameter corresponding to `_POSIX_GETPW_R_SIZE_MAX`.

`_SC_LOGIN_NAME_MAX`

> Inquire about the parameter corresponding to `_POSIX_LOGIN_NAME_MAX`.

`_SC_TTY_NAME_MAX`

> Inquire about the parameter corresponding to `_POSIX_TTY_NAME_MAX`.

`_SC_THREAD_DESTRUCTOR_ITERATIONS`

> Inquire about the parameter corresponding to `_POSIX_THREAD_DESTRUCTOR_`
> `ITERATIONS`.

`_SC_THREAD_KEYS_MAX`

> Inquire about the parameter corresponding to `_POSIX_THREAD_KEYS_MAX`.

`_SC_THREAD_STACK_MIN`

> Inquire about the parameter corresponding to `_POSIX_THREAD_STACK_MIN`.

`_SC_THREAD_THREADS_MAX`

> Inquire about the parameter corresponding to `_POSIX_THREAD_THREADS_MAX`.

`_SC_THREAD_ATTR_STACKADDR`

> Inquire about the parameter corresponding to
> a `_POSIX_THREAD_ATTR_STACKADDR`.

`_SC_THREAD_ATTR_STACKSIZE`

> Inquire about the parameter corresponding to
> `_POSIX_THREAD_ATTR_STACKSIZE`.

`_SC_THREAD_PRIORITY_SCHEDULING`

> Inquire about the parameter corresponding to `_POSIX_THREAD_PRIORITY_`
> `SCHEDULING`.

`_SC_THREAD_PRIO_INHERIT`

> Inquire about the parameter corresponding to `_POSIX_THREAD_PRIO_INHERIT`.

`_SC_THREAD_PRIO_PROTECT`

> Inquire about the parameter corresponding to `_POSIX_THREAD_PRIO_PROTECT`.

`_SC_THREAD_PROCESS_SHARED`

> Inquire about the parameter corresponding to `_POSIX_THREAD_PROCESS_SHARED`.

`_SC_2_C_DEV`

> Inquire about whether the system has the POSIX.2 C compiler command, `c89`.

`_SC_2_FORT_DEV`

> Inquire about whether the system has the POSIX.2 Fortran compiler command, `fort77`.

`_SC_2_FORT_RUN`

> Inquire about whether the system has the POSIX.2 `asa` command to interpret Fortran carriage control.

`_SC_2_LOCALEDEF`

> Inquire about whether the system has the POSIX.2 `localedef` command.

`_SC_2_SW_DEV`

> Inquire about whether the system has the POSIX.2 commands `ar`, `make`, and `strip`.

`_SC_BC_BASE_MAX`

> Inquire about the maximum value of `obase` in the `bc` utility.

`_SC_BC_DIM_MAX`

> Inquire about the maximum size of an array in the `bc` utility.

`_SC_BC_SCALE_MAX`

> Inquire about the maximum value of `scale` in the `bc` utility.

`_SC_BC_STRING_MAX`

> Inquire about the maximum size of a string constant in the `bc` utility.

`_SC_COLL_WEIGHTS_MAX`

> Inquire about the maximum number of weights that can necessarily be used in defining the collating sequence for a locale.

`_SC_EXPR_NEST_MAX`

> Inquire about the maximum number of expressions nested within parentheses when using the `expr` utility.

`_SC_LINE_MAX`

> Inquire about the maximum size of a text line that the POSIX.2 text utilities can handle.

`_SC_EQUIV_CLASS_MAX`

> Inquire about the maximum number of weights that can be assigned to an entry of the `LC_COLLATE` category 'order' keyword in a locale definition. The GNU C Library does not presently support locale definitions.

`_SC_VERSION`

> Inquire about the version number of POSIX.1 that the library and kernel support.

`_SC_2_VERSION`

> Inquire about the version number of POSIX.2 that the system utilities support.

`_SC_PAGESIZE`

> Inquire about the virtual memory page size of the machine. `getpagesize` returns the same value (see Section 22.4.2 [How to get information about the memory subsystem?], page 648).

`_SC_NPROCESSORS_CONF`

> Inquire about the number of configured processors.

`_SC_NPROCESSORS_ONLN`

> Inquire about the number of processors online.

`_SC_PHYS_PAGES`

> Inquire about the number of physical pages in the system.

`_SC_AVPHYS_PAGES`

> Inquire about the number of available physical pages in the system.

`_SC_ATEXIT_MAX`

> Inquire about the number of functions which can be registered as termination functions for `atexit`; see Section 25.7.3 [Cleanups on Exit], page 746.

`_SC_XOPEN_VERSION`

> Inquire about the parameter corresponding to `_XOPEN_VERSION`.

`_SC_XOPEN_XCU_VERSION`

> Inquire about the parameter corresponding to `_XOPEN_XCU_VERSION`.

`_SC_XOPEN_UNIX`

> Inquire about the parameter corresponding to `_XOPEN_UNIX`.

`_SC_XOPEN_REALTIME`

> Inquire about the parameter corresponding to `_XOPEN_REALTIME`.

`_SC_XOPEN_REALTIME_THREADS`

> Inquire about the parameter corresponding to `_XOPEN_REALTIME_THREADS`.

`_SC_XOPEN_LEGACY`

> Inquire about the parameter corresponding to `_XOPEN_LEGACY`.

`_SC_XOPEN_CRYPT`

> Inquire about the parameter corresponding to `_XOPEN_CRYPT`.

`_SC_XOPEN_ENH_I18N`

> Inquire about the parameter corresponding to `_XOPEN_ENH_I18N`.

`_SC_XOPEN_SHM`

> Inquire about the parameter corresponding to `_XOPEN_SHM`.

`_SC_XOPEN_XPG2`

> Inquire about the parameter corresponding to `_XOPEN_XPG2`.

`_SC_XOPEN_XPG3`

> Inquire about the parameter corresponding to `_XOPEN_XPG3`.

`_SC_XOPEN_XPG4`

> Inquire about the parameter corresponding to `_XOPEN_XPG4`.

`_SC_CHAR_BIT`

> Inquire about the number of bits in a variable of type `char`.

`_SC_CHAR_MAX`

> Inquire about the maximum value which can be stored in a variable of type `char`.

`_SC_CHAR_MIN`

> Inquire about the minimum value which can be stored in a variable of type `char`.

`_SC_INT_MAX`

> Inquire about the maximum value which can be stored in a variable of type `int`.

`_SC_INT_MIN`

> Inquire about the minimum value which can be stored in a variable of type `int`.

`_SC_LONG_BIT`

> Inquire about the number of bits in a variable of type `long int`.

`_SC_WORD_BIT`

> Inquire about the number of bits in a variable of a register word.

`_SC_MB_LEN_MAX`

> Inquire the maximum length of a multi-byte representation of a wide character value.

`_SC_NZERO`

> Inquire about the value used to internally represent the zero priority level for the process execution.

`SC_SSIZE_MAX`

> Inquire about the maximum value which can be stored in a variable of type `ssize_t`.

`_SC_SCHAR_MAX`

> Inquire about the maximum value which can be stored in a variable of type `signed char`.

`_SC_SCHAR_MIN`

> Inquire about the minimum value which can be stored in a variable of type `signed char`.

`_SC_SHRT_MAX`

> Inquire about the maximum value which can be stored in a variable of type `short int`.

_SC_SHRT_MIN
> Inquire about the minimum value which can be stored in a variable of type short int.

_SC_UCHAR_MAX
> Inquire about the maximum value which can be stored in a variable of type unsigned char.

_SC_UINT_MAX
> Inquire about the maximum value which can be stored in a variable of type unsigned int.

_SC_ULONG_MAX
> Inquire about the maximum value which can be stored in a variable of type unsigned long int.

_SC_USHRT_MAX
> Inquire about the maximum value which can be stored in a variable of type unsigned short int.

_SC_NL_ARGMAX
> Inquire about the parameter corresponding to NL_ARGMAX.

_SC_NL_LANGMAX
> Inquire about the parameter corresponding to NL_LANGMAX.

_SC_NL_MSGMAX
> Inquire about the parameter corresponding to NL_MSGMAX.

_SC_NL_NMAX
> Inquire about the parameter corresponding to NL_NMAX.

_SC_NL_SETMAX
> Inquire about the parameter corresponding to NL_SETMAX.

_SC_NL_TEXTMAX
> Inquire about the parameter corresponding to NL_TEXTMAX.

### 32.4.3 Examples of sysconf

We recommend that you first test for a macro definition for the parameter you are interested in, and call sysconf only if the macro is not defined. For example, here is how to test whether job control is supported:

```
int
have_job_control (void)
{
#ifdef _POSIX_JOB_CONTROL
  return 1;
#else
  int value = sysconf (_SC_JOB_CONTROL);
  if (value < 0)
    /* If the system is that badly wedged,
       there's no use trying to go on.  */
    fatal (strerror (errno));
  return value;
#endif
}
```

Here is how to get the value of a numeric limit:

```
int
get_child_max ()
{
#ifdef CHILD_MAX
  return CHILD_MAX;
#else
  int value = sysconf (_SC_CHILD_MAX);
  if (value < 0)
    fatal (strerror (errno));
  return value;
#endif
}
```

# 32.5 Minimum Values for General Capacity Limits

Here are the names for the POSIX minimum upper bounds for the system limit parameters. The significance of these values is that you can safely push to these limits without checking whether the particular system you are using can go that far.

`_POSIX_AIO_LISTIO_MAX`

> The most restrictive limit permitted by POSIX for the maximum number of I/O operations that can be specified in a list I/O call. The value of this constant is 2; thus you can add up to two new entries of the list of outstanding operations.

`_POSIX_AIO_MAX`

> The most restrictive limit permitted by POSIX for the maximum number of outstanding asynchronous I/O operations. The value of this constant is 1. So you cannot expect that you can issue more than one operation and immediately continue with the normal work, receiving the notifications asynchronously.

`_POSIX_ARG_MAX`

> The value of this macro is the most restrictive limit permitted by POSIX for the maximum combined length of the *argv* and *environ* arguments that can be passed to the **exec** functions. Its value is 4096.

`_POSIX_CHILD_MAX`

> The value of this macro is the most restrictive limit permitted by POSIX for the maximum number of simultaneous processes per real user ID. Its value is 6.

`_POSIX_NGROUPS_MAX`

> The value of this macro is the most restrictive limit permitted by POSIX for the maximum number of supplementary group IDs per process. Its value is 0.

`_POSIX_OPEN_MAX`

> The value of this macro is the most restrictive limit permitted by POSIX for the maximum number of files that a single process can have open simultaneously. Its value is 16.

`_POSIX_SSIZE_MAX`

> The value of this macro is the most restrictive limit permitted by POSIX for the maximum value that can be stored in an object of type **ssize_t**. Its value is 32767.

_POSIX_STREAM_MAX

> The value of this macro is the most restrictive limit permitted by POSIX for the maximum number of streams that a single process can have open simultaneously. Its value is 8.

_POSIX_TZNAME_MAX

> The value of this macro is the most restrictive limit permitted by POSIX for the maximum length of a time zone name. Its value is 3.

_POSIX2_RE_DUP_MAX

> The value of this macro is the most restrictive limit permitted by POSIX for the numbers used in the '\{min,max\}' construct in a regular expression. Its value is 255.

## 32.6 Limits on File System Capacity

The POSIX.1 standard specifies a number of parameters that describe the limitations of the file system. It's possible for the system to have a fixed, uniform limit for a parameter, but this isn't the usual case. On most systems, it's possible for different file systems (and, for some parameters, even different files) to have different maximum limits. For example, this is very likely if you use NFS to mount some of the file systems from other machines.

Each of the following macros is defined in limits.h only if the system has a fixed, uniform limit for the parameter in question. If the system allows different file systems or files to have different limits, then the macro is undefined; use pathconf or fpathconf to find out the limit that applies to a particular file. See Section 32.9 [Using pathconf], page 853.

Each parameter also has another macro, with a name starting with '_POSIX', which gives the lowest value that the limit is allowed to have on *any* POSIX system. See Section 32.8 [Minimum Values for File System Limits], page 852.

int LINK_MAX                                                              [Macro]

> The uniform system limit (if any) for the number of names for a given file. See Section 14.4 [Hard Links], page 392.

int MAX_CANON                                                            [Macro]

> The uniform system limit (if any) for the amount of text in a line of input when input editing is enabled. See Section 17.3 [Two Styles of Input: Canonical or Not], page 478.

int MAX_INPUT                                                            [Macro]

> The uniform system limit (if any) for the total number of characters typed ahead as input. See Section 17.2 [I/O Queues], page 478.

int NAME_MAX                                                             [Macro]

> The uniform system limit (if any) for the length of a file name component, not including the terminating null character.
>
> **Portability Note:** On some systems, the GNU C Library defines NAME_MAX, but does not actually enforce this limit.

**int PATH_MAX**                                                                     [Macro]

The uniform system limit (if any) for the length of an entire file name (that is, the argument given to system calls such as `open`), including the terminating null character.

**Portability Note:** The GNU C Library does not enforce this limit even if `PATH_MAX` is defined.

**int PIPE_BUF**                                                                     [Macro]

The uniform system limit (if any) for the number of bytes that can be written atomically to a pipe. If multiple processes are writing to the same pipe simultaneously, output from different processes might be interleaved in chunks of this size. See Chapter 15 [Pipes and FIFOs], page 424.

These are alternative macro names for some of the same information.

**int MAXNAMLEN**                                                               [Macro]

This is the BSD name for `NAME_MAX`. It is defined in `dirent.h`.

**int FILENAME_MAX**                                                          [Macro]

The value of this macro is an integer constant expression that represents the maximum length of a file name string. It is defined in `stdio.h`.

Unlike `PATH_MAX`, this macro is defined even if there is no actual limit imposed. In such a case, its value is typically a very large number. **This is always the case on GNU/Hurd systems.**

**Usage Note:** Don't use `FILENAME_MAX` as the size of an array in which to store a file name! You can't possibly make an array that big! Use dynamic allocation (see Section 3.2 [Allocating Storage For Program Data], page 40) instead.

## 32.7 Optional Features in File Support

POSIX defines certain system-specific options in the system calls for operating on files. Some systems support these options and others do not. Since these options are provided in the kernel, not in the library, simply using the GNU C Library does not guarantee that any of these features is supported; it depends on the system you are using. They can also vary between file systems on a single machine.

This section describes the macros you can test to determine whether a particular option is supported on your machine. If a given macro is defined in `unistd.h`, then its value says whether the corresponding feature is supported. (A value of −1 indicates no; any other value indicates yes.) If the macro is undefined, it means particular files may or may not support the feature.

Since all the machines that support the GNU C Library also support NFS, one can never make a general statement about whether all file systems support the `_POSIX_CHOWN_RESTRICTED` and `_POSIX_NO_TRUNC` features. So these names are never defined as macros in the GNU C Library.

**int _POSIX_CHOWN_RESTRICTED**                                               [Macro]

If this option is in effect, the `chown` function is restricted so that the only changes permitted to nonprivileged processes is to change the group owner of a file to either be the effective group ID of the process, or one of its supplementary group IDs. See Section 14.9.4 [File Owner], page 406.

`int _POSIX_NO_TRUNC`                                                    [Macro]

>  If this option is in effect, file name components longer than `NAME_MAX` generate an `ENAMETOOLONG` error. Otherwise, file name components that are too long are silently truncated.

`unsigned char _POSIX_VDISABLE`                                          [Macro]

>  This option is only meaningful for files that are terminal devices. If it is enabled, then handling for special control characters can be disabled individually. See Section 17.4.9 [Special Characters], page 490.

If one of these macros is undefined, that means that the option might be in effect for some files and not for others. To inquire about a particular file, call `pathconf` or `fpathconf`. See Section 32.9 [Using `pathconf`], page 853.

## 32.8 Minimum Values for File System Limits

Here are the names for the POSIX minimum upper bounds for some of the above parameters. The significance of these values is that you can safely push to these limits without checking whether the particular system you are using can go that far. In most cases GNU systems do not have these strict limitations. The actual limit should be requested if necessary.

`_POSIX_LINK_MAX`

>  The most restrictive limit permitted by POSIX for the maximum value of a file's link count. The value of this constant is 8; thus, you can always make up to eight names for a file without running into a system limit.

`_POSIX_MAX_CANON`

>  The most restrictive limit permitted by POSIX for the maximum number of bytes in a canonical input line from a terminal device. The value of this constant is 255.

`_POSIX_MAX_INPUT`

>  The most restrictive limit permitted by POSIX for the maximum number of bytes in a terminal device input queue (or typeahead buffer). See Section 17.4.4 [Input Modes], page 482. The value of this constant is 255.

`_POSIX_NAME_MAX`

>  The most restrictive limit permitted by POSIX for the maximum number of bytes in a file name component. The value of this constant is 14.

`_POSIX_PATH_MAX`

>  The most restrictive limit permitted by POSIX for the maximum number of bytes in a file name. The value of this constant is 256.

`_POSIX_PIPE_BUF`

>  The most restrictive limit permitted by POSIX for the maximum number of bytes that can be written atomically to a pipe. The value of this constant is 512.

`SYMLINK_MAX`

>  Maximum number of bytes in a symbolic link.

POSIX_REC_INCR_XFER_SIZE
>	Recommended increment for file transfer sizes between the POSIX_REC_MIN_
>	XFER_SIZE and POSIX_REC_MAX_XFER_SIZE values.

POSIX_REC_MAX_XFER_SIZE
>	Maximum recommended file transfer size.

POSIX_REC_MIN_XFER_SIZE
>	Minimum recommended file transfer size.

POSIX_REC_XFER_ALIGN
>	Recommended file transfer buffer alignment.

## 32.9 Using pathconf

When your machine allows different files to have different values for a file system parameter, you can use the functions in this section to find out the value that applies to any particular file.

These functions and the associated constants for the *parameter* argument are declared in the header file unistd.h.

long int pathconf (*const char \*filename*, *int parameter*)  [Function]
>	Preliminary: | MT-Safe | AS-Unsafe lock heap | AC-Unsafe lock fd mem | See Section 1.2.2.1 [POSIX Safety Concepts], page 2.
>
>	This function is used to inquire about the limits that apply to the file named *filename*.
>
>	The *parameter* argument should be one of the '_PC_' constants listed below.
>
>	The normal return value from pathconf is the value you requested. A value of −1 is returned both if the implementation does not impose a limit, and in case of an error. In the former case, errno is not set, while in the latter case, errno is set to indicate the cause of the problem. So the only way to use this function robustly is to store 0 into errno just before calling it.
>
>	Besides the usual file name errors (see Section 11.2.3 [File Name Errors], page 246), the following error condition is defined for this function:
>
>	EINVAL	The value of *parameter* is invalid, or the implementation doesn't support the *parameter* for the specific file.

long int fpathconf (*int filedes*, *int parameter*)  [Function]
>	Preliminary: | MT-Safe | AS-Unsafe lock heap | AC-Unsafe lock fd mem | See Section 1.2.2.1 [POSIX Safety Concepts], page 2.
>
>	This is just like pathconf except that an open file descriptor is used to specify the file for which information is requested, instead of a file name.
>
>	The following errno error conditions are defined for this function:
>
>	EBADF	The *filedes* argument is not a valid file descriptor.
>
>	EINVAL	The value of *parameter* is invalid, or the implementation doesn't support the *parameter* for the specific file.

Here are the symbolic constants that you can use as the *parameter* argument to `pathconf` and `fpathconf`. The values are all integer constants.

`_PC_LINK_MAX`

> Inquire about the value of `LINK_MAX`.

`_PC_MAX_CANON`

> Inquire about the value of `MAX_CANON`.

`_PC_MAX_INPUT`

> Inquire about the value of `MAX_INPUT`.

`_PC_NAME_MAX`

> Inquire about the value of `NAME_MAX`.

`_PC_PATH_MAX`

> Inquire about the value of `PATH_MAX`.

`_PC_PIPE_BUF`

> Inquire about the value of `PIPE_BUF`.

`_PC_CHOWN_RESTRICTED`

> Inquire about the value of `_POSIX_CHOWN_RESTRICTED`.

`_PC_NO_TRUNC`

> Inquire about the value of `_POSIX_NO_TRUNC`.

`_PC_VDISABLE`

> Inquire about the value of `_POSIX_VDISABLE`.

`_PC_SYNC_IO`

> Inquire about the value of `_POSIX_SYNC_IO`.

`_PC_ASYNC_IO`

> Inquire about the value of `_POSIX_ASYNC_IO`.

`_PC_PRIO_IO`

> Inquire about the value of `_POSIX_PRIO_IO`.

`_PC_FILESIZEBITS`

> Inquire about the availability of large files on the filesystem.

`_PC_REC_INCR_XFER_SIZE`

> Inquire about the value of `POSIX_REC_INCR_XFER_SIZE`.

`_PC_REC_MAX_XFER_SIZE`

> Inquire about the value of `POSIX_REC_MAX_XFER_SIZE`.

`_PC_REC_MIN_XFER_SIZE`

> Inquire about the value of `POSIX_REC_MIN_XFER_SIZE`.

`_PC_REC_XFER_ALIGN`

> Inquire about the value of `POSIX_REC_XFER_ALIGN`.

**Portability Note:** On some systems, the GNU C Library does not enforce `_PC_NAME_MAX` or `_PC_PATH_MAX` limits.

## 32.10  Utility Program Capacity Limits

The POSIX.2 standard specifies certain system limits that you can access through `sysconf` that apply to utility behavior rather than the behavior of the library or the operating system.

The GNU C Library defines macros for these limits, and `sysconf` returns values for them if you ask; but these values convey no meaningful information. They are simply the smallest values that POSIX.2 permits.

**int BC_BASE_MAX**                                                                [Macro]
 The largest value of `obase` that the `bc` utility is guaranteed to support.

**int BC_DIM_MAX**                                                                 [Macro]
 The largest number of elements in one array that the `bc` utility is guaranteed to support.

**int BC_SCALE_MAX**                                                               [Macro]
 The largest value of `scale` that the `bc` utility is guaranteed to support.

**int BC_STRING_MAX**                                                              [Macro]
 The largest number of characters in one string constant that the `bc` utility is guaranteed to support.

**int COLL_WEIGHTS_MAX**                                                           [Macro]
 The largest number of weights that can necessarily be used in defining the collating sequence for a locale.

**int EXPR_NEST_MAX**                                                              [Macro]
 The maximum number of expressions that can be nested within parenthesis by the `expr` utility.

**int LINE_MAX**                                                                   [Macro]
 The largest text line that the text-oriented POSIX.2 utilities can support. (If you are using the GNU versions of these utilities, then there is no actual limit except that imposed by the available virtual memory, but there is no way that the library can tell you this.)

**int EQUIV_CLASS_MAX**                                                            [Macro]
 The maximum number of weights that can be assigned to an entry of the `LC_COLLATE` category 'order' keyword in a locale definition. The GNU C Library does not presently support locale definitions.

## 32.11  Minimum Values for Utility Limits

`_POSIX2_BC_BASE_MAX`
 The most restrictive limit permitted by POSIX.2 for the maximum value of `obase` in the `bc` utility. Its value is 99.

`_POSIX2_BC_DIM_MAX`
 The most restrictive limit permitted by POSIX.2 for the maximum size of an array in the `bc` utility. Its value is 2048.

_POSIX2_BC_SCALE_MAX

> The most restrictive limit permitted by POSIX.2 for the maximum value of scale in the bc utility. Its value is 99.

_POSIX2_BC_STRING_MAX

> The most restrictive limit permitted by POSIX.2 for the maximum size of a string constant in the bc utility. Its value is 1000.

_POSIX2_COLL_WEIGHTS_MAX

> The most restrictive limit permitted by POSIX.2 for the maximum number of weights that can necessarily be used in defining the collating sequence for a locale. Its value is 2.

_POSIX2_EXPR_NEST_MAX

> The most restrictive limit permitted by POSIX.2 for the maximum number of expressions nested within parenthesis when using the expr utility. Its value is 32.

_POSIX2_LINE_MAX

> The most restrictive limit permitted by POSIX.2 for the maximum size of a text line that the text utilities can handle. Its value is 2048.

_POSIX2_EQUIV_CLASS_MAX

> The most restrictive limit permitted by POSIX.2 for the maximum number of weights that can be assigned to an entry of the LC_COLLATE category 'order' keyword in a locale definition. Its value is 2. The GNU C Library does not presently support locale definitions.

## 32.12 String-Valued Parameters

POSIX.2 defines a way to get string-valued parameters from the operating system with the function confstr:

size_t confstr (*int* **parameter**, *char *buf*, *size_t* **len**)                           [Function]
> Preliminary: | MT-Safe | AS-Safe | AC-Safe | See Section 1.2.2.1 [POSIX Safety Concepts], page 2.

> This function reads the value of a string-valued system parameter, storing the string into *len* bytes of memory space starting at *buf*. The *parameter* argument should be one of the '_CS_' symbols listed below.

> The normal return value from confstr is the length of the string value that you asked for. If you supply a null pointer for *buf*, then confstr does not try to store the string; it just returns its length. A value of 0 indicates an error.

> If the string you asked for is too long for the buffer (that is, longer than len - 1), then confstr stores just that much (leaving room for the terminating null character). You can tell that this has happened because confstr returns a value greater than or equal to *len*.

> The following errno error conditions are defined for this function:

> EINVAL     The value of the *parameter* is invalid.

Currently there is just one parameter you can read with `confstr`:

`_CS_PATH`      This parameter's value is the recommended default path for searching for executable files. This is the path that a user has by default just after logging in.

`_CS_LFS_CFLAGS`

The returned string specifies which additional flags must be given to the C compiler if a source is compiled using the `_LARGEFILE_SOURCE` feature select macro; see Section 1.3.4 [Feature Test Macros], page 15.

`_CS_LFS_LDFLAGS`

The returned string specifies which additional flags must be given to the linker if a source is compiled using the `_LARGEFILE_SOURCE` feature select macro; see Section 1.3.4 [Feature Test Macros], page 15.

`_CS_LFS_LIBS`

The returned string specifies which additional libraries must be linked to the application if a source is compiled using the `_LARGEFILE_SOURCE` feature select macro; see Section 1.3.4 [Feature Test Macros], page 15.

`_CS_LFS_LINTFLAGS`

The returned string specifies which additional flags must be given to the lint tool if a source is compiled using the `_LARGEFILE_SOURCE` feature select macro; see Section 1.3.4 [Feature Test Macros], page 15.

`_CS_LFS64_CFLAGS`

The returned string specifies which additional flags must be given to the C compiler if a source is compiled using the `_LARGEFILE64_SOURCE` feature select macro; see Section 1.3.4 [Feature Test Macros], page 15.

`_CS_LFS64_LDFLAGS`

The returned string specifies which additional flags must be given to the linker if a source is compiled using the `_LARGEFILE64_SOURCE` feature select macro; see Section 1.3.4 [Feature Test Macros], page 15.

`_CS_LFS64_LIBS`

The returned string specifies which additional libraries must be linked to the application if a source is compiled using the `_LARGEFILE64_SOURCE` feature select macro; see Section 1.3.4 [Feature Test Macros], page 15.

`_CS_LFS64_LINTFLAGS`

The returned string specifies which additional flags must be given to the lint tool if a source is compiled using the `_LARGEFILE64_SOURCE` feature select macro; see Section 1.3.4 [Feature Test Macros], page 15.

The way to use `confstr` without any arbitrary limit on string size is to call it twice: first call it to get the length, allocate the buffer accordingly, and then call `confstr` again to fill the buffer, like this:

```
char *
get_default_path (void)
{
  size_t len = confstr (_CS_PATH, NULL, 0);
  char *buffer = (char *) xmalloc (len);

  if (confstr (_CS_PATH, buf, len + 1) == 0)
    {
      free (buffer);
      return NULL;
    }

  return buffer;
}
```

# 33 DES Encryption and Password Handling

On many systems, it is unnecessary to have any kind of user authentication; for instance, a workstation which is not connected to a network probably does not need any user authentication, because to use the machine an intruder must have physical access.

Sometimes, however, it is necessary to be sure that a user is authorized to use some service a machine provides—for instance, to log in as a particular user id (see Chapter 30 [Users and Groups], page 791). One traditional way of doing this is for each user to choose a secret *password*; then, the system can ask someone claiming to be a user what the user's password is, and if the person gives the correct password then the system can grant the appropriate privileges.

If all the passwords are just stored in a file somewhere, then this file has to be very carefully protected. To avoid this, passwords are run through a *one-way function*, a function which makes it difficult to work out what its input was by looking at its output, before storing in the file.

The GNU C Library provides a one-way function that is compatible with the behavior of the `crypt` function introduced in FreeBSD 2.0. It supports two one-way algorithms: one based on the MD5 message-digest algorithm that is compatible with modern BSD systems, and the other based on the Data Encryption Standard (DES) that is compatible with Unix systems.

It also provides support for Secure RPC, and some library functions that can be used to perform normal DES encryption. The `AUTH_DES` authentication flavor in Secure RPC, as provided by the GNU C Library, uses DES and does not comply with FIPS 140-2 nor does any other use of DES within the GNU C Library. It is recommended that Secure RPC should not be used for systems that need to comply with FIPS 140-2 since all flavors of encrypted authentication use normal DES.

## 33.1 Legal Problems

Because of the continuously changing state of the law, it's not possible to provide a definitive survey of the laws affecting cryptography. Instead, this section warns you of some of the known trouble spots; this may help you when you try to find out what the laws of your country are.

Some countries require that you have a licence to use, possess, or import cryptography. These countries are believed to include Byelorussia, Burma, India, Indonesia, Israel, Kazakhstan, Pakistan, Russia, and Saudi Arabia.

Some countries restrict the transmission of encrypted messages by radio; some telecommunications carriers restrict the transmission of encrypted messages over their network.

Many countries have some form of export control for encryption software. The Wassenaar Arrangement is a multilateral agreement between 33 countries (Argentina, Australia, Austria, Belgium, Bulgaria, Canada, the Czech Republic, Denmark, Finland, France, Germany, Greece, Hungary, Ireland, Italy, Japan, Luxembourg, the Netherlands, New Zealand, Norway, Poland, Portugal, the Republic of Korea, Romania, the Russian Federation, the Slovak Republic, Spain, Sweden, Switzerland, Turkey, Ukraine, the United Kingdom and the United States) which restricts some kinds of encryption exports. Different countries apply the arrangement in different ways; some do not allow the exception for certain kinds of "public domain" software (which would include this library), some only restrict the export of software in tangible form, and others impose significant additional restrictions.

The United States has additional rules. This software would generally be exportable under 15 CFR 740.13(e), which permits exports of "encryption source code" which is "publicly available" and which is "not subject to an express agreement for the payment of a licensing fee or royalty for commercial production or sale of any product developed with the source code" to most countries.

The rules in this area are continuously changing. If you know of any information in this manual that is out-of-date, please report it to the bug database. See Section C.5 [Reporting Bugs], page 1002.

## 33.2 Reading Passwords

When reading in a password, it is desirable to avoid displaying it on the screen, to help keep it secret. The following function handles this in a convenient way.

char * getpass (*const char \*prompt*)                                          [Function]
    Preliminary: | MT-Unsafe term | AS-Unsafe heap lock corrupt | AC-Unsafe term lock corrupt | See Section 1.2.2.1 [POSIX Safety Concepts], page 2.

    getpass outputs *prompt*, then reads a string in from the terminal without echoing it. It tries to connect to the real terminal, /dev/tty, if possible, to encourage users not to put plaintext passwords in files; otherwise, it uses stdin and stderr. getpass also disables the INTR, QUIT, and SUSP characters on the terminal using the ISIG terminal attribute (see Section 17.4.7 [Local Modes], page 486). The terminal is flushed before and after getpass, so that characters of a mistyped password are not accidentally visible.

    In other C libraries, getpass may only return the first PASS_MAX bytes of a password. The GNU C Library has no limit, so PASS_MAX is undefined.

    The prototype for this function is in unistd.h.  PASS_MAX would be defined in limits.h.

This precise set of operations may not suit all possible situations. In this case, it is recommended that users write their own getpass substitute. For instance, a very simple substitute is as follows:

```
#include <termios.h>
#include <stdio.h>

ssize_t
my_getpass (char **lineptr, size_t *n, FILE *stream)
{
  struct termios old, new;
  int nread;

  /* Turn echoing off and fail if we can't. */
  if (tcgetattr (fileno (stream), &old) != 0)
    return -1;
  new = old;
  new.c_lflag &= ~ECHO;
  if (tcsetattr (fileno (stream), TCSAFLUSH, &new) != 0)
```

```
    return -1;

/* Read the password. */
nread = getline (lineptr, n, stream);

/* Restore terminal. */
(void) tcsetattr (fileno (stream), TCSAFLUSH, &old);

    return nread;
}
```

The substitute takes the same parameters as `getline` (see Section 12.9 [Line-Oriented Input], page 264); the user must print any prompt desired.

## 33.3 Encrypting Passwords

`char * crypt` (*const char *key, const char *salt*)                [Function]
> Preliminary: | MT-Unsafe race:crypt | AS-Unsafe corrupt lock heap dlopen | AC-Unsafe lock mem | See Section 1.2.2.1 [POSIX Safety Concepts], page 2.

The `crypt` function takes a password, *key*, as a string, and a *salt* character array which is described below, and returns a printable ASCII string which starts with another salt. It is believed that, given the output of the function, the best way to find a *key* that will produce that output is to guess values of *key* until the original value of *key* is found.

The *salt* parameter does two things. Firstly, it selects which algorithm is used, the MD5-based one or the DES-based one. Secondly, it makes life harder for someone trying to guess passwords against a file containing many passwords; without a *salt*, an intruder can make a guess, run `crypt` on it once, and compare the result with all the passwords. With a *salt*, the intruder must run `crypt` once for each different salt.

For the MD5-based algorithm, the *salt* should consist of the string $1$, followed by up to 8 characters, terminated by either another $ or the end of the string. The result of `crypt` will be the *salt*, followed by a $ if the salt didn't end with one, followed by 22 characters from the alphabet ./0-9A-Za-z, up to 34 characters total. Every character in the *key* is significant.

For the DES-based algorithm, the *salt* should consist of two characters from the alphabet ./0-9A-Za-z, and the result of `crypt` will be those two characters followed by 11 more from the same alphabet, 13 in total. Only the first 8 characters in the *key* are significant.

The MD5-based algorithm has no limit on the useful length of the password used, and is slightly more secure. It is therefore preferred over the DES-based algorithm.

When the user enters their password for the first time, the *salt* should be set to a new string which is reasonably random. To verify a password against the result of a previous call to `crypt`, pass the result of the previous call as the *salt*.

The following short program is an example of how to use `crypt` the first time a password is entered. Note that the *salt* generation is just barely acceptable; in particular, it is not unique between machines, and in many applications it would not be acceptable to let an attacker know what time the user's password was last set.

```c
#include <stdio.h>
#include <time.h>
#include <unistd.h>
#include <crypt.h>

int
main(void)
{
  unsigned long seed[2];
  char salt[] = "$1$........";
  const char *const seedchars =
    "./0123456789ABCDEFGHIJKLMNOPQRST"
    "UVWXYZabcdefghijklmnopqrstuvwxyz";
  char *password;
  int i;

  /* Generate a (not very) random seed.
     You should do it better than this... */
  seed[0] = time(NULL);
  seed[1] = getpid() ^ (seed[0] >> 14 & 0x30000);

  /* Turn it into printable characters from 'seedchars'. */
  for (i = 0; i < 8; i++)
    salt[3+i] = seedchars[(seed[i/5] >> (i%5)*6) & 0x3f];

  /* Read in the user's password and encrypt it. */
  password = crypt(getpass("Password:"), salt);

  /* Print the results. */
  puts(password);
  return 0;
}
```

The next program shows how to verify a password. It prompts the user for a password and prints "Access granted." if the user types GNU libc manual.

```c
#include <stdio.h>
#include <string.h>
#include <unistd.h>
#include <crypt.h>

int
main(void)
{
  /* Hashed form of "GNU libc manual". */
  const char *const pass = "$1$/iSaq7rB$EoUw5jPPvAPECNaaWzMK/";

  char *result;
  int ok;

  /* Read in the user's password and encrypt it,
     passing the expected password in as the salt. */
  result = crypt(getpass("Password:"), pass);

  /* Test the result. */
  ok = strcmp (result, pass) == 0;
```

```
    puts(ok ? "Access granted." : "Access denied.");
    return ok ? 0 : 1;
}
```

**char \* crypt_r** (*const char \*key, const char \*salt, struct crypt_data \**     [Function]
    *data*)

> Preliminary: | MT-Safe | AS-Unsafe corrupt lock heap dlopen | AC-Unsafe lock
> mem | See Section 1.2.2.1 [POSIX Safety Concepts], page 2.
>
> The `crypt_r` function does the same thing as `crypt`, but takes an extra parame-
> ter which includes space for its result (among other things), so it can be reentrant.
> `data->initialized` must be cleared to zero before the first time `crypt_r` is called.
>
> The `crypt_r` function is a GNU extension.

The `crypt` and `crypt_r` functions are prototyped in the header `crypt.h`.

## 33.4 DES Encryption

The Data Encryption Standard is described in the US Government Federal Information
Processing Standards (FIPS) 46-3 published by the National Institute of Standards and
Technology. The DES has been very thoroughly analyzed since it was developed in the late
1970s, and no new significant flaws have been found.

However, the DES uses only a 56-bit key (plus 8 parity bits), and a machine has been
built in 1998 which can search through all possible keys in about 6 days, which cost about
US$200000; faster searches would be possible with more money. This makes simple DES
insecure for most purposes, and NIST no longer permits new US government systems to
use simple DES.

For serious encryption functionality, it is recommended that one of the many free encryption libraries be used instead of these routines.

The DES is a reversible operation which takes a 64-bit block and a 64-bit key, and
produces another 64-bit block. Usually the bits are numbered so that the most-significant
bit, the first bit, of each block is numbered 1.

Under that numbering, every 8th bit of the key (the 8th, 16th, and so on) is not used
by the encryption algorithm itself. But the key must have odd parity; that is, out of bits 1
through 8, and 9 through 16, and so on, there must be an odd number of '1' bits, and this
completely specifies the unused bits.

**void setkey** (*const char \*key*)                                      [Function]

> Preliminary: | MT-Unsafe race:crypt | AS-Unsafe corrupt lock | AC-Unsafe lock |
> See Section 1.2.2.1 [POSIX Safety Concepts], page 2.
>
> The `setkey` function sets an internal data structure to be an expanded form of *key*.
> *key* is specified as an array of 64 bits each stored in a `char`, the first bit is `key[0]`
> and the 64th bit is `key[63]`. The *key* should have the correct parity.

**void encrypt** (*char \*block, int edflag*)                            [Function]

> Preliminary: | MT-Unsafe race:crypt | AS-Unsafe corrupt lock | AC-Unsafe lock |
> See Section 1.2.2.1 [POSIX Safety Concepts], page 2.
>
> The `encrypt` function encrypts *block* if *edflag* is 0, otherwise it decrypts *block*, using
> a key previously set by `setkey`. The result is placed in *block*.

Like setkey, *block* is specified as an array of 64 bits each stored in a char, but there are no parity bits in *block*.

void setkey_r (*const char \*key, struct crypt_data \* data*)                    [Function]
void encrypt_r (*char \*block, int edflag, struct crypt_data \* data*)          [Function]
>    Preliminary:  |  MT-Safe   |  AS-Unsafe corrupt lock  |  AC-Unsafe lock  |  See Section 1.2.2.1 [POSIX Safety Concepts], page 2.

>    These are reentrant versions of setkey and encrypt. The only difference is the extra parameter, which stores the expanded version of *key*. Before calling setkey_r the first time, data->initialized must be cleared to zero.

The setkey_r and encrypt_r functions are GNU extensions. setkey, encrypt, setkey_r, and encrypt_r are defined in crypt.h.

int ecb_crypt (*char \*key, char \*blocks, unsigned len, unsigned mode*)    [Function]
>    Preliminary: | MT-Safe | AS-Safe | AC-Safe | See Section 1.2.2.1 [POSIX Safety Concepts], page 2.

>    The function ecb_crypt encrypts or decrypts one or more blocks using DES. Each block is encrypted independently.

>    The *blocks* and the *key* are stored packed in 8-bit bytes, so that the first bit of the key is the most-significant bit of key[0] and the 63rd bit of the key is stored as the least-significant bit of key[7]. The *key* should have the correct parity.

>    *len* is the number of bytes in *blocks*. It should be a multiple of 8 (so that there is a whole number of blocks to encrypt). *len* is limited to a maximum of DES_MAXDATA bytes.

>    The result of the encryption replaces the input in *blocks*.

>    The *mode* parameter is the bitwise OR of two of the following:

DES_ENCRYPT
>    This constant, used in the *mode* parameter, specifies that *blocks* is to be encrypted.

DES_DECRYPT
>    This constant, used in the *mode* parameter, specifies that *blocks* is to be decrypted.

DES_HW    This constant, used in the *mode* parameter, asks to use a hardware device. If no hardware device is available, encryption happens anyway, but in software.

DES_SW    This constant, used in the *mode* parameter, specifies that no hardware device is to be used.

>    The result of the function will be one of these values:

DESERR_NONE
>    The encryption succeeded.

DESERR_NOHWDEVICE
>    The encryption succeeded, but there was no hardware device available.

DESERR_HWERROR

> The encryption failed because of a hardware problem.

DESERR_BADPARAM

> The encryption failed because of a bad parameter, for instance *len* is not a multiple of 8 or *len* is larger than DES_MAXDATA.

int DES_FAILED (*int* **err**)                                                                    [Function]
> Preliminary: | MT-Safe | AS-Safe | AC-Safe | See Section 1.2.2.1 [POSIX Safety Concepts], page 2.

> This macro returns 1 if *err* is a 'success' result code from ecb_crypt or cbc_crypt, and 0 otherwise.

int cbc_crypt (*char* ***key**, *char* ***blocks**, *unsigned* **len**, *unsigned* **mode**,         [Function]
      *char* ***ivec**)
> Preliminary: | MT-Safe | AS-Safe | AC-Safe | See Section 1.2.2.1 [POSIX Safety Concepts], page 2.

> The function cbc_crypt encrypts or decrypts one or more blocks using DES in Cipher Block Chaining mode.

> For encryption in CBC mode, each block is exclusive-ored with *ivec* before being encrypted, then *ivec* is replaced with the result of the encryption, then the next block is processed. Decryption is the reverse of this process.

> This has the advantage that blocks which are the same before being encrypted are very unlikely to be the same after being encrypted, making it much harder to detect patterns in the data.

> Usually, *ivec* is set to 8 random bytes before encryption starts. Then the 8 random bytes are transmitted along with the encrypted data (without themselves being encrypted), and passed back in as *ivec* for decryption. Another possibility is to set *ivec* to 8 zeroes initially, and have the first the block encrypted consist of 8 random bytes.

> Otherwise, all the parameters are similar to those for ecb_crypt.

void des_setparity (*char* ***key**)                                                               [Function]
> Preliminary: | MT-Safe | AS-Safe | AC-Safe | See Section 1.2.2.1 [POSIX Safety Concepts], page 2.

> The function des_setparity changes the 64-bit *key*, stored packed in 8-bit bytes, to have odd parity by altering the low bits of each byte.

The ecb_crypt, cbc_crypt, and des_setparity functions and their accompanying macros are all defined in the header rpc/des_crypt.h.

# 34 Debugging support

Applications are usually debugged using dedicated debugger programs. But sometimes this is not possible and, in any case, it is useful to provide the developer with as much information as possible at the time the problems are experienced. For this reason a few functions are provided which a program can use to help the developer more easily locate the problem.

## 34.1 Backtraces

A *backtrace* is a list of the function calls that are currently active in a thread. The usual way to inspect a backtrace of a program is to use an external debugger such as gdb. However, sometimes it is useful to obtain a backtrace programmatically from within a program, e.g., for the purposes of logging or diagnostics.

The header file `execinfo.h` declares three functions that obtain and manipulate backtraces of the current thread.

**int backtrace** (*void **buffer*, *int size*)                                   [Function]
> Preliminary: | MT-Safe | AS-Unsafe init heap dlopen plugin lock | AC-Unsafe init mem lock fd | See Section 1.2.2.1 [POSIX Safety Concepts], page 2.
>
> The `backtrace` function obtains a backtrace for the current thread, as a list of pointers, and places the information into *buffer*. The argument *size* should be the number of `void *` elements that will fit into *buffer*. The return value is the actual number of entries of *buffer* that are obtained, and is at most *size*.
>
> The pointers placed in *buffer* are actually return addresses obtained by inspecting the stack, one return address per stack frame.
>
> Note that certain compiler optimizations may interfere with obtaining a valid backtrace. Function inlining causes the inlined function to not have a stack frame; tail call optimization replaces one stack frame with another; frame pointer elimination will stop `backtrace` from interpreting the stack contents correctly.

**char ** backtrace_symbols** (*void *const *buffer*, *int size*)               [Function]
> Preliminary: | MT-Safe | AS-Unsafe heap | AC-Unsafe mem lock | See Section 1.2.2.1 [POSIX Safety Concepts], page 2.
>
> The `backtrace_symbols` function translates the information obtained from the `backtrace` function into an array of strings. The argument *buffer* should be a pointer to an array of addresses obtained via the `backtrace` function, and *size* is the number of entries in that array (the return value of `backtrace`).
>
> The return value is a pointer to an array of strings, which has *size* entries just like the array *buffer*. Each string contains a printable representation of the corresponding element of *buffer*. It includes the function name (if this can be determined), an offset into the function, and the actual return address (in hexadecimal).
>
> Currently, the function name and offset only be obtained on systems that use the ELF binary format for programs and libraries. On other systems, only the hexadecimal return address will be present. Also, you may need to pass additional flags to the linker to make the function names available to the program. (For example, on systems using GNU ld, you must pass (`-rdynamic`.)

The return value of `backtrace_symbols` is a pointer obtained via the `malloc` function, and it is the responsibility of the caller to `free` that pointer. Note that only the return value need be freed, not the individual strings.

The return value is `NULL` if sufficient memory for the strings cannot be obtained.

`void backtrace_symbols_fd` (*void \*const \*buffer*, *int size*, *int fd*)        [Function]
Preliminary: | MT-Safe | AS-Safe | AC-Unsafe lock | See Section 1.2.2.1 [POSIX Safety Concepts], page 2.

The `backtrace_symbols_fd` function performs the same translation as the function `backtrace_symbols` function. Instead of returning the strings to the caller, it writes the strings to the file descriptor *fd*, one per line. It does not use the `malloc` function, and can therefore be used in situations where that function might fail.

The following program illustrates the use of these functions. Note that the array to contain the return addresses returned by `backtrace` is allocated on the stack. Therefore code like this can be used in situations where the memory handling via `malloc` does not work anymore (in which case the `backtrace_symbols` has to be replaced by a `backtrace_symbols_fd` call as well). The number of return addresses is normally not very large. Even complicated programs rather seldom have a nesting level of more than, say, 50 and with 200 possible entries probably all programs should be covered.

```
#include <execinfo.h>
#include <stdio.h>
#include <stdlib.h>

/* Obtain a backtrace and print it to stdout. */
void
print_trace (void)
{
  void *array[10];
  size_t size;
  char **strings;
  size_t i;

  size = backtrace (array, 10);
  strings = backtrace_symbols (array, size);

  printf ("Obtained %zd stack frames.\n", size);

  for (i = 0; i < size; i++)
     printf ("%s\n", strings[i]);

  free (strings);
}

/* A dummy function to make the backtrace more interesting. */
void
dummy_function (void)
{
  print_trace ();
}

int
main (void)
```

```
{
  dummy_function ();
  return 0;
}
```

# 35 POSIX Threads

This chapter describes the GNU C Library POSIX Thread implementation.

## 35.1 Thread-specific Data

The GNU C Library implements functions to allow users to create and manage data specific to a thread. Such data may be destroyed at thread exit, if a destructor is provided. The following functions are defined:

**int pthread_key_create** (*pthread_key_t \*key*, *void*                    [Function]
    (*\*destructor*)(*void\**))
    Preliminary: | MT-Safe | AS-Safe | AC-Safe | See Section 1.2.2.1 [POSIX Safety Concepts], page 2.

    Create a thread-specific data key for the calling thread, referenced by *key*.

    Objects declared with the C++11 **thread_local** keyword are destroyed before thread-specific data, so they should not be used in thread-specific data destructors or even as members of the thread-specific data, since the latter is passed as an argument to the destructor function.

**int pthread_key_delete** (*pthread_key_t key*)                            [Function]
    Preliminary: | MT-Safe | AS-Safe | AC-Safe | See Section 1.2.2.1 [POSIX Safety Concepts], page 2.

    Destroy the thread-specific data *key* in the calling thread. The destructor for the thread-specific data is not called during destruction, nor is it called during thread exit.

**void \*pthread_getspecific** (*pthread_key_t key*)                        [Function]
    Preliminary: | MT-Safe | AS-Safe | AC-Safe | See Section 1.2.2.1 [POSIX Safety Concepts], page 2.

    Return the thread-specific data associated with *key* in the calling thread.

**int pthread_setspecific** (*pthread_key_t key*, *const void \*value*)     [Function]
    Preliminary: | MT-Safe | AS-Unsafe corrupt heap | AC-Unsafe corrupt mem | See Section 1.2.2.1 [POSIX Safety Concepts], page 2.

    Associate the thread-specific *value* with *key* in the calling thread.

## 35.2 Non-POSIX Extensions

In addition to implementing the POSIX API for threads, the GNU C Library provides additional functions and interfaces to provide functionality not specified in the standard.

### 35.2.1 Setting Process-wide defaults for thread attributes

The GNU C Library provides non-standard API functions to set and get the default attributes used in the creation of threads in a process.

int **pthread_getattr_default_np** (*pthread_attr_t* **\*attr**)                    [Function]
    Preliminary: | MT-Safe | AS-Unsafe lock | AC-Unsafe lock | See Section 1.2.2.1
    [POSIX Safety Concepts], page 2.

    Get the default attribute values and set *attr* to match. This function returns 0 on
    success and a non-zero error code on failure.

int **pthread_setattr_default_np** (*pthread_attr_t* **\*attr**)                    [Function]
    Preliminary: | MT-Safe | AS-Unsafe heap lock | AC-Unsafe lock mem | See
    Section 1.2.2.1 [POSIX Safety Concepts], page 2.

    Set the default attribute values to match the values in *attr*. The function returns 0
    on success and a non-zero error code on failure. The following error codes are defined
    for this function:

    EINVAL      At least one of the values in *attr* does not qualify as valid for the attributes
                or the stack address is set in the attribute.

    ENOMEM      The system does not have sufficient memory.

# 36 Internal probes

In order to aid in debugging and monitoring internal behavior, the GNU C Library exposes nearly-zero-overhead SystemTap probes marked with the `libc` provider.

These probes are not part of the GNU C Library stable ABI, and they are subject to change or removal across releases. Our only promise with regard to them is that, if we find a need to remove or modify the arguments of a probe, the modified probe will have a different name, so that program monitors relying on the old probe will not get unexpected arguments.

## 36.1 Memory Allocation Probes

These probes are designed to signal relatively unusual situations within the virtual memory subsystem of the GNU C Library.

**memory_sbrk_more** (*void \*$arg1, size_t $arg2*)                                              [Probe]
> This probe is triggered after the main arena is extended by calling `sbrk`. Argument *$arg1* is the additional size requested to `sbrk`, and *$arg2* is the pointer that marks the end of the `sbrk` area, returned in response to the request.

**memory_sbrk_less** (*void \*$arg1, size_t $arg2*)                                              [Probe]
> This probe is triggered after the size of the main arena is decreased by calling `sbrk`. Argument *$arg1* is the size released by `sbrk` (the positive value, rather than the negative value passed to `sbrk`), and *$arg2* is the pointer that marks the end of the `sbrk` area, returned in response to the request.

**memory_heap_new** (*void \*$arg1, size_t $arg2*)                                               [Probe]
> This probe is triggered after a new heap is `mmap`ed. Argument *$arg1* is a pointer to the base of the memory area, where the `heap_info` data structure is held, and *$arg2* is the size of the heap.

**memory_heap_free** (*void \*$arg1, size_t $arg2*)                                              [Probe]
> This probe is triggered *before* (unlike the other sbrk and heap probes) a heap is completely removed via `munmap`. Argument *$arg1* is a pointer to the heap, and *$arg2* is the size of the heap.

**memory_heap_more** (*void \*$arg1, size_t $arg2*)                                              [Probe]
> This probe is triggered after a trailing portion of an `mmap`ed heap is extended. Argument *$arg1* is a pointer to the heap, and *$arg2* is the new size of the heap.

**memory_heap_less** (*void \*$arg1, size_t $arg2*)                                              [Probe]
> This probe is triggered after a trailing portion of an `mmap`ed heap is released. Argument *$arg1* is a pointer to the heap, and *$arg2* is the new size of the heap.

**memory_malloc_retry** (*size_t $arg1*)                                                         [Probe]
**memory_realloc_retry** (*size_t $arg1, void \*$arg2*)                                          [Probe]
**memory_memalign_retry** (*size_t $arg1, size_t $arg2*)                                         [Probe]
**memory_calloc_retry** (*size_t $arg1*)                                                         [Probe]
> These probes are triggered when the corresponding functions fail to obtain the requested amount of memory from the arena in use, before they call `arena_get_retry`

to select an alternate arena in which to retry the allocation. Argument *$arg1* is the amount of memory requested by the user; in the `calloc` case, that is the total size computed from both function arguments. In the `realloc` case, *$arg2* is the pointer to the memory area being resized. In the `memalign` case, *$arg2* is the alignment to be used for the request, which may be stricter than the value passed to the `memalign` function. A `memalign` probe is also used by functions `posix_memalign, valloc` and `pvalloc`.

Note that the argument order does *not* match that of the corresponding two-argument functions, so that in all of these probes the user-requested allocation size is in *$arg1*.

**memory_arena_retry** (*size_t $arg1, void *$arg2*)                          [Probe]

This probe is triggered within `arena_get_retry` (the function called to select the alternate arena in which to retry an allocation that failed on the first attempt), before the selection of an alternate arena. This probe is redundant, but much easier to use when it's not important to determine which of the various memory allocation functions is failing to allocate on the first try. Argument *$arg1* is the same as in the function-specific probes, except for extra room for padding introduced by functions that have to ensure stricter alignment. Argument *$arg2* is the arena in which allocation failed.

**memory_arena_new** (*void *$arg1, size_t $arg2*)                           [Probe]

This probe is triggered when `malloc` allocates and initializes an additional arena (not the main arena), but before the arena is assigned to the running thread or inserted into the internal linked list of arenas. The arena's `malloc_state` internal data structure is located at *$arg1*, within a newly-allocated heap big enough to hold at least *$arg2* bytes.

**memory_arena_reuse** (*void *$arg1, void *$arg2*)                          [Probe]

This probe is triggered when `malloc` has just selected an existing arena to reuse, and (temporarily) reserved it for exclusive use. Argument *$arg1* is a pointer to the newly-selected arena, and *$arg2* is a pointer to the arena previously used by that thread.

This occurs within `reused_arena`, right after the mutex mentioned in probe `memory_arena_reuse_wait` is acquired; argument *$arg1* will point to the same arena. In this configuration, this will usually only occur once per thread. The exception is when a thread first selected the main arena, but a subsequent allocation from it fails: then, and only then, may we switch to another arena to retry that allocations, and for further allocations within that thread.

**memory_arena_reuse_wait** (*void *$arg1, void *$arg2, void *$arg3*)       [Probe]

This probe is triggered when `malloc` is about to wait for an arena to become available for reuse. Argument *$arg1* holds a pointer to the mutex the thread is going to wait on, *$arg2* is a pointer to a newly-chosen arena to be reused, and *$arg3* is a pointer to the arena previously used by that thread.

This occurs within `reused_arena`, when a thread first tries to allocate memory or needs a retry after a failure to allocate from the main arena, there isn't any free arena, the maximum number of arenas has been reached, and an existing arena was chosen for reuse, but its mutex could not be immediately acquired. The mutex in *$arg1* is the mutex of the selected arena.

**memory_arena_reuse_free_list** (*void \*$arg1*) [Probe]

This probe is triggered when `malloc` has chosen an arena that is in the free list for use by a thread, within the `get_free_list` function. The argument *$arg1* holds a pointer to the selected arena.

**memory_mallopt** (*int $arg1, int $arg2*) [Probe]

This probe is triggered when function `mallopt` is called to change `malloc` internal configuration parameters, before any change to the parameters is made. The arguments *$arg1* and *$arg2* are the ones passed to the `mallopt` function.

**memory_mallopt_mxfast** (*int $arg1, int $arg2*) [Probe]

This probe is triggered shortly after the `memory_mallopt` probe, when the parameter to be changed is `M_MXFAST`, and the requested value is in an acceptable range. Argument *$arg1* is the requested value, and *$arg2* is the previous value of this `malloc` parameter.

**memory_mallopt_trim_threshold** (*int $arg1, int $arg2, int $arg3*) [Probe]

This probe is triggere shortly after the `memory_mallopt` probe, when the parameter to be changed is `M_TRIM_THRESHOLD`. Argument *$arg1* is the requested value, *$arg2* is the previous value of this `malloc` parameter, and *$arg3* is nonzero if dynamic threshold adjustment was already disabled.

**memory_mallopt_top_pad** (*int $arg1, int $arg2, int $arg3*) [Probe]

This probe is triggered shortly after the `memory_mallopt` probe, when the parameter to be changed is `M_TOP_PAD`. Argument *$arg1* is the requested value, *$arg2* is the previous value of this `malloc` parameter, and *$arg3* is nonzero if dynamic threshold adjustment was already disabled.

**memory_mallopt_mmap_threshold** (*int $arg1, int $arg2, int $arg3*) [Probe]

This probe is triggered shortly after the `memory_mallopt` probe, when the parameter to be changed is `M_MMAP_THRESHOLD`, and the requested value is in an acceptable range. Argument *$arg1* is the requested value, *$arg2* is the previous value of this `malloc` parameter, and *$arg3* is nonzero if dynamic threshold adjustment was already disabled.

**memory_mallopt_mmap_max** (*int $arg1, int $arg2, int $arg3*) [Probe]

This probe is triggered shortly after the `memory_mallopt` probe, when the parameter to be changed is `M_MMAP_MAX`. Argument *$arg1* is the requested value, *$arg2* is the previous value of this `malloc` parameter, and *$arg3* is nonzero if dynamic threshold adjustment was already disabled.

**memory_mallopt_check_action** (*int $arg1, int $arg2*) [Probe]

This probe is triggered shortly after the `memory_mallopt` probe, when the parameter to be changed is `M_CHECK_ACTION`. Argument *$arg1* is the requested value, and *$arg2* is the previous value of this `malloc` parameter.

**memory_mallopt_perturb** (*int $arg1, int $arg2*) [Probe]

This probe is triggered shortly after the `memory_mallopt` probe, when the parameter to be changed is `M_PERTURB`. Argument *$arg1* is the requested value, and *$arg2* is the previous value of this `malloc` parameter.

**memory_mallopt_arena_test** (*int $arg1*, *int $arg2*)                            [Probe]

 > This probe is triggered shortly after the `memory_mallopt` probe, when the parameter to be changed is `M_ARENA_TEST`, and the requested value is in an acceptable range. Argument *$arg1* is the requested value, and *$arg2* is the previous value of this `malloc` parameter.

**memory_mallopt_arena_max** (*int $arg1*, *int $arg2*)                             [Probe]

 > This probe is triggered shortly after the `memory_mallopt` probe, when the parameter to be changed is `M_ARENA_MAX`, and the requested value is in an acceptable range. Argument *$arg1* is the requested value, and *$arg2* is the previous value of this `malloc` parameter.

**memory_mallopt_free_dyn_thresholds** (*int $arg1*, *int $arg2*)                   [Probe]

 > This probe is triggered when function `free` decides to adjust the dynamic brk/mmap thresholds. Argument *$arg1* and *$arg2* are the adjusted mmap and trim thresholds, respectively.

## 36.2 Mathematical Function Probes

Some mathematical functions fall back to multiple precision arithmetic for some inputs to get last bit precision for their return values. This multiple precision fallback is much slower than the default algorithms and may have a significant impact on application performance. The systemtap probe markers described in this section may help you determine if your application calls mathematical functions with inputs that may result in multiple-precision arithmetic.

Unless explicitly mentioned otherwise, a precision of 1 implies 24 bits of precision in the mantissa of the multiple precision number. Hence, a precision level of 32 implies 768 bits of precision in the mantissa.

**slowexp_p6** (*double $arg1*, *double $arg2*)                                     [Probe]

 > This probe is triggered when the `exp` function is called with an input that results in multiple precision computation with precision 6. Argument *$arg1* is the input value and *$arg2* is the computed output.

**slowexp_p32** (*double $arg1*, *double $arg2*)                                    [Probe]

 > This probe is triggered when the `exp` function is called with an input that results in multiple precision computation with precision 32. Argument *$arg1* is the input value and *$arg2* is the computed output.

**slowpow_p10** (*double $arg1*, *double $arg2*, *double $arg3*, *double $arg4*)    [Probe]

 > This probe is triggered when the `pow` function is called with inputs that result in multiple precision computation with precision 10. Arguments *$arg1* and *$arg2* are the input values, *$arg3* is the value computed in the fast phase of the algorithm and *$arg4* is the final accurate value.

**slowpow_p32** (*double $arg1*, *double $arg2*, *double $arg3*, *double $arg4*)    [Probe]

 > This probe is triggered when the `pow` function is called with an input that results in multiple precision computation with precision 32. Arguments *$arg1* and *$arg2* are the input values, *$arg3* is the value computed in the fast phase of the algorithm and *$arg4* is the final accurate value.

slowlog (*int $arg1*, *double $arg2*, *double $arg3*)                        [Probe]
> This probe is triggered when the `log` function is called with an input that results in multiple precision computation. Argument *$arg1* is the precision with which the computation succeeded. Argument *$arg2* is the input and *$arg3* is the computed output.

slowlog_inexact (*int $arg1*, *double $arg2*, *double $arg3*)                 [Probe]
> This probe is triggered when the `log` function is called with an input that results in multiple precision computation and none of the multiple precision computations result in an accurate result. Argument *$arg1* is the maximum precision with which computations were performed. Argument *$arg2* is the input and *$arg3* is the computed output.

slowatan2 (*int $arg1*, *double $arg2*, *double $arg3*, *double $arg4*)       [Probe]
> This probe is triggered when the `atan2` function is called with an input that results in multiple precision computation. Argument *$arg1* is the precision with which computation succeeded. Arguments *$arg2* and *$arg3* are inputs to the `atan2` function and *$arg4* is the computed result.

slowatan2_inexact (*int $arg1*, *double $arg2*, *double $arg3*, *double* *$arg4*)  [Probe]
> This probe is triggered when the `atan` function is called with an input that results in multiple precision computation and none of the multiple precision computations result in an accurate result. Argument *$arg1* is the maximum precision with which computations were performed. Arguments *$arg2* and *$arg3* are inputs to the `atan2` function and *$arg4* is the computed result.

slowatan (*int $arg1*, *double $arg2*, *double $arg3*)                        [Probe]
> This probe is triggered when the `atan` function is called with an input that results in multiple precision computation. Argument *$arg1* is the precision with which computation succeeded. Argument *$arg2* is the input to the `atan` function and *$arg3* is the computed result.

slowatan_inexact (*int $arg1*, *double $arg2*, *double $arg3*)                [Probe]
> This probe is triggered when the `atan` function is called with an input that results in multiple precision computation and none of the multiple precision computations result in an accurate result. Argument *$arg1* is the maximum precision with which computations were performed. Argument *$arg2* is the input to the `atan` function and *$arg3* is the computed result.

slowtan (*double $arg1*, *double $arg2*)                                      [Probe]
> This probe is triggered when the `tan` function is called with an input that results in multiple precision computation with precision 32. Argument *$arg1* is the input to the function and *$arg2* is the computed result.

slowasin (*double $arg1*, *double $arg2*)                                     [Probe]
> This probe is triggered when the `asin` function is called with an input that results in multiple precision computation with precision 32. Argument *$arg1* is the input to the function and *$arg2* is the computed result.

slowacos (*double $arg1*, *double $arg2*)                                          [Probe]

    This probe is triggered when the acos function is called with an input that results in multiple precision computation with precision 32. Argument *$arg1* is the input to the function and *$arg2* is the computed result.

slowsin (*double $arg1*, *double $arg2*)                                           [Probe]

    This probe is triggered when the sin function is called with an input that results in multiple precision computation with precision 32. Argument *$arg1* is the input to the function and *$arg2* is the computed result.

slowcos (*double $arg1*, *double $arg2*)                                           [Probe]

    This probe is triggered when the cos function is called with an input that results in multiple precision computation with precision 32. Argument *$arg1* is the input to the function and *$arg2* is the computed result.

slowsin_dx (*double $arg1*, *double $arg2*, *double $arg3*)                         [Probe]

    This probe is triggered when the sin function is called with an input that results in multiple precision computation with precision 32. Argument *$arg1* is the input to the function, *$arg2* is the error bound of *$arg1* and *$arg3* is the computed result.

slowcos_dx (*double $arg1*, *double $arg2*, *double $arg3*)                         [Probe]

    This probe is triggered when the cos function is called with an input that results in multiple precision computation with precision 32. Argument *$arg1* is the input to the function, *$arg2* is the error bound of *$arg1* and *$arg3* is the computed result.

## 36.3 Non-local Goto Probes

These probes are used to signal calls to setjmp, sigsetjmp, longjmp or siglongjmp.

setjmp (*void *$arg1*, *int $arg2*, *void *$arg3*)                                  [Probe]

    This probe is triggered whenever setjmp or sigsetjmp is called. Argument *$arg1* is a pointer to the jmp_buf passed as the first argument of setjmp or sigsetjmp, *$arg2* is the second argument of sigsetjmp or zero if this is a call to setjmp and *$arg3* is a pointer to the return address that will be stored in the jmp_buf.

longjmp (*void *$arg1*, *int $arg2*, *void *$arg3*)                                 [Probe]

    This probe is triggered whenever longjmp or siglongjmp is called. Argument *$arg1* is a pointer to the jmp_buf passed as the first argument of longjmp or siglongjmp, *$arg2* is the return value passed as the second argument of longjmp or siglongjmp and *$arg3* is a pointer to the return address longjmp or siglongjmp will return to.

    The longjmp probe is triggered at a point where the registers have not yet been restored to the values in the jmp_buf and unwinding will show a call stack including the caller of longjmp or siglongjmp.

longjmp_target (*void *$arg1*, *int $arg2*, *void *$arg3*)                          [Probe]

    This probe is triggered under the same conditions and with the same arguments as the longjmp probe.

    The longjmp_target probe is triggered at a point where the registers have been restored to the values in the jmp_buf and unwinding will show a call stack including the caller of setjmp or sigsetjmp.

# Appendix A  C Language Facilities in the Library

Some of the facilities implemented by the C library really should be thought of as parts of the C language itself. These facilities ought to be documented in the C Language Manual, not in the library manual; but since we don't have the language manual yet, and documentation for these features has been written, we are publishing it here.

## A.1  Explicitly Checking Internal Consistency

When you're writing a program, it's often a good idea to put in checks at strategic places for "impossible" errors or violations of basic assumptions. These kinds of checks are helpful in debugging problems with the interfaces between different parts of the program, for example.

The **assert** macro, defined in the header file **assert.h**, provides a convenient way to abort the program while printing a message about where in the program the error was detected.

Once you think your program is debugged, you can disable the error checks performed by the **assert** macro by recompiling with the macro **NDEBUG** defined. This means you don't actually have to change the program source code to disable these checks.

But disabling these consistency checks is undesirable unless they make the program significantly slower. All else being equal, more error checking is good no matter who is running the program. A wise user would rather have a program crash, visibly, than have it return nonsense without indicating anything might be wrong.

**void assert (*int expression*)**                                                    [Macro]
    Preliminary: | MT-Safe | AS-Unsafe heap corrupt | AC-Unsafe mem lock corrupt | See Section 1.2.2.1 [POSIX Safety Concepts], page 2.

    Verify the programmer's belief that *expression* is nonzero at this point in the program.

    If **NDEBUG** is not defined, **assert** tests the value of *expression*. If it is false (zero), **assert** aborts the program (see Section 25.7.4 [Aborting a Program], page 747) after printing a message of the form:

```
file:linenum: function: Assertion `expression' failed.
```

    on the standard error stream **stderr** (see Section 12.2 [Standard Streams], page 248). The filename and line number are taken from the C preprocessor macros **__FILE__** and **__LINE__** and specify where the call to **assert** was made. When using the GNU C compiler, the name of the function which calls **assert** is taken from the built-in variable **__PRETTY_FUNCTION__**; with older compilers, the function name and following colon are omitted.

    If the preprocessor macro **NDEBUG** is defined before **assert.h** is included, the **assert** macro is defined to do absolutely nothing.

    **Warning:** Even the argument expression *expression* is not evaluated if **NDEBUG** is in effect. So never use **assert** with arguments that involve side effects. For example, **assert (++i > 0);** is a bad idea, because i will not be incremented if **NDEBUG** is defined.

Sometimes the "impossible" condition you want to check for is an error return from an operating system function. Then it is useful to display not only where the program crashes, but also what error was returned. The **assert_perror** macro makes this easy.

void **assert_perror** (*int errnum*)                                         [Macro]

> Preliminary: | MT-Safe | AS-Unsafe heap corrupt | AC-Unsafe mem lock corrupt
> | See Section 1.2.2.1 [POSIX Safety Concepts], page 2.
>
> Similar to **assert**, but verifies that *errnum* is zero.
>
> If NDEBUG is not defined, **assert_perror** tests the value of *errnum*. If it is nonzero,
> **assert_perror** aborts the program after printing a message of the form:
>
> > `file:linenum: function: error text`
>
> on the standard error stream. The file name, line number, and function name are as
> for **assert**. The error text is the result of **strerror (*errnum*)**. See Section 2.3 [Error
> Messages], page 33.
>
> Like **assert**, if NDEBUG is defined before **assert.h** is included, the **assert_perror**
> macro does absolutely nothing. It does not evaluate the argument, so *errnum* should
> not have any side effects. It is best for *errnum* to be just a simple variable reference;
> often it will be **errno**.
>
> This macro is a GNU extension.

**Usage note:** The **assert** facility is designed for detecting *internal inconsistency*; it is
not suitable for reporting invalid input or improper usage by the *user* of the program.

The information in the diagnostic messages printed by the **assert** and **assert_perror**
macro is intended to help you, the programmer, track down the cause of a bug, but is
not really useful for telling a user of your program why his or her input was invalid or
why a command could not be carried out. What's more, your program should not abort
when given invalid input, as **assert** would do—it should exit with nonzero status (see
Section 25.7.2 [Exit Status], page 745) after printing its error messages, or perhaps read
another command or move on to the next input file.

See Section 2.3 [Error Messages], page 33, for information on printing error messages for
problems that *do not* represent bugs in the program.

## A.2 Variadic Functions

ISO C defines a syntax for declaring a function to take a variable number or type of arguments. (Such functions are referred to as *varargs functions* or *variadic functions*.) However,
the language itself provides no mechanism for such functions to access their non-required
arguments; instead, you use the variable arguments macros defined in **stdarg.h**.

This section describes how to declare variadic functions, how to write them, and how to
call them properly.

**Compatibility Note:** Many older C dialects provide a similar, but incompatible, mechanism for defining functions with variable numbers of arguments, using **varargs.h**.

### A.2.1 Why Variadic Functions are Used

Ordinary C functions take a fixed number of arguments. When you define a function, you
specify the data type for each argument. Every call to the function should supply the
expected number of arguments, with types that can be converted to the specified ones.
Thus, if the function 'foo' is declared with **int foo (int, char *);** then you must call it
with two arguments, a number (any kind will do) and a string pointer.

But some functions perform operations that can meaningfully accept an unlimited number of arguments.

In some cases a function can handle any number of values by operating on all of them as a block. For example, consider a function that allocates a one-dimensional array with `malloc` to hold a specified set of values. This operation makes sense for any number of values, as long as the length of the array corresponds to that number. Without facilities for variable arguments, you would have to define a separate function for each possible array size.

The library function `printf` (see Section 12.12 [Formatted Output], page 270) is an example of another class of function where variable arguments are useful. This function prints its arguments (which can vary in type as well as number) under the control of a format template string.

These are good reasons to define a *variadic* function which can handle as many arguments as the caller chooses to pass.

Some functions such as `open` take a fixed set of arguments, but occasionally ignore the last few. Strict adherence to ISO C requires these functions to be defined as variadic; in practice, however, the GNU C compiler and most other C compilers let you define such a function to take a fixed set of arguments—the most it can ever use—and then only *declare* the function as variadic (or not declare its arguments at all!).

## A.2.2 How Variadic Functions are Defined and Used

Defining and using a variadic function involves three steps:

- *Define* the function as variadic, using an ellipsis ('`...`') in the argument list, and using special macros to access the variable arguments. See Section A.2.2.2 [Receiving the Argument Values], page 880.

- *Declare* the function as variadic, using a prototype with an ellipsis ('`...`'), in all the files which call it. See Section A.2.2.1 [Syntax for Variable Arguments], page 879.

- *Call* the function by writing the fixed arguments followed by the additional variable arguments. See Section A.2.2.4 [Calling Variadic Functions], page 881.

## A.2.2.1 Syntax for Variable Arguments

A function that accepts a variable number of arguments must be declared with a prototype that says so. You write the fixed arguments as usual, and then tack on '`...`' to indicate the possibility of additional arguments. The syntax of ISO C requires at least one fixed argument before the '`...`'. For example,

```
int
func (const char *a, int b, ...)
{
  . . .
}
```

defines a function `func` which returns an `int` and takes two required arguments, a `const char *` and an `int`. These are followed by any number of anonymous arguments.

**Portability note:** For some C compilers, the last required argument must not be declared `register` in the function definition. Furthermore, this argument's type must be *self-promoting*: that is, the default promotions must not change its type. This rules out array and function types, as well as `float`, `char` (whether signed or not) and `short int` (whether signed or not). This is actually an ISO C requirement.

## A.2.2.2 Receiving the Argument Values

Ordinary fixed arguments have individual names, and you can use these names to access their values. But optional arguments have no names—nothing but '`...`'. How can you access them?

The only way to access them is sequentially, in the order they were written, and you must use special macros from `stdarg.h` in the following three step process:

1. You initialize an argument pointer variable of type `va_list` using `va_start`. The argument pointer when initialized points to the first optional argument.

2. You access the optional arguments by successive calls to `va_arg`. The first call to `va_arg` gives you the first optional argument, the next call gives you the second, and so on.

   You can stop at any time if you wish to ignore any remaining optional arguments. It is perfectly all right for a function to access fewer arguments than were supplied in the call, but you will get garbage values if you try to access too many arguments.

3. You indicate that you are finished with the argument pointer variable by calling `va_end`.

   (In practice, with most C compilers, calling `va_end` does nothing. This is always true in the GNU C compiler. But you might as well call `va_end` just in case your program is someday compiled with a peculiar compiler.)

See Section A.2.2.5 [Argument Access Macros], page 881, for the full definitions of `va_start`, `va_arg` and `va_end`.

Steps 1 and 3 must be performed in the function that accepts the optional arguments. However, you can pass the `va_list` variable as an argument to another function and perform all or part of step 2 there.

You can perform the entire sequence of three steps multiple times within a single function invocation. If you want to ignore the optional arguments, you can do these steps zero times.

You can have more than one argument pointer variable if you like. You can initialize each variable with `va_start` when you wish, and then you can fetch arguments with each argument pointer as you wish. Each argument pointer variable will sequence through the same set of argument values, but at its own pace.

**Portability note:** With some compilers, once you pass an argument pointer value to a subroutine, you must not keep using the same argument pointer value after that subroutine returns. For full portability, you should just pass it to `va_end`. This is actually an ISO C requirement, but most ANSI C compilers work happily regardless.

## A.2.2.3 How Many Arguments Were Supplied

There is no general way for a function to determine the number and type of the optional arguments it was called with. So whoever designs the function typically designs a convention for the caller to specify the number and type of arguments. It is up to you to define an appropriate calling convention for each variadic function, and write all calls accordingly.

One kind of calling convention is to pass the number of optional arguments as one of the fixed arguments. This convention works provided all of the optional arguments are of the same type.

A similar alternative is to have one of the required arguments be a bit mask, with a bit for each possible purpose for which an optional argument might be supplied. You would test the bits in a predefined sequence; if the bit is set, fetch the value of the next argument, otherwise use a default value.

A required argument can be used as a pattern to specify both the number and types of the optional arguments. The format string argument to `printf` is one example of this (see Section 12.12.7 [Formatted Output Functions], page 278).

Another possibility is to pass an "end marker" value as the last optional argument. For example, for a function that manipulates an arbitrary number of pointer arguments, a null pointer might indicate the end of the argument list. (This assumes that a null pointer isn't otherwise meaningful to the function.) The `execl` function works in just this way; see Section 26.5 [Executing a File], page 752.

## A.2.2.4 Calling Variadic Functions

You don't have to do anything special to call a variadic function. Just put the arguments (required arguments, followed by optional ones) inside parentheses, separated by commas, as usual. But you must declare the function with a prototype and know how the argument values are converted.

In principle, functions that are *defined* to be variadic must also be *declared* to be variadic using a function prototype whenever you call them. (See Section A.2.2.1 [Syntax for Variable Arguments], page 879, for how.) This is because some C compilers use a different calling convention to pass the same set of argument values to a function depending on whether that function takes variable arguments or fixed arguments.

In practice, the GNU C compiler always passes a given set of argument types in the same way regardless of whether they are optional or required. So, as long as the argument types are self-promoting, you can safely omit declaring them. Usually it is a good idea to declare the argument types for variadic functions, and indeed for all functions. But there are a few functions which it is extremely convenient not to have to declare as variadic—for example, `open` and `printf`.

Since the prototype doesn't specify types for optional arguments, in a call to a variadic function the *default argument promotions* are performed on the optional argument values. This means the objects of type `char` or `short int` (whether signed or not) are promoted to either `int` or `unsigned int`, as appropriate; and that objects of type `float` are promoted to type `double`. So, if the caller passes a `char` as an optional argument, it is promoted to an `int`, and the function can access it with `va_arg (ap, int)`.

Conversion of the required arguments is controlled by the function prototype in the usual way: the argument expression is converted to the declared argument type as if it were being assigned to a variable of that type.

## A.2.2.5 Argument Access Macros

Here are descriptions of the macros used to retrieve variable arguments. These macros are defined in the header file `stdarg.h`.

`va_list`                                                              [Data Type]
     The type `va_list` is used for argument pointer variables.

**void va_start** (*va_list* **ap**, *last-required*)                                    [Macro]
> Preliminary: | MT-Safe | AS-Safe | AC-Safe | See Section 1.2.2.1 [POSIX Safety
> Concepts], page 2.
>
> This macro initializes the argument pointer variable *ap* to point to the first of the
> optional arguments of the current function; *last-required* must be the last required
> argument to the function.

*type* **va_arg** (*va_list* **ap**, *type*)                                             [Macro]
> Preliminary: | MT-Safe race:ap | AS-Safe | AC-Unsafe corrupt | See Section 1.2.2.1
> [POSIX Safety Concepts], page 2.
>
> The **va_arg** macro returns the value of the next optional argument, and modifies the
> value of *ap* to point to the subsequent argument. Thus, successive uses of **va_arg**
> return successive optional arguments.
>
> The type of the value returned by **va_arg** is *type* as specified in the call. *type* must
> be a self-promoting type (not **char** or **short int** or **float**) that matches the type of
> the actual argument.

**void va_end** (*va_list* **ap**)                                                       [Macro]
> Preliminary: | MT-Safe | AS-Safe | AC-Safe | See Section 1.2.2.1 [POSIX Safety
> Concepts], page 2.
>
> This ends the use of *ap*. After a **va_end** call, further **va_arg** calls with the same *ap*
> may not work. You should invoke **va_end** before returning from the function in which
> **va_start** was invoked with the same *ap* argument.
>
> In the GNU C Library, **va_end** does nothing, and you need not ever use it except for
> reasons of portability.

Sometimes it is necessary to parse the list of parameters more than once or one wants
to remember a certain position in the parameter list. To do this, one will have to make a
copy of the current value of the argument. But **va_list** is an opaque type and one cannot
necessarily assign the value of one variable of type **va_list** to another variable of the same
type.

**void va_copy** (*va_list* **dest**, *va_list* **src**)                                 [Macro]
**void __va_copy** (*va_list* **dest**, *va_list* **src**)                               [Macro]
> Preliminary: | MT-Safe | AS-Safe | AC-Safe | See Section 1.2.2.1 [POSIX Safety
> Concepts], page 2.
>
> The **va_copy** macro allows copying of objects of type **va_list** even if this is not
> an integral type. The argument pointer in *dest* is initialized to point to the same
> argument as the pointer in *src*.
>
> This macro was added in ISO C99. When building for strict conformance to ISO
> C90 ('gcc -ansi'), it is not available. The macro **__va_copy** is available as a GNU
> extension in any standards mode; before GCC 3.0, it was the only macro for this
> functionality.

If you want to use **va_copy** and be portable to pre-C99 systems, you should always be
prepared for the possibility that this macro will not be available. On architectures where
a simple assignment is invalid, hopefully **va_copy** *will* be available, so one should always
write something like this if concerned about pre-C99 portability:

```
{
  va_list ap, save;
  ...
#ifdef va_copy
  va_copy (save, ap);
#else
  save = ap;
#endif
  ...
}
```

## A.2.3 Example of a Variadic Function

Here is a complete sample function that accepts a variable number of arguments. The first argument to the function is the count of remaining arguments, which are added up and the result returned. While trivial, this function is sufficient to illustrate how to use the variable arguments facility.

```
#include <stdarg.h>
#include <stdio.h>

int
add_em_up (int count,...)
{
  va_list ap;
  int i, sum;

  va_start (ap, count);          /* Initialize the argument list. */

  sum = 0;
  for (i = 0; i < count; i++)
    sum += va_arg (ap, int);     /* Get the next argument value. */

  va_end (ap);                   /* Clean up. */
  return sum;
}

int
main (void)
{
  /* This call prints 16. */
  printf ("%d\n", add_em_up (3, 5, 5, 6));

  /* This call prints 55. */
  printf ("%d\n", add_em_up (10, 1, 2, 3, 4, 5, 6, 7, 8, 9, 10));

  return 0;
}
```

## A.3 Null Pointer Constant

The null pointer constant is guaranteed not to point to any real object. You can assign it to any pointer variable since it has type void *. The preferred way to write a null pointer constant is with NULL.

**void * NULL**                                                                 [Macro]

    This is a null pointer constant.

You can also use 0 or (void *)0 as a null pointer constant, but using NULL is cleaner because it makes the purpose of the constant more evident.

If you use the null pointer constant as a function argument, then for complete portability you should make sure that the function has a prototype declaration. Otherwise, if the target machine has two different pointer representations, the compiler won't know which representation to use for that argument. You can avoid the problem by explicitly casting the constant to the proper pointer type, but we recommend instead adding a prototype for the function you are calling.

## A.4 Important Data Types

The result of subtracting two pointers in C is always an integer, but the precise data type varies from C compiler to C compiler. Likewise, the data type of the result of sizeof also varies between compilers. ISO defines standard aliases for these two types, so you can refer to them in a portable fashion. They are defined in the header file stddef.h.

ptrdiff_t                                                              [Data Type]
> This is the signed integer type of the result of subtracting two pointers. For example, with the declaration char *p1, *p2;, the expression p2 - p1 is of type ptrdiff_t. This will probably be one of the standard signed integer types (short int, int or long int), but might be a nonstandard type that exists only for this purpose.

size_t                                                                 [Data Type]
> This is an unsigned integer type used to represent the sizes of objects. The result of the sizeof operator is of this type, and functions such as malloc (see Section 3.2.2 [Unconstrained Allocation], page 42) and memcpy (see Section 5.4 [Copying and Concatenation], page 91) accept arguments of this type to specify object sizes. On systems using the GNU C Library, this will be unsigned int or unsigned long int.
>
> **Usage Note:** size_t is the preferred way to declare any arguments or variables that hold the size of an object.

**Compatibility Note:** Implementations of C before the advent of ISO C generally used unsigned int for representing object sizes and int for pointer subtraction results. They did not necessarily define either size_t or ptrdiff_t. Unix systems did define size_t, in sys/types.h, but the definition was usually a signed type.

## A.5 Data Type Measurements

Most of the time, if you choose the proper C data type for each object in your program, you need not be concerned with just how it is represented or how many bits it uses. When you do need such information, the C language itself does not provide a way to get it. The header files limits.h and float.h contain macros which give you this information in full detail.

### A.5.1 Computing the Width of an Integer Data Type

The most common reason that a program needs to know how many bits are in an integer type is for using an array of long int as a bit vector. You can access the bit at index $n$ with

```
vector[n / LONGBITS] & (1 << (n % LONGBITS))
```
provided you define LONGBITS as the number of bits in a long int.

There is no operator in the C language that can give you the number of bits in an integer data type. But you can compute it from the macro CHAR_BIT, defined in the header file limits.h.

CHAR_BIT    This is the number of bits in a char—eight, on most systems. The value has type int.

You can compute the number of bits in any data type type like this:
```
sizeof (type) * CHAR_BIT
```

## A.5.2 Range of an Integer Type

Suppose you need to store an integer value which can range from zero to one million. Which is the smallest type you can use? There is no general rule; it depends on the C compiler and target machine. You can use the 'MIN' and 'MAX' macros in limits.h to determine which type will work.

Each signed integer type has a pair of macros which give the smallest and largest values that it can hold. Each unsigned integer type has one such macro, for the maximum value; the minimum value is, of course, zero.

The values of these macros are all integer constant expressions. The 'MAX' and 'MIN' macros for char and short int types have values of type int. The 'MAX' and 'MIN' macros for the other types have values of the same type described by the macro—thus, ULONG_MAX has type unsigned long int.

SCHAR_MIN
          This is the minimum value that can be represented by a signed char.

SCHAR_MAX
UCHAR_MAX
          These are the maximum values that can be represented by a signed char and unsigned char, respectively.

CHAR_MIN
          This is the minimum value that can be represented by a char. It's equal to SCHAR_MIN if char is signed, or zero otherwise.

CHAR_MAX
          This is the maximum value that can be represented by a char. It's equal to SCHAR_MAX if char is signed, or UCHAR_MAX otherwise.

SHRT_MIN
          This is the minimum value that can be represented by a signed short int. On most machines that the GNU C Library runs on, short integers are 16-bit quantities.

SHRT_MAX
USHRT_MAX
          These are the maximum values that can be represented by a signed short int and unsigned short int, respectively.

INT_MIN

> This is the minimum value that can be represented by a `signed int`. On most machines that the GNU C Library runs on, an `int` is a 32-bit quantity.

INT_MAX
UINT_MAX

> These are the maximum values that can be represented by, respectively, the type `signed int` and the type `unsigned int`.

LONG_MIN

> This is the minimum value that can be represented by a `signed long int`. On most machines that the GNU C Library runs on, `long` integers are 32-bit quantities, the same size as `int`.

LONG_MAX
ULONG_MAX

> These are the maximum values that can be represented by a `signed long int` and `unsigned long int`, respectively.

LLONG_MIN

> This is the minimum value that can be represented by a `signed long long int`. On most machines that the GNU C Library runs on, `long long` integers are 64-bit quantities.

LLONG_MAX
ULLONG_MAX

> These are the maximum values that can be represented by a `signed long long int` and `unsigned long long int`, respectively.

LONG_LONG_MIN
LONG_LONG_MAX
ULONG_LONG_MAX

> These are obsolete names for `LLONG_MIN`, `LLONG_MAX`, and `ULLONG_MAX`. They are only available if `_GNU_SOURCE` is defined (see Section 1.3.4 [Feature Test Macros], page 15). In GCC versions prior to 3.0, these were the only names available.

WCHAR_MAX

> This is the maximum value that can be represented by a `wchar_t`. See Section 6.1 [Introduction to Extended Characters], page 127.

The header file `limits.h` also defines some additional constants that parameterize various operating system and file system limits. These constants are described in Chapter 32 [System Configuration Parameters], page 838.

## A.5.3 Floating Type Macros

The specific representation of floating point numbers varies from machine to machine. Because floating point numbers are represented internally as approximate quantities, algorithms for manipulating floating point data often need to take account of the precise details of the machine's floating point representation.

Some of the functions in the C library itself need this information; for example, the algorithms for printing and reading floating point numbers (see Chapter 12 [Input/Output on Streams], page 248) and for calculating trigonometric and irrational functions (see Chapter 19 [Mathematics], page 511) use it to avoid round-off error and loss of accuracy. User programs that implement numerical analysis techniques also often need this information in order to minimize or compute error bounds.

The header file `float.h` describes the format used by your machine.

## A.5.3.1 Floating Point Representation Concepts

This section introduces the terminology for describing floating point representations.

You are probably already familiar with most of these concepts in terms of scientific or exponential notation for floating point numbers. For example, the number `123456.0` could be expressed in exponential notation as `1.23456e+05`, a shorthand notation indicating that the mantissa `1.23456` is multiplied by the base `10` raised to power `5`.

More formally, the internal representation of a floating point number can be characterized in terms of the following parameters:

- The *sign* is either `-1` or `1`.

- The *base* or *radix* for exponentiation, an integer greater than 1. This is a constant for a particular representation.

- The *exponent* to which the base is raised. The upper and lower bounds of the exponent value are constants for a particular representation.

  Sometimes, in the actual bits representing the floating point number, the exponent is *biased* by adding a constant to it, to make it always be represented as an unsigned quantity. This is only important if you have some reason to pick apart the bit fields making up the floating point number by hand, which is something for which the GNU C Library provides no support. So this is ignored in the discussion that follows.

- The *mantissa* or *significand* is an unsigned integer which is a part of each floating point number.

- The *precision* of the mantissa. If the base of the representation is $b$, then the precision is the number of base-$b$ digits in the mantissa. This is a constant for a particular representation.

  Many floating point representations have an implicit *hidden bit* in the mantissa. This is a bit which is present virtually in the mantissa, but not stored in memory because its value is always 1 in a normalized number. The precision figure (see above) includes any hidden bits.

  Again, the GNU C Library provides no facilities for dealing with such low-level aspects of the representation.

The mantissa of a floating point number represents an implicit fraction whose denominator is the base raised to the power of the precision. Since the largest representable mantissa is one less than this denominator, the value of the fraction is always strictly less than 1. The mathematical value of a floating point number is then the product of this fraction, the sign, and the base raised to the exponent.

We say that the floating point number is *normalized* if the fraction is at least $1/b$, where $b$ is the base. In other words, the mantissa would be too large to fit if it were multiplied by the base. Non-normalized numbers are sometimes called *denormal*; they contain less precision than the representation normally can hold.

If the number is not normalized, then you can subtract 1 from the exponent while multiplying the mantissa by the base, and get another floating point number with the same value. *Normalization* consists of doing this repeatedly until the number is normalized. Two distinct normalized floating point numbers cannot be equal in value.

(There is an exception to this rule: if the mantissa is zero, it is considered normalized. Another exception happens on certain machines where the exponent is as small as the representation can hold. Then it is impossible to subtract 1 from the exponent, so a number may be normalized even if its fraction is less than $1/b$.)

## A.5.3.2 Floating Point Parameters

These macro definitions can be accessed by including the header file `float.h` in your program.

Macro names starting with 'FLT_' refer to the `float` type, while names beginning with 'DBL_' refer to the `double` type and names beginning with 'LDBL_' refer to the `long double` type. (If GCC does not support `long double` as a distinct data type on a target machine then the values for the 'LDBL_' constants are equal to the corresponding constants for the `double` type.)

Of these macros, only `FLT_RADIX` is guaranteed to be a constant expression. The other macros listed here cannot be reliably used in places that require constant expressions, such as '`#if`' preprocessing directives or in the dimensions of static arrays.

Although the ISO C standard specifies minimum and maximum values for most of these parameters, the GNU C implementation uses whatever values describe the floating point representation of the target machine. So in principle GNU C actually satisfies the ISO C requirements only if the target machine is suitable. In practice, all the machines currently supported are suitable.

FLT_ROUNDS

> This value characterizes the rounding mode for floating point addition. The following values indicate standard rounding modes:
>
> | | |
> |---|---|
> | -1 | The mode is indeterminable. |
> | 0 | Rounding is towards zero. |
> | 1 | Rounding is to the nearest number. |
> | 2 | Rounding is towards positive infinity. |
> | 3 | Rounding is towards negative infinity. |
>
> Any other value represents a machine-dependent nonstandard rounding mode.
>
> On most machines, the value is 1, in accordance with the IEEE standard for floating point.
>
> Here is a table showing how certain values round for each possible value of `FLT_ROUNDS`, if the other aspects of the representation match the IEEE single-precision standard.

|            | 0    | 1          | 2          | 3          |
|------------|------|------------|------------|------------|
| 1.00000003 | 1.0  | 1.0        | 1.00000012 | 1.0        |
| 1.00000007 | 1.0  | 1.00000012 | 1.00000012 | 1.0        |
| -1.00000003| -1.0 | -1.0       | -1.0       | -1.00000012|
| -1.00000007| -1.0 | -1.00000012| -1.0       | -1.00000012|

`FLT_RADIX`

This is the value of the base, or radix, of the exponent representation. This is guaranteed to be a constant expression, unlike the other macros described in this section. The value is 2 on all machines we know of except the IBM 360 and derivatives.

`FLT_MANT_DIG`

This is the number of base-`FLT_RADIX` digits in the floating point mantissa for the `float` data type. The following expression yields 1.0 (even though mathematically it should not) due to the limited number of mantissa digits:

```
float radix = FLT_RADIX;
```

```
1.0f + 1.0f / radix / radix / ... / radix
```

where `radix` appears `FLT_MANT_DIG` times.

`DBL_MANT_DIG`
`LDBL_MANT_DIG`

This is the number of base-`FLT_RADIX` digits in the floating point mantissa for the data types `double` and `long double`, respectively.

`FLT_DIG`

This is the number of decimal digits of precision for the `float` data type. Technically, if $p$ and $b$ are the precision and base (respectively) for the representation, then the decimal precision $q$ is the maximum number of decimal digits such that any floating point number with $q$ base 10 digits can be rounded to a floating point number with $p$ base $b$ digits and back again, without change to the $q$ decimal digits.

The value of this macro is supposed to be at least 6, to satisfy ISO C.

`DBL_DIG`
`LDBL_DIG`

These are similar to `FLT_DIG`, but for the data types `double` and `long double`, respectively. The values of these macros are supposed to be at least 10.

`FLT_MIN_EXP`

This is the smallest possible exponent value for type `float`. More precisely, is the minimum negative integer such that the value `FLT_RADIX` raised to this power minus 1 can be represented as a normalized floating point number of type `float`.

`DBL_MIN_EXP`
`LDBL_MIN_EXP`

These are similar to `FLT_MIN_EXP`, but for the data types `double` and `long double`, respectively.

FLT_MIN_10_EXP

> This is the minimum negative integer such that 10 raised to this power minus 1 can be represented as a normalized floating point number of type `float`. This is supposed to be -37 or even less.

DBL_MIN_10_EXP

LDBL_MIN_10_EXP

> These are similar to `FLT_MIN_10_EXP`, but for the data types `double` and `long double`, respectively.

FLT_MAX_EXP

> This is the largest possible exponent value for type `float`. More precisely, this is the maximum positive integer such that value `FLT_RADIX` raised to this power minus 1 can be represented as a floating point number of type `float`.

DBL_MAX_EXP

LDBL_MAX_EXP

> These are similar to `FLT_MAX_EXP`, but for the data types `double` and `long double`, respectively.

FLT_MAX_10_EXP

> This is the maximum positive integer such that 10 raised to this power minus 1 can be represented as a normalized floating point number of type `float`. This is supposed to be at least 37.

DBL_MAX_10_EXP

LDBL_MAX_10_EXP

> These are similar to `FLT_MAX_10_EXP`, but for the data types `double` and `long double`, respectively.

FLT_MAX

> The value of this macro is the maximum number representable in type `float`. It is supposed to be at least 1E+37. The value has type `float`.
>
> The smallest representable number is - `FLT_MAX`.

DBL_MAX

LDBL_MAX

> These are similar to `FLT_MAX`, but for the data types `double` and `long double`, respectively. The type of the macro's value is the same as the type it describes.

FLT_MIN

> The value of this macro is the minimum normalized positive floating point number that is representable in type `float`. It is supposed to be no more than 1E-37.

DBL_MIN

LDBL_MIN

> These are similar to `FLT_MIN`, but for the data types `double` and `long double`, respectively. The type of the macro's value is the same as the type it describes.

FLT_EPSILON

> This is the difference between 1 and the smallest floating point number of type `float` that is greater than 1. It's supposed to be no greater than 1E-5.

```
DBL_EPSILON
LDBL_EPSILON
```
These are similar to `FLT_EPSILON`, but for the data types `double` and `long double`, respectively. The type of the macro's value is the same as the type it describes. The values are not supposed to be greater than `1E-9`.

## A.5.3.3 IEEE Floating Point

Here is an example showing how the floating type measurements come out for the most common floating point representation, specified by the *IEEE Standard for Binary Floating Point Arithmetic (ANSI/IEEE Std 754-1985)*. Nearly all computers designed since the 1980s use this format.

The IEEE single-precision float representation uses a base of 2. There is a sign bit, a mantissa with 23 bits plus one hidden bit (so the total precision is 24 base-2 digits), and an 8-bit exponent that can represent values in the range -125 to 128, inclusive.

So, for an implementation that uses this representation for the `float` data type, appropriate values for the corresponding parameters are:

```
FLT_RADIX                   2
FLT_MANT_DIG               24
FLT_DIG                     6
FLT_MIN_EXP              -125
FLT_MIN_10_EXP            -37
FLT_MAX_EXP              128
FLT_MAX_10_EXP           +38
FLT_MIN        1.17549435E-38F
FLT_MAX        3.40282347E+38F
FLT_EPSILON    1.19209290E-07F
```

Here are the values for the `double` data type:

```
DBL_MANT_DIG              53
DBL_DIG                   15
DBL_MIN_EXP            -1021
DBL_MIN_10_EXP          -307
DBL_MAX_EXP             1024
DBL_MAX_10_EXP           308
DBL_MAX     1.7976931348623157E+308
DBL_MIN     2.2250738585072014E-308
DBL_EPSILON 2.2204460492503131E-016
```

## A.5.4 Structure Field Offset Measurement

You can use `offsetof` to measure the location within a structure type of a particular structure member.

**size_t offsetof (*type*, *member*)**                                    [Macro]

Preliminary: | MT-Safe | AS-Safe | AC-Safe | See Section 1.2.2.1 [POSIX Safety Concepts], page 2.

This expands to an integer constant expression that is the offset of the structure member named *member* in the structure type *type*. For example, `offsetof (struct s, elem)` is the offset, in bytes, of the member `elem` in a `struct s`.

This macro won't work if *member* is a bit field; you get an error from the C compiler in that case.

# Appendix B  Summary of Library Facilities

This appendix is a complete list of the facilities declared within the header files supplied with the GNU C Library. Each entry also lists the standard or other source from which each facility is derived, and tells you where in the manual you can find more information about how to use it.

`long int a64l (const char *string)`
> stdlib.h (XPG): Section 5.11 [Encode Binary Data], page 121.

`void abort (void)`
> stdlib.h (ISO): Section 25.7.4 [Aborting a Program], page 747.

`int abs (int number)`
> stdlib.h (ISO): Section 20.8.1 [Absolute Value], page 574.

`int accept (int socket, struct sockaddr *addr, socklen_t *length_ptr)`
> sys/socket.h (BSD): Section 16.9.3 [Accepting Connections], page 457.

`int access (const char *filename, int how)`
> unistd.h (POSIX.1): Section 14.9.8 [Testing Permission to Access a File], page 412.

`ACCOUNTING`
> utmp.h (SVID): Section 30.12.1 [Manipulating the User Accounting Database], page 802.

`double acos (double x)`
> math.h (ISO): Section 19.3 [Inverse Trigonometric Functions], page 514.

`float acosf (float x)`
> math.h (ISO): Section 19.3 [Inverse Trigonometric Functions], page 514.

`double acosh (double x)`
> math.h (ISO): Section 19.5 [Hyperbolic Functions], page 520.

`float acoshf (float x)`
> math.h (ISO): Section 19.5 [Hyperbolic Functions], page 520.

`long double acoshl (long double x)`
> math.h (ISO): Section 19.5 [Hyperbolic Functions], page 520.

`long double acosl (long double x)`
> math.h (ISO): Section 19.3 [Inverse Trigonometric Functions], page 514.

`int addmntent (FILE *stream, const struct mntent *mnt)`
> mntent.h (BSD): Section 31.3.1.2 [The mtab file], page 828.

`int adjtime (const struct timeval *delta, struct timeval *olddelta)`
> sys/time.h (BSD): Section 21.4.2 [High-Resolution Calendar], page 600.

`int adjtimex (struct timex *timex)`
> sys/timex.h (GNU): Section 21.4.2 [High-Resolution Calendar], page 600.

`AF_FILE`
> sys/socket.h (GNU): Section 16.3.1 [Address Formats], page 431.

`AF_INET`
> sys/socket.h (BSD): Section 16.3.1 [Address Formats], page 431.

`AF_INET6`
> sys/socket.h (IPv6 Basic API): Section 16.3.1 [Address Formats], page 431.

`AF_LOCAL`
> sys/socket.h (POSIX): Section 16.3.1 [Address Formats], page 431.

`AF_UNIX`

   `sys/socket.h` (BSD, Unix98): Section 16.3.1 [Address Formats], page 431.

`AF_UNSPEC`

   `sys/socket.h` (BSD): Section 16.3.1 [Address Formats], page 431.

`int aio_cancel (int fildes, struct aiocb *aiocbp)`

   `aio.h` (POSIX.1b): Section 13.10.4 [Cancellation of AIO Operations], page 356.

`int aio_cancel64 (int fildes, struct aiocb64 *aiocbp)`

   `aio.h` (Unix98): Section 13.10.4 [Cancellation of AIO Operations], page 356.

`int aio_error (const struct aiocb *aiocbp)`

   `aio.h` (POSIX.1b): Section 13.10.2 [Getting the Status of AIO Operations], page 353.

`int aio_error64 (const struct aiocb64 *aiocbp)`

   `aio.h` (Unix98): Section 13.10.2 [Getting the Status of AIO Operations], page 353.

`int aio_fsync (int op, struct aiocb *aiocbp)`

   `aio.h` (POSIX.1b): Section 13.10.3 [Getting into a Consistent State], page 354.

`int aio_fsync64 (int op, struct aiocb64 *aiocbp)`

   `aio.h` (Unix98): Section 13.10.3 [Getting into a Consistent State], page 354.

`void aio_init (const struct aioinit *init)`

   `aio.h` (GNU): Section 13.10.5 [How to optimize the AIO implementation], page 358.

`int aio_read (struct aiocb *aiocbp)`

   `aio.h` (POSIX.1b): Section 13.10.1 [Asynchronous Read and Write Operations], page 349.

`int aio_read64 (struct aiocb64 *aiocbp)`

   `aio.h` (Unix98): Section 13.10.1 [Asynchronous Read and Write Operations], page 349.

`ssize_t aio_return (struct aiocb *aiocbp)`

   `aio.h` (POSIX.1b): Section 13.10.2 [Getting the Status of AIO Operations], page 353.

`ssize_t aio_return64 (struct aiocb64 *aiocbp)`

   `aio.h` (Unix98): Section 13.10.2 [Getting the Status of AIO Operations], page 353.

`int aio_suspend (const struct aiocb *const list[], int nent, const struct timespec *timeout)`

   `aio.h` (POSIX.1b): Section 13.10.3 [Getting into a Consistent State], page 354.

`int aio_suspend64 (const struct aiocb64 *const list[], int nent, const struct timespec *timeout)`

   `aio.h` (Unix98): Section 13.10.3 [Getting into a Consistent State], page 354.

`int aio_write (struct aiocb *aiocbp)`

   `aio.h` (POSIX.1b): Section 13.10.1 [Asynchronous Read and Write Operations], page 349.

`int aio_write64 (struct aiocb64 *aiocbp)`

   `aio.h` (Unix98): Section 13.10.1 [Asynchronous Read and Write Operations], page 349.

`unsigned int alarm (unsigned int seconds)`

   `unistd.h` (POSIX.1): Section 21.5 [Setting an Alarm], page 625.

`void * aligned_alloc (size_t alignment, size_t size)`

   `stdlib.h` (stdlib.h): Section 3.2.2.7 [Allocating Aligned Memory Blocks], page 46.

`void * alloca (size_t size)`

   `stdlib.h` (GNU, BSD): Section 3.2.5 [Automatic Storage with Variable Size], page 69.

`int alphasort (const struct dirent **a, const struct dirent **b)`

   `dirent.h` (BSD/SVID): Section 14.2.6 [Scanning the Content of a Directory], page 385.

`int alphasort64 (const struct dirent64 **a, const struct dirent **b)`

   `dirent.h` (GNU): Section 14.2.6 [Scanning the Content of a Directory], page 385.

`tcflag_t ALTWERASE`

   `termios.h` (BSD): Section 17.4.7 [Local Modes], page 486.

int ARG_MAX
>        limits.h (POSIX.1): Section 32.1 [General Capacity Limits], page 838.

error_t argp_err_exit_status
>        argp.h (GNU): Section 25.3.2 [Argp Global Variables], page 715.

void argp_error (const struct argp_state *state, const char *fmt, ...)
>        argp.h (GNU): Section 25.3.5.3 [Functions For Use in Argp Parsers], page 722.

int ARGP_ERR_UNKNOWN
>        argp.h (GNU): Section 25.3.5 [Argp Parser Functions], page 718.

void argp_failure (const struct argp_state *state, int status, int errnum, const char *fmt, ...)
>        argp.h (GNU): Section 25.3.5.3 [Functions For Use in Argp Parsers], page 722.

void argp_help (const struct argp *argp, FILE *stream, unsigned flags, char *name)
>        argp.h (GNU): Section 25.3.9 [The argp_help Function], page 726.

ARGP_IN_ORDER
>        argp.h (GNU): Section 25.3.7 [Flags for argp_parse], page 724.

ARGP_KEY_ARG
>        argp.h (GNU): Section 25.3.5.1 [Special Keys for Argp Parser Functions], page 719.

ARGP_KEY_ARGS
>        argp.h (GNU): Section 25.3.5.1 [Special Keys for Argp Parser Functions], page 719.

ARGP_KEY_END
>        argp.h (GNU): Section 25.3.5.1 [Special Keys for Argp Parser Functions], page 719.

ARGP_KEY_ERROR
>        argp.h (GNU): Section 25.3.5.1 [Special Keys for Argp Parser Functions], page 719.

ARGP_KEY_FINI
>        argp.h (GNU): Section 25.3.5.1 [Special Keys for Argp Parser Functions], page 719.

ARGP_KEY_HELP_ARGS_DOC
>        argp.h (GNU): Section 25.3.8.1 [Special Keys for Argp Help Filter Functions], page 725.

ARGP_KEY_HELP_DUP_ARGS_NOTE
>        argp.h (GNU): Section 25.3.8.1 [Special Keys for Argp Help Filter Functions], page 725.

ARGP_KEY_HELP_EXTRA
>        argp.h (GNU): Section 25.3.8.1 [Special Keys for Argp Help Filter Functions], page 725.

ARGP_KEY_HELP_HEADER
>        argp.h (GNU): Section 25.3.8.1 [Special Keys for Argp Help Filter Functions], page 725.

ARGP_KEY_HELP_POST_DOC
>        argp.h (GNU): Section 25.3.8.1 [Special Keys for Argp Help Filter Functions], page 725.

ARGP_KEY_HELP_PRE_DOC
>        argp.h (GNU): Section 25.3.8.1 [Special Keys for Argp Help Filter Functions], page 725.

ARGP_KEY_INIT
>        argp.h (GNU): Section 25.3.5.1 [Special Keys for Argp Parser Functions], page 719.

ARGP_KEY_NO_ARGS
>        argp.h (GNU): Section 25.3.5.1 [Special Keys for Argp Parser Functions], page 719.

ARGP_KEY_SUCCESS
>        argp.h (GNU): Section 25.3.5.1 [Special Keys for Argp Parser Functions], page 719.

ARGP_LONG_ONLY
>        argp.h (GNU): Section 25.3.7 [Flags for argp_parse], page 724.

ARGP_NO_ARGS
>        argp.h (GNU): Section 25.3.7 [Flags for argp_parse], page 724.

ARGP_NO_ERRS
                argp.h (GNU): Section 25.3.7 [Flags for argp_parse], page 724.

ARGP_NO_EXIT
                argp.h (GNU): Section 25.3.7 [Flags for argp_parse], page 724.

ARGP_NO_HELP
                argp.h (GNU): Section 25.3.7 [Flags for argp_parse], page 724.

error_t argp_parse (const struct argp *argp, int argc, char **argv, unsigned flags, int
*arg_index, void *input)
                argp.h (GNU): Section 25.3 [Parsing Program Options with Argp], page 714.

ARGP_PARSE_ARGV0
                argp.h (GNU): Section 25.3.7 [Flags for argp_parse], page 724.

const char * argp_program_bug_address
                argp.h (GNU): Section 25.3.2 [Argp Global Variables], page 715.

const char * argp_program_version
                argp.h (GNU): Section 25.3.2 [Argp Global Variables], page 715.

argp_program_version_hook
                argp.h (GNU): Section 25.3.2 [Argp Global Variables], page 715.

ARGP_SILENT
                argp.h (GNU): Section 25.3.7 [Flags for argp_parse], page 724.

void argp_state_help (const struct argp_state *state, FILE *stream, unsigned flags)
                argp.h (GNU): Section 25.3.5.3 [Functions For Use in Argp Parsers], page 722.

void argp_usage (const struct argp_state *state)
                argp.h (GNU): Section 25.3.5.3 [Functions For Use in Argp Parsers], page 722.

error_t argz_add (char **argz, size_t *argz_len, const char *str)
                argz.h (GNU): Section 5.12.1 [Argz Functions], page 123.

error_t argz_add_sep (char **argz, size_t *argz_len, const char *str, int delim)
                argz.h (GNU): Section 5.12.1 [Argz Functions], page 123.

error_t argz_append (char **argz, size_t *argz_len, const char *buf, size_t buf_len)
                argz.h (GNU): Section 5.12.1 [Argz Functions], page 123.

size_t argz_count (const char *argz, size_t arg_len)
                argz.h (GNU): Section 5.12.1 [Argz Functions], page 123.

error_t argz_create (char *const argv[], char **argz, size_t *argz_len)
                argz.h (GNU): Section 5.12.1 [Argz Functions], page 123.

error_t argz_create_sep (const char *string, int sep, char **argz, size_t *argz_len)
                argz.h (GNU): Section 5.12.1 [Argz Functions], page 123.

void argz_delete (char **argz, size_t *argz_len, char *entry)
                argz.h (GNU): Section 5.12.1 [Argz Functions], page 123.

void argz_extract (const char *argz, size_t argz_len, char **argv)
                argz.h (GNU): Section 5.12.1 [Argz Functions], page 123.

error_t argz_insert (char **argz, size_t *argz_len, char *before, const char *entry)
                argz.h (GNU): Section 5.12.1 [Argz Functions], page 123.

char * argz_next (const char *argz, size_t argz_len, const char *entry)
                argz.h (GNU): Section 5.12.1 [Argz Functions], page 123.

error_t argz_replace (char **argz, size_t *argz_len, const char *str, const char *with,
unsigned *replace_count)
                argz.h (GNU): Section 5.12.1 [Argz Functions], page 123.

void argz_stringify (char *argz, size_t len, int sep)
         argz.h (GNU): Section 5.12.1 [Argz Functions], page 123.

char * asctime (const struct tm *brokentime)
         time.h (ISO): Section 21.4.5 [Formatting Calendar Time], page 608.

char * asctime_r (const struct tm *brokentime, char *buffer)
         time.h (POSIX.1c): Section 21.4.5 [Formatting Calendar Time], page 608.

double asin (double x)
         math.h (ISO): Section 19.3 [Inverse Trigonometric Functions], page 514.

float asinf (float x)
         math.h (ISO): Section 19.3 [Inverse Trigonometric Functions], page 514.

double asinh (double x)
         math.h (ISO): Section 19.5 [Hyperbolic Functions], page 520.

float asinhf (float x)
         math.h (ISO): Section 19.5 [Hyperbolic Functions], page 520.

long double asinhl (long double x)
         math.h (ISO): Section 19.5 [Hyperbolic Functions], page 520.

long double asinl (long double x)
         math.h (ISO): Section 19.3 [Inverse Trigonometric Functions], page 514.

int asprintf (char **ptr, const char *template, ...)
         stdio.h (GNU): Section 12.12.8 [Dynamically Allocating Formatted Output], page 281.

void assert (int expression)
         assert.h (ISO): Section A.1 [Explicitly Checking Internal Consistency], page 877.

void assert_perror (int errnum)
         assert.h (GNU): Section A.1 [Explicitly Checking Internal Consistency], page 877.

double atan (double x)
         math.h (ISO): Section 19.3 [Inverse Trigonometric Functions], page 514.

double atan2 (double y, double x)
         math.h (ISO): Section 19.3 [Inverse Trigonometric Functions], page 514.

float atan2f (float y, float x)
         math.h (ISO): Section 19.3 [Inverse Trigonometric Functions], page 514.

long double atan2l (long double y, long double x)
         math.h (ISO): Section 19.3 [Inverse Trigonometric Functions], page 514.

float atanf (float x)
         math.h (ISO): Section 19.3 [Inverse Trigonometric Functions], page 514.

double atanh (double x)
         math.h (ISO): Section 19.5 [Hyperbolic Functions], page 520.

float atanhf (float x)
         math.h (ISO): Section 19.5 [Hyperbolic Functions], page 520.

long double atanhl (long double x)
         math.h (ISO): Section 19.5 [Hyperbolic Functions], page 520.

long double atanl (long double x)
         math.h (ISO): Section 19.3 [Inverse Trigonometric Functions], page 514.

int atexit (void (*function) (void))
         stdlib.h (ISO): Section 25.7.3 [Cleanups on Exit], page 746.

double atof (const char *string)
         stdlib.h (ISO): Section 20.11.2 [Parsing of Floats], page 589.

`int atoi (const char *string)`
> `stdlib.h` (ISO): Section 20.11.1 [Parsing of Integers], page 585.

`long int atol (const char *string)`
> `stdlib.h` (ISO): Section 20.11.1 [Parsing of Integers], page 585.

`long long int atoll (const char *string)`
> `stdlib.h` (ISO): Section 20.11.1 [Parsing of Integers], page 585.

`B0`
> `termios.h` (POSIX.1): Section 17.4.8 [Line Speed], page 489.

`B110`
> `termios.h` (POSIX.1): Section 17.4.8 [Line Speed], page 489.

`B115200`
> `termios.h` (GNU): Section 17.4.8 [Line Speed], page 489.

`B1200`
> `termios.h` (POSIX.1): Section 17.4.8 [Line Speed], page 489.

`B134`
> `termios.h` (POSIX.1): Section 17.4.8 [Line Speed], page 489.

`B150`
> `termios.h` (POSIX.1): Section 17.4.8 [Line Speed], page 489.

`B1800`
> `termios.h` (POSIX.1): Section 17.4.8 [Line Speed], page 489.

`B19200`
> `termios.h` (POSIX.1): Section 17.4.8 [Line Speed], page 489.

`B200`
> `termios.h` (POSIX.1): Section 17.4.8 [Line Speed], page 489.

`B230400`
> `termios.h` (GNU): Section 17.4.8 [Line Speed], page 489.

`B2400`
> `termios.h` (POSIX.1): Section 17.4.8 [Line Speed], page 489.

`B300`
> `termios.h` (POSIX.1): Section 17.4.8 [Line Speed], page 489.

`B38400`
> `termios.h` (POSIX.1): Section 17.4.8 [Line Speed], page 489.

`B460800`
> `termios.h` (GNU): Section 17.4.8 [Line Speed], page 489.

`B4800`
> `termios.h` (POSIX.1): Section 17.4.8 [Line Speed], page 489.

`B50`
> `termios.h` (POSIX.1): Section 17.4.8 [Line Speed], page 489.

`B57600`
> `termios.h` (GNU): Section 17.4.8 [Line Speed], page 489.

`B600`
> `termios.h` (POSIX.1): Section 17.4.8 [Line Speed], page 489.

**B75**

        `termios.h` (POSIX.1): Section 17.4.8 [Line Speed], page 489.

**B9600**

        `termios.h` (POSIX.1): Section 17.4.8 [Line Speed], page 489.

`int backtrace (void **buffer, int size)`

        `execinfo.h` (GNU): Section 34.1 [Backtraces], page 866.

`char ** backtrace_symbols (void *const *buffer, int size)`

        `execinfo.h` (GNU): Section 34.1 [Backtraces], page 866.

`void backtrace_symbols_fd (void *const *buffer, int size, int fd)`

        `execinfo.h` (GNU): Section 34.1 [Backtraces], page 866.

`char * basename (char *path)`

        `libgen.h` (XPG): Section 5.8 [Finding Tokens in a String], page 115.

`char * basename (const char *filename)`

        `string.h` (GNU): Section 5.8 [Finding Tokens in a String], page 115.

`int BC_BASE_MAX`

        `limits.h` (POSIX.2): Section 32.10 [Utility Program Capacity Limits], page 855.

`int BC_DIM_MAX`

        `limits.h` (POSIX.2): Section 32.10 [Utility Program Capacity Limits], page 855.

`int bcmp (const void *a1, const void *a2, size_t size)`

        `string.h` (BSD): Section 5.5 [String/Array Comparison], page 102.

`void bcopy (const void *from, void *to, size_t size)`

        `string.h` (BSD): Section 5.4 [Copying and Concatenation], page 91.

`int BC_SCALE_MAX`

        `limits.h` (POSIX.2): Section 32.10 [Utility Program Capacity Limits], page 855.

`int BC_STRING_MAX`

        `limits.h` (POSIX.2): Section 32.10 [Utility Program Capacity Limits], page 855.

`int bind (int socket, struct sockaddr *addr, socklen_t length)`

        `sys/socket.h` (BSD): Section 16.3.2 [Setting the Address of a Socket], page 433.

`char * bindtextdomain (const char *domainname, const char *dirname)`

        `libintl.h` (GNU): Section 8.2.1.2 [How to determine which catalog to be used], page 200.

`char * bind_textdomain_codeset (const char *domainname, const char *codeset)`

        `libintl.h` (GNU): Section 8.2.1.4 [How to specify the output character set **gettext** uses], page 206.

**blkcnt64_t**

        `sys/types.h` (Unix98): Section 14.9.1 [The meaning of the File Attributes], page 399.

**blkcnt_t**

        `sys/types.h` (Unix98): Section 14.9.1 [The meaning of the File Attributes], page 399.

**BOOT_TIME**

        `utmp.h` (SVID): Section 30.12.1 [Manipulating the User Accounting Database], page 802.

**BOOT_TIME**

        `utmpx.h` (XPG4.2): Section 30.12.2 [XPG User Accounting Database Functions], page 807.

`int brk (void *addr)`

        `unistd.h` (BSD): Section 3.3 [Resizing the Data Segment], page 72.

`tcflag_t BRKINT`

        `termios.h` (POSIX.1): Section 17.4.4 [Input Modes], page 482.

void * bsearch (const void *key, const void *array, size_t count, size_t size, comparison_fn_t compare)

> stdlib.h (ISO): Section 9.2 [Array Search Function], page 212.

wint_t btowc (int c)

> wchar.h (ISO): Section 6.3.3 [Converting Single Characters], page 133.

int BUFSIZ

> stdio.h (ISO): Section 12.20.3 [Controlling Which Kind of Buffering], page 311.

void bzero (void *block, size_t size)

> string.h (BSD): Section 5.4 [Copying and Concatenation], page 91.

double cabs (complex double z)

> complex.h (ISO): Section 20.8.1 [Absolute Value], page 574.

float cabsf (complex float z)

> complex.h (ISO): Section 20.8.1 [Absolute Value], page 574.

long double cabsl (complex long double z)

> complex.h (ISO): Section 20.8.1 [Absolute Value], page 574.

complex double cacos (complex double z)

> complex.h (ISO): Section 19.3 [Inverse Trigonometric Functions], page 514.

complex float cacosf (complex float z)

> complex.h (ISO): Section 19.3 [Inverse Trigonometric Functions], page 514.

complex double cacosh (complex double z)

> complex.h (ISO): Section 19.5 [Hyperbolic Functions], page 520.

complex float cacoshf (complex float z)

> complex.h (ISO): Section 19.5 [Hyperbolic Functions], page 520.

complex long double cacoshl (complex long double z)

> complex.h (ISO): Section 19.5 [Hyperbolic Functions], page 520.

complex long double cacosl (complex long double z)

> complex.h (ISO): Section 19.3 [Inverse Trigonometric Functions], page 514.

void * calloc (size_t count, size_t eltsize)

> malloc.h, stdlib.h (ISO): Section 3.2.2.5 [Allocating Cleared Space], page 45.

char * canonicalize_file_name (const char *name)

> stdlib.h (GNU): Section 14.5 [Symbolic Links], page 393.

double carg (complex double z)

> complex.h (ISO): Section 20.10 [Projections, Conjugates, and Decomposing of Complex Numbers], page 583.

float cargf (complex float z)

> complex.h (ISO): Section 20.10 [Projections, Conjugates, and Decomposing of Complex Numbers], page 583.

long double cargl (complex long double z)

> complex.h (ISO): Section 20.10 [Projections, Conjugates, and Decomposing of Complex Numbers], page 583.

complex double casin (complex double z)

> complex.h (ISO): Section 19.3 [Inverse Trigonometric Functions], page 514.

complex float casinf (complex float z)

> complex.h (ISO): Section 19.3 [Inverse Trigonometric Functions], page 514.

complex double casinh (complex double z)

> complex.h (ISO): Section 19.5 [Hyperbolic Functions], page 520.

`complex float casinhf (complex float z)`
> `complex.h` (ISO): Section 19.5 [Hyperbolic Functions], page 520.

`complex long double casinhl (complex long double z)`
> `complex.h` (ISO): Section 19.5 [Hyperbolic Functions], page 520.

`complex long double casinl (complex long double z)`
> `complex.h` (ISO): Section 19.3 [Inverse Trigonometric Functions], page 514.

`complex double catan (complex double z)`
> `complex.h` (ISO): Section 19.3 [Inverse Trigonometric Functions], page 514.

`complex float catanf (complex float z)`
> `complex.h` (ISO): Section 19.3 [Inverse Trigonometric Functions], page 514.

`complex double catanh (complex double z)`
> `complex.h` (ISO): Section 19.5 [Hyperbolic Functions], page 520.

`complex float catanhf (complex float z)`
> `complex.h` (ISO): Section 19.5 [Hyperbolic Functions], page 520.

`complex long double catanhl (complex long double z)`
> `complex.h` (ISO): Section 19.5 [Hyperbolic Functions], page 520.

`complex long double catanl (complex long double z)`
> `complex.h` (ISO): Section 19.3 [Inverse Trigonometric Functions], page 514.

`nl_catd catopen (const char *cat_name, int flag)`
> `nl_types.h` (X/Open): Section 8.1.1 [The `catgets` function family], page 188.

`int cbc_crypt (char *key, char *blocks, unsigned len, unsigned mode, char *ivec)`
> `rpc/des_crypt.h` (SUNRPC): Section 33.4 [DES Encryption], page 863.

`double cbrt (double x)`
> `math.h` (BSD): Section 19.4 [Exponentiation and Logarithms], page 515.

`float cbrtf (float x)`
> `math.h` (BSD): Section 19.4 [Exponentiation and Logarithms], page 515.

`long double cbrtl (long double x)`
> `math.h` (BSD): Section 19.4 [Exponentiation and Logarithms], page 515.

`complex double ccos (complex double z)`
> `complex.h` (ISO): Section 19.2 [Trigonometric Functions], page 512.

`complex float ccosf (complex float z)`
> `complex.h` (ISO): Section 19.2 [Trigonometric Functions], page 512.

`complex double ccosh (complex double z)`
> `complex.h` (ISO): Section 19.5 [Hyperbolic Functions], page 520.

`complex float ccoshf (complex float z)`
> `complex.h` (ISO): Section 19.5 [Hyperbolic Functions], page 520.

`complex long double ccoshl (complex long double z)`
> `complex.h` (ISO): Section 19.5 [Hyperbolic Functions], page 520.

`complex long double ccosl (complex long double z)`
> `complex.h` (ISO): Section 19.2 [Trigonometric Functions], page 512.

`cc_t`
> `termios.h` (POSIX.1): Section 17.4.1 [Terminal Mode Data Types], page 479.

`tcflag_t CCTS_OFLOW`
> `termios.h` (BSD): Section 17.4.6 [Control Modes], page 485.

`double ceil (double x)`
> `math.h` (ISO): Section 20.8.3 [Rounding Functions], page 576.

`float ceilf (float x)`
> `math.h` (ISO): Section 20.8.3 [Rounding Functions], page 576.

`long double ceill (long double x)`
> `math.h` (ISO): Section 20.8.3 [Rounding Functions], page 576.

`complex double cexp (complex double z)`
> `complex.h` (ISO): Section 19.4 [Exponentiation and Logarithms], page 515.

`complex float cexpf (complex float z)`
> `complex.h` (ISO): Section 19.4 [Exponentiation and Logarithms], page 515.

`complex long double cexpl (complex long double z)`
> `complex.h` (ISO): Section 19.4 [Exponentiation and Logarithms], page 515.

`speed_t cfgetispeed (const struct termios *termios-p)`
> `termios.h` (POSIX.1): Section 17.4.8 [Line Speed], page 489.

`speed_t cfgetospeed (const struct termios *termios-p)`
> `termios.h` (POSIX.1): Section 17.4.8 [Line Speed], page 489.

`void cfmakeraw (struct termios *termios-p)`
> `termios.h` (BSD): Section 17.4.10 [Noncanonical Input], page 494.

`void cfree (void *ptr)`
> `stdlib.h` (Sun): Section 3.2.2.3 [Freeing Memory Allocated with `malloc`], page 43.

`int cfsetispeed (struct termios *termios-p, speed_t speed)`
> `termios.h` (POSIX.1): Section 17.4.8 [Line Speed], page 489.

`int cfsetospeed (struct termios *termios-p, speed_t speed)`
> `termios.h` (POSIX.1): Section 17.4.8 [Line Speed], page 489.

`int cfsetspeed (struct termios *termios-p, speed_t speed)`
> `termios.h` (BSD): Section 17.4.8 [Line Speed], page 489.

`CHAR_BIT`
> `limits.h` (ISO): Section A.5.1 [Computing the Width of an Integer Data Type], page 884.

`CHAR_MAX`
> `limits.h` (ISO): Section A.5.2 [Range of an Integer Type], page 885.

`CHAR_MIN`
> `limits.h` (ISO): Section A.5.2 [Range of an Integer Type], page 885.

`int chdir (const char *filename)`
> `unistd.h` (POSIX.1): Section 14.1 [Working Directory], page 377.

`int CHILD_MAX`
> `limits.h` (POSIX.1): Section 32.1 [General Capacity Limits], page 838.

`int chmod (const char *filename, mode_t mode)`
> `sys/stat.h` (POSIX.1): Section 14.9.7 [Assigning File Permissions], page 410.

`int chown (const char *filename, uid_t owner, gid_t group)`
> `unistd.h` (POSIX.1): Section 14.9.4 [File Owner], page 406.

`tcflag_t CIGNORE`
> `termios.h` (BSD): Section 17.4.6 [Control Modes], page 485.

`double cimag (complex double z)`
> `complex.h` (ISO): Section 20.10 [Projections, Conjugates, and Decomposing of Complex Numbers], page 583.

`float cimagf (complex float z)`
> `complex.h` (ISO): Section 20.10 [Projections, Conjugates, and Decomposing of Complex Numbers], page 583.

`long double cimagl (complex long double z)`
> `complex.h` (ISO): Section 20.10 [Projections, Conjugates, and Decomposing of Complex Numbers], page 583.

`int clearenv (void)`
> `stdlib.h` (GNU): Section 25.4.1 [Environment Access], page 738.

`void clearerr (FILE *stream)`
> `stdio.h` (ISO): Section 12.16 [Recovering from errors], page 303.

`void clearerr_unlocked (FILE *stream)`
> `stdio.h` (GNU): Section 12.16 [Recovering from errors], page 303.

`int CLK_TCK`
> `time.h` (POSIX.1): Section 21.3.2 [Processor Time Inquiry], page 598.

`tcflag_t CLOCAL`
> `termios.h` (POSIX.1): Section 17.4.6 [Control Modes], page 485.

`clock_t clock (void)`
> `time.h` (ISO): Section 21.3.1 [CPU Time Inquiry], page 597.

`int CLOCKS_PER_SEC`
> `time.h` (ISO): Section 21.3.1 [CPU Time Inquiry], page 597.

`clock_t`
> `time.h` (ISO): Section 21.3.1 [CPU Time Inquiry], page 597.

`complex double clog (complex double z)`
> `complex.h` (ISO): Section 19.4 [Exponentiation and Logarithms], page 515.

`complex double clog10 (complex double z)`
> `complex.h` (GNU): Section 19.4 [Exponentiation and Logarithms], page 515.

`complex float clog10f (complex float z)`
> `complex.h` (GNU): Section 19.4 [Exponentiation and Logarithms], page 515.

`complex long double clog10l (complex long double z)`
> `complex.h` (GNU): Section 19.4 [Exponentiation and Logarithms], page 515.

`complex float clogf (complex float z)`
> `complex.h` (ISO): Section 19.4 [Exponentiation and Logarithms], page 515.

`complex long double clogl (complex long double z)`
> `complex.h` (ISO): Section 19.4 [Exponentiation and Logarithms], page 515.

`int close (int filedes)`
> `unistd.h` (POSIX.1): Section 13.1 [Opening and Closing Files], page 323.

`int closedir (DIR *dirstream)`
> `dirent.h` (POSIX.1): Section 14.2.3 [Reading and Closing a Directory Stream], page 382.

`void closelog (void)`
> `syslog.h` (BSD): Section 18.2.3 [closelog], page 509.

`int COLL_WEIGHTS_MAX`
> `limits.h` (POSIX.2): Section 32.10 [Utility Program Capacity Limits], page 855.

`size_t confstr (int parameter, char *buf, size_t len)`
> `unistd.h` (POSIX.2): Section 32.12 [String-Valued Parameters], page 856.

`complex double conj (complex double z)`
> `complex.h` (ISO): Section 20.10 [Projections, Conjugates, and Decomposing of Complex Numbers], page 583.

`complex float conjf (complex float z)`
> `complex.h` (ISO): Section 20.10 [Projections, Conjugates, and Decomposing of Complex Numbers], page 583.

`complex long double conjl (complex long double z)`
> `complex.h` (ISO): Section 20.10 [Projections, Conjugates, and Decomposing of Complex Numbers], page 583.

`int connect (int socket, struct sockaddr *addr, socklen_t length)`
> `sys/socket.h` (BSD): Section 16.9.1 [Making a Connection], page 456.

`cookie_close_function_t`
> `stdio.h` (GNU): Section 12.21.2.2 [Custom Stream Hook Functions], page 317.

`cookie_io_functions_t`
> `stdio.h` (GNU): Section 12.21.2.1 [Custom Streams and Cookies], page 316.

`cookie_read_function_t`
> `stdio.h` (GNU): Section 12.21.2.2 [Custom Stream Hook Functions], page 317.

`cookie_seek_function_t`
> `stdio.h` (GNU): Section 12.21.2.2 [Custom Stream Hook Functions], page 317.

`cookie_write_function_t`
> `stdio.h` (GNU): Section 12.21.2.2 [Custom Stream Hook Functions], page 317.

`double copysign (double x, double y)`
> `math.h` (ISO): Section 20.8.5 [Setting and modifying single bits of FP values], page 579.

`float copysignf (float x, float y)`
> `math.h` (ISO): Section 20.8.5 [Setting and modifying single bits of FP values], page 579.

`long double copysignl (long double x, long double y)`
> `math.h` (ISO): Section 20.8.5 [Setting and modifying single bits of FP values], page 579.

`double cos (double x)`
> `math.h` (ISO): Section 19.2 [Trigonometric Functions], page 512.

`float cosf (float x)`
> `math.h` (ISO): Section 19.2 [Trigonometric Functions], page 512.

`double cosh (double x)`
> `math.h` (ISO): Section 19.5 [Hyperbolic Functions], page 520.

`float coshf (float x)`
> `math.h` (ISO): Section 19.5 [Hyperbolic Functions], page 520.

`long double coshl (long double x)`
> `math.h` (ISO): Section 19.5 [Hyperbolic Functions], page 520.

`long double cosl (long double x)`
> `math.h` (ISO): Section 19.2 [Trigonometric Functions], page 512.

`complex double cpow (complex double base, complex double power)`
> `complex.h` (ISO): Section 19.4 [Exponentiation and Logarithms], page 515.

`complex float cpowf (complex float base, complex float power)`
> `complex.h` (ISO): Section 19.4 [Exponentiation and Logarithms], page 515.

`complex long double cpowl (complex long double base, complex long double power)`
> `complex.h` (ISO): Section 19.4 [Exponentiation and Logarithms], page 515.

`complex double cproj (complex double z)`
> `complex.h` (ISO): Section 20.10 [Projections, Conjugates, and Decomposing of Complex Numbers], page 583.

`complex float cprojf (complex float z)`
> `complex.h` (ISO): Section 20.10 [Projections, Conjugates, and Decomposing of Complex Numbers], page 583.

`complex long double cprojl (complex long double z)`
> `complex.h` (ISO): Section 20.10 [Projections, Conjugates, and Decomposing of Complex Numbers], page 583.

void CPU_CLR (int *cpu*, cpu_set_t *set*)
> sched.h (GNU): Section 22.3.5 [Limiting execution to certain CPUs], page 645.

int CPU_ISSET (int *cpu*, const cpu_set_t *set*)
> sched.h (GNU): Section 22.3.5 [Limiting execution to certain CPUs], page 645.

void CPU_SET (int *cpu*, cpu_set_t *set*)
> sched.h (GNU): Section 22.3.5 [Limiting execution to certain CPUs], page 645.

int CPU_SETSIZE
> sched.h (GNU): Section 22.3.5 [Limiting execution to certain CPUs], page 645.

cpu_set_t
> sched.h (GNU): Section 22.3.5 [Limiting execution to certain CPUs], page 645.

void CPU_ZERO (cpu_set_t *set*)
> sched.h (GNU): Section 22.3.5 [Limiting execution to certain CPUs], page 645.

tcflag_t CREAD
> termios.h (POSIX.1): Section 17.4.6 [Control Modes], page 485.

double creal (complex double *z*)
> complex.h (ISO): Section 20.10 [Projections, Conjugates, and Decomposing of Complex Numbers], page 583.

float crealf (complex float *z*)
> complex.h (ISO): Section 20.10 [Projections, Conjugates, and Decomposing of Complex Numbers], page 583.

long double creall (complex long double *z*)
> complex.h (ISO): Section 20.10 [Projections, Conjugates, and Decomposing of Complex Numbers], page 583.

int creat (const char *filename*, mode_t *mode*)
> fcntl.h (POSIX.1): Section 13.1 [Opening and Closing Files], page 323.

int creat64 (const char *filename*, mode_t *mode*)
> fcntl.h (Unix98): Section 13.1 [Opening and Closing Files], page 323.

tcflag_t CRTS_IFLOW
> termios.h (BSD): Section 17.4.6 [Control Modes], page 485.

char * crypt (const char *key*, const char *salt*)
> crypt.h (BSD, SVID): Section 33.3 [Encrypting Passwords], page 861.

char * crypt_r (const char *key*, const char *salt*, struct crypt_data * *data*)
> crypt.h (GNU): Section 33.3 [Encrypting Passwords], page 861.

tcflag_t CS5
> termios.h (POSIX.1): Section 17.4.6 [Control Modes], page 485.

tcflag_t CS6
> termios.h (POSIX.1): Section 17.4.6 [Control Modes], page 485.

tcflag_t CS7
> termios.h (POSIX.1): Section 17.4.6 [Control Modes], page 485.

tcflag_t CS8
> termios.h (POSIX.1): Section 17.4.6 [Control Modes], page 485.

complex double csin (complex double *z*)
> complex.h (ISO): Section 19.2 [Trigonometric Functions], page 512.

complex float csinf (complex float *z*)
> complex.h (ISO): Section 19.2 [Trigonometric Functions], page 512.

complex double csinh (complex double *z*)
> complex.h (ISO): Section 19.5 [Hyperbolic Functions], page 520.

`complex float csinhf (complex float z)`
    complex.h (ISO): Section 19.5 [Hyperbolic Functions], page 520.

`complex long double csinhl (complex long double z)`
    complex.h (ISO): Section 19.5 [Hyperbolic Functions], page 520.

`complex long double csinl (complex long double z)`
    complex.h (ISO): Section 19.2 [Trigonometric Functions], page 512.

`tcflag_t CSIZE`
    termios.h (POSIX.1): Section 17.4.6 [Control Modes], page 485.

`_CS_LFS64_CFLAGS`
    unistd.h (Unix98): Section 32.12 [String-Valued Parameters], page 856.

`_CS_LFS64_LDFLAGS`
    unistd.h (Unix98): Section 32.12 [String-Valued Parameters], page 856.

`_CS_LFS64_LIBS`
    unistd.h (Unix98): Section 32.12 [String-Valued Parameters], page 856.

`_CS_LFS64_LINTFLAGS`
    unistd.h (Unix98): Section 32.12 [String-Valued Parameters], page 856.

`_CS_LFS_CFLAGS`
    unistd.h (Unix98): Section 32.12 [String-Valued Parameters], page 856.

`_CS_LFS_LDFLAGS`
    unistd.h (Unix98): Section 32.12 [String-Valued Parameters], page 856.

`_CS_LFS_LIBS`
    unistd.h (Unix98): Section 32.12 [String-Valued Parameters], page 856.

`_CS_LFS_LINTFLAGS`
    unistd.h (Unix98): Section 32.12 [String-Valued Parameters], page 856.

`_CS_PATH`
    unistd.h (POSIX.2): Section 32.12 [String-Valued Parameters], page 856.

`complex double csqrt (complex double z)`
    complex.h (ISO): Section 19.4 [Exponentiation and Logarithms], page 515.

`complex float csqrtf (complex float z)`
    complex.h (ISO): Section 19.4 [Exponentiation and Logarithms], page 515.

`complex long double csqrtl (complex long double z)`
    complex.h (ISO): Section 19.4 [Exponentiation and Logarithms], page 515.

`tcflag_t CSTOPB`
    termios.h (POSIX.1): Section 17.4.6 [Control Modes], page 485.

`complex double ctan (complex double z)`
    complex.h (ISO): Section 19.2 [Trigonometric Functions], page 512.

`complex float ctanf (complex float z)`
    complex.h (ISO): Section 19.2 [Trigonometric Functions], page 512.

`complex double ctanh (complex double z)`
    complex.h (ISO): Section 19.5 [Hyperbolic Functions], page 520.

`complex float ctanhf (complex float z)`
    complex.h (ISO): Section 19.5 [Hyperbolic Functions], page 520.

`complex long double ctanhl (complex long double z)`
    complex.h (ISO): Section 19.5 [Hyperbolic Functions], page 520.

`complex long double ctanl (complex long double z)`
    complex.h (ISO): Section 19.2 [Trigonometric Functions], page 512.

char * ctermid (char *string)
> stdio.h (POSIX.1): Section 28.7.1 [Identifying the Controlling Terminal], page 778.

char * ctime (const time_t *time)
> time.h (ISO): Section 21.4.5 [Formatting Calendar Time], page 608.

char * ctime_r (const time_t *time, char *buffer)
> time.h (POSIX.1c): Section 21.4.5 [Formatting Calendar Time], page 608.

char * cuserid (char *string)
> stdio.h (POSIX.1): Section 30.11 [Identifying Who Logged In], page 801.

int daylight
> time.h (SVID): Section 21.4.8 [Functions and Variables for Time Zones], page 624.

DBL_DIG
> float.h (ISO): Section A.5.3.2 [Floating Point Parameters], page 888.

DBL_EPSILON
> float.h (ISO): Section A.5.3.2 [Floating Point Parameters], page 888.

DBL_MANT_DIG
> float.h (ISO): Section A.5.3.2 [Floating Point Parameters], page 888.

DBL_MAX
> float.h (ISO): Section A.5.3.2 [Floating Point Parameters], page 888.

DBL_MAX_10_EXP
> float.h (ISO): Section A.5.3.2 [Floating Point Parameters], page 888.

DBL_MAX_EXP
> float.h (ISO): Section A.5.3.2 [Floating Point Parameters], page 888.

DBL_MIN
> float.h (ISO): Section A.5.3.2 [Floating Point Parameters], page 888.

DBL_MIN_10_EXP
> float.h (ISO): Section A.5.3.2 [Floating Point Parameters], page 888.

DBL_MIN_EXP
> float.h (ISO): Section A.5.3.2 [Floating Point Parameters], page 888.

char * dcgettext (const char *domainname, const char *msgid, int category)
> libintl.h (GNU): Section 8.2.1.1 [What has to be done to translate a message?], page 198.

char * dcngettext (const char *domain, const char *msgid1, const char *msgid2, unsigned long int n, int category)
> libintl.h (GNU): Section 8.2.1.3 [Additional functions for more complicated situations], page 202.

DEAD_PROCESS
> utmp.h (SVID): Section 30.12.1 [Manipulating the User Accounting Database], page 802.

DEAD_PROCESS
> utmpx.h (XPG4.2): Section 30.12.2 [XPG User Accounting Database Functions], page 807.

_DEFAULT_SOURCE
> (GNU): Section 1.3.4 [Feature Test Macros], page 15.

DES_DECRYPT
> rpc/des_crypt.h (SUNRPC): Section 33.4 [DES Encryption], page 863.

DES_ENCRYPT
> rpc/des_crypt.h (SUNRPC): Section 33.4 [DES Encryption], page 863.

DESERR_BADPARAM
> rpc/des_crypt.h (SUNRPC): Section 33.4 [DES Encryption], page 863.

`DESERR_HWERROR`
> `rpc/des_crypt.h` (SUNRPC): Section 33.4 [DES Encryption], page 863.

`DESERR_NOHWDEVICE`
> `rpc/des_crypt.h` (SUNRPC): Section 33.4 [DES Encryption], page 863.

`DESERR_NONE`
> `rpc/des_crypt.h` (SUNRPC): Section 33.4 [DES Encryption], page 863.

`int DES_FAILED (int err)`
> `rpc/des_crypt.h` (SUNRPC): Section 33.4 [DES Encryption], page 863.

`DES_HW`
> `rpc/des_crypt.h` (SUNRPC): Section 33.4 [DES Encryption], page 863.

`void des_setparity (char *key)`
> `rpc/des_crypt.h` (SUNRPC): Section 33.4 [DES Encryption], page 863.

`DES_SW`
> `rpc/des_crypt.h` (SUNRPC): Section 33.4 [DES Encryption], page 863.

`dev_t`
> `sys/types.h` (POSIX.1): Section 14.9.1 [The meaning of the File Attributes], page 399.

`char * dgettext (const char *domainname, const char *msgid)`
> `libintl.h` (GNU): Section 8.2.1.1 [What has to be done to translate a message?], page 198.

`double difftime (time_t time1, time_t time0)`
> `time.h` (ISO): Section 21.2 [Elapsed Time], page 595.

`DIR`
> `dirent.h` (POSIX.1): Section 14.2.2 [Opening a Directory Stream], page 381.

`int dirfd (DIR *dirstream)`
> `dirent.h` (GNU): Section 14.2.2 [Opening a Directory Stream], page 381.

`char * dirname (char *path)`
> `libgen.h` (XPG): Section 5.8 [Finding Tokens in a String], page 115.

`div_t div (int numerator, int denominator)`
> `stdlib.h` (ISO): Section 20.2 [Integer Division], page 560.

`div_t`
> `stdlib.h` (ISO): Section 20.2 [Integer Division], page 560.

`char * dngettext (const char *domain, const char *msgid1, const char *msgid2, unsigned long int n)`
> `libintl.h` (GNU): Section 8.2.1.3 [Additional functions for more complicated situations], page 202.

`double drand48 (void)`
> `stdlib.h` (SVID): Section 19.8.3 [SVID Random Number Function], page 553.

`int drand48_r (struct drand48_data *buffer, double *result)`
> `stdlib.h` (GNU): Section 19.8.3 [SVID Random Number Function], page 553.

`double drem (double numerator, double denominator)`
> `math.h` (BSD): Section 20.8.4 [Remainder Functions], page 578.

`float dremf (float numerator, float denominator)`
> `math.h` (BSD): Section 20.8.4 [Remainder Functions], page 578.

`long double dreml (long double numerator, long double denominator)`
> `math.h` (BSD): Section 20.8.4 [Remainder Functions], page 578.

`mode_t DTTOIF (int dtype)`
> `dirent.h` (BSD): Section 14.2.1 [Format of a Directory Entry], page 379.

int dup (int *old*)

        unistd.h (POSIX.1): Section 13.12 [Duplicating Descriptors], page 360.

int dup2 (int *old*, int *new*)

        unistd.h (POSIX.1): Section 13.12 [Duplicating Descriptors], page 360.

int E2BIG

        errno.h (POSIX.1: Argument list too long): Section 2.2 [Error Codes], page 23.

int EACCES

        errno.h (POSIX.1: Permission denied): Section 2.2 [Error Codes], page 23.

int EADDRINUSE

        errno.h (BSD: Address already in use): Section 2.2 [Error Codes], page 23.

int EADDRNOTAVAIL

        errno.h (BSD: Cannot assign requested address): Section 2.2 [Error Codes], page 23.

int EADV

        errno.h (Linux???: Advertise error): Section 2.2 [Error Codes], page 23.

int EAFNOSUPPORT

        errno.h (BSD: Address family not supported by protocol): Section 2.2 [Error Codes], page 23.

int EAGAIN

        errno.h (POSIX.1: Resource temporarily unavailable): Section 2.2 [Error Codes], page 23.

int EALREADY

        errno.h (BSD: Operation already in progress): Section 2.2 [Error Codes], page 23.

int EAUTH

        errno.h (BSD: Authentication error): Section 2.2 [Error Codes], page 23.

int EBACKGROUND

        errno.h (GNU: Inappropriate operation for background process): Section 2.2 [Error Codes], page 23.

int EBADE

        errno.h (Linux???: Invalid exchange): Section 2.2 [Error Codes], page 23.

int EBADF

        errno.h (POSIX.1: Bad file descriptor): Section 2.2 [Error Codes], page 23.

int EBADFD

        errno.h (Linux???: File descriptor in bad state): Section 2.2 [Error Codes], page 23.

int EBADMSG

        errno.h (XOPEN: Bad message): Section 2.2 [Error Codes], page 23.

int EBADR

        errno.h (Linux???: Invalid request descriptor): Section 2.2 [Error Codes], page 23.

int EBADRPC

        errno.h (BSD: RPC struct is bad): Section 2.2 [Error Codes], page 23.

int EBADRQC

        errno.h (Linux???: Invalid request code): Section 2.2 [Error Codes], page 23.

int EBADSLT

        errno.h (Linux???: Invalid slot): Section 2.2 [Error Codes], page 23.

int EBFONT

        errno.h (Linux???: Bad font file format): Section 2.2 [Error Codes], page 23.

int EBUSY

        `errno.h` (POSIX.1: Device or resource busy): Section 2.2 [Error Codes], page 23.

int ECANCELED

        `errno.h` (POSIX.1: Operation canceled): Section 2.2 [Error Codes], page 23.

int ecb_crypt (char *`key`, char *`blocks`, unsigned `len`, unsigned `mode`)

        `rpc/des_crypt.h` (SUNRPC): Section 33.4 [DES Encryption], page 863.

int ECHILD

        `errno.h` (POSIX.1: No child processes): Section 2.2 [Error Codes], page 23.

tcflag_t ECHO

        `termios.h` (POSIX.1): Section 17.4.7 [Local Modes], page 486.

tcflag_t ECHOCTL

        `termios.h` (BSD): Section 17.4.7 [Local Modes], page 486.

tcflag_t ECHOE

        `termios.h` (POSIX.1): Section 17.4.7 [Local Modes], page 486.

tcflag_t ECHOK

        `termios.h` (POSIX.1): Section 17.4.7 [Local Modes], page 486.

tcflag_t ECHOKE

        `termios.h` (BSD): Section 17.4.7 [Local Modes], page 486.

tcflag_t ECHONL

        `termios.h` (POSIX.1): Section 17.4.7 [Local Modes], page 486.

tcflag_t ECHOPRT

        `termios.h` (BSD): Section 17.4.7 [Local Modes], page 486.

int ECHRNG

        `errno.h` (Linux???: Channel number out of range): Section 2.2 [Error Codes], page 23.

int ECOMM

        `errno.h` (Linux???: Communication error on send): Section 2.2 [Error Codes], page 23.

int ECONNABORTED

        `errno.h` (BSD: Software caused connection abort): Section 2.2 [Error Codes], page 23.

int ECONNREFUSED

        `errno.h` (BSD: Connection refused): Section 2.2 [Error Codes], page 23.

int ECONNRESET

        `errno.h` (BSD: Connection reset by peer): Section 2.2 [Error Codes], page 23.

char * ecvt (double `value`, int `ndigit`, int *`decpt`, int *`neg`)

        `stdlib.h` (SVID, Unix98): Section 20.12 [Old-fashioned System V number-to-string functions], page 591.

int ecvt_r (double `value`, int `ndigit`, int *`decpt`, int *`neg`, char *`buf`, size_t `len`)

        `stdlib.h` (GNU): Section 20.12 [Old-fashioned System V number-to-string functions], page 591.

int ED

        `errno.h` (GNU: ?): Section 2.2 [Error Codes], page 23.

int EDEADLK

        `errno.h` (POSIX.1: Resource deadlock avoided): Section 2.2 [Error Codes], page 23.

int EDEADLOCK

        `errno.h` (Linux???: File locking deadlock error): Section 2.2 [Error Codes], page 23.

int EDESTADDRREQ

        `errno.h` (BSD: Destination address required): Section 2.2 [Error Codes], page 23.

int EDIED

>    errno.h (GNU: Translator died): Section 2.2 [Error Codes], page 23.

int EDOM

>    errno.h (ISO: Numerical argument out of domain): Section 2.2 [Error Codes], page 23.

int EDOTDOT

>    errno.h (Linux???: RFS specific error): Section 2.2 [Error Codes], page 23.

int EDQUOT

>    errno.h (BSD: Disk quota exceeded): Section 2.2 [Error Codes], page 23.

int EEXIST

>    errno.h (POSIX.1: File exists): Section 2.2 [Error Codes], page 23.

int EFAULT

>    errno.h (POSIX.1: Bad address): Section 2.2 [Error Codes], page 23.

int EFBIG

>    errno.h (POSIX.1: File too large): Section 2.2 [Error Codes], page 23.

int EFTYPE

>    errno.h (BSD: Inappropriate file type or format): Section 2.2 [Error Codes], page 23.

int EGRATUITOUS

>    errno.h (GNU: Gratuitous error): Section 2.2 [Error Codes], page 23.

int EGREGIOUS

>    errno.h (GNU: You really blew it this time): Section 2.2 [Error Codes], page 23.

int EHOSTDOWN

>    errno.h (BSD: Host is down): Section 2.2 [Error Codes], page 23.

int EHOSTUNREACH

>    errno.h (BSD: No route to host): Section 2.2 [Error Codes], page 23.

int EHWPOISON

>    errno.h (Linux: Memory page has hardware error): Section 2.2 [Error Codes], page 23.

int EIDRM

>    errno.h (XOPEN: Identifier removed): Section 2.2 [Error Codes], page 23.

int EIEIO

>    errno.h (GNU: Computer bought the farm): Section 2.2 [Error Codes], page 23.

int EILSEQ

>    errno.h (ISO: Invalid or incomplete multibyte or wide character): Section 2.2 [Error Codes], page 23.

int EINPROGRESS

>    errno.h (BSD: Operation now in progress): Section 2.2 [Error Codes], page 23.

int EINTR

>    errno.h (POSIX.1: Interrupted system call): Section 2.2 [Error Codes], page 23.

int EINVAL

>    errno.h (POSIX.1: Invalid argument): Section 2.2 [Error Codes], page 23.

int EIO

>    errno.h (POSIX.1: Input/output error): Section 2.2 [Error Codes], page 23.

int EISCONN

>    errno.h (BSD: Transport endpoint is already connected): Section 2.2 [Error Codes], page 23.

`int EISDIR`

>       `errno.h` (POSIX.1: Is a directory): Section 2.2 [Error Codes], page 23.

`int EISNAM`

>       `errno.h` (Linux???: Is a named type file): Section 2.2 [Error Codes], page 23.

`int EKEYEXPIRED`

>       `errno.h` (Linux: Key has expired): Section 2.2 [Error Codes], page 23.

`int EKEYREJECTED`

>       `errno.h` (Linux: Key was rejected by service): Section 2.2 [Error Codes], page 23.

`int EKEYREVOKED`

>       `errno.h` (Linux: Key has been revoked): Section 2.2 [Error Codes], page 23.

`int EL2HLT`

>       `errno.h` (Obsolete: Level 2 halted): Section 2.2 [Error Codes], page 23.

`int EL2NSYNC`

>       `errno.h` (Obsolete: Level 2 not synchronized): Section 2.2 [Error Codes], page 23.

`int EL3HLT`

>       `errno.h` (Obsolete: Level 3 halted): Section 2.2 [Error Codes], page 23.

`int EL3RST`

>       `errno.h` (Obsolete: Level 3 reset): Section 2.2 [Error Codes], page 23.

`int ELIBACC`

>       `errno.h` (Linux???: Can not access a needed shared library): Section 2.2 [Error Codes], page 23.

`int ELIBBAD`

>       `errno.h` (Linux???: Accessing a corrupted shared library): Section 2.2 [Error Codes], page 23.

`int ELIBEXEC`

>       `errno.h` (Linux???: Cannot exec a shared library directly): Section 2.2 [Error Codes], page 23.

`int ELIBMAX`

>       `errno.h` (Linux???: Attempting to link in too many shared libraries): Section 2.2 [Error Codes], page 23.

`int ELIBSCN`

>       `errno.h` (Linux???: .lib section in a.out corrupted): Section 2.2 [Error Codes], page 23.

`int ELNRNG`

>       `errno.h` (Linux???: Link number out of range): Section 2.2 [Error Codes], page 23.

`int ELOOP`

>       `errno.h` (BSD: Too many levels of symbolic links): Section 2.2 [Error Codes], page 23.

`int EMEDIUMTYPE`

>       `errno.h` (Linux???: Wrong medium type): Section 2.2 [Error Codes], page 23.

`int EMFILE`

>       `errno.h` (POSIX.1: Too many open files): Section 2.2 [Error Codes], page 23.

`int EMLINK`

>       `errno.h` (POSIX.1: Too many links): Section 2.2 [Error Codes], page 23.

`EMPTY`

>       `utmp.h` (SVID): Section 30.12.1 [Manipulating the User Accounting Database], page 802.

`EMPTY`

>       `utmpx.h` (XPG4.2): Section 30.12.2 [XPG User Accounting Database Functions], page 807.

int EMSGSIZE
>           errno.h (BSD: Message too long): Section 2.2 [Error Codes], page 23.

int EMULTIHOP
>           errno.h (XOPEN: Multihop attempted): Section 2.2 [Error Codes], page 23.

int ENAMETOOLONG
>           errno.h (POSIX.1: File name too long): Section 2.2 [Error Codes], page 23.

int ENAVAIL
>           errno.h (Linux???: No XENIX semaphores available): Section 2.2 [Error Codes], page 23.

void encrypt (char *block, int edflag)
>           crypt.h (BSD, SVID): Section 33.4 [DES Encryption], page 863.

void encrypt_r (char *block, int edflag, struct crypt_data * data)
>           crypt.h (GNU): Section 33.4 [DES Encryption], page 863.

void endfsent (void)
>           fstab.h (BSD): Section 31.3.1.1 [The fstab file], page 825.

void endgrent (void)
>           grp.h (SVID, BSD): Section 30.14.3 [Scanning the List of All Groups], page 815.

void endhostent (void)
>           netdb.h (BSD): Section 16.6.2.4 [Host Names], page 443.

int endmntent (FILE *stream)
>           mntent.h (BSD): Section 31.3.1.2 [The mtab file], page 828.

void endnetent (void)
>           netdb.h (BSD): Section 16.13 [Networks Database], page 475.

void endnetgrent (void)
>           netdb.h (BSD): Section 30.16.2 [Looking up one Netgroup], page 818.

void endprotoent (void)
>           netdb.h (BSD): Section 16.6.6 [Protocols Database], page 450.

void endpwent (void)
>           pwd.h (SVID, BSD): Section 30.13.3 [Scanning the List of All Users], page 812.

void endservent (void)
>           netdb.h (BSD): Section 16.6.4 [The Services Database], page 448.

void endutent (void)
>           utmp.h (SVID): Section 30.12.1 [Manipulating the User Accounting Database], page 802.

void endutxent (void)
>           utmpx.h (XPG4.2): Section 30.12.2 [XPG User Accounting Database Functions], page 807.

int ENEEDAUTH
>           errno.h (BSD: Need authenticator): Section 2.2 [Error Codes], page 23.

int ENETDOWN
>           errno.h (BSD: Network is down): Section 2.2 [Error Codes], page 23.

int ENETRESET
>           errno.h (BSD: Network dropped connection on reset): Section 2.2 [Error Codes], page 23.

int ENETUNREACH
>           errno.h (BSD: Network is unreachable): Section 2.2 [Error Codes], page 23.

int ENFILE
>           errno.h (POSIX.1: Too many open files in system): Section 2.2 [Error Codes], page 23.

int ENOANO
>           errno.h (Linux???: No anode): Section 2.2 [Error Codes], page 23.

int ENOBUFS

        `errno.h` (BSD: No buffer space available): Section 2.2 [Error Codes], page 23.

int ENOCSI

        `errno.h` (Linux???: No CSI structure available): Section 2.2 [Error Codes], page 23.

int ENODATA

        `errno.h` (XOPEN: No data available): Section 2.2 [Error Codes], page 23.

int ENODEV

        `errno.h` (POSIX.1: No such device): Section 2.2 [Error Codes], page 23.

int ENOENT

        `errno.h` (POSIX.1: No such file or directory): Section 2.2 [Error Codes], page 23.

int ENOEXEC

        `errno.h` (POSIX.1: Exec format error): Section 2.2 [Error Codes], page 23.

int ENOKEY

        `errno.h` (Linux: Required key not available): Section 2.2 [Error Codes], page 23.

int ENOLCK

        `errno.h` (POSIX.1: No locks available): Section 2.2 [Error Codes], page 23.

int ENOLINK

        `errno.h` (XOPEN: Link has been severed): Section 2.2 [Error Codes], page 23.

int ENOMEDIUM

        `errno.h` (Linux???: No medium found): Section 2.2 [Error Codes], page 23.

int ENOMEM

        `errno.h` (POSIX.1: Cannot allocate memory): Section 2.2 [Error Codes], page 23.

int ENOMSG

        `errno.h` (XOPEN: No message of desired type): Section 2.2 [Error Codes], page 23.

int ENONET

        `errno.h` (Linux???: Machine is not on the network): Section 2.2 [Error Codes], page 23.

int ENOPKG

        `errno.h` (Linux???: Package not installed): Section 2.2 [Error Codes], page 23.

int ENOPROTOOPT

        `errno.h` (BSD: Protocol not available): Section 2.2 [Error Codes], page 23.

int ENOSPC

        `errno.h` (POSIX.1: No space left on device): Section 2.2 [Error Codes], page 23.

int ENOSR

        `errno.h` (XOPEN: Out of streams resources): Section 2.2 [Error Codes], page 23.

int ENOSTR

        `errno.h` (XOPEN: Device not a stream): Section 2.2 [Error Codes], page 23.

int ENOSYS

        `errno.h` (POSIX.1: Function not implemented): Section 2.2 [Error Codes], page 23.

int ENOTBLK

        `errno.h` (BSD: Block device required): Section 2.2 [Error Codes], page 23.

int ENOTCONN

        `errno.h` (BSD: Transport endpoint is not connected): Section 2.2 [Error Codes], page 23.

int ENOTDIR

>    errno.h (POSIX.1: Not a directory): Section 2.2 [Error Codes], page 23.

int ENOTEMPTY

>    errno.h (POSIX.1: Directory not empty): Section 2.2 [Error Codes], page 23.

int ENOTNAM

>    errno.h (Linux???: Not a XENIX named type file): Section 2.2 [Error Codes], page 23.

int ENOTRECOVERABLE

>    errno.h (Linux: State not recoverable): Section 2.2 [Error Codes], page 23.

int ENOTSOCK

>    errno.h (BSD: Socket operation on non-socket): Section 2.2 [Error Codes], page 23.

int ENOTSUP

>    errno.h (POSIX.1: Not supported): Section 2.2 [Error Codes], page 23.

int ENOTTY

>    errno.h (POSIX.1: Inappropriate ioctl for device): Section 2.2 [Error Codes], page 23.

int ENOTUNIQ

>    errno.h (Linux???: Name not unique on network): Section 2.2 [Error Codes], page 23.

char ** environ

>    unistd.h (POSIX.1): Section 25.4.1 [Environment Access], page 738.

error_t envz_add (char **envz, size_t *envz_len, const char *name, const char *value)

>    envz.h (GNU): Section 5.12.2 [Envz Functions], page 125.

char * envz_entry (const char *envz, size_t envz_len, const char *name)

>    envz.h (GNU): Section 5.12.2 [Envz Functions], page 125.

char * envz_get (const char *envz, size_t envz_len, const char *name)

>    envz.h (GNU): Section 5.12.2 [Envz Functions], page 125.

error_t envz_merge (char **envz, size_t *envz_len, const char *envz2, size_t envz2_len, int
override)

>    envz.h (GNU): Section 5.12.2 [Envz Functions], page 125.

void envz_remove (char **envz, size_t *envz_len, const char *name)

>    envz.h (GNU): Section 5.12.2 [Envz Functions], page 125.

void envz_strip (char **envz, size_t *envz_len)

>    envz.h (GNU): Section 5.12.2 [Envz Functions], page 125.

int ENXIO

>    errno.h (POSIX.1: No such device or address): Section 2.2 [Error Codes], page 23.

int EOF

>    stdio.h (ISO): Section 12.15 [End-Of-File and Errors], page 302.

int EOPNOTSUPP

>    errno.h (BSD: Operation not supported): Section 2.2 [Error Codes], page 23.

int EOVERFLOW

>    errno.h (XOPEN: Value too large for defined data type): Section 2.2 [Error Codes], page 23.

int EOWNERDEAD

>    errno.h (Linux: Owner died): Section 2.2 [Error Codes], page 23.

int EPERM

>    errno.h (POSIX.1: Operation not permitted): Section 2.2 [Error Codes], page 23.

int EPFNOSUPPORT

>    errno.h (BSD: Protocol family not supported): Section 2.2 [Error Codes], page 23.

int EPIPE

> errno.h (POSIX.1: Broken pipe): Section 2.2 [Error Codes], page 23.

int EPROCLIM

> errno.h (BSD: Too many processes): Section 2.2 [Error Codes], page 23.

int EPROCUNAVAIL

> errno.h (BSD: RPC bad procedure for program): Section 2.2 [Error Codes], page 23.

int EPROGMISMATCH

> errno.h (BSD: RPC program version wrong): Section 2.2 [Error Codes], page 23.

int EPROGUNAVAIL

> errno.h (BSD: RPC program not available): Section 2.2 [Error Codes], page 23.

int EPROTO

> errno.h (XOPEN: Protocol error): Section 2.2 [Error Codes], page 23.

int EPROTONOSUPPORT

> errno.h (BSD: Protocol not supported): Section 2.2 [Error Codes], page 23.

int EPROTOTYPE

> errno.h (BSD: Protocol wrong type for socket): Section 2.2 [Error Codes], page 23.

int EQUIV_CLASS_MAX

> limits.h (POSIX.2): Section 32.10 [Utility Program Capacity Limits], page 855.

double erand48 (unsigned short int *xsubi*[3])

> stdlib.h (SVID): Section 19.8.3 [SVID Random Number Function], page 553.

int erand48_r (unsigned short int *xsubi*[3], struct drand48_data *buffer*, double *result*)

> stdlib.h (GNU): Section 19.8.3 [SVID Random Number Function], page 553.

int ERANGE

> errno.h (ISO: Numerical result out of range): Section 2.2 [Error Codes], page 23.

int EREMCHG

> errno.h (Linux???: Remote address changed): Section 2.2 [Error Codes], page 23.

int EREMOTE

> errno.h (BSD: Object is remote): Section 2.2 [Error Codes], page 23.

int EREMOTEIO

> errno.h (Linux???: Remote I/O error): Section 2.2 [Error Codes], page 23.

int ERESTART

> errno.h (Linux???: Interrupted system call should be restarted): Section 2.2 [Error Codes], page 23.

double erf (double *x*)

> math.h (SVID): Section 19.6 [Special Functions], page 522.

double erfc (double *x*)

> math.h (SVID): Section 19.6 [Special Functions], page 522.

float erfcf (float *x*)

> math.h (SVID): Section 19.6 [Special Functions], page 522.

long double erfcl (long double *x*)

> math.h (SVID): Section 19.6 [Special Functions], page 522.

float erff (float *x*)

> math.h (SVID): Section 19.6 [Special Functions], page 522.

int ERFKILL

> errno.h (Linux: Operation not possible due to RF-kill): Section 2.2 [Error Codes], page 23.

`long double erfl (long double x)`
> `math.h` (SVID): Section 19.6 [Special Functions], page 522.

`int EROFS`

> `errno.h` (POSIX.1: Read-only file system): Section 2.2 [Error Codes], page 23.

`int ERPCMISMATCH`

> `errno.h` (BSD: RPC version wrong): Section 2.2 [Error Codes], page 23.

`void err (int status, const char *format, ...)`
> `err.h` (BSD): Section 2.3 [Error Messages], page 33.

`volatile int errno`

> `errno.h` (ISO): Section 2.1 [Checking for Errors], page 22.

`void error (int status, int errnum, const char *format, ...)`
> `error.h` (GNU): Section 2.3 [Error Messages], page 33.

`void error_at_line (int status, int errnum, const char *fname, unsigned int lineno, const char *format, ...)`
> `error.h` (GNU): Section 2.3 [Error Messages], page 33.

`unsigned int error_message_count`

> `error.h` (GNU): Section 2.3 [Error Messages], page 33.

`int error_one_per_line`

> `error.h` (GNU): Section 2.3 [Error Messages], page 33.

`void errx (int status, const char *format, ...)`
> `err.h` (BSD): Section 2.3 [Error Messages], page 33.

`int ESHUTDOWN`

> `errno.h` (BSD: Cannot send after transport endpoint shutdown): Section 2.2 [Error Codes], page 23.

`int ESOCKTNOSUPPORT`

> `errno.h` (BSD: Socket type not supported): Section 2.2 [Error Codes], page 23.

`int ESPIPE`

> `errno.h` (POSIX.1: Illegal seek): Section 2.2 [Error Codes], page 23.

`int ESRCH`

> `errno.h` (POSIX.1: No such process): Section 2.2 [Error Codes], page 23.

`int ESRMNT`

> `errno.h` (Linux???: Srmount error): Section 2.2 [Error Codes], page 23.

`int ESTALE`

> `errno.h` (BSD: Stale file handle): Section 2.2 [Error Codes], page 23.

`int ESTRPIPE`

> `errno.h` (Linux???: Streams pipe error): Section 2.2 [Error Codes], page 23.

`int ETIME`

> `errno.h` (XOPEN: Timer expired): Section 2.2 [Error Codes], page 23.

`int ETIMEDOUT`

> `errno.h` (BSD: Connection timed out): Section 2.2 [Error Codes], page 23.

`int ETOOMANYREFS`

> `errno.h` (BSD: Too many references: cannot splice): Section 2.2 [Error Codes], page 23.

`int ETXTBSY`

> `errno.h` (BSD: Text file busy): Section 2.2 [Error Codes], page 23.

`int EUCLEAN`

> `errno.h` (Linux???: Structure needs cleaning): Section 2.2 [Error Codes], page 23.

int EUNATCH

> errno.h (Linux???: Protocol driver not attached): Section 2.2 [Error Codes], page 23.

int EUSERS

> errno.h (BSD: Too many users): Section 2.2 [Error Codes], page 23.

int EWOULDBLOCK

> errno.h (BSD: Operation would block): Section 2.2 [Error Codes], page 23.

int EXDEV

> errno.h (POSIX.1: Invalid cross-device link): Section 2.2 [Error Codes], page 23.

int execl (const char *filename, const char *arg0, ...)
> unistd.h (POSIX.1): Section 26.5 [Executing a File], page 752.

int execle (const char *filename, const char *arg0, ..., char *const env[])
> unistd.h (POSIX.1): Section 26.5 [Executing a File], page 752.

int execlp (const char *filename, const char *arg0, ...)
> unistd.h (POSIX.1): Section 26.5 [Executing a File], page 752.

int execv (const char *filename, char *const argv[])
> unistd.h (POSIX.1): Section 26.5 [Executing a File], page 752.

int execve (const char *filename, char *const argv[], char *const env[])
> unistd.h (POSIX.1): Section 26.5 [Executing a File], page 752.

int execvp (const char *filename, char *const argv[])
> unistd.h (POSIX.1): Section 26.5 [Executing a File], page 752.

int EXFULL

> errno.h (Linux???: Exchange full): Section 2.2 [Error Codes], page 23.

void _Exit (int status)
> stdlib.h (ISO): Section 25.7.5 [Termination Internals], page 747.

void _exit (int status)
> unistd.h (POSIX.1): Section 25.7.5 [Termination Internals], page 747.

void exit (int status)
> stdlib.h (ISO): Section 25.7.1 [Normal Termination], page 745.

int EXIT_FAILURE
> stdlib.h (ISO): Section 25.7.2 [Exit Status], page 745.

int EXIT_SUCCESS
> stdlib.h (ISO): Section 25.7.2 [Exit Status], page 745.

double exp (double x)
> math.h (ISO): Section 19.4 [Exponentiation and Logarithms], page 515.

double exp10 (double x)
> math.h (GNU): Section 19.4 [Exponentiation and Logarithms], page 515.

float exp10f (float x)
> math.h (GNU): Section 19.4 [Exponentiation and Logarithms], page 515.

long double exp10l (long double x)
> math.h (GNU): Section 19.4 [Exponentiation and Logarithms], page 515.

double exp2 (double x)
> math.h (ISO): Section 19.4 [Exponentiation and Logarithms], page 515.

float exp2f (float x)
> math.h (ISO): Section 19.4 [Exponentiation and Logarithms], page 515.

long double exp2l (long double x)
> math.h (ISO): Section 19.4 [Exponentiation and Logarithms], page 515.

float expf (float *x*)
> math.h (ISO): Section 19.4 [Exponentiation and Logarithms], page 515.

long double expl (long double *x*)
> math.h (ISO): Section 19.4 [Exponentiation and Logarithms], page 515.

double expm1 (double *x*)
> math.h (ISO): Section 19.4 [Exponentiation and Logarithms], page 515.

float expm1f (float *x*)
> math.h (ISO): Section 19.4 [Exponentiation and Logarithms], page 515.

long double expm1l (long double *x*)
> math.h (ISO): Section 19.4 [Exponentiation and Logarithms], page 515.

int EXPR_NEST_MAX
> limits.h (POSIX.2): Section 32.10 [Utility Program Capacity Limits], page 855.

double fabs (double *number*)
> math.h (ISO): Section 20.8.1 [Absolute Value], page 574.

float fabsf (float *number*)
> math.h (ISO): Section 20.8.1 [Absolute Value], page 574.

long double fabsl (long double *number*)
> math.h (ISO): Section 20.8.1 [Absolute Value], page 574.

size_t __fbufsize (FILE *\*stream*)
> stdio_ext.h (GNU): Section 12.20.3 [Controlling Which Kind of Buffering], page 311.

int fchdir (int *filedes*)
> unistd.h (XPG): Section 14.1 [Working Directory], page 377.

int fchmod (int *filedes*, mode_t *mode*)
> sys/stat.h (BSD): Section 14.9.7 [Assigning File Permissions], page 410.

int fchown (int *filedes*, uid_t *owner*, gid_t *group*)
> unistd.h (BSD): Section 14.9.4 [File Owner], page 406.

int fclose (FILE *\*stream*)
> stdio.h (ISO): Section 12.4 [Closing Streams], page 253.

int fcloseall (void)
> stdio.h (GNU): Section 12.4 [Closing Streams], page 253.

int fcntl (int *filedes*, int *command*, ...)
> fcntl.h (POSIX.1): Section 13.11 [Control Operations on Files], page 359.

char * fcvt (double *value*, int *ndigit*, int *\*decpt*, int *\*neg*)
> stdlib.h (SVID, Unix98): Section 20.12 [Old-fashioned System V number-to-string functions], page 591.

int fcvt_r (double *value*, int *ndigit*, int *\*decpt*, int *\*neg*, char *\*buf*, size_t *len*)
> stdlib.h (SVID, Unix98): Section 20.12 [Old-fashioned System V number-to-string functions], page 591.

int fdatasync (int *fildes*)
> unistd.h (POSIX): Section 13.9 [Synchronizing I/O operations], page 345.

int FD_CLOEXEC
> fcntl.h (POSIX.1): Section 13.13 [File Descriptor Flags], page 361.

void FD_CLR (int *filedes*, fd_set *\*set*)
> sys/types.h (BSD): Section 13.8 [Waiting for Input or Output], page 342.

double fdim (double *x*, double *y*)
> math.h (ISO): Section 20.8.7 [Miscellaneous FP arithmetic functions], page 582.

float fdimf (float *x*, float *y*)
>math.h (ISO): Section 20.8.7 [Miscellaneous FP arithmetic functions], page 582.

long double fdiml (long double *x*, long double *y*)
>math.h (ISO): Section 20.8.7 [Miscellaneous FP arithmetic functions], page 582.

int FD_ISSET (int *filedes*, const fd_set *\*set*)
>sys/types.h (BSD): Section 13.8 [Waiting for Input or Output], page 342.

FILE * fdopen (int *filedes*, const char *\*opentype*)
>stdio.h (POSIX.1): Section 13.4 [Descriptors and Streams], page 333.

DIR * fdopendir (int *fd*)
>dirent.h (GNU): Section 14.2.2 [Opening a Directory Stream], page 381.

void FD_SET (int *filedes*, fd_set *\*set*)
>sys/types.h (BSD): Section 13.8 [Waiting for Input or Output], page 342.

fd_set
>sys/types.h (BSD): Section 13.8 [Waiting for Input or Output], page 342.

int FD_SETSIZE
>sys/types.h (BSD): Section 13.8 [Waiting for Input or Output], page 342.

int F_DUPFD
>fcntl.h (POSIX.1): Section 13.12 [Duplicating Descriptors], page 360.

void FD_ZERO (fd_set *\*set*)
>sys/types.h (BSD): Section 13.8 [Waiting for Input or Output], page 342.

int feclearexcept (int *excepts*)
>fenv.h (ISO): Section 20.5.3 [Examining the FPU status word], page 567.

int fedisableexcept (int *excepts*)
>fenv.h (GNU): Section 20.7 [Floating-Point Control Functions], page 571.

FE_DIVBYZERO
>fenv.h (ISO): Section 20.5.3 [Examining the FPU status word], page 567.

FE_DOWNWARD
>fenv.h (ISO): Section 20.6 [Rounding Modes], page 570.

int feenableexcept (int *excepts*)
>fenv.h (GNU): Section 20.7 [Floating-Point Control Functions], page 571.

int fegetenv (fenv_t *\*envp*)
>fenv.h (ISO): Section 20.7 [Floating-Point Control Functions], page 571.

int fegetexcept (void)
>fenv.h (GNU): Section 20.7 [Floating-Point Control Functions], page 571.

int fegetexceptflag (fexcept_t *\*flagp*, int *excepts*)
>fenv.h (ISO): Section 20.5.3 [Examining the FPU status word], page 567.

int fegetround (void)
>fenv.h (ISO): Section 20.6 [Rounding Modes], page 570.

int feholdexcept (fenv_t *\*envp*)
>fenv.h (ISO): Section 20.7 [Floating-Point Control Functions], page 571.

FE_INEXACT
>fenv.h (ISO): Section 20.5.3 [Examining the FPU status word], page 567.

FE_INVALID
>fenv.h (ISO): Section 20.5.3 [Examining the FPU status word], page 567.

int feof (FILE *\*stream*)
>stdio.h (ISO): Section 12.15 [End-Of-File and Errors], page 302.

```
int feof_unlocked (FILE *stream)
```
        `stdio.h` (GNU): Section 12.15 [End-Of-File and Errors], page 302.

```
FE_OVERFLOW
```
        `fenv.h` (ISO): Section 20.5.3 [Examining the FPU status word], page 567.

```
int feraiseexcept (int excepts)
```
        `fenv.h` (ISO): Section 20.5.3 [Examining the FPU status word], page 567.

```
int ferror (FILE *stream)
```
        `stdio.h` (ISO): Section 12.15 [End-Of-File and Errors], page 302.

```
int ferror_unlocked (FILE *stream)
```
        `stdio.h` (GNU): Section 12.15 [End-Of-File and Errors], page 302.

```
int fesetenv (const fenv_t *envp)
```
        `fenv.h` (ISO): Section 20.7 [Floating-Point Control Functions], page 571.

```
int fesetexceptflag (const fexcept_t *flagp, int excepts)
```
        `fenv.h` (ISO): Section 20.5.3 [Examining the FPU status word], page 567.

```
int fesetround (int round)
```
        `fenv.h` (ISO): Section 20.6 [Rounding Modes], page 570.

```
int fetestexcept (int excepts)
```
        `fenv.h` (ISO): Section 20.5.3 [Examining the FPU status word], page 567.

```
FE_TONEAREST
```
        `fenv.h` (ISO): Section 20.6 [Rounding Modes], page 570.

```
FE_TOWARDZERO
```
        `fenv.h` (ISO): Section 20.6 [Rounding Modes], page 570.

```
FE_UNDERFLOW
```
        `fenv.h` (ISO): Section 20.5.3 [Examining the FPU status word], page 567.

```
int feupdateenv (const fenv_t *envp)
```
        `fenv.h` (ISO): Section 20.7 [Floating-Point Control Functions], page 571.

```
FE_UPWARD
```
        `fenv.h` (ISO): Section 20.6 [Rounding Modes], page 570.

```
int fflush (FILE *stream)
```
        `stdio.h` (ISO): Section 12.20.2 [Flushing Buffers], page 310.

```
int fflush_unlocked (FILE *stream)
```
        `stdio.h` (POSIX): Section 12.20.2 [Flushing Buffers], page 310.

```
int fgetc (FILE *stream)
```
        `stdio.h` (ISO): Section 12.8 [Character Input], page 262.

```
int fgetc_unlocked (FILE *stream)
```
        `stdio.h` (POSIX): Section 12.8 [Character Input], page 262.

```
int F_GETFD
```
        `fcntl.h` (POSIX.1): Section 13.13 [File Descriptor Flags], page 361.

```
int F_GETFL
```
        `fcntl.h` (POSIX.1): Section 13.14.4 [Getting and Setting File Status Flags], page 367.

```
struct group * fgetgrent (FILE *stream)
```
        `grp.h` (SVID): Section 30.14.3 [Scanning the List of All Groups], page 815.

```
int fgetgrent_r (FILE *stream, struct group *result_buf, char *buffer, size_t buflen, struct
group **result)
```
        `grp.h` (GNU): Section 30.14.3 [Scanning the List of All Groups], page 815.

int F_GETLK
> fcntl.h (POSIX.1): Section 13.15 [File Locks], page 368.

int F_GETOWN
> fcntl.h (BSD): Section 13.18 [Interrupt-Driven Input], page 375.

int fgetpos (FILE *stream, fpos_t *position)
> stdio.h (ISO): Section 12.19 [Portable File-Position Functions], page 307.

int fgetpos64 (FILE *stream, fpos64_t *position)
> stdio.h (Unix98): Section 12.19 [Portable File-Position Functions], page 307.

struct passwd * fgetpwent (FILE *stream)
> pwd.h (SVID): Section 30.13.3 [Scanning the List of All Users], page 812.

int fgetpwent_r (FILE *stream, struct passwd *result_buf, char *buffer, size_t buflen, struct passwd **result)
> pwd.h (GNU): Section 30.13.3 [Scanning the List of All Users], page 812.

char * fgets (char *s, int count, FILE *stream)
> stdio.h (ISO): Section 12.9 [Line-Oriented Input], page 264.

char * fgets_unlocked (char *s, int count, FILE *stream)
> stdio.h (GNU): Section 12.9 [Line-Oriented Input], page 264.

wint_t fgetwc (FILE *stream)
> wchar.h (ISO): Section 12.8 [Character Input], page 262.

wint_t fgetwc_unlocked (FILE *stream)
> wchar.h (GNU): Section 12.8 [Character Input], page 262.

wchar_t * fgetws (wchar_t *ws, int count, FILE *stream)
> wchar.h (ISO): Section 12.9 [Line-Oriented Input], page 264.

wchar_t * fgetws_unlocked (wchar_t *ws, int count, FILE *stream)
> wchar.h (GNU): Section 12.9 [Line-Oriented Input], page 264.

FILE
> stdio.h (ISO): Section 12.1 [Streams], page 248.

int FILENAME_MAX
> stdio.h (ISO): Section 32.6 [Limits on File System Capacity], page 850.

int fileno (FILE *stream)
> stdio.h (POSIX.1): Section 13.4 [Descriptors and Streams], page 333.

int fileno_unlocked (FILE *stream)
> stdio.h (GNU): Section 13.4 [Descriptors and Streams], page 333.

int finite (double x)
> math.h (BSD): Section 20.4 [Floating-Point Number Classification Functions], page 563.

int finitef (float x)
> math.h (BSD): Section 20.4 [Floating-Point Number Classification Functions], page 563.

int finitel (long double x)
> math.h (BSD): Section 20.4 [Floating-Point Number Classification Functions], page 563.

int __flbf (FILE *stream)
> stdio_ext.h (GNU): Section 12.20.3 [Controlling Which Kind of Buffering], page 311.

void flockfile (FILE *stream)
> stdio.h (POSIX): Section 12.5 [Streams and Threads], page 254.

double floor (double x)
> math.h (ISO): Section 20.8.3 [Rounding Functions], page 576.

float floorf (float x)
> math.h (ISO): Section 20.8.3 [Rounding Functions], page 576.

`long double floorl (long double x)`
>        math.h (ISO): Section 20.8.3 [Rounding Functions], page 576.

`FLT_DIG`
>        float.h (ISO): Section A.5.3.2 [Floating Point Parameters], page 888.

`FLT_EPSILON`
>        float.h (ISO): Section A.5.3.2 [Floating Point Parameters], page 888.

`FLT_MANT_DIG`
>        float.h (ISO): Section A.5.3.2 [Floating Point Parameters], page 888.

`FLT_MAX`
>        float.h (ISO): Section A.5.3.2 [Floating Point Parameters], page 888.

`FLT_MAX_10_EXP`
>        float.h (ISO): Section A.5.3.2 [Floating Point Parameters], page 888.

`FLT_MAX_EXP`
>        float.h (ISO): Section A.5.3.2 [Floating Point Parameters], page 888.

`FLT_MIN`
>        float.h (ISO): Section A.5.3.2 [Floating Point Parameters], page 888.

`FLT_MIN_10_EXP`
>        float.h (ISO): Section A.5.3.2 [Floating Point Parameters], page 888.

`FLT_MIN_EXP`
>        float.h (ISO): Section A.5.3.2 [Floating Point Parameters], page 888.

`FLT_RADIX`
>        float.h (ISO): Section A.5.3.2 [Floating Point Parameters], page 888.

`FLT_ROUNDS`
>        float.h (ISO): Section A.5.3.2 [Floating Point Parameters], page 888.

`void _flushlbf (void)`
>        stdio_ext.h (GNU): Section 12.20.2 [Flushing Buffers], page 310.

`tcflag_t FLUSHO`
>        termios.h (BSD): Section 17.4.7 [Local Modes], page 486.

`double fma (double x, double y, double z)`
>        math.h (ISO): Section 20.8.7 [Miscellaneous FP arithmetic functions], page 582.

`float fmaf (float x, float y, float z)`
>        math.h (ISO): Section 20.8.7 [Miscellaneous FP arithmetic functions], page 582.

`long double fmal (long double x, long double y, long double z)`
>        math.h (ISO): Section 20.8.7 [Miscellaneous FP arithmetic functions], page 582.

`double fmax (double x, double y)`
>        math.h (ISO): Section 20.8.7 [Miscellaneous FP arithmetic functions], page 582.

`float fmaxf (float x, float y)`
>        math.h (ISO): Section 20.8.7 [Miscellaneous FP arithmetic functions], page 582.

`long double fmaxl (long double x, long double y)`
>        math.h (ISO): Section 20.8.7 [Miscellaneous FP arithmetic functions], page 582.

`FILE * fmemopen (void *buf, size_t size, const char *opentype)`
>        stdio.h (GNU): Section 12.21.1 [String Streams], page 314.

`double fmin (double x, double y)`
>        math.h (ISO): Section 20.8.7 [Miscellaneous FP arithmetic functions], page 582.

`float fminf (float x, float y)`
>        math.h (ISO): Section 20.8.7 [Miscellaneous FP arithmetic functions], page 582.

long double fminl (long double *x*, long double *y*)
>math.h (ISO): Section 20.8.7 [Miscellaneous FP arithmetic functions], page 582.

double fmod (double *numerator*, double *denominator*)
>math.h (ISO): Section 20.8.4 [Remainder Functions], page 578.

float fmodf (float *numerator*, float *denominator*)
>math.h (ISO): Section 20.8.4 [Remainder Functions], page 578.

long double fmodl (long double *numerator*, long double *denominator*)
>math.h (ISO): Section 20.8.4 [Remainder Functions], page 578.

int fmtmsg (long int *classification*, const char *\*label*, int *severity*, const char *\*text*, const char *\*action*, const char *\*tag*)
>fmtmsg.h (XPG): Section 12.22.1 [Printing Formatted Messages], page 318.

int fnmatch (const char *\*pattern*, const char *\*string*, int *flags*)
>fnmatch.h (POSIX.2): Section 10.1 [Wildcard Matching], page 222.

FNM_CASEFOLD
>fnmatch.h (GNU): Section 10.1 [Wildcard Matching], page 222.

FNM_EXTMATCH
>fnmatch.h (GNU): Section 10.1 [Wildcard Matching], page 222.

FNM_FILE_NAME
>fnmatch.h (GNU): Section 10.1 [Wildcard Matching], page 222.

FNM_LEADING_DIR
>fnmatch.h (GNU): Section 10.1 [Wildcard Matching], page 222.

FNM_NOESCAPE
>fnmatch.h (POSIX.2): Section 10.1 [Wildcard Matching], page 222.

FNM_PATHNAME
>fnmatch.h (POSIX.2): Section 10.1 [Wildcard Matching], page 222.

FNM_PERIOD
>fnmatch.h (POSIX.2): Section 10.1 [Wildcard Matching], page 222.

int F_OFD_SETLK
>fcntl.h (POSIX.1): Section 13.16 [Open File Description Locks], page 371.

int F_OFD_SETLKW
>fcntl.h (POSIX.1): Section 13.16 [Open File Description Locks], page 371.

int F_OK
>unistd.h (POSIX.1): Section 14.9.8 [Testing Permission to Access a File], page 412.

FILE * fopen (const char *\*filename*, const char *\*opentype*)
>stdio.h (ISO): Section 12.3 [Opening Streams], page 249.

FILE * fopen64 (const char *\*filename*, const char *\*opentype*)
>stdio.h (Unix98): Section 12.3 [Opening Streams], page 249.

FILE * fopencookie (void *\*cookie*, const char *\*opentype*, cookie_io_functions_t *io-functions*)
>stdio.h (GNU): Section 12.21.2.1 [Custom Streams and Cookies], page 316.

int FOPEN_MAX
>stdio.h (ISO): Section 12.3 [Opening Streams], page 249.

pid_t fork (void)
>unistd.h (POSIX.1): Section 26.4 [Creating a Process], page 751.

int forkpty (int *\*amaster*, char *\*name*, const struct termios *\*termp*, const struct winsize *\*winp*)
>pty.h (BSD): Section 17.8.2 [Opening a Pseudo-Terminal Pair], page 502.

long int fpathconf (int *filedes*, int *parameter*)
>unistd.h (POSIX.1): Section 32.9 [Using pathconf], page 853.

int fpclassify (*float-type x*)
> math.h (ISO): Section 20.4 [Floating-Point Number Classification Functions], page 563.

FPE_DECOVF_TRAP
> signal.h (BSD): Section 24.2.1 [Program Error Signals], page 663.

FPE_FLTDIV_FAULT
> signal.h (BSD): Section 24.2.1 [Program Error Signals], page 663.

FPE_FLTDIV_TRAP
> signal.h (BSD): Section 24.2.1 [Program Error Signals], page 663.

FPE_FLTOVF_FAULT
> signal.h (BSD): Section 24.2.1 [Program Error Signals], page 663.

FPE_FLTOVF_TRAP
> signal.h (BSD): Section 24.2.1 [Program Error Signals], page 663.

FPE_FLTUND_FAULT
> signal.h (BSD): Section 24.2.1 [Program Error Signals], page 663.

FPE_FLTUND_TRAP
> signal.h (BSD): Section 24.2.1 [Program Error Signals], page 663.

FPE_INTDIV_TRAP
> signal.h (BSD): Section 24.2.1 [Program Error Signals], page 663.

FPE_INTOVF_TRAP
> signal.h (BSD): Section 24.2.1 [Program Error Signals], page 663.

size_t __fpending (FILE *stream*)
> stdio_ext.h (GNU): Section 12.20.3 [Controlling Which Kind of Buffering], page 311.

FPE_SUBRNG_TRAP
> signal.h (BSD): Section 24.2.1 [Program Error Signals], page 663.

int FP_ILOGB0
> math.h (ISO): Section 19.4 [Exponentiation and Logarithms], page 515.

int FP_ILOGBNAN
> math.h (ISO): Section 19.4 [Exponentiation and Logarithms], page 515.

fpos64_t
> stdio.h (Unix98): Section 12.19 [Portable File-Position Functions], page 307.

fpos_t
> stdio.h (ISO): Section 12.19 [Portable File-Position Functions], page 307.

int fprintf (FILE *stream*, const char *template*, ...)
> stdio.h (ISO): Section 12.12.7 [Formatted Output Functions], page 278.

void __fpurge (FILE *stream*)
> stdio_ext.h (GNU): Section 12.20.2 [Flushing Buffers], page 310.

int fputc (int *c*, FILE *stream*)
> stdio.h (ISO): Section 12.7 [Simple Output by Characters or Lines], page 259.

int fputc_unlocked (int *c*, FILE *stream*)
> stdio.h (POSIX): Section 12.7 [Simple Output by Characters or Lines], page 259.

int fputs (const char *s*, FILE *stream*)
> stdio.h (ISO): Section 12.7 [Simple Output by Characters or Lines], page 259.

int fputs_unlocked (const char *s*, FILE *stream*)
> stdio.h (GNU): Section 12.7 [Simple Output by Characters or Lines], page 259.

wint_t fputwc (wchar_t *wc*, FILE *stream*)
> wchar.h (ISO): Section 12.7 [Simple Output by Characters or Lines], page 259.

wint_t fputwc_unlocked (wchar_t *wc*, FILE **stream*)
>       wchar.h (POSIX): Section 12.7 [Simple Output by Characters or Lines], page 259.

int fputws (const wchar_t **ws*, FILE **stream*)
>       wchar.h (ISO): Section 12.7 [Simple Output by Characters or Lines], page 259.

int fputws_unlocked (const wchar_t **ws*, FILE **stream*)
>       wchar.h (GNU): Section 12.7 [Simple Output by Characters or Lines], page 259.

F_RDLCK
>       fcntl.h (POSIX.1): Section 13.15 [File Locks], page 368.

size_t fread (void **data*, size_t *size*, size_t *count*, FILE **stream*)
>       stdio.h (ISO): Section 12.11 [Block Input/Output], page 268.

int __freadable (FILE **stream*)
>       stdio_ext.h (GNU): Section 12.3 [Opening Streams], page 249.

int __freading (FILE **stream*)
>       stdio_ext.h (GNU): Section 12.3 [Opening Streams], page 249.

size_t fread_unlocked (void **data*, size_t *size*, size_t *count*, FILE **stream*)
>       stdio.h (GNU): Section 12.11 [Block Input/Output], page 268.

void free (void **ptr*)
>       malloc.h, stdlib.h (ISO): Section 3.2.2.3 [Freeing Memory Allocated with malloc], page 43.

__free_hook
>       malloc.h (GNU): Section 3.2.2.10 [Memory Allocation Hooks], page 50.

FILE * freopen (const char **filename*, const char **opentype*, FILE **stream*)
>       stdio.h (ISO): Section 12.3 [Opening Streams], page 249.

FILE * freopen64 (const char **filename*, const char **opentype*, FILE **stream*)
>       stdio.h (Unix98): Section 12.3 [Opening Streams], page 249.

double frexp (double *value*, int **exponent*)
>       math.h (ISO): Section 20.8.2 [Normalization Functions], page 574.

float frexpf (float *value*, int **exponent*)
>       math.h (ISO): Section 20.8.2 [Normalization Functions], page 574.

long double frexpl (long double *value*, int **exponent*)
>       math.h (ISO): Section 20.8.2 [Normalization Functions], page 574.

int fscanf (FILE **stream*, const char **template*, ...)
>       stdio.h (ISO): Section 12.14.8 [Formatted Input Functions], page 300.

int fseek (FILE **stream*, long int *offset*, int *whence*)
>       stdio.h (ISO): Section 12.18 [File Positioning], page 305.

int fseeko (FILE **stream*, off_t *offset*, int *whence*)
>       stdio.h (Unix98): Section 12.18 [File Positioning], page 305.

int fseeko64 (FILE **stream*, off64_t *offset*, int *whence*)
>       stdio.h (Unix98): Section 12.18 [File Positioning], page 305.

int F_SETFD
>       fcntl.h (POSIX.1): Section 13.13 [File Descriptor Flags], page 361.

int F_SETFL
>       fcntl.h (POSIX.1): Section 13.14.4 [Getting and Setting File Status Flags], page 367.

int F_SETLK
>       fcntl.h (POSIX.1): Section 13.15 [File Locks], page 368.

int F_SETLKW
>       fcntl.h (POSIX.1): Section 13.15 [File Locks], page 368.

```
int __fsetlocking (FILE *stream, int type)
          stdio_ext.h (GNU): Section 12.5 [Streams and Threads], page 254.

int F_SETOWN
          fcntl.h (BSD): Section 13.18 [Interrupt-Driven Input], page 375.

int fsetpos (FILE *stream, const fpos_t *position)
          stdio.h (ISO): Section 12.19 [Portable File-Position Functions], page 307.

int fsetpos64 (FILE *stream, const fpos64_t *position)
          stdio.h (Unix98): Section 12.19 [Portable File-Position Functions], page 307.

int fstat (int filedes, struct stat *buf)
          sys/stat.h (POSIX.1): Section 14.9.2 [Reading the Attributes of a File], page 403.

int fstat64 (int filedes, struct stat64 *buf)
          sys/stat.h (Unix98): Section 14.9.2 [Reading the Attributes of a File], page 403.

int fsync (int fildes)
          unistd.h (POSIX): Section 13.9 [Synchronizing I/O operations], page 345.

long int ftell (FILE *stream)
          stdio.h (ISO): Section 12.18 [File Positioning], page 305.

off_t ftello (FILE *stream)
          stdio.h (Unix98): Section 12.18 [File Positioning], page 305.

off64_t ftello64 (FILE *stream)
          stdio.h (Unix98): Section 12.18 [File Positioning], page 305.

int ftruncate (int fd, off_t length)
          unistd.h (POSIX): Section 14.9.10 [File Size], page 415.

int ftruncate64 (int id, off64_t length)
          unistd.h (Unix98): Section 14.9.10 [File Size], page 415.

int ftrylockfile (FILE *stream)
          stdio.h (POSIX): Section 12.5 [Streams and Threads], page 254.

int ftw (const char *filename, __ftw_func_t func, int descriptors)
          ftw.h (SVID): Section 14.3 [Working with Directory Trees], page 388.

int ftw64 (const char *filename, __ftw64_func_t func, int descriptors)
          ftw.h (Unix98): Section 14.3 [Working with Directory Trees], page 388.

__ftw64_func_t
          ftw.h (GNU): Section 14.3 [Working with Directory Trees], page 388.

__ftw_func_t
          ftw.h (GNU): Section 14.3 [Working with Directory Trees], page 388.

F_UNLCK
          fcntl.h (POSIX.1): Section 13.15 [File Locks], page 368.

void funlockfile (FILE *stream)
          stdio.h (POSIX): Section 12.5 [Streams and Threads], page 254.

int futimes (int fd, const struct timeval tvp[2])
          sys/time.h (BSD): Section 14.9.9 [File Times], page 413.

int fwide (FILE *stream, int mode)
          wchar.h (ISO): Section 12.6 [Streams in Internationalized Applications], page 257.

int fwprintf (FILE *stream, const wchar_t *template, ...)
          wchar.h (ISO): Section 12.12.7 [Formatted Output Functions], page 278.

int __fwritable (FILE *stream)
          stdio_ext.h (GNU): Section 12.3 [Opening Streams], page 249.
```

size_t fwrite (const void *data, size_t size, size_t count, FILE *stream)
>        stdio.h (ISO): Section 12.11 [Block Input/Output], page 268.

size_t fwrite_unlocked (const void *data, size_t size, size_t count, FILE *stream)
>        stdio.h (GNU): Section 12.11 [Block Input/Output], page 268.

int __fwriting (FILE *stream)
>        stdio_ext.h (GNU): Section 12.3 [Opening Streams], page 249.

F_WRLCK
>        fcntl.h (POSIX.1): Section 13.15 [File Locks], page 368.

int fwscanf (FILE *stream, const wchar_t *template, ...)
>        wchar.h (ISO): Section 12.14.8 [Formatted Input Functions], page 300.

double gamma (double x)
>        math.h (SVID): Section 19.6 [Special Functions], page 522.

float gammaf (float x)
>        math.h (SVID): Section 19.6 [Special Functions], page 522.

long double gammal (long double x)
>        math.h (SVID): Section 19.6 [Special Functions], page 522.

void (*__gconv_end_fct) (struct gconv_step *)
>        gconv.h (GNU): Section 6.5.4 [The iconv Implementation in the GNU C Library], page 155.

int (*__gconv_fct) (struct __gconv_step *, struct __gconv_step_data *, const char **, const char *, size_t *, int)
>        gconv.h (GNU): Section 6.5.4 [The iconv Implementation in the GNU C Library], page 155.

int (*__gconv_init_fct) (struct __gconv_step *)
>        gconv.h (GNU): Section 6.5.4 [The iconv Implementation in the GNU C Library], page 155.

char * gcvt (double value, int ndigit, char *buf)
>        stdlib.h (SVID, Unix98): Section 20.12 [Old-fashioned System V number-to-string functions], page 591.

unsigned long int getauxval (unsigned long int type)
>        sys/auxv.h (sys/auxv.h): Section 25.5 [Auxiliary Vector], page 742.

long int get_avphys_pages (void)
>        sys/sysinfo.h (GNU): Section 22.4.2 [How to get information about the memory subsystem?], page 648.

int getc (FILE *stream)
>        stdio.h (ISO): Section 12.8 [Character Input], page 262.

int getchar (void)
>        stdio.h (ISO): Section 12.8 [Character Input], page 262.

int getchar_unlocked (void)
>        stdio.h (POSIX): Section 12.8 [Character Input], page 262.

int getcontext (ucontext_t *ucp)
>        ucontext.h (SVID): Section 23.4 [Complete Context Control], page 655.

int getc_unlocked (FILE *stream)
>        stdio.h (POSIX): Section 12.8 [Character Input], page 262.

char * get_current_dir_name (void)
>        unistd.h (GNU): Section 14.1 [Working Directory], page 377.

char * getcwd (char *buffer, size_t size)
>        unistd.h (POSIX.1): Section 14.1 [Working Directory], page 377.

struct tm * getdate (const char *string)
>        time.h (Unix98): Section 21.4.6.2 [A More User-friendly Way to Parse Times and Dates], page 619.

getdate_err
>	time.h (Unix98): Section 21.4.6.2 [A More User-friendly Way to Parse Times and Dates], page 619.

int getdate_r (const char *string, struct tm *tp)
>	time.h (GNU): Section 21.4.6.2 [A More User-friendly Way to Parse Times and Dates], page 619.

ssize_t getdelim (char **lineptr, size_t *n, int delimiter, FILE *stream)
>	stdio.h (GNU): Section 12.9 [Line-Oriented Input], page 264.

int getdomainnname (char *name, size_t length)
>	unistd.h (???): Section 31.1 [Host Identification], page 821.

gid_t getegid (void)
>	unistd.h (POSIX.1): Section 30.5 [Reading the Persona of a Process], page 793.

char * getenv (const char *name)
>	stdlib.h (ISO): Section 25.4.1 [Environment Access], page 738.

uid_t geteuid (void)
>	unistd.h (POSIX.1): Section 30.5 [Reading the Persona of a Process], page 793.

struct fstab * getfsent (void)
>	fstab.h (BSD): Section 31.3.1.1 [The fstab file], page 825.

struct fstab * getfsfile (const char *name)
>	fstab.h (BSD): Section 31.3.1.1 [The fstab file], page 825.

struct fstab * getfsspec (const char *name)
>	fstab.h (BSD): Section 31.3.1.1 [The fstab file], page 825.

gid_t getgid (void)
>	unistd.h (POSIX.1): Section 30.5 [Reading the Persona of a Process], page 793.

struct group * getgrent (void)
>	grp.h (SVID, BSD): Section 30.14.3 [Scanning the List of All Groups], page 815.

int getgrent_r (struct group *result_buf, char *buffer, size_t buflen, struct group **result)
>	grp.h (GNU): Section 30.14.3 [Scanning the List of All Groups], page 815.

struct group * getgrgid (gid_t gid)
>	grp.h (POSIX.1): Section 30.14.2 [Looking Up One Group], page 814.

int getgrgid_r (gid_t gid, struct group *result_buf, char *buffer, size_t buflen, struct group **result)
>	grp.h (POSIX.1c): Section 30.14.2 [Looking Up One Group], page 814.

struct group * getgrnam (const char *name)
>	grp.h (SVID, BSD): Section 30.14.2 [Looking Up One Group], page 814.

int getgrnam_r (const char *name, struct group *result_buf, char *buffer, size_t buflen, struct group **result)
>	grp.h (POSIX.1c): Section 30.14.2 [Looking Up One Group], page 814.

int getgrouplist (const char *user, gid_t group, gid_t *groups, int *ngroups)
>	grp.h (BSD): Section 30.7 [Setting the Group IDs], page 795.

int getgroups (int count, gid_t *groups)
>	unistd.h (POSIX.1): Section 30.5 [Reading the Persona of a Process], page 793.

struct hostent * gethostbyaddr (const void *addr, socklen_t length, int format)
>	netdb.h (BSD): Section 16.6.2.4 [Host Names], page 443.

int gethostbyaddr_r (const void *addr, socklen_t length, int format, struct hostent *restrict result_buf, char *restrict buf, size_t buflen, struct hostent **restrict result, int *restrict h_errnop)
>	netdb.h (GNU): Section 16.6.2.4 [Host Names], page 443.

`struct hostent * gethostbyname (const char *name)`
>    `netdb.h` (BSD): Section 16.6.2.4 [Host Names], page 443.

`struct hostent * gethostbyname2 (const char *name, int af)`
>    `netdb.h` (IPv6 Basic API): Section 16.6.2.4 [Host Names], page 443.

`int gethostbyname2_r (const char *name, int af, struct hostent *restrict result_buf, char *restrict buf, size_t buflen, struct hostent **restrict result, int *restrict h_errnop)`
>    `netdb.h` (GNU): Section 16.6.2.4 [Host Names], page 443.

`int gethostbyname_r (const char *restrict name, struct hostent *restrict result_buf, char *restrict buf, size_t buflen, struct hostent **restrict result, int *restrict h_errnop)`
>    `netdb.h` (GNU): Section 16.6.2.4 [Host Names], page 443.

`struct hostent * gethostent (void)`
>    `netdb.h` (BSD): Section 16.6.2.4 [Host Names], page 443.

`long int gethostid (void)`
>    `unistd.h` (BSD): Section 31.1 [Host Identification], page 821.

`int gethostname (char *name, size_t size)`
>    `unistd.h` (BSD): Section 31.1 [Host Identification], page 821.

`int getitimer (int which, struct itimerval *old)`
>    `sys/time.h` (BSD): Section 21.5 [Setting an Alarm], page 625.

`ssize_t getline (char **lineptr, size_t *n, FILE *stream)`
>    `stdio.h` (GNU): Section 12.9 [Line-Oriented Input], page 264.

`int getloadavg (double loadavg[], int nelem)`
>    `stdlib.h` (BSD): Section 22.5 [Learn about the processors available], page 650.

`char * getlogin (void)`
>    `unistd.h` (POSIX.1): Section 30.11 [Identifying Who Logged In], page 801.

`struct mntent * getmntent (FILE *stream)`
>    `mntent.h` (BSD): Section 31.3.1.2 [The `mtab` file], page 828.

`struct mntent * getmntent_r (FILE *stream, struct mntent *result, char *buffer, int bufsize)`
>    `mntent.h` (BSD): Section 31.3.1.2 [The `mtab` file], page 828.

`struct netent * getnetbyaddr (uint32_t net, int type)`
>    `netdb.h` (BSD): Section 16.13 [Networks Database], page 475.

`struct netent * getnetbyname (const char *name)`
>    `netdb.h` (BSD): Section 16.13 [Networks Database], page 475.

`struct netent * getnetent (void)`
>    `netdb.h` (BSD): Section 16.13 [Networks Database], page 475.

`int getnetgrent (char **hostp, char **userp, char **domainp)`
>    `netdb.h` (BSD): Section 30.16.2 [Looking up one Netgroup], page 818.

`int getnetgrent_r (char **hostp, char **userp, char **domainp, char *buffer, size_t buflen)`
>    `netdb.h` (GNU): Section 30.16.2 [Looking up one Netgroup], page 818.

`int get_nprocs (void)`
>    `sys/sysinfo.h` (GNU): Section 22.5 [Learn about the processors available], page 650.

`int get_nprocs_conf (void)`
>    `sys/sysinfo.h` (GNU): Section 22.5 [Learn about the processors available], page 650.

`int getopt (int argc, char *const *argv, const char *options)`
>    `unistd.h` (POSIX.2): Section 25.2.1 [Using the `getopt` function], page 707.

`int getopt_long (int argc, char *const *argv, const char *shortopts, const struct option *longopts, int *indexptr)`
>    `getopt.h` (GNU): Section 25.2.3 [Parsing Long Options with `getopt_long`], page 710.

int getopt_long_only (int argc, char *const *argv, const char *shortopts, const struct option *longopts, int *indexptr)
> getopt.h (GNU): Section 25.2.3 [Parsing Long Options with getopt_long], page 710.

int getpagesize (void)
> unistd.h (BSD): Section 22.4.2 [How to get information about the memory subsystem?], page 648.

char * getpass (const char *prompt)
> unistd.h (BSD): Section 33.2 [Reading Passwords], page 860.

int getpeername (int socket, struct sockaddr *addr, socklen_t *length-ptr)
> sys/socket.h (BSD): Section 16.9.4 [Who is Connected to Me?], page 459.

int getpgid (pid_t pid)
> unistd.h (POSIX.1): Section 28.7.2 [Process Group Functions], page 778.

pid_t getpgrp (void)
> unistd.h (POSIX.1): Section 28.7.2 [Process Group Functions], page 778.

long int get_phys_pages (void)
> sys/sysinfo.h (GNU): Section 22.4.2 [How to get information about the memory subsystem?], page 648.

pid_t getpid (void)
> unistd.h (POSIX.1): Section 26.3 [Process Identification], page 750.

pid_t getppid (void)
> unistd.h (POSIX.1): Section 26.3 [Process Identification], page 750.

int getpriority (int class, int id)
> sys/resource.h (BSD,POSIX): Section 22.3.4.2 [Functions For Traditional Scheduling], page 644.

struct protoent * getprotobyname (const char *name)
> netdb.h (BSD): Section 16.6.6 [Protocols Database], page 450.

struct protoent * getprotobynumber (int protocol)
> netdb.h (BSD): Section 16.6.6 [Protocols Database], page 450.

struct protoent * getprotoent (void)
> netdb.h (BSD): Section 16.6.6 [Protocols Database], page 450.

int getpt (void)
> stdlib.h (GNU): Section 17.8.1 [Allocating Pseudo-Terminals], page 500.

struct passwd * getpwent (void)
> pwd.h (POSIX.1): Section 30.13.3 [Scanning the List of All Users], page 812.

int getpwent_r (struct passwd *result_buf, char *buffer, size_t buflen, struct passwd **result)
> pwd.h (GNU): Section 30.13.3 [Scanning the List of All Users], page 812.

struct passwd * getpwnam (const char *name)
> pwd.h (POSIX.1): Section 30.13.2 [Looking Up One User], page 811.

int getpwnam_r (const char *name, struct passwd *result_buf, char *buffer, size_t buflen, struct passwd **result)
> pwd.h (POSIX.1c): Section 30.13.2 [Looking Up One User], page 811.

struct passwd * getpwuid (uid_t uid)
> pwd.h (POSIX.1): Section 30.13.2 [Looking Up One User], page 811.

int getpwuid_r (uid_t uid, struct passwd *result_buf, char *buffer, size_t buflen, struct passwd **result)
> pwd.h (POSIX.1c): Section 30.13.2 [Looking Up One User], page 811.

int getrlimit (int resource, struct rlimit *rlp)
> sys/resource.h (BSD): Section 22.2 [Limiting Resource Usage], page 632.

int getrlimit64 (int *resource*, struct rlimit64 *rlp*)
        sys/resource.h (Unix98): Section 22.2 [Limiting Resource Usage], page 632.

int getrusage (int *processes*, struct rusage *rusage*)
        sys/resource.h (BSD): Section 22.1 [Resource Usage], page 630.

char * gets (char *s*)
        stdio.h (ISO): Section 12.9 [Line-Oriented Input], page 264.

struct servent * getservbyname (const char *name*, const char *proto*)
        netdb.h (BSD): Section 16.6.4 [The Services Database], page 448.

struct servent * getservbyport (int *port*, const char *proto*)
        netdb.h (BSD): Section 16.6.4 [The Services Database], page 448.

struct servent * getservent (void)
        netdb.h (BSD): Section 16.6.4 [The Services Database], page 448.

pid_t getsid (pid_t *pid*)
        unistd.h (SVID): Section 28.7.2 [Process Group Functions], page 778.

int getsockname (int *socket*, struct sockaddr *addr*, socklen_t *length-ptr*)
        sys/socket.h (BSD): Section 16.3.3 [Reading the Address of a Socket], page 433.

int getsockopt (int *socket*, int *level*, int *optname*, void *optval*, socklen_t *optlen-ptr*)
        sys/socket.h (BSD): Section 16.12.1 [Socket Option Functions], page 472.

int getsubopt (char **optionp*, char *const *tokens*, char **valuep*)
        stdlib.h (stdlib.h): Section 25.3.12.1 [Parsing of Suboptions], page 736.

char * gettext (const char *msgid*)
        libintl.h (GNU): Section 8.2.1.1 [What has to be done to translate a message?], page 198.

int gettimeofday (struct timeval *tp*, struct timezone *tzp*)
        sys/time.h (BSD): Section 21.4.2 [High-Resolution Calendar], page 600.

uid_t getuid (void)
        unistd.h (POSIX.1): Section 30.5 [Reading the Persona of a Process], page 793.

mode_t getumask (void)
        sys/stat.h (GNU): Section 14.9.7 [Assigning File Permissions], page 410.

struct utmp * getutent (void)
        utmp.h (SVID): Section 30.12.1 [Manipulating the User Accounting Database], page 802.

int getutent_r (struct utmp *buffer*, struct utmp **result*)
        utmp.h (GNU): Section 30.12.1 [Manipulating the User Accounting Database], page 802.

struct utmp * getutid (const struct utmp *id*)
        utmp.h (SVID): Section 30.12.1 [Manipulating the User Accounting Database], page 802.

int getutid_r (const struct utmp *id*, struct utmp *buffer*, struct utmp **result*)
        utmp.h (GNU): Section 30.12.1 [Manipulating the User Accounting Database], page 802.

struct utmp * getutline (const struct utmp *line*)
        utmp.h (SVID): Section 30.12.1 [Manipulating the User Accounting Database], page 802.

int getutline_r (const struct utmp *line*, struct utmp *buffer*, struct utmp **result*)
        utmp.h (GNU): Section 30.12.1 [Manipulating the User Accounting Database], page 802.

int getutmp (const struct utmpx *utmpx*, struct utmp *utmp*)
        utmp.h (GNU): Section 30.12.2 [XPG User Accounting Database Functions], page 807.

int getutmpx (const struct utmp *utmp*, struct utmpx *utmpx*)
        utmp.h (GNU): Section 30.12.2 [XPG User Accounting Database Functions], page 807.

struct utmpx * getutxent (void)
        utmpx.h (XPG4.2): Section 30.12.2 [XPG User Accounting Database Functions], page 807.

struct utmpx * getutxid (const struct utmpx *id)
>       utmpx.h (XPG4.2): Section 30.12.2 [XPG User Accounting Database Functions], page 807.

struct utmpx * getutxline (const struct utmpx *line)
>       utmpx.h (XPG4.2): Section 30.12.2 [XPG User Accounting Database Functions], page 807.

int getw (FILE *stream)
>       stdio.h (SVID): Section 12.8 [Character Input], page 262.

wint_t getwc (FILE *stream)
>       wchar.h (ISO): Section 12.8 [Character Input], page 262.

wint_t getwchar (void)
>       wchar.h (ISO): Section 12.8 [Character Input], page 262.

wint_t getwchar_unlocked (void)
>       wchar.h (GNU): Section 12.8 [Character Input], page 262.

wint_t getwc_unlocked (FILE *stream)
>       wchar.h (GNU): Section 12.8 [Character Input], page 262.

char * getwd (char *buffer)
>       unistd.h (BSD): Section 14.1 [Working Directory], page 377.

gid_t
>       sys/types.h (POSIX.1): Section 30.5 [Reading the Persona of a Process], page 793.

int glob (const char *pattern, int flags, int (*errfunc) (const char *filename, int error-code), glob_t *vector-ptr)
>       glob.h (POSIX.2): Section 10.2.1 [Calling glob], page 223.

int glob64 (const char *pattern, int flags, int (*errfunc) (const char *filename, int error-code), glob64_t *vector-ptr)
>       glob.h (GNU): Section 10.2.1 [Calling glob], page 223.

glob64_t
>       glob.h (GNU): Section 10.2.1 [Calling glob], page 223.

GLOB_ABORTED
>       glob.h (POSIX.2): Section 10.2.1 [Calling glob], page 223.

GLOB_ALTDIRFUNC
>       glob.h (GNU): Section 10.2.3 [More Flags for Globbing], page 228.

GLOB_APPEND
>       glob.h (POSIX.2): Section 10.2.2 [Flags for Globbing], page 227.

GLOB_BRACE
>       glob.h (GNU): Section 10.2.3 [More Flags for Globbing], page 228.

GLOB_DOOFFS
>       glob.h (POSIX.2): Section 10.2.2 [Flags for Globbing], page 227.

GLOB_ERR
>       glob.h (POSIX.2): Section 10.2.2 [Flags for Globbing], page 227.

void globfree (glob_t *pglob)
>       glob.h (POSIX.2): Section 10.2.3 [More Flags for Globbing], page 228.

void globfree64 (glob64_t *pglob)
>       glob.h (GNU): Section 10.2.3 [More Flags for Globbing], page 228.

GLOB_MAGCHAR
>       glob.h (GNU): Section 10.2.3 [More Flags for Globbing], page 228.

GLOB_MARK
>       glob.h (POSIX.2): Section 10.2.2 [Flags for Globbing], page 227.

GLOB_NOCHECK

> glob.h (POSIX.2): Section 10.2.2 [Flags for Globbing], page 227.

GLOB_NOESCAPE

> glob.h (POSIX.2): Section 10.2.2 [Flags for Globbing], page 227.

GLOB_NOMAGIC

> glob.h (GNU): Section 10.2.3 [More Flags for Globbing], page 228.

GLOB_NOMATCH

> glob.h (POSIX.2): Section 10.2.1 [Calling glob], page 223.

GLOB_NOSORT

> glob.h (POSIX.2): Section 10.2.2 [Flags for Globbing], page 227.

GLOB_NOSPACE

> glob.h (POSIX.2): Section 10.2.1 [Calling glob], page 223.

GLOB_ONLYDIR

> glob.h (GNU): Section 10.2.3 [More Flags for Globbing], page 228.

GLOB_PERIOD

> glob.h (GNU): Section 10.2.3 [More Flags for Globbing], page 228.

glob_t

> glob.h (POSIX.2): Section 10.2.1 [Calling glob], page 223.

GLOB_TILDE

> glob.h (GNU): Section 10.2.3 [More Flags for Globbing], page 228.

GLOB_TILDE_CHECK

> glob.h (GNU): Section 10.2.3 [More Flags for Globbing], page 228.

struct tm * gmtime (const time_t *time)
> time.h (ISO): Section 21.4.3 [Broken-down Time], page 602.

struct tm * gmtime_r (const time_t *time, struct tm *resultp)
> time.h (POSIX.1c): Section 21.4.3 [Broken-down Time], page 602.

_GNU_SOURCE

> (GNU): Section 1.3.4 [Feature Test Macros], page 15.

int grantpt (int filedes)
> stdlib.h (SVID, XPG4.2): Section 17.8.1 [Allocating Pseudo-Terminals], page 500.

int gsignal (int signum)
> signal.h (SVID): Section 24.6.1 [Signaling Yourself], page 688.

int gtty (int filedes, struct sgttyb *attributes)
> sgtty.h (BSD): Section 17.5 [BSD Terminal Modes], page 496.

char * hasmntopt (const struct mntent *mnt, const char *opt)
> mntent.h (BSD): Section 31.3.1.2 [The mtab file], page 828.

int hcreate (size_t nel)
> search.h (SVID): Section 9.5 [The hsearch function.], page 216.

int hcreate_r (size_t nel, struct hsearch_data *htab)
> search.h (GNU): Section 9.5 [The hsearch function.], page 216.

void hdestroy (void)
> search.h (SVID): Section 9.5 [The hsearch function.], page 216.

void hdestroy_r (struct hsearch_data *htab)
> search.h (GNU): Section 9.5 [The hsearch function.], page 216.

HOST_NOT_FOUND

> netdb.h (BSD): Section 16.6.2.4 [Host Names], page 443.

ENTRY * hsearch (ENTRY *item*, ACTION *action*)
> search.h (SVID): Section 9.5 [The **hsearch** function.], page 216.

int hsearch_r (ENTRY *item*, ACTION *action*, ENTRY **retval*, struct hsearch_data **htab*)
> search.h (GNU): Section 9.5 [The **hsearch** function.], page 216.

uint32_t htonl (uint32_t *hostlong*)
> netinet/in.h (BSD): Section 16.6.5 [Byte Order Conversion], page 449.

uint16_t htons (uint16_t *hostshort*)
> netinet/in.h (BSD): Section 16.6.5 [Byte Order Conversion], page 449.

double HUGE_VAL
> math.h (ISO): Section 20.5.4 [Error Reporting by Mathematical Functions], page 569.

float HUGE_VALF
> math.h (ISO): Section 20.5.4 [Error Reporting by Mathematical Functions], page 569.

long double HUGE_VALL
> math.h (ISO): Section 20.5.4 [Error Reporting by Mathematical Functions], page 569.

tcflag_t HUPCL
> termios.h (POSIX.1): Section 17.4.6 [Control Modes], page 485.

double hypot (double *x*, double *y*)
> math.h (ISO): Section 19.4 [Exponentiation and Logarithms], page 515.

float hypotf (float *x*, float *y*)
> math.h (ISO): Section 19.4 [Exponentiation and Logarithms], page 515.

long double hypotl (long double *x*, long double *y*)
> math.h (ISO): Section 19.4 [Exponentiation and Logarithms], page 515.

tcflag_t ICANON
> termios.h (POSIX.1): Section 17.4.7 [Local Modes], page 486.

size_t iconv (iconv_t *cd*, char **inbuf*, size_t **inbytesleft*, char **outbuf*, size_t **outbytesleft*)
> iconv.h (XPG2): Section 6.5.1 [Generic Character Set Conversion Interface], page 149.

int iconv_close (iconv_t *cd*)
> iconv.h (XPG2): Section 6.5.1 [Generic Character Set Conversion Interface], page 149.

iconv_t iconv_open (const char **tocode*, const char **fromcode*)
> iconv.h (XPG2): Section 6.5.1 [Generic Character Set Conversion Interface], page 149.

iconv_t
> iconv.h (XPG2): Section 6.5.1 [Generic Character Set Conversion Interface], page 149.

tcflag_t ICRNL
> termios.h (POSIX.1): Section 17.4.4 [Input Modes], page 482.

tcflag_t IEXTEN
> termios.h (POSIX.1): Section 17.4.7 [Local Modes], page 486.

void if_freenameindex (struct if_nameindex **ptr*)
> net/if.h (IPv6 basic API): Section 16.4 [Interface Naming], page 434.

char * if_indextoname (unsigned int *ifindex*, char **ifname*)
> net/if.h (IPv6 basic API): Section 16.4 [Interface Naming], page 434.

struct if_nameindex * if_nameindex (void)
> net/if.h (IPv6 basic API): Section 16.4 [Interface Naming], page 434.

unsigned int if_nametoindex (const char **ifname*)
> net/if.h (IPv6 basic API): Section 16.4 [Interface Naming], page 434.

size_t IFNAMSIZ
> net/if.h (net/if.h): Section 16.4 [Interface Naming], page 434.

int IFTODT (mode_t *mode*)

> dirent.h (BSD): Section 14.2.1 [Format of a Directory Entry], page 379.

tcflag_t IGNBRK

> termios.h (POSIX.1): Section 17.4.4 [Input Modes], page 482.

tcflag_t IGNCR

> termios.h (POSIX.1): Section 17.4.4 [Input Modes], page 482.

tcflag_t IGNPAR

> termios.h (POSIX.1): Section 17.4.4 [Input Modes], page 482.

int ilogb (double *x*)

> math.h (ISO): Section 19.4 [Exponentiation and Logarithms], page 515.

int ilogbf (float *x*)

> math.h (ISO): Section 19.4 [Exponentiation and Logarithms], page 515.

int ilogbl (long double *x*)

> math.h (ISO): Section 19.4 [Exponentiation and Logarithms], page 515.

intmax_t imaxabs (intmax_t *number*)

> inttypes.h (ISO): Section 20.8.1 [Absolute Value], page 574.

tcflag_t IMAXBEL

> termios.h (BSD): Section 17.4.4 [Input Modes], page 482.

imaxdiv_t imaxdiv (intmax_t *numerator*, intmax_t *denominator*)

> inttypes.h (ISO): Section 20.2 [Integer Division], page 560.

imaxdiv_t

> inttypes.h (ISO): Section 20.2 [Integer Division], page 560.

struct in6_addr in6addr_any

> netinet/in.h (IPv6 basic API): Section 16.6.2.2 [Host Address Data Type], page 440.

struct in6_addr in6addr_loopback

> netinet/in.h (IPv6 basic API): Section 16.6.2.2 [Host Address Data Type], page 440.

uint32_t INADDR_ANY

> netinet/in.h (BSD): Section 16.6.2.2 [Host Address Data Type], page 440.

uint32_t INADDR_BROADCAST

> netinet/in.h (BSD): Section 16.6.2.2 [Host Address Data Type], page 440.

uint32_t INADDR_LOOPBACK

> netinet/in.h (BSD): Section 16.6.2.2 [Host Address Data Type], page 440.

uint32_t INADDR_NONE

> netinet/in.h (BSD): Section 16.6.2.2 [Host Address Data Type], page 440.

char * index (const char *string*, int *c*)

> string.h (BSD): Section 5.7 [Search Functions], page 110.

uint32_t inet_addr (const char *name*)

> arpa/inet.h (BSD): Section 16.6.2.3 [Host Address Functions], page 441.

int inet_aton (const char *name*, struct in_addr *addr*)

> arpa/inet.h (BSD): Section 16.6.2.3 [Host Address Functions], page 441.

uint32_t inet_lnaof (struct in_addr *addr*)

> arpa/inet.h (BSD): Section 16.6.2.3 [Host Address Functions], page 441.

struct in_addr inet_makeaddr (uint32_t *net*, uint32_t *local*)

> arpa/inet.h (BSD): Section 16.6.2.3 [Host Address Functions], page 441.

uint32_t inet_netof (struct in_addr *addr*)

> arpa/inet.h (BSD): Section 16.6.2.3 [Host Address Functions], page 441.

`uint32_t inet_network (const char *name)`
>        arpa/inet.h (BSD): Section 16.6.2.3 [Host Address Functions], page 441.

`char * inet_ntoa (struct in_addr addr)`
>        arpa/inet.h (BSD): Section 16.6.2.3 [Host Address Functions], page 441.

`const char * inet_ntop (int af, const void *cp, char *buf, socklen_t len)`
>        arpa/inet.h (IPv6 basic API): Section 16.6.2.3 [Host Address Functions], page 441.

`int inet_pton (int af, const char *cp, void *buf)`
>        arpa/inet.h (IPv6 basic API): Section 16.6.2.3 [Host Address Functions], page 441.

`float INFINITY`
>        math.h (ISO): Section 20.5.2 [Infinity and NaN], page 566.

`int initgroups (const char *user, gid_t group)`
>        grp.h (BSD): Section 30.7 [Setting the Group IDs], page 795.

`INIT_PROCESS`
>        utmp.h (SVID): Section 30.12.1 [Manipulating the User Accounting Database], page 802.

`INIT_PROCESS`
>        utmpx.h (XPG4.2): Section 30.12.2 [XPG User Accounting Database Functions], page 807.

`char * initstate (unsigned int seed, char *state, size_t size)`
>        stdlib.h (BSD): Section 19.8.2 [BSD Random Number Functions], page 551.

`int initstate_r (unsigned int seed, char *restrict statebuf, size_t statelen, struct random_data *restrict buf)`
>        stdlib.h (GNU): Section 19.8.2 [BSD Random Number Functions], page 551.

`tcflag_t INLCR`
>        termios.h (POSIX.1): Section 17.4.4 [Input Modes], page 482.

`int innetgr (const char *netgroup, const char *host, const char *user, const char *domain)`
>        netdb.h (BSD): Section 30.16.3 [Testing for Netgroup Membership], page 820.

`ino64_t`
>        sys/types.h (Unix98): Section 14.9.1 [The meaning of the File Attributes], page 399.

`ino_t`
>        sys/types.h (POSIX.1): Section 14.9.1 [The meaning of the File Attributes], page 399.

`tcflag_t INPCK`
>        termios.h (POSIX.1): Section 17.4.4 [Input Modes], page 482.

`INT_MAX`
>        limits.h (ISO): Section A.5.2 [Range of an Integer Type], page 885.

`INT_MIN`
>        limits.h (ISO): Section A.5.2 [Range of an Integer Type], page 885.

`int ioctl (int filedes, int command, ...)`
>        sys/ioctl.h (BSD): Section 13.19 [Generic I/O Control operations], page 375.

`int _IOFBF`
>        stdio.h (ISO): Section 12.20.3 [Controlling Which Kind of Buffering], page 311.

`int _IOLBF`
>        stdio.h (ISO): Section 12.20.3 [Controlling Which Kind of Buffering], page 311.

`int _IONBF`
>        stdio.h (ISO): Section 12.20.3 [Controlling Which Kind of Buffering], page 311.

`int IPPORT_RESERVED`
>        netinet/in.h (BSD): Section 16.6.3 [Internet Ports], page 447.

int IPPORT_USERRESERVED
        netinet/in.h (BSD): Section 16.6.3 [Internet Ports], page 447.

int isalnum (int c)
        ctype.h (ISO): Section 4.1 [Classification of Characters], page 77.

int isalpha (int c)
        ctype.h (ISO): Section 4.1 [Classification of Characters], page 77.

int isascii (int c)
        ctype.h (SVID, BSD): Section 4.1 [Classification of Characters], page 77.

int isatty (int filedes)
        unistd.h (POSIX.1): Section 17.1 [Identifying Terminals], page 477.

int isblank (int c)
        ctype.h (ISO): Section 4.1 [Classification of Characters], page 77.

int iscntrl (int c)
        ctype.h (ISO): Section 4.1 [Classification of Characters], page 77.

int isdigit (int c)
        ctype.h (ISO): Section 4.1 [Classification of Characters], page 77.

int isfinite (float-type x)
        math.h (ISO): Section 20.4 [Floating-Point Number Classification Functions], page 563.

int isgraph (int c)
        ctype.h (ISO): Section 4.1 [Classification of Characters], page 77.

int isgreater (real-floating x, real-floating y)
        math.h (ISO): Section 20.8.6 [Floating-Point Comparison Functions], page 580.

int isgreaterequal (real-floating x, real-floating y)
        math.h (ISO): Section 20.8.6 [Floating-Point Comparison Functions], page 580.

tcflag_t ISIG
        termios.h (POSIX.1): Section 17.4.7 [Local Modes], page 486.

int isinf (double x)
        math.h (BSD): Section 20.4 [Floating-Point Number Classification Functions], page 563.

int isinff (float x)
        math.h (BSD): Section 20.4 [Floating-Point Number Classification Functions], page 563.

int isinfl (long double x)
        math.h (BSD): Section 20.4 [Floating-Point Number Classification Functions], page 563.

int isless (real-floating x, real-floating y)
        math.h (ISO): Section 20.8.6 [Floating-Point Comparison Functions], page 580.

int islessequal (real-floating x, real-floating y)
        math.h (ISO): Section 20.8.6 [Floating-Point Comparison Functions], page 580.

int islessgreater (real-floating x, real-floating y)
        math.h (ISO): Section 20.8.6 [Floating-Point Comparison Functions], page 580.

int islower (int c)
        ctype.h (ISO): Section 4.1 [Classification of Characters], page 77.

int isnan (float-type x)
        math.h (ISO): Section 20.4 [Floating-Point Number Classification Functions], page 563.

int isnan (double x)
        math.h (BSD): Section 20.4 [Floating-Point Number Classification Functions], page 563.

int isnanf (float x)
        math.h (BSD): Section 20.4 [Floating-Point Number Classification Functions], page 563.

`int isnanl (long double x)`
> `math.h` (BSD): Section 20.4 [Floating-Point Number Classification Functions], page 563.

`int isnormal (float-type x)`
> `math.h` (ISO): Section 20.4 [Floating-Point Number Classification Functions], page 563.

`_ISOC99_SOURCE`
> (GNU): Section 1.3.4 [Feature Test Macros], page 15.

`int isprint (int c)`
> `ctype.h` (ISO): Section 4.1 [Classification of Characters], page 77.

`int ispunct (int c)`
> `ctype.h` (ISO): Section 4.1 [Classification of Characters], page 77.

`int issignaling (float-type x)`
> `math.h` (GNU): Section 20.4 [Floating-Point Number Classification Functions], page 563.

`int isspace (int c)`
> `ctype.h` (ISO): Section 4.1 [Classification of Characters], page 77.

`tcflag_t ISTRIP`
> `termios.h` (POSIX.1): Section 17.4.4 [Input Modes], page 482.

`int isunordered (real-floating x, real-floating y)`
> `math.h` (ISO): Section 20.8.6 [Floating-Point Comparison Functions], page 580.

`int isupper (int c)`
> `ctype.h` (ISO): Section 4.1 [Classification of Characters], page 77.

`int iswalnum (wint_t wc)`
> `wctype.h` (ISO): Section 4.3 [Character class determination for wide characters], page 80.

`int iswalpha (wint_t wc)`
> `wctype.h` (ISO): Section 4.3 [Character class determination for wide characters], page 80.

`int iswblank (wint_t wc)`
> `wctype.h` (ISO): Section 4.3 [Character class determination for wide characters], page 80.

`int iswcntrl (wint_t wc)`
> `wctype.h` (ISO): Section 4.3 [Character class determination for wide characters], page 80.

`int iswctype (wint_t wc, wctype_t desc)`
> `wctype.h` (ISO): Section 4.3 [Character class determination for wide characters], page 80.

`int iswdigit (wint_t wc)`
> `wctype.h` (ISO): Section 4.3 [Character class determination for wide characters], page 80.

`int iswgraph (wint_t wc)`
> `wctype.h` (ISO): Section 4.3 [Character class determination for wide characters], page 80.

`int iswlower (wint_t wc)`
> `ctype.h` (ISO): Section 4.3 [Character class determination for wide characters], page 80.

`int iswprint (wint_t wc)`
> `wctype.h` (ISO): Section 4.3 [Character class determination for wide characters], page 80.

`int iswpunct (wint_t wc)`
> `wctype.h` (ISO): Section 4.3 [Character class determination for wide characters], page 80.

`int iswspace (wint_t wc)`
> `wctype.h` (ISO): Section 4.3 [Character class determination for wide characters], page 80.

`int iswupper (wint_t wc)`
> `wctype.h` (ISO): Section 4.3 [Character class determination for wide characters], page 80.

`int iswxdigit (wint_t wc)`
> `wctype.h` (ISO): Section 4.3 [Character class determination for wide characters], page 80.

int isxdigit (int *c*)
> ctype.h (ISO): Section 4.1 [Classification of Characters], page 77.

ITIMER_PROF
> sys/time.h (BSD): Section 21.5 [Setting an Alarm], page 625.

ITIMER_REAL
> sys/time.h (BSD): Section 21.5 [Setting an Alarm], page 625.

ITIMER_VIRTUAL
> sys/time.h (BSD): Section 21.5 [Setting an Alarm], page 625.

tcflag_t IXANY
> termios.h (BSD): Section 17.4.4 [Input Modes], page 482.

tcflag_t IXOFF
> termios.h (POSIX.1): Section 17.4.4 [Input Modes], page 482.

tcflag_t IXON
> termios.h (POSIX.1): Section 17.4.4 [Input Modes], page 482.

double j0 (double *x*)
> math.h (SVID): Section 19.6 [Special Functions], page 522.

float j0f (float *x*)
> math.h (SVID): Section 19.6 [Special Functions], page 522.

long double j0l (long double *x*)
> math.h (SVID): Section 19.6 [Special Functions], page 522.

double j1 (double *x*)
> math.h (SVID): Section 19.6 [Special Functions], page 522.

float j1f (float *x*)
> math.h (SVID): Section 19.6 [Special Functions], page 522.

long double j1l (long double *x*)
> math.h (SVID): Section 19.6 [Special Functions], page 522.

jmp_buf
> setjmp.h (ISO): Section 23.2 [Details of Non-Local Exits], page 653.

double jn (int *n*, double *x*)
> math.h (SVID): Section 19.6 [Special Functions], page 522.

float jnf (int *n*, float *x*)
> math.h (SVID): Section 19.6 [Special Functions], page 522.

long double jnl (int *n*, long double *x*)
> math.h (SVID): Section 19.6 [Special Functions], page 522.

long int jrand48 (unsigned short int *xsubi*[3])
> stdlib.h (SVID): Section 19.8.3 [SVID Random Number Function], page 553.

int jrand48_r (unsigned short int *xsubi*[3], struct drand48_data *\*buffer*, long int *\*result*)
> stdlib.h (GNU): Section 19.8.3 [SVID Random Number Function], page 553.

int kill (pid_t *pid*, int *signum*)
> signal.h (POSIX.1): Section 24.6.2 [Signaling Another Process], page 689.

int killpg (int *pgid*, int *signum*)
> signal.h (BSD): Section 24.6.2 [Signaling Another Process], page 689.

char * l64a (long int *n*)
> stdlib.h (XPG): Section 5.11 [Encode Binary Data], page 121.

long int labs (long int *number*)
> stdlib.h (ISO): Section 20.8.1 [Absolute Value], page 574.

LANG

> `locale.h` (ISO): Section 7.3 [Locale Categories], page 170.

LC_ALL

> `locale.h` (ISO): Section 7.3 [Locale Categories], page 170.

LC_COLLATE

> `locale.h` (ISO): Section 7.3 [Locale Categories], page 170.

LC_CTYPE

> `locale.h` (ISO): Section 7.3 [Locale Categories], page 170.

LC_MESSAGES

> `locale.h` (XOPEN): Section 7.3 [Locale Categories], page 170.

LC_MONETARY

> `locale.h` (ISO): Section 7.3 [Locale Categories], page 170.

LC_NUMERIC

> `locale.h` (ISO): Section 7.3 [Locale Categories], page 170.

`void lcong48 (unsigned short int param[7])`

> `stdlib.h` (SVID): Section 19.8.3 [SVID Random Number Function], page 553.

`int lcong48_r (unsigned short int param[7], struct drand48_data *buffer)`

> `stdlib.h` (GNU): Section 19.8.3 [SVID Random Number Function], page 553.

`int L_ctermid`

> `stdio.h` (POSIX.1): Section 28.7.1 [Identifying the Controlling Terminal], page 778.

LC_TIME

> `locale.h` (ISO): Section 7.3 [Locale Categories], page 170.

`int L_cuserid`

> `stdio.h` (POSIX.1): Section 30.11 [Identifying Who Logged In], page 801.

`double ldexp (double value, int exponent)`

> `math.h` (ISO): Section 20.8.2 [Normalization Functions], page 574.

`float ldexpf (float value, int exponent)`

> `math.h` (ISO): Section 20.8.2 [Normalization Functions], page 574.

`long double ldexpl (long double value, int exponent)`

> `math.h` (ISO): Section 20.8.2 [Normalization Functions], page 574.

`ldiv_t ldiv (long int numerator, long int denominator)`

> `stdlib.h` (ISO): Section 20.2 [Integer Division], page 560.

`ldiv_t`

> `stdlib.h` (ISO): Section 20.2 [Integer Division], page 560.

`void * lfind (const void *key, const void *base, size_t *nmemb, size_t size, comparison_fn_t compar)`

> `search.h` (SVID): Section 9.2 [Array Search Function], page 212.

`double lgamma (double x)`

> `math.h` (SVID): Section 19.6 [Special Functions], page 522.

`float lgammaf (float x)`

> `math.h` (SVID): Section 19.6 [Special Functions], page 522.

`float lgammaf_r (float x, int *signp)`

> `math.h` (XPG): Section 19.6 [Special Functions], page 522.

`long double lgammal (long double x)`

> `math.h` (SVID): Section 19.6 [Special Functions], page 522.

```
long double lgammal_r (long double x, int *signp)
```
math.h (XPG): Section 19.6 [Special Functions], page 522.

```
double lgamma_r (double x, int *signp)
```
math.h (XPG): Section 19.6 [Special Functions], page 522.

```
L_INCR
```
sys/file.h (BSD): Section 12.18 [File Positioning], page 305.

```
int LINE_MAX
```
limits.h (POSIX.2): Section 32.10 [Utility Program Capacity Limits], page 855.

```
int link (const char *oldname, const char *newname)
```
unistd.h (POSIX.1): Section 14.4 [Hard Links], page 392.

```
int LINK_MAX
```
limits.h, (optional) (POSIX.1): Section 32.6 [Limits on File System Capacity], page 850.

```
int lio_listio (int mode, struct aiocb *const list[], int nent, struct sigevent *sig)
```
aio.h (POSIX.1b): Section 13.10.1 [Asynchronous Read and Write Operations], page 349.

```
int lio_listio64 (int mode, struct aiocb64 *const list[], int nent, struct sigevent *sig)
```
aio.h (Unix98): Section 13.10.1 [Asynchronous Read and Write Operations], page 349.

```
int listen (int socket, int n)
```
sys/socket.h (BSD): Section 16.9.2 [Listening for Connections], page 457.

```
long long int llabs (long long int number)
```
stdlib.h (ISO): Section 20.8.1 [Absolute Value], page 574.

```
lldiv_t lldiv (long long int numerator, long long int denominator)
```
stdlib.h (ISO): Section 20.2 [Integer Division], page 560.

```
lldiv_t
```
stdlib.h (ISO): Section 20.2 [Integer Division], page 560.

```
LLONG_MAX
```
limits.h (ISO): Section A.5.2 [Range of an Integer Type], page 885.

```
LLONG_MIN
```
limits.h (ISO): Section A.5.2 [Range of an Integer Type], page 885.

```
long long int llrint (double x)
```
math.h (ISO): Section 20.8.3 [Rounding Functions], page 576.

```
long long int llrintf (float x)
```
math.h (ISO): Section 20.8.3 [Rounding Functions], page 576.

```
long long int llrintl (long double x)
```
math.h (ISO): Section 20.8.3 [Rounding Functions], page 576.

```
long long int llround (double x)
```
math.h (ISO): Section 20.8.3 [Rounding Functions], page 576.

```
long long int llroundf (float x)
```
math.h (ISO): Section 20.8.3 [Rounding Functions], page 576.

```
long long int llroundl (long double x)
```
math.h (ISO): Section 20.8.3 [Rounding Functions], page 576.

```
struct lconv * localeconv (void)
```
locale.h (ISO): Section 7.7.1 [localeconv: It is portable but . . .], page 175.

```
struct tm * localtime (const time_t *time)
```
time.h (ISO): Section 21.4.3 [Broken-down Time], page 602.

```
struct tm * localtime_r (const time_t *time, struct tm *resultp)
```
time.h (POSIX.1c): Section 21.4.3 [Broken-down Time], page 602.

double log (double x)
> math.h (ISO): Section 19.4 [Exponentiation and Logarithms], page 515.

double log10 (double x)
> math.h (ISO): Section 19.4 [Exponentiation and Logarithms], page 515.

float log10f (float x)
> math.h (ISO): Section 19.4 [Exponentiation and Logarithms], page 515.

long double log10l (long double x)
> math.h (ISO): Section 19.4 [Exponentiation and Logarithms], page 515.

double log1p (double x)
> math.h (ISO): Section 19.4 [Exponentiation and Logarithms], page 515.

float log1pf (float x)
> math.h (ISO): Section 19.4 [Exponentiation and Logarithms], page 515.

long double log1pl (long double x)
> math.h (ISO): Section 19.4 [Exponentiation and Logarithms], page 515.

double log2 (double x)
> math.h (ISO): Section 19.4 [Exponentiation and Logarithms], page 515.

float log2f (float x)
> math.h (ISO): Section 19.4 [Exponentiation and Logarithms], page 515.

long double log2l (long double x)
> math.h (ISO): Section 19.4 [Exponentiation and Logarithms], page 515.

double logb (double x)
> math.h (ISO): Section 19.4 [Exponentiation and Logarithms], page 515.

float logbf (float x)
> math.h (ISO): Section 19.4 [Exponentiation and Logarithms], page 515.

long double logbl (long double x)
> math.h (ISO): Section 19.4 [Exponentiation and Logarithms], page 515.

float logf (float x)
> math.h (ISO): Section 19.4 [Exponentiation and Logarithms], page 515.

void login (const struct utmp *entry)
> utmp.h (BSD): Section 30.12.3 [Logging In and Out], page 809.

LOGIN_PROCESS
> utmp.h (SVID): Section 30.12.1 [Manipulating the User Accounting Database], page 802.

LOGIN_PROCESS
> utmpx.h (XPG4.2): Section 30.12.2 [XPG User Accounting Database Functions], page 807.

int login_tty (int filedes)
> utmp.h (BSD): Section 30.12.3 [Logging In and Out], page 809.

long double logl (long double x)
> math.h (ISO): Section 19.4 [Exponentiation and Logarithms], page 515.

int logout (const char *ut_line)
> utmp.h (BSD): Section 30.12.3 [Logging In and Out], page 809.

void logwtmp (const char *ut_line, const char *ut_name, const char *ut_host)
> utmp.h (BSD): Section 30.12.3 [Logging In and Out], page 809.

void longjmp (jmp_buf state, int value)
> setjmp.h (ISO): Section 23.2 [Details of Non-Local Exits], page 653.

LONG_LONG_MAX
> limits.h (GNU): Section A.5.2 [Range of an Integer Type], page 885.

LONG_LONG_MIN
          `limits.h` (GNU): Section A.5.2 [Range of an Integer Type], page 885.

LONG_MAX
          `limits.h` (ISO): Section A.5.2 [Range of an Integer Type], page 885.

LONG_MIN
          `limits.h` (ISO): Section A.5.2 [Range of an Integer Type], page 885.

`long int lrand48 (void)`
          `stdlib.h` (SVID): Section 19.8.3 [SVID Random Number Function], page 553.

`int lrand48_r (struct drand48_data *buffer, long int *result)`
          `stdlib.h` (GNU): Section 19.8.3 [SVID Random Number Function], page 553.

`long int lrint (double x)`
          `math.h` (ISO): Section 20.8.3 [Rounding Functions], page 576.

`long int lrintf (float x)`
          `math.h` (ISO): Section 20.8.3 [Rounding Functions], page 576.

`long int lrintl (long double x)`
          `math.h` (ISO): Section 20.8.3 [Rounding Functions], page 576.

`long int lround (double x)`
          `math.h` (ISO): Section 20.8.3 [Rounding Functions], page 576.

`long int lroundf (float x)`
          `math.h` (ISO): Section 20.8.3 [Rounding Functions], page 576.

`long int lroundl (long double x)`
          `math.h` (ISO): Section 20.8.3 [Rounding Functions], page 576.

`void * lsearch (const void *key, void *base, size_t *nmemb, size_t size, comparison_fn_t compar)`
          `search.h` (SVID): Section 9.2 [Array Search Function], page 212.

`off_t lseek (int filedes, off_t offset, int whence)`
          `unistd.h` (POSIX.1): Section 13.3 [Setting the File Position of a Descriptor], page 331.

`off64_t lseek64 (int filedes, off64_t offset, int whence)`
          `unistd.h` (Unix98): Section 13.3 [Setting the File Position of a Descriptor], page 331.

L_SET
          `sys/file.h` (BSD): Section 12.18 [File Positioning], page 305.

`int lstat (const char *filename, struct stat *buf)`
          `sys/stat.h` (BSD): Section 14.9.2 [Reading the Attributes of a File], page 403.

`int lstat64 (const char *filename, struct stat64 *buf)`
          `sys/stat.h` (Unix98): Section 14.9.2 [Reading the Attributes of a File], page 403.

`int L_tmpnam`
          `stdio.h` (ISO): Section 14.11 [Temporary Files], page 419.

`int lutimes (const char *filename, const struct timeval tvp[2])`
          `sys/time.h` (BSD): Section 14.9.9 [File Times], page 413.

L_XTND
          `sys/file.h` (BSD): Section 12.18 [File Positioning], page 305.

`int madvise (void *addr, size_t length, int advice)`
          `sys/mman.h` (POSIX): Section 13.7 [Memory-mapped I/O], page 337.

`void makecontext (ucontext_t *ucp, void (*func) (void), int argc, ...)`
          `ucontext.h` (SVID): Section 23.4 [Complete Context Control], page 655.

`struct mallinfo mallinfo (void)`
          `malloc.h` (SVID): Section 3.2.2.11 [Statistics for Memory Allocation with `malloc`], page 52.

void * malloc (size_t *size*)
> malloc.h, stdlib.h (ISO): Section 3.2.2.1 [Basic Memory Allocation], page 42.

__malloc_hook
> malloc.h (GNU): Section 3.2.2.10 [Memory Allocation Hooks], page 50.

__malloc_initialize_hook
> malloc.h (GNU): Section 3.2.2.10 [Memory Allocation Hooks], page 50.

int MAX_CANON
> limits.h (POSIX.1): Section 32.6 [Limits on File System Capacity], page 850.

int MAX_INPUT
> limits.h (POSIX.1): Section 32.6 [Limits on File System Capacity], page 850.

int MAXNAMLEN
> dirent.h (BSD): Section 32.6 [Limits on File System Capacity], page 850.

int MAXSYMLINKS
> sys/param.h (BSD): Section 14.5 [Symbolic Links], page 393.

int MB_CUR_MAX
> stdlib.h (ISO): Section 6.3.1 [Selecting the conversion and its properties], page 131.

int mblen (const char *string*, size_t *size*)
> stdlib.h (ISO): Section 6.4.1 [Non-reentrant Conversion of Single Characters], page 144.

int MB_LEN_MAX
> limits.h (ISO): Section 6.3.1 [Selecting the conversion and its properties], page 131.

size_t mbrlen (const char *restrict *s*, size_t *n*, mbstate_t *ps*)
> wchar.h (ISO): Section 6.3.3 [Converting Single Characters], page 133.

size_t mbrtowc (wchar_t *restrict *pwc*, const char *restrict *s*, size_t *n*, mbstate_t *restrict *ps*)
> wchar.h (ISO): Section 6.3.3 [Converting Single Characters], page 133.

int mbsinit (const mbstate_t *ps*)
> wchar.h (ISO): Section 6.3.2 [Representing the state of the conversion], page 132.

size_t mbsnrtowcs (wchar_t *restrict *dst*, const char **restrict *src*, size_t *nmc*, size_t *len*, mbstate_t *restrict *ps*)
> wchar.h (GNU): Section 6.3.4 [Converting Multibyte and Wide Character Strings], page 139.

size_t mbsrtowcs (wchar_t *restrict *dst*, const char **restrict *src*, size_t *len*, mbstate_t *restrict *ps*)
> wchar.h (ISO): Section 6.3.4 [Converting Multibyte and Wide Character Strings], page 139.

mbstate_t
> wchar.h (ISO): Section 6.3.2 [Representing the state of the conversion], page 132.

size_t mbstowcs (wchar_t *wstring*, const char *string*, size_t *size*)
> stdlib.h (ISO): Section 6.4.2 [Non-reentrant Conversion of Strings], page 146.

int mbtowc (wchar_t *restrict *result*, const char *restrict *string*, size_t *size*)
> stdlib.h (ISO): Section 6.4.1 [Non-reentrant Conversion of Single Characters], page 144.

int mcheck (void (*abortfn*) (enum mcheck_status *status*))
> mcheck.h (GNU): Section 3.2.2.9 [Heap Consistency Checking], page 48.

tcflag_t MDMBUF
> termios.h (BSD): Section 17.4.6 [Control Modes], page 485.

void * memalign (size_t *boundary*, size_t *size*)
> malloc.h (BSD): Section 3.2.2.7 [Allocating Aligned Memory Blocks], page 46.

__memalign_hook
> malloc.h (GNU): Section 3.2.2.10 [Memory Allocation Hooks], page 50.

void * memccpy (void *restrict *to*, const void *restrict *from*, int *c*, size_t *size*)
         string.h (SVID): Section 5.4 [Copying and Concatenation], page 91.

void * memchr (const void **block*, int *c*, size_t *size*)
         string.h (ISO): Section 5.7 [Search Functions], page 110.

int memcmp (const void **a1*, const void **a2*, size_t *size*)
         string.h (ISO): Section 5.5 [String/Array Comparison], page 102.

void * memcpy (void *restrict *to*, const void *restrict *from*, size_t *size*)
         string.h (ISO): Section 5.4 [Copying and Concatenation], page 91.

void * memfrob (void **mem*, size_t *length*)
         string.h (GNU): Section 5.10 [Trivial Encryption], page 120.

void * memmem (const void **haystack*, size_t *haystack-len*,
const void **needle*, size_t *needle-len*)
         string.h (GNU): Section 5.7 [Search Functions], page 110.

void * memmove (void **to*, const void **from*, size_t *size*)
         string.h (ISO): Section 5.4 [Copying and Concatenation], page 91.

void * mempcpy (void *restrict *to*, const void *restrict *from*, size_t *size*)
         string.h (GNU): Section 5.4 [Copying and Concatenation], page 91.

void * memrchr (const void **block*, int *c*, size_t *size*)
         string.h (GNU): Section 5.7 [Search Functions], page 110.

void * memset (void **block*, int *c*, size_t *size*)
         string.h (ISO): Section 5.4 [Copying and Concatenation], page 91.

int mkdir (const char **filename*, mode_t *mode*)
         sys/stat.h (POSIX.1): Section 14.8 [Creating Directories], page 398.

char * mkdtemp (char **template*)
         stdlib.h (BSD): Section 14.11 [Temporary Files], page 419.

int mkfifo (const char **filename*, mode_t *mode*)
         sys/stat.h (POSIX.1): Section 15.3 [FIFO Special Files], page 427.

int mknod (const char **filename*, mode_t *mode*, dev_t *dev*)
         sys/stat.h (BSD): Section 14.10 [Making Special Files], page 419.

int mkstemp (char **template*)
         stdlib.h (BSD): Section 14.11 [Temporary Files], page 419.

char * mktemp (char **template*)
         stdlib.h (Unix): Section 14.11 [Temporary Files], page 419.

time_t mktime (struct tm **brokentime*)
         time.h (ISO): Section 21.4.3 [Broken-down Time], page 602.

int mlock (const void **addr*, size_t *len*)
         sys/mman.h (POSIX.1b): Section 3.4.3 [Functions To Lock And Unlock Pages], page 74.

int mlockall (int *flags*)
         sys/mman.h (POSIX.1b): Section 3.4.3 [Functions To Lock And Unlock Pages], page 74.

void * mmap (void **address*, size_t *length*, int *protect*, int *flags*, int *filedes*, off_t *offset*)
         sys/mman.h (POSIX): Section 13.7 [Memory-mapped I/O], page 337.

void * mmap64 (void **address*, size_t *length*, int *protect*, int *flags*, int *filedes*, off64_t
*offset*)
         sys/mman.h (LFS): Section 13.7 [Memory-mapped I/O], page 337.

mode_t
         sys/types.h (POSIX.1): Section 14.9.1 [The meaning of the File Attributes], page 399.

double modf (double *value*, double *\*integer-part*)
> math.h (ISO): Section 20.8.3 [Rounding Functions], page 576.

float modff (float *value*, float *\*integer-part*)
> math.h (ISO): Section 20.8.3 [Rounding Functions], page 576.

long double modfl (long double *value*, long double *\*integer-part*)
> math.h (ISO): Section 20.8.3 [Rounding Functions], page 576.

int mount (const char *\*special_file*, const char *\*dir*, const char *\*fstype*, unsigned long int *options*, const void *\*data*)
> sys/mount.h (SVID, BSD): Section 31.3.2 [Mount, Unmount, Remount], page 831.

long int mrand48 (void)
> stdlib.h (SVID): Section 19.8.3 [SVID Random Number Function], page 553.

int mrand48_r (struct drand48_data *\*buffer*, long int *\*result*)
> stdlib.h (GNU): Section 19.8.3 [SVID Random Number Function], page 553.

void * mremap (void *\*address*, size_t *length*, size_t *new_length*, int *flag*)
> sys/mman.h (GNU): Section 13.7 [Memory-mapped I/O], page 337.

int MSG_DONTROUTE
> sys/socket.h (BSD): Section 16.9.5.3 [Socket Data Options], page 461.

int MSG_OOB
> sys/socket.h (BSD): Section 16.9.5.3 [Socket Data Options], page 461.

int MSG_PEEK
> sys/socket.h (BSD): Section 16.9.5.3 [Socket Data Options], page 461.

int msync (void *\*address*, size_t *length*, int *flags*)
> sys/mman.h (POSIX): Section 13.7 [Memory-mapped I/O], page 337.

void mtrace (void)
> mcheck.h (GNU): Section 3.2.3.1 [How to install the tracing functionality], page 54.

int munlock (const void *\*addr*, size_t *len*)
> sys/mman.h (POSIX.1b): Section 3.4.3 [Functions To Lock And Unlock Pages], page 74.

int munlockall (void)
> sys/mman.h (POSIX.1b): Section 3.4.3 [Functions To Lock And Unlock Pages], page 74.

int munmap (void *\*addr*, size_t *length*)
> sys/mman.h (POSIX): Section 13.7 [Memory-mapped I/O], page 337.

void muntrace (void)
> mcheck.h (GNU): Section 3.2.3.1 [How to install the tracing functionality], page 54.

int NAME_MAX
> limits.h (POSIX.1): Section 32.6 [Limits on File System Capacity], page 850.

float NAN
> math.h (GNU): Section 20.5.2 [Infinity and NaN], page 566.

double nan (const char *\*tagp*)
> math.h (ISO): Section 20.8.5 [Setting and modifying single bits of FP values], page 579.

float nanf (const char *\*tagp*)
> math.h (ISO): Section 20.8.5 [Setting and modifying single bits of FP values], page 579.

long double nanl (const char *\*tagp*)
> math.h (ISO): Section 20.8.5 [Setting and modifying single bits of FP values], page 579.

int nanosleep (const struct timespec *\*requested_time*, struct timespec *\*remaining*)
> time.h (POSIX.1): Section 21.6 [Sleeping], page 628.

`int NCCS`

> `termios.h` (POSIX.1): Section 17.4.1 [Terminal Mode Data Types], page 479.

`double nearbyint (double x)`

> `math.h` (ISO): Section 20.8.3 [Rounding Functions], page 576.

`float nearbyintf (float x)`

> `math.h` (ISO): Section 20.8.3 [Rounding Functions], page 576.

`long double nearbyintl (long double x)`

> `math.h` (ISO): Section 20.8.3 [Rounding Functions], page 576.

`NEW_TIME`

> `utmp.h` (SVID): Section 30.12.1 [Manipulating the User Accounting Database], page 802.

`NEW_TIME`

> `utmpx.h` (XPG4.2): Section 30.12.2 [XPG User Accounting Database Functions], page 807.

`double nextafter (double x, double y)`

> `math.h` (ISO): Section 20.8.5 [Setting and modifying single bits of FP values], page 579.

`float nextafterf (float x, float y)`

> `math.h` (ISO): Section 20.8.5 [Setting and modifying single bits of FP values], page 579.

`long double nextafterl (long double x, long double y)`

> `math.h` (ISO): Section 20.8.5 [Setting and modifying single bits of FP values], page 579.

`double nexttoward (double x, long double y)`

> `math.h` (ISO): Section 20.8.5 [Setting and modifying single bits of FP values], page 579.

`float nexttowardf (float x, long double y)`

> `math.h` (ISO): Section 20.8.5 [Setting and modifying single bits of FP values], page 579.

`long double nexttowardl (long double x, long double y)`

> `math.h` (ISO): Section 20.8.5 [Setting and modifying single bits of FP values], page 579.

`int nftw (const char *filename, __nftw_func_t func, int descriptors, int flag)`

> `ftw.h` (XPG4.2): Section 14.3 [Working with Directory Trees], page 388.

`int nftw64 (const char *filename, __nftw64_func_t func, int descriptors, int flag)`

> `ftw.h` (Unix98): Section 14.3 [Working with Directory Trees], page 388.

`__nftw64_func_t`

> `ftw.h` (GNU): Section 14.3 [Working with Directory Trees], page 388.

`__nftw_func_t`

> `ftw.h` (GNU): Section 14.3 [Working with Directory Trees], page 388.

`char * ngettext (const char *msgid1, const char *msgid2, unsigned long int n)`

> `libintl.h` (GNU): Section 8.2.1.3 [Additional functions for more complicated situations], page 202.

`int NGROUPS_MAX`

> `limits.h` (POSIX.1): Section 32.1 [General Capacity Limits], page 838.

`int nice (int increment)`

> `unistd.h` (BSD): Section 22.3.4.2 [Functions For Traditional Scheduling], page 644.

`nlink_t`

> `sys/types.h` (POSIX.1): Section 14.9.1 [The meaning of the File Attributes], page 399.

`char * nl_langinfo (nl_item item)`

> `langinfo.h` (XOPEN): Section 7.7.2 [Pinpoint Access to Locale Data], page 178.

`NO_ADDRESS`

> `netdb.h` (BSD): Section 16.6.2.4 [Host Names], page 443.

`tcflag_t NOFLSH`
> `termios.h` (POSIX.1): Section 17.4.7 [Local Modes], page 486.

`tcflag_t NOKERNINFO`
> `termios.h`, (optional) (BSD): Section 17.4.7 [Local Modes], page 486.

`NO_RECOVERY`
> `netdb.h` (BSD): Section 16.6.2.4 [Host Names], page 443.

`long int nrand48 (unsigned short int xsubi[3])`
> `stdlib.h` (SVID): Section 19.8.3 [SVID Random Number Function], page 553.

`int nrand48_r (unsigned short int xsubi[3], struct drand48_data *buffer, long int *result)`
> `stdlib.h` (GNU): Section 19.8.3 [SVID Random Number Function], page 553.

`int NSIG`
> `signal.h` (BSD): Section 24.2 [Standard Signals], page 663.

`uint32_t ntohl (uint32_t netlong)`
> `netinet/in.h` (BSD): Section 16.6.5 [Byte Order Conversion], page 449.

`uint16_t ntohs (uint16_t netshort)`
> `netinet/in.h` (BSD): Section 16.6.5 [Byte Order Conversion], page 449.

`int ntp_adjtime (struct timex *tptr)`
> `sys/timex.h` (GNU): Section 21.4.4 [High Accuracy Clock], page 605.

`int ntp_gettime (struct ntptimeval *tptr)`
> `sys/timex.h` (GNU): Section 21.4.4 [High Accuracy Clock], page 605.

`void * NULL`
> `stddef.h` (ISO): Section A.3 [Null Pointer Constant], page 883.

`int O_ACCMODE`
> `fcntl.h` (POSIX.1): Section 13.14.1 [File Access Modes], page 363.

`int O_APPEND`
> `fcntl.h` (POSIX.1): Section 13.14.3 [I/O Operating Modes], page 366.

`int O_ASYNC`
> `fcntl.h` (BSD): Section 13.14.3 [I/O Operating Modes], page 366.

`void obstack_1grow (struct obstack *obstack-ptr, char c)`
> `obstack.h` (GNU): Section 3.2.4.6 [Growing Objects], page 62.

`void obstack_1grow_fast (struct obstack *obstack-ptr, char c)`
> `obstack.h` (GNU): Section 3.2.4.7 [Extra Fast Growing Objects], page 64.

`int obstack_alignment_mask (struct obstack *obstack-ptr)`
> `obstack.h` (GNU): Section 3.2.4.9 [Alignment of Data in Obstacks], page 67.

`void * obstack_alloc (struct obstack *obstack-ptr, int size)`
> `obstack.h` (GNU): Section 3.2.4.3 [Allocation in an Obstack], page 60.

`obstack_alloc_failed_handler`
> `obstack.h` (GNU): Section 3.2.4.2 [Preparing for Using Obstacks], page 59.

`void * obstack_base (struct obstack *obstack-ptr)`
> `obstack.h` (GNU): Section 3.2.4.8 [Status of an Obstack], page 66.

`void obstack_blank (struct obstack *obstack-ptr, int size)`
> `obstack.h` (GNU): Section 3.2.4.6 [Growing Objects], page 62.

`void obstack_blank_fast (struct obstack *obstack-ptr, int size)`
> `obstack.h` (GNU): Section 3.2.4.7 [Extra Fast Growing Objects], page 64.

`int obstack_chunk_size (struct obstack *obstack-ptr)`
> `obstack.h` (GNU): Section 3.2.4.10 [Obstack Chunks], page 67.

void * obstack_copy (struct obstack *obstack-ptr, void *address, int size)
        obstack.h (GNU): Section 3.2.4.3 [Allocation in an Obstack], page 60.

void * obstack_copy0 (struct obstack *obstack-ptr, void *address, int size)
        obstack.h (GNU): Section 3.2.4.3 [Allocation in an Obstack], page 60.

void * obstack_finish (struct obstack *obstack-ptr)
        obstack.h (GNU): Section 3.2.4.6 [Growing Objects], page 62.

void obstack_free (struct obstack *obstack-ptr, void *object)
        obstack.h (GNU): Section 3.2.4.4 [Freeing Objects in an Obstack], page 61.

void obstack_grow (struct obstack *obstack-ptr, void *data, int size)
        obstack.h (GNU): Section 3.2.4.6 [Growing Objects], page 62.

void obstack_grow0 (struct obstack *obstack-ptr, void *data, int size)
        obstack.h (GNU): Section 3.2.4.6 [Growing Objects], page 62.

int obstack_init (struct obstack *obstack-ptr)
        obstack.h (GNU): Section 3.2.4.2 [Preparing for Using Obstacks], page 59.

void obstack_int_grow (struct obstack *obstack-ptr, int data)
        obstack.h (GNU): Section 3.2.4.6 [Growing Objects], page 62.

void obstack_int_grow_fast (struct obstack *obstack-ptr, int data)
        obstack.h (GNU): Section 3.2.4.7 [Extra Fast Growing Objects], page 64.

void * obstack_next_free (struct obstack *obstack-ptr)
        obstack.h (GNU): Section 3.2.4.8 [Status of an Obstack], page 66.

int obstack_object_size (struct obstack *obstack-ptr)
        obstack.h (GNU): Section 3.2.4.6 [Growing Objects], page 62.

int obstack_object_size (struct obstack *obstack-ptr)
        obstack.h (GNU): Section 3.2.4.8 [Status of an Obstack], page 66.

int obstack_printf (struct obstack *obstack, const char *template, ...)
        stdio.h (GNU): Section 12.12.8 [Dynamically Allocating Formatted Output], page 281.

void obstack_ptr_grow (struct obstack *obstack-ptr, void *data)
        obstack.h (GNU): Section 3.2.4.6 [Growing Objects], page 62.

void obstack_ptr_grow_fast (struct obstack *obstack-ptr, void *data)
        obstack.h (GNU): Section 3.2.4.7 [Extra Fast Growing Objects], page 64.

int obstack_room (struct obstack *obstack-ptr)
        obstack.h (GNU): Section 3.2.4.7 [Extra Fast Growing Objects], page 64.

int obstack_vprintf (struct obstack *obstack, const char *template, va_list ap)
        stdio.h (GNU): Section 12.12.9 [Variable Arguments Output Functions], page 281.

int O_CREAT
        fcntl.h (POSIX.1): Section 13.14.2 [Open-time Flags], page 364.

int O_EXCL
        fcntl.h (POSIX.1): Section 13.14.2 [Open-time Flags], page 364.

int O_EXEC
        fcntl.h, (optional) (GNU): Section 13.14.1 [File Access Modes], page 363.

int O_EXLOCK
        fcntl.h, (optional) (BSD): Section 13.14.2 [Open-time Flags], page 364.

off64_t
        sys/types.h (Unix98): Section 13.3 [Setting the File Position of a Descriptor], page 331.

size_t offsetof (type, member)
        stddef.h (ISO): Section A.5.4 [Structure Field Offset Measurement], page 891.

off_t

> sys/types.h (POSIX.1): Section 13.3 [Setting the File Position of a Descriptor], page 331.

int O_FSYNC

> fcntl.h (BSD): Section 13.14.3 [I/O Operating Modes], page 366.

int O_IGNORE_CTTY

> fcntl.h, (optional) (GNU): Section 13.14.2 [Open-time Flags], page 364.

OLD_TIME

> utmp.h (SVID): Section 30.12.1 [Manipulating the User Accounting Database], page 802.

OLD_TIME

> utmpx.h (XPG4.2): Section 30.12.2 [XPG User Accounting Database Functions], page 807.

int O_NDELAY

> fcntl.h (BSD): Section 13.14.3 [I/O Operating Modes], page 366.

int on_exit (void (*function)(int status, void *arg), void *arg)
> stdlib.h (SunOS): Section 25.7.3 [Cleanups on Exit], page 746.

tcflag_t ONLCR

> termios.h (POSIX.1): Section 17.4.5 [Output Modes], page 484.

int O_NOATIME

> fcntl.h (GNU): Section 13.14.3 [I/O Operating Modes], page 366.

int O_NOCTTY

> fcntl.h (POSIX.1): Section 13.14.2 [Open-time Flags], page 364.

tcflag_t ONOEOT

> termios.h, (optional) (BSD): Section 17.4.5 [Output Modes], page 484.

int O_NOLINK

> fcntl.h, (optional) (GNU): Section 13.14.2 [Open-time Flags], page 364.

int O_NONBLOCK

> fcntl.h (POSIX.1): Section 13.14.2 [Open-time Flags], page 364.

int O_NONBLOCK

> fcntl.h (POSIX.1): Section 13.14.3 [I/O Operating Modes], page 366.

int O_NOTRANS

> fcntl.h, (optional) (GNU): Section 13.14.2 [Open-time Flags], page 364.

int open (const char *filename, int flags[, mode_t mode])
> fcntl.h (POSIX.1): Section 13.1 [Opening and Closing Files], page 323.

int open64 (const char *filename, int flags[, mode_t mode])
> fcntl.h (Unix98): Section 13.1 [Opening and Closing Files], page 323.

DIR * opendir (const char *dirname)
> dirent.h (POSIX.1): Section 14.2.2 [Opening a Directory Stream], page 381.

void openlog (const char *ident, int option, int facility)
> syslog.h (BSD): Section 18.2.1 [openlog], page 505.

int OPEN_MAX

> limits.h (POSIX.1): Section 32.1 [General Capacity Limits], page 838.

FILE * open_memstream (char **ptr, size_t *sizeloc)
> stdio.h (GNU): Section 12.21.1 [String Streams], page 314.

int openpty (int *amaster, int *aslave, char *name, const struct termios *termp, const struct winsize *winp)
> pty.h (BSD): Section 17.8.2 [Opening a Pseudo-Terminal Pair], page 502.

`tcflag_t OPOST`

> `termios.h` (POSIX.1): Section 17.4.5 [Output Modes], page 484.

`char * optarg`

> `unistd.h` (POSIX.2): Section 25.2.1 [Using the **getopt** function], page 707.

`int opterr`

> `unistd.h` (POSIX.2): Section 25.2.1 [Using the **getopt** function], page 707.

`int optind`

> `unistd.h` (POSIX.2): Section 25.2.1 [Using the **getopt** function], page 707.

`OPTION_ALIAS`

> `argp.h` (GNU): Section 25.3.4.1 [Flags for Argp Options], page 717.

`OPTION_ARG_OPTIONAL`

> `argp.h` (GNU): Section 25.3.4.1 [Flags for Argp Options], page 717.

`OPTION_DOC`

> `argp.h` (GNU): Section 25.3.4.1 [Flags for Argp Options], page 717.

`OPTION_HIDDEN`

> `argp.h` (GNU): Section 25.3.4.1 [Flags for Argp Options], page 717.

`OPTION_NO_USAGE`

> `argp.h` (GNU): Section 25.3.4.1 [Flags for Argp Options], page 717.

`int optopt`

> `unistd.h` (POSIX.2): Section 25.2.1 [Using the **getopt** function], page 707.

`int O_RDONLY`

> `fcntl.h` (POSIX.1): Section 13.14.1 [File Access Modes], page 363.

`int O_RDWR`

> `fcntl.h` (POSIX.1): Section 13.14.1 [File Access Modes], page 363.

`int O_READ`

> `fcntl.h`, `(optional)` (GNU): Section 13.14.1 [File Access Modes], page 363.

`int O_SHLOCK`

> `fcntl.h`, `(optional)` (BSD): Section 13.14.2 [Open-time Flags], page 364.

`int O_SYNC`

> `fcntl.h` (BSD): Section 13.14.3 [I/O Operating Modes], page 366.

`int O_TRUNC`

> `fcntl.h` (POSIX.1): Section 13.14.2 [Open-time Flags], page 364.

`int O_WRITE`

> `fcntl.h`, `(optional)` (GNU): Section 13.14.1 [File Access Modes], page 363.

`int O_WRONLY`

> `fcntl.h` (POSIX.1): Section 13.14.1 [File Access Modes], page 363.

`tcflag_t OXTABS`

> `termios.h`, `(optional)` (BSD): Section 17.4.5 [Output Modes], page 484.

`PA_CHAR`

> `printf.h` (GNU): Section 12.12.10 [Parsing a Template String], page 284.

`PA_DOUBLE`

> `printf.h` (GNU): Section 12.12.10 [Parsing a Template String], page 284.

`PA_FLAG_LONG`

> `printf.h` (GNU): Section 12.12.10 [Parsing a Template String], page 284.

PA_FLAG_LONG_DOUBLE
             `printf.h` (GNU): Section 12.12.10 [Parsing a Template String], page 284.

PA_FLAG_LONG_LONG
             `printf.h` (GNU): Section 12.12.10 [Parsing a Template String], page 284.

int PA_FLAG_MASK
             `printf.h` (GNU): Section 12.12.10 [Parsing a Template String], page 284.

PA_FLAG_PTR
             `printf.h` (GNU): Section 12.12.10 [Parsing a Template String], page 284.

PA_FLAG_SHORT
             `printf.h` (GNU): Section 12.12.10 [Parsing a Template String], page 284.

PA_FLOAT
             `printf.h` (GNU): Section 12.12.10 [Parsing a Template String], page 284.

PA_INT
             `printf.h` (GNU): Section 12.12.10 [Parsing a Template String], page 284.

PA_LAST
             `printf.h` (GNU): Section 12.12.10 [Parsing a Template String], page 284.

PA_POINTER
             `printf.h` (GNU): Section 12.12.10 [Parsing a Template String], page 284.

tcflag_t PARENB
             `termios.h` (POSIX.1): Section 17.4.6 [Control Modes], page 485.

tcflag_t PARMRK
             `termios.h` (POSIX.1): Section 17.4.4 [Input Modes], page 482.

tcflag_t PARODD
             `termios.h` (POSIX.1): Section 17.4.6 [Control Modes], page 485.

size_t parse_printf_format (const char *template, size_t n, int *argtypes)
             `printf.h` (GNU): Section 12.12.10 [Parsing a Template String], page 284.

PA_STRING
             `printf.h` (GNU): Section 12.12.10 [Parsing a Template String], page 284.

long int pathconf (const char *filename, int parameter)
             `unistd.h` (POSIX.1): Section 32.9 [Using **pathconf**], page 853.

int PATH_MAX
             `limits.h` (POSIX.1): Section 32.6 [Limits on File System Capacity], page 850.

int pause (void)
             `unistd.h` (POSIX.1): Section 24.8.1 [Using **pause**], page 699.

_PC_ASYNC_IO
             `unistd.h` (POSIX.1): Section 32.9 [Using **pathconf**], page 853.

_PC_CHOWN_RESTRICTED
             `unistd.h` (POSIX.1): Section 32.9 [Using **pathconf**], page 853.

_PC_FILESIZEBITS
             `unistd.h` (LFS): Section 32.9 [Using **pathconf**], page 853.

_PC_LINK_MAX
             `unistd.h` (POSIX.1): Section 32.9 [Using **pathconf**], page 853.

int pclose (FILE *stream)
             `stdio.h` (POSIX.2, SVID, BSD): Section 15.2 [Pipe to a Subprocess], page 426.

_PC_MAX_CANON
             `unistd.h` (POSIX.1): Section 32.9 [Using **pathconf**], page 853.

`_PC_MAX_INPUT`
> `unistd.h` (POSIX.1): Section 32.9 [Using `pathconf`], page 853.

`_PC_NAME_MAX`
> `unistd.h` (POSIX.1): Section 32.9 [Using `pathconf`], page 853.

`_PC_NO_TRUNC`
> `unistd.h` (POSIX.1): Section 32.9 [Using `pathconf`], page 853.

`_PC_PATH_MAX`
> `unistd.h` (POSIX.1): Section 32.9 [Using `pathconf`], page 853.

`_PC_PIPE_BUF`
> `unistd.h` (POSIX.1): Section 32.9 [Using `pathconf`], page 853.

`_PC_PRIO_IO`
> `unistd.h` (POSIX.1): Section 32.9 [Using `pathconf`], page 853.

`_PC_REC_INCR_XFER_SIZE`
> `unistd.h` (POSIX.1): Section 32.9 [Using `pathconf`], page 853.

`_PC_REC_MAX_XFER_SIZE`
> `unistd.h` (POSIX.1): Section 32.9 [Using `pathconf`], page 853.

`_PC_REC_MIN_XFER_SIZE`
> `unistd.h` (POSIX.1): Section 32.9 [Using `pathconf`], page 853.

`_PC_REC_XFER_ALIGN`
> `unistd.h` (POSIX.1): Section 32.9 [Using `pathconf`], page 853.

`_PC_SYNC_IO`
> `unistd.h` (POSIX.1): Section 32.9 [Using `pathconf`], page 853.

`_PC_VDISABLE`
> `unistd.h` (POSIX.1): Section 32.9 [Using `pathconf`], page 853.

`tcflag_t PENDIN`
> `termios.h` (BSD): Section 17.4.7 [Local Modes], page 486.

`void perror (const char *message)`
> `stdio.h` (ISO): Section 2.3 [Error Messages], page 33.

`int PF_FILE`
> `sys/socket.h` (GNU): Section 16.5.2 [Details of Local Namespace], page 435.

`int PF_INET`
> `sys/socket.h` (BSD): Section 16.6 [The Internet Namespace], page 437.

`int PF_INET6`
> `sys/socket.h` (X/Open): Section 16.6 [The Internet Namespace], page 437.

`int PF_LOCAL`
> `sys/socket.h` (POSIX): Section 16.5.2 [Details of Local Namespace], page 435.

`int PF_UNIX`
> `sys/socket.h` (BSD): Section 16.5.2 [Details of Local Namespace], page 435.

`pid_t`
> `sys/types.h` (POSIX.1): Section 26.3 [Process Identification], page 750.

`int pipe (int filedes[2])`
> `unistd.h` (POSIX.1): Section 15.1 [Creating a Pipe], page 424.

`int PIPE_BUF`
> `limits.h` (POSIX.1): Section 32.6 [Limits on File System Capacity], page 850.

`FILE * popen (const char *command, const char *mode)`
> `stdio.h` (POSIX.2, SVID, BSD): Section 15.2 [Pipe to a Subprocess], page 426.

`_POSIX2_BC_BASE_MAX`
>        `limits.h` (POSIX.2): Section 32.11 [Minimum Values for Utility Limits], page 855.

`_POSIX2_BC_DIM_MAX`
>        `limits.h` (POSIX.2): Section 32.11 [Minimum Values for Utility Limits], page 855.

`_POSIX2_BC_SCALE_MAX`
>        `limits.h` (POSIX.2): Section 32.11 [Minimum Values for Utility Limits], page 855.

`_POSIX2_BC_STRING_MAX`
>        `limits.h` (POSIX.2): Section 32.11 [Minimum Values for Utility Limits], page 855.

`int _POSIX2_C_DEV`
>        `unistd.h` (POSIX.2): Section 32.2 [Overall System Options], page 839.

`_POSIX2_COLL_WEIGHTS_MAX`
>        `limits.h` (POSIX.2): Section 32.11 [Minimum Values for Utility Limits], page 855.

`long int _POSIX2_C_VERSION`
>        `unistd.h` (POSIX.2): Section 32.3 [Which Version of POSIX is Supported], page 840.

`_POSIX2_EQUIV_CLASS_MAX`
>        `limits.h` (POSIX.2): Section 32.11 [Minimum Values for Utility Limits], page 855.

`_POSIX2_EXPR_NEST_MAX`
>        `limits.h` (POSIX.2): Section 32.11 [Minimum Values for Utility Limits], page 855.

`int _POSIX2_FORT_DEV`
>        `unistd.h` (POSIX.2): Section 32.2 [Overall System Options], page 839.

`int _POSIX2_FORT_RUN`
>        `unistd.h` (POSIX.2): Section 32.2 [Overall System Options], page 839.

`_POSIX2_LINE_MAX`
>        `limits.h` (POSIX.2): Section 32.11 [Minimum Values for Utility Limits], page 855.

`int _POSIX2_LOCALEDEF`
>        `unistd.h` (POSIX.2): Section 32.2 [Overall System Options], page 839.

`_POSIX2_RE_DUP_MAX`
>        `limits.h` (POSIX.2): Section 32.5 [Minimum Values for General Capacity Limits], page 849.

`int _POSIX2_SW_DEV`
>        `unistd.h` (POSIX.2): Section 32.2 [Overall System Options], page 839.

`_POSIX_AIO_LISTIO_MAX`
>        `limits.h` (POSIX.1): Section 32.5 [Minimum Values for General Capacity Limits], page 849.

`_POSIX_AIO_MAX`
>        `limits.h` (POSIX.1): Section 32.5 [Minimum Values for General Capacity Limits], page 849.

`_POSIX_ARG_MAX`
>        `limits.h` (POSIX.1): Section 32.5 [Minimum Values for General Capacity Limits], page 849.

`_POSIX_CHILD_MAX`
>        `limits.h` (POSIX.1): Section 32.5 [Minimum Values for General Capacity Limits], page 849.

`int _POSIX_CHOWN_RESTRICTED`
>        `unistd.h` (POSIX.1): Section 32.7 [Optional Features in File Support], page 851.

`_POSIX_C_SOURCE`
>        (POSIX.2): Section 1.3.4 [Feature Test Macros], page 15.

`int _POSIX_JOB_CONTROL`
>        `unistd.h` (POSIX.1): Section 32.2 [Overall System Options], page 839.

`_POSIX_LINK_MAX`
>        `limits.h` (POSIX.1): Section 32.8 [Minimum Values for File System Limits], page 852.

long double pow10l (long double *x*)
>       math.h (GNU): Section 19.4 [Exponentiation and Logarithms], page 515.

float powf (float *base*, float *power*)
>       math.h (ISO): Section 19.4 [Exponentiation and Logarithms], page 515.

long double powl (long double *base*, long double *power*)
>       math.h (ISO): Section 19.4 [Exponentiation and Logarithms], page 515.

ssize_t pread (int *filedes*, void *\*buffer*, size_t *size*, off_t *offset*)
>       unistd.h (Unix98): Section 13.2 [Input and Output Primitives], page 326.

ssize_t pread64 (int *filedes*, void *\*buffer*, size_t *size*, off64_t *offset*)
>       unistd.h (Unix98): Section 13.2 [Input and Output Primitives], page 326.

int printf (const char *\*template*, ...)
>       stdio.h (ISO): Section 12.12.7 [Formatted Output Functions], page 278.

printf_arginfo_function
>       printf.h (GNU): Section 12.13.3 [Defining the Output Handler], page 289.

printf_function
>       printf.h (GNU): Section 12.13.3 [Defining the Output Handler], page 289.

int printf_size (FILE *\*fp*, const struct printf_info *\*info*, const void *const *\*args*)
>       printf.h (GNU): Section 12.13.5 [Predefined printf Handlers], page 291.

int printf_size_info (const struct printf_info *\*info*, size_t *n*, int *\*argtypes*)
>       printf.h (GNU): Section 12.13.5 [Predefined printf Handlers], page 291.

PRIO_MAX
>       sys/resource.h (BSD): Section 22.3.4.2 [Functions For Traditional Scheduling], page 644.

PRIO_MIN
>       sys/resource.h (BSD): Section 22.3.4.2 [Functions For Traditional Scheduling], page 644.

PRIO_PGRP
>       sys/resource.h (BSD): Section 22.3.4.2 [Functions For Traditional Scheduling], page 644.

PRIO_PROCESS
>       sys/resource.h (BSD): Section 22.3.4.2 [Functions For Traditional Scheduling], page 644.

PRIO_USER
>       sys/resource.h (BSD): Section 22.3.4.2 [Functions For Traditional Scheduling], page 644.

char * program_invocation_name
>       errno.h (GNU): Section 2.3 [Error Messages], page 33.

char * program_invocation_short_name
>       errno.h (GNU): Section 2.3 [Error Messages], page 33.

void psignal (int *signum*, const char *\*message*)
>       signal.h (BSD): Section 24.2.8 [Signal Messages], page 671.

int pthread_getattr_default_np (pthread_attr_t *\*attr*)
>       pthread.h (GNU): Section 35.2.1 [Setting Process-wide defaults for thread attributes], page 869.

void *pthread_getspecific (pthread_key_t *key*)
>       pthread.h (POSIX): Section 35.1 [Thread-specific Data], page 869.

int pthread_key_create (pthread_key_t *\*key*, void (*\*destructor*)(void*))
>       pthread.h (POSIX): Section 35.1 [Thread-specific Data], page 869.

int pthread_key_delete (pthread_key_t *key*)
>       pthread.h (POSIX): Section 35.1 [Thread-specific Data], page 869.

int pthread_setattr_default_np (pthread_attr_t *attr)
> pthread.h (GNU): Section 35.2.1 [Setting Process-wide defaults for thread attributes], page 869.

int pthread_setspecific (pthread_key_t key, const void *value)
> pthread.h (POSIX): Section 35.1 [Thread-specific Data], page 869.

char * P_tmpdir
> stdio.h (SVID): Section 14.11 [Temporary Files], page 419.

ptrdiff_t
> stddef.h (ISO): Section A.4 [Important Data Types], page 884.

char * ptsname (int filedes)
> stdlib.h (SVID, XPG4.2): Section 17.8.1 [Allocating Pseudo-Terminals], page 500.

int ptsname_r (int filedes, char *buf, size_t len)
> stdlib.h (GNU): Section 17.8.1 [Allocating Pseudo-Terminals], page 500.

int putc (int c, FILE *stream)
> stdio.h (ISO): Section 12.7 [Simple Output by Characters or Lines], page 259.

int putchar (int c)
> stdio.h (ISO): Section 12.7 [Simple Output by Characters or Lines], page 259.

int putchar_unlocked (int c)
> stdio.h (POSIX): Section 12.7 [Simple Output by Characters or Lines], page 259.

int putc_unlocked (int c, FILE *stream)
> stdio.h (POSIX): Section 12.7 [Simple Output by Characters or Lines], page 259.

int putenv (char *string)
> stdlib.h (SVID): Section 25.4.1 [Environment Access], page 738.

int putpwent (const struct passwd *p, FILE *stream)
> pwd.h (SVID): Section 30.13.4 [Writing a User Entry], page 813.

int puts (const char *s)
> stdio.h (ISO): Section 12.7 [Simple Output by Characters or Lines], page 259.

struct utmp * pututline (const struct utmp *utmp)
> utmp.h (SVID): Section 30.12.1 [Manipulating the User Accounting Database], page 802.

struct utmpx * pututxline (const struct utmpx *utmp)
> utmpx.h (XPG4.2): Section 30.12.2 [XPG User Accounting Database Functions], page 807.

int putw (int w, FILE *stream)
> stdio.h (SVID): Section 12.7 [Simple Output by Characters or Lines], page 259.

wint_t putwc (wchar_t wc, FILE *stream)
> wchar.h (ISO): Section 12.7 [Simple Output by Characters or Lines], page 259.

wint_t putwchar (wchar_t wc)
> wchar.h (ISO): Section 12.7 [Simple Output by Characters or Lines], page 259.

wint_t putwchar_unlocked (wchar_t wc)
> wchar.h (GNU): Section 12.7 [Simple Output by Characters or Lines], page 259.

wint_t putwc_unlocked (wchar_t wc, FILE *stream)
> wchar.h (GNU): Section 12.7 [Simple Output by Characters or Lines], page 259.

ssize_t pwrite (int filedes, const void *buffer, size_t size, off_t offset)
> unistd.h (Unix98): Section 13.2 [Input and Output Primitives], page 326.

ssize_t pwrite64 (int filedes, const void *buffer, size_t size, off64_t offset)
> unistd.h (Unix98): Section 13.2 [Input and Output Primitives], page 326.

char * qecvt (long double *value*, int *ndigit*, int *decpt*, int *neg*)
>    stdlib.h (GNU): Section 20.12 [Old-fashioned System V number-to-string functions], page 591.

int qecvt_r (long double *value*, int *ndigit*, int *decpt*, int *neg*, char *buf*, size_t *len*)
>    stdlib.h (GNU): Section 20.12 [Old-fashioned System V number-to-string functions], page 591.

char * qfcvt (long double *value*, int *ndigit*, int *decpt*, int *neg*)
>    stdlib.h (GNU): Section 20.12 [Old-fashioned System V number-to-string functions], page 591.

int qfcvt_r (long double *value*, int *ndigit*, int *decpt*, int *neg*, char *buf*, size_t *len*)
>    stdlib.h (GNU): Section 20.12 [Old-fashioned System V number-to-string functions], page 591.

char * qgcvt (long double *value*, int *ndigit*, char *buf*)
>    stdlib.h (GNU): Section 20.12 [Old-fashioned System V number-to-string functions], page 591.

void qsort (void *array, size_t *count*, size_t *size*, comparison_fn_t *compare*)
>    stdlib.h (ISO): Section 9.3 [Array Sort Function], page 213.

int raise (int *signum*)
>    signal.h (ISO): Section 24.6.1 [Signaling Yourself], page 688.

int rand (void)
>    stdlib.h (ISO): Section 19.8.1 [ISO C Random Number Functions], page 550.

int RAND_MAX
>    stdlib.h (ISO): Section 19.8.1 [ISO C Random Number Functions], page 550.

long int random (void)
>    stdlib.h (BSD): Section 19.8.2 [BSD Random Number Functions], page 551.

int random_r (struct random_data *restrict *buf*, int32_t *restrict *result*)
>    stdlib.h (GNU): Section 19.8.2 [BSD Random Number Functions], page 551.

int rand_r (unsigned int *seed*)
>    stdlib.h (POSIX.1): Section 19.8.1 [ISO C Random Number Functions], page 550.

void * rawmemchr (const void *block*, int *c*)
>    string.h (GNU): Section 5.7 [Search Functions], page 110.

ssize_t read (int *filedes*, void *buffer*, size_t *size*)
>    unistd.h (POSIX.1): Section 13.2 [Input and Output Primitives], page 326.

struct dirent * readdir (DIR *dirstream*)
>    dirent.h (POSIX.1): Section 14.2.3 [Reading and Closing a Directory Stream], page 382.

struct dirent64 * readdir64 (DIR *dirstream*)
>    dirent.h (LFS): Section 14.2.3 [Reading and Closing a Directory Stream], page 382.

int readdir64_r (DIR *dirstream*, struct dirent64 *entry*, struct dirent64 **result*)
>    dirent.h (LFS): Section 14.2.3 [Reading and Closing a Directory Stream], page 382.

int readdir_r (DIR *dirstream*, struct dirent *entry*, struct dirent **result*)
>    dirent.h (GNU): Section 14.2.3 [Reading and Closing a Directory Stream], page 382.

ssize_t readlink (const char *filename*, char *buffer*, size_t *size*)
>    unistd.h (BSD): Section 14.5 [Symbolic Links], page 393.

ssize_t readv (int *filedes*, const struct iovec *vector*, int *count*)
>    sys/uio.h (BSD): Section 13.6 [Fast Scatter-Gather I/O], page 336.

void * realloc (void *ptr*, size_t *newsize*)
>    malloc.h, stdlib.h (ISO): Section 3.2.2.4 [Changing the Size of a Block], page 44.

__realloc_hook
>        malloc.h (GNU): Section 3.2.2.10 [Memory Allocation Hooks], page 50.

char * realpath (const char *restrict *name*, char *restrict *resolved*)
>        stdlib.h (XPG): Section 14.5 [Symbolic Links], page 393.

ssize_t recv (int *socket*, void *\*buffer*, size_t *size*, int *flags*)
>        sys/socket.h (BSD): Section 16.9.5.2 [Receiving Data], page 460.

ssize_t recvfrom (int *socket*, void *\*buffer*, size_t *size*, int *flags*, struct sockaddr *\*addr*,
socklen_t *\*length-ptr*)
>        sys/socket.h (BSD): Section 16.10.2 [Receiving Datagrams], page 468.

ssize_t recvmsg (int *socket*, struct msghdr *\*message*, int *flags*)
>        sys/socket.h (BSD): Section 16.10.2 [Receiving Datagrams], page 468.

int RE_DUP_MAX
>        limits.h (POSIX.2): Section 32.1 [General Capacity Limits], page 838.

_REENTRANT

>        (GNU): Section 1.3.4 [Feature Test Macros], page 15.

REG_BADBR

>        regex.h (POSIX.2): Section 10.3.1 [POSIX Regular Expression Compilation], page 231.

REG_BADPAT

>        regex.h (POSIX.2): Section 10.3.1 [POSIX Regular Expression Compilation], page 231.

REG_BADRPT

>        regex.h (POSIX.2): Section 10.3.1 [POSIX Regular Expression Compilation], page 231.

int regcomp (regex_t *restrict *compiled*, const char *restrict *pattern*, int *cflags*)
>        regex.h (POSIX.2): Section 10.3.1 [POSIX Regular Expression Compilation], page 231.

REG_EBRACE

>        regex.h (POSIX.2): Section 10.3.1 [POSIX Regular Expression Compilation], page 231.

REG_EBRACK

>        regex.h (POSIX.2): Section 10.3.1 [POSIX Regular Expression Compilation], page 231.

REG_ECOLLATE
>        regex.h (POSIX.2): Section 10.3.1 [POSIX Regular Expression Compilation], page 231.

REG_ECTYPE

>        regex.h (POSIX.2): Section 10.3.1 [POSIX Regular Expression Compilation], page 231.

REG_EESCAPE

>        regex.h (POSIX.2): Section 10.3.1 [POSIX Regular Expression Compilation], page 231.

REG_EPAREN

>        regex.h (POSIX.2): Section 10.3.1 [POSIX Regular Expression Compilation], page 231.

REG_ERANGE

>        regex.h (POSIX.2): Section 10.3.1 [POSIX Regular Expression Compilation], page 231.

size_t regerror (int *errcode*, const regex_t *restrict *compiled*, char *restrict *buffer*, size_t
*length*)
>        regex.h (POSIX.2): Section 10.3.6 [POSIX Regexp Matching Cleanup], page 235.

REG_ESPACE

>        regex.h (POSIX.2): Section 10.3.3 [Matching a Compiled POSIX Regular Expression],
>        page 233.

REG_ESPACE

>        regex.h (POSIX.2): Section 10.3.1 [POSIX Regular Expression Compilation], page 231.

REG_ESUBREG

> regex.h (POSIX.2): Section 10.3.1 [POSIX Regular Expression Compilation], page 231.

int regexec (const regex_t *restrict *compiled*, const char *restrict *string*, size_t *nmatch*, regmatch_t *matchptr*[restrict], int *eflags*)

> regex.h (POSIX.2): Section 10.3.3 [Matching a Compiled POSIX Regular Expression], page 233.

regex_t

> regex.h (POSIX.2): Section 10.3.1 [POSIX Regular Expression Compilation], page 231.

REG_EXTENDED

> regex.h (POSIX.2): Section 10.3.2 [Flags for POSIX Regular Expressions], page 232.

void regfree (regex_t *compiled*)

> regex.h (POSIX.2): Section 10.3.6 [POSIX Regexp Matching Cleanup], page 235.

REG_ICASE

> regex.h (POSIX.2): Section 10.3.2 [Flags for POSIX Regular Expressions], page 232.

int register_printf_function (int *spec*, printf_function *handler-function*, printf_arginfo_function *arginfo-function*)

> printf.h (GNU): Section 12.13.1 [Registering New Conversions], page 287.

regmatch_t

> regex.h (POSIX.2): Section 10.3.4 [Match Results with Subexpressions], page 234.

REG_NEWLINE

> regex.h (POSIX.2): Section 10.3.2 [Flags for POSIX Regular Expressions], page 232.

REG_NOMATCH

> regex.h (POSIX.2): Section 10.3.3 [Matching a Compiled POSIX Regular Expression], page 233.

REG_NOSUB

> regex.h (POSIX.2): Section 10.3.2 [Flags for POSIX Regular Expressions], page 232.

REG_NOTBOL

> regex.h (POSIX.2): Section 10.3.3 [Matching a Compiled POSIX Regular Expression], page 233.

REG_NOTEOL

> regex.h (POSIX.2): Section 10.3.3 [Matching a Compiled POSIX Regular Expression], page 233.

regoff_t

> regex.h (POSIX.2): Section 10.3.4 [Match Results with Subexpressions], page 234.

double remainder (double *numerator*, double *denominator*)

> math.h (BSD): Section 20.8.4 [Remainder Functions], page 578.

float remainderf (float *numerator*, float *denominator*)

> math.h (BSD): Section 20.8.4 [Remainder Functions], page 578.

long double remainderl (long double *numerator*, long double *denominator*)

> math.h (BSD): Section 20.8.4 [Remainder Functions], page 578.

int remove (const char *filename*)

> stdio.h (ISO): Section 14.6 [Deleting Files], page 396.

int rename (const char *oldname*, const char *newname*)

> stdio.h (ISO): Section 14.7 [Renaming Files], page 397.

void rewind (FILE *stream*)

> stdio.h (ISO): Section 12.18 [File Positioning], page 305.

```
void rewinddir (DIR *dirstream)
        dirent.h (POSIX.1): Section 14.2.5 [Random Access in a Directory Stream], page 385.
char * rindex (const char *string, int c)
        string.h (BSD): Section 5.7 [Search Functions], page 110.
double rint (double x)
        math.h (ISO): Section 20.8.3 [Rounding Functions], page 576.
float rintf (float x)
        math.h (ISO): Section 20.8.3 [Rounding Functions], page 576.
long double rintl (long double x)
        math.h (ISO): Section 20.8.3 [Rounding Functions], page 576.
rlim_t RLIM_INFINITY
        sys/resource.h (BSD): Section 22.2 [Limiting Resource Usage], page 632.
RLIMIT_AS
        sys/resource.h (Unix98): Section 22.2 [Limiting Resource Usage], page 632.
RLIMIT_CORE
        sys/resource.h (BSD): Section 22.2 [Limiting Resource Usage], page 632.
RLIMIT_CPU
        sys/resource.h (BSD): Section 22.2 [Limiting Resource Usage], page 632.
RLIMIT_DATA
        sys/resource.h (BSD): Section 22.2 [Limiting Resource Usage], page 632.
RLIMIT_FSIZE
        sys/resource.h (BSD): Section 22.2 [Limiting Resource Usage], page 632.
RLIMIT_MEMLOCK
        sys/resource.h (BSD): Section 22.2 [Limiting Resource Usage], page 632.
RLIMIT_NOFILE
        sys/resource.h (BSD): Section 22.2 [Limiting Resource Usage], page 632.
RLIMIT_NPROC
        sys/resource.h (BSD): Section 22.2 [Limiting Resource Usage], page 632.
RLIMIT_RSS
        sys/resource.h (BSD): Section 22.2 [Limiting Resource Usage], page 632.
RLIMIT_STACK
        sys/resource.h (BSD): Section 22.2 [Limiting Resource Usage], page 632.
RLIM_NLIMITS
        sys/resource.h (BSD): Section 22.2 [Limiting Resource Usage], page 632.
int rmdir (const char *filename)
        unistd.h (POSIX.1): Section 14.6 [Deleting Files], page 396.
int R_OK
        unistd.h (POSIX.1): Section 14.9.8 [Testing Permission to Access a File], page 412.
double round (double x)
        math.h (ISO): Section 20.8.3 [Rounding Functions], page 576.
float roundf (float x)
        math.h (ISO): Section 20.8.3 [Rounding Functions], page 576.
long double roundl (long double x)
        math.h (ISO): Section 20.8.3 [Rounding Functions], page 576.
int rpmatch (const char *response)
        stdlib.h (stdlib.h): Section 7.9 [Yes-or-No Questions], page 187.
```

RUN_LVL

> `utmp.h` (SVID): Section 30.12.1 [Manipulating the User Accounting Database], page 802.

RUN_LVL

> `utmpx.h` (XPG4.2): Section 30.12.2 [XPG User Accounting Database Functions], page 807.

RUSAGE_CHILDREN

> `sys/resource.h` (BSD): Section 22.1 [Resource Usage], page 630.

RUSAGE_SELF

> `sys/resource.h` (BSD): Section 22.1 [Resource Usage], page 630.

int SA_NOCLDSTOP

> `signal.h` (POSIX.1): Section 24.3.5 [Flags for `sigaction`], page 676.

int SA_ONSTACK

> `signal.h` (BSD): Section 24.3.5 [Flags for `sigaction`], page 676.

int SA_RESTART

> `signal.h` (BSD): Section 24.3.5 [Flags for `sigaction`], page 676.

void *sbrk (ptrdiff_t *delta*)

> `unistd.h` (BSD): Section 3.3 [Resizing the Data Segment], page 72.

_SC_2_C_DEV

> `unistd.h` (POSIX.2): Section 32.4.2 [Constants for `sysconf` Parameters], page 841.

_SC_2_FORT_DEV

> `unistd.h` (POSIX.2): Section 32.4.2 [Constants for `sysconf` Parameters], page 841.

_SC_2_FORT_RUN

> `unistd.h` (POSIX.2): Section 32.4.2 [Constants for `sysconf` Parameters], page 841.

_SC_2_LOCALEDEF

> `unistd.h` (POSIX.2): Section 32.4.2 [Constants for `sysconf` Parameters], page 841.

_SC_2_SW_DEV

> `unistd.h` (POSIX.2): Section 32.4.2 [Constants for `sysconf` Parameters], page 841.

_SC_2_VERSION

> `unistd.h` (POSIX.2): Section 32.4.2 [Constants for `sysconf` Parameters], page 841.

_SC_AIO_LISTIO_MAX

> `unistd.h` (POSIX.1): Section 32.4.2 [Constants for `sysconf` Parameters], page 841.

_SC_AIO_MAX

> `unistd.h` (POSIX.1): Section 32.4.2 [Constants for `sysconf` Parameters], page 841.

_SC_AIO_PRIO_DELTA_MAX

> `unistd.h` (POSIX.1): Section 32.4.2 [Constants for `sysconf` Parameters], page 841.

double scalb (double *value*, double *exponent*)

> `math.h` (BSD): Section 20.8.2 [Normalization Functions], page 574.

float scalbf (float *value*, float *exponent*)

> `math.h` (BSD): Section 20.8.2 [Normalization Functions], page 574.

long double scalbl (long double *value*, long double *exponent*)

> `math.h` (BSD): Section 20.8.2 [Normalization Functions], page 574.

double scalbln (double *x*, long int *n*)

> `math.h` (BSD): Section 20.8.2 [Normalization Functions], page 574.

float scalblnf (float *x*, long int *n*)

> `math.h` (BSD): Section 20.8.2 [Normalization Functions], page 574.

long double scalblnl (long double *x*, long int *n*)

> `math.h` (BSD): Section 20.8.2 [Normalization Functions], page 574.

`double scalbn (double x, int n)`
> `math.h` (BSD): Section 20.8.2 [Normalization Functions], page 574.

`float scalbnf (float x, int n)`
> `math.h` (BSD): Section 20.8.2 [Normalization Functions], page 574.

`long double scalbnl (long double x, int n)`
> `math.h` (BSD): Section 20.8.2 [Normalization Functions], page 574.

`int scandir (const char *dir, struct dirent ***namelist, int (*selector) (const struct dirent *), int (*cmp) (const struct dirent **, const struct dirent **))`
> `dirent.h` (BSD/SVID): Section 14.2.6 [Scanning the Content of a Directory], page 385.

`int scandir64 (const char *dir, struct dirent64 ***namelist, int (*selector) (const struct dirent64 *), int (*cmp) (const struct dirent64 **, const struct dirent64 **))`
> `dirent.h` (GNU): Section 14.2.6 [Scanning the Content of a Directory], page 385.

`int scanf (const char *template, ...)`
> `stdio.h` (ISO): Section 12.14.8 [Formatted Input Functions], page 300.

`_SC_ARG_MAX`
> `unistd.h` (POSIX.1): Section 32.4.2 [Constants for `sysconf` Parameters], page 841.

`_SC_ASYNCHRONOUS_IO`
> `unistd.h` (POSIX.1): Section 32.4.2 [Constants for `sysconf` Parameters], page 841.

`_SC_ATEXIT_MAX`
> `unistd.h` (GNU): Section 32.4.2 [Constants for `sysconf` Parameters], page 841.

`_SC_AVPHYS_PAGES`
> `unistd.h` (GNU): Section 32.4.2 [Constants for `sysconf` Parameters], page 841.

`_SC_BC_BASE_MAX`
> `unistd.h` (POSIX.2): Section 32.4.2 [Constants for `sysconf` Parameters], page 841.

`_SC_BC_DIM_MAX`
> `unistd.h` (POSIX.2): Section 32.4.2 [Constants for `sysconf` Parameters], page 841.

`_SC_BC_SCALE_MAX`
> `unistd.h` (POSIX.2): Section 32.4.2 [Constants for `sysconf` Parameters], page 841.

`_SC_BC_STRING_MAX`
> `unistd.h` (POSIX.2): Section 32.4.2 [Constants for `sysconf` Parameters], page 841.

`_SC_CHAR_BIT`
> `unistd.h` (X/Open): Section 32.4.2 [Constants for `sysconf` Parameters], page 841.

`_SC_CHARCLASS_NAME_MAX`
> `unistd.h` (GNU): Section 32.4.2 [Constants for `sysconf` Parameters], page 841.

`_SC_CHAR_MAX`
> `unistd.h` (X/Open): Section 32.4.2 [Constants for `sysconf` Parameters], page 841.

`_SC_CHAR_MIN`
> `unistd.h` (X/Open): Section 32.4.2 [Constants for `sysconf` Parameters], page 841.

`_SC_CHILD_MAX`
> `unistd.h` (POSIX.1): Section 32.4.2 [Constants for `sysconf` Parameters], page 841.

`_SC_CLK_TCK`
> `unistd.h` (POSIX.1): Section 32.4.2 [Constants for `sysconf` Parameters], page 841.

`_SC_COLL_WEIGHTS_MAX`
> `unistd.h` (POSIX.2): Section 32.4.2 [Constants for `sysconf` Parameters], page 841.

`_SC_DELAYTIMER_MAX`
> `unistd.h` (POSIX.1): Section 32.4.2 [Constants for `sysconf` Parameters], page 841.

**_SC_EQUIV_CLASS_MAX**

> `unistd.h` (POSIX.2): Section 32.4.2 [Constants for `sysconf` Parameters], page 841.

**_SC_EXPR_NEST_MAX**

> `unistd.h` (POSIX.2): Section 32.4.2 [Constants for `sysconf` Parameters], page 841.

**_SC_FSYNC**

> `unistd.h` (POSIX.1): Section 32.4.2 [Constants for `sysconf` Parameters], page 841.

**_SC_GETGR_R_SIZE_MAX**

> `unistd.h` (POSIX.1): Section 32.4.2 [Constants for `sysconf` Parameters], page 841.

**_SC_GETPW_R_SIZE_MAX**

> `unistd.h` (POSIX.1): Section 32.4.2 [Constants for `sysconf` Parameters], page 841.

**SCHAR_MAX**

> `limits.h` (ISO): Section A.5.2 [Range of an Integer Type], page 885.

**SCHAR_MIN**

> `limits.h` (ISO): Section A.5.2 [Range of an Integer Type], page 885.

**int sched_getaffinity (pid_t *pid*, size_t *cpusetsize*, cpu_set_t *\*cpuset*)**

> `sched.h` (GNU): Section 22.3.5 [Limiting execution to certain CPUs], page 645.

**int sched_getparam (pid_t *pid*, struct sched_param *\*param*)**

> `sched.h` (POSIX): Section 22.3.3 [Basic Scheduling Functions], page 639.

**int sched_get_priority_max (int *policy*)**

> `sched.h` (POSIX): Section 22.3.3 [Basic Scheduling Functions], page 639.

**int sched_get_priority_min (int *policy*)**

> `sched.h` (POSIX): Section 22.3.3 [Basic Scheduling Functions], page 639.

**int sched_getscheduler (pid_t *pid*)**

> `sched.h` (POSIX): Section 22.3.3 [Basic Scheduling Functions], page 639.

**int sched_rr_get_interval (pid_t *pid*, struct timespec *\*interval*)**

> `sched.h` (POSIX): Section 22.3.3 [Basic Scheduling Functions], page 639.

**int sched_setaffinity (pid_t *pid*, size_t *cpusetsize*, const cpu_set_t *\*cpuset*)**

> `sched.h` (GNU): Section 22.3.5 [Limiting execution to certain CPUs], page 645.

**int sched_setparam (pid_t *pid*, const struct sched_param *\*param*)**

> `sched.h` (POSIX): Section 22.3.3 [Basic Scheduling Functions], page 639.

**int sched_setscheduler (pid_t *pid*, int *policy*, const struct sched_param *\*param*)**

> `sched.h` (POSIX): Section 22.3.3 [Basic Scheduling Functions], page 639.

**int sched_yield (void)**

> `sched.h` (POSIX): Section 22.3.3 [Basic Scheduling Functions], page 639.

**_SC_INT_MAX**

> `unistd.h` (X/Open): Section 32.4.2 [Constants for `sysconf` Parameters], page 841.

**_SC_INT_MIN**

> `unistd.h` (X/Open): Section 32.4.2 [Constants for `sysconf` Parameters], page 841.

**_SC_JOB_CONTROL**

> `unistd.h` (POSIX.1): Section 32.4.2 [Constants for `sysconf` Parameters], page 841.

**_SC_LINE_MAX**

> `unistd.h` (POSIX.2): Section 32.4.2 [Constants for `sysconf` Parameters], page 841.

**_SC_LOGIN_NAME_MAX**

> `unistd.h` (POSIX.1): Section 32.4.2 [Constants for `sysconf` Parameters], page 841.

**_SC_LONG_BIT**

> `unistd.h` (X/Open): Section 32.4.2 [Constants for `sysconf` Parameters], page 841.

_SC_MAPPED_FILES
            unistd.h (POSIX.1): Section 32.4.2 [Constants for sysconf Parameters], page 841.

_SC_MB_LEN_MAX
            unistd.h (X/Open): Section 32.4.2 [Constants for sysconf Parameters], page 841.

_SC_MEMLOCK
            unistd.h (POSIX.1): Section 32.4.2 [Constants for sysconf Parameters], page 841.

_SC_MEMLOCK_RANGE
            unistd.h (POSIX.1): Section 32.4.2 [Constants for sysconf Parameters], page 841.

_SC_MEMORY_PROTECTION
            unistd.h (POSIX.1): Section 32.4.2 [Constants for sysconf Parameters], page 841.

_SC_MESSAGE_PASSING
            unistd.h (POSIX.1): Section 32.4.2 [Constants for sysconf Parameters], page 841.

_SC_MQ_OPEN_MAX
            unistd.h (POSIX.1): Section 32.4.2 [Constants for sysconf Parameters], page 841.

_SC_MQ_PRIO_MAX
            unistd.h (POSIX.1): Section 32.4.2 [Constants for sysconf Parameters], page 841.

_SC_NGROUPS_MAX
            unistd.h (POSIX.1): Section 32.4.2 [Constants for sysconf Parameters], page 841.

_SC_NL_ARGMAX
            unistd.h (X/Open): Section 32.4.2 [Constants for sysconf Parameters], page 841.

_SC_NL_LANGMAX
            unistd.h (X/Open): Section 32.4.2 [Constants for sysconf Parameters], page 841.

_SC_NL_MSGMAX
            unistd.h (X/Open): Section 32.4.2 [Constants for sysconf Parameters], page 841.

_SC_NL_NMAX
            unistd.h (X/Open): Section 32.4.2 [Constants for sysconf Parameters], page 841.

_SC_NL_SETMAX
            unistd.h (X/Open): Section 32.4.2 [Constants for sysconf Parameters], page 841.

_SC_NL_TEXTMAX
            unistd.h (X/Open): Section 32.4.2 [Constants for sysconf Parameters], page 841.

_SC_NPROCESSORS_CONF
            unistd.h (GNU): Section 32.4.2 [Constants for sysconf Parameters], page 841.

_SC_NPROCESSORS_ONLN
            unistd.h (GNU): Section 32.4.2 [Constants for sysconf Parameters], page 841.

_SC_NZERO
            unistd.h (X/Open): Section 32.4.2 [Constants for sysconf Parameters], page 841.

_SC_OPEN_MAX
            unistd.h (POSIX.1): Section 32.4.2 [Constants for sysconf Parameters], page 841.

_SC_PAGESIZE
            unistd.h (GNU): Section 32.4.2 [Constants for sysconf Parameters], page 841.

_SC_PHYS_PAGES
            unistd.h (GNU): Section 32.4.2 [Constants for sysconf Parameters], page 841.

_SC_PII
            unistd.h (POSIX.1g): Section 32.4.2 [Constants for sysconf Parameters], page 841.

_SC_PII_INTERNET
            unistd.h (POSIX.1g): Section 32.4.2 [Constants for sysconf Parameters], page 841.

_SC_PII_INTERNET_DGRAM
        unistd.h (POSIX.1g): Section 32.4.2 [Constants for sysconf Parameters], page 841.

_SC_PII_INTERNET_STREAM
        unistd.h (POSIX.1g): Section 32.4.2 [Constants for sysconf Parameters], page 841.

_SC_PII_OSI
        unistd.h (POSIX.1g): Section 32.4.2 [Constants for sysconf Parameters], page 841.

_SC_PII_OSI_CLTS
        unistd.h (POSIX.1g): Section 32.4.2 [Constants for sysconf Parameters], page 841.

_SC_PII_OSI_COTS
        unistd.h (POSIX.1g): Section 32.4.2 [Constants for sysconf Parameters], page 841.

_SC_PII_OSI_M
        unistd.h (POSIX.1g): Section 32.4.2 [Constants for sysconf Parameters], page 841.

_SC_PII_SOCKET
        unistd.h (POSIX.1g): Section 32.4.2 [Constants for sysconf Parameters], page 841.

_SC_PII_XTI
        unistd.h (POSIX.1g): Section 32.4.2 [Constants for sysconf Parameters], page 841.

_SC_PRIORITIZED_IO
        unistd.h (POSIX.1): Section 32.4.2 [Constants for sysconf Parameters], page 841.

_SC_PRIORITY_SCHEDULING
        unistd.h (POSIX.1): Section 32.4.2 [Constants for sysconf Parameters], page 841.

_SC_REALTIME_SIGNALS
        unistdh.h (POSIX.1): Section 32.4.2 [Constants for sysconf Parameters], page 841.

_SC_RTSIG_MAX
        unistd.h (POSIX.1): Section 32.4.2 [Constants for sysconf Parameters], page 841.

_SC_SAVED_IDS
        unistd.h (POSIX.1): Section 32.4.2 [Constants for sysconf Parameters], page 841.

_SC_SCHAR_MAX
        unistd.h (X/Open): Section 32.4.2 [Constants for sysconf Parameters], page 841.

_SC_SCHAR_MIN
        unistd.h (X/Open): Section 32.4.2 [Constants for sysconf Parameters], page 841.

_SC_SELECT
        unistd.h (POSIX.1g): Section 32.4.2 [Constants for sysconf Parameters], page 841.

_SC_SEMAPHORES
        unistd.h (POSIX.1): Section 32.4.2 [Constants for sysconf Parameters], page 841.

_SC_SEM_NSEMS_MAX
        unistd.h (POSIX.1): Section 32.4.2 [Constants for sysconf Parameters], page 841.

_SC_SEM_VALUE_MAX
        unistd.h (POSIX.1): Section 32.4.2 [Constants for sysconf Parameters], page 841.

_SC_SHARED_MEMORY_OBJECTS
        unistd.h (POSIX.1): Section 32.4.2 [Constants for sysconf Parameters], page 841.

_SC_SHRT_MAX
        unistd.h (X/Open): Section 32.4.2 [Constants for sysconf Parameters], page 841.

_SC_SHRT_MIN
        unistd.h (X/Open): Section 32.4.2 [Constants for sysconf Parameters], page 841.

_SC_SIGQUEUE_MAX
        unistd.h (POSIX.1): Section 32.4.2 [Constants for sysconf Parameters], page 841.

SC_SSIZE_MAX

> unistd.h (X/Open): Section 32.4.2 [Constants for sysconf Parameters], page 841.

_SC_STREAM_MAX

> unistd.h (POSIX.1): Section 32.4.2 [Constants for sysconf Parameters], page 841.

_SC_SYNCHRONIZED_IO

> unistd.h (POSIX.1): Section 32.4.2 [Constants for sysconf Parameters], page 841.

_SC_THREAD_ATTR_STACKADDR

> unistd.h (POSIX.1): Section 32.4.2 [Constants for sysconf Parameters], page 841.

_SC_THREAD_ATTR_STACKSIZE

> unistd.h (POSIX.1): Section 32.4.2 [Constants for sysconf Parameters], page 841.

_SC_THREAD_DESTRUCTOR_ITERATIONS

> unistd.h (POSIX.1): Section 32.4.2 [Constants for sysconf Parameters], page 841.

_SC_THREAD_KEYS_MAX

> unistd.h (POSIX.1): Section 32.4.2 [Constants for sysconf Parameters], page 841.

_SC_THREAD_PRIO_INHERIT

> unistd.h (POSIX.1): Section 32.4.2 [Constants for sysconf Parameters], page 841.

_SC_THREAD_PRIO_PROTECT

> unistd.h (POSIX.1): Section 32.4.2 [Constants for sysconf Parameters], page 841.

_SC_THREAD_PRIORITY_SCHEDULING

> unistd.h (POSIX.1): Section 32.4.2 [Constants for sysconf Parameters], page 841.

_SC_THREAD_PROCESS_SHARED

> unistd.h (POSIX.1): Section 32.4.2 [Constants for sysconf Parameters], page 841.

_SC_THREADS

> unistd.h (POSIX.1): Section 32.4.2 [Constants for sysconf Parameters], page 841.

_SC_THREAD_SAFE_FUNCTIONS

> unistd.h (POSIX.1): Section 32.4.2 [Constants for sysconf Parameters], page 841.

_SC_THREAD_STACK_MIN

> unistd.h (POSIX.1): Section 32.4.2 [Constants for sysconf Parameters], page 841.

_SC_THREAD_THREADS_MAX

> unistd.h (POSIX.1): Section 32.4.2 [Constants for sysconf Parameters], page 841.

_SC_TIMER_MAX

> unistd.h (POSIX.1): Section 32.4.2 [Constants for sysconf Parameters], page 841.

_SC_TIMERS

> unistd.h (POSIX.1): Section 32.4.2 [Constants for sysconf Parameters], page 841.

_SC_T_IOV_MAX

> unistd.h (POSIX.1g): Section 32.4.2 [Constants for sysconf Parameters], page 841.

_SC_TTY_NAME_MAX

> unistd.h (POSIX.1): Section 32.4.2 [Constants for sysconf Parameters], page 841.

_SC_TZNAME_MAX

> unistd.h (POSIX.1): Section 32.4.2 [Constants for sysconf Parameters], page 841.

_SC_UCHAR_MAX

> unistd.h (X/Open): Section 32.4.2 [Constants for sysconf Parameters], page 841.

_SC_UINT_MAX

> unistd.h (X/Open): Section 32.4.2 [Constants for sysconf Parameters], page 841.

_SC_UIO_MAXIOV

> unistd.h (POSIX.1g): Section 32.4.2 [Constants for sysconf Parameters], page 841.

_SC_ULONG_MAX
          unistd.h (X/Open): Section 32.4.2 [Constants for sysconf Parameters], page 841.

_SC_USHRT_MAX
          unistd.h (X/Open): Section 32.4.2 [Constants for sysconf Parameters], page 841.

_SC_VERSION
          unistd.h (POSIX.1): Section 32.4.2 [Constants for sysconf Parameters], page 841.

_SC_VERSION
          unistd.h (POSIX.2): Section 32.4.2 [Constants for sysconf Parameters], page 841.

_SC_WORD_BIT
          unistd.h (X/Open): Section 32.4.2 [Constants for sysconf Parameters], page 841.

_SC_XOPEN_CRYPT
          unistd.h (X/Open): Section 32.4.2 [Constants for sysconf Parameters], page 841.

_SC_XOPEN_ENH_I18N
          unistd.h (X/Open): Section 32.4.2 [Constants for sysconf Parameters], page 841.

_SC_XOPEN_LEGACY
          unistd.h (X/Open): Section 32.4.2 [Constants for sysconf Parameters], page 841.

_SC_XOPEN_REALTIME
          unistd.h (X/Open): Section 32.4.2 [Constants for sysconf Parameters], page 841.

_SC_XOPEN_REALTIME_THREADS
          unistd.h (X/Open): Section 32.4.2 [Constants for sysconf Parameters], page 841.

_SC_XOPEN_SHM
          unistd.h (X/Open): Section 32.4.2 [Constants for sysconf Parameters], page 841.

_SC_XOPEN_UNIX
          unistd.h (X/Open): Section 32.4.2 [Constants for sysconf Parameters], page 841.

_SC_XOPEN_VERSION
          unistd.h (X/Open): Section 32.4.2 [Constants for sysconf Parameters], page 841.

_SC_XOPEN_XCU_VERSION
          unistd.h (X/Open): Section 32.4.2 [Constants for sysconf Parameters], page 841.

_SC_XOPEN_XPG2
          unistd.h (X/Open): Section 32.4.2 [Constants for sysconf Parameters], page 841.

_SC_XOPEN_XPG3
          unistd.h (X/Open): Section 32.4.2 [Constants for sysconf Parameters], page 841.

_SC_XOPEN_XPG4
          unistd.h (X/Open): Section 32.4.2 [Constants for sysconf Parameters], page 841.

char * secure_getenv (const char *name)
          stdlib.h (GNU): Section 25.4.1 [Environment Access], page 738.

unsigned short int * seed48 (unsigned short int seed16v[3])
          stdlib.h (SVID): Section 19.8.3 [SVID Random Number Function], page 553.

int seed48_r (unsigned short int seed16v[3], struct drand48_data *buffer)
          stdlib.h (GNU): Section 19.8.3 [SVID Random Number Function], page 553.

int SEEK_CUR
          stdio.h (ISO): Section 12.18 [File Positioning], page 305.

void seekdir (DIR *dirstream, long int pos)
          dirent.h (BSD): Section 14.2.5 [Random Access in a Directory Stream], page 385.

int SEEK_END
          stdio.h (ISO): Section 12.18 [File Positioning], page 305.

int SEEK_SET
>          stdio.h (ISO): Section 12.18 [File Positioning], page 305.

int select (int *nfds*, fd_set *read-fds*, fd_set *write-fds*, fd_set *except-fds*, struct timeval *timeout*)
>          sys/types.h (BSD): Section 13.8 [Waiting for Input or Output], page 342.

ssize_t send (int *socket*, const void *buffer*, size_t *size*, int *flags*)
>          sys/socket.h (BSD): Section 16.9.5.1 [Sending Data], page 459.

ssize_t sendmsg (int *socket*, const struct msghdr *message*, int *flags*)
>          sys/socket.h (BSD): Section 16.10.2 [Receiving Datagrams], page 468.

ssize_t sendto (int *socket*, const void *buffer*, size_t *size*, int *flags*, struct sockaddr *addr*, socklen_t *length*)
>          sys/socket.h (BSD): Section 16.10.1 [Sending Datagrams], page 467.

void setbuf (FILE *stream*, char *buf*)
>          stdio.h (ISO): Section 12.20.3 [Controlling Which Kind of Buffering], page 311.

void setbuffer (FILE *stream*, char *buf*, size_t *size*)
>          stdio.h (BSD): Section 12.20.3 [Controlling Which Kind of Buffering], page 311.

int setcontext (const ucontext_t *ucp*)
>          ucontext.h (SVID): Section 23.4 [Complete Context Control], page 655.

int setdomainname (const char *name*, size_t *length*)
>          unistd.h (???): Section 31.1 [Host Identification], page 821.

int setegid (gid_t *newgid*)
>          unistd.h (POSIX.1): Section 30.7 [Setting the Group IDs], page 795.

int setenv (const char *name*, const char *value*, int *replace*)
>          stdlib.h (BSD): Section 25.4.1 [Environment Access], page 738.

int seteuid (uid_t *neweuid*)
>          unistd.h (POSIX.1): Section 30.6 [Setting the User ID], page 794.

int setfsent (void)
>          fstab.h (BSD): Section 31.3.1.1 [The fstab file], page 825.

int setgid (gid_t *newgid*)
>          unistd.h (POSIX.1): Section 30.7 [Setting the Group IDs], page 795.

void setgrent (void)
>          grp.h (SVID, BSD): Section 30.14.3 [Scanning the List of All Groups], page 815.

int setgroups (size_t *count*, const gid_t *groups*)
>          grp.h (BSD): Section 30.7 [Setting the Group IDs], page 795.

void sethostent (int *stayopen*)
>          netdb.h (BSD): Section 16.6.2.4 [Host Names], page 443.

int sethostid (long int *id*)
>          unistd.h (BSD): Section 31.1 [Host Identification], page 821.

int sethostname (const char *name*, size_t *length*)
>          unistd.h (BSD): Section 31.1 [Host Identification], page 821.

int setitimer (int *which*, const struct itimerval *new*, struct itimerval *old*)
>          sys/time.h (BSD): Section 21.5 [Setting an Alarm], page 625.

int setjmp (jmp_buf *state*)
>          setjmp.h (ISO): Section 23.2 [Details of Non-Local Exits], page 653.

void setkey (const char *key*)
>          crypt.h (BSD, SVID): Section 33.4 [DES Encryption], page 863.

void setkey_r (const char *key, struct crypt_data * data)
        crypt.h (GNU): Section 33.4 [DES Encryption], page 863.

void setlinebuf (FILE *stream)
        stdio.h (BSD): Section 12.20.3 [Controlling Which Kind of Buffering], page 311.

char * setlocale (int category, const char *locale)
        locale.h (ISO): Section 7.4 [How Programs Set the Locale], page 171.

int setlogmask (int mask)
        syslog.h (BSD): Section 18.2.4 [setlogmask], page 510.

FILE * setmntent (const char *file, const char *mode)
        mntent.h (BSD): Section 31.3.1.2 [The mtab file], page 828.

void setnetent (int stayopen)
        netdb.h (BSD): Section 16.13 [Networks Database], page 475.

int setnetgrent (const char *netgroup)
        netdb.h (BSD): Section 30.16.2 [Looking up one Netgroup], page 818.

int setpgid (pid_t pid, pid_t pgid)
        unistd.h (POSIX.1): Section 28.7.2 [Process Group Functions], page 778.

int setpgrp (pid_t pid, pid_t pgid)
        unistd.h (BSD): Section 28.7.2 [Process Group Functions], page 778.

int setpriority (int class, int id, int niceval)
        sys/resource.h (BSD,POSIX): Section 22.3.4.2 [Functions For Traditional Scheduling],
        page 644.

void setprotoent (int stayopen)
        netdb.h (BSD): Section 16.6.6 [Protocols Database], page 450.

void setpwent (void)
        pwd.h (SVID, BSD): Section 30.13.3 [Scanning the List of All Users], page 812.

int setregid (gid_t rgid, gid_t egid)
        unistd.h (BSD): Section 30.7 [Setting the Group IDs], page 795.

int setreuid (uid_t ruid, uid_t euid)
        unistd.h (BSD): Section 30.6 [Setting the User ID], page 794.

int setrlimit (int resource, const struct rlimit *rlp)
        sys/resource.h (BSD): Section 22.2 [Limiting Resource Usage], page 632.

int setrlimit64 (int resource, const struct rlimit64 *rlp)
        sys/resource.h (Unix98): Section 22.2 [Limiting Resource Usage], page 632.

void setservent (int stayopen)
        netdb.h (BSD): Section 16.6.4 [The Services Database], page 448.

pid_t setsid (void)
        unistd.h (POSIX.1): Section 28.7.2 [Process Group Functions], page 778.

int setsockopt (int socket, int level, int optname, const void *optval, socklen_t optlen)
        sys/socket.h (BSD): Section 16.12.1 [Socket Option Functions], page 472.

char * setstate (char *state)
        stdlib.h (BSD): Section 19.8.2 [BSD Random Number Functions], page 551.

int setstate_r (char *restrict statebuf, struct random_data *restrict buf)
        stdlib.h (GNU): Section 19.8.2 [BSD Random Number Functions], page 551.

int settimeofday (const struct timeval *tp, const struct timezone *tzp)
        sys/time.h (BSD): Section 21.4.2 [High-Resolution Calendar], page 600.

int setuid (uid_t newuid)
        unistd.h (POSIX.1): Section 30.6 [Setting the User ID], page 794.

void setutent (void)
>        utmp.h (SVID): Section 30.12.1 [Manipulating the User Accounting Database], page 802.

void setutxent (void)
>        utmpx.h (XPG4.2): Section 30.12.2 [XPG User Accounting Database Functions], page 807.

int setvbuf (FILE *stream, char *buf, int mode, size_t size)
>        stdio.h (ISO): Section 12.20.3 [Controlling Which Kind of Buffering], page 311.

int shm_open (const char *name, int oflag, mode_t mode)
>        sys/mman.h (POSIX): Section 13.7 [Memory-mapped I/O], page 337.

SHRT_MAX
>        limits.h (ISO): Section A.5.2 [Range of an Integer Type], page 885.

SHRT_MIN
>        limits.h (ISO): Section A.5.2 [Range of an Integer Type], page 885.

int shutdown (int socket, int how)
>        sys/socket.h (BSD): Section 16.8.2 [Closing a Socket], page 454.

S_IEXEC
>        sys/stat.h (BSD): Section 14.9.5 [The Mode Bits for Access Permission], page 408.

S_IFBLK
>        sys/stat.h (BSD): Section 14.9.3 [Testing the Type of a File], page 404.

S_IFCHR
>        sys/stat.h (BSD): Section 14.9.3 [Testing the Type of a File], page 404.

S_IFDIR
>        sys/stat.h (BSD): Section 14.9.3 [Testing the Type of a File], page 404.

S_IFIFO
>        sys/stat.h (BSD): Section 14.9.3 [Testing the Type of a File], page 404.

S_IFLNK
>        sys/stat.h (BSD): Section 14.9.3 [Testing the Type of a File], page 404.

int S_IFMT
>        sys/stat.h (BSD): Section 14.9.3 [Testing the Type of a File], page 404.

S_IFREG
>        sys/stat.h (BSD): Section 14.9.3 [Testing the Type of a File], page 404.

S_IFSOCK
>        sys/stat.h (BSD): Section 14.9.3 [Testing the Type of a File], page 404.

int SIGABRT
>        signal.h (ISO): Section 24.2.1 [Program Error Signals], page 663.

int sigaction (int signum, const struct sigaction *restrict action, struct sigaction *restrict old-action)
>        signal.h (POSIX.1): Section 24.3.2 [Advanced Signal Handling], page 674.

int sigaddset (sigset_t *set, int signum)
>        signal.h (POSIX.1): Section 24.7.2 [Signal Sets], page 693.

int SIGALRM
>        signal.h (POSIX.1): Section 24.2.3 [Alarm Signals], page 667.

int sigaltstack (const stack_t *restrict stack, stack_t *restrict oldstack)
>        signal.h (XPG): Section 24.9 [Using a Separate Signal Stack], page 701.

`sig_atomic_t`
> `signal.h` (ISO): Section 24.4.7.2 [Atomic Types], page 686.

`SIG_BLOCK`
> `signal.h` (POSIX.1): Section 24.7.3 [Process Signal Mask], page 694.

`int sigblock (int mask)`
> `signal.h` (BSD): Section 24.10 [BSD Signal Handling], page 703.

`int SIGBUS`
> `signal.h` (BSD): Section 24.2.1 [Program Error Signals], page 663.

`int SIGCHLD`
> `signal.h` (POSIX.1): Section 24.2.5 [Job Control Signals], page 668.

`int SIGCLD`
> `signal.h` (SVID): Section 24.2.5 [Job Control Signals], page 668.

`int SIGCONT`
> `signal.h` (POSIX.1): Section 24.2.5 [Job Control Signals], page 668.

`int sigdelset (sigset_t *set, int signum)`
> `signal.h` (POSIX.1): Section 24.7.2 [Signal Sets], page 693.

`int sigemptyset (sigset_t *set)`
> `signal.h` (POSIX.1): Section 24.7.2 [Signal Sets], page 693.

`int SIGEMT`
> `signal.h` (BSD): Section 24.2.1 [Program Error Signals], page 663.

`sighandler_t SIG_ERR`
> `signal.h` (ISO): Section 24.3.1 [Basic Signal Handling], page 672.

`int sigfillset (sigset_t *set)`
> `signal.h` (POSIX.1): Section 24.7.2 [Signal Sets], page 693.

`int SIGFPE`
> `signal.h` (ISO): Section 24.2.1 [Program Error Signals], page 663.

`sighandler_t`
> `signal.h` (GNU): Section 24.3.1 [Basic Signal Handling], page 672.

`int SIGHUP`
> `signal.h` (POSIX.1): Section 24.2.2 [Termination Signals], page 666.

`int SIGILL`
> `signal.h` (ISO): Section 24.2.1 [Program Error Signals], page 663.

`int SIGINFO`
> `signal.h` (BSD): Section 24.2.7 [Miscellaneous Signals], page 670.

`int SIGINT`
> `signal.h` (ISO): Section 24.2.2 [Termination Signals], page 666.

`int siginterrupt (int signum, int failflag)`
> `signal.h` (XPG): Section 24.10 [BSD Signal Handling], page 703.

`int SIGIO`
> `signal.h` (BSD): Section 24.2.4 [Asynchronous I/O Signals], page 667.

`int SIGIOT`
> `signal.h` (Unix): Section 24.2.1 [Program Error Signals], page 663.

`int sigismember (const sigset_t *set, int signum)`
> `signal.h` (POSIX.1): Section 24.7.2 [Signal Sets], page 693.

`sigjmp_buf`

> `setjmp.h` (POSIX.1): Section 23.3 [Non-Local Exits and Signals], page 654.

`int SIGKILL`

> `signal.h` (POSIX.1): Section 24.2.2 [Termination Signals], page 666.

`void siglongjmp (sigjmp_buf state, int value)`

> `setjmp.h` (POSIX.1): Section 23.3 [Non-Local Exits and Signals], page 654.

`int SIGLOST`

> `signal.h` (GNU): Section 24.2.6 [Operation Error Signals], page 669.

`int sigmask (int signum)`

> `signal.h` (BSD): Section 24.10 [BSD Signal Handling], page 703.

`sighandler_t signal (int signum, sighandler_t action)`

> `signal.h` (ISO): Section 24.3.1 [Basic Signal Handling], page 672.

`int signbit (float-type x)`

> `math.h` (ISO): Section 20.8.5 [Setting and modifying single bits of FP values], page 579.

`double significand (double x)`

> `math.h` (BSD): Section 20.8.2 [Normalization Functions], page 574.

`float significandf (float x)`

> `math.h` (BSD): Section 20.8.2 [Normalization Functions], page 574.

`long double significandl (long double x)`

> `math.h` (BSD): Section 20.8.2 [Normalization Functions], page 574.

`int sigpause (int mask)`

> `signal.h` (BSD): Section 24.10 [BSD Signal Handling], page 703.

`int sigpending (sigset_t *set)`

> `signal.h` (POSIX.1): Section 24.7.6 [Checking for Pending Signals], page 697.

`int SIGPIPE`

> `signal.h` (POSIX.1): Section 24.2.6 [Operation Error Signals], page 669.

`int SIGPOLL`

> `signal.h` (SVID): Section 24.2.4 [Asynchronous I/O Signals], page 667.

`int sigprocmask (int how, const sigset_t *restrict set, sigset_t *restrict oldset)`

> `signal.h` (POSIX.1): Section 24.7.3 [Process Signal Mask], page 694.

`int SIGPROF`

> `signal.h` (BSD): Section 24.2.3 [Alarm Signals], page 667.

`int SIGQUIT`

> `signal.h` (POSIX.1): Section 24.2.2 [Termination Signals], page 666.

`int SIGSEGV`

> `signal.h` (ISO): Section 24.2.1 [Program Error Signals], page 663.

`int sigsetjmp (sigjmp_buf state, int savesigs)`

> `setjmp.h` (POSIX.1): Section 23.3 [Non-Local Exits and Signals], page 654.

`SIG_SETMASK`

> `signal.h` (POSIX.1): Section 24.7.3 [Process Signal Mask], page 694.

`int sigsetmask (int mask)`

> `signal.h` (BSD): Section 24.10 [BSD Signal Handling], page 703.

`sigset_t`

> `signal.h` (POSIX.1): Section 24.7.2 [Signal Sets], page 693.

```
int sigstack (struct sigstack *stack, struct sigstack *oldstack)
```
    `signal.h` (BSD): Section 24.9 [Using a Separate Signal Stack], page 701.

```
int SIGSTOP
```
    `signal.h` (POSIX.1): Section 24.2.5 [Job Control Signals], page 668.

```
int sigsuspend (const sigset_t *set)
```
    `signal.h` (POSIX.1): Section 24.8.3 [Using `sigsuspend`], page 700.

```
int SIGSYS
```
    `signal.h` (Unix): Section 24.2.1 [Program Error Signals], page 663.

```
int SIGTERM
```
    `signal.h` (ISO): Section 24.2.2 [Termination Signals], page 666.

```
int SIGTRAP
```
    `signal.h` (BSD): Section 24.2.1 [Program Error Signals], page 663.

```
int SIGTSTP
```
    `signal.h` (POSIX.1): Section 24.2.5 [Job Control Signals], page 668.

```
int SIGTTIN
```
    `signal.h` (POSIX.1): Section 24.2.5 [Job Control Signals], page 668.

```
int SIGTTOU
```
    `signal.h` (POSIX.1): Section 24.2.5 [Job Control Signals], page 668.

```
SIG_UNBLOCK
```
    `signal.h` (POSIX.1): Section 24.7.3 [Process Signal Mask], page 694.

```
int SIGURG
```
    `signal.h` (BSD): Section 24.2.4 [Asynchronous I/O Signals], page 667.

```
int SIGUSR1
```
    `signal.h` (POSIX.1): Section 24.2.7 [Miscellaneous Signals], page 670.

```
int SIGUSR2
```
    `signal.h` (POSIX.1): Section 24.2.7 [Miscellaneous Signals], page 670.

```
int SIGVTALRM
```
    `signal.h` (BSD): Section 24.2.3 [Alarm Signals], page 667.

```
int SIGWINCH
```
    `signal.h` (BSD): Section 24.2.7 [Miscellaneous Signals], page 670.

```
int SIGXCPU
```
    `signal.h` (BSD): Section 24.2.6 [Operation Error Signals], page 669.

```
int SIGXFSZ
```
    `signal.h` (BSD): Section 24.2.6 [Operation Error Signals], page 669.

```
double sin (double x)
```
    `math.h` (ISO): Section 19.2 [Trigonometric Functions], page 512.

```
void sincos (double x, double *sinx, double *cosx)
```
    `math.h` (GNU): Section 19.2 [Trigonometric Functions], page 512.

```
void sincosf (float x, float *sinx, float *cosx)
```
    `math.h` (GNU): Section 19.2 [Trigonometric Functions], page 512.

```
void sincosl (long double x, long double *sinx, long double *cosx)
```
    `math.h` (GNU): Section 19.2 [Trigonometric Functions], page 512.

```
float sinf (float x)
```
    `math.h` (ISO): Section 19.2 [Trigonometric Functions], page 512.

`double sinh (double x)`
> `math.h` (ISO): Section 19.5 [Hyperbolic Functions], page 520.

`float sinhf (float x)`
> `math.h` (ISO): Section 19.5 [Hyperbolic Functions], page 520.

`long double sinhl (long double x)`
> `math.h` (ISO): Section 19.5 [Hyperbolic Functions], page 520.

`long double sinl (long double x)`
> `math.h` (ISO): Section 19.2 [Trigonometric Functions], page 512.

`S_IREAD`

> `sys/stat.h` (BSD): Section 14.9.5 [The Mode Bits for Access Permission], page 408.

`S_IRGRP`

> `sys/stat.h` (POSIX.1): Section 14.9.5 [The Mode Bits for Access Permission], page 408.

`S_IROTH`

> `sys/stat.h` (POSIX.1): Section 14.9.5 [The Mode Bits for Access Permission], page 408.

`S_IRUSR`

> `sys/stat.h` (POSIX.1): Section 14.9.5 [The Mode Bits for Access Permission], page 408.

`S_IRWXG`

> `sys/stat.h` (POSIX.1): Section 14.9.5 [The Mode Bits for Access Permission], page 408.

`S_IRWXO`

> `sys/stat.h` (POSIX.1): Section 14.9.5 [The Mode Bits for Access Permission], page 408.

`S_IRWXU`

> `sys/stat.h` (POSIX.1): Section 14.9.5 [The Mode Bits for Access Permission], page 408.

`int S_ISBLK (mode_t m)`
> `sys/stat.h` (POSIX): Section 14.9.3 [Testing the Type of a File], page 404.

`int S_ISCHR (mode_t m)`
> `sys/stat.h` (POSIX): Section 14.9.3 [Testing the Type of a File], page 404.

`int S_ISDIR (mode_t m)`
> `sys/stat.h` (POSIX): Section 14.9.3 [Testing the Type of a File], page 404.

`int S_ISFIFO (mode_t m)`
> `sys/stat.h` (POSIX): Section 14.9.3 [Testing the Type of a File], page 404.

`S_ISGID`

> `sys/stat.h` (POSIX): Section 14.9.5 [The Mode Bits for Access Permission], page 408.

`int S_ISLNK (mode_t m)`
> `sys/stat.h` (GNU): Section 14.9.3 [Testing the Type of a File], page 404.

`int S_ISREG (mode_t m)`
> `sys/stat.h` (POSIX): Section 14.9.3 [Testing the Type of a File], page 404.

`int S_ISSOCK (mode_t m)`
> `sys/stat.h` (GNU): Section 14.9.3 [Testing the Type of a File], page 404.

`S_ISUID`

> `sys/stat.h` (POSIX): Section 14.9.5 [The Mode Bits for Access Permission], page 408.

`S_ISVTX`

> `sys/stat.h` (BSD): Section 14.9.5 [The Mode Bits for Access Permission], page 408.

`S_IWGRP`

> `sys/stat.h` (POSIX.1): Section 14.9.5 [The Mode Bits for Access Permission], page 408.

S_IWOTH

>      sys/stat.h (POSIX.1): Section 14.9.5 [The Mode Bits for Access Permission], page 408.

S_IWRITE

>      sys/stat.h (BSD): Section 14.9.5 [The Mode Bits for Access Permission], page 408.

S_IWUSR

>      sys/stat.h (POSIX.1): Section 14.9.5 [The Mode Bits for Access Permission], page 408.

S_IXGRP

>      sys/stat.h (POSIX.1): Section 14.9.5 [The Mode Bits for Access Permission], page 408.

S_IXOTH

>      sys/stat.h (POSIX.1): Section 14.9.5 [The Mode Bits for Access Permission], page 408.

S_IXUSR

>      sys/stat.h (POSIX.1): Section 14.9.5 [The Mode Bits for Access Permission], page 408.

size_t

>      stddef.h (ISO): Section A.4 [Important Data Types], page 884.

unsigned int sleep (unsigned int seconds)
>      unistd.h (POSIX.1): Section 21.6 [Sleeping], page 628.

int snprintf (char *s, size_t size, const char *template, ...)
>      stdio.h (GNU): Section 12.12.7 [Formatted Output Functions], page 278.

SO_BROADCAST

>      sys/socket.h (BSD): Section 16.12.2 [Socket-Level Options], page 473.

int SOCK_DGRAM

>      sys/socket.h (BSD): Section 16.2 [Communication Styles], page 430.

int socket (int namespace, int style, int protocol)
>      sys/socket.h (BSD): Section 16.8.1 [Creating a Socket], page 453.

int socketpair (int namespace, int style, int protocol, int filedes[2])
>      sys/socket.h (BSD): Section 16.8.3 [Socket Pairs], page 455.

int SOCK_RAW

>      sys/socket.h (BSD): Section 16.2 [Communication Styles], page 430.

int SOCK_RDM

>      sys/socket.h (BSD): Section 16.2 [Communication Styles], page 430.

int SOCK_SEQPACKET

>      sys/socket.h (BSD): Section 16.2 [Communication Styles], page 430.

int SOCK_STREAM

>      sys/socket.h (BSD): Section 16.2 [Communication Styles], page 430.

SO_DEBUG

>      sys/socket.h (BSD): Section 16.12.2 [Socket-Level Options], page 473.

SO_DONTROUTE

>      sys/socket.h (BSD): Section 16.12.2 [Socket-Level Options], page 473.

SO_ERROR

>      sys/socket.h (BSD): Section 16.12.2 [Socket-Level Options], page 473.

SO_KEEPALIVE

>      sys/socket.h (BSD): Section 16.12.2 [Socket-Level Options], page 473.

SO_LINGER

>      sys/socket.h (BSD): Section 16.12.2 [Socket-Level Options], page 473.

`int SOL_SOCKET`
> `sys/socket.h` (BSD): Section 16.12.2 [Socket-Level Options], page 473.

`SO_OOBINLINE`
> `sys/socket.h` (BSD): Section 16.12.2 [Socket-Level Options], page 473.

`SO_RCVBUF`
> `sys/socket.h` (BSD): Section 16.12.2 [Socket-Level Options], page 473.

`SO_REUSEADDR`
> `sys/socket.h` (BSD): Section 16.12.2 [Socket-Level Options], page 473.

`SO_SNDBUF`
> `sys/socket.h` (BSD): Section 16.12.2 [Socket-Level Options], page 473.

`SO_STYLE`
> `sys/socket.h` (GNU): Section 16.12.2 [Socket-Level Options], page 473.

`SO_TYPE`
> `sys/socket.h` (BSD): Section 16.12.2 [Socket-Level Options], page 473.

`speed_t`
> `termios.h` (POSIX.1): Section 17.4.8 [Line Speed], page 489.

`int sprintf (char *s, const char *template, ...)`
> `stdio.h` (ISO): Section 12.12.7 [Formatted Output Functions], page 278.

`double sqrt (double x)`
> `math.h` (ISO): Section 19.4 [Exponentiation and Logarithms], page 515.

`float sqrtf (float x)`
> `math.h` (ISO): Section 19.4 [Exponentiation and Logarithms], page 515.

`long double sqrtl (long double x)`
> `math.h` (ISO): Section 19.4 [Exponentiation and Logarithms], page 515.

`void srand (unsigned int seed)`
> `stdlib.h` (ISO): Section 19.8.1 [ISO C Random Number Functions], page 550.

`void srand48 (long int seedval)`
> `stdlib.h` (SVID): Section 19.8.3 [SVID Random Number Function], page 553.

`int srand48_r (long int seedval, struct drand48_data *buffer)`
> `stdlib.h` (GNU): Section 19.8.3 [SVID Random Number Function], page 553.

`void srandom (unsigned int seed)`
> `stdlib.h` (BSD): Section 19.8.2 [BSD Random Number Functions], page 551.

`int srandom_r (unsigned int seed, struct random_data *buf)`
> `stdlib.h` (GNU): Section 19.8.2 [BSD Random Number Functions], page 551.

`int sscanf (const char *s, const char *template, ...)`
> `stdio.h` (ISO): Section 12.14.8 [Formatted Input Functions], page 300.

`sighandler_t ssignal (int signum, sighandler_t action)`
> `signal.h` (SVID): Section 24.3.1 [Basic Signal Handling], page 672.

`ssize_t SSIZE_MAX`
> `limits.h` (POSIX.1): Section 32.1 [General Capacity Limits], page 838.

`ssize_t`
> `unistd.h` (POSIX.1): Section 13.2 [Input and Output Primitives], page 326.

`stack_t`
> `signal.h` (XPG): Section 24.9 [Using a Separate Signal Stack], page 701.

`int stat (const char *filename, struct stat *buf)`
> `sys/stat.h` (POSIX.1): Section 14.9.2 [Reading the Attributes of a File], page 403.

`int stat64 (const char *filename, struct stat64 *buf)`
> `sys/stat.h` (Unix98): Section 14.9.2 [Reading the Attributes of a File], page 403.

`FILE * stderr`
> `stdio.h` (ISO): Section 12.2 [Standard Streams], page 248.

`STDERR_FILENO`
> `unistd.h` (POSIX.1): Section 13.4 [Descriptors and Streams], page 333.

`FILE * stdin`
> `stdio.h` (ISO): Section 12.2 [Standard Streams], page 248.

`STDIN_FILENO`
> `unistd.h` (POSIX.1): Section 13.4 [Descriptors and Streams], page 333.

`FILE * stdout`
> `stdio.h` (ISO): Section 12.2 [Standard Streams], page 248.

`STDOUT_FILENO`
> `unistd.h` (POSIX.1): Section 13.4 [Descriptors and Streams], page 333.

`int stime (const time_t *newtime)`
> `time.h` (SVID, XPG): Section 21.4.1 [Simple Calendar Time], page 599.

`char * stpcpy (char *restrict to, const char *restrict from)`
> `string.h` (Unknown origin): Section 5.4 [Copying and Concatenation], page 91.

`char * stpncpy (char *restrict to, const char *restrict from, size_t size)`
> `string.h` (GNU): Section 5.4 [Copying and Concatenation], page 91.

`int strcasecmp (const char *s1, const char *s2)`
> `string.h` (BSD): Section 5.5 [String/Array Comparison], page 102.

`char * strcasestr (const char *haystack, const char *needle)`
> `string.h` (GNU): Section 5.7 [Search Functions], page 110.

`char * strcat (char *restrict to, const char *restrict from)`
> `string.h` (ISO): Section 5.4 [Copying and Concatenation], page 91.

`char * strchr (const char *string, int c)`
> `string.h` (ISO): Section 5.7 [Search Functions], page 110.

`char * strchrnul (const char *string, int c)`
> `string.h` (GNU): Section 5.7 [Search Functions], page 110.

`int strcmp (const char *s1, const char *s2)`
> `string.h` (ISO): Section 5.5 [String/Array Comparison], page 102.

`int strcoll (const char *s1, const char *s2)`
> `string.h` (ISO): Section 5.6 [Collation Functions], page 106.

`char * strcpy (char *restrict to, const char *restrict from)`
> `string.h` (ISO): Section 5.4 [Copying and Concatenation], page 91.

`size_t strcspn (const char *string, const char *stopset)`
> `string.h` (ISO): Section 5.7 [Search Functions], page 110.

`char * strdup (const char *s)`
> `string.h` (SVID): Section 5.4 [Copying and Concatenation], page 91.

`char * strdupa (const char *s)`
> `string.h` (GNU): Section 5.4 [Copying and Concatenation], page 91.

`int STREAM_MAX`
> `limits.h` (POSIX.1): Section 32.1 [General Capacity Limits], page 838.

char * strerror (int errnum)
        string.h (ISO): Section 2.3 [Error Messages], page 33.

char * strerror_r (int errnum, char *buf, size_t n)
        string.h (GNU): Section 2.3 [Error Messages], page 33.

char * strfry (char *string)
        string.h (GNU): Section 5.9 [strfry], page 120.

size_t strftime (char *s, size_t size, const char *template, const struct tm *brokentime)
        time.h (ISO): Section 21.4.5 [Formatting Calendar Time], page 608.

size_t strlen (const char *s)
        string.h (ISO): Section 5.3 [String Length], page 89.

int strncasecmp (const char *s1, const char *s2, size_t n)
        string.h (BSD): Section 5.5 [String/Array Comparison], page 102.

char * strncat (char *restrict to, const char *restrict from, size_t size)
        string.h (ISO): Section 5.4 [Copying and Concatenation], page 91.

int strncmp (const char *s1, const char *s2, size_t size)
        string.h (ISO): Section 5.5 [String/Array Comparison], page 102.

char * strncpy (char *restrict to, const char *restrict from, size_t size)
        string.h (ISO): Section 5.4 [Copying and Concatenation], page 91.

char * strndup (const char *s, size_t size)
        string.h (GNU): Section 5.4 [Copying and Concatenation], page 91.

char * strndupa (const char *s, size_t size)
        string.h (GNU): Section 5.4 [Copying and Concatenation], page 91.

size_t strnlen (const char *s, size_t maxlen)
        string.h (GNU): Section 5.3 [String Length], page 89.

char * strpbrk (const char *string, const char *stopset)
        string.h (ISO): Section 5.7 [Search Functions], page 110.

char * strptime (const char *s, const char *fmt, struct tm *tp)
        time.h (XPG4): Section 21.4.6.1 [Interpret string according to given format], page 614.

char * strrchr (const char *string, int c)
        string.h (ISO): Section 5.7 [Search Functions], page 110.

char * strsep (char **string_ptr, const char *delimiter)
        string.h (BSD): Section 5.8 [Finding Tokens in a String], page 115.

char * strsignal (int signum)
        string.h (GNU): Section 24.2.8 [Signal Messages], page 671.

size_t strspn (const char *string, const char *skipset)
        string.h (ISO): Section 5.7 [Search Functions], page 110.

char * strstr (const char *haystack, const char *needle)
        string.h (ISO): Section 5.7 [Search Functions], page 110.

double strtod (const char *restrict string, char **restrict tailptr)
        stdlib.h (ISO): Section 20.11.2 [Parsing of Floats], page 589.

float strtof (const char *string, char **tailptr)
        stdlib.h (ISO): Section 20.11.2 [Parsing of Floats], page 589.

intmax_t strtoimax (const char *restrict string, char **restrict tailptr, int base)
        inttypes.h (ISO): Section 20.11.1 [Parsing of Integers], page 585.

char * strtok (char *restrict newstring, const char *restrict delimiters)
        string.h (ISO): Section 5.8 [Finding Tokens in a String], page 115.

char * strtok_r (char *newstring, const char *delimiters, char **save_ptr)
        string.h (POSIX): Section 5.8 [Finding Tokens in a String], page 115.

long int strtol (const char *restrict string, char **restrict tailptr, int base)
        stdlib.h (ISO): Section 20.11.1 [Parsing of Integers], page 585.

long double strtold (const char *string, char **tailptr)
        stdlib.h (ISO): Section 20.11.2 [Parsing of Floats], page 589.

long long int strtoll (const char *restrict string, char **restrict tailptr, int base)
        stdlib.h (ISO): Section 20.11.1 [Parsing of Integers], page 585.

long long int strtoq (const char *restrict string, char **restrict tailptr, int base)
        stdlib.h (BSD): Section 20.11.1 [Parsing of Integers], page 585.

unsigned long int strtoul (const char *retrict string, char **restrict tailptr, int base)
        stdlib.h (ISO): Section 20.11.1 [Parsing of Integers], page 585.

unsigned long long int strtoull (const char *restrict string, char **restrict tailptr, int base)
        stdlib.h (ISO): Section 20.11.1 [Parsing of Integers], page 585.

uintmax_t strtoumax (const char *restrict string, char **restrict tailptr, int base)
        inttypes.h (ISO): Section 20.11.1 [Parsing of Integers], page 585.

unsigned long long int strtouq (const char *restrict string, char **restrict tailptr, int base)
        stdlib.h (BSD): Section 20.11.1 [Parsing of Integers], page 585.

struct aiocb
        aio.h (POSIX.1b): Section 13.10 [Perform I/O Operations in Parallel], page 346.

struct aiocb64
        aio.h (POSIX.1b): Section 13.10 [Perform I/O Operations in Parallel], page 346.

struct aioinit
        aio.h (GNU): Section 13.10.5 [How to optimize the AIO implementation], page 358.

struct argp
        argp.h (GNU): Section 25.3.3 [Specifying Argp Parsers], page 715.

struct argp_child
        argp.h (GNU): Section 25.3.6 [Combining Multiple Argp Parsers], page 724.

struct argp_option
        argp.h (GNU): Section 25.3.4 [Specifying Options in an Argp Parser], page 716.

struct argp_state
        argp.h (GNU): Section 25.3.5.2 [Argp Parsing State], page 721.

struct dirent
        dirent.h (POSIX.1): Section 14.2.1 [Format of a Directory Entry], page 379.

struct exit_status
        utmp.h (SVID): Section 30.12.1 [Manipulating the User Accounting Database], page 802.

struct flock
        fcntl.h (POSIX.1): Section 13.15 [File Locks], page 368.

struct fstab
        fstab.h (BSD): Section 31.3.1.1 [The fstab file], page 825.

struct FTW
        ftw.h (XPG4.2): Section 14.3 [Working with Directory Trees], page 388.

struct __gconv_step
        gconv.h (GNU): Section 6.5.4 [The iconv Implementation in the GNU C Library], page 155.

struct __gconv_step_data
        gconv.h (GNU): Section 6.5.4 [The iconv Implementation in the GNU C Library], page 155.

`struct group`
> `grp.h` (POSIX.1): Section 30.14.1 [The Data Structure for a Group], page 814.

`struct hostent`
> `netdb.h` (BSD): Section 16.6.2.4 [Host Names], page 443.

`struct if_nameindex`
> `net/if.h` (IPv6 basic API): Section 16.4 [Interface Naming], page 434.

`struct in6_addr`
> `netinet/in.h` (IPv6 basic API): Section 16.6.2.2 [Host Address Data Type], page 440.

`struct in_addr`
> `netinet/in.h` (BSD): Section 16.6.2.2 [Host Address Data Type], page 440.

`struct iovec`
> `sys/uio.h` (BSD): Section 13.6 [Fast Scatter-Gather I/O], page 336.

`struct itimerval`
> `sys/time.h` (BSD): Section 21.5 [Setting an Alarm], page 625.

`struct lconv`
> `locale.h` (ISO): Section 7.7.1 [`localeconv`: It is portable but . . .], page 175.

`struct linger`
> `sys/socket.h` (BSD): Section 16.12.2 [Socket-Level Options], page 473.

`struct mallinfo`
> `malloc.h` (GNU): Section 3.2.2.11 [Statistics for Memory Allocation with `malloc`], page 52.

`struct mntent`
> `mntent.h` (BSD): Section 31.3.1.2 [The `mtab` file], page 828.

`struct msghdr`
> `sys/socket.h` (BSD): Section 16.10.2 [Receiving Datagrams], page 468.

`struct netent`
> `netdb.h` (BSD): Section 16.13 [Networks Database], page 475.

`struct obstack`
> `obstack.h` (GNU): Section 3.2.4.1 [Creating Obstacks], page 58.

`struct option`
> `getopt.h` (GNU): Section 25.2.3 [Parsing Long Options with `getopt_long`], page 710.

`struct passwd`
> `pwd.h` (POSIX.1): Section 30.13.1 [The Data Structure that Describes a User], page 810.

`struct printf_info`
> `printf.h` (GNU): Section 12.13.2 [Conversion Specifier Options], page 287.

`struct protoent`
> `netdb.h` (BSD): Section 16.6.6 [Protocols Database], page 450.

`struct random_data`
> `stdlib.h` (GNU): Section 19.8.2 [BSD Random Number Functions], page 551.

`struct rlimit`
> `sys/resource.h` (BSD): Section 22.2 [Limiting Resource Usage], page 632.

`struct rlimit64`
> `sys/resource.h` (Unix98): Section 22.2 [Limiting Resource Usage], page 632.

`struct rusage`
> `sys/resource.h` (BSD): Section 22.1 [Resource Usage], page 630.

`struct sched_param`
> `sched.h` (POSIX): Section 22.3.3 [Basic Scheduling Functions], page 639.

struct servent
          netdb.h (BSD): Section 16.6.4 [The Services Database], page 448.

struct sgttyb
          termios.h (BSD): Section 17.5 [BSD Terminal Modes], page 496.

struct sigaction
          signal.h (POSIX.1): Section 24.3.2 [Advanced Signal Handling], page 674.

struct sigstack
          signal.h (BSD): Section 24.9 [Using a Separate Signal Stack], page 701.

struct sockaddr
          sys/socket.h (BSD): Section 16.3.1 [Address Formats], page 431.

struct sockaddr_in
          netinet/in.h (BSD): Section 16.6.1 [Internet Socket Address Formats], page 438.

struct sockaddr_un
          sys/un.h (BSD): Section 16.5.2 [Details of Local Namespace], page 435.

struct stat
          sys/stat.h (POSIX.1): Section 14.9.1 [The meaning of the File Attributes], page 399.

struct stat64
          sys/stat.h (LFS): Section 14.9.1 [The meaning of the File Attributes], page 399.

struct termios
          termios.h (POSIX.1): Section 17.4.1 [Terminal Mode Data Types], page 479.

struct timespec
          sys/time.h (POSIX.1): Section 21.2 [Elapsed Time], page 595.

struct timeval
          sys/time.h (BSD): Section 21.2 [Elapsed Time], page 595.

struct timezone
          sys/time.h (BSD): Section 21.4.2 [High-Resolution Calendar], page 600.

struct tm
          time.h (ISO): Section 21.4.3 [Broken-down Time], page 602.

struct tms
          sys/times.h (POSIX.1): Section 21.3.2 [Processor Time Inquiry], page 598.

struct utimbuf
          utime.h (POSIX.1): Section 14.9.9 [File Times], page 413.

struct utsname
          sys/utsname.h (POSIX.1): Section 31.2 [Platform Type Identification], page 823.

int strverscmp (const char *s1, const char *s2)
          string.h (GNU): Section 5.5 [String/Array Comparison], page 102.

size_t strxfrm (char *restrict to, const char *restrict from, size_t size)
          string.h (ISO): Section 5.6 [Collation Functions], page 106.

int stty (int filedes, const struct sgttyb *attributes)
          sgtty.h (BSD): Section 17.5 [BSD Terminal Modes], page 496.

int S_TYPEISMQ (struct stat *s)
          sys/stat.h (POSIX): Section 14.9.3 [Testing the Type of a File], page 404.

int S_TYPEISSEM (struct stat *s)
          sys/stat.h (POSIX): Section 14.9.3 [Testing the Type of a File], page 404.

int S_TYPEISSHM (struct stat *s)
          sys/stat.h (POSIX): Section 14.9.3 [Testing the Type of a File], page 404.

int SUN_LEN (struct sockaddr_un * ptr)
>        sys/un.h (BSD): Section 16.5.2 [Details of Local Namespace], page 435.

int swapcontext (ucontext_t *restrict oucp, const ucontext_t *restrict ucp)
>        ucontext.h (SVID): Section 23.4 [Complete Context Control], page 655.

int swprintf (wchar_t *s, size_t size, const wchar_t *template, ...)
>        wchar.h (GNU): Section 12.12.7 [Formatted Output Functions], page 278.

int swscanf (const wchar_t *ws, const wchar_t *template, ...)
>        wchar.h (ISO): Section 12.14.8 [Formatted Input Functions], page 300.

int symlink (const char *oldname, const char *newname)
>        unistd.h (BSD): Section 14.5 [Symbolic Links], page 393.

SYMLINK_MAX
>        limits.h (POSIX.1): Section 32.8 [Minimum Values for File System Limits], page 852.

void sync (void)
>        unistd.h (X/Open): Section 13.9 [Synchronizing I/O operations], page 345.

long int syscall (long int sysno, ...)
>        unistd.h (???): Section 25.6 [System Calls], page 743.

long int sysconf (int parameter)
>        unistd.h (POSIX.1): Section 32.4.1 [Definition of sysconf], page 841.

int sysctl (int *names, int nlen, void *oldval, size_t *oldlenp, void *newval, size_t newlen)
>        sys/sysctl.h (BSD): Section 31.4 [System Parameters], page 835.

void syslog (int facility_priority, const char *format, ...)
>        syslog.h (BSD): Section 18.2.2 [syslog, vsyslog], page 507.

int system (const char *command)
>        stdlib.h (ISO): Section 26.1 [Running a Command], page 749.

sighandler_t sysv_signal (int signum, sighandler_t action)
>        signal.h (GNU): Section 24.3.1 [Basic Signal Handling], page 672.

double tan (double x)
>        math.h (ISO): Section 19.2 [Trigonometric Functions], page 512.

float tanf (float x)
>        math.h (ISO): Section 19.2 [Trigonometric Functions], page 512.

double tanh (double x)
>        math.h (ISO): Section 19.5 [Hyperbolic Functions], page 520.

float tanhf (float x)
>        math.h (ISO): Section 19.5 [Hyperbolic Functions], page 520.

long double tanhl (long double x)
>        math.h (ISO): Section 19.5 [Hyperbolic Functions], page 520.

long double tanl (long double x)
>        math.h (ISO): Section 19.2 [Trigonometric Functions], page 512.

int tcdrain (int filedes)
>        termios.h (POSIX.1): Section 17.6 [Line Control Functions], page 497.

tcflag_t
>        termios.h (POSIX.1): Section 17.4.1 [Terminal Mode Data Types], page 479.

int tcflow (int filedes, int action)
>        termios.h (POSIX.1): Section 17.6 [Line Control Functions], page 497.

int tcflush (int filedes, int queue)
>        termios.h (POSIX.1): Section 17.6 [Line Control Functions], page 497.

```
int tcgetattr (int filedes, struct termios *termios-p)
```
   termios.h (POSIX.1): Section 17.4.2 [Terminal Mode Functions], page 480.

```
pid_t tcgetpgrp (int filedes)
```
   unistd.h (POSIX.1): Section 28.7.3 [Functions for Controlling Terminal Access], page 780.

```
pid_t tcgetsid (int fildes)
```
   termios.h (Unix98): Section 28.7.3 [Functions for Controlling Terminal Access], page 780.

```
TCSADRAIN
```
   termios.h (POSIX.1): Section 17.4.2 [Terminal Mode Functions], page 480.

```
TCSAFLUSH
```
   termios.h (POSIX.1): Section 17.4.2 [Terminal Mode Functions], page 480.

```
TCSANOW
```
   termios.h (POSIX.1): Section 17.4.2 [Terminal Mode Functions], page 480.

```
TCSASOFT
```
   termios.h (BSD): Section 17.4.2 [Terminal Mode Functions], page 480.

```
int tcsendbreak (int filedes, int duration)
```
   termios.h (POSIX.1): Section 17.6 [Line Control Functions], page 497.

```
int tcsetattr (int filedes, int when, const struct termios *termios-p)
```
   termios.h (POSIX.1): Section 17.4.2 [Terminal Mode Functions], page 480.

```
int tcsetpgrp (int filedes, pid_t pgid)
```
   unistd.h (POSIX.1): Section 28.7.3 [Functions for Controlling Terminal Access], page 780.

```
void * tdelete (const void *key, void **rootp, comparison_fn_t compar)
```
   search.h (SVID): Section 9.6 [The tsearch function.], page 219.

```
void tdestroy (void *vroot, __free_fn_t freefct)
```
   search.h (GNU): Section 9.6 [The tsearch function.], page 219.

```
long int telldir (DIR *dirstream)
```
   dirent.h (BSD): Section 14.2.5 [Random Access in a Directory Stream], page 385.

```
TEMP_FAILURE_RETRY (expression)
```
   unistd.h (GNU): Section 24.5 [Primitives Interrupted by Signals], page 687.

```
char * tempnam (const char *dir, const char *prefix)
```
   stdio.h (SVID): Section 14.11 [Temporary Files], page 419.

```
char * textdomain (const char *domainname)
```
   libintl.h (GNU): Section 8.2.1.2 [How to determine which catalog to be used], page 200.

```
void * tfind (const void *key, void *const *rootp, comparison_fn_t compar)
```
   search.h (SVID): Section 9.6 [The tsearch function.], page 219.

```
double tgamma (double x)
```
   math.h (XPG, ISO): Section 19.6 [Special Functions], page 522.

```
float tgammaf (float x)
```
   math.h (XPG, ISO): Section 19.6 [Special Functions], page 522.

```
long double tgammal (long double x)
```
   math.h (XPG, ISO): Section 19.6 [Special Functions], page 522.

```
time_t time (time_t *result)
```
   time.h (ISO): Section 21.4.1 [Simple Calendar Time], page 599.

```
time_t timegm (struct tm *brokentime)
```
   time.h (???): Section 21.4.3 [Broken-down Time], page 602.

```
time_t timelocal (struct tm *brokentime)
```
   time.h (???): Section 21.4.3 [Broken-down Time], page 602.

clock_t times (struct tms *buffer)
>           sys/times.h (POSIX.1): Section 21.3.2 [Processor Time Inquiry], page 598.

time_t
>           time.h (ISO): Section 21.4.1 [Simple Calendar Time], page 599.

long int timezone
>           time.h (SVID): Section 21.4.8 [Functions and Variables for Time Zones], page 624.

FILE * tmpfile (void)
>           stdio.h (ISO): Section 14.11 [Temporary Files], page 419.

FILE * tmpfile64 (void)
>           stdio.h (Unix98): Section 14.11 [Temporary Files], page 419.

int TMP_MAX
>           stdio.h (ISO): Section 14.11 [Temporary Files], page 419.

char * tmpnam (char *result)
>           stdio.h (ISO): Section 14.11 [Temporary Files], page 419.

char * tmpnam_r (char *result)
>           stdio.h (GNU): Section 14.11 [Temporary Files], page 419.

int toascii (int c)
>           ctype.h (SVID, BSD): Section 4.2 [Case Conversion], page 79.

int _tolower (int c)
>           ctype.h (SVID): Section 4.2 [Case Conversion], page 79.

int tolower (int c)
>           ctype.h (ISO): Section 4.2 [Case Conversion], page 79.

tcflag_t TOSTOP
>           termios.h (POSIX.1): Section 17.4.7 [Local Modes], page 486.

int _toupper (int c)
>           ctype.h (SVID): Section 4.2 [Case Conversion], page 79.

int toupper (int c)
>           ctype.h (ISO): Section 4.2 [Case Conversion], page 79.

wint_t towctrans (wint_t wc, wctrans_t desc)
>           wctype.h (ISO): Section 4.5 [Mapping of wide characters.], page 85.

wint_t towlower (wint_t wc)
>           wctype.h (ISO): Section 4.5 [Mapping of wide characters.], page 85.

wint_t towupper (wint_t wc)
>           wctype.h (ISO): Section 4.5 [Mapping of wide characters.], page 85.

double trunc (double x)
>           math.h (ISO): Section 20.8.3 [Rounding Functions], page 576.

int truncate (const char *filename, off_t length)
>           unistd.h (X/Open): Section 14.9.10 [File Size], page 415.

int truncate64 (const char *name, off64_t length)
>           unistd.h (Unix98): Section 14.9.10 [File Size], page 415.

float truncf (float x)
>           math.h (ISO): Section 20.8.3 [Rounding Functions], page 576.

long double truncl (long double x)
>           math.h (ISO): Section 20.8.3 [Rounding Functions], page 576.

TRY_AGAIN
>           netdb.h (BSD): Section 16.6.2.4 [Host Names], page 443.

```
void * tsearch (const void *key, void **rootp, comparison_fn_t compar)
        search.h (SVID): Section 9.6 [The tsearch function.], page 219.

char * ttyname (int filedes)
        unistd.h (POSIX.1): Section 17.1 [Identifying Terminals], page 477.

int ttyname_r (int filedes, char *buf, size_t len)
        unistd.h (POSIX.1): Section 17.1 [Identifying Terminals], page 477.

void twalk (const void *root, __action_fn_t action)
        search.h (SVID): Section 9.6 [The tsearch function.], page 219.

char * tzname [2]
        time.h (POSIX.1): Section 21.4.8 [Functions and Variables for Time Zones], page 624.

int TZNAME_MAX
        limits.h (POSIX.1): Section 32.1 [General Capacity Limits], page 838.

void tzset (void)
        time.h (POSIX.1): Section 21.4.8 [Functions and Variables for Time Zones], page 624.

UCHAR_MAX
        limits.h (ISO): Section A.5.2 [Range of an Integer Type], page 885.

ucontext_t
        ucontext.h (SVID): Section 23.4 [Complete Context Control], page 655.

uid_t
        sys/types.h (POSIX.1): Section 30.5 [Reading the Persona of a Process], page 793.

UINT_MAX
        limits.h (ISO): Section A.5.2 [Range of an Integer Type], page 885.

long int ulimit (int cmd, ...)
        ulimit.h (BSD): Section 22.2 [Limiting Resource Usage], page 632.

ULLONG_MAX
        limits.h (ISO): Section A.5.2 [Range of an Integer Type], page 885.

ULONG_LONG_MAX
        limits.h (GNU): Section A.5.2 [Range of an Integer Type], page 885.

ULONG_MAX
        limits.h (ISO): Section A.5.2 [Range of an Integer Type], page 885.

mode_t umask (mode_t mask)
        sys/stat.h (POSIX.1): Section 14.9.7 [Assigning File Permissions], page 410.

int umount (const char *file)
        sys/mount.h (SVID, GNU): Section 31.3.2 [Mount, Unmount, Remount], page 831.

int umount2 (const char *file, int flags)
        sys/mount.h (GNU): Section 31.3.2 [Mount, Unmount, Remount], page 831.

int uname (struct utsname *info)
        sys/utsname.h (POSIX.1): Section 31.2 [Platform Type Identification], page 823.

int ungetc (int c, FILE *stream)
        stdio.h (ISO): Section 12.10.2 [Using ungetc To Do Unreading], page 267.

wint_t ungetwc (wint_t wc, FILE *stream)
        wchar.h (ISO): Section 12.10.2 [Using ungetc To Do Unreading], page 267.

union wait
        sys/wait.h (BSD): Section 26.8 [BSD Process Wait Functions], page 758.
```

int unlink (const char *filename)
        unistd.h (POSIX.1): Section 14.6 [Deleting Files], page 396.

int unlockpt (int filedes)
        stdlib.h (SVID, XPG4.2): Section 17.8.1 [Allocating Pseudo-Terminals], page 500.

int unsetenv (const char *name)
        stdlib.h (BSD): Section 25.4.1 [Environment Access], page 738.

void updwtmp (const char *wtmp_file, const struct utmp *utmp)
        utmp.h (SVID): Section 30.12.1 [Manipulating the User Accounting Database], page 802.

USER_PROCESS
        utmp.h (SVID): Section 30.12.1 [Manipulating the User Accounting Database], page 802.

USER_PROCESS
        utmpx.h (XPG4.2): Section 30.12.2 [XPG User Accounting Database Functions], page 807.

USHRT_MAX
        limits.h (ISO): Section A.5.2 [Range of an Integer Type], page 885.

int utime (const char *filename, const struct utimbuf *times)
        utime.h (POSIX.1): Section 14.9.9 [File Times], page 413.

int utimes (const char *filename, const struct timeval tvp[2])
        sys/time.h (BSD): Section 14.9.9 [File Times], page 413.

int utmpname (const char *file)
        utmp.h (SVID): Section 30.12.1 [Manipulating the User Accounting Database], page 802.

int utmpxname (const char *file)
        utmpx.h (XPG4.2): Section 30.12.2 [XPG User Accounting Database Functions], page 807.

type va_arg (va_list ap, type)
        stdarg.h (ISO): Section A.2.2.5 [Argument Access Macros], page 881.

void va_copy (va_list dest, va_list src)
        stdarg.h (ISO): Section A.2.2.5 [Argument Access Macros], page 881.

void va_end (va_list ap)
        stdarg.h (ISO): Section A.2.2.5 [Argument Access Macros], page 881.

va_list
        stdarg.h (ISO): Section A.2.2.5 [Argument Access Macros], page 881.

void * valloc (size_t size)
        malloc.h, stdlib.h (BSD): Section 3.2.2.7 [Allocating Aligned Memory Blocks], page 46.

int vasprintf (char **ptr, const char *template, va_list ap)
        stdio.h (GNU): Section 12.12.9 [Variable Arguments Output Functions], page 281.

void va_start (va_list ap, last-required)
        stdarg.h (ISO): Section A.2.2.5 [Argument Access Macros], page 881.

int VDISCARD
        termios.h (BSD): Section 17.4.9.4 [Other Special Characters], page 494.

int VDSUSP
        termios.h (BSD): Section 17.4.9.2 [Characters that Cause Signals], page 492.

int VEOF
        termios.h (POSIX.1): Section 17.4.9.1 [Characters for Input Editing], page 490.

int VEOL
        termios.h (POSIX.1): Section 17.4.9.1 [Characters for Input Editing], page 490.

int VEOL2
        termios.h (BSD): Section 17.4.9.1 [Characters for Input Editing], page 490.

int VERASE

>       termios.h (POSIX.1): Section 17.4.9.1 [Characters for Input Editing], page 490.

void verr (int *status*, const char *\*format*, va_list *ap*)
>       err.h (BSD): Section 2.3 [Error Messages], page 33.

void verrx (int *status*, const char *\*format*, va_list *ap*)
>       err.h (BSD): Section 2.3 [Error Messages], page 33.

int versionsort (const struct dirent *\*a*, const struct dirent *\*b*)
>       dirent.h (GNU): Section 14.2.6 [Scanning the Content of a Directory], page 385.

int versionsort64 (const struct dirent64 *\*a*, const struct dirent64 *\*b*)
>       dirent.h (GNU): Section 14.2.6 [Scanning the Content of a Directory], page 385.

pid_t vfork (void)
>       unistd.h (BSD): Section 26.4 [Creating a Process], page 751.

int vfprintf (FILE *\*stream*, const char *\*template*, va_list *ap*)
>       stdio.h (ISO): Section 12.12.9 [Variable Arguments Output Functions], page 281.

int vfscanf (FILE *\*stream*, const char *\*template*, va_list *ap*)
>       stdio.h (ISO): Section 12.14.9 [Variable Arguments Input Functions], page 301.

int vfwprintf (FILE *\*stream*, const wchar_t *\*template*, va_list *ap*)
>       wchar.h (ISO): Section 12.12.9 [Variable Arguments Output Functions], page 281.

int vfwscanf (FILE *\*stream*, const wchar_t *\*template*, va_list *ap*)
>       wchar.h (ISO): Section 12.14.9 [Variable Arguments Input Functions], page 301.

int VINTR

>       termios.h (POSIX.1): Section 17.4.9.2 [Characters that Cause Signals], page 492.

int VKILL

>       termios.h (POSIX.1): Section 17.4.9.1 [Characters for Input Editing], page 490.

int vlimit (int *resource*, int *limit*)
>       sys/vlimit.h (BSD): Section 22.2 [Limiting Resource Usage], page 632.

int VLNEXT

>       termios.h (BSD): Section 17.4.9.4 [Other Special Characters], page 494.

int VMIN

>       termios.h (POSIX.1): Section 17.4.10 [Noncanonical Input], page 494.

void (*error_print_progname) (void)
>       error.h (GNU): Section 2.3 [Error Messages], page 33.

int vprintf (const char *\*template*, va_list *ap*)
>       stdio.h (ISO): Section 12.12.9 [Variable Arguments Output Functions], page 281.

int VQUIT

>       termios.h (POSIX.1): Section 17.4.9.2 [Characters that Cause Signals], page 492.

int VREPRINT

>       termios.h (BSD): Section 17.4.9.1 [Characters for Input Editing], page 490.

int vscanf (const char *\*template*, va_list *ap*)
>       stdio.h (ISO): Section 12.14.9 [Variable Arguments Input Functions], page 301.

int vsnprintf (char *\*s*, size_t *size*, const char *\*template*, va_list *ap*)
>       stdio.h (GNU): Section 12.12.9 [Variable Arguments Output Functions], page 281.

int vsprintf (char *\*s*, const char *\*template*, va_list *ap*)
>       stdio.h (ISO): Section 12.12.9 [Variable Arguments Output Functions], page 281.

`int vsscanf (const char *s, const char *template, va_list ap)`
> `stdio.h` (ISO): Section 12.14.9 [Variable Arguments Input Functions], page 301.

`int VSTART`
> `termios.h` (POSIX.1): Section 17.4.9.3 [Special Characters for Flow Control], page 493.

`int VSTATUS`
> `termios.h` (BSD): Section 17.4.9.4 [Other Special Characters], page 494.

`int VSTOP`
> `termios.h` (POSIX.1): Section 17.4.9.3 [Special Characters for Flow Control], page 493.

`int VSUSP`
> `termios.h` (POSIX.1): Section 17.4.9.2 [Characters that Cause Signals], page 492.

`int vswprintf (wchar_t *s, size_t size, const wchar_t *template, va_list ap)`
> `wchar.h` (GNU): Section 12.12.9 [Variable Arguments Output Functions], page 281.

`int vswscanf (const wchar_t *s, const wchar_t *template, va_list ap)`
> `wchar.h` (ISO): Section 12.14.9 [Variable Arguments Input Functions], page 301.

`void vsyslog (int facility_priority, const char *format, va_list arglist)`
> `syslog.h` (BSD): Section 18.2.2 [syslog, vsyslog], page 507.

`int VTIME`
> `termios.h` (POSIX.1): Section 17.4.10 [Noncanonical Input], page 494.

`int vtimes (struct vtimes *current, struct vtimes *child)`
> `sys/vtimes.h` (sys/vtimes.h): Section 22.1 [Resource Usage], page 630.

`void vwarn (const char *format, va_list ap)`
> `err.h` (BSD): Section 2.3 [Error Messages], page 33.

`void vwarnx (const char *format, va_list ap)`
> `err.h` (BSD): Section 2.3 [Error Messages], page 33.

`int VWERASE`
> `termios.h` (BSD): Section 17.4.9.1 [Characters for Input Editing], page 490.

`int vwprintf (const wchar_t *template, va_list ap)`
> `wchar.h` (ISO): Section 12.12.9 [Variable Arguments Output Functions], page 281.

`int vwscanf (const wchar_t *template, va_list ap)`
> `wchar.h` (ISO): Section 12.14.9 [Variable Arguments Input Functions], page 301.

`pid_t wait (int *status-ptr)`
> `sys/wait.h` (POSIX.1): Section 26.6 [Process Completion], page 755.

`pid_t wait3 (union wait *status-ptr, int options, struct rusage *usage)`
> `sys/wait.h` (BSD): Section 26.8 [BSD Process Wait Functions], page 758.

`pid_t wait4 (pid_t pid, int *status-ptr, int options, struct rusage *usage)`
> `sys/wait.h` (BSD): Section 26.6 [Process Completion], page 755.

`pid_t waitpid (pid_t pid, int *status-ptr, int options)`
> `sys/wait.h` (POSIX.1): Section 26.6 [Process Completion], page 755.

`void warn (const char *format, ...)`
> `err.h` (BSD): Section 2.3 [Error Messages], page 33.

`void warnx (const char *format, ...)`
> `err.h` (BSD): Section 2.3 [Error Messages], page 33.

`WCHAR_MAX`
> `limits.h` (GNU): Section A.5.2 [Range of an Integer Type], page 885.

wint_t WCHAR_MAX
            wchar.h (ISO): Section 6.1 [Introduction to Extended Characters], page 127.

wint_t WCHAR_MIN
            wchar.h (ISO): Section 6.1 [Introduction to Extended Characters], page 127.

wchar_t
            stddef.h (ISO): Section 6.1 [Introduction to Extended Characters], page 127.

int WCOREDUMP (int *status*)
            sys/wait.h (BSD): Section 26.7 [Process Completion Status], page 757.

wchar_t * wcpcpy (wchar_t *restrict *wto*, const wchar_t *restrict *wfrom*)
            wchar.h (GNU): Section 5.4 [Copying and Concatenation], page 91.

wchar_t * wcpncpy (wchar_t *restrict *wto*, const wchar_t *restrict *wfrom*, size_t *size*)
            wchar.h (GNU): Section 5.4 [Copying and Concatenation], page 91.

size_t wcrtomb (char *restrict *s*, wchar_t *wc*, mbstate_t *restrict *ps*)
            wchar.h (ISO): Section 6.3.3 [Converting Single Characters], page 133.

int wcscasecmp (const wchar_t *ws1*, const wchar_t *ws2*)
            wchar.h (GNU): Section 5.5 [String/Array Comparison], page 102.

wchar_t * wcscat (wchar_t *restrict *wto*, const wchar_t *restrict *wfrom*)
            wchar.h (ISO): Section 5.4 [Copying and Concatenation], page 91.

wchar_t * wcschr (const wchar_t *wstring*, int *wc*)
            wchar.h (ISO): Section 5.7 [Search Functions], page 110.

wchar_t * wcschrnul (const wchar_t *wstring*, wchar_t *wc*)
            wchar.h (GNU): Section 5.7 [Search Functions], page 110.

int wcscmp (const wchar_t *ws1*, const wchar_t *ws2*)
            wchar.h (ISO): Section 5.5 [String/Array Comparison], page 102.

int wcscoll (const wchar_t *ws1*, const wchar_t *ws2*)
            wchar.h (ISO): Section 5.6 [Collation Functions], page 106.

wchar_t * wcscpy (wchar_t *restrict *wto*, const wchar_t *restrict *wfrom*)
            wchar.h (ISO): Section 5.4 [Copying and Concatenation], page 91.

size_t wcscspn (const wchar_t *wstring*, const wchar_t *stopset*)
            wchar.h (ISO): Section 5.7 [Search Functions], page 110.

wchar_t * wcsdup (const wchar_t *ws*)
            wchar.h (GNU): Section 5.4 [Copying and Concatenation], page 91.

size_t wcsftime (wchar_t *s*, size_t *size*, const wchar_t *template*, const struct tm *brokentime*)
            time.h (ISO/Amend1): Section 21.4.5 [Formatting Calendar Time], page 608.

size_t wcslen (const wchar_t *ws*)
            wchar.h (ISO): Section 5.3 [String Length], page 89.

int wcsncasecmp (const wchar_t *ws1*, const wchar_t *s2*, size_t *n*)
            wchar.h (GNU): Section 5.5 [String/Array Comparison], page 102.

wchar_t * wcsncat (wchar_t *restrict *wto*, const wchar_t *restrict *wfrom*, size_t *size*)
            wchar.h (ISO): Section 5.4 [Copying and Concatenation], page 91.

int wcsncmp (const wchar_t *ws1*, const wchar_t *ws2*, size_t *size*)
            wchar.h (ISO): Section 5.5 [String/Array Comparison], page 102.

wchar_t * wcsncpy (wchar_t *restrict *wto*, const wchar_t *restrict *wfrom*, size_t *size*)
            wchar.h (ISO): Section 5.4 [Copying and Concatenation], page 91.

size_t wcsnlen (const wchar_t *ws*, size_t *maxlen*)
            wchar.h (GNU): Section 5.3 [String Length], page 89.

`size_t wcsnrtombs (char *restrict dst, const wchar_t **restrict src, size_t nwc, size_t len, mbstate_t *restrict ps)`
> `wchar.h` (GNU): Section 6.3.4 [Converting Multibyte and Wide Character Strings], page 139.

`wchar_t * wcspbrk (const wchar_t *wstring, const wchar_t *stopset)`
> `wchar.h` (ISO): Section 5.7 [Search Functions], page 110.

`wchar_t * wcsrchr (const wchar_t *wstring, wchar_t c)`
> `wchar.h` (ISO): Section 5.7 [Search Functions], page 110.

`size_t wcsrtombs (char *restrict dst, const wchar_t **restrict src, size_t len, mbstate_t *restrict ps)`
> `wchar.h` (ISO): Section 6.3.4 [Converting Multibyte and Wide Character Strings], page 139.

`size_t wcsspn (const wchar_t *wstring, const wchar_t *skipset)`
> `wchar.h` (ISO): Section 5.7 [Search Functions], page 110.

`wchar_t * wcsstr (const wchar_t *haystack, const wchar_t *needle)`
> `wchar.h` (ISO): Section 5.7 [Search Functions], page 110.

`double wcstod (const wchar_t *restrict string, wchar_t **restrict tailptr)`
> `wchar.h` (ISO): Section 20.11.2 [Parsing of Floats], page 589.

`float wcstof (const wchar_t *string, wchar_t **tailptr)`
> `stdlib.h` (ISO): Section 20.11.2 [Parsing of Floats], page 589.

`intmax_t wcstoimax (const wchar_t *restrict string, wchar_t **restrict tailptr, int base)`
> `wchar.h` (ISO): Section 20.11.1 [Parsing of Integers], page 585.

`wchar_t * wcstok (wchar_t *newstring, const wchar_t *delimiters, wchar_t **save_ptr)`
> `wchar.h` (ISO): Section 5.8 [Finding Tokens in a String], page 115.

`long int wcstol (const wchar_t *restrict string, wchar_t **restrict tailptr, int base)`
> `wchar.h` (ISO): Section 20.11.1 [Parsing of Integers], page 585.

`long double wcstold (const wchar_t *string, wchar_t **tailptr)`
> `stdlib.h` (ISO): Section 20.11.2 [Parsing of Floats], page 589.

`long long int wcstoll (const wchar_t *restrict string, wchar_t **restrict tailptr, int base)`
> `wchar.h` (ISO): Section 20.11.1 [Parsing of Integers], page 585.

`size_t wcstombs (char *string, const wchar_t *wstring, size_t size)`
> `stdlib.h` (ISO): Section 6.4.2 [Non-reentrant Conversion of Strings], page 146.

`long long int wcstoq (const wchar_t *restrict string, wchar_t **restrict tailptr, int base)`
> `wchar.h` (GNU): Section 20.11.1 [Parsing of Integers], page 585.

`unsigned long int wcstoul (const wchar_t *restrict string, wchar_t **restrict tailptr, int base)`
> `wchar.h` (ISO): Section 20.11.1 [Parsing of Integers], page 585.

`unsigned long long int wcstoull (const wchar_t *restrict string, wchar_t **restrict tailptr, int base)`
> `wchar.h` (ISO): Section 20.11.1 [Parsing of Integers], page 585.

`uintmax_t wcstoumax (const wchar_t *restrict string, wchar_t **restrict tailptr, int base)`
> `wchar.h` (ISO): Section 20.11.1 [Parsing of Integers], page 585.

`unsigned long long int wcstouq (const wchar_t *restrict string, wchar_t **restrict tailptr, int base)`
> `wchar.h` (GNU): Section 20.11.1 [Parsing of Integers], page 585.

`wchar_t * wcswcs (const wchar_t *haystack, const wchar_t *needle)`
> `wchar.h` (XPG): Section 5.7 [Search Functions], page 110.

`size_t wcsxfrm (wchar_t *restrict wto, const wchar_t *wfrom, size_t size)`
> `wchar.h` (ISO): Section 5.6 [Collation Functions], page 106.

`int wctob (wint_t c)`
> `wchar.h` (ISO): Section 6.3.3 [Converting Single Characters], page 133.

`int wctomb (char *string, wchar_t wchar)`
> `stdlib.h` (ISO): Section 6.4.1 [Non-reentrant Conversion of Single Characters], page 144.

`wctrans_t wctrans (const char *property)`
> `wctype.h` (ISO): Section 4.5 [Mapping of wide characters.], page 85.

`wctrans_t`
> `wctype.h` (ISO): Section 4.5 [Mapping of wide characters.], page 85.

`wctype_t wctype (const char *property)`
> `wctype.h` (ISO): Section 4.3 [Character class determination for wide characters], page 80.

`wctype_t`
> `wctype.h` (ISO): Section 4.3 [Character class determination for wide characters], page 80.

`int WEOF`
> `wchar.h` (ISO): Section 12.15 [End-Of-File and Errors], page 302.

`wint_t WEOF`
> `wchar.h` (ISO): Section 6.1 [Introduction to Extended Characters], page 127.

`int WEXITSTATUS (int status)`
> `sys/wait.h` (POSIX.1): Section 26.7 [Process Completion Status], page 757.

`int WIFEXITED (int status)`
> `sys/wait.h` (POSIX.1): Section 26.7 [Process Completion Status], page 757.

`int WIFSIGNALED (int status)`
> `sys/wait.h` (POSIX.1): Section 26.7 [Process Completion Status], page 757.

`int WIFSTOPPED (int status)`
> `sys/wait.h` (POSIX.1): Section 26.7 [Process Completion Status], page 757.

`wint_t`
> `wchar.h` (ISO): Section 6.1 [Introduction to Extended Characters], page 127.

`wchar_t * wmemchr (const wchar_t *block, wchar_t wc, size_t size)`
> `wchar.h` (ISO): Section 5.7 [Search Functions], page 110.

`int wmemcmp (const wchar_t *a1, const wchar_t *a2, size_t size)`
> `wchar.h` (ISO): Section 5.5 [String/Array Comparison], page 102.

`wchar_t * wmemcpy (wchar_t *restrict wto, const wchar_t *restrict wfrom, size_t size)`
> `wchar.h` (ISO): Section 5.4 [Copying and Concatenation], page 91.

`wchar_t * wmemmove (wchar_t *wto, const wchar_t *wfrom, size_t size)`
> `wchar.h` (ISO): Section 5.4 [Copying and Concatenation], page 91.

`wchar_t * wmempcpy (wchar_t *restrict wto, const wchar_t *restrict wfrom, size_t size)`
> `wchar.h` (GNU): Section 5.4 [Copying and Concatenation], page 91.

`wchar_t * wmemset (wchar_t *block, wchar_t wc, size_t size)`
> `wchar.h` (ISO): Section 5.4 [Copying and Concatenation], page 91.

`int W_OK`
> `unistd.h` (POSIX.1): Section 14.9.8 [Testing Permission to Access a File], page 412.

`int wordexp (const char *words, wordexp_t *word-vector-ptr, int flags)`
> `wordexp.h` (POSIX.2): Section 10.4.2 [Calling `wordexp`], page 237.

`wordexp_t`
> `wordexp.h` (POSIX.2): Section 10.4.2 [Calling `wordexp`], page 237.

void wordfree (wordexp_t *word-vector-ptr)
        wordexp.h (POSIX.2): Section 10.4.2 [Calling wordexp], page 237.

int wprintf (const wchar_t *template, ...)
        wchar.h (ISO): Section 12.12.7 [Formatted Output Functions], page 278.

WRDE_APPEND
        wordexp.h (POSIX.2): Section 10.4.3 [Flags for Word Expansion], page 238.

WRDE_BADCHAR
        wordexp.h (POSIX.2): Section 10.4.2 [Calling wordexp], page 237.

WRDE_BADVAL
        wordexp.h (POSIX.2): Section 10.4.2 [Calling wordexp], page 237.

WRDE_CMDSUB
        wordexp.h (POSIX.2): Section 10.4.2 [Calling wordexp], page 237.

WRDE_DOOFFS
        wordexp.h (POSIX.2): Section 10.4.3 [Flags for Word Expansion], page 238.

WRDE_NOCMD
        wordexp.h (POSIX.2): Section 10.4.3 [Flags for Word Expansion], page 238.

WRDE_NOSPACE
        wordexp.h (POSIX.2): Section 10.4.2 [Calling wordexp], page 237.

WRDE_REUSE
        wordexp.h (POSIX.2): Section 10.4.3 [Flags for Word Expansion], page 238.

WRDE_SHOWERR
        wordexp.h (POSIX.2): Section 10.4.3 [Flags for Word Expansion], page 238.

WRDE_SYNTAX
        wordexp.h (POSIX.2): Section 10.4.2 [Calling wordexp], page 237.

WRDE_UNDEF
        wordexp.h (POSIX.2): Section 10.4.3 [Flags for Word Expansion], page 238.

ssize_t write (int filedes, const void *buffer, size_t size)
        unistd.h (POSIX.1): Section 13.2 [Input and Output Primitives], page 326.

ssize_t writev (int filedes, const struct iovec *vector, int count)
        sys/uio.h (BSD): Section 13.6 [Fast Scatter-Gather I/O], page 336.

int wscanf (const wchar_t *template, ...)
        wchar.h (ISO): Section 12.14.8 [Formatted Input Functions], page 300.

int WSTOPSIG (int status)
        sys/wait.h (POSIX.1): Section 26.7 [Process Completion Status], page 757.

int WTERMSIG (int status)
        sys/wait.h (POSIX.1): Section 26.7 [Process Completion Status], page 757.

int X_OK
        unistd.h (POSIX.1): Section 14.9.8 [Testing Permission to Access a File], page 412.

_XOPEN_SOURCE
        (X/Open): Section 1.3.4 [Feature Test Macros], page 15.

_XOPEN_SOURCE_EXTENDED
        (X/Open): Section 1.3.4 [Feature Test Macros], page 15.

double y0 (double x)
        math.h (SVID): Section 19.6 [Special Functions], page 522.

float y0f (float x)
        math.h (SVID): Section 19.6 [Special Functions], page 522.

`long double y0l (long double x)`
> `math.h` (SVID): Section 19.6 [Special Functions], page 522.

`double y1 (double x)`
> `math.h` (SVID): Section 19.6 [Special Functions], page 522.

`float y1f (float x)`
> `math.h` (SVID): Section 19.6 [Special Functions], page 522.

`long double y1l (long double x)`
> `math.h` (SVID): Section 19.6 [Special Functions], page 522.

`double yn (int n, double x)`
> `math.h` (SVID): Section 19.6 [Special Functions], page 522.

`float ynf (int n, float x)`
> `math.h` (SVID): Section 19.6 [Special Functions], page 522.

`long double ynl (int n, long double x)`
> `math.h` (SVID): Section 19.6 [Special Functions], page 522.

# Appendix C Installing the GNU C Library

Before you do anything else, you should read the FAQ at `http://sourceware.org/glibc/wiki/FAQ`. It answers common questions and describes problems you may experience with compilation and installation.

Features can be added to the GNU C Library via *add-on* bundles. These are separate tar files, which you unpack into the top level of the source tree. Then you give `configure` the '`--enable-add-ons`' option to activate them, and they will be compiled into the library.

You will need recent versions of several GNU tools: definitely GCC and GNU Make, and possibly others. See Section C.3 [Recommended Tools for Compilation], page 1000, below.

## C.1 Configuring and compiling the GNU C Library

The GNU C Library cannot be compiled in the source directory. You must build it in a separate build directory. For example, if you have unpacked the GNU C Library sources in `/src/gnu/glibc-version`, create a directory `/src/gnu/glibc-build` to put the object files in. This allows removing the whole build directory in case an error occurs, which is the safest way to get a fresh start and should always be done.

From your object directory, run the shell script `configure` located at the top level of the source tree. In the scenario above, you'd type

```
$ ../glibc-version/configure args...
```

Please note that even though you're building in a separate build directory, the compilation may need to create or modify files and directories in the source directory.

`configure` takes many options, but the only one that is usually mandatory is '`--prefix`'. This option tells `configure` where you want the GNU C Library installed. This defaults to `/usr/local`, but the normal setting to install as the standard system library is '`--prefix=/usr`' for GNU/Linux systems and '`--prefix=`' (an empty prefix) for GNU/Hurd systems.

It may also be useful to set the *CC* and *CFLAGS* variables in the environment when running `configure`. *CC* selects the C compiler that will be used, and *CFLAGS* sets optimization options for the compiler.

The following list describes all of the available options for `configure`:

'`--prefix=directory`'
> Install machine-independent data files in subdirectories of *directory*. The default is to install in `/usr/local`.

'`--exec-prefix=directory`'
> Install the library and other machine-dependent files in subdirectories of *directory*. The default is to the '`--prefix`' directory if that option is specified, or `/usr/local` otherwise.

'`--with-headers=directory`'
> Look for kernel header files in *directory*, not `/usr/include`. The GNU C Library needs information from the kernel's header files describing the interface to the kernel. The GNU C Library will normally look in `/usr/include` for them, but if you specify this option, it will look in *DIRECTORY* instead.

This option is primarily of use on a system where the headers in `/usr/include` come from an older version of the GNU C Library. Conflicts can occasionally happen in this case. You can also use this option if you want to compile the GNU C Library with a newer set of kernel headers than the ones found in `/usr/include`.

'`--enable-add-ons[=`*`list`*`]`'

Specify add-on packages to include in the build. If this option is specified with no list, it enables all the add-on packages it finds in the main source directory; this is the default behavior. You may specify an explicit list of add-ons to use in *list*, separated by spaces or commas (if you use spaces, remember to quote them from the shell). Each add-on in *list* can be an absolute directory name or can be a directory name relative to the main source directory, or relative to the build directory (that is, the current working directory). For example, '`--enable-add-ons=nptl,../glibc-libidn-`*`version`*'.

'`--enable-kernel=`*`version`*'

This option is currently only useful on GNU/Linux systems. The *version* parameter should have the form X.Y.Z and describes the smallest version of the Linux kernel the generated library is expected to support. The higher the *version* number is, the less compatibility code is added, and the faster the code gets.

'`--with-binutils=`*`directory`*'

Use the binutils (assembler and linker) in *`directory`*, not the ones the C compiler would default to. You can use this option if the default binutils on your system cannot deal with all the constructs in the GNU C Library. In that case, `configure` will detect the problem and suppress these constructs, so that the library will still be usable, but functionality may be lost—for example, you can't build a shared libc with old binutils.

'`--without-fp`'

Use this option if your computer lacks hardware floating-point support and your operating system does not emulate an FPU.

'`--disable-shared`'

Don't build shared libraries even if it is possible. Not all systems support shared libraries; you need ELF support and (currently) the GNU linker.

'`--disable-profile`'

Don't build libraries with profiling information. You may want to use this option if you don't plan to do profiling.

'`--enable-static-nss`'

Compile static versions of the NSS (Name Service Switch) libraries. This is not recommended because it defeats the purpose of NSS; a program linked statically with the NSS libraries cannot be dynamically reconfigured to use a different name database.

'--without-tls'

> By default the C library is built with support for thread-local storage if the used tools support it. By using '--without-tls' this can be prevented though there generally is no reason since it creates compatibility problems.

'--enable-hardcoded-path-in-tests'

> By default, dynamic tests are linked to run with the installed C library. This option hardcodes the newly built C library path in dynamic tests so that they can be invoked directly.

'--enable-lock-elision=yes'

> Enable lock elision for pthread mutexes by default.

'--enable-pt_chown'

> The file pt_chown is a helper binary for grantpt (see Section 17.8.1 [Allocating Pseudo-Terminals], page 500) that is installed setuid root to fix up pseudo-terminal ownership. It is not built by default because systems using the Linux kernel are commonly built with the devpts filesystem enabled and mounted at /dev/pts, which manages pseudo-terminal ownership automatically. By using '--enable-pt_chown', you may build pt_chown and install it setuid and owned by root. The use of pt_chown introduces additional security risks to the system and you should enable it only if you understand and accept those risks.

'--disable-werror'

> By default, the GNU C Library is built with -Werror. If you wish to build without this option (for example, if building with a newer version of GCC than this version of the GNU C Library was tested with, so new warnings cause the build with -Werror to fail), you can configure with --disable-werror.

'--disable-mathvec'

> By default for x86_64, the GNU C Library is built with vector math library. Use this option to disable vector math library.

'--build=build-system'
'--host=host-system'

> These options are for cross-compiling. If you specify both options and build-system is different from host-system, configure will prepare to cross-compile the GNU C Library from build-system to be used on host-system. You'll probably need the '--with-headers' option too, and you may have to override configure's selection of the compiler and/or binutils.

> If you only specify '--host', configure will prepare for a native compile but use what you specify instead of guessing what your system is. This is most useful to change the CPU submodel. For example, if configure guesses your machine as i686-pc-linux-gnu but you want to compile a library for 586es, give '--host=i586-pc-linux-gnu' or just '--host=i586-linux' and add the appropriate compiler flags ('-mcpu=i586' will do the trick) to CFLAGS.

> If you specify just '--build', configure will get confused.

'--with-pkgversion=version'

> Specify a description, possibly including a build number or build date, of the binaries being built, to be included in --version output from programs in-

stalled with the GNU C Library. For example, `--with-pkgversion='FooBar GNU/Linux glibc build 123'`. The default value is 'GNU libc'.

'`--with-bugurl=`*url*'

Specify the URL that users should visit if they wish to report a bug, to be included in `--help` output from programs installed with the GNU C Library. The default value refers to the main bug-reporting information for the GNU C Library.

To build the library and related programs, type `make`. This will produce a lot of output, some of which may look like errors from `make` but isn't. Look for error messages from `make` containing '`***`'. Those indicate that something is seriously wrong.

The compilation process can take a long time, depending on the configuration and the speed of your machine. Some complex modules may take a very long time to compile, as much as several minutes on slower machines. Do not panic if the compiler appears to hang.

If you want to run a parallel make, simply pass the '`-j`' option with an appropriate numeric parameter to `make`. You need a recent GNU `make` version, though.

To build and run test programs which exercise some of the library facilities, type `make check`. If it does not complete successfully, do not use the built library, and report a bug after verifying that the problem is not already known. See Section C.5 [Reporting Bugs], page 1002, for instructions on reporting bugs. Note that some of the tests assume they are not being run by `root`. We recommend you compile and test the GNU C Library as an unprivileged user.

Before reporting bugs make sure there is no problem with your system. The tests (and later installation) use some pre-existing files of the system such as `/etc/passwd`, `/etc/nsswitch.conf` and others. These files must all contain correct and sensible content.

Normally, `make check` will run all the tests before reporting all problems found and exiting with error status if any problems occurred. You can specify '`stop-on-test-failure=y`' when running `make check` to make the test run stop and exit with an error status immediately when a failure occurs.

To format the *GNU C Library Reference Manual* for printing, type `make dvi`. You need a working TeX installation to do this. The distribution builds the on-line formatted version of the manual, as Info files, as part of the build process. You can build them manually with `make info`.

The library has a number of special-purpose configuration parameters which you can find in `Makeconfig`. These can be overwritten with the file `configparms`. To change them, create a `configparms` in your build directory and add values as appropriate for your system. The file is included and parsed by `make` and has to follow the conventions for makefiles.

It is easy to configure the GNU C Library for cross-compilation by setting a few variables in `configparms`. Set `CC` to the cross-compiler for the target you configured the library for; it is important to use this same `CC` value when running `configure`, like this: '`CC=`*target*`-gcc` `configure` *target*'. Set `BUILD_CC` to the compiler to use for programs run on the build system as part of compiling the library. You may need to set `AR` to cross-compiling versions of `ar` if the native tools are not configured to work with object files for the target you configured for. When cross-compiling the GNU C Library, it may be tested using '`make check test-wrapper="`*srcdir*`/scripts/cross-test-ssh.sh` *hostname*`"`', where *srcdir* is the absolute directory name for the main source directory and *hostname* is the host name of a system that can run the newly built binaries of the GNU C Library. The source and build directories must be visible at the same locations on both the build system and *hostname*.

In general, when testing the GNU C Library, 'test-wrapper' may be set to the name and arguments of any program to run newly built binaries. This program must preserve the arguments to the binary being run, its working directory and the standard input, output and error file descriptors. If 'test-wrapper env' will not work to run a program with environment variables set, then 'test-wrapper-env' must be set to a program that runs a newly built program with environment variable assignments in effect, those assignments being specified as 'var=value' before the name of the program to be run. If multiple assignments to the same variable are specified, the last assignment specified must take precedence. Similarly, if 'test-wrapper env -i' will not work to run a program with an environment completely empty of variables except those directly assigned, then 'test-wrapper-env-only' must be set; its use has the same syntax as 'test-wrapper-env', the only difference in its semantics being starting with an empty set of environment variables rather than the ambient set.

## C.2 Installing the C Library

To install the library and its header files, and the Info files of the manual, type **make install**. This will build things, if necessary, before installing them; however, you should still compile everything first. If you are installing the GNU C Library as your primary C library, we recommend that you shut the system down to single-user mode first, and reboot afterward. This minimizes the risk of breaking things when the library changes out from underneath.

'make install' will do the entire job of upgrading from a previous installation of the GNU C Library version 2.x. There may sometimes be headers left behind from the previous installation, but those are generally harmless. If you want to avoid leaving headers behind you can do things in the following order.

You must first build the library ('make'), optionally check it ('make check'), switch the include directories and then install ('make install'). The steps must be done in this order. Not moving the directory before install will result in an unusable mixture of header files from both libraries, but configuring, building, and checking the library requires the ability to compile and run programs against the old library. The new /usr/include, after switching the include directories and before installing the library should contain the Linux headers, but nothing else. If you do this, you will need to restore any headers from libraries other than the GNU C Library yourself after installing the library.

You can install the GNU C Library somewhere other than where you configured it to go by setting the DESTDIR GNU standard make variable on the command line for 'make install'. The value of this variable is prepended to all the paths for installation. This is useful when setting up a chroot environment or preparing a binary distribution. The directory should be specified with an absolute file name. Installing with the **prefix** and **exec_prefix** GNU standard make variables set is not supported.

The GNU C Library includes a daemon called **nscd**, which you may or may not want to run. **nscd** caches name service lookups; it can dramatically improve performance with NIS+, and may help with DNS as well.

One auxiliary program, `/usr/libexec/pt_chown`, is installed setuid `root` if the '`--enable-pt_chown`' configuration option is used. This program is invoked by the `grantpt` function; it sets the permissions on a pseudoterminal so it can be used by the calling process. If you are using a Linux kernel with the `devpts` filesystem enabled and mounted at `/dev/pts`, you don't need this program.

After installation you might want to configure the timezone and locale installation of your system. The GNU C Library comes with a locale database which gets configured with `localedef`. For example, to set up a German locale with name `de_DE`, simply issue the command '`localedef -i de_DE -f ISO-8859-1 de_DE`'. To configure all locales that are supported by the GNU C Library, you can issue from your build directory the command '`make localedata/install-locales`'.

To configure the locally used timezone, set the `TZ` environment variable. The script `tzselect` helps you to select the right value. As an example, for Germany, `tzselect` would tell you to use '`TZ='Europe/Berlin''`. For a system wide installation (the given paths are for an installation with '`--prefix=/usr`'), link the timezone file which is in `/usr/share/zoneinfo` to the file `/etc/localtime`. For Germany, you might execute '`ln -s /usr/share/zoneinfo/Europe/Berlin /etc/localtime`'.

## C.3 Recommended Tools for Compilation

We recommend installing the following GNU tools before attempting to build the GNU C Library:

- GNU `make` 3.79 or newer

  You need the latest version of GNU `make`. Modifying the GNU C Library to work with other `make` programs would be so difficult that we recommend you port GNU `make` instead. **Really.** We recommend GNU `make` version 3.79. All earlier versions have severe bugs or lack features.

- GCC 4.6 or newer

  GCC 4.6 or higher is required. In general it is recommended to use the newest version of the compiler that is known to work for building the GNU C Library, as newer compilers usually produce better code. As of release time, GCC 4.9.2 is the newest compiler verified to work to build the GNU C Library.

  You can use whatever compiler you like to compile programs that use the GNU C Library.

  Check the FAQ for any special compiler issues on particular platforms.

- GNU `binutils` 2.22 or later

  You must use GNU `binutils` (as and ld) to build the GNU C Library. No other assembler or linker has the necessary functionality at the moment. As of release time, GNU `binutils` 2.25 is the newest verified to work to build the GNU C Library.

- GNU `texinfo` 4.7 or later

  To correctly translate and install the Texinfo documentation you need this version of the `texinfo` package. Earlier versions do not understand all the tags used in the document, and the installation mechanism for the info files is not present or works differently. As of release time, `texinfo` 5.2 is the newest verified to work to build the GNU C Library.

- GNU `awk` 3.1.2, or higher

  `awk` is used in several places to generate files. Some `gawk` extensions are used, including the `asorti` function, which was introduced in version 3.1.2 of `gawk`.

- Perl 5

  Perl is not required, but it is used if present to test the installation. We may decide to use it elsewhere in the future.

- GNU `sed` 3.02 or newer

  `Sed` is used in several places to generate files. Most scripts work with any version of `sed`. The known exception is the script `po2test.sed` in the `intl` subdirectory which is used to generate `msgs.h` for the test suite. This script works correctly only with GNU `sed` 3.02. If you like to run the test suite, you should definitely upgrade `sed`.

If you change any of the `configure.ac` files you will also need

- GNU `autoconf` 2.69 (exactly)

and if you change any of the message translation files you will need

- GNU `gettext` 0.10.36 or later

If you wish to regenerate the `yacc` parser code in the `intl` subdirectory you will need

- GNU `bison` 2.7 or later

You may also need these packages if you upgrade your source tree using patches, although we try to avoid this.

## C.4 Specific advice for GNU/Linux systems

If you are installing the GNU C Library on GNU/Linux systems, you need to have the header files from a 2.6.32 or newer kernel around for reference. These headers must be installed using 'make headers_install'; the headers present in the kernel source directory are not suitable for direct use by the GNU C Library. You do not need to use that kernel, just have its headers installed where the GNU C Library can access them, referred to here as *install-directory*. The easiest way to do this is to unpack it in a directory such as /usr/src/linux-*version*. In that directory, run 'make headers_install INSTALL_HDR_PATH=*install-directory*'. Finally, configure the GNU C Library with the option '--with-headers=*install-directory*/include'. Use the most recent kernel you can get your hands on. (If you are cross-compiling the GNU C Library, you need to specify 'ARCH=*architecture*' in the 'make headers_install' command, where *architecture* is the architecture name used by the Linux kernel, such as 'x86' or 'powerpc'.)

After installing the GNU C Library, you may need to remove or rename directories such as /usr/include/linux and /usr/include/asm, and replace them with copies of directories such as `linux` and `asm` from *install-directory*/include. All directories present in *install-directory*/include should be copied, except that the GNU C Library provides its own version of /usr/include/scsi; the files provided by the kernel should be copied without replacing those provided by the GNU C Library. The `linux`, `asm` and `asm-generic` directories are required to compile programs using the GNU C Library; the other directories describe interfaces to the kernel but are not required if not compiling programs using those interfaces. You do not need to copy kernel headers if you did not specify an alternate kernel header source using '--with-headers'.

The Filesystem Hierarchy Standard for GNU/Linux systems expects some components of the GNU C Library installation to be in /lib and some in /usr/lib. This is handled automatically if you configure the GNU C Library with '--prefix=/usr'. If you set some other prefix or allow it to default to /usr/local, then all the components are installed there.

## C.5 Reporting Bugs

There are probably bugs in the GNU C Library. There are certainly errors and omissions in this manual. If you report them, they will get fixed. If you don't, no one will ever know about them and they will remain unfixed for all eternity, if not longer.

It is a good idea to verify that the problem has not already been reported. Bugs are documented in two places: The file BUGS describes a number of well known bugs and the central GNU C Library bug tracking system has a WWW interface at http://sourceware. org/bugzilla/. The WWW interface gives you access to open and closed reports. A closed report normally includes a patch or a hint on solving the problem.

To report a bug, first you must find it. With any luck, this will be the hard part. Once you've found a bug, make sure it's really a bug. A good way to do this is to see if the GNU C Library behaves the same way some other C library does. If so, probably you are wrong and the libraries are right (but not necessarily). If not, one of the libraries is probably wrong. It might not be the GNU C Library. Many historical Unix C libraries permit things that we don't, such as closing a file twice.

If you think you have found some way in which the GNU C Library does not conform to the ISO and POSIX standards (see Section 1.2 [Standards and Portability], page 1), that is definitely a bug. Report it!

Once you're sure you've found a bug, try to narrow it down to the smallest test case that reproduces the problem. In the case of a C library, you really only need to narrow it down to one library function call, if possible. This should not be too difficult.

The final step when you have a simple test case is to report the bug. Do this at http://www.gnu.org/software/libc/bugs.html.

If you are not sure how a function should behave, and this manual doesn't tell you, that's a bug in the manual. Report that too! If the function's behavior disagrees with the manual, then either the library or the manual has a bug, so report the disagreement. If you find any errors or omissions in this manual, please report them to the bug database. If you refer to specific sections of the manual, please include the section names for easier identification.

# Appendix D  Library Maintenance

## D.1  Adding New Functions

The process of building the library is driven by the makefiles, which make heavy use of special features of GNU `make`. The makefiles are very complex, and you probably don't want to try to understand them. But what they do is fairly straightforward, and only requires that you define a few variables in the right places.

The library sources are divided into subdirectories, grouped by topic.

The `string` subdirectory has all the string-manipulation functions, `math` has all the mathematical functions, etc.

Each subdirectory contains a simple makefile, called `Makefile`, which defines a few `make` variables and then includes the global makefile `Rules` with a line like:

```
include ../Rules
```

The basic variables that a subdirectory makefile defines are:

`subdir`      The name of the subdirectory, for example `stdio`. This variable **must** be defined.

`headers`     The names of the header files in this section of the library, such as `stdio.h`.

`routines`
`aux`         The names of the modules (source files) in this section of the library. These should be simple names, such as '`strlen`' (rather than complete file names, such as `strlen.c`). Use `routines` for modules that define functions in the library, and `aux` for auxiliary modules containing things like data definitions. But the values of `routines` and `aux` are just concatenated, so there really is no practical difference.

`tests`       The names of test programs for this section of the library. These should be simple names, such as '`tester`' (rather than complete file names, such as `tester.c`). '`make tests`' will build and run all the test programs. If a test program needs input, put the test data in a file called *test-program*`.input`; it will be given to the test program on its standard input. If a test program wants to be run with arguments, put the arguments (all on a single line) in a file called *test-program*`.args`. Test programs should exit with zero status when the test passes, and nonzero status when the test indicates a bug in the library or error in building.

`others`      The names of "other" programs associated with this section of the library. These are programs which are not tests per se, but are other small programs included with the library. They are built by '`make others`'.

`install-lib`
`install-data`
`install`     Files to be installed by '`make install`'. Files listed in '`install-lib`' are installed in the directory specified by '`libdir`' in `configparms` or `Makeconfig` (see Appendix C [Installing the GNU C Library], page 995). Files listed in `install-data` are installed in the directory specified by '`datadir`' in

configparms or Makeconfig. Files listed in `install` are installed in the directory specified by 'bindir' in configparms or Makeconfig.

distribute

Other files from this subdirectory which should be put into a distribution tar file. You need not list here the makefile itself or the source and header files listed in the other standard variables. Only define `distribute` if there are files used in an unusual way that should go into the distribution.

generated

Files which are generated by `Makefile` in this subdirectory. These files will be removed by 'make clean', and they will never go into a distribution.

extra-objs

Extra object files which are built by `Makefile` in this subdirectory. This should be a list of file names like `foo.o`; the files will actually be found in whatever directory object files are being built in. These files will be removed by 'make clean'. This variable is used for secondary object files needed to build `others` or `tests`.

## D.1.1 Platform-specific types, macros and functions

It's sometimes necessary to provide nonstandard, platform-specific features to developers. The C library is traditionally the lowest library layer, so it makes sense for it to provide these low-level features. However, including these features in the C library may be a disadvantage if another package provides them as well as there will be two conflicting versions of them. Also, the features won't be available to projects that do not use the GNU C Library but use other GNU tools, like GCC.

The current guidelines are:

- If the header file provides features that only make sense on a particular machine architecture and have nothing to do with an operating system, then the features should ultimately be provided as GCC built-in functions. Until then, the GNU C Library may provide them in the header file. When the GCC built-in functions become available, those provided in the header file should be made conditionally available prior to the GCC version in which the built-in function was made available.

- If the header file provides features that are specific to an operating system, both GCC and the GNU C Library could provide it, but the GNU C Library is preferred as it already has a lot of information about the operating system.

- If the header file provides features that are specific to an operating system but used by the GNU C Library, then the GNU C Library should provide them.

The general solution for providing low-level features is to export them as follows:

- A nonstandard, low-level header file that defines macros and inline functions should be called sys/platform/*name*.h.

- Each header file's name should include the platform name, to avoid users thinking there is anything in common between different the header files for different platforms. For example, a sys/platform/*arch*.h name such as sys/platform/ppc.h is better than sys/platform.h.

- A platform-specific header file provided by the GNU C Library should coordinate with GCC such that compiler built-in versions of the functions and macros are preferred if available. This means that user programs will only ever need to include `sys/platform/arch.h`, keeping the same names of types, macros, and functions for convenience and portability.

- Each included symbol must have the prefix `__arch_`, such as `__ppc_get_timebase`.

The easiest way to provide a header file is to add it to the `sysdep_headers` variable. For example, the combination of Linux-specific header files on PowerPC could be provided like this:

```
sysdep_headers += sys/platform/ppc.h
```

Then ensure that you have added a `sys/platform/ppc.h` header file in the machine-specific directory, e.g., `sysdeps/powerpc/sys/platform/ppc.h`.

## D.2 Porting the GNU C Library

The GNU C Library is written to be easily portable to a variety of machines and operating systems. Machine- and operating system-dependent functions are well separated to make it easy to add implementations for new machines or operating systems. This section describes the layout of the library source tree and explains the mechanisms used to select machine-dependent code to use.

All the machine-dependent and operating system-dependent files in the library are in the subdirectory `sysdeps` under the top-level library source directory. This directory contains a hierarchy of subdirectories (see Section D.2.1 [Layout of the `sysdeps` Directory Hierarchy], page 1007).

Each subdirectory of `sysdeps` contains source files for a particular machine or operating system, or for a class of machine or operating system (for example, systems by a particular vendor, or all machines that use IEEE 754 floating-point format). A configuration specifies an ordered list of these subdirectories. Each subdirectory implicitly appends its parent directory to the list. For example, specifying the list `unix/bsd/vax` is equivalent to specifying the list `unix/bsd/vax unix/bsd unix`. A subdirectory can also specify that it implies other subdirectories which are not directly above it in the directory hierarchy. If the file `Implies` exists in a subdirectory, it lists other subdirectories of `sysdeps` which are appended to the list, appearing after the subdirectory containing the `Implies` file. Lines in an `Implies` file that begin with a '#' character are ignored as comments. For example, `unix/bsd/Implies` contains:

```
# BSD has Internet-related things.
unix/inet
```

and `unix/Implies` contains:

```
posix
```

So the final list is `unix/bsd/vax unix/bsd unix/inet unix posix`.

`sysdeps` has a "special" subdirectory called `generic`. It is always implicitly appended to the list of subdirectories, so you needn't put it in an `Implies` file, and you should not create any subdirectories under it intended to be new specific categories. `generic` serves two purposes. First, the makefiles do not bother to look for a system-dependent version of a file that's not in `generic`. This means that any system-dependent source file must have an analogue in `generic`, even if the routines defined by that file are not implemented on other platforms. Second, the `generic` version of a system-dependent file is used if the makefiles do not find a version specific to the system you're compiling for.

If it is possible to implement the routines in a `generic` file in machine-independent C, using only other machine-independent functions in the C library, then you should do so. Otherwise, make them stubs. A *stub* function is a function which cannot be implemented on a particular machine or operating system. Stub functions always return an error, and set `errno` to `ENOSYS` (Function not implemented). See Chapter 2 [Error Reporting], page 22. If you define a stub function, you must place the statement `stub_warning(function)`, where *function* is the name of your function, after its definition. This causes the function to be listed in the installed `<gnu/stubs.h>`, and makes GNU ld warn when the function is used.

Some rare functions are only useful on specific systems and aren't defined at all on others; these do not appear anywhere in the system-independent source code or makefiles (including the `generic` directory), only in the system-dependent `Makefile` in the specific system's subdirectory.

If you come across a file that is in one of the main source directories (`string`, `stdio`, etc.), and you want to write a machine- or operating system-dependent version of it, move the file into `sysdeps/generic` and write your new implementation in the appropriate system-specific subdirectory. Note that if a file is to be system-dependent, it **must not** appear in one of the main source directories.

There are a few special files that may exist in each subdirectory of `sysdeps`:

`Makefile`

> A makefile for this machine or operating system, or class of machine or operating system. This file is included by the library makefile `Makerules`, which is used by the top-level makefile and the subdirectory makefiles. It can change the variables set in the including makefile or add new rules. It can use GNU `make` conditional directives based on the variable 'subdir' (see above) to select different sets of variables and rules for different sections of the library. It can also set the `make` variable 'sysdep-routines', to specify extra modules to be included in the library. You should use 'sysdep-routines' rather than adding modules to 'routines' because the latter is used in determining what to distribute for each subdirectory of the main source tree.
>
> Each makefile in a subdirectory in the ordered list of subdirectories to be searched is included in order. Since several system-dependent makefiles may be included, each should append to 'sysdep-routines' rather than simply setting it:
>
> ```
> sysdep-routines := $(sysdep-routines) foo bar
> ```

`Subdirs`

> This file contains the names of new whole subdirectories under the top-level library source tree that should be included for this system. These subdirectories are treated just like the system-independent subdirectories in the library source tree, such as `stdio` and `math`.
>
> Use this when there are completely new sets of functions and header files that should go into the library for the system this subdirectory of `sysdeps` implements. For example, `sysdeps/unix/inet/Subdirs` contains `inet`; the `inet`

directory contains various network-oriented operations which only make sense to put in the library on systems that support the Internet.

`configure`

>   This file is a shell script fragment to be run at configuration time. The top-level `configure` script uses the shell . command to read the `configure` file in each system-dependent directory chosen, in order. The `configure` files are often generated from `configure.ac` files using Autoconf.
>
>   A system-dependent `configure` script will usually add things to the shell variables 'DEFS' and 'config_vars'; see the top-level `configure` script for details. The script can check for '*--with-package*' options that were passed to the top-level `configure`. For an option '*--with-package=value*' `configure` sets the shell variable '`with_package`' (with any dashes in *package* converted to underscores) to *value*; if the option is just '*--with-package*' (no argument), then it sets '`with_package`' to 'yes'.

`configure.ac`

>   This file is an Autoconf input fragment to be processed into the file `configure` in this subdirectory. See Section "Introduction" in *Autoconf: Generating Automatic Configuration Scripts*, for a description of Autoconf. You should write either `configure` or `configure.ac`, but not both. The first line of `configure.ac` should invoke the m4 macro 'GLIBC_PROVIDES'. This macro does several AC_PROVIDE calls for Autoconf macros which are used by the top-level `configure` script; without this, those macros might be invoked again unnecessarily by Autoconf.

That is the general system for how system-dependencies are isolated. The next section explains how to decide what directories in **sysdeps** to use. Section D.2.2 [Porting the GNU C Library to Unix Systems], page 1009, has some tips on porting the library to Unix variants.

## D.2.1 Layout of the sysdeps Directory Hierarchy

A GNU configuration name has three parts: the CPU type, the manufacturer's name, and the operating system. `configure` uses these to pick the list of system-dependent directories to look for. If the '*--nfp*' option is *not* passed to `configure`, the directory *machine*/fpu is also used. The operating system often has a *base operating system*; for example, if the operating system is 'Linux', the base operating system is 'unix/sysv'. The algorithm used to pick the list of directories is simple: `configure` makes a list of the base operating system, manufacturer, CPU type, and operating system, in that order. It then concatenates all these together with slashes in between, to produce a directory name; for example, the configuration 'i686-linux-gnu' results in unix/sysv/linux/i386/i686. `configure` then tries removing each element of the list in turn, so unix/sysv/linux and unix/sysv are also tried, among others. Since the precise version number of the operating system is often not important, and it would be very inconvenient, for example, to have identical irix6.2 and irix6.3 directories, `configure` tries successively less specific operating system names by removing trailing suffixes starting with a period.

As an example, here is the complete list of directories that would be tried for the configuration 'i686-linux-gnu' (with the `crypt` and `linuxthreads` add-on):

```
sysdeps/i386/elf
crypt/sysdeps/unix
linuxthreads/sysdeps/unix/sysv/linux
linuxthreads/sysdeps/pthread
linuxthreads/sysdeps/unix/sysv
linuxthreads/sysdeps/unix
linuxthreads/sysdeps/i386/i686
linuxthreads/sysdeps/i386
linuxthreads/sysdeps/pthread/no-cmpxchg
sysdeps/unix/sysv/linux/i386
sysdeps/unix/sysv/linux
sysdeps/gnu
sysdeps/unix/common
sysdeps/unix/mman
sysdeps/unix/inet
sysdeps/unix/sysv/i386/i686
sysdeps/unix/sysv/i386
sysdeps/unix/sysv
sysdeps/unix/i386
sysdeps/unix
sysdeps/posix
sysdeps/i386/i686
sysdeps/i386/i486
sysdeps/libm-i387/i686
sysdeps/i386/fpu
sysdeps/libm-i387
sysdeps/i386
sysdeps/wordsize-32
sysdeps/ieee754
sysdeps/libm-ieee754
sysdeps/generic
```

Different machine architectures are conventionally subdirectories at the top level of the `sysdeps` directory tree. For example, `sysdeps/sparc` and `sysdeps/m68k`. These contain files specific to those machine architectures, but not specific to any particular operating system. There might be subdirectories for specializations of those architectures, such as `sysdeps/m68k/68020`. Code which is specific to the floating-point coprocessor used with a particular machine should go in `sysdeps/machine/fpu`.

There are a few directories at the top level of the `sysdeps` hierarchy that are not for particular machine architectures.

generic     As described above (see Section D.2 [Porting the GNU C Library], page 1005), this is the subdirectory that every configuration implicitly uses after all others.

ieee754     This directory is for code using the IEEE 754 floating-point format, where the C type `float` is IEEE 754 single-precision format, and `double` is IEEE 754 double-precision format. Usually this directory is referred to in the `Implies` file in a machine architecture-specific directory, such as `m68k/Implies`.

libm-ieee754

This directory contains an implementation of a mathematical library usable on platforms which use IEEE 754 conformant floating-point arithmetic.

libm-i387

This is a special case. Ideally the code should be in `sysdeps/i386/fpu` but for various reasons it is kept aside.

posix       This directory contains implementations of things in the library in terms of POSIX.1 functions. This includes some of the POSIX.1 functions themselves. Of course, POSIX.1 cannot be completely implemented in terms of itself, so a configuration using just `posix` cannot be complete.

unix        This is the directory for Unix-like things. See Section D.2.2 [Porting the GNU C Library to Unix Systems], page 1009. `unix` implies `posix`. There are some special-purpose subdirectories of `unix`:

unix/common

        This directory is for things common to both BSD and System V release 4. Both `unix/bsd` and `unix/sysv/sysv4` imply `unix/common`.

unix/inet

        This directory is for `socket` and related functions on Unix systems. `unix/inet/Subdirs` enables the `inet` top-level subdirectory. `unix/common` implies `unix/inet`.

mach       This is the directory for things based on the Mach microkernel from CMU (including GNU/Hurd systems). Other basic operating systems (VMS, for example) would have their own directories at the top level of the `sysdeps` hierarchy, parallel to `unix` and `mach`.

## D.2.2 Porting the GNU C Library to Unix Systems

Most Unix systems are fundamentally very similar. There are variations between different machines, and variations in what facilities are provided by the kernel. But the interface to the operating system facilities is, for the most part, pretty uniform and simple.

The code for Unix systems is in the directory `unix`, at the top level of the `sysdeps` hierarchy. This directory contains subdirectories (and subdirectory trees) for various Unix variants.

The functions which are system calls in most Unix systems are implemented in assembly code, which is generated automatically from specifications in files named `syscalls.list`. There are several such files, one in `sysdeps/unix` and others in its subdirectories. Some special system calls are implemented in files that are named with a suffix of '.S'; for example, `_exit.S`. Files ending in '.S' are run through the C preprocessor before being fed to the assembler.

These files all use a set of macros that should be defined in `sysdep.h`. The `sysdep.h` file in `sysdeps/unix` partially defines them; a `sysdep.h` file in another directory must finish defining them for the particular machine and operating system variant. See `sysdeps/unix/sysdep.h` and the machine-specific `sysdep.h` implementations to see what these macros are and what they should do.

The system-specific makefile for the `unix` directory (`sysdeps/unix/Makefile`) gives rules to generate several files from the Unix system you are building the library on (which is assumed to be the target system you are building the library *for*). All the generated files are put in the directory where the object files are kept; they should not affect the source tree itself. The files generated are `ioctls.h`, `errnos.h`, `sys/param.h`, and `errlist.c` (for the `stdio` section of the library).

# Appendix E Platform-specific facilities

The GNU C Library can provide machine-specific functionality.

## E.1 PowerPC-specific Facilities

Facilities specific to PowerPC that are not specific to a particular operating system are declared in `sys/platform/ppc.h`.

**uint64_t __ppc_get_timebase** (*void*)                                          [Function]
> Preliminary: | MT-Safe | AS-Safe | AC-Safe | See Section 1.2.2.1 [POSIX Safety Concepts], page 2.
>
> Read the current value of the Time Base Register.
>
> The *Time Base Register* is a 64-bit register that stores a monotonically incremented value updated at a system-dependent frequency that may be different from the processor frequency. More information is available in *Power ISA 2.06b - Book II - Section 5.2*.
>
> `__ppc_get_timebase` uses the processor's time base facility directly without requiring assistance from the operating system, so it is very efficient.

**uint64_t __ppc_get_timebase_freq** (*void*)                                     [Function]
> Preliminary: | MT-Unsafe init | AS-Unsafe corrupt:init | AC-Unsafe corrupt:init | See Section 1.2.2.1 [POSIX Safety Concepts], page 2.
>
> Read the current frequency at which the Time Base Register is updated.
>
> This frequency is not related to the processor clock or the bus clock. It is also possible that this frequency is not constant. More information is available in *Power ISA 2.06b - Book II - Section 5.2*.

The following functions provide hints about the usage of resources that are shared with other processors. They can be used, for example, if a program waiting on a lock intends to divert the shared resources to be used by other processors. More information is available in *Power ISA 2.06b - Book II - Section 3.2*.

**void __ppc_yield** (*void*)                                                     [Function]
> Preliminary: | MT-Safe | AS-Safe | AC-Safe | See Section 1.2.2.1 [POSIX Safety Concepts], page 2.
>
> Provide a hint that performance will probably be improved if shared resources dedicated to the executing processor are released for use by other processors.

**void __ppc_mdoio** (*void*)                                                     [Function]
> Preliminary: | MT-Safe | AS-Safe | AC-Safe | See Section 1.2.2.1 [POSIX Safety Concepts], page 2.
>
> Provide a hint that performance will probably be improved if shared resources dedicated to the executing processor are released until all outstanding storage accesses to caching-inhibited storage have been completed.

`void __ppc_mdoom` (*void*)                                          [Function]
> Preliminary: | MT-Safe | AS-Safe | AC-Safe | See Section 1.2.2.1 [POSIX Safety Concepts], page 2.
>
> Provide a hint that performance will probably be improved if shared resources dedicated to the executing processor are released until all outstanding storage accesses to cacheable storage for which the data is not in the cache have been completed.

`void __ppc_set_ppr_med` (*void*)                                    [Function]
> Preliminary: | MT-Safe | AS-Safe | AC-Safe | See Section 1.2.2.1 [POSIX Safety Concepts], page 2.
>
> Set the Program Priority Register to medium value (default).
>
> The *Program Priority Register* (PPR) is a 64-bit register that controls the program's priority. By adjusting the PPR value the programmer may improve system throughput by causing the system resources to be used more efficiently, especially in contention situations. The three unprivileged states available are covered by the functions `__ppc_set_ppr_med` (medium – default), `__ppc_set_ppc_low` (low) and `__ppc_set_ppc_med_low` (medium low). More information available in *Power ISA 2.06b - Book II - Section 3.1.*

`void __ppc_set_ppr_low` (*void*)                                    [Function]
> Preliminary: | MT-Safe | AS-Safe | AC-Safe | See Section 1.2.2.1 [POSIX Safety Concepts], page 2.
>
> Set the Program Priority Register to low value.

`void __ppc_set_ppr_med_low` (*void*)                                [Function]
> Preliminary: | MT-Safe | AS-Safe | AC-Safe | See Section 1.2.2.1 [POSIX Safety Concepts], page 2.
>
> Set the Program Priority Register to medium low value.

# Appendix F  Contributors to the GNU C Library

The GNU C Library project would like to thank its many contributors. Without them the project would not have been nearly as successful as it has been. Any omissions in this list are accidental. Feel free to file a bug in bugzilla if you have been left out or some of your contributions are not listed. Please keep this list in alphabetical order.

- Ryan S. Arnold for his improvements for Linux on PowerPC and his direction as FSF Project Steward for the GNU C Library.
- Miles Bader for writing the `argp` argument-parsing package, and the `argz`/`envz` interfaces.
- Jeff Bailey for his maintainership of the HPPA architecture.
- Petr Baudis for bug fixes and testing.
- Stephen R. van den Berg for contributing a highly-optimized `strstr` function.
- Ondrej Bilka for contributing optimized string routines for x64 and various fixes.
- Eric Blake for adding O(n) implementations of `memmem`, `strstr` and `strcasestr`.
- Philip Blundell for the ports to Linux/ARM (`arm-ANYTHING-linuxaout`) and ARM standalone (`arm-ANYTHING-none`), as well as for parts of the IPv6 support code.
- Per Bothner for the implementation of the `libio` library which is used to implement `stdio` functions.
- Mark Brown for his direction as part of the GNU C Library steering committee.
- Thomas Bushnell for his contributions to Hurd.
- Wilco Dijkstra for various fixes.
- Liubov Dmitrieva for optimzed string and math functions on x86-64 and x86.
- Ulrich Drepper for his many contributions in almost all parts of the GNU C Library, including:
  - internationalization support, including the `locale` and `localedef` utilities.
  - Linux i386/ELF support
  - the `hsearch` and `drand48` families of functions, reentrant '...`_r`' versions of the `random` family; System V shared memory and IPC support code
  - several highly-optimized string functions for ix86 processors
  - many math functions
  - the character conversion functions (`iconv`)
  - the `ftw` and `nftw` functions
  - the floating-point printing function used by `printf` and friends and the floating-point reading function used by `scanf`, `strtod` and friends
  - the `catgets` support and the entire suite of multi-byte and wide-character support functions (`wctype.h`, `wchar.h`, etc.).
  - versioning of objects on the symbol level
- Richard Earnshaw for continued support and fixes to the various ARM machine files.
- Paul Eggert for the `mktime` function and for his direction as part of the GNU C Library steering committee.

- Steve Ellcey for various fixes.

- Tulio Magno Quites Machado Filho for adding a new class of installed headers for low-level platform-specific functionality and one such for PowerPC.

- Mike Frysinger for his maintaining of the IA64 architecture and for testing and bug fixing.

- Michael Glad for the DES encryption function `crypt` and related functions.

- Wolfram Gloger for contributing the memory allocation functions functions `malloc`, `realloc` and `free` and related code.

- Torbjörn Granlund for fast implementations of many of the string functions (`memcpy`, `strlen`, etc.).

- Michael J. Haertel for writing the merge sort function `qsort` and malloc checking functions like `mcheck`.

- Bruno Haible for his improvements to the `iconv` and locale implementations.

- Richard Henderson for the port to Linux on Alpha (`alpha-anything-linux`).

- David Holsgrove for the port to Linux on MicroBlaze.

- Daniel Jacobowitz for various fixes and enhancements.

- Andreas Jaeger for the port to Linux on x86-64 (`x86_64-anything-linux` and his work on Linux for MIPS (`mips-anything-linux`), implementing the `ldconfig` program, providing a test suite for the math library and for his direction as part of the GNU C Library steering committee.

- Aurelien Jarno for various fixes.

- Jakub Jelinek for implementing a number of checking functions and for his direction as part of the GNU C Library steering committee.

- Geoffrey Keating for the port to Linux on PowerPC (`powerpc-anything-linux`).

- Brendan Kehoe for contributing the port to the MIPS DECStation running Ultrix 4 (`mips-dec-ultrix4`) and the port to the DEC Alpha running OSF/1 (`alpha-dec-osf1`).

- Mark Kettenis for implementing the `utmpx` interface and an utmp daemon, and for a Hesiod NSS module.

- Andi Kleen for implementing pthreads lock elision with TSX.

- Kazumoto Kojima for the port of the Mach and Hurd code to the MIPS architecture (`mips-anything-gnu`) and for his work on the SH architecture.

- Andreas Krebbel for his work on Linux for s390 and s390x.

- Thorsten Kukuk for providing an implementation for NIS (YP) and NIS+, securelevel 0, 1 and 2 and for the implementation for a caching daemon for NSS (`nscd`).

- Jeff Law for various fixes.

- Doug Lea for contributing the memory allocation functions functions `malloc`, `realloc` and `free` and related code.

- Chris Leonard for various fixes and enhancements to localedata.

- Stefan Liebler for various fixes.

- Hongjiu Lu for providing the support for a Linux 32-bit runtime environment under x86-64 (x32), for porting to Linux on IA64, for improved string functions, a framework for testing IFUNC implementations, and many bug fixes.

- Luis Machado for optimized functions on PowerPC.

- David J. MacKenzie for his contribution to the `getopt` function and writing the `tar.h` header.

- Greg McGary for adding runtime support for bounds checking.

- Roland McGrath for writing most of the GNU C Library originally, for his work on the Hurd port, his direction as part of the GNU C Library steering committee and as FSF Project Steward for the GNU C Library, and for many bug fixes and reviewing of contributions.

- Allan McRae for various fixes.

- Jason Merrill for the port to the Sequent Symmetry running Dynix version 3 (`i386-sequent-bsd`).

- Chris Metcalf for the port to Linux/Tile (`tilegx-anything-linux` and `tilepro-anything-linux`).

- David Miller for contributing the port to Linux/Sparc (`sparc*-anything-linux`).

- Alan Modra for his improvements for Linux on PowerPC.

- David Mosberger-Tang for contributing the port to Linux/Alpha (`alpha-anything-linux`).

- Stephen Moshier for implementing some 128-bit long double format math functions.

- Stephen Munroe for his port to Linux on PowerPC64 (`powerpc64-anything-linux`) and for adding optimized implementations for PowerPC.

- Joseph S. Myers for numerous bug fixes for the libm functions, for his maintainership of the ARM and MIPS architectures, improving cross-compilation and cross-testing of the GNU C Library, expanded coverage of conformtest, merging the ports/ subdirectory into the GNU C Library main repository and his direction as FSF Project Steward for the GNU C Library.

- Will Newton for contributing some optimized string functions and pointer encryption support for ARM and various fixes.

- Carlos O'Donell for his maintainership of the HPPA architecture, for maintaining the GNU C Library web pages and wiki, for his direction as FSF Project Steward for the GNU C Library and various bug fixes.

- Alexandre Oliva for adding TLS descriptors for LD and GD on x86 and x86-64, for the am33 port, for completing the MIPS n64/n32/o32 multilib port, for thread-safety, async-signal safety and async-cancellation safety documentation in the manual, for his direction as FSF Project Maintainer and for various fixes.

- Paul Pluzhnikov for various fixes.

- Marek Polacek for various fixes.

- Siddhesh Poyarekar for various fixes and an implementation of a framework for performance benchmarking of functions.

- Tom Quinn for contributing the startup code to support SunOS shared libraries and the port to SGI machines running Irix 4 (`mips-sgi-irix4`).

- Torvald Riegel for the implementation of a new semaphore algorithm.
- Pravin Satpute for writing sorting rules for some Indian languages.
- Douglas C. Schmidt for writing the quick sort function used as a fallback by `qsort`.
- Will Schmidt for optimized string functions on PowerPC.
- Andreas Schwab for the port to Linux/m68k (`m68k-anything-linux`) and for his direction as part of the GNU C Library steering committee.
- Martin Schwidefsky for porting to Linux on s390 (`s390-anything-linux`) and s390x (`s390x-anything-linux`).
- Thomas Schwinge for his contribution to Hurd and the SH architecture.
- Carlos Eduardo Seo for optimized functions on PowerPC.
- Marcus Shawcroft for contributing the AArch64 port.
- Franz Sirl for various fixes.
- Jes Sorensen for porting to Linux on IA64 (`ia64-anything-linux`).
- Richard Stallman for his contribution to the `getopt` function.
- Alfred M. Szmidt for various fixes.
- Ian Lance Taylor for contributing the port to the MIPS DECStation running Ultrix 4 (`mips-dec-ultrix4`).
- Samuel Thibault for improving the Hurd port.
- Tim Waugh for the implementation of the POSIX.2 `wordexp` function family.
- Eric Youngdale for implementing versioning of objects on the symbol level.
- Adhemerval Zanella for optimized functions on PowerPC.

Some code in the GNU C Library comes from other projects and might be under a different license:

- The timezone support code is derived from the public-domain timezone package by Arthur David Olson and his many contributors.
- Some of the support code for Mach is taken from Mach 3.0 by CMU; the file if_ppp.h is also copyright by CMU, but under a different license; see the file `LICENSES` for the text of the licenses.
- The random number generation functions `random`, `srandom`, `setstate` and `initstate`, which are also the basis for the `rand` and `srand` functions, were written by Earl T. Cohen for the University of California at Berkeley and are copyrighted by the Regents of the University of California. They have undergone minor changes to fit into the GNU C Library and to fit the ISO C standard, but the functional code is Berkeley's.
- The Internet-related code (most of the `inet` subdirectory) and several other miscellaneous functions and header files have been included from 4.4 BSD with little or no modification. The copying permission notice for this code can be found in the file `LICENSES` in the source distribution.
- The `getaddrinfo` and `getnameinfo` functions and supporting code were written by Craig Metz; see the file `LICENSES` for details on their licensing.
- The DNS resolver code is taken directly from BIND 4.9.5, which includes copyrighted code from UC Berkeley and from Digital Equipment Corporation. See the file `LICENSES` for the text of the DEC license.

- The code to support Sun RPC is taken verbatim from Sun's RPCSRC-4.0 distribution; see the file LICENSES for the text of the license.

- The math functions are taken from fdlibm-5.1 by Sun Microsystems, as modified by J.T. Conklin, Ian Lance Taylor, Ulrich Drepper, Andreas Schwab, and Roland McGrath.

- Many of the IEEE 64-bit double precision math functions (in the sysdeps/ieee754/dbl-64 subdirectory) come from the IBM Accurate Mathematical Library, contributed by IBM.

- Many of the IA64 math functions are taken from a collection of "Highly Optimized Mathematical Functions for Itanium" that Intel makes available under a free license; see the file LICENSES for details.

# Appendix  G  Free Software Needs Free Documentation

The biggest deficiency in the free software community today is not in the software—it is the lack of good free documentation that we can include with the free software. Many of our most important programs do not come with free reference manuals and free introductory texts. Documentation is an essential part of any software package; when an important free software package does not come with a free manual and a free tutorial, that is a major gap. We have many such gaps today.

Consider Perl, for instance. The tutorial manuals that people normally use are non-free. How did this come about? Because the authors of those manuals published them with restrictive terms—no copying, no modification, source files not available—which exclude them from the free software world.

That wasn't the first time this sort of thing happened, and it was far from the last. Many times we have heard a GNU user eagerly describe a manual that he is writing, his intended contribution to the community, only to learn that he had ruined everything by signing a publication contract to make it non-free.

Free documentation, like free software, is a matter of freedom, not price. The problem with the non-free manual is not that publishers charge a price for printed copies—that in itself is fine. (The Free Software Foundation sells printed copies of manuals, too.) The problem is the restrictions on the use of the manual. Free manuals are available in source code form, and give you permission to copy and modify. Non-free manuals do not allow this.

The criteria of freedom for a free manual are roughly the same as for free software. Redistribution (including the normal kinds of commercial redistribution) must be permitted, so that the manual can accompany every copy of the program, both on-line and on paper.

Permission for modification of the technical content is crucial too. When people modify the software, adding or changing features, if they are conscientious they will change the manual too—so they can provide accurate and clear documentation for the modified program. A manual that leaves you no choice but to write a new manual to document a changed version of the program is not really available to our community.

Some kinds of limits on the way modification is handled are acceptable. For example, requirements to preserve the original author's copyright notice, the distribution terms, or the list of authors, are ok. It is also no problem to require modified versions to include notice that they were modified. Even entire sections that may not be deleted or changed are acceptable, as long as they deal with nontechnical topics (like this one). These kinds of restrictions are acceptable because they don't obstruct the community's normal use of the manual.

However, it must be possible to modify all the *technical* content of the manual, and then distribute the result in all the usual media, through all the usual channels. Otherwise, the restrictions obstruct the use of the manual, it is not free, and we need another manual to replace it.

Please spread the word about this issue. Our community continues to lose manuals to proprietary publishing. If we spread the word that free software needs free reference manuals and free tutorials, perhaps the next person who wants to contribute by writing documentation will realize, before it is too late, that only free manuals contribute to the free software community.

If you are writing documentation, please insist on publishing it under the GNU Free Documentation License or another free documentation license. Remember that this decision requires your approval—you don't have to let the publisher decide. Some commercial publishers will use a free license if you insist, but they will not propose the option; it is up to you to raise the issue and say firmly that this is what you want. If the publisher you are dealing with refuses, please try other publishers. If you're not sure whether a proposed license is free, write to `licensing@gnu.org`.

You can encourage commercial publishers to sell more free, copylefted manuals and tutorials by buying them, and particularly by buying copies from the publishers that paid for their writing or for major improvements. Meanwhile, try to avoid buying non-free documentation at all. Check the distribution terms of a manual before you buy it, and insist that whoever seeks your business must respect your freedom. Check the history of the book, and try reward the publishers that have paid or pay the authors to work on it.

The Free Software Foundation maintains a list of free documentation published by other publishers, at `http://www.fsf.org/doc/other-free-books.html`.

# Appendix H  GNU Lesser General Public License

Version 2.1, February 1999

Copyright © 1991, 1999 Free Software Foundation, Inc.
51 Franklin Street, Fifth Floor, Boston, MA 02110-1301, USA

Everyone is permitted to copy and distribute verbatim copies
of this license document, but changing it is not allowed.

[This is the first released version of the Lesser GPL. It also counts
as the successor of the GNU Library Public License, version 2, hence the
version number 2.1.]

## Preamble

The licenses for most software are designed to take away your freedom to share and change it. By contrast, the GNU General Public Licenses are intended to guarantee your freedom to share and change free software—to make sure the software is free for all its users.

This license, the Lesser General Public License, applies to some specially designated software—typically libraries—of the Free Software Foundation and other authors who decide to use it. You can use it too, but we suggest you first think carefully about whether this license or the ordinary General Public License is the better strategy to use in any particular case, based on the explanations below.

When we speak of free software, we are referring to freedom of use, not price. Our General Public Licenses are designed to make sure that you have the freedom to distribute copies of free software (and charge for this service if you wish); that you receive source code or can get it if you want it; that you can change the software and use pieces of it in new free programs; and that you are informed that you can do these things.

To protect your rights, we need to make restrictions that forbid distributors to deny you these rights or to ask you to surrender these rights. These restrictions translate to certain responsibilities for you if you distribute copies of the library or if you modify it.

For example, if you distribute copies of the library, whether gratis or for a fee, you must give the recipients all the rights that we gave you. You must make sure that they, too, receive or can get the source code. If you link other code with the library, you must provide complete object files to the recipients, so that they can relink them with the library after making changes to the library and recompiling it. And you must show them these terms so they know their rights.

We protect your rights with a two-step method: (1) we copyright the library, and (2) we offer you this license, which gives you legal permission to copy, distribute and/or modify the library.

To protect each distributor, we want to make it very clear that there is no warranty for the free library. Also, if the library is modified by someone else and passed on, the recipients should know that what they have is not the original version, so that the original author's reputation will not be affected by problems that might be introduced by others.

Finally, software patents pose a constant threat to the existence of any free program. We wish to make sure that a company cannot effectively restrict the users of a free program by obtaining a restrictive license from a patent holder. Therefore, we insist that any patent license obtained for a version of the library must be consistent with the full freedom of use specified in this license.

Most GNU software, including some libraries, is covered by the ordinary GNU General Public License. This license, the GNU Lesser General Public License, applies to certain designated libraries, and is quite different from the ordinary General Public License. We use this license for certain libraries in order to permit linking those libraries into non-free programs.

When a program is linked with a library, whether statically or using a shared library, the combination of the two is legally speaking a combined work, a derivative of the original library. The ordinary General Public License therefore permits such linking only if the entire combination fits its criteria of freedom. The Lesser General Public License permits more lax criteria for linking other code with the library.

We call this license the *Lesser* General Public License because it does *Less* to protect the user's freedom than the ordinary General Public License. It also provides other free software developers Less of an advantage over competing non-free programs. These disadvantages are the reason we use the ordinary General Public License for many libraries. However, the Lesser license provides advantages in certain special circumstances.

For example, on rare occasions, there may be a special need to encourage the widest possible use of a certain library, so that it becomes a de-facto standard. To achieve this, non-free programs must be allowed to use the library. A more frequent case is that a free library does the same job as widely used non-free libraries. In this case, there is little to gain by limiting the free library to free software only, so we use the Lesser General Public License.

In other cases, permission to use a particular library in non-free programs enables a greater number of people to use a large body of free software. For example, permission to use the GNU C Library in non-free programs enables many more people to use the whole GNU operating system, as well as its variant, the GNU/Linux operating system.

Although the Lesser General Public License is Less protective of the users' freedom, it does ensure that the user of a program that is linked with the Library has the freedom and the wherewithal to run that program using a modified version of the Library.

The precise terms and conditions for copying, distribution and modification follow. Pay close attention to the difference between a "work based on the library" and a "work that uses the library". The former contains code derived from the library, whereas the latter must be combined with the library in order to run.

## TERMS AND CONDITIONS FOR COPYING, DISTRIBUTION AND MODIFICATION

0. This License Agreement applies to any software library or other program which contains a notice placed by the copyright holder or other authorized party saying it may be distributed under the terms of this Lesser General Public License (also called "this License"). Each licensee is addressed as "you".

   A "library" means a collection of software functions and/or data prepared so as to be conveniently linked with application programs (which use some of those functions and data) to form executables.

The "Library", below, refers to any such software library or work which has been distributed under these terms. A "work based on the Library" means either the Library or any derivative work under copyright law: that is to say, a work containing the Library or a portion of it, either verbatim or with modifications and/or translated straightforwardly into another language. (Hereinafter, translation is included without limitation in the term "modification".)

"Source code" for a work means the preferred form of the work for making modifications to it. For a library, complete source code means all the source code for all modules it contains, plus any associated interface definition files, plus the scripts used to control compilation and installation of the library.

Activities other than copying, distribution and modification are not covered by this License; they are outside its scope. The act of running a program using the Library is not restricted, and output from such a program is covered only if its contents constitute a work based on the Library (independent of the use of the Library in a tool for writing it). Whether that is true depends on what the Library does and what the program that uses the Library does.

1. You may copy and distribute verbatim copies of the Library's complete source code as you receive it, in any medium, provided that you conspicuously and appropriately publish on each copy an appropriate copyright notice and disclaimer of warranty; keep intact all the notices that refer to this License and to the absence of any warranty; and distribute a copy of this License along with the Library.

   You may charge a fee for the physical act of transferring a copy, and you may at your option offer warranty protection in exchange for a fee.

2. You may modify your copy or copies of the Library or any portion of it, thus forming a work based on the Library, and copy and distribute such modifications or work under the terms of Section 1 above, provided that you also meet all of these conditions:

   a. The modified work must itself be a software library.

   b. You must cause the files modified to carry prominent notices stating that you changed the files and the date of any change.

   c. You must cause the whole of the work to be licensed at no charge to all third parties under the terms of this License.

   d. If a facility in the modified Library refers to a function or a table of data to be supplied by an application program that uses the facility, other than as an argument passed when the facility is invoked, then you must make a good faith effort to ensure that, in the event an application does not supply such function or table, the facility still operates, and performs whatever part of its purpose remains meaningful.

      (For example, a function in a library to compute square roots has a purpose that is entirely well-defined independent of the application. Therefore, Subsection 2d requires that any application-supplied function or table used by this function must be optional: if the application does not supply it, the square root function must still compute square roots.)

   These requirements apply to the modified work as a whole. If identifiable sections of that work are not derived from the Library, and can be reasonably considered independent and separate works in themselves, then this License, and its terms, do not apply to those sections when you distribute them as separate works. But when you distribute the same sections as part of a whole which is a work based on the Library, the distribution of the whole must be on the terms of this License, whose permissions for other licensees extend to the entire whole, and thus to each and every part regardless of who wrote it.

Thus, it is not the intent of this section to claim rights or contest your rights to work written entirely by you; rather, the intent is to exercise the right to control the distribution of derivative or collective works based on the Library.

In addition, mere aggregation of another work not based on the Library with the Library (or with a work based on the Library) on a volume of a storage or distribution medium does not bring the other work under the scope of this License.

3. You may opt to apply the terms of the ordinary GNU General Public License instead of this License to a given copy of the Library. To do this, you must alter all the notices that refer to this License, so that they refer to the ordinary GNU General Public License, version 2, instead of to this License. (If a newer version than version 2 of the ordinary GNU General Public License has appeared, then you can specify that version instead if you wish.) Do not make any other change in these notices.

   Once this change is made in a given copy, it is irreversible for that copy, so the ordinary GNU General Public License applies to all subsequent copies and derivative works made from that copy.

   This option is useful when you wish to copy part of the code of the Library into a program that is not a library.

4. You may copy and distribute the Library (or a portion or derivative of it, under Section 2) in object code or executable form under the terms of Sections 1 and 2 above provided that you accompany it with the complete corresponding machine-readable source code, which must be distributed under the terms of Sections 1 and 2 above on a medium customarily used for software interchange.

   If distribution of object code is made by offering access to copy from a designated place, then offering equivalent access to copy the source code from the same place satisfies the requirement to distribute the source code, even though third parties are not compelled to copy the source along with the object code.

5. A program that contains no derivative of any portion of the Library, but is designed to work with the Library by being compiled or linked with it, is called a "work that uses the Library". Such a work, in isolation, is not a derivative work of the Library, and therefore falls outside the scope of this License.

   However, linking a "work that uses the Library" with the Library creates an executable that is a derivative of the Library (because it contains portions of the Library), rather than a "work that uses the library". The executable is therefore covered by this License. Section 6 states terms for distribution of such executables.

   When a "work that uses the Library" uses material from a header file that is part of the Library, the object code for the work may be a derivative work of the Library even though the source code is not. Whether this is true is especially significant if the work can be linked without the Library, or if the work is itself a library. The threshold for this to be true is not precisely defined by law.

If such an object file uses only numerical parameters, data structure layouts and accessors, and small macros and small inline functions (ten lines or less in length), then the use of the object file is unrestricted, regardless of whether it is legally a derivative work. (Executables containing this object code plus portions of the Library will still fall under Section 6.)

Otherwise, if the work is a derivative of the Library, you may distribute the object code for the work under the terms of Section 6. Any executables containing that work also fall under Section 6, whether or not they are linked directly with the Library itself.

6. As an exception to the Sections above, you may also combine or link a "work that uses the Library" with the Library to produce a work containing portions of the Library, and distribute that work under terms of your choice, provided that the terms permit modification of the work for the customer's own use and reverse engineering for debugging such modifications.

   You must give prominent notice with each copy of the work that the Library is used in it and that the Library and its use are covered by this License. You must supply a copy of this License. If the work during execution displays copyright notices, you must include the copyright notice for the Library among them, as well as a reference directing the user to the copy of this License. Also, you must do one of these things:

   a. Accompany the work with the complete corresponding machine-readable source code for the Library including whatever changes were used in the work (which must be distributed under Sections 1 and 2 above); and, if the work is an executable linked with the Library, with the complete machine-readable "work that uses the Library", as object code and/or source code, so that the user can modify the Library and then relink to produce a modified executable containing the modified Library. (It is understood that the user who changes the contents of definitions files in the Library will not necessarily be able to recompile the application to use the modified definitions.)

   b. Use a suitable shared library mechanism for linking with the Library. A suitable mechanism is one that (1) uses at run time a copy of the library already present on the user's computer system, rather than copying library functions into the executable, and (2) will operate properly with a modified version of the library, if the user installs one, as long as the modified version is interface-compatible with the version that the work was made with.

   c. Accompany the work with a written offer, valid for at least three years, to give the same user the materials specified in Subsection 6a, above, for a charge no more than the cost of performing this distribution.

   d. If distribution of the work is made by offering access to copy from a designated place, offer equivalent access to copy the above specified materials from the same place.

   e. Verify that the user has already received a copy of these materials or that you have already sent this user a copy.

   For an executable, the required form of the "work that uses the Library" must include any data and utility programs needed for reproducing the executable from it. However, as a special exception, the materials to be distributed need not include anything that is normally distributed (in either source or binary form) with the major components (compiler, kernel, and so on) of the operating system on which the executable runs, unless that component itself accompanies the executable.

It may happen that this requirement contradicts the license restrictions of other proprietary libraries that do not normally accompany the operating system. Such a contradiction means you cannot use both them and the Library together in an executable that you distribute.

7. You may place library facilities that are a work based on the Library side-by-side in a single library together with other library facilities not covered by this License, and distribute such a combined library, provided that the separate distribution of the work based on the Library and of the other library facilities is otherwise permitted, and provided that you do these two things:

   a. Accompany the combined library with a copy of the same work based on the Library, uncombined with any other library facilities. This must be distributed under the terms of the Sections above.

   b. Give prominent notice with the combined library of the fact that part of it is a work based on the Library, and explaining where to find the accompanying uncombined form of the same work.

8. You may not copy, modify, sublicense, link with, or distribute the Library except as expressly provided under this License. Any attempt otherwise to copy, modify, sublicense, link with, or distribute the Library is void, and will automatically terminate your rights under this License. However, parties who have received copies, or rights, from you under this License will not have their licenses terminated so long as such parties remain in full compliance.

9. You are not required to accept this License, since you have not signed it. However, nothing else grants you permission to modify or distribute the Library or its derivative works. These actions are prohibited by law if you do not accept this License. Therefore, by modifying or distributing the Library (or any work based on the Library), you indicate your acceptance of this License to do so, and all its terms and conditions for copying, distributing or modifying the Library or works based on it.

10. Each time you redistribute the Library (or any work based on the Library), the recipient automatically receives a license from the original licensor to copy, distribute, link with or modify the Library subject to these terms and conditions. You may not impose any further restrictions on the recipients' exercise of the rights granted herein. You are not responsible for enforcing compliance by third parties with this License.

11. If, as a consequence of a court judgment or allegation of patent infringement or for any other reason (not limited to patent issues), conditions are imposed on you (whether by court order, agreement or otherwise) that contradict the conditions of this License, they do not excuse you from the conditions of this License. If you cannot distribute so as to satisfy simultaneously your obligations under this License and any other pertinent obligations, then as a consequence you may not distribute the Library at all. For example, if a patent license would not permit royalty-free redistribution of the Library by all those who receive copies directly or indirectly through you, then the only way you could satisfy both it and this License would be to refrain entirely from distribution of the Library.

If any portion of this section is held invalid or unenforceable under any particular circumstance, the balance of the section is intended to apply, and the section as a whole is intended to apply in other circumstances.

It is not the purpose of this section to induce you to infringe any patents or other property right claims or to contest validity of any such claims; this section has the sole purpose of protecting the integrity of the free software distribution system which is implemented by public license practices. Many people have made generous contributions to the wide range of software distributed through that system in reliance on consistent application of that system; it is up to the author/donor to decide if he or she is willing to distribute software through any other system and a licensee cannot impose that choice.

This section is intended to make thoroughly clear what is believed to be a consequence of the rest of this License.

12. If the distribution and/or use of the Library is restricted in certain countries either by patents or by copyrighted interfaces, the original copyright holder who places the Library under this License may add an explicit geographical distribution limitation excluding those countries, so that distribution is permitted only in or among countries not thus excluded. In such case, this License incorporates the limitation as if written in the body of this License.

13. The Free Software Foundation may publish revised and/or new versions of the Lesser General Public License from time to time. Such new versions will be similar in spirit to the present version, but may differ in detail to address new problems or concerns.

Each version is given a distinguishing version number. If the Library specifies a version number of this License which applies to it and "any later version", you have the option of following the terms and conditions either of that version or of any later version published by the Free Software Foundation. If the Library does not specify a license version number, you may choose any version ever published by the Free Software Foundation.

14. If you wish to incorporate parts of the Library into other free programs whose distribution conditions are incompatible with these, write to the author to ask for permission. For software which is copyrighted by the Free Software Foundation, write to the Free Software Foundation; we sometimes make exceptions for this. Our decision will be guided by the two goals of preserving the free status of all derivatives of our free software and of promoting the sharing and reuse of software generally.

**NO WARRANTY**

15. BECAUSE THE LIBRARY IS LICENSED FREE OF CHARGE, THERE IS NO WARRANTY FOR THE LIBRARY, TO THE EXTENT PERMITTED BY APPLICABLE LAW. EXCEPT WHEN OTHERWISE STATED IN WRITING THE COPYRIGHT HOLDERS AND/OR OTHER PARTIES PROVIDE THE LIBRARY "AS IS" WITHOUT WARRANTY OF ANY KIND, EITHER EXPRESSED OR IMPLIED, INCLUDING, BUT NOT LIMITED TO, THE IMPLIED WARRANTIES OF MERCHANTABILITY AND FITNESS FOR A PARTICULAR PURPOSE. THE ENTIRE RISK AS TO THE QUALITY AND PERFORMANCE OF THE LIBRARY IS WITH YOU. SHOULD THE LIBRARY PROVE DEFECTIVE, YOU ASSUME THE COST OF ALL NECESSARY SERVICING, REPAIR OR CORRECTION.

16. IN NO EVENT UNLESS REQUIRED BY APPLICABLE LAW OR AGREED TO IN

WRITING WILL ANY COPYRIGHT HOLDER, OR ANY OTHER PARTY WHO
MAY MODIFY AND/OR REDISTRIBUTE THE LIBRARY AS PERMITTED
ABOVE, BE LIABLE TO YOU FOR DAMAGES, INCLUDING ANY GENERAL,
SPECIAL, INCIDENTAL OR CONSEQUENTIAL DAMAGES ARISING OUT OF
THE USE OR INABILITY TO USE THE LIBRARY (INCLUDING BUT NOT
LIMITED TO LOSS OF DATA OR DATA BEING RENDERED INACCURATE OR
LOSSES SUSTAINED BY YOU OR THIRD PARTIES OR A FAILURE OF THE
LIBRARY TO OPERATE WITH ANY OTHER SOFTWARE), EVEN IF SUCH
HOLDER OR OTHER PARTY HAS BEEN ADVISED OF THE POSSIBILITY OF
SUCH DAMAGES.

## END OF TERMS AND CONDITIONS

## How to Apply These Terms to Your New Libraries

If you develop a new library, and you want it to be of the greatest possible use to the public, we recommend making it free software that everyone can redistribute and change. You can do so by permitting redistribution under these terms (or, alternatively, under the terms of the ordinary General Public License).

To apply these terms, attach the following notices to the library. It is safest to attach them to the start of each source file to most effectively convey the exclusion of warranty; and each file should have at least the "copyright" line and a pointer to where the full notice is found.

```
one line to give the library's name and an idea of what it does.
Copyright (C) year  name of author

This library is free software; you can redistribute it and/or modify it
under the terms of the GNU Lesser General Public License as published by
the Free Software Foundation; either version 2.1 of the License, or (at
your option) any later version.

This library is distributed in the hope that it will be useful, but
WITHOUT ANY WARRANTY; without even the implied warranty of
MERCHANTABILITY or FITNESS FOR A PARTICULAR PURPOSE.  See the GNU
Lesser General Public License for more details.

You should have received a copy of the GNU Lesser General Public
License along with this library; if not, write to the Free Software
Foundation, Inc., 51 Franklin Street, Fifth Floor, Boston, MA 02110-1301,
USA.
```

Also add information on how to contact you by electronic and paper mail.

You should also get your employer (if you work as a programmer) or your school, if any, to sign a "copyright disclaimer" for the library, if necessary. Here is a sample; alter the names:

```
Yoyodyne, Inc., hereby disclaims all copyright interest in the library
'Frob' (a library for tweaking knobs) written by James Random Hacker.

signature of Ty Coon, 1 April 1990
Ty Coon, President of Vice
```

That's all there is to it!

# Appendix I  GNU Free Documentation License

Version 1.3, 3 November 2008

Copyright © 2000, 2001, 2002, 2007, 2008 Free Software Foundation, Inc.
http://fsf.org/

Everyone is permitted to copy and distribute verbatim copies
of this license document, but changing it is not allowed.

0. PREAMBLE

The purpose of this License is to make a manual, textbook, or other functional and useful document *free* in the sense of freedom: to assure everyone the effective freedom to copy and redistribute it, with or without modifying it, either commercially or non-commercially. Secondarily, this License preserves for the author and publisher a way to get credit for their work, while not being considered responsible for modifications made by others.

This License is a kind of "copyleft", which means that derivative works of the document must themselves be free in the same sense. It complements the GNU General Public License, which is a copyleft license designed for free software.

We have designed this License in order to use it for manuals for free software, because free software needs free documentation: a free program should come with manuals providing the same freedoms that the software does. But this License is not limited to software manuals; it can be used for any textual work, regardless of subject matter or whether it is published as a printed book. We recommend this License principally for works whose purpose is instruction or reference.

1. APPLICABILITY AND DEFINITIONS

This License applies to any manual or other work, in any medium, that contains a notice placed by the copyright holder saying it can be distributed under the terms of this License. Such a notice grants a world-wide, royalty-free license, unlimited in duration, to use that work under the conditions stated herein. The "Document", below, refers to any such manual or work. Any member of the public is a licensee, and is addressed as "you". You accept the license if you copy, modify or distribute the work in a way requiring permission under copyright law.

A "Modified Version" of the Document means any work containing the Document or a portion of it, either copied verbatim, or with modifications and/or translated into another language.

A "Secondary Section" is a named appendix or a front-matter section of the Document that deals exclusively with the relationship of the publishers or authors of the Document to the Document's overall subject (or to related matters) and contains nothing that could fall directly within that overall subject. (Thus, if the Document is in part a textbook of mathematics, a Secondary Section may not explain any mathematics.) The relationship could be a matter of historical connection with the subject or with related matters, or of legal, commercial, philosophical, ethical or political position regarding them.

The "Invariant Sections" are certain Secondary Sections whose titles are designated, as being those of Invariant Sections, in the notice that says that the Document is released under this License. If a section does not fit the above definition of Secondary then it is not allowed to be designated as Invariant. The Document may contain zero Invariant Sections. If the Document does not identify any Invariant Sections then there are none.

The "Cover Texts" are certain short passages of text that are listed, as Front-Cover Texts or Back-Cover Texts, in the notice that says that the Document is released under this License. A Front-Cover Text may be at most 5 words, and a Back-Cover Text may be at most 25 words.

A "Transparent" copy of the Document means a machine-readable copy, represented in a format whose specification is available to the general public, that is suitable for revising the document straightforwardly with generic text editors or (for images composed of pixels) generic paint programs or (for drawings) some widely available drawing editor, and that is suitable for input to text formatters or for automatic translation to a variety of formats suitable for input to text formatters. A copy made in an otherwise Transparent file format whose markup, or absence of markup, has been arranged to thwart or discourage subsequent modification by readers is not Transparent. An image format is not Transparent if used for any substantial amount of text. A copy that is not "Transparent" is called "Opaque".

Examples of suitable formats for Transparent copies include plain ASCII without markup, Texinfo input format, LaTeX input format, SGML or XML using a publicly available DTD, and standard-conforming simple HTML, PostScript or PDF designed for human modification. Examples of transparent image formats include PNG, XCF and JPG. Opaque formats include proprietary formats that can be read and edited only by proprietary word processors, SGML or XML for which the DTD and/or processing tools are not generally available, and the machine-generated HTML, PostScript or PDF produced by some word processors for output purposes only.

The "Title Page" means, for a printed book, the title page itself, plus such following pages as are needed to hold, legibly, the material this License requires to appear in the title page. For works in formats which do not have any title page as such, "Title Page" means the text near the most prominent appearance of the work's title, preceding the beginning of the body of the text.

The "publisher" means any person or entity that distributes copies of the Document to the public.

A section "Entitled XYZ" means a named subunit of the Document whose title either is precisely XYZ or contains XYZ in parentheses following text that translates XYZ in another language. (Here XYZ stands for a specific section name mentioned below, such as "Acknowledgements", "Dedications", "Endorsements", or "History".) To "Preserve the Title" of such a section when you modify the Document means that it remains a section "Entitled XYZ" according to this definition.

The Document may include Warranty Disclaimers next to the notice which states that this License applies to the Document. These Warranty Disclaimers are considered to be included by reference in this License, but only as regards disclaiming warranties: any other implication that these Warranty Disclaimers may have is void and has no effect on the meaning of this License.

2. VERBATIM COPYING

You may copy and distribute the Document in any medium, either commercially or noncommercially, provided that this License, the copyright notices, and the license notice saying this License applies to the Document are reproduced in all copies, and that you add no other conditions whatsoever to those of this License. You may not use technical measures to obstruct or control the reading or further copying of the copies you make or distribute. However, you may accept compensation in exchange for copies. If you distribute a large enough number of copies you must also follow the conditions in section 3.

You may also lend copies, under the same conditions stated above, and you may publicly display copies.

3. COPYING IN QUANTITY

If you publish printed copies (or copies in media that commonly have printed covers) of the Document, numbering more than 100, and the Document's license notice requires Cover Texts, you must enclose the copies in covers that carry, clearly and legibly, all these Cover Texts: Front-Cover Texts on the front cover, and Back-Cover Texts on the back cover. Both covers must also clearly and legibly identify you as the publisher of these copies. The front cover must present the full title with all words of the title equally prominent and visible. You may add other material on the covers in addition. Copying with changes limited to the covers, as long as they preserve the title of the Document and satisfy these conditions, can be treated as verbatim copying in other respects.

If the required texts for either cover are too voluminous to fit legibly, you should put the first ones listed (as many as fit reasonably) on the actual cover, and continue the rest onto adjacent pages.

If you publish or distribute Opaque copies of the Document numbering more than 100, you must either include a machine-readable Transparent copy along with each Opaque copy, or state in or with each Opaque copy a computer-network location from which the general network-using public has access to download using public-standard network protocols a complete Transparent copy of the Document, free of added material. If you use the latter option, you must take reasonably prudent steps, when you begin distribution of Opaque copies in quantity, to ensure that this Transparent copy will remain thus accessible at the stated location until at least one year after the last time you distribute an Opaque copy (directly or through your agents or retailers) of that edition to the public.

It is requested, but not required, that you contact the authors of the Document well before redistributing any large number of copies, to give them a chance to provide you with an updated version of the Document.

4. MODIFICATIONS

You may copy and distribute a Modified Version of the Document under the conditions of sections 2 and 3 above, provided that you release the Modified Version under precisely this License, with the Modified Version filling the role of the Document, thus licensing distribution and modification of the Modified Version to whoever possesses a copy of it. In addition, you must do these things in the Modified Version:

A. Use in the Title Page (and on the covers, if any) a title distinct from that of the Document, and from those of previous versions (which should, if there were any, be listed in the History section of the Document). You may use the same title as a previous version if the original publisher of that version gives permission.

B.  List on the Title Page, as authors, one or more persons or entities responsible for authorship of the modifications in the Modified Version, together with at least five of the principal authors of the Document (all of its principal authors, if it has fewer than five), unless they release you from this requirement.

C.  State on the Title page the name of the publisher of the Modified Version, as the publisher.

D.  Preserve all the copyright notices of the Document.

E.  Add an appropriate copyright notice for your modifications adjacent to the other copyright notices.

F.  Include, immediately after the copyright notices, a license notice giving the public permission to use the Modified Version under the terms of this License, in the form shown in the Addendum below.

G.  Preserve in that license notice the full lists of Invariant Sections and required Cover Texts given in the Document's license notice.

H.  Include an unaltered copy of this License.

I.  Preserve the section Entitled "History", Preserve its Title, and add to it an item stating at least the title, year, new authors, and publisher of the Modified Version as given on the Title Page. If there is no section Entitled "History" in the Document, create one stating the title, year, authors, and publisher of the Document as given on its Title Page, then add an item describing the Modified Version as stated in the previous sentence.

J.  Preserve the network location, if any, given in the Document for public access to a Transparent copy of the Document, and likewise the network locations given in the Document for previous versions it was based on. These may be placed in the "History" section. You may omit a network location for a work that was published at least four years before the Document itself, or if the original publisher of the version it refers to gives permission.

K.  For any section Entitled "Acknowledgements" or "Dedications", Preserve the Title of the section, and preserve in the section all the substance and tone of each of the contributor acknowledgements and/or dedications given therein.

L.  Preserve all the Invariant Sections of the Document, unaltered in their text and in their titles. Section numbers or the equivalent are not considered part of the section titles.

M.  Delete any section Entitled "Endorsements". Such a section may not be included in the Modified Version.

N.  Do not retitle any existing section to be Entitled "Endorsements" or to conflict in title with any Invariant Section.

O.  Preserve any Warranty Disclaimers.

If the Modified Version includes new front-matter sections or appendices that qualify as Secondary Sections and contain no material copied from the Document, you may at your option designate some or all of these sections as invariant. To do this, add their titles to the list of Invariant Sections in the Modified Version's license notice. These titles must be distinct from any other section titles.

You may add a section Entitled "Endorsements", provided it contains nothing but endorsements of your Modified Version by various parties—for example, statements of peer review or that the text has been approved by an organization as the authoritative definition of a standard.

You may add a passage of up to five words as a Front-Cover Text, and a passage of up to 25 words as a Back-Cover Text, to the end of the list of Cover Texts in the Modified Version. Only one passage of Front-Cover Text and one of Back-Cover Text may be added by (or through arrangements made by) any one entity. If the Document already includes a cover text for the same cover, previously added by you or by arrangement made by the same entity you are acting on behalf of, you may not add another; but you may replace the old one, on explicit permission from the previous publisher that added the old one.

The author(s) and publisher(s) of the Document do not by this License give permission to use their names for publicity for or to assert or imply endorsement of any Modified Version.

5. COMBINING DOCUMENTS

You may combine the Document with other documents released under this License, under the terms defined in section 4 above for modified versions, provided that you include in the combination all of the Invariant Sections of all of the original documents, unmodified, and list them all as Invariant Sections of your combined work in its license notice, and that you preserve all their Warranty Disclaimers.

The combined work need only contain one copy of this License, and multiple identical Invariant Sections may be replaced with a single copy. If there are multiple Invariant Sections with the same name but different contents, make the title of each such section unique by adding at the end of it, in parentheses, the name of the original author or publisher of that section if known, or else a unique number. Make the same adjustment to the section titles in the list of Invariant Sections in the license notice of the combined work.

In the combination, you must combine any sections Entitled "History" in the various original documents, forming one section Entitled "History"; likewise combine any sections Entitled "Acknowledgements", and any sections Entitled "Dedications". You must delete all sections Entitled "Endorsements."

6. COLLECTIONS OF DOCUMENTS

You may make a collection consisting of the Document and other documents released under this License, and replace the individual copies of this License in the various documents with a single copy that is included in the collection, provided that you follow the rules of this License for verbatim copying of each of the documents in all other respects.

You may extract a single document from such a collection, and distribute it individually under this License, provided you insert a copy of this License into the extracted document, and follow this License in all other respects regarding verbatim copying of that document.

7. AGGREGATION WITH INDEPENDENT WORKS

A compilation of the Document or its derivatives with other separate and independent documents or works, in or on a volume of a storage or distribution medium, is called an "aggregate" if the copyright resulting from the compilation is not used to limit the legal rights of the compilation's users beyond what the individual works permit. When the Document is included in an aggregate, this License does not apply to the other works in the aggregate which are not themselves derivative works of the Document.

If the Cover Text requirement of section 3 is applicable to these copies of the Document, then if the Document is less than one half of the entire aggregate, the Document's Cover Texts may be placed on covers that bracket the Document within the aggregate, or the electronic equivalent of covers if the Document is in electronic form. Otherwise they must appear on printed covers that bracket the whole aggregate.

8. TRANSLATION

Translation is considered a kind of modification, so you may distribute translations of the Document under the terms of section 4. Replacing Invariant Sections with translations requires special permission from their copyright holders, but you may include translations of some or all Invariant Sections in addition to the original versions of these Invariant Sections. You may include a translation of this License, and all the license notices in the Document, and any Warranty Disclaimers, provided that you also include the original English version of this License and the original versions of those notices and disclaimers. In case of a disagreement between the translation and the original version of this License or a notice or disclaimer, the original version will prevail.

If a section in the Document is Entitled "Acknowledgements", "Dedications", or "History", the requirement (section 4) to Preserve its Title (section 1) will typically require changing the actual title.

9. TERMINATION

You may not copy, modify, sublicense, or distribute the Document except as expressly provided under this License. Any attempt otherwise to copy, modify, sublicense, or distribute it is void, and will automatically terminate your rights under this License.

However, if you cease all violation of this License, then your license from a particular copyright holder is reinstated (a) provisionally, unless and until the copyright holder explicitly and finally terminates your license, and (b) permanently, if the copyright holder fails to notify you of the violation by some reasonable means prior to 60 days after the cessation.

Moreover, your license from a particular copyright holder is reinstated permanently if the copyright holder notifies you of the violation by some reasonable means, this is the first time you have received notice of violation of this License (for any work) from that copyright holder, and you cure the violation prior to 30 days after your receipt of the notice.

Termination of your rights under this section does not terminate the licenses of parties who have received copies or rights from you under this License. If your rights have been terminated and not permanently reinstated, receipt of a copy of some or all of the same material does not give you any rights to use it.

10. FUTURE REVISIONS OF THIS LICENSE

The Free Software Foundation may publish new, revised versions of the GNU Free Documentation License from time to time. Such new versions will be similar in spirit to the present version, but may differ in detail to address new problems or concerns. See `http://www.gnu.org/copyleft/`.

Each version of the License is given a distinguishing version number. If the Document specifies that a particular numbered version of this License "or any later version" applies to it, you have the option of following the terms and conditions either of that specified version or of any later version that has been published (not as a draft) by the Free Software Foundation. If the Document does not specify a version number of this License, you may choose any version ever published (not as a draft) by the Free Software Foundation. If the Document specifies that a proxy can decide which future versions of this License can be used, that proxy's public statement of acceptance of a version permanently authorizes you to choose that version for the Document.

11. RELICENSING

"Massive Multiauthor Collaboration Site" (or "MMC Site") means any World Wide Web server that publishes copyrightable works and also provides prominent facilities for anybody to edit those works. A public wiki that anybody can edit is an example of such a server. A "Massive Multiauthor Collaboration" (or "MMC") contained in the site means any set of copyrightable works thus published on the MMC site.

"CC-BY-SA" means the Creative Commons Attribution-Share Alike 3.0 license published by Creative Commons Corporation, a not-for-profit corporation with a principal place of business in San Francisco, California, as well as future copyleft versions of that license published by that same organization.

"Incorporate" means to publish or republish a Document, in whole or in part, as part of another Document.

An MMC is "eligible for relicensing" if it is licensed under this License, and if all works that were first published under this License somewhere other than this MMC, and subsequently incorporated in whole or in part into the MMC, (1) had no cover texts or invariant sections, and (2) were thus incorporated prior to November 1, 2008.

The operator of an MMC Site may republish an MMC contained in the site under CC-BY-SA on the same site at any time before August 1, 2009, provided the MMC is eligible for relicensing.

# ADDENDUM: How to use this License for your documents

To use this License in a document you have written, include a copy of the License in the document and put the following copyright and license notices just after the title page:

```
Copyright (C)  year  your name.
Permission is granted to copy, distribute and/or modify this document
under the terms of the GNU Free Documentation License, Version 1.3
or any later version published by the Free Software Foundation;
with no Invariant Sections, no Front-Cover Texts, and no Back-Cover
Texts.  A copy of the license is included in the section entitled ''GNU
Free Documentation License''.
```

If you have Invariant Sections, Front-Cover Texts and Back-Cover Texts, replace the "with...Texts." line with this:

```
with the Invariant Sections being list their titles, with
the Front-Cover Texts being list, and with the Back-Cover Texts
being list.
```

If you have Invariant Sections without Cover Texts, or some other combination of the three, merge those two alternatives to suit the situation.

If your document contains nontrivial examples of program code, we recommend releasing these examples in parallel under your choice of free software license, such as the GNU General Public License, to permit their use in free software.

# Concept Index

# Type Index

# Function and Macro Index

## Q

## R

## S

## Y

# Variable and Constant Macro Index

# A

## B

## C

## D

# F

# Program and File Index

www.ingramcontent.com/pod-product-compliance
Lightning Source LLC
LaVergne TN
LVHW060132070326
832902LV00018B/2753